Peter Staveley was born in 1949 in Leamington Spa and educated at Rugby School, then South Bank and Southampton Universities respectively. After a career in sales and marketing within the oil and logistics industries and a long-time dabble in genealogy, he took early retirement and moved to Tuscany to focus upon his greatest passion: history. After 50 years of study, he is the archetypal autodidactic historian, with a particular fondness for the medieval period, World War II and, of course, Robin Hood. Outside of this, he enjoys producing his own extra virgin olive oil, travelling, cat-wrangling and improving upon his English longbow archery skills.

This book is dedicated to all those who believe Robin Hood to be a symbol of the spirit of the common man standing up against tyranny and injustice – representing hope for the oppressed, but achieved with a generous helping of courtesy and good humour.

Peter Staveley

ROBIN UNHOODED

And the Death of a King

AUSTIN MACAULEY PUBLISHERS™

LONDON ⋆ CAMBRIDGE ⋆ NEW YORK ⋆ SHARJAH

A CIP catalogue record for this title is available from the British Library.

ISBN 9781035835737 (Paperback)
ISBN 9781035835744 (Hardback)
ISBN 9781035835751 (ePub e-book)

www.austinmacauley.com

First Published 2024
Austin Macauley Publishers Ltd®
1 Canada Square
Canary Wharf
London
E14 5AA

Table of Contents

List of Illustrations   **9**

Preface   **12**

Part I   **19**

Chapter 1: Birth of a Legend   *21*

Chapter 2: What's in a Name?   *31*

Chapter 3: An Earlier Man   *48*

Chapter 4: Unhooding the Legend   *61*

Chapter 5: Treachery and Downfall   *88*

Chapter 6: The Making of...an Outlawed Noble or Noble Outlaw?   *98*

Chapter 7: Forest Life and Friends   *113*

Chapter 8: The Poor Man's Hero   *149*

Chapter 9: The Nemeses   *157*

Part II: The Death of a King   **199**

Introduction   *201*

Chapter 1: A New King   *209*

Chapter 2: A Possible Plot   *226*

Chapter 3: Henry's Inner Circle   *237*

Chapter 4: The Other Suspects   *254*

Chapter 5: Omens and Portents and Doom—Oh My!   *267*

Chapter 6: The Deathly Forest   *278*

Chapter 7: The Not-so-Deathly Hunt   *284*

Chapter 8: The Red King Falls   *305*

Chapter 9: The Next Hours   *324*

Chapter 10: The Next Days   *335*

Chapter 11: The Next Years—and the 'Clare Benefit'   *350*

Chapter 12: The Nun, the Princess, the Son, the Shrine and the Letter…   *367*

Chapter 13: The Death of Robin: A Treacherous Nun and Red Roger   *390*

Chapter 14: Conclusions   *424*

Appendices   **445**

Appendix 1   *447*

Appendix 2.1: (Part 1)   *448*

Appendix 2.1: (Part 2)   *450*

Appendix 2.2   *451*

Appendix 3   *452*

Appendix 4   *458*

Appendix 5   *459*

Appendix 6   *460*

Appendix 7   *462*

Appendix 8   *469*

Appendix 9   *485*

Appendix 9a   *486*

Appendix 10   *488*

Appendix 11   *499*

Appendix 12   *503*

Bibliography and Primary Resources   **508**

List of Illustrations

Frontispiece: Robin Hood on a horse (woodcut, c.1500–10 with later coloration).

Part I

1. Extract from Piers Ploughman mentioning Robin Hood c.1377
2. Extract from Memoranda Roll of 1262 showing name change to Willi. Robehood
3. The Justice Pipe Roll for 1225 showing the debt owed by Rob Hod, fugitive.
4. Statue of Waltheof on the front of Crowland Abbey
5. The death of Earl Siward
6. Extract from the Hallam entry in the Domesday Book
7. Reconstruction of an Anglo-Saxon long hall
8. Municipal seal of the Borough of Huntingdon
9. Packhorse Bridge over the River Rivelin
10. Little John's great bow photographed in the early 1950s
11. Alabaster effigy of Matilda Fitzwalter
12. a) Hood Brook and b) Robin Hood's Cave
13. The proud Bishop of Hereford
14. Extract from Domesday showing Roger de Busli's control over Waltheof's lands.
15. Handcoloured engraving of Tickhill Castle in the 16th century
16. Peveril Castle ruins today
17. Property holdings of Ralph FitzHubert
18. Robin beheads Guy of Gisborne

Part II

19. William Rufus shot by an arrow in the forest

20. Tomb of William the Conqueror

21. The 3 sons of William the Conqueror—Robert, William and Henry

22. Depiction of William Rufus

23. Pope Urban preaching at the Council of Clermont

24. Robert Curthose at the siege of Antioch

25. 12th century fresco of a royal hunting party

26. The Vexin and Picardy links of the plotters

27. Map showing the Duchies and Countships of France

28. The sun setting over Canterton Glen

29. Victorian image of the death of William Rufus

30. Par Force hunting a great stag with hounds

31. Hand-split oak deer-fence or 'Pale'

32. Dismounted archers at a 'bow and stable' hunt

33. Aerial view of the Malwood Lodge plateau today

34. View over the New Forest from Castle Malwood

35. The Perche-Montdidier family and its links to Beaumont, l'Aigle, Warenne, etc.

36. Entrance up to Malwood Lodge from Minstead

37. The Rufus Stone

38. Looking south-west up the slope of Malwood Walk in Canterton Glen

39. Looking due west up the slope of Malwood Walk from the King's position

40. The King's position and Tyrell's position

41. The 'Death Zone' showing possible positions of the parties

42. Arrow fletchings and points

43. Robin shooting from a tree depicted on new £2 coins

44. View to the King's position from base of Robin's tree

45. Purkis taking the body of Rufus to Winchester

46. Tyrell's Ford, the shallow crossing of the River Avon

47. Henry confronted by William de Breteuil at Winchester treasury

48. The Coronation Charter of Liberties of Henry I

49. The Coronation of Henry I

50. Letter from Archbishop Anselm to Athelits, Abbess of Romsey, 1102

51. A surviving 12th century preserved heart reliquary

52. The Passing of Robin Hood, Painting by N. C. Wyeth, 1917

53. The King pardons Robin and his Merry Men

54. 18th century sketch of Robin Hood's grave—now missing

55. The Prioress greets Robin at the Priory door

56. Robin shoots his final arrow from his deathbed helped by Little John

57. Images of Kimberworth motte and Bailey castle

58. Ecclesfield Priory

59. Location of the Priory, St Mary's church and Robin's final arrow

Appendices

60. Possible site of Robin Hood's grave in Ecclesfield Churchyard

61. Reconstruction of a Viking Longhouse in Denmark

62. Remains of Roger de Busli's castle at Laughton-en-le-Morthen

63. Places associated with Ecclesfield Priory

64. Very early image of an English longbow, back quiver and hunting dog

65. An English longbow made from a single piece of yew

66. 11th century carved stone image of a longbow

67. Carved stone image of a longbow archer at Colchester Castle

68. Depiction of a 14th century tournament mêlée

69. May Day Morris Dancers with Pole and pipe and taborer.

70. Image of Robin Hood in the early 17th century May Day revels

71. The 'Green Man' font at Stow Minster and Robin Hood statue, Nottingham.

Preface

In 1956, as a small boy of 7, I would walk back home from primary school with my friend Robert. About twice a week, I would stop off at his house for tea. His mother made delicious crisp sandwiches but, more importantly, Robert's family had a television, which we did not. Consisting of a small black and white screen in a large walnut cabinet with just 2 channels, we would look forward, with eager anticipation, to the 'show' that teatime. Our outright favourite—far better than *The Lone Ranger, Rin Tin Tin, Fury, Zorro* or *Champion the Wonder Horse*, was the ITV series *The Adventures of Robin Hood*, starring sturdy Richard Greene as the eponymous hero (and latterly, a very young Paul Eddington as Will Scarlet).[1]

My pulse would quicken as each episode began with the rousing call of a hunting horn and an arrow piercing a tree. This 1950s Robin Hood was the embodiment of decency and, bizarrely, no robberies were committed! To those of us brought up with such stirring, romantic and adventurous tales, or to anyone who has savoured the many books, TV shows and films of the last 80 years or so, Robin Hood is deeply entrenched in our hearts and imaginations. In truth, since the publication of Walter Scott's 'Ivanhoe' in the mid-19th century, the lure and transmission of the Robin Hood tales had been centred on the children's market, both for books[2] and latterly, films and TV. It was not really until the

---

[1] We were briefly seduced by Davy Crockett, 'King of the Wild Frontier', starring Fess Parker in the Disney mini-series on ITV and later feature film. It was the worldwide media and merchandise phenomena of 1955/6 (with famously catchy theme tune) that resulted in children rampaging around their gardens in replica coonskin fur hats, buckskin jackets and rifles, instead of feathered caps and bows and arrows. Despite an heroic death at the Battle of the Alamo, unlike Robin Hood his popularity was fleeting.

[2] Most notably *The Merry Adventures of Robin Hood of Great Renown in Nottinghamshire*, a very popular and successful 1883 novel by the American author and

alluring, mystical and more earthy 1980s ITV *Robin of Sherwood* series[3] that a whole new, more adult, generation was re-awakened to the legend, leading to a flurry of further Hollywood movie interpretations.[4]

In a setting centuries ago, the main roads and forests seem to have been awash with vagabonds, highwaymen and thieves. Yet while a sprinkling of tales of other historic outlaws have survived, they pale in comparison to the worldwide legend of Robin Hood who has become the undisputed ideal model of the outlaw hero. Maybe his story has endured because of bravery, clever disguises, archery prowess and an ability to evade capture by the Norman nemesis. Or maybe it is because he represents our timeless, unquenchable desire for a better society: the fierce yeoman standing up against the greedy bishops and ruthless sheriffs in medieval ballads; the mischievous 'Lord of Misrule' of the 15th century May Games, challenging the authority of the State; the Warner brothers depression era 1938 subtly anti-Nazi, pro-Roosevelt's New Deal version (starring Errol Flynn); and the Richard Greene series I grew up with in the 1950s.

This ran for 6 years and 143 episodes, many written by Americans Ring Lardner Jr.[5] and Ian McLellan Hunter, who were both blacklisted as probable communists in the Hollywood McCarthyite witch-hunts and moved to England…no doubt with sympathy for anti-establishment outlaws helping out the proletariat! In fact, in November, 1953, during the height of the McCarthy era, Robin Hood and his band of 'merry outlaws' made headlines in the USA when a certain Mrs J. White of the Indiana Textbook Commission called for a ban of Robin Hood, in all school books and libraries, for promoting

---

illustrator Howard Pyle, who took his basic material from the original medieval ballads and wove it into a coherent adventure story for children.

[3] Many readers will recall the three very popular and gritty (oft-repeated), *Robin of Sherwood* ITV series that ran from 1984–86, penned by Richard Carpenter, with its haunting Clannad theme tune, starring Michael Praed and then Jason Connery, or possibly the less successful three BBC series of *Robin Hood* starring Jonas Armstrong, 2006–09. At a rough count, there have been around 80 films and small-screen adaptations of the legend over the last century or so.

[4] Like Frankenstein's monster, Sherlock Holmes and soon Mickey Mouse, Robin Hood has no copyright protection and anyone can make a film or book about them without incurring those rights costs, which is very appealing to film and TV producers.

[5] Lardner won two Oscars for his screenplays, for *Woman of the Year* (1942) and *M.A.S.H.* (1970).

communism—because 'he stole from the rich to give to the poor'! Thankfully this ridiculous attempt to censor Robin Hood failed.

So, who was this mysterious and great English folklore hero that spawned a deluge of literary, creative and generally politicised outpourings? He is one of only 10 characters—including King Arthur, Merlin and King Lear—profiled in *The Dictionary of National Biography* (*DNB*) since 1891 yet not proven to be real. Sidney Lee, the editor of this first DNB edition, was emphatic that Robin Hood was solely the stuff of make-believe, stating '*evidence of historical existence, although very voluminous, will not bear scholarly examination*'. He also went on to posit the link between the name Hood and the Germanic folklore elf *Hödeken,* though given the absence of any traces of magic or the supernatural in the Robin Hood ballads, this proposition has not been taken up by modern scholars. However—in the 2004 DNB update—Robin is recognised as a possible historical subject, for whom there is a sketchy biography. Throughout this book I shall reference the works of 19th century antiquarian and historian, Joseph Hunter. Hunter, a firm believer in a real Robin, had some strong words for those un-patriotic scholars who would deny Robin Hood's reality:

'*Trusting to the plain sense of my countrymen, I dismiss these theorists to that limbo of vanity, there to live with all those who would make all remote history fable, who would make us believe that everything which is good in England is a mere copy of something originated in countries eastwards to our own, and who would deny to the English nation in past ages all skill and all advancement in literature or in the arts of sculpture and architecture*'.[6]

If you were to line up all the books ever written about Robin Hood, you would fill a large floor-to-ceiling bookcase.[7] I know this to be true because I own a lot of them! The volume of literature on this famous English legend, both fiction and non-fiction, proves 2 things: First, he holds a compelling grip on all, indeed, worldwide recognition—be they writers, readers, bloggers, aficionados, academics, historians and the public in general;[8] and second, that despite valiant

---

[6] *Critical and Historical Tracts*, Joseph Hunter, London, John Russell Smith, 1850, p.3.

[7] There are over 1000 fiction and non-fiction books held in the British Library covering various aspects of the Robin Hood legend.

[8] Survey by Cottages and Castles. Sept. 2021: Under Legends and Myths, Robin Hood equals the Loch Ness monster 'Nessie' in UK Google searches, averaging 60,500 per

efforts and extravagant dust jacket claims, no-one has yet been able to advocate irrefutable solutions to the intriguing mysteries of his true origins, identity and demise.

On this point, the simple fact is that the further back you go in time to study a moment in history, the sparser and more questionable the sources become, making the establishment of an indisputable truth extremely problematic. Increasingly, deduction, detection and interpretation come into play. We are talking about a period several hundred years ago, almost a thousand, so any surviving documents are extremely limited. Those that do exist were generally written some years later, often by people who were not there (simply being copies of earlier versions), and usually contain a bias or particular agenda, be it political, religious or simply to entertain. Every nugget that is unearthed needs to be questioned. If there are 2 versions of the same event, they cannot both be right, but they might both be wrong. Then again, one of them might be right.

The author Geoffrey Singman, despite admitting that the pursuit of Robin's true identity holds allure to even the most fervent cynic, describes the search for him as: "*…the perennial will-o'-the-wisp of Robin Hood studies.*"[9] Or in the somewhat more harsher opinion of Stephen Knight, professor of English literature at Cardiff University and leading light among the current cadre of literary scholars of the Robin Hood legend, who treat the ballad texts solely as examples of late medieval literature: "*…the search for the real outlaw is vulgar empiricism*"[10]

Knight firmly believes Robin Hood to be a mythic name and a literary creation—but everyone is entitled to their own opinion. So, stubbornly rejecting all of the suggested origins of him just being a 'ballad muse' or 'hero of ritual drama' and resolutely brushing aside any charges of 'vulgarity' and perceived 'wispiness', I entered into this rabbit hole of a subject—the only thing I am completely sure of is that my words will not be the last on the matter. Alas, I have not found—in the National Archives, British Library or some dusty

---

month. However, globally, Robin is way out in front as the world's most searched legend, with an astonishing 888,300 searches on average per month (double those for King Arthur in second place).
https://www.cottages-and-castles.co.uk/guides/most-popular-uk-legends.
[9] *Robin Hood: The Shaping of the Legend*, Jeffrey L. Singman, Greenwood Press, 1998.
[10] '*In search of the real Robin Hood*', *Mail and Guardian* (Africa), Stephen Moss, 11 May 2010.

cathedral's vaults—an indisputable medieval manuscript that solves the mystery once and for all. Nevertheless, in order to produce my own unique conclusions, I have delved, undaunted, into and/or reinterpreted all known material, plus considered additional sources that have been missed or dismissed by previous writers. In conclusion, what I offer is somewhat radical, certainly original and, dare I say, rather convincing.

Granted, I am not a professional historian or university academic, but solely following that noble British tradition of the self-taught amateur.[11] This book is the result of a slow gestation of more than 2 decades of research, historical detection and analysis by an inquisitive mind. Where appropriate, I provide further academic references in Footnotes, Appendices and a Bibliography. As such, it is a serious investigative, quasi-academic, study into both the legend of Robin Hood and the death of King William II of England, aka William Rufus— two conundrums that, as we shall see, are interconnected. In addition, I endeavour to answer what is perhaps the even more important and intriguing question—if there was one single highwayman out of which the whole legend began, what was that 'something' in the legend and its themes which began to appeal first to medieval Englishmen, then in later centuries to the whole world?

Above all, however, I have endeavoured to create an enjoyable read. You do not need a history degree to have some fun here—just a sense of curiosity, a love of mysteries and an open mind.

As I lead you on this adventure, I ask you to keep in mind the following: the truth is often more complex than it first appears to be, but that does not mean it is impossible to find. Throughout this labour of love, I've been reminded of a quote by Henry David Thoreau, American author, poet, philosopher and activist. In November 1850, when writing in his *Journal* about public suspicions that, in an 1849 strike, dairymen were watering down supplies, he suggested:

"Some circumstantial evidence is very strong, as when you find a trout in the milk."

---

[11] In the same manner as Victorian palaeontologist Mary Anning and more recently amateur researcher Philippa Langley, of the Richard III Society, who approached Leicester City Council and the University of Leicester Archaeological Services to propose an excavation of the Greyfriars Social Services car park site, leading to the discovery of his skeleton in 2012.

It is said that the honest historian '*affirms what is true, avoids what is false and respects the uncertain*'[12]. To that end I have endeavoured to be as diligent as possible in the research and presentation of all the material within the covers of this book and have constantly had the words of Charles Dickens in mind...

'I have no need to observe that I do not wilfully or negligently mislead my readers, and that before I wrote that description I took pains to investigate the subject'.

Charles Dickens
Preface to Bleak House

---

[12] *Henry I*, Warren Hollister, Yale Uni. Press, 2001, chap. 2, p.30

Depiction of Robin Hood, from '*A Lytell Geste of Robyn Hode*'
A woodcut (later colouration) - printed in c.1495 by Antwerp printer
Gerhaert Leeu, but first used by English printer Richard Pynson in the
Prologue of his c.1492 edition of Chaucer's Canterbury Tales
as a depiction of the Squire's Yeoman.
Public domain image

Lythe and listin gentilmen
That be of frebore blode
I shall you tel of a gode yeoman
His name was Robyn Hode

The opening stanza from *A Lytell Geste of Robyn Hode*
(Printer: Wynkyn de Worde, *c.*1506)

Part I

Chapter 1
Birth of a Legend

"After all, I believe that legends and myths are largely made of truth."
~ J. R. R. Tolkien, The Letters of J. R. R. Tolkien

The character Robin Hood has been stealing our attention for hundreds of years. Is he simply the result of someone's romantic or political ideals, the amalgam of several heroes and the invention of a lively-minded medieval storyteller? Perhaps he derives from one of the pagan creations attached to the medieval May Games—like the Green Man, Jack-in-the-Green, John Barleycorn or Robin Goodfellow—a heathen lord of springtime and fertility, a folklore forest spirit made immortal? Maybe he is linked to the likes of the Aryan sun god, the blind archer Hödr or a form of the god Odin from Norse mythology, although such interpretations do strain credulity. Or perhaps, just perhaps, he was a real man.[13]

Certainly, when ancient references become legends, legends become a quest. An earnest search for the authentic Robin began nearly 2 centuries ago and has intensified in the last few decades but this mysterious hero has seemingly proved impossible to run to ground. The key question of *when* he might have been active is now as hotly contested as the nature of his identity, or the *who*. Most consider a period spanning around 150 years, from the end of the 12th to the mid-14th centuries. This expansive timeframe has resulted in the continual publication of claims to have solved the mystery. But *where* and *how* did it all begin?

The first literary reference to Robin Hood is well-known to be in William Langland's poetic eschatological and allegorical masterpiece, *Piers Plowman,*

---

[13] Because this study is firmly coming down on the side of a real person, the matter of the folkloric study of the Robin Hood legend is not ignored but has been restricted to Appendix 10. A 2021 Sky History survey gave a figure of 29% of people believing Robin was a real person (and 40% for King Arthur).

that dates to c.1377–9. Written in Middle English, but in a West Midland dialect, Passus VIII[14] of Piers Ploughman tells the tale of Sloth (*Sleuthe*), a lazy drunken parish priest, who admits that he cannot perfectly recite the Paternoster (the Latin version of the Lord's Prayer), but adds:

'*Ich can* [I know the] *rymes of* **Robyn Hode** *and of Randolf, Erl* [Earl]) *of Chestre*'

PASSUS VIII.

Incipit passus octauus.

CONFESSIO ACCIDIE.

THO cam Sleuthe al by-slobered · with two slymed eyen.
'Ich most sitte to be shryuen,' quath he · 'or elles shal ich nappe.
Ich may nouht stonde ne stoupe · ne with-oute stoule knele.
Were ich brouhte in my bed · bote my taylende hit made,   4
Sholde no ryngynge do me ryse · tyl ich were rype to dyne.'
Benedicite he by-gan with a bolke · and hus brest knokede,
Rascled and remed · and routte at the laste.
'What a-wake, renk,' quath Repentaunce · 'rape the to shryfte!'
* 'Sholde ich deye,' quath he, 'by this daye · ich drede me sore, 9
Ich can nouht parfytliche my *pater-noster* · as the prest hit seggeth.
Ich can rymes of Robyn Hode · and of Randolf, erl of Chestre,
Ac of oure lord ne of oure lady · the lest that euere was maked.

1. Extract from *The Vision of William concerning Piers The Plowman* (1393) by William Langland (Ed. Rev. W. Skeat) Clarendon Press, 1886

Use of © image granted under licence by Oxford University Press

This priestly admission clearly suggests that such 'rhymes' were already well-known throughout the land. In fact, to be recognisable as stories learnt by heart, and by a priest, they must have been established for *some considerable time*. Precisely when that was and what those now lost stories contained is, frustratingly, not known but presumably very popular ballads/poems are being referenced.

---

[14] Section, canto or division, like chapter, particularly used in medieval stories and poems.

However, what is definite is that these Robin Hood ballads were obviously in *oral* circulation by the second half of the 14th century, the precise period when Latin and Norman French were superseded by the revival of 'English' (by Chaucer, Langland and others) as the new literary style. Such ballads were more along the lines of epic poems rather than songs, being spoken or chanted in verse rather than sung, though perhaps the later 16th/17th century ballads had some musical accompaniment when performed in public. Significantly, unlike other medieval tales, the Robin Hood ballads are in Middle English, a version of the English language used between the mid-12th and late 15th centuries. Although the earliest surviving written versions of Robin Hood ballads date from the late 15th century, their linguistic features and the social background depicted in them, suggest that they were composed and set in the 13th or early 14th centuries and linguists have also observed that they are written in a distinct northern dialect.

This does not preclude the possibility that the real man, if indeed there was a real man, could have lived some time before this—a historic figure alive far earlier than the ballads suggest and simply the subject of oral tales. In fact, given the limits of the 13th century balladeers' historical knowledge and the desirability to provide a backdrop familiar with their audience—the common man—it seems entirely plausible that they plucked Robin Hood from his original timeframe, composed these rhyming ballads around the many oral stories and dropped him into a contemporary setting to suit their own convenience and agenda, using a language that the paying crowd understood.[15] It is often pointed out by academic researchers that one of the prime reasons the Robin Hood stories have survived the test of time was the balladeers' ability to adapt them to any era and avoid ascribing them to any particular historical period.[16] In our post-industrial world where within a century the technology of electricity, cars, planes, televisions,

---

[15] Just as Shakespeare had clocks chiming in his play, *Julius Caesar.* and the Queen playing billiards in his *Anthony and Cleopatra*—both inventions from many centuries later! Similarly, later 17th and 18th century pictorial depictions of Robin Hood stories almost always depict the protagonists wearing contemporary clothing of that period.

[16] Never better exemplified than by a new Canadian eight-episode, one-hour, contemporary re-imagining of the Robin Hood legend, '*Robyn Hood*', set to premiere in 2023, that follows fearless heroine and rap artist, Robyn Loxley and her anti-authoritarian masked hip-hop band, 'The Hood', as they call out injustices and fight for freedom and equality in the city of New Nottingham.
https://www.imdb.com/title/tt20918756/?ref_=nm_flmg_act_1

computers, telecommunications, the internet and weaponry[17] (to name but a few) have changed life beyond all recognition from my parents, let alone my grandparents, it is hard for us to comprehend that for the medieval feudal peasants, life in 1100 was essentially still pretty much the same for their descendants 3 centuries later, in 1400—virtually nothing had changed in their essentially simple agrarian existence of the changing seasons.[18] Hence to suggest the backdrop for the ballads is the 13th century, without there being any reference to specific historical events, is just guesswork as they may well relate to any era during these centuries and indeed, earlier.

One of the few things that everyone seems agreed upon, is that the precious remaining fragments of ballads (thought by scholars to be a fraction of the original oral legend and of a far larger corpus of tales[19]) do not represent great literature, with the possible exception of Child Ballad 119: *Robin Hood and the Monk*, dating from c.1450, a brief tale but believed to be one of the oldest and the only one set in Sherwood Forest (also Nottingham, and now preserved in Cambridge University Library).

Then Robyn goes to Notyngham,
Hym selfe mornyng (*grieving*) allone,
And Litull John to mery Scherwode,
The pathes he knew ilkone (*every one*) (stanza 16)

---

[17] The unchanging bow and arrow, lance, spear and sword cover this whole period. Cannons were not used in England until the mid-14th century (Battle of Crécy, 1346), and the first 'gun' or 'arquebus' did not appear in England until the first half of the 15th century, with muskets and the one-handed flintlock/wheel-lock pistol not until the mid-16th century.

[18] The Black Death in the mid-14th century, in which perhaps up to 50% of the population died within a few years, gave the process of emancipation a huge push forward. 'Unfree tenancies' were already on the way out when the Peasants' Revolt demanded their abolition in 1389, with Richard II famously agreeing and then reneging on his word. ("Serfs you are, and serfs you shall remain.") They were extremely rare by 1500.

[19] Recent research using statistical methods by a team of European researchers, and published in the journal *Science* (17 Feb 2022, Vol 375, Issue 6582), suggests that more than 90% per cent of medieval manuscripts in English containing chivalric and heroic narratives have been lost—and huge numbers of other kinds of texts have also vanished across the ages.

The 'Child Ballads' is the colloquial name given to a group of 305 English and Scottish ballads collected in the 19th century by American scholar and folklorist, Francis James Child, who as an 'unbeliever' said that *'Robin Hood is absolutely a creation of the ballad-muse'*.[20] Almost 40 of these Ballads (nos.117–154) feature Robin Hood and are referenced by these numbers throughout this book. Douglas Grey called Ballad 119 *'an excellent piece of vivid narrative'*[21] and George Orwell once declared in an essay that it was the finest poem in the English language. In general though, literary opinion is that they are too long and confusing, lacking depth, subtlety and vocabulary and laced with unsophisticated and uninventive imagery. All of which would suggest that the original writers of the ballads, who translated the oral tales into poetry, were generally men of lower status and limited education.

The ballads' construction—built on a narrative around the four-line stanza (verse) that generally rhymes in lines 2 and 4, ABCB—also shows influence from the French *lai* and *carole*, which is hardly surprising as early medieval minstrels were linked to the great Norman aristocracies and travelled widely, including to the continent. It seems likely that these simple oral tales, told in taverns, marketplaces, fairs and around village greens and firesides, would have been in the vernacular and constantly updated with minor language changes—slowly, over the centuries—for the better understanding of the contemporary audience. In just the same way, we do not think it odd that when Errol Flynn, Sean Connery, Kevin Costner, Russell Crowe and Taron Egerton spoke in their respective recent cinematic renderings of *Robin Hood*, it was not in the 14th century English of Chaucer or an even earlier era, as that would have been virtually impossible for 20th/21st century ears to understand (though the source of Kevin Costner's accent remains an eternal mystery!). The question can legitimately be asked—do the details in the surviving ballads reflect back to social conditions in a hypothetical time associated with the original Robin Hood, or do they merely contain those memories prevalent at the time (unknown) of that ballad's later composition? It seems likely that the truth lies in a mixture of both possibilities. I am convinced of one thing for certain, if the ballads were produced today, they would carry the tag of *'This story is based on* (or *inspired*

---

[20] *The English and Scottish Popular Ballads,* Ed. Francis James Child, pub. Houghton Mifflin, Boston and New York, 1890, III, p.42.

[21] *'The Robin Hood Poems'. Poetica: An international journal of linguistic and literary studies,* 18, Douglas Gray, Tokyo (1984), pp. 1–39.

by) actual events. In certain cases, incidents, characters and timelines have been changed for dramatic purposes'. What cannot be disputed is the view of Robin Hood literary academic Professor Stephen Knight, who concluded that the retention of these ballad tales was a feat of public memory only matched by the stories of King Arthur.

At the very core of the legend is the first of Child's collection to feature our eponymous hero, Ballad 117: *A Gest of Robyn Hode*,[22] printed in several versions between 1492 and 1534 but most likely written down c.1450 in manuscript form (though no original manuscript version actually survives) and given a vague setting, perhaps sometime in the early 1300s.[23] The popularity of the Robin Hood tale is striking as these very early printers, such as Caxton or Wynkyn de Worde, only printed books (then a very expensive process) that they thought would have mass appeal rather than taking risks on obscure or seemingly strange, innovative texts; such that along with *The Gest,* ripping yarns like *Sir Gawain and the Green Knight,* the *'Fables of Aesop',* Malory's *Le Morte d'Arthur* and Chaucer's *Canterbury Tales* were all the 'best sellers' of their day.

The Gest itself, is an epic made up of 456 x 4-line 'stanzas' or verses (total 1824 lines) divided into 8 'fyttes' or chapters.[24] It draws together 5 separate tales with a single connecting narrative and seemingly moves in a roughly

---

[22] A *Gest,* meaning 'Deeds' (nothing to do with either a 'guest' or 'jest') was a romantic tale of exploits passed on by oral tradition over the centuries. These stories were performed to the public at a time when almost everyone was illiterate and the itinerant balladeer/storyteller was very popular, being one of the very few forms of entertainment, hence they continued for generations. These storytellers were also very likely illiterate and in the ballads themselves, no one ever reads or writes.

[23] It is generally accepted that the version by English printer Richard Pynson, from c.1495, must take pride of place as the earliest surviving printed edition. However, where Pynson acquired his copy-text remains a continuing and frustrating mystery, as no surviving handwritten manuscripts of the texts have ever been discovered. The most complete surviving printed edition is that attributed to the one-time assistant of William Caxton; namely, Wynkyn de Worde's *A Lytell Geste of Robyn Hode* (Cambridge University Library, Sel.5.18.), thought to date from 1506. The best surviving edition was printed by Jan Von Doesbroch in Antwerp around 1510, now in the National Library of Scotland, Edinburgh.

[24] Professor Knight (*Robin Hood: A Complete Study of the English Outlaw, 1994*) points out that while it sounds better to call the story '*The Gest*', the proper title is '*A Gest*', being one of many Robin Hood tales.

chronological order—the first of which, involving a knight, is the only other considered to be 'well-written'. Additionally, much of the topography of Barnsdale in South Yorkshire, as described in *The Gest,* is unerringly accurate. In the ballad we meet the intrepid leader of a band of between 20–140 (up to 200 in some tales) outlawed men—living a wild and free life in the woods and helping an impoverished knight, rather than plundering the rich in order to give to the poor, though their financial reserves seem significant. Most research into Robin Hood begins with a reading and study of *The Gest*. Indeed, I reference it throughout.

Equally important is the source document for Child: the *Percy Folio*. In 1765, Thomas Percy, Bishop of Dromore in County Down, Northern Ireland, used a salvaged manuscript to compile his *Reliques of Ancient Poetry*. Although the manuscript itself was put together in the 17th century, some of its material goes back well into the 12th century. Preserved in the *Folio* (and as Child Ballad versions) are 8 early ballads on Robin Hood, the most notable and oldest being the 'holy trinity' of: *Robin Hood and Guy of Gisborne (Child 118); Robin Hood's Death (Child 120)*; and *Robin Hood and the Curtal Friar (Child 123)*.

Tragically, the manuscript was not well looked after. Its previous owners, probably regarding the Middle English and border dialect as incomprehensible and worthless, allowed housemaids to use some pages to start fires! Once rescued, Percy had the manuscript bound, but the bookbinder inflicted additional damage in trimming the sheets, losing first or last lines on many pages. Furthermore, Percy treated it badly, writing notes upon it and tearing out some pages after binding. All this makes it very difficult to date them precisely (likely 15th century and before) or even to read them in totality. However, the 520 pages and fragments that do still exist (in the British Library) form a solid foundation to the legend. Together with *The Gest* and *Robin Hood and the Monk*, these 5 epics provide an almost coherent story.

And so a legend evolved. It is worth bearing in mind that these ballads are the only surviving medieval stories (or fragments of stories)—there may have been hundreds more, including those from much earlier or never recorded, lost to time and voice. It surely has to be accepted though, that some strands of the true history of our hero are somewhere embodied into these few surviving ballad tales. They are, after all, the 'primary source' and without them there is no legend. It seems unarguable that all the various literary streams converged over long periods of time into more unified narratives, undoubtedly embellished by the balladeers, but that still display some key elements of the various original source materials. However, as medievalist and author Jeffrey Singman astutely observed:

> '*Robin Hood scholarship has been hindered by too close a reliance on the surviving texts as a means of understanding the pre-modern Robin Hood tradition*'.[25]

Essentially, the ballads form the core of the legend but it is unwise to set too much store into some of the precise details provided, particularly those of later centuries. What we do know is that by the 15th century, there were developed, complex and sometimes conflicting narratives of a courteous, devout gentleman[26]; a cunning, cheeky joker; a master of disguise; a vicious killer (particularly in the older tales); a skilled archer ('*One of the best that ever bore a bow*',[27]) and swordsman; a nature lover; an audacious, fearless man among men; a leader commanding great loyalty from his band; and a freedom fighter, or at least an outlaw, who if not seeking justice for his people, anarchically led a crime wave from the forests of Barnsdale[28] and outwitted the local sheriffs.

> Robyn *stode* in Bernesdale (stood)
> And *lenyd hym to* a tree (leaned against)
> And *bi hym* stode Litell John (next to him)
> A gode yeoman was he.

---

[25] *Robin Hood: The Shaping of the Legend*, Jeffrey L. Singman, Greenwood Press, 1998. p.5

[26] Robin has a particular devotion to the Virgin Mary. His contemporary, whose love of Mary exceeds even Robin's devotion (via his prayers and Marian writings), was Anselm, Archbishop of Canterbury and the connection between them is worth noting for events unfolding in Part II.

[27] *Robin Hood and the Potter*, Child Ballad 121. 2nd stanza.

[28] Barnsdale, or Barnsdale Forest, is an area of South Yorkshire that now falls within the Whitley Ward of Wakefield Metropolitan Council. Although an ill-defined area, historically Barnsdale is part of the West Riding of Yorkshire midway between Doncaster and Pontefract centring on Barnsdale Bar and the villages of Skelbrooke and Hampole, even including Wentbridge and as far as Wakefield in some descriptions. It has always been much more lightly wooded than Sherwood Forest but was never a royal forest thus not subject to Forest Law.

And also dyd gode *Scathelock* (Scarlet)

And Much, the miller's son

(3rd /4th(part) stanzas of The Gest of Robin Hood: Child Ballad 117)

Many surviving tales of proven real outlaw heroes of the medieval era, such as Hereward the Wake, Fulk FitzWarin and Eustace the Monk (a French pirate), bear striking similarities to Robin[29], particularly to his skills of disguise as in *Robin Hood and the Potter* (Child Ballad 121). Virtually all experts agree that the later balladeers and writers ascribed the same tales to more than one man, which makes untangling the facts and true origins somewhat tricky. This was a common medieval practice, in much the same way as Chaucer, in his 14th century *Canterbury Tales,* borrowed portions, sometimes very large portions, from earlier stories. The one significant difference, though, between the tales of Robin and those of other outlaws is that the latter were all produced in either Latin or French. As mentioned earlier, there is no evidence that the stories of Robin Hood were ever produced or told in anything other than (Middle) English.

But is it likely that Robin is older still? There are firm foundations to the claim that the legend was already alive and well in the 13th century. Some historians and authors, like the late Cambridge Professor of Medieval History, James C. Holt—arguably the most renowned expert on Hood—prefer an early real Robin. Holt had a number of research-based arguments for believing that the legend originated in the early decades of the 13th century at the latest.[30] His central reasoning was the appearance of 'Robinhood' surnames (and their variations) around the end of the 13th century that gave rise to men, especially criminals, taking the name as a form of honorific, the label of a heroic outlaw whose crimes were justified in the eyes of the general populace. Holt believed that the real man had been lost in the mists of time itself, but that his genesis could be traced to the activities of genuine outlaws.

---

[29] Though one English chronicler of the time condemns Eustace as 'a shameful man and a wicked pirate' which is hardly the image given of Robin.

[30] *Robin Hood*, Professor J.C. Holt, Thames and Hudson, 1982. (2nd edition 1989, 3rd edition 2011). Although now 40 years old, this study by Professor Holt (1922–2014) was updated and revised in two further editions and is generally considered the current 'go to' academic study on the legend of Robin Hood, by a highly respected medieval historian from Cambridge University.

With documented people and historical events emerging from the mists of my research, I dare to go further back than Holt or anyone else, quite a bit further…but more on that later.

The wonderful thing about the evolution of the Robin Hood story is that it has come to mean so many things to so many people: the triumph of good over evil; a principled kind of thief; the romance of Robin and Marian; outlaws pursuing their beliefs in defiance of authority; the kinship of a merry band in the forest; and pagan connections to nature, to name but a few. One has a plethora of medieval imagery to choose from—English longbows, archery contests, murders, robberies, hunting, castles and kings, ballads, court rolls and faded manuscripts—resulting in a wonderfully heady mix that fuels the questions:

Is there a real life underlying all this? If so, who are our potential suspects?

Chapter 2
What's in a Name?

While the vivid spirit of Robin Hood lives on, hard historical evidence is more elusive. No surviving record of any real person from 'contemporary' history ever mentions his name, or suggests they had met. Just how far the stories reflect fact—in the essence of ballads, rhymes and possibly prose stories as well, now lost to the ages, chaos and destruction of the Reformation and the English Civil War—is unknown. Therefore, all any of us can do is examine what evidence we have, play detective and eliminate suspects.

Before we discuss the possibilities, it is important to understand the state of early medieval documentation. Almost the entire populace of England was illiterate, including the first Norman king, William the Conqueror and probably William II, 'Rufus' his son. What little information and news that there was, came most readily on Sundays via the local priest. Sermons containing commentary on current events, as well as spiritual guidance, were often the only regular, if biased, local source of news. The vast majority of folk rarely, if ever, travelled more than a few miles from their village, perhaps to sell surplus produce at the town market, attend a fair and maybe be dragged off to war in the borders of Wales, Scotland and Normandy. Hard agricultural labour, caring for livestock, putting food on the table, avoiding illness and injury and going to church constituted the bulk of everyday life for the average peasant.

There was no form of public transport (horses were the preserve of the wealthy) and roads, save the remnants of the old Roman network, were effectively non-existent; just cart tracks or old footpaths virtually impassable in wet weather. The spread of news, such as it was, came in spoken form, down the tavern and in market squares, from itinerant travellers like skilled tradesmen (tilers, thatchers, masons etc), pilgrims, messengers, storytellers, entertainers, returning soldiers and staff at the great castles overhearing conversations. In a nutshell, the medieval populace lived their lives locally and orally without access to writing materials nor skills in writing or reading, neither of which receive mention in the ballads.[31] As such, very few names were ever recorded. There were no birth, death or marriage certificates. Non-official documents—those not relating to royals/nobility, financial or legal matters—were sparse. Those we know of were usually scribed by the hand of monks and government clerks (who were generally clerics as well). In addition, texts—be they court or financial records—used phonetic spellings of names that varied wildly and written in Latin. As any of you who have studied Robin Hood or any historical character will already know, this leaves us with tens of possibilities. Both Robert and its derivative, Robin/Robyn, were not just common but entirely interchangeable. The surname Hood (Hod, Hode, Hude etc.) was also not unusual, especially in South Yorkshire. One man, if he warranted use of ink, could legitimately have a dozen 'names'.

Add to this, the backdrop. Early medieval England was a society racked from top to bottom by violence and repression. The masses spent their lives toiling on the land in feudal servitude, exploited by the nobility and church officials through tithes and taxed to the hilt by the Crown through the presiding sheriff of the area, a position that embodied all the most hated qualities in medieval Anglo-Norman society. It was a time fraught with frequent rebellions, poor peasants press-ganged into military service and crippling tax payments imposed by their all-powerful landlords to finance their lavish lifestyles and wars either for or against the king's armies. Even the simple gathering of dead branches for

---

[31] In the early centuries of medieval England there were, in essence, no books, newspapers (none until the 17th century!), magazines, manuals, postal service, signposts, adverts, etc. hence the need to read was not imperative and if you were one of the clever, important and wealthy people who did make use of the written word, like a king, sheriff, theologian or an intellectual, you would use a scribe/secretary (based in your 'Scriptorium'), who would write down what you dictated—and read letters on your behalf. Henry I was probably the first literate monarch and a key Royal Household official was 'Master of the Writing Office'. Paper, rather than the very expensive animal based parchment/vellum, did not become widely available until the 15th century. Reading, writing and books were almost exclusively the preserve of the great religious houses.

firewood required 'estovers'—a grant to villagers from the landlord[32]—and the simple picking of berries in the forest (if in an area under the jurisdiction of 'Forest Law') was highly illegal.[33] Many starved, yet lived next to royal forests literally teeming with food, where the penalty for poaching was torture and death. The newly introduced severe Norman Forest Law was extremely unpopular among all sections of society, but it achieved its purpose of retaining vast areas of semi-wild landscape over which the king and his court could hunt. The very wildness of this land made forests the perfect places for fugitives to hide out. This was a time when becoming an outlaw or choosing the life of a vagrant were the only chances of freedom from servile tyranny. In his famous 'Reliques of Ancient English Poetry' (1765), Thomas Percy declared that *'the severity of those tyrannical forest laws, that were introduced by our Norman kings, and the great temptation of breaking them by such as lived near the royal forests, must constantly have occasioned great numbers of outlaws'.*

Under these conditions, it becomes easy to see the appeal of an outlaw hero who not only embodies all those famed qualities detailed earlier and escapes such oppression, but also returns to protect the weak, to right wrongs, bring justice, is chivalric to women, Christian in principle but not 'of the church' and takes revenge on the invading tyrants over whom he always triumphs in the end. Only

---

[32] These estovers often came with the restriction *'By hook or by crook'*—permitting limited, dead branch and kindling collection using only a billhook (a curved cutting tool, like a small sickle/machete) and shepherd's crook. No saws allowed!

[33] **Forest Law** protected the 'vert and venison'. The 'venison' i.e. the noble animals of the chase—red, fallow and roe deer and wild boar—but also hare, wolf, fox, marten, pheasant and partridge; and the 'vert'—the greenery and habitat that sustained them. The concept of 'forest' within the jurisdiction known as Forest Law was just a technical term, as it meant any land that was covered by the Law. Indeed, the areas under royal protection also covered any large open spaces that would support game, with bracken, scrubland, marsh and heather covered heathland included, not just woods—even some urban areas were covered by the Law. In fact forests were multi-use areas encompassing a significant amount of tilled and pasture land, rather than woodland alone. Such law had been common practice in Normandy and France but was entirely unknown in Anglo-Saxon England, where Royal Forests had existed but gave fairly liberal rights and access to the general population. The importation of this new law, the Anglo-Saxon Chronicle makes clear when reporting the Conqueror's actions, was one of the most deplored and hated aspects of the Norman Conquest and hence its significance to the life and times of Robin Hood.

once in *The Gest* is Robin described as 'gentle', but seventeen times he is said to be 'courteous'. Importantly, it also becomes easy to see how a popular, established outlaw's name could be adopted by others, either in homage, as an act of rebellion, as a devious way to remain anonymous or simply in jest.

In fact, the mimicry/taking of Robin's name became so serious, that a law was passed in Scotland to curtail it. The *Regiam Majestatem* is the earliest surviving work giving a comprehensive digest of the Laws of Scotland. The precise date is not known but around 1320–25 as it was written as early as the reign of Robert the Bruce (1306–1329), although later than 1318 as a statute from that year was included in it. Within this document, we read under civic crimes:

If any provest, baillie, counsel, or communitie, chose
Robert Hude, litell John, Abbot of Unreason, Queens of May, the choosers
shall tyne their freedom for 5 years; and shall be punished at the king's will: and
the acceptor of such an office, shall be banished forth from the Realme.

And under 'percuniall' (monetary) crimes:

...all persons, quha? A landwort, or within a burgh, chooses Robert Hude
shall pay 10 pounds and shall be warded, induring the king's pleasure.

Five years in prison, royal punishment, huge fines of 10 pounds, banishment from Scotland…this was all serious stuff. With Robert Hood and Little John clearly established characters in Scotland at this time, not only does it show how widespread the names had become amongst common folk and how grievous the problem for the authorities, but also surely that in order to be so infamous, and bound into law, so far away from the original source—another kingdom—must have taken time and surely implies that these were 'real' people, not balladic inventions.

Who could have warranted such attention and held it for so long? 'Discoveries' of the real identity of Robin have been numerous and varying; some bold, some plausible, most now entirely dismissed. I cannot attempt any unhooding of my own before examining the main claims to our legend so far, most based on rational attempts, as accurate historical scholarship improved over the last 150 years, to account for Robin Hood based on the study of authentic documents.

Robyn/Robert Hood

In 1852, Joseph Hunter, a clergyman and 'assistant keeper of public records', published No.4 of his *Critical and Historical Tracts* entitled: *The Great Hero of the ancient Minstrelsy of England, Robin Hood*, in which he claimed to offer 'proof' of a real Robin Hood from the early 14th century. At the very end of the 6th Fytte of *The Gest* (Stanza 353, line 1412), a 'comely' king named Edward travels around the country. He meets Robin Hood and pardons him. Robin then goes to work in his court. 15 months later, he is broke, bored and returns to his outlaw life for 22 years. Although there are no more specifics on the king, Edward II was said to have been handsome and he did travel extensively throughout England. Details of the king's 'progress' in *The Gest* do match a journey made to Nottingham by Edward II between April and November of 1323, the year after the Lancastrian Revolt which had culminated in the royalist victory at the Battle of Boroughbridge.

Hunter discovered (in documents preserved in the *Exchequer Records* containing accounts of the expenses of the king's household) a 'Robyn Hood' serving as 'chamber valet' or 'porter' to the king's court between 24 March—22 November 1324, for 3 pence a day. In the last court entry, after periods of absence, Robyn was paid off with 5 shillings because '*he can no longer work*'; a status that is not explained but maybe implies decrepitude through age, maybe illness (given his absences) or perhaps some physical disability. However, this 'Robyn' seems to have been in the right place at the right time, and in the right sort of job for the Hood of the early ballad. Hunter went on to speculate that this Robyn Hood was the same as Robert Hood, a tenant of Wakefield, Yorkshire, who is mentioned in 1316–17. Wakefield[34] is only 10 miles from Barnsdale, the stamping ground of the legend identified in *The Gest*. What's more, Robert's wife was named Matilda; the true name of Maid Marian in 2 Elizabethan plays. A later writer also discovered that Robert, like Robin in some tales, might well have been the son of a forester named Adam (in the somewhat later 18th century Child Ballad 149: *Robin Hood's Birth, Breeding, Valour and Marriage*, Adam was a forester to Earl John de Warenne). Thus Hunter, and others after him, speculated that Robert Hood of Wakefield was one of the rebels involved in the 1322 uprising against King Edward II led by Thomas, Earl of Lancaster and that

---

[34] See Appendix 1, map pins 6 and 11

he was outlawed and later pardoned by the king who notably visited Nottingham in November 1323.

However, there is no tradition that has Robin being born in Wakefield, no connection to the Earl of Lancaster or the Battle of Boroughbridge or the great outlaw working as a menial servant to the King. There is also no proof that Robert and Robyn were the same person, that either of them were Lancastrian rebels or that they were outlaws. To make matters worse for the theory, a record turned up showing that this 'Robyn Hood' was in the king's service on 27 June 1323; i.e. **before** the king's trip to Nottingham, such that J.C. Holt writes:

'*This one reference destroys the coincidence of detail which made Hunter's argument seem so attractive*'. (Holt, 1989, p.50).[35]

If indeed Mr Hode could 'no longer work' due to old age, then the likelihood of him being able to have participated in the rebellion just a year or so earlier might be questioned but then again his retirement might have emanated from injury sustained in battle. In any event, he certainly does not seem in a fit state for a further 22 years of outlawry!

Overall, the key flaw in Hunter's project (and that of others) was his dedication to the ballads as holders of vital historic clues. Admittedly, such clues do exist but they are never specific enough, such that they could well refer to events hundreds of years apart. The other real issue not to be ignored, that as we shall see, applies to numerous other candidates, is the appearance of various 'Robin Hoods' in the record, well before the early 1300s. Indeed, even his appearance in Scottish law, as mentioned above, quite clearly shows Robin is a very well established and significant figure prior to any visit of Edward II to Nottingham in 1323…The overall conclusion probably must be that this lowly servant was simply called Robyn Hood and had no connection at all to our outlaw.

---

[35] Prof. Holt discovered, from an ultraviolet scan of the expenses of the king's household (*Journal de la Chambre*), this payment was made to a 'Robyn Hode'. The very idea that Robin Hood was a 'porter', carrying goods and bags for rich people is in itself equally unlikely and slightly depressing. In later medieval times this role became a royal 'groom porter', who was responsible for '*the Inspection of the King's Lodgings, and took care that they are provided with Tables, Chairs, Firing etc. Also to provide Cards, Dice etc. and decide disputes which arise in Gaming*'. This role does also not ring true of Robin who, I am sure, if he was ever employed by the King it would have been as a royal forester, keeper or huntsman—not a furniture remover or croupier!

Robert Dore/Hode

In 2012, there was a flurry of publicity surrounding a discovery in the National Archives at Kew, from the late 14th century, by 2 researchers, David Pilling and Rob Lynley. The duo had found a pardon given by King Richard II after the Peasants' Revolt in York, which stated:

'*Robert Dore of Wadsley, otherwise known as Robert Hode, given the king's pardon on 22 May 1382*'. (Roll of King's Pardons 4–5, 1382)

However, given the number of documents featuring a Robin Hood (or variation) in the same period (and earlier), it would seem just another instance of a rebel taking on the alias for themselves, a practice that had been going on for over 150 years. Of greater significance perhaps, is that the village of Wadsley is only a mile from that of the village of Loxley, near Sheffield, a location, which as we shall see, has very long-held folkloric connections to our hero—something local man Robert Dore was undoubtedly only all too aware of back in the 1300s.

Indeed, if he had originated from the 14th century, as the above and many others suggest, then where is he? State records and monastic chronicles by this later time frame were not insignificant. Yet despite his obvious fame and notoriety—the 'stuff of legend'—he seems not to have met (nor been the subject matter for) even one reputable scribe who records a meeting, writes about him in any letters, manuscripts or other accounts that could be directly attributed to the much talked-about outlaw. Why not? We have 2 possibilities: Either Robin never existed in reality; or he was from an earlier time, perhaps much earlier—and has never been found.

Roger Godberd

One of the most recent claims, by the late David Baldwin in *Robin Hood: The English Outlaw Unmasked*,[36] expands Brian Benison's poorly referenced earlier work,[37] and, more particularly, that of Professor Holt.[38] Baldwin proffers a timeframe first mooted by 15th century Scottish chronicler Walter Bower, who, under the year 1266, records, in Latin, Robin Hood as a '*famosus siccarius*'

---

[36] 2010, Amberley Publishing, ISBN: 8601410278908.

[37] *Robin Hood, The Real Story*, Brian Benison, Self-published, 2004.

[38] *Robin Hood*, J.C. Holt, Thames and Hudson, 1982.

(well-known cut-throat).[39] Baldwin thinks this to be the 13th century rebel Roger Godberd (c.1240–90)—a *'leader and captain of malefactors'* who fought on the side of Simon de Montfort in his notorious rebellion of the mid-1260s against Henry III, was outlawed after the Battle of Evesham in 1265 and subsequently led a renegade campaign. All this nearly 60 years prior to Hunter's 'groom' candidate.

Godberd is a seductive candidate for a number of reasons and hence has garnered a solid core of recent support. He had once been in the garrison of Nottingham Castle but after being outlawed looks to have retreated to Sherwood Forest with a group of defectors from around 1265 until his capture in 1272 (approximately 7 years, not the 22 recorded in *The Gest*). He was a prisoner in Nottingham Castle but escaped, helped, along with his outlaw band, by a sympathetic knight Sir Richard Foliot (often likened to Sir Richard at the Lee from *The Gest*).

However, Godberd's life of constant criminal activity, robberies and indiscriminate killings is at variance with Robin Hood's principle of not bothering 'good fellows', and fails to match the description in the lines 7–8 of *The Gest*, *'so courteous an outlaw as he was, 'one was otherwise never found'*— his courtesy being referenced a further sixteen times in *The Gest*. Essentially, his criminal lifestyle seems unlikely to have accrued him the great love, sympathy and adoration of the masses that Robin warranted, leading to his legendary status. Furthermore, there is no mention of Godberd ever being an archer, let alone a great one; he was involved in a major rebellion against the crown—far beyond the action of a modest highwayman cum outlaw with seemingly no interest in national politics. All records of Godberd centre on Leicestershire, Wiltshire and Nottinghamshire and are disconnected from Barnsdale and Yorkshire, the clear locale in the early ballads. He is also a good friend of Reginald de Grey, better known as the Sheriff of Nottingham—an unlikely pairing given the legend! Records indicate that they are on good terms, and contrary to the folk tales, the locals respect the sheriff. In truth, there is absolutely nothing in the surviving ballads to suggest that Robin had the slightest concern with the political issues of the Barons' Wars (or any wars), as straightforward highway robbery, gentlemanly or otherwise, was really his thing—snaffling people off the road,

---

[39] *Scotichronicon.* Walter Bower, 1440–1447, 16 vols. This chronicle was written is Latin, and the word used for 'murderer, or cutthroat' was *sicarius*. [Hence the Spanish and Italian *sicario*, meaning 'hitman'.]

saying mass, giving them a slap-up meal, then making them pay thousands of pounds for the privilege. In fact, he truly takes no position with regard to the feudal faction fights which made up so much of medieval politics. So, there is no reference to Godberd being an archer and also not so good for his claim, is that nowhere is there found any reference to him ever taking the name of 'Robin Hood' or being described as such by the courts or officialdom, which if there had been, would clearly make Baldwin's claim for him somewhat stronger, but which eventually just withers on the vine.[40]

As further evidenced by the fact that after Godberd's trial, he spent 3 years in London gaols and was pardoned by the new king, Edward I, under a general amnesty and lived out his life peaceably—which doesn't fit with the ballad's treacherous abbess and 'Red Roger' conspiring in his famously grisly demise of being bled to death in a priory. Baldwin also claimed, without evidence, that in St Nicholas' churchyard, Loxley, Warwickshire, an unmarked stone grave slab carved with a sword, belongs to Roger Godberd/Robin Hood. Perhaps most damning of all though, to this and other later candidates, is the entirely separate action of a court clerk in Berkshire in 1262, 3 years before the exploits of Godberd (see below shortly), strongly indicating that Robin Hood was already a well-known legend with recorded use of the name as early as 1225 making Godberd about 70+ years old at the time of his antics and trial, which seems very unlikely indeed.

---

[40] Another candidate who warranted a whole book (Sean McGlynn, *Robin Hood, a True Legend*, Sharpe Books, 2018) **but was never called 'Robin Hood'** was William of Cassingham (or Willikin of the Weald, died 1257) a country squire of Cassingham (now Kensham) in Kent. William supported King John against the French Prince Louis, when he invaded England in support of the barons in the First Barons War from mid-1216 to mid-1217. He raised a rabble army of up to 1000 archers and inflicted much damage on the French, particularly in an ambush at Lewes in May 1217. William operated in Kent and Sussex not Barnsdale, fought for only sixteen months—not the twenty or more years of the legend, waged military war not thieving along the highway, did not use disguises or battle with the Sheriff or church officials—overall, apart from having a bow, his story bears little or no resemblance to the ballads and lifetime of the legendary outlaw.—and why would the composition of the ballads be in a northern dialect?

William 'Robehod' Le Fevre

While not a true Robin Hood contender, a rather interesting recorded criminal was uncovered in 1984 by David Crook, the former assistant record keeper at the Public Record Office (now National Archives). A man named William, son of Robert Le Fevre (of whom we know nothing more), was indicted at Reading court for larceny in 1261. He turned up again in the King's Remembrancer's Memoranda Roll for Berkshire the following year, indicted with 2 other men and 2 women for forming a criminal gang of armed robbers. Nothing too interesting in that yet. But what is curious is that this William le Fevre now has the surname *Robehod* entered in the subsequent record. Exactly why this change was made by the court clerk is unclear, but firstly it suggests that the name is somehow appropriate to the condition of a fugitive and secondly, that it was adopted in a place nowhere near to Robin's Barnsdale in Yorkshire or Sherwood in Nottinghamshire, would both indicate that the legend was already going strong by the mid-13th century and so well-known as far south as Berkshire by 1262 that court officials seem happy to use it as a recognisable pseudonym.

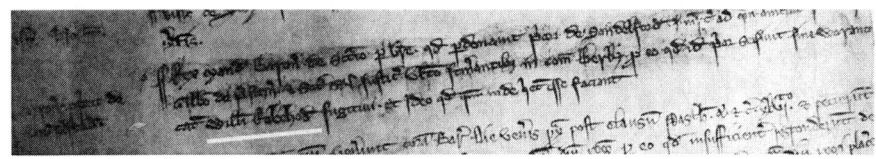

2. The name change 'Willi Robehod', underlined in white
Extract of the Memoranda Roll, Easter Communia 45–46, Henry III, Easter
1262, from The National Archives document E/159/36
Reprint permission under the Open Govt. Licence

Robert FitzOoth

Another name that floats about is that of Robert FitzOoth. FitzOoth was a Norman claimant to the Earldom of Huntingdon who was supposedly born c.1160 and died in 1247, making him a contemporary of King John and King Richard (as well as perhaps one of the oldest men to die in medieval England!). Some reference works—notably the 18th century antiquary Joseph Ritson's *Robin Hood: A Collection of all the Ancient Poems, Songs, and Ballads, now extant relative to that celebrated English Outlaw, to which are prefixed*

Historical Anecdotes of his Life—actually cite these dates for Robin Hood. However, it is now generally accepted that Ritson relied on, or gave weight to, a number of unreliable sources. Sceptics also point out that contemporary records contain no mention of a rebellious nobleman named Robert FitzOoth, let alone a Robin Hood. Also, the legend's popularity with people at the lower end of the social spectrum who had little interest in nobility seems incongruous. Above all, the name first appeared in somewhat eccentric English antiquarian Dr William Stukeley's *Paleographica Britannica* in 1746, which was an entirely spurious pedigree of people, places and titles. It is now considered a totally fake construction that hoodwinked many for a while with its inventive fabrications (reinforcing the King Richard/Prince John era), but is now readily dismissed.

Robert de Kyme

Following on from this, a certain Jim Lees from Nottingham, who died in 2001, was regarded as an authority on the legend and known locally as 'Mr Robin Hood'. He used the Stukeley pedigree in his book *The Quest for Robin Hood* (Temple Press, 1987) in which he tried to prove Robin Hood was in fact a Robert de Kyme, born around 1205 at Bilborough, a knight outlawed in 1226 and again in 1265, after the Battle of Evesham and linked to the FitzOoth family and the Earls of Huntingdon. The invented nature of these pedigrees, disparaged by Holt and others, make the whole basis for such claims not just weak but fanciful. Certainly the idea of a 13th century knight having outstanding archery skills (of which we hear nothing) is less than likely and does not seem to come close to connecting to our elusive yeoman hero.

Robert Hood

This is not the first *recorded* Hood who is a criminal (though not a proven outlaw), as sometime between 1213 and 1216 a Robert Hood, servant of Alexander Neckam, the Abbot of Cirencester, killed Ralph of Cirencester in the abbot's garden (some 200 miles south of Barnsdale, in Gloucestershire). At this time, during King John's reign, the country was awash with outlaw gangs, thieves and criminals and the murder rate soared, so this name on a legal record could easily be another 'name assumption'. However, most researchers and historians suspect that it was simply his actual name and not an epithet.

Rob Hod/Rob Hood/Hobbehod

Now we get to one of the most popular contenders giving credence to an early date. In the mid-1930s, an entry was famously discovered in the 1226 records of the York Assizes by Professor L.V.D. Owen, and in 1936, in his article *Robin Hood in the Light of Research*,[41] a certain 'Rob Hod' makes his first appearance, as a debtor. The Justice 'Pipe Rolls'[42] for 1225 (Michaelmas) include the entry:

3. *'Idem vicecomes debet xxxij. s. et. vj. d. de catallis Rob Hod fug'.*
[The sheriff is owed 32 shillings and sixpence[43] of the chattels of
Rob Hod, fugitive]
From The National Archives, document E372/70

David Crook (the former National Archives man), informs us that the name appears in 9 successive Pipe Rolls from 1226 to 1234:

Six times as Rob Hod (1226/27 and 1230–1234);

Twice (in 1227 and 1228) as Hobbehod. ('Hob/Hobbe' is another medieval English variant of Robert/Robin); and once (in 1229/30) as Rob Hood.

In 1227, 'St Peter' is inserted in the margin of the roll next to his name, and again in 1234, when the name is also preceded by a cross (this was an **X**, not a religious †). By the following year, it had been removed from the roll. The cross

---

[41] *The Times, Trade and Engineering Supplement*, xxxviii, no 864 (new series), February 1936, p. xxix

[42] The majority of Pipe Rolls were essentially accounting documents—records of yearly audits, accounts and payments presented to the Treasury by sheriffs and other royal officials. Their owed their name to the shape they took, as the various sheets were affixed to each other and then rolled tightly, resembling a pipe, for storage.

[43] Financial comparisons are difficult, but a 12th century archer who carried the King's bow, a *Constitutio Domus Regis*, received 5d a day, the same as the staff position of 'huntsman'. Considering that inflation was practically zero, 32s 6d might represent some two to three months' salary in 1225; an amount similar to numerous others listed on the same roll.

could suggest that the debt had been written off, or finally paid, although this could also be a signal that a summons was put in place. J. C. Holt mentions the marginal note in his book, and declares that this debt was due from the Liberty of St Peter's York, and that '*Hobbehod or Rob Hod must therefore have been a tenant of the archbishopric*'.(p.54) Although it is also worth noting that none of the lands of the Archbishop of York were in the Wakefield, Barnsdale or Hallamshire areas of South Yorkshire most often associated with our elusive hero.

Some entries in the rolls actually have 'utlagii' (outlaw) instead of 'fugitivi' written after the name. We do not know for sure what his crimes were as we do not have a surviving plea roll that may have given details of the charges against him, but we can assume that it was connected to the unpaid debts. In essence, if a debtor failed to turn up to court 5 consecutive times, then his assets, or 'chattels', could be seized by the authorities and sold to help settle the debt, along with him being declared 'outlawed'.

Although never mentioned in the ballads, unpaid 'debt' is sometimes mooted as the origins of Robin's outlaw life. The amount detailed—32s 6d—was similar to others noted in the same roll against other felons, so clearly it was not an unusual amount and, with a modern value of a few thousand pounds, hardly a king's ransom. In fact, document experts have now interpreted the margin notes as an indication that the debt was eventually paid off which, if true, would make this singular record a somewhat anticlimactic end to someone supposed to be the champion of outlaws putting 2 fingers up to authority for twenty-two years!

I think that this man gets a number of votes purely because he is the earliest reference to a Hood outlaw and that he is mentioned in more than one document. In fact, those 9 repeat entries for one debtor bearing a plausible name are the only original record to date establishing a Rob Hood who is known to have fled jurisdiction. Prior to this date, there is virtually no written record to look at, so it is hardly surprising that many get excited about our 1225 suspect.

Holt initially believed that the strong choice for the real Robin Hood '*lies between Robert Hod, the Yorkshire outlaw of 1225, and some member of the Hood family of Wakefield and its neighbourhood*'. However in the postscript of his second edition (1988) he reassessed the possible 'biography': Robin active in the 1190s, an outlaw in 1225, allegedly dead in 1247 (an epitaph left/made up? By Robert Gale, Dean of York, in 1702)—a timeframe which retrospectively conveniently matches the 22 years spent in the 'greenwood' in *The Gest*. Holt concluded by admitting that 'believing' that this Robin Hood was the historical outlaw required much faith, and observed: '...*in a tendentious fashion, it can all be made to work...yet there are good reasons for not relying on such a neat and easy solution'*. He in fact concluded by saying '*either the Hoods of Wakefield gave Robin to the world, or they absorbed the tale of the outlaw into their family traditions, or their neighbours and descendants came to associate the 2. Of these the last is the most likely*'[44]

Opinions vary, but ultimately most commentators now agree that the debtor cannot be attached to Robin Hood of the legend. An affordable sum owed for some rent to the church landlord is hardly legendary action stuff compared to lore details of loaning a knight and robbing a bishop of hundreds of thousands of pounds and killing the sheriff and his men. It is just one man and one rather common debt, possibly it was his real name or, more likely, he was using an already popular sobriquet. Think back (or rather slightly forwards) to the criminal William le Fevre, whose name was changed to Robehod in 1262.

As an aside, the fashion of name-dropping Robin seems to have persisted for centuries, including in the legal sphere, as is clear from a record some 200 years later, in Tutbury, Staffordshire, 1439. According to an official account, a criminal called Piers Venables, of nearby Aston: '...*gathered and assembled unto hym many misdoers beynge of his clothinge and, in manere of insurrection, wente into the wodes in that contre,* **like as it hadde be Robyn Hode and his meyne**'.—a phraseology that certainly seems to imply real persons are being referenced. It is a tag frequently still used by the media today to imply justifiable crime or tax.

Robert Wetherby

Following on from this, it is suggested by some, particularly David Crook, that Rob Hod was actually Robert Wetherby, 'an outlaw and evildoer' hunted by the Sheriff of Yorkshire and hanged in 1225. Crook's theory is that the tale of the hunting down of Robert Hod/Robert of Wetherby rapidly spread, carried up and down the Great North Road, and within a generation Robe Hod and Robhod had become colloquial names for an outlaw. This, though, would seem unlikely

---

[44] *Robin Hood*, J. C. Holt, Thames and Hudson, 1989, p.51.

and indeed ghostly, given Hod's appearance in later censuses up to 9 years after Wetherby's hanging took place…

Robynhood, Robynhod, Robert Hode and All the Rest

The name evolved just as the legend did. The rather odd conjoined surname 'Robynhood' was to be found from quite a widespread area of south-east England, Sussex in particular, although this is thought to be more to do with judicial records from this era and area both surviving and being studied in the last few years. One particular record has gathered interest—the East Sussex Tax Roll for 1296—showing a man called Gilbert Robynhood in the village of Fletching, happily paying his taxes and seemingly living a non-criminal life. There is a logical explanation for this rather distant early Sussex connection. Two great baronial Norman families of de Warenne (father d.1088 and son c.1070–1138, both called William, 1st and 2nd Earls of Surrey) and de Mortain both held vast swathes of territory dead centre in the bullseye of Robin Hood country. The Warennes held the Manor of Conisbrough (plus many more manors in this area between Sheffield and Doncaster) and at the same time, Robert, Count of Mortain (c.1031-c.1095), half-brother of William the Conqueror, also held extensive lands and manors throughout Barnsdale. More significantly though, they both also held even larger estates in Sussex in the south of England; the Warennes had the vast area known as the 'Rape of Lewes', near to where the village of Fletching lies and de Mortain had the adjacent and equally large, 'Rape of Pevensey', in which Fletching actually lies.[45]

Fletching is mentioned in *Domesday Book* (1086)—the comprehensive survey of England and parts of Wales (listing land ownership both at the time of the Conquest in 1066 and in 1085) as ordered by William the Conqueror. As the name implies, Fletching was significantly associated with the production of bows, and more particularly arrows (a 'fletcher' being an arrow-maker). One can well understand why, 2 centuries later, Fletching man Gilbert may have adopted this Robynhood surname, living most likely in the service of either de Warenne or de Mortain, perhaps an arrow-maker himself, and wishing to be associated with the heroic English archer from their area of Yorkshire. It goes a long way to explain how the stories became legend, migrating south in the later decades of

---

[45] 'Rapes' were six administrative subdivisions of Sussex, each with a castle and lord, all considered to be of strategic importance on the south coast.

the 11th century and thereafter, through the voices of the minstrels and retainers attached to those noble households who may have had first-hand experience of the 'activities' of Robin Hood. These minstrels were the pop singers of their day and there is later evidence that, just like modern stars, they also 'went on tour'.

Gilbert was not alone, as further 13th century examples of the Robynhood surname have now been unearthed, all dated between 1261 and 1296 (a high proportion of whom were suspected or outlawed criminals), as well as 14th century examples from Sussex in 1332 and 1381. Subsequently, even more records of the name have been brought to light: 2 in Huntingdonshire; 2 from Hampshire; one each from the counties of Suffolk, Essex and Berkshire; and a lady, Katherine Robynhod, from London, 1325. (Cawthorne[46], p.50; Holt, pp.52 and 187).

If Gilbert and others were already assuming Robin's name in the south of England as early as the second half of the 13th century, and the Berkshire court clerk was changing 'Le Fevre' to 'Robehod' in 1262, then the exploits of our hero were obviously well-established a long time prior to the reign of Edward II.

As the years roll by, from time to time the discovery of some documentary fragment pertaining to a 'Hood', emerges. Most recently, in 2009, Dr Julian Luxford, professor of Art History at the University of St Andrew's, was researching a completely different topic and he stumbled across a marginal (foot)note in a copy of the *Polychronicon*, a chronicle of English and world history written in the 1340s by Ralph Higdon, a monk of St Werburgh, in Chester. This particular copy was owned by Eton College and is thought to date from around 1420. The reference he found to our legendary figure had been added as a Latin inscription by an unknown monk from around 1460, believed to have been from Witham Priory in Somerset.

The notation is on a page that places Robin Hood in Edward I's reign, thus supporting the belief that his legend is of late 13th century origin as with the tale of Robert Godberd discussed earlier. A translation of the short inscription, which contains only twenty-three words in Latin, reads:

'Around this time, according to popular opinion, a certain outlaw named Robin Hood, with his accomplices, infested Sherwood and other law-abiding areas of England with continuous robberies'.

---

[46] *Robin Hood, the True History Behind the Legend,* Nigel Cawthorne, Constable and Robinson, 2010.

A further recent translation suggests the Latin word for 'region' does not mean 'regions' or 'areas' here, but *'royalty'* and translates the last line as *'...stole constantly from the faithful (servants) of the king of England at Sherwood...'*. One feels such targeted theft from presumably the sheriff, his reeves and tax collectors, does put him one step up from being just a 'rapacious cut-throat'!

However, nobody knows what the monk's source was for his comment, but the fact that he used the phrase *'according to popular opinion'* has led historians to conclude that it may have been nothing more than simple word of mouth 'hearsay' and oral history without any factual basis. The original 14th century *Chronichron* itself makes no reference to Robin Hood and the footnote was, of course, written some 120 years later, and 200 years after the date suggested for Robin Hood in the reign of Edward I. The monk's notation was added not long before *The Gest* went into print, at a time when Robin Hood was already a popular figure of legend from the May Games and can thus hardly be considered a contemporary record. Although of interest, as an English (rather than Scottish) 15th century reference to a real, rather than purely fictional Robin Hood, it does not really convince anyone with regard to defining Robin's era and even Dr Luxford himself is unconvinced this entry refers to the original Robin.

Indeed, this continual use of the outlaw alias through many centuries casts doubt on every mention of the name. As Professor Holt succinctly concluded:

'The search for Robin Hood ends in obscurity created by its own fame. Real people move in the shadows, their crimes revealed before the courts, **but by borrowing his reputation they dissolved his identity'.** And his overall conclusion of the many candidates put forward is *'...there is a quiversful of possible Robin Hoods. Even the likeliest is little better than a shot in the gloaming'.* He did at least concede that to discover who he might have been *'...is inseparable from who he was thought to have been: any search for a man involves an analysis of the legend'.*

To have a chance at finding our archer in the greenwood, we need to walk further and deeper into the past and the legend...while remembering the immortal words of Sherlock Holmes, the famous fictional detective.

'The world is full of obvious things which nobody by any chance ever observes' (Conan Doyle, A., *The Hound of the Baskervilles*, Chapter 3).

Chapter 3
An Earlier Man

"There is good argument that the earlier the Hood, the more likely he is to be the right man."
~ **Nick Rennison**[47]

The true origins of Robin may only be found in voices now lost. Does this mean our search must end here, with the last scraps of parchment bearing his name? Paper does not create life, it merely records it. It is just as likely there were real Hoods (or real outlaws adopting the name Hood) living pre-1225, in a time with no documents to specifically identify them. This, then, is surely an opportunity for us to think laterally, to focus elsewhere.

Apart from minstrel renderings, written later in the form of a few key ballads, early sources frequently alluded to the 'rimes', 'tales' or 'romances' of Robin Hood. This strongly suggests a corpus far larger, and older, than what is still in existence. However, where we find legends, we also find medieval moralists who disapproved of the ribaudiers, jesters, histriones and jongleurs,[48] entertaining gentry and the lower classes alike, at festivals, fairs and markets, with their profane stories, rhymes, dissolute innuendo, disrespectful jokes and insistent cries (for money): *'for largesse, for largesse!'*. Many were little better than vagabonds and beggars, leading good Christians and law-abiding subjects astray.

One reason for the lack, or loss, of words on the legend, apart from deterioration and destruction over time, may well be the fact that the Robin Hood stories were picked out by the authorities for special condemnation. There is a

---

[47] *Robin Hood, Myth, History and Culture*, Nick Rennison, Oldcastle Books, 2012.
[48] Jongleurs were itinerant performers who did not usually compose original stories. They often performed the minstrel's songs/poems: singing, playing instruments, dancing, recitation and even juggling and acrobatics.

long string of complaints, primarily by the church, from the time of Langland's *Piers Ploughman* through to the Reformation and beyond. Fears were that they distracted men—primarily young, unmarried, unpropertied men—from their devotions and appealed to the crude populace, the 'great unwashed' or '*stolidum vulgus*' to use the Latin phrase of 15th century historian, Walter Bower. Such behaviour seems to be closely linked to sexual shenanigans and excessive consumption of alcohol on public high days and holidays. Sloth's familiarity with minstrel tales of Robin Hood, yet lack of knowledge of things spiritual, reflects the concern of the church for the souls of people who could readily recite popular and ribald poems by heart but not psalms and prayers.

However, what ballads we do have, along with the Pipe Rolls from 1225 in the reign of Henry III, nearly a century before the most likely *Gest* king, Edward II, indicate that the legend dates back earlier still. What I am absolutely certain of, is the enormous chasm of time between the origins of Robin and today. Words based on legends that finally ended up in 14th century poems, plays and 15th century printed epics, alongside aliases recorded in the 13th century, could simply not have happened overnight.

Everyone has their favourite theory as to the identity of Robin Hood, including, of course, that he never actually existed. Within the writings at our disposal, the lack of known historical characters, or mentions of a specific date or even a time period, is ammunition used by those who believe that the legend was simply the *invention* of balladeers and storytellers. But what about *re-invention*?

The line between fact and fiction is dimly drawn in early folk literature but most—be they of Troy, King Arthur or Beowulf—seem to have origins, however faint and elusive, in actual history. Indeed, the Robin I favour is related to, and associated with, real, proven characters living a century before many early placements, and over 2 centuries before some—in fact over 900 years ago.

The challenge, as with any early historical investigation, is in establishing the most likely version of the truth and, more subversively, acknowledging that there is often real history behind fiction and perhaps, equally, that there are falsehoods in official records.

Truth in Fiction

Of what remains, most scholars now insist that the medieval ballads cannot be relied on for historical facts. However, there are a few references and clues evolved from real events, places and people, some of which may settle outside of the most popular theories but are, nonetheless, valid.

The Gest of Robin Hood (Child Ballad 117) is arguably the most renowned ballad of all. It pays to remind ourselves that this late medieval reworking of oral tales was committed to paper up to 300 years after the Prince John/King Richard timeframe and 400 years after 'my' Robin existed. Incidentally, this is much the same time span as that between the life of Jesus of Nazareth (c.5BC-33AD) and the writing of the *Codex Sinaiticus* (c.350AD) which contains the oldest complete copy of the New Testament…and approximately 2 billion Christians worldwide believe in that being about real people!

Those who have studied the ballads at length agree that elements of error, let alone artistic licence, inevitably crept into the stories over time. The simple truth is that the poetic interpretation of gleemen, minstrels and storytellers, who themselves were not educated men, meant versions of the word-of-mouth events evolved without the greatest concern for historical accuracy. Plot lines, actions and incidents are endlessly repeated, mixed and varied, and probably real stories of later outlaws were retrospectively attributed to Robin Hood.

In the main tales, the 'Merry Men' go into Nottingham in disguise and fool the sheriff, there are archery competitions, hair-raising rescues and pitched battles between Robin's and the sheriff's men. In the 8 most well-known stories, a sheriff dies 3 times (one hanged, one beheaded by Robin and one shot by Little John), a monk is robbed twice and the king intervenes a couple of times. There were probably many more storylines and variations in circulation than have survived in writing.

This highlights my point about the flexible and thus troublesome nature of any study of early history. What can be dismissed as fantasy or falsehood, what can be accepted as truth, if anything, and what can be cherry-picked or bent to suit a writer's theories or findings? Most is open to interpretation by us, just as it was by the balladeers.

A good example of this is the king contemporary to Robin's time. In *The Gest*, as we know, he is described as 'comely' and 'Edward'[49]. However, historians Hilton Kelliher and Stephen Knight found different kings in their studies of *The Forresters Manuscript*[50] which was discovered in 1993 and contained 21 ballads dated about 1670.[51] In those were 3 pieces naming the king as 'Richard' and at least 2 pointing to a 'Henry'. What seems apparent from this is that balladeers were quite happy to update details of the tales to keep them topical, including the name of the reigning monarch such that who is to say the King Edward mentioned was not already an update of an earlier monarch. It is, though, the latter of these names that weaves into my version. Not, as Robert Waltz recently surmised: *'presumably Henry II, although Henry III is not an unreasonable possibility'*[52]—but Henry I. He was a monarch whose many attributes—in terms of personality, physicality and mentality—could be described as 'comely', certainly to the ladies as he fathered around 24 illegitimate children with many aristocratic beauties of the day—several of them married! He was preceded by his brother William Rufus, preceded again by their father, William the Conqueror. Robin, I believe, would have lived through the reign of all 3 of these first Norman monarchs. More on that later.

Whichever king one believes reigned at his time, it was unlikely that Robin intended to have any dealings with him. He led an outlaw band of 'Merry Men' in the wild almost ungovernable north of England, ranging in number from 20–200; hardly an army worthy of upsetting the Crown. Unlike the Northumbrian Earl rebellions of the late 1060s, and the activities of other recorded rebels— from Hereward the Wake and Eadric 'the Wild' in the 11th century, to Fulk FitzWarin, Eustace Monk, William Wallace and Simon de Montfort in the 12th

---

[49] It is now thought by some scholars that the 'Comely King Edward' of *The Gest* was a line stolen by the writer from a political poem (*poem IV*) written about 1339 by Lawrence Minor during the invasion of France by Edward III, whose opening line is *'Edward oure cumly king'*.

[50] *Robin Hood: The Forresters Manuscript: British Library Additional MS 71158*, Hilton Kelliher and Stephen Knight, D.S. Brewer, 1998.

[51] The 38 surviving traditional ballads relating to Robin Hood cover a wide timeframe. The later 17th century ones borrow much from the earlier, and move away from any medieval reality. The popularity of these and other 'outlaw ballads' was seen as legitimising peasant protest.

[52] *The Gest of Robyn Hode: A Critical and Textual Commentary*, Robert Waltz, 2013.

and 13th centuries—there is nothing in the legend or the original ballads to infer that Robin and his men were resistance fighters, as some suggest.[53] They were simply outlaws and highwaymen, not part of rebel armies, but perhaps seeking freedom for themselves, escape from a legal system that lacked moral authority and certainly being a wretched thorn in the side of the royal administration, nobles and corrupt church officials of Barnsdale, Sherwood and their environs. You are never going to perform a *coup d'état* with 150 men, against a king who can raise an army of 10,000+, no matter how good an archer, courteous and charismatic you are!

The idea that a king, with many pressing priorities (like wars with France, the Welsh, the Scots, plus troublesome popes, barons and archbishops etc., let alone the hunting and feasting), would have time to intervene personally in the forest shenanigans of maybe 150 Yorkshiremen, requires more than a willing suspension of disbelief. In any event, sheriffs, and their private armed retinues, were delegated precisely such tasks. If the king of England really was donning disguises and bobbing in and out of Barnsdale Forest to find an outlaw, surely the monastic scribes, clerks and historical chroniclers of the day would have put quill to parchment to record these dramatic events…but not a word was written, as far as we know. What is possible, indeed likely, is that it was indeed the king's representative or 'agent', i.e. the sheriff or his subordinate—the local castle governor/constable/castellan/deputy sheriff, who was doing the bobbing and that the storytellers and balladeers spiced the facts up with 'royalty'[54] for their audience.

There is no doubt, as entertainment pieces, rather than history lessons, the ballads were embellished and amended through time. A literary comparison can be made with the fictional detective, Sherlock Holmes. Many identifiably iconic features of the man and stories—his deerstalker hat, the Aberdeen cape, his pipe and the persistent London fog—do not feature in any of the original Conan Doyle texts, but were the inventions of early illustrator, Sydney Paget and

---

[53] For example, the advocates of Roger Godberd who fought against Henry III in 1265, and also supporters of the Robyn Hood character who maybe rebelled against Edward II in 1322.

[54] Sean Connery appearing in an uncredited cameo as King Richard I 'the Lionheart' to marry Robin and Marian in the final scene of the film 'Robin Hood, Prince of Thieves' (1991) is a classic modern example of this practice. He was paid $250,000 to utter a few lines of script and one day's work!

enthusiastically adopted by the later film-makers. The pipe's transition to a curved meerschaum and the renowned phrase, '*Elementary, my dear Watson*' are both attributable to American actor William Gillette, who portrayed Holmes in early 20th century theatrical productions. Alan Werner, Curator of the Museum of London and its recent Sherlock exhibition in 2014, mused:

"*Ever since he* [Sherlock] *first appeared, there's been a more or less non-stop drip of re-invention*s."

He could just as well have been speaking about Robin Hood.

We can also draw an analogy with a real-life Spanish hero. In his short book, *The Gest of Robyn Hode: A Critical and Textual Commentary* (2013), Robert Waltz makes a valid and critical comparison between *The Gest* and *El Poema del Cid* [The Poem of the Cid]. In a similar construction, it tells of Castilian hero Rodrigo Díaz de Vivar, better known as El Cid, and takes place during the *Reconquista*, or Christian Reconquest of Spain from the Islamic Moors. Born around 1043, El Cid died in 1099, very similar to the dates I am to propose for Robin. El Cid was also a robber, an outlaw, a minor noble; he sought reconciliation, helped the people, was loyal to his companions and there is no mention of a romance. He did perhaps lack the courteous nature and chivalric principles of Robin. The key difference between them is that Robin restricted himself to robberies from the forests of Barnsdale and Sherwood, whereas El Cid was a significant commander and military leader under the sovereign of Castile and other dynasties, the self-styled 'Prince of Valencia', and hence was much more likely to be (and indeed was) recorded officially as well as poetically, in the manner of Hereward the Wake. However, like *The Gest*, the Spanish poem sanitises Cid (in reality a duplicitous mercenary who worked for both sides and whoever paid the most), making him the greatest national hero, immortalised in song, folk tales, film, plays and even video games. Sound familiar to our, possibly contemporary, legend?

Most authors on the subject, myself included, agree that by the time Robin arrives in the 15th century, he is a composite character forged from several outlaws, and their tales, over the centuries. In the present day, he is more complex still. Phillips and Keatman[55] propose that the modern version is an amalgam of at least 3 different people, whom they describe as:

---

[55] *Robin Hood: The Man behind the Myth*, Graham Phillips and Martin Keatman, 1995, Michael O'Mara.

1) the Robin Hood of *The Gest* and other early ballads
2) the Renaissance Robin Hood
3) an earlier hero of Loxley, or 'the third man' as they call him.

The Ballad Robin is the Barnsdale outlaw, hijacking travellers, killing without sentiment. With the Sheriff of Nottingham as his nemesis (though Barnsdale is in Yorkshire), this Robin ends up being buried at Kirklees Priory. The most likely candidate for this man, they suggest, is the Robert Hod of Wakefield, uncovered by Joseph Hunter in 1852, as being on the king's staff in late 1323. The case was made for him having taken part in the Lancashire Rebellion of 1322 (whose perpetrators did indeed feud with the Sheriff of Nottingham), being outlawed, then pardoned by the king and taken into royal service during his visit to Nottingham in November 1323. Phillips and Keatman still believed this Robert Hod to be 'the man' we are looking for, despite there being the ultraviolet scan/evidence to the contrary (see footnote 35), showing him as employed in June that year, several months prior to the king's visit plus copious evidence to demonstrate that the Robin Hood legend was in full swing well before these dates.

The Renaissance Robin, of the later prose tales and plays, looks like a composite of the Ballad Robin, the mythical Gamelyn[56] and the historical outlaw Fulk FitzWarine. This is made more complicated by the fact that many of Fulk's tales were themselves a mixture of those of King Arthur and previous Robin Hood stories.[57]

Phillips and Keatman then go on to propose that the 'original' Robin, the man of Loxley, was a certain Sir Robert FitzOdo (a name often confused with Norman claimant Robert FitzOoth). Furthermore, they suggest that Loxley is the so-named village around 5 miles east of Stratford-upon-Avon, being in

---

[56] *'The Tale of Gamelyn'*, a Middle English ancestral romance and swashbuckling outlaw yarn, has been variously dated from 1340 to 1370. It is the earliest known ballad about a 'forest outlaw', and may have been inspired by now-lost tales of Robin Hood and/or contributed to the later ballads of him.

[57] *Fouke le Fitz Waryn*: The stories, written anonymously in Old French prose, survive in a miscellany of works in Latin, French, and English, dating from c. 1325–40. The manuscript—British Library, Royal 12.C.XII—contains some sixty pieces. The text of *Fouke le Fitz Waryn*, occupying folios 33–61, is based on a lost late-thirteenth-century verse romance.

Warwickshire, not Yorkshire. This Warwickshire man was discovered in 1864 by J.R. Planche[58] who suggests that FitzOdo was descended from William the Conqueror's half-brother, Bishop Odo. FitzOdo is said to have lived in the time of King John and Richard I and looks to have been disinherited in the reign of the latter. Little more is known of him, but his life contains certain parallels with versions of the Robin Hood legend: he lived in the late 12th century and the reign of King Richard, was disinherited and outlawed, might have been called Robert Ode and, last but not least, was Lord of Loxley, albeit the one in Warwickshire not Yorkshire. However, with all his research, Planche failed to prove that Robert Fitz Odo was ever an outlaw, or in any way associated with the Robin Hood of legend.

The essence of what these authors conclude holds some gravitas. Tales of the Wakefield rebel, the outlaw Fulk and perhaps other characters (particularly Roger Godberd, who Phillips and Keatman ignore completely!) were mingled and merged to develop a vibrant life of their own, with roots planted in history. As for FitzOdo, I remain unconvinced. Due to my own historic discoveries, I propose instead that the 'third man'—the real Robin of Locksley/Loxley and true origin of the legend—can be found in a different place and even earlier time.

Fiction in Truth

As we have seen, during the last 50-odd years, many researchers have beavered away producing a handful of official documents referencing Hood families in Wakefield, or unconnected strangers taking the name, generally between the early 1200s and early 1300s. As the claims of later Robins have, to all intents, now been dismissed by historians, documentary proof and timeline logic, we have been left with a focus on the oldest known sources.

The earliest known *historical* text that quotes Robin Hood is the *Metrical* or *Orygynale Chronicle,* scribed at the monastery of Loch Leven in 1420 by Scottish Prior, Andrew of Wyntoun. For the year 1283, he entered the following, although no reference source was given for something being quoted nearly 150 years beforehand:

---

[58] *A Ramble with Robin Hood*, J. R. Planche, Report of the Association of Architects, 1864.

"Lytil Jhone and Robyne Hude
Wayth-men were commendit gud
In Yngilwode and Bernysdale
Thai oysyd all this tyme thare trawale."

Little John and Robin Hood
Robbers who were praised as good
In Inglewood[59] and Barnsdale
They used to do this as their work."

In 1445, 25 years after Prior Andrew, comes another reference from Scotland (that also mentions Little John, Barnsdale and the sheriff), this from Walter Bower, historian and Abbot of St Colomb, in his Latin *Scotichronicon,* a continuation of the earlier work *Chronica Gentis Scotorum* by his teacher and cleric/historian, John of Fordun. In this, Bower places Robin in 1266, earlier than Prior Andrew's dates and a year or so after Simon de Montfort's death at the Battle of Evesham during his failed rebellion against Henry III.

"Then arose the famous cut-throat, Robert Hood, as well as Little John,
together with their accomplices from among the dispossessed, whom the vulgar
masses are so inordinately fond of celebrating both in tragedy and comedy."[60]

Bower does at least apply a more vicious tenor to the outlaw band rather than the softer 'courteous, good-humoured cudgelings' dished out in the ballads of later centuries. It is interesting to note that these earliest chroniclers of the 14th and 15th centuries were Scottish. It is also interesting to note that although there is no documentary evidence given of how either Bower or Prior Andrew came to select the 13th century dates for our protagonist, their writings were the very first to establish Robin as a 'historic' figure, not a character who existed solely

---

[59] Inglewood forest near Carlisle is the setting for the Cumberland bandits, *Adam Bell, Clym of the Clough and William of Cloudesley* (Child ballad 116) and dates to a similar period to the printed *Gest of Robin Hood.* It includes many similarities to the early ballad action of *Robin Hood and the Monk.*

[60] The celebrations to which he refers are the plays, dances and sports etc. attached to 'Robin Hood' that had become popular features of the May Day festivities by the mid-15th century.

in ballads—they seem certain he was a real person and not just a character from fiction.

A third later Scotsman, gives us an even earlier date. John Major (or Mair), 16th century philosopher and historian, writing in his *Historia Majoris Britanniæ* (1521), again without any confirmation of his sources, created a 'life' for Robin by entering his birth date as 1160, his activities around 1193–94 and dying, at the ripe old age of 87 on the very specific 24th December 1247—suspiciously, the same date also given on a spurious gravestone at Kirklees Priory. He was the first to provide the timeframe of the reigns of Richard the Lionheart and Prince (later King) John. He chronicled a Robin who robbed abbots, defended women and had a band of 100 men, condemning his acts but calling him the 'humanest' of robbers. He gave him the title '*dux*' of robbers (Latin for 'leader' or 'chief' and the derivation of the title 'duke'). Importantly, he is one of the earliest references to suggest that Robin was of noble birth and again, his overall suggestion is that he was a real person.

This leads us to the beginnings of a documented Robin and more questions about reliability of sources. The paucity of records for the pre-Tudor period cannot be stressed enough here; *Domesday Book* (1086) is the only surviving public record from the 11th century. When we get to the late 13th century—200 years after the time we are concerned with—we still don't know the names of 2 of King Edward I's children, for example.[61] If royalty wasn't recorded (or those records haven't survived), what hope do we have for outlaws?

By chance, if an outlaw ended up with his name in early records, details of his crimes would likely not have been included. The majority of Pipe Rolls were not judicial records, they primarily recorded financial payments, accounts, debts owed and disbursements made—hardly the stuff of serious criminals and vicious murderers.

However, if the crimes associated with Robin—stealing and eating the king's deer, robbing churchmen and barons, kidnapping people for ransom or shooting arrows into the sheriff and his men—were documented anywhere, they would be in the judicial, not the accounting records.

Now here's the rub…until the Chancery Records began in the reign of King John (1199–1216), the Pipe Rolls were the only continuous set of records kept by the English government. The first surviving Wakefield Court Rolls that

---

[61] *Edward I,* Michael Prestwich, University of California Press, 1988.

covered the prime Barnsdale area of interest did not start until 1274. The King's Remembrancer's Memoranda Rolls for Berkshire were just 12 years prior (1262). They consist of records made in the Exchequer, of which only a couple of earlier pieces remain, from the time of King John in 1216.

Listed below are the earliest surviving sources of court records that we have, most of which are in fragmentary form in the National Archives at Kew in London. These documents are the more likely places to maybe find mention of outlaws and more specifically, the one named Robin Hood.

1. Early Plea and Essoin Rolls, from 1194
2. Curia Regis Rolls 1196–1272 (Curia Regis Rolls series, 7 vols. HMSO)
3. Pleas before the King or his Justices 1198–1212 (4 vols. Seldon Society)
4. Records of the Court of King's Bench and Coroners Court records, from 1194
5. Select Pleas of the Crown 1200–1225 (Seldon Society 1888)
6. Eyre Rolls, from 1201
7. Exchequer of Pleas, from 1218
8. Yorkshire Assize Rolls, for the reigns of King John and King Henry III, from 1215 (*Yorkshire Archaeological and Historical Society Record Series* vol. 44, 1911)
9. Court of King's Bench records, scraps from 1272, more after 1323
10. Court of Common Pleas, scraps from 1200, more after 1273
11. Court rolls of the manor of Wakefield, vol i, 1274–1297 (*Yorkshire Archaeological and Historical Society Record Series* vol. 29, 1901)

Many expert researchers and professional archivists, far more qualified than I, have pawed over the remnants of these manuscripts. The only mention of anyone bearing Robin Hood's name is in no. 8—the much-debated '**Rob Hood fugitive**' reference from 1225, dug out by Professor Owen in the 1930s and discussed earlier. As we know, some have suggested that this felon is the real fellow—Robin. Some argue that since there is a dearth, indeed a void, of references prior to the early 1200s, then the basis for the legend must have started at about that time. This is why the era of Richard the Lionheart and his brother, the later King John (reigning consecutively from 1189–1216) is so often given as the timeframe for Robin. Indeed, this is the period of his current 'biography' in the latest *Oxford Dictionary of National Biography (2004).*

Of course, it is tempting to believe that this fugitive is our man, as the earliest known reference; the oldest genuine 'proof' of a criminal Robin Hood. This is what every writer on the subject of Robin Hood dreams of. This is the Holy Grail. But what are the chances of him actually being recorded? According to legend Robin is captured by the sheriff from time to time, but he always escapes and is never brought to trial in any ballad. If there was a real man behind this and if he was never caught or brought to justice, then surely nothing would have been written in court documents. Others believe, by a stroke of coincidence, that it was simply his real name. But we now know that the fashion of name-dropping/adoption was very real and lasted for centuries.

If instead it is taken that the 'Rob Hood' nickname is just that—a nickname—then given the limited state of communications in 1225, especially amongst common folk, we are left with 2 possibilities: an almost impossibly rapid spread of the outlaw legend or, more likely; that stories of Robin Hood were already popular from the earliest of times, being told and enjoyed for a century or more.

There are just a few public record fragments pre-1225. The earliest surviving non-'royal' Pipe Rolls modelled on those of the royal administration, are those of the Bishop of Winchester, and relate to the accounting year 1208/9. Although the earliest surviving Exchequer Pipe Rolls date from 1130, late in the reign of Henry I, it is clear from their construction that they were being produced by the Exchequer before then, as the 1130 roll is clearly a quite developed document; it shows fluidity in its use of accounts and continuity from previous years. It would seem that earlier examples have simply not survived. One fragmentary extract from a Pipe Roll of 1124 has been found—in a 14th century manuscript now in the Cotton Library at the British Museum—but contains nothing of import. Exactly when the Pipe Rolls began to be produced is debated among historians, but most hold that they date from Henry I's time (1100–1135). Nothing either survives, or was produced, from the previous reign of his brother William II, 'Rufus', in the 11th century. 1154 is the generally accepted date of the first continuous series of public records, under the first Plantagenet king, Henry II (1154–1189), grandson of Henry I. Indeed, the seeds of the modern justice system were sown by Henry II, who established a jury of 12 local knights to settle disputes over the ownership of land. Henry II first chose 5 members of his personal household—two clergy and 3 lay—"to hear all the complaints of the realm and to do right." This, supervised by the king and 'wise men' of the realm, was the origin of the Court of Common Pleas. Eventually, a new permanent court, the Court of the King's Bench, evolved, becoming the most senior criminal court in England, exercising supervisory jurisdiction over all inferior criminal courts. However, apart from a few scraps of Common Plea records from around 1200 onwards, the surviving plea rolls of the King's Bench division between the crown and a 'subject' are really only available from the early part of the 14th century, so all in all, from 100 to more than 200+ years after I suggest Robin was operating.

As far as we know, there simply isn't any older documentation for us to discover. For the possibility of an earlier Robin from mid-11th century to mid-12th century, an absence of evidence in the public record—of a Hooded Holy Grail—has led to a frustrating lack of debate on this possibility. Until now.

To quote author and self-proclaimed Robin Hood expert, Graham Phillips, from a 2010 video production...

"To try and find the real Robin Hood, what you've got to do is find the earliest reference to Robin Hood, whether it's fictional or in historical record."
Graham Phillips—National Geographic Mystery Files (Robin Hood)

Frankly, I am not convinced even doing that would provide an unquestionable answer to the mystery, as I am sure he was active, maybe a century before (surviving) records began. Indeed, this is the vital flaw in previous searches for Robin in surviving authentic historical documents—he is not there to be found, being from an earlier time...

Chapter 4
Unhooding the Legend

"At least, one thing seems to have been established in the last 15 years or so—that the real Robin Hood, if there was one, was considerably earlier than has traditionally been thought."
~ **R.B. Dobson[62], Professor of Medieval History, Universities of Cambridge and York (1997)**

Professor Dobson clearly supported the underlying thrust of the previous chapters—that an earlier real character is not only possible but probable. I have lived with my favoured candidate for the man at the source of the great legend for more than 2 decades. I know him well. Conversely, you have, thus far, only received teasers and inferences, so without further ado, let us remove the hood. Beneath, we find:

The illegitimate son (c.1058—c.1103) of Anglo-Danish nobleman Waltheof II (c.1041—d.1076). Earl of Huntingdon and Earl of Northumbria.

It is now agreed in academia that a letter, written in 1102 (by someone generally recognised as the keenest philosophical and theological mind of his time and a pivotal figure in early medieval Europe), regarding an unnamed deceased man and his son was referring to Waltheof and his son. Furthermore, we know that Waltheof's only marriage produced just 2 legitimate daughters (we know their names and much about their lives) so this son was illegitimate, 'a

---

[62] Leading authority on the legend of Robin Hood and co-author of *Rymes of Robyn Hood: An Introduction to the English Outlaw,* R.B. Dobson, and J. Taylor (Heinemann, 1976).

bastard'. But before we can connect the dots, we must examine the dots themselves.

4. Statue, believed to be of Waltheof, on the west front
of Crowland Abbey (now the parish church of Crowland), Lincolnshire
Photograph courtesy of Eleanor Parker

I first came across the intriguing Waltheof II over 20 years ago while researching my own family history as a millennium project, which led me back to the lives of the 11th century Northumbrian Earls of the great House of Bamburgh. Later, when I started my research on this book, Waltheof's name cropped up again—in a passing reference on a message board—as a potential suspect, or at least progenitor, to Robin's real identity and regrettably his name is somewhat tarnished by appearing at the top of that spurious pedigree concocted by William Stukeley back in 1746. In addition, a late 11th century Robin was sporadically mentioned on some forums and websites, although neither Waltheof nor a Norman/Saxon/Danish Robin were ever expanded upon or connected. This is, I believe, the first study to pursue this in some detail.[63]

Although no identifiable geopolitical or military events are referenced within *The Gest* which might have given a clue to the setting of the tales, and the Anglo-Saxon vs. Norman narrative does not feature by name in the early ballads, the overall tenor of a subjugated nation under victorious and oppressive lords and masters is apparent. There is no doubt that 18th century literary and historical scholars such as Thomas Percy and Joseph Ritson certainly over egged the element of Saxon resistance to the Norman Conquest in their link to the legend, this leading to the first steps, in the 19th century, of Robin's reconstruction as a Saxon hero, particularly by Sir Walter Scott in his novel Ivanhoe.

Stephen Knight, one of the foremost modern scholars on Robin Hood, a literary historian whose work has shaped much of the current Robin Hood debate, argues for an origin in power struggles, in which Robin can stand for any group in conflict with another group holding authority.[64] This implies a conflict between peasants and the nobility in the earlier legends. The renowned French historian Augustin Thierry, in his 1825 work,[65] was perhaps the first to promulgate such an idea but his belief that the Robin Hood legends were products of nationalism is not universally accepted.

Be that as it may, the level of disdain and contempt that the Normans held for the English and the indignities the latter had to suffer, in those early decades following the Conquest, are hard to appreciate and may well have formed an element of the driving force behind the motivation of the original Robin. Perhaps it was more along the lines suggested by Maurice Keen, professor of Medieval History at Balliol College, Oxford, who suggested that the legends arose out of 'intense tribal loyalty' and 'arrogance' of the Anglo-Saxons versus their Norman

---

[63] Of all the fictional stories, there is one set just after the Norman Conquest in the Conqueror's and Waltheof's day (early 1070's) at the time of Hereward the Wake (*'Sherwood'* by Parke Godwin, Avon Books, 1991). Godwin's Robin is depicted as a minor Saxon thegn called Edward Aelredson and Waltheof also features significantly but they are not blood related.

[64] *Robin Hood: A Complete Study of the English Outlaw,* Stephen Knight (Oxford: Blackwell Publishers, 1994). p.5

[65] *L'Histoire de la conquête de l'Angleterre par les Normands (History of the Conquest of England by the Normans);* Augustin Thierry, 1825, 3 vols.; translated from the seventh Paris edition, by William Hazlitt (London: H.G. Bohn, 1856). 2 vols.

conquerors.[66] It is interesting that following further research by Keen, he somewhat changed his view. In the updated introduction of the 1977 version of his book, he described the context of the ballads as '*an age plagued by lack of governance*' and explained that, in his view, it was this lack of governance, and not social unrest, that produced the Robin Hood ballads. There is no question that for the first twenty to thirty years, post Hastings, the governance of Northumbria and Yorkshire was only nominal to say the least.

However, I am not promoting Robin and his men as rebels fighting back as discontented agrarian peasants or downtrodden Saxons rebelling against their oppressors—but simply men who had been outlawed 'in absentia', just highwaymen, kidnappers and thieves—but with a targeted audience of corrupt churchmen and government officers. The deprivations of the populace are well related by French historian Augustin Thierry when describing the travels or 'progresses' of the court of William Rufus around the country over thirty years after Hastings, as depicted by the contemporary chronicler, Eadmer.

Wherever the Norman king was passing, in his progresses through England, the servants and soldiers in his train were accustomed to ravage the country. When they could not wholly consume the provisions of various kinds, which they found in the houses of the English, they had them carried to the neighbouring market by the proprietor himself, and obliged him to sell the same for their profit.

At other times, they would burn them for their pastime, and when they found an overplus of strong drink they used it to wash their horses feet. "Their ill usage of the fathers of families, their insults to the wives and daughters," according to the historian of that day, "were too shameful to relate; so that on the first rumour of the king's approach everyone would fly from his dwelling and retreat, with whatever he could save, to the depths of the forests and into desert places."[67]

Whether Thierry was influenced by the fictitious pen of Sir Walter Scott, or vice versa, is unknown, but in Scott's famous 1819 novel, *Ivanhoe,* set in the late twelfth century, he certainly popularised the premise in advocating that Robin was a Saxon freedom fighter following which writers converted Robin into '*a breaker of chains imposed by the slave master (William the Conqueror), an*

---

[66] *The Outlaws of Medieval Legend,* Maurice Keen (Routledge, 1961).

[67] Eadmer's *Historia novorum in Anglia,* first edited by John Selden in 1623 (p.94)

unparliamentary re-distributor, a great reformer, a forerunner of Wycliffe, and, ultimately, a dangerous Socialist'.[68]

Scott's influence upon subsequent treatments of Robin Hood can scarcely be exaggerated. Virtually every text written after 1820 features the conflict between the Saxons and Normans and its racialist overtones as a prominent motif and the time frame of King Richard, Prince John and the Crusades, erroneously or otherwise, has become embedded in the national psyche (being post 1154 this is technically the Plantagenet era, not Norman). Nowadays this is the audience's expectation and Hollywood happily obliges. However, as history always reminds us, the stories we know are rarely the stories that are true.

As an author well versed in medieval history, Scott would certainly have been aware of the fact that by the end of the twelfth century, through intermarriage, domesticity and the passage of nearly 150 years since the Battle of Hastings, the Saxons and Normans had become almost entirely assimilated—although not in the last quarter of the eleventh. Robin's cause seems much more driven by rebellion against any corrupt, unjust authority rather than 'Norman' per se, and indeed, the early ballads suggest throughout that he would fight heroically to defend true kingship.

Waltheof is often described as the last great Anglo-Saxon thegn.[69] He was the younger son of Siward Bjornsson, Earl of Northumbria, better known as either 'Siward the Great' or 'Siward the Strong'. Siward was a highborn Dane (of unclear origins) and Waltheof was not Anglo-Saxon but Anglo-Danish, from the noble House of Bamburgh into which Siward had married (Ælfflæd, the daughter of Earl Ealdred—Appendix 2.1). This was the Northumbrian aristocracy of Anglo-Saxon origin (later Anglo-Scandinavian) which had ruled the wild districts of the north of England (Bernicia—Northumbria, and Deira—Yorkshire) as kings for 400 years since Ida the Flame Bearer in 550, through to Eric of York (known as Eric 'Bloodaxe') in 954 and thereafter as Earls, since

---

[68] *'The Historic Robin Hood', The Journal of American Folklore;* William E. Simeone, Vol. 66, No. 262 (October-December 1953), pp. 303–308

[69] Thegn (also Thane, Thayn, thegn) is commonly used to describe an aristocratic retainer of the king or a nobleman in Anglo-Saxon England. There was a distinct difference in status though between a thegn and a 'royal' thegn, of which Waltheof was the latter. He held 106 manors from the King in 1066 and had recently been elevated to the Earldom of Huntingdon and Northampton.

U(c)htred 'the Bold' (Waltheof's great-grandfather. Appendix 2.1) in 1006.[70] His name, Waltheof, was borne by his maternal great-great-grandfather, Waltheof I, high-reeve and ealdorman of Northumbria in the late 10th century and father of Uchtred the Bold. They were also closely linked through political marriages to the Royal House of Scotland, with whom they were constantly at war over the ill-defined border territories like Lothian, Strathclyde and Cumbria. Known references to this father and son—in terms of physical description, personality, leadership and warrior skills—perfectly match those of our hero.

In 1887, a somewhat obscure Victorian writer and author called Eleanor Stredder (b.1835) wrote a short article entitled *Who was Robin Hood?*.[71] Within those few pages, Miss Stredder makes the earliest claim I have found, outside the spurious Stukeley pedigree, for Robin being a descendant of the House of Bamburgh. Her suggestion was that Robin was probably the great-grandson of Waltheof, being the grandson of his daughter Maud and her second husband, King David of Scotland, 8th Earl of Huntingdon. Miss Stredder found significance in a number of ballads describing Robin blowing his horn after slaying a deer. In Anglo-Saxon law, a legitimate hunter would sound his horn to declare his presence, so as not to be confused with a poacher. Stredder concluded this act was Robin's assertion that he was no thief, but rightful heir to the lands of his ancestors in Hallamshire, as the Earl of Huntingdon—an assertion that might equally apply in the case of a wronged and illegitimate only son of Waltheof II…

Ms Stredder was an author of fiction and not a qualified historian, hence her suggestions may appear somewhat tenuous and a lack of evidence cannot be denied, but is a lineage to Waltheof entirely fanciful? Recently, American historian Dr Stephanie Barczewski was somewhat dismissive of Ms Stredder's

---

[70] Eric of York was the last Danish king of Northumbria; after his death in 954, Eadred of Wessex stripped the kingdom of its independent status and made the land part of England. The region was then disputed between England and Scotland for half a century before being roughly divided down the River Tweed, with Uctred the Bold becoming the first Earl of Northumbria in 1006, in what became, for two centuries, a somewhat autonomous self-governing part of the kingdom with its own distinct identity, subsequently excluded from the Domesday survey of 1086.

[71] *'Who was Robin Hood'*, Notes and Queries, E. Stredder, Series 7, Vol III, April 1887

claim, calling it, "Just as outlandish as Stukeley's had been"[72]—but I have to disagree. Given the lack of records linking them by name, it is impossible for me, just as for other theorists, to prove my hypothesis beyond all doubt. Then again, it is equally difficult for it to be so readily dismissed based on the amount of circumstantial evidence being brought to the table. If the illegitimate son of Waltheof, born c.1058, was indeed the original Robin Hood, then he would have been approximately 28 years old—and an outlaw for at least 6 of those—by the time the oldest surviving public record in England, *Domesday Book* (1086), was produced. It is thus hardly surprising we have little or no chance of finding reference to him.

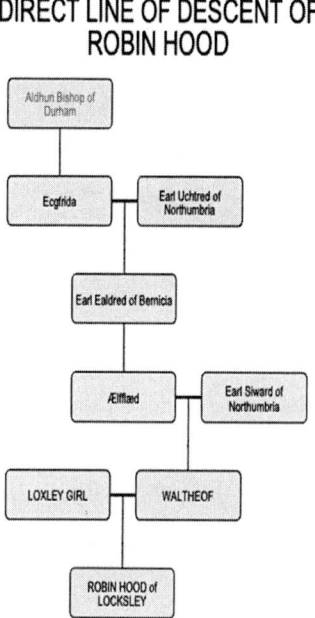

DIRECT LINE OF DESCENT OF ROBIN HOOD

A Legend's Lineage: Robin's Possible Family Tree
Given in full in Appendix 2.1

---

[72] *Myth and National Identity in Nineteenth-Century Britain: 'The Legends of King Arthur and Robin Hood'*, Stephanie Barczewski (Oxford University Press, 2000), p.139.

With that in mind, below are the various strands, some new, some old, that have been woven together to bring the story to life in the late 11th century. These include reasoned analysis and identification of many of the key characters associated with the legend, such as the Sheriff of Nottingham, Maid Marian, Guy of Gisborne, Friar Tuck, Sir Richard at the Lee and the treacherous abbess and her accomplice, Red Roger. Maybe they add up to something. I leave it to you to decide if the sum of all these parts possibly, or dare I saw, probably, equals the life of the real man behind the legend.

Grandfather: Siward (c.1020–d.1055)

Waltheof's father was a great magnate and soldier called Siward the Great (or the Strong), becoming the Earl of Northumbria[73] under Edward the Confessor in 1041 (by murdering the incumbent, Eadwulf III—his wife's uncle!), who essentially ruled, or at least contained, that wild and ungovernable area of northern England on behalf of the king. Siward's exact origins are unclear, he is believed to have been of highborn Scandinavian birth and, no doubt due to his great size and blond hair, legend suggests a genealogy claiming he was the descendant of his grandmother and a polar bear, a commonplace piece of Germanic folklore! He came to prominence by marrying Aelflaed, daughter of Earl Ealdred II and granddaughter of Earl Uchtred of the ancient House of Bamburgh, whose kings had ruled Northumbria from their great castle, their 'caput baroniae', since 550AD. Siward and Aelflaed's first son, Osbjorn, natural heir to the Earldom of Northumbria, was born c.1037. Waltheof's mother, Aelflaed, died at some point in his childhood, maybe in his childbirth c.1041, and Siward remarried[74], a lady called Godgifu whose lineage is unknown, but she also predeceased him. Siward is believed to have had close links to the Scottish monarchy and chronicler John of Fordun[75] suggested that Suthen, the

---

[73] This Earldom had been an amalgam of the kingdoms of Northumberland (Bernicia) and Yorkshire (Deira) since 954AD, i.e. land north of the River Humber.

[74] *"The second marriage is known from a grant she* [Godifu] *made of territory around Stamford, Lincolnshire, to Peterborough Abbey."* W. M. Aird on 'Siward, Earl of Northumbria' (d.1055), ODNB.

[75] *Chronica Gentis Scotorum*, John of Fordun, c.1380. Also the *Chronicle of the Kings of Alba* (a 13th century version survives, the original was most probably written in the early 11th century) giving Duncan's wife the Gaelic name 'Suthen'.

wife of King Duncan I, may well have been a relative of Siward. Most modern academics believe she was his sister, or at least his cousin. King Duncan I (murdered by Macbeth in 1040) and Suthen were the parents of Malcolm III, who was King of Scotland for 35 years, from 1058–1093; significantly, a period that covers virtually the whole of my Robin's life.

Siward was said to have been mentally strong and physically imposing—referred to in various chronicles as '*Siward the Strong*', '*the mighty Earl of Northumbria*' and '*almost a giant in stature*'.[76] He was, however, despite some murderous qualities, renowned as much for his goodness and piety as for his valour, having been converted to Christianity by King Edward the Confessor himself. At the time of King Edward, Siward was perhaps the most powerful man in England, save the King—indeed he was Edward's right-hand man in the wild north, famed for its independent spirit.

If my theory is correct, Siward would have died 3 years or so before Robin was born. In 1055, he succumbed to a fatal illness (most likely dysentery or smallpox). According to chronicler Henry of Huntingdon (c.1135), upon his deathbed Siward requested, as a Danish warrior, that his end be fitting for such a valiant soldier, who having not died gloriously in battle, should at least die upright like a soldier and so he was duly clothed in his armour, with battle-axe and shield in hand and gave up his spirit with honour.

---

[76] *Historia Anglorum*, Henry of Huntingdon c.1129–1154, first printed by Sir Henry Sackvile in 1596.

5. A 19th century representation of Earl Siward readying for death in
The Death of Earl Siward **by James Smetham, 1861.**
Public domain image out of copyright

Father: Waltheof II[77] (c.1041–1076)

Siward and Aelflaed's surviving younger son, Waltheof, was tall and well-built like his father, he was strong and courageous in battle, devout and with an engaging personality. How do we know all this? Fortunately, for the purposes of my research, there are extensive details on Waltheof from a number of the most respected and reliable chroniclers of the 11th and 12th centuries, namely Orderic

---

[77] Waltheof is often designated 'II'. Waltheof I, after whom he was named, was his great-great-grandfather (d.circa 1006), the father of Earl Uchtred.

Vitalis, William of Malmesbury, Simeon of Durham[78] and Henry of Huntingdon, along with the biography of his life produced by the monks of Ely, the *Vita Waldevi*.[79] Orderic described him as 'a handsome man of splendid physique'.

Although we know precisely when Waltheof died—as the only 'English' nobleman to have been executed by William the Conqueror—the date of his birth is not recorded. This was not unusual in pre-Conquest Britain, even for people of very high status, but based on certain events in his life, we can hazard an intelligent guess. Some suggest as late as c.1050, but a birth year of c.1041/2 seems most probable based on key facts, logic and what was customary at the time, namely: the age gap between Waltheof and his brother (4 years difference rather than 14), the year he became Earl of Huntingdon (at 24, he would be deemed mature enough; whereas at 14 he would not); and the depth of his ecclesiastical education (unlikely if his teachings were curtailed at c.4 years old upon the death of his father and assumption of responsibilities of an heir).

According to the chroniclers, Waltheof was, like his father, matchless as a warrior but somewhat politically naïve and easily manipulated. Common for the younger son(s) of nobles, he was educated with a view to a life within the church[80]. Deeply devout, he later qualified as a lay person to sit on the Synods of Walcher, Bishop of Durham, and was able to recite all 150 psalms from memory (noted by Orderic Vitalis, who thought him admirable and said he had *'gifts in which, in the lay order, he delighted to a remarkable degree'.*). However, in 1055, that life course changed when his father died, just a year after his elder (and only) brother Osbjorn had died, when aged about 18, when fighting,

---

[78] His great height and extraordinary 'vigour' of body—*nervosus lacertis, robustis pectore et procerus Coto corpore*—being recorded by Simeon of Durham in *Symeonis Opera*, p.219 and by William of Malmesbury in *Gesta Regum*, I, pp.468–9, 'He had great strength of arm, powerful chest muscles, his whole frame tough and tall'.

[79] *Historia Ecclesiastica,* Orderic Vitalis c.1127; *Historia ecclesiastica gentis Anglorum*, William of Malmesbury 1125; *Historia regum Anglorum et Dacorum*, Simeon of Durham 1129; *Historia Anglorum*, Henry of Huntingdon c.1135; *Historia novorum in Anglia: Vita et passio Waldevi comitis,* unnamed Ely Abbey monk(s) early 12th c.

[80] This was most likely when aged 8–14 between 1049–1055 under Æthelric, who was Bishop of Durham from 1042 to 1056 when he resigned within a year of the death of Earl Siward, who had been one of the bishop's main supporters and to whom he owed his advancement. He retired to Peterborough Abbey, where he remained until the Norman Conquest. He was arrested by King William I after May 1070 and died in captivity at Westminster in 1072.

alongside their father to depose Macbeth in the 1054 battle known variously as the 'Battle of the Seven Sleepers' or the 'Battle of Dunsinane'.[81] Under Anglo-Danish custom, the 'rites of manhood' could not be claimed until the age of 15, and Waltheof, likely 13 or 14, was just too young to be considered for his father Siward's position as Earl of Northumbria. Instead, the earldom was unwisely granted by Edward the Confessor to Tostig (brother of Harold Godwinson; later King Harold) who, for the next 10 years, ruled ruthlessly over Northumbria until his banishment and exile in 1065.

Away from the chroniclers' eyes, it is during this period in the late 1050s when, as a teenager, after his father's death, Waltheof is most likely to have fathered his son, probably with a girl of non-noble blood. More on this later (apologies, dear reader, but for now we move on to Waltheof's documented adulthood).

In 1064, Earl Tostig oversaw the murder of 2 important young royal thegns—Gamal (Waltheof's 1st cousin—son of his aunt Aetheldrytha and her husband Orm—Appendix 2.1) and Ulf—who were visiting him under 'safe conduct'. These murders were the final straw for the Northumbrians. Tostig was deposed in 1065, outlawed and exiled to Flanders staying with his brother-in-law, Count Baldwin, but perishing a year later at the Battle of Stamford Bridge, along with his Norwegian Viking cohort, King Harold Hardrada, following their alliance and failed joint attempt to seize the English crown. The Mercian Earl Morcar, most likely instrumental in Tostig's earlier removal, was given the Earldom of Northumbria by King Edward the Confessor. Waltheof, now aged around 23–24, although old enough to hold the title, was not considered acceptable owing to a remarkable lingering family feud (discussed in detail later in this chapter). However, no doubt to placate him, King Edward hived off the southerly part of the Northumbrian lands, Middle Anglia, and—importantly for our story—created a new minor earldom, 'of Huntingdon and Northampton'—consisting of significant parts of those shires and elements of Bedfordshire, Rutland and Cambridgeshire—which he gave to Waltheof in 1065.[82] The significance of this earldom, and its connection to Robin, will soon become clear.

---

[81] Macbeth was finally deposed as King, and killed, at the Battle of Lumphanan fought in August 1057, between him and the future King Malcolm III, Canmore. See Appx. 2.2 for more detail.

[82] Details of the earldom taken from Waltheof's entry in *Encyclopedia Britannica*. Although its veracity can be questioned, the Croyland Chronicle and separate references

Like many Northern nobles, who fought and survived the battles of Fulford and Stamford Bridge, the newly-titled Earl Waltheof would likely **not** have travelled all the way south with Harold for the Battle of Hastings in Kent.[83] From the surviving written records, it is difficult to precisely chart his life for the 3 years after this, aged about 25–28. However, after the Hastings defeat, following the advice of the Witan—the Anglo-Saxon royal council—and to avoid further slaughter, Waltheof clearly acquiesced and submitted to William, thereby prospering under the new King, the Conqueror. He retained his Midland estates and his Earldom of Huntingdon and Northampton was to be re-confirmed in 1070 by the Conqueror, following the final defeat of the English rebels at York.

What we do know is that in the immediate aftermath of Hastings, in March 1067, William returned to Normandy with a huge amount of booty and treasure from his first 6 months of Conquest, taking Waltheof with him, seemingly as an honoured guest or 'Prominente', along with Edgar the Ætheling, Earls (and brothers) Edwin and Morcar, Archbishop Stigand and others. (William of Poitiers noted that in Normandy the personal beauty and long flowing hair of the young Englishmen astonished the Normans and French.[84]). In reality, they were hostages; a supposedly shrewd move by William to lessen the chance of rebellion in his absence, especially considering that firm Norman 'control' of Britain had barely extended north of the River Thames at this time. In reality, their absence seems to have made for more anarchy in England, not less. However, either by force of personality or political manoeuvring during his 9 months at the Norman Court, Waltheof became quite a favourite of the Conqueror and one of very few indigenous nobles to have retained power in the post-Conquest period. Here, he may well have first met his future wife, the 15/16 year-old Judith de Lens, the

---

recorded that Waltheof received the Earldom of Huntingdon and Northampton, when attaining manhood, as far back as 1056 following his father's death and being reconfirmed by the Conqueror in 1070 following the rebels defeat at York and his marriage to Judith de Lens. The 1065 date, though, following the exile and forfeit of lands by Tostig, seems the most credible.

[83] Various poems of Skaldic verse, composed soon after Hastings, suggest he, along with Earls Edwin and Morcar, may well have been at the earlier battles of Fulford and Stamford Bridge—the three battles that were collectively said '*to have lost England*'.

[84] *Gesta Willelmi Ducis Normannorum et Regis Anglorum*, ed. J. A. Giles, London, 1845, p. 156.

niece of King William[85], and he most certainly would have spent time with young Edgar Ætheling—Saxon prince, grandson of Edmund Ironside (briefly King of England 1016), and later figurehead of the various Northumbrian rebellions.

In December 1067, William returned to England, ostensibly to arrange for the coronation of his queen (Matilda of Flanders) the following year, but also to stem worrying rumours of rebellion in the West Country.[86] Like the uprisings in the Welsh Marches and Kent crushed by previous regents, William quashed Exeter promptly, with ringleaders fleeing and citizens submitting. His English 'guests' either returned with him at this time or joined him early in the new year for the coronation ceremony in May 1068. There were now serious rumblings emerging from Mercia and Northumbria and more significantly, a rumoured supporting invasion from King Swein of Denmark. For a few months, from the relative calm and safety of his residence in the East Midlands, Waltheof made a reasonable show of being a vassal to the king, bearing witness to a handful of royal writs and charters. However, surely he must have been ruffled by the royal insistence of 2 new Norman castles to be built on his estates (at Huntingdon and Cambridge[87]), added to the fact that he had now been passed over twice for his father's Earldom of Northumbria, where rumours of revolt were growing.

To put more fuel on the fire, later the same year, Earl Gospatric[88] led a failed fiasco of a rebellion around York and had to flee with Edgar Ætheling and other

---

[85] Judith (b.1053) was the daughter of William the Conqueror's sister, Adelaide (Adeliza), Countess of Aumale and her second husband, Lambert II, Count of Lens (he died in battle aged 24 when Judith was a baby). William the Conqueror was thus her uncle and she was *first* cousin to the three royal brothers, Prince Henry, King Rufus and Duke Robert Curthose.

[86] The revolt was around Exeter, an uprising thought to be centred on Countess Gytha, wife of Earl Godwin, and mother of both Edith, consort of the Confessor and also the late King Harold and Tostig. She lived there after Hastings in 1067, prior to going into exile in Scandinavia.

[87] These motte and bailey castles, along with Warwick, Nottingham and Lincoln had been constructed in 1068 following the failed uprising by Earls Edwin and Morcar along with Edgar Ætheling.

[88] Like Waltheof (a great-grandson), Earl Gospatric was also directly descended from Earl Uchtred (a grandson) but from Ucthred's third marriage to Ælfgifu, the royal Saxon daughter of King Æthelred 'the Unready'. After his victory at Hastings, William the Conqueror first appointed Copsi, a supporter of the late Earl Tostig, as Earl of Bernicia in the spring of 1067. Copsi was dead within five weeks, killed by Oswulf, another

rebel leaders back to the safety of the Scottish Court of King Malcolm III Canmore (Gaelic for 'Great Chief'). King William replaced him as earl with a loyal Norman, Robert de Comines, who was arrogant and rapacious, and— within months—was murdered by the rebels during a raid on Durham in January 1069 (along with the massacre of 700–900 of his men). No doubt inspired by the ongoing English resistance, in spring 1069 Waltheof made his way north— collecting and exhorting rebel fighters on the way (the surviving Yorkshire thegns and their housecarls[89])—to join the main protagonists then 'in retreat' at the court of King Malcolm in Scotland. In the following 6 months or so, he took part in the Northern Resistance against the Normans, later aided by a Danish invasion fleet sent by King Swein in September '69.

The final major English v Norman battle, at York in September 1069, is unsurprisingly well-documented. Chronicler William of Malmesbury, described York under Waltheof's gang as 'a warm nest for tyranny' (*nidum tirranidis*).[90] Although 3,000 Normans are said to have been slaughtered (50 by Waltheof alone—with his great battle-axe), it eventually led to the rebels' defeat (and the retreat of their Danish allies, having been bribed by King William with large quantities of gold and silver). Then followed the 'Harrying[91] of the North' as the Conqueror sought his vengeance, with as many as 100,000 people or more perishing through genocide, famine and disease. By early 1070, both Waltheof and Earl Gospatric submitted to William, Waltheof publicly at the king's Easter crown-wearing ceremony in Winchester. Far from being punished, he was then surprisingly reinstated to his earldom in Huntingdon castle and a marriage to William's 18-year-old niece Judith de Lens was shrewdly arranged by King

---

grandson of Uchtred, who installed himself as Earl (see Appendix 2.1). Oswulf was killed in the autumn by bandits after less than six months as Earl.

Gospatric, who had a plausible claim to the Earldom, given he was related to both Oswulf and Uchtred, offered King William a large amount of money to be granted the Earldom of Bernicia. The King, who was in the process of raising heavy taxes, somewhat unwisely, accepted.

[89] Housecarls were the retainers or bodyguards of royalty, the nobility and thegns. Whilst not a military elite, they were well trained and had better weapons than the usual manservants.

[90] *Gesta Regum Anglorum, I, pp.462–3*, William of Malmesbury.

[91] Harrying or harrowing: to persistently carry out attacks on a territory, to ravage and devastate, as in war. To burn all crops and houses, kill all livestock and population. What today we call a 'scorched earth' policy coupled with 'ethnic cleansing'.

William in an endeavour to mould this popular native magnate into a Norman loyalist who could maintain control of the unruly northern territories.[92] Meanwhile, Earl Gospatric—to whom William had surprisingly restored the title following 'the harrying'—was still rebelling. In 1072, William defeated and banished him for the final time.[93] That same year, the seemingly trusty and submissive Waltheof, him of the magnetic personality, thus finally received his father's Earldom of Northumbria—from the all-conquering Norman king.

Now a powerful northern Earl, Waltheof decided to snuff out the final ashes of one of the longest running feuds ever recorded, lest they reignite—a feud of lingering family enmities that played a part in him being denied the earldom 7 years earlier, back in 1065 and again in 1067. Indeed, it was the only feud detailed at length in both *The Anglo-Saxon Chronicle* and *De Obsessione Dunelmi*.[94] It started right back in 1016 with the murder of Waltheof's great-grandfather Earl Uchtred, who was hacked to death in the court of King Cnut along with forty of his retainers. The man actually responsible (with Cnut's blessing) was a fellow called Thurbrand 'the Hold' and what followed was a series of tit-for-tat 'blood-feud' killings over 4 generations that lasted for an

---

[92] Perhaps the most unique feature of this marriage is that it was of an aristocratic Norman woman to an elite English native male—this was extremely rare—though the reverse was quite common. The Saxons were regarded as second class citizens and even though her husband was ennobled, she would have felt some stigma and possible resentment, as her contemporaries were likely to have held the union against her.

[93] Initially exiled in Scotland, next Flanders and then back to Scotland, where he was granted Dunbar Castle by his cousin King Malcolm III—he died soon after in 1073.

[94] The Anglo-Saxon Chronicle is a remarkable collection of annals in Old English chronicling the history of the Anglo-Saxons. Significantly, it was **not** an official record kept by the crown but compiled by monks in certain monasteries and at times openly criticised the rulers of the day. The original manuscript was created in the 9th century during the reign of Alfred the Great (871–899). Multiple copies were made of that one original and then distributed to monasteries across England, where they were independently updated. In one case, the Chronicle was still being actively updated in 1154. Nine manuscripts survive though none of them is the original version—seven in the British Library and the other two in the Bodleian Library at Oxford and the Parker Library of Corpus Christi College, Cambridge.

The *De obsessione Dunelmi* ("On the siege of Durham"), is an historical work written in the north of England during the Anglo-Norman period, almost certainly at Durham monastery and probably in the late 11th or early 12th century.

astonishing 57 years and assumed all the elements of one of the great Icelandic or Scandinavian sagas. Finally, in the winter of 1073–74, when Robin was about 16 years old, it culminated in the massacre of most of the sons and grandsons of Carl (son of Thurbrand, and sometimes recorded as 'Karli') during a family feast in Settrington, North Yorkshire (about 3 miles east of Malton), engineered by Waltheof and his housecarls.[95] Bear in mind, these same men had, back in 1069, fought shoulder to shoulder with him against the Normans at York and possibly even earlier at the battles of Fulford and Stamford Bridge. But family retribution would have been ingrained in this descendant of Vikings—it was just a matter of timing for final revenge and the feud to be ended.

For the next couple of years after the massacre, Earl Waltheof enjoyed relative peace with 2 earldoms to run, witnessing some royal documents, 2 castles to build in Durham and the Welsh Marches, synods to attend in Durham with the bishop and to be a father to 2 young daughters and spend some time with his engaging teenage son, fast becoming a man. However, by 1076, his entanglement with an infamous Anglo-Norman uprising resulted in his controversial execution; an event that is intricately tied into our story, as we shall see.

Modern historians consider the 11th and 12th century chronicles detailing his life as a reliable source. So, if the above is a reasonable summation of Waltheof's movements, then those of his offspring (and indeed the mother of his son) can only be guessed at. I would say take a leap of faith but take it as just a little step, for I believe it will pay off later.

Mother: A maid of Loxley?

Loxley is first associated with Robin's birth in an anonymous prose story forming part of the Sloane Manuscripts[96] which suggest he was 'of noble blood'.

---

[95]This gathering would have been in the manor house of Carl's son, Thurbrand who held the manor in 1066 (named after his grandfather who had instigated the feud). After his death in the massacre it was handed to a Norman, Béranger de Tosny who held it at Domesday in 1086. (The grandson of his uncle Roger, one Ralph III de Tosny, married Alice, the younger daughter of Waltheof c.1102—see appendix 2.1)

[96] The Sloane Manuscripts are a collection of medieval documents formed by physician Sir Hans Sloane (1660–1753) and purchased at his death by an Act of Parliament, which also established the British Museum to curate them. Now housed in the British Library,

Within this collection exist 5 and a half pages of a crudely written prose story from c.1600, adding up to the earliest surviving attempt to document the full life and career of the outlaw:

"Robin Hood was borne at Lockesley [Loxley]*, in Yorkeshire…in the days of Henry the second, about the yeare 1160; but lyved tyll the latter end of Richard the Fyrst."*

While much of this 'record' was actually taken from early stories and so the dates and details are certainly questionable, the location—not mentioned in the ballads—is an interesting one. It is here that the foundations of Robin's traditional birthplace were said to be still visible in Bar-Wood just outside the village of Loxley in 1637, where surveyor John Harrison noted:

"Little Haggas croft wherein is ye foundation of a house or cottage where Robin Hood was born; this piece is compassed about with Loxley Firth and contains 2 Roods and 13 square perches." [97]

Nearly 400 years and many references later, it is still considered a viable birthplace which, in turn means it is a viable place to find Robin's mother. Today, Loxley is a village 4 miles north-west of the centre of modern-day Sheffield, edging towards the Peak District. It should be noted that at the time of Domesday, in 1086, the manor of Sheffield itself consisted solely of 3 ploughlands, no houses and zero population! In the 11th century, Loxley was one of 16 small hamlets, together comprising historic Hallamshire. The somewhat petty debate of whether Robin was from Yorkshire or Nottinghamshire (mostly between respective council officials and MPs!) was recently re-ignited with the publishing of a book in association with Sheffield Council, *'Reclaiming Robin Hood'* (Independent Publishing Network, 2021), by teacher/historian Dan Eaton and Dr David Clarke, folklore professor at Sheffield Hallam University. In it, they lay out their strong claim on Loxley and their discovery of an ancient stone cross marker purportedly pinpointing his birthplace in Little Haggas croft as

---

they have been described as the greatest collection ever assembled by a single individual, not just in quantity and variety but in the exceptional quality of the items.

[97] *Exact and Perfect Survey and View of the Manor of Sheffield and other Lands*, John Harrison, 1637

identified by Harrison back in 1637—albeit this is still almost 600 years after the date of Robin's birth being proposed as 1058.

But putting all contemporary arguments aside—what is Waltheof's connection here?

**6. Extract from the Hallam entry in *Domesday Book*
showing reference to Waltheof's aula**
Image courtesy of *www.opendomesday.org*
Anna Powell-Smith, Professor John Palmer and George Slater

Going back to *Domesday Book,* we know that a large hall, or '*aula*', had been built by the Earls of Northumbria in the manor of Hallam, though the settlement of Hallam itself has frustratingly become lost over time and its precise whereabouts remains a mystery and subject of much conjecture. The whole Hallam district was over 720 sq. miles in overall size, accounting for it being sometimes referred to as a 'shire' (this is 5 times the size of the county of Rutland). This *aula* (probably made of timber with a thatch or wood shingle roof—see Illustrations 7 and 60) would have been used both as a hunting lodge and as a court, administering justice over his mini fiefdom—the sixteen hamlets of Hallamshire (regrettably not individually named in Domesday) and its 3000 acres of cultivated land[98] and numerous hunting grounds like Loxley and Rivelin Chases. It was also conveniently precisely halfway between Huntingdon and Durham. From an academic translation of the *Domesday* entry (see fig.6 above):

'*In Hallam, one manor with its 16 hamlets, there are 29 carucates to be taxed. There Earl Waltheof had an aula*'.

---

[98] Because Waltheof died prior to Domesday 1086, an accurate record of his total landholdings at his death in 1076 is unclear. However in 1066 he was Lord of over 100 manors stretching from North Yorkshire down to Essex. Hallam was one of the largest with a population of c.150+. His widow, Judith, held 193 manors in 1086.

While Waltheof was Earl of Huntingdon and Middle Anglia at this time, he was simply Lord of Hallam—a sizeable manor that straddled the border between the kingdoms of Mercia and Northumbria in Yorkshire (Deira as was) and not part of his earldom. Pre-Conquest, like most nobles, he held, as a royal thegn, many lordships, and as tenant-in-chief, across England—106 places according to *Domesday,* mostly in the East Midlands but stretching from North Yorkshire down to Essex. These he continued to hold after the Conquest up to his execution in 1076. He actually had very little to the far north, save a few manors of little value in the North Riding, the exception being this large holding of Hallam, which included Loxley amongst the 16 hamlets of which it was comprised, being in South Yorkshire near the borders of Derbyshire and Nottinghamshire. We also know from the *Domesday* records that Hallam was the only manor owned by the family to include a significant building and can sensibly conclude that, upon the deaths of his brother Osbjorn and his father Siward, his education at Durham then ended (c.1055) and when the unpleasant Tostig assumed the Earldom of Northumbria soon after, Hallam was very probably the place Waltheof retreated to for the next 10 years. Here he would have spent much of his time, from the age of 13/14, until being granted, by Edward the Confessor, the Midland lands of the exiled Tostig and the Earldom of Huntingdon and Northampton in 1065, when aged about 24, just a year prior to the Battle of Hastings.

As a court serving the families of those hamlets, the Hallam *aula* would have been accessible to all on foot. Due to the deteriorating nature of its building materials, its actual site has sadly never been identified beyond doubt, but Hallam Head, Bolsterstone, High Bradfield and Sheffield[99] have all been put forward as possibilities and are further discussed in detail in Appendix 3.

---

[99] It is important to note that at the time of Domesday, in 1086, the manor of Sheffield consisted solely of three ploughlands—literally 'field by the (river) Sheaf', which historically formed part of the border separating the Anglo-Saxon kingdoms of Mercia and Northumbria. A ploughland was an area that could nominally be ploughed by a plough team of eight oxen in a single agricultural year—approx. 120–140 acres. So about 400 acres of fields that had no houses and no recorded inhabitants! The town of Sheffield only started to emerge after 1103 when the new Lord of the Manor, William de Lovetot, built his castle there at the confluence of the rivers Sheaf and Don. In comparison, in 1086 Nottingham had a recorded 165 households (population c.1000–1500) and was divided into two separately administered boroughs, one 'Norman French', around the castle, and the other 'Anglo-Saxon English', with the Market Square in between.

However, if my theory is to be believed, then there is every likelihood that it was the place of Robin's conception. With this in mind, we can propose 3 possible candidates for Robin's mother:

Firstly, she may have been the daughter of a neighbouring landowner whose manors abutted those of Waltheof. The prime candidate is a lesser thegn called Healfdene (often simplified to Aldene) who we know from *Domesday* had 69 manors and looked after Waltheof's interests in his absence. He may have lived in one of his own manors, as just a mile or 2 from Bradfield is one of his Domesday manors of 1066, a place called Ughill (a residence and road that still exist to this day) or similarly that of Wadsley manor, just a mile from Loxley itself. If young Waltheof invited local landowners to his *aula* for a hunting party, would Healfdene have brought his daughter along with the hope of matchmaking?

A second possibility is that she was the daughter of one of Waltheof's tenant farmers from the 16 hamlets comprising the Hallamshire lordship. Again we know from *Domesday* that this comprised 33 families. But would someone so far down the pecking order of society ever have had occasion to meet a highborn and powerful noble, son of the late earl? This leads us to my final and preferred option.

7. A 20m-long reconstructed Anglo-Saxon Long Hall
(made by re-enactment group Regia Anglorum)—similar to the *aula* of Waltheof, though his may have had defensive features like a ditch and timber palisade.
Permission for © photo granted by Alan Tidy

What we know, from later history, is that there was a long lineage of estate managers from the Loxley (Lokeslay/Lockesley/Locksley) family[100]—named after their village, like so many Old English surnames (such as my own). These managers, called bailiffs or reeves (managing the resources of the forests and hunting chases while taking care of the aula) would always be in residence during visits by their Lord (or as mentioned above, more permanent residence), in order to attend to him, his entourage and his officials. They would also be responsible for organising medieval deer hunts for the nobility, quite a complex, sophisticated and labour-intensive job, needing highly qualified staff, aside from organising all the usual domestic household retainers like cooks and housemaids etc. needed to cater for the elite. Records show the Loxleys to have been reeves and bailiffs in Bradfield, a huge hunting estate for the Lord of Hallam that ran from Ecclesall, Sandygate, Fulwood, Rivelin Chase, Stannington, Loxley Chase[101], Wadsley and Shirecliffe, westwood to the boundaries of Bradfield in the Low Peak District, some 7000 acres or more[102]. It is very likely that the estate manager/chief hunter and man responsible for the foresters, Loxley, would have brought along his daughter to help him with such important events. As a local girl living walking distance from Waltheof's *aula*, my preferred candidate is definitely several notches down the social ladder, but if her father was responsible for the maintenance of the Lord's *aula* and hunting grounds, a man

---

[100] *An Account of the Loxleys of Hallamshire*, F. L. Preston, 1966 (Local Studies Section of Sheffield City Library, reference 929.2 LOXL SST) details manuscripts from Thomas de Lokeslay, the Bailiff of Bradfield in 1399, and his son John, Reeve of Bradfield in 1417 and again (perhaps his son John) in 1439 to 1443.

[101] Chases were private woodland within the estates of barons, knights, lords, sheriffs or religious houses, i.e. not royal land directly owned by the king. At their zenith, there were 70 royal forests in medieval times, maybe just as many private 'chases' and more than 1900 fenced deer parks. Forest Law gave the right of 'free chase' to its lord, the exclusive right to hunt not only venison, but all wild animals in a forest or chase. *Agricultural History Review. 'Deer and deer farming in medieval England'*. Jean Birrell. 1992. Vol 40, Part 2.

[102] *Historic Hallamshire*, David Hey, Landmark, 2002 and *Hallamshire. The History and Topography of the Parish of Sheffield in the County of York,* Joseph Hunter (Folio, 1819), Chapter 2. In Domesday, the total woodland in Hallam is recorded as 3 x 3 leagues. A league on land is 4 miles, so the area of Hallam extended to some 144 sq. miles or 92,000 acres. This is about 60% of the size of the New Forest in Norman times and exactly the same size as the New Forest National Park is today.

of the yeoman class (maybe even his chief huntsman), regular liaisons with young Waltheof were much more likely than with a girl of lower or higher status.

Writing 6 decades later, chronicler Henry of Huntingdon described Waltheof as a '*parvulus*' ('child') in 1055—the year of his father's death. At around 13 or 14, the handsome and rich young teenage nobleman found himself fatherless, motherless and brotherless and rattling around his family estate for several years before he was thrown into the maelstrom of English politics with the Norman invasion. One can only imagine how lonely he was in those years and how appealing a friendly, pretty local girl would have been.

Teenage fling or true young love, we do not know, but a future together would have been impossible. Marriages of persons of high birth were almost always politically contrived—as we know, Waltheof was to make just such a union in 1070/1—to Judith, the Norman niece of the king, William the Conqueror.

Son: Robin—or More Likely, Robert (c.1058–1103)

From the 14th century onwards, both real-life chroniclers, playwrights and storytellers have variously described Robin Hood as a disinherited nobleman. While this is detailed further in Chapter 6, for now it leads us to the central core of my hypothesis. I suggest that Waltheof's 'roll in the hay' behind the Hallam aula with the Loxley lass occurred in c.1057 when the young future Earl of Northumbria was around 16–17, and that a rather famous son was the result the following year, born, perhaps, in his mother's humble family cottage, Little Haggas Croft, in the surroundings of 'Loxley Firth' and 'Loxley Common'.

It is very likely that Robin was originally called Robert, or 'Hrodberht'—the 2 names were entirely interchangeable at this time. (While the Norman name Robert came with the Conquest, the Old English 'Hrodberht' was already in use.) If he did use a surname, it would have simply been 'De Lokeslay' or maybe 'FitzWaltheof'. (The prefix 'Fitz' originally meant illegitimate 'son of', usually of a highborn person, but later nobles often incorporated it into their own surnames to simply mean 'son of'—in Scotland and Ireland it is 'Mac' (Gaelic).) As most experts agree, the name 'Robin Hood' was likely a pseudonym or alias adopted later—common practice amongst outlaws. But perhaps, in our Robin's case, it was to mask any association to his father, the only English nobleman executed for treason by the king and was, in itself, a name which implied disguise, secrecy and a 'cloaking' of the body.

Although 'bastard' is used as a general insult today, or to describe a child born to non-marital unions, it still has echoes of shame and sin despite being largely free of the kind of stigma once attached to it. However, prior to the 13th century, legitimate marriage or its absence was not the key factor in determining quality of birth. Instead, what mattered was the social status of the parents. If both parties were noble then, regardless of whether they were married, a child could be deemed worthy of inheriting parents' lands, properties and titles.[103] This was even the case with offspring between noble and non-noble. A good example here is William the Conqueror himself. Often referred to as 'William the Bastard'[104], he was born to Robert II, Duke of Normandy and Herleva (the daughter of Fulbert of Falaise[105], who was either a tanner or an undertaker/embalmer—opinion is divided—but later made the Duke's 'Chamberlain'!) to whom Duke Robert clearly was not married. William never doubted his legitimacy to the lands and titles and was recognised by his father as his heir. Robin may have hoped for the same treatment, but as his mother most likely was non-noble *and* his titled father was executed as a traitor (historically a traitor's lands were forfeit—in Waltheof's case, they passed to his Norman widow, Judith), his chances would have evaporated.

So how would this 'bastard' boy have survived throughout a turbulent period of battles, genocide, famine and pestilence that may well have killed his mother and the Loxley family? The first explanation assumes that he had a close relationship with his father and that in 1068, around 10 years old, he was taken to Normandy by Waltheof when 'guests' of the Conqueror. Children were rarely, if ever, mentioned by chroniclers (royals aside), though the children of nobles as young as 5 were taken as hostages by the Normans. If he did go, it is likely he

---

[103] King Henry I had many illegitimate children who were all treated very favourably with lands, titles, positions and marriages.

[104] In a Royal Proclamation drawn up in 1069 to transfer some property, the wording is actually given as...*Ego Wil(el)mus cognomine Bastardus Rex Anglie* (I, William, surnamed Bastard, King of England) such that clearly no shame attached to the use of the title. (from 'Alain Le Roux et Alain Le Noir, Comtes de Bretagne'—Annales de Bretagne, André Wilmart (1928): p.581.)

[105] This detail from early 12th-century additions made by Orderic Vitalis to his *Gesta Normannorum Ducum*.

played with, and perhaps was educated alongside the king's young son, William Rufus, similar in age to himself[106]. Was the interaction of these boys a reason for William to act so favourably towards Waltheof (including his leniency shown after his first rebellion)? It seems as good a reason as any. If the boy was with his father in Normandy, it is likely he returned to England with Waltheof and lived with him for a year or so in Huntingdon, then subsequently moved to the safety of the Scottish Court prior to the bloody insurrections and subsequent harrying of late 1069–70, returning home after his father's submission to the king in spring 1070.

The second possibility, which I prefer, is that his father had been unwilling or, more likely, unable to take him to Normandy, so he remained in Hallam, living for nearly 2 years with the many deposed Yorkshire thegns (friends of his father) and their housecarls in the woods and marshes of the Wild West Riding (like those with Hereward in the Fens of East Anglia). To the Normans, they were known as '*silvatici*' (of the woods, wild) and to the English, 'green men'. These thegns had strong Danish heritage and lived by the Norse axiom of '*joyous and liberal everyone should be, until the hour of his death*'.[107] Maybe young Robin stayed under their protection as a 'green boy'. But if he had any kind of relationship with his father, in all likelihood, he would have been scooped up by Waltheof in 1069, on his journey north to join the rebels in the Scottish Court and then, as with the first possibility, returned when it was safe the following year.

Either way, aged about 11, he may well have spent several months at the court of King Malcolm becoming acquainted with the 2 English princesses ensconced there; Margaret—soon to marry King Malcolm—and her sister Christina, both in their early twenties and the granddaughters of Edmund Ironside (King of England for 7 months back in 1016). He would also have observed close-up, those renowned characters from history like the 1069 rebels Earls Gospatric, Edwin and Morcar also Siward Barn, Arnketil and the sons of Carl, as well as Prince Edgar Atheling. Princess Christina (c.22) in particular would likely have taken care of him, perhaps even educated him a little, as she

---

[106] It is even possible they were taught at Caen Abbey school by Abbot Lanfranc, the future Archbishop of Canterbury in 1070 and who became a close friend and patron of Waltheof.

[107] Taken from *The Hávamál* (*'Sayings of the High One'*), a series of Old Norse poems from the Viking age, mainly attributed to their supreme god, Odin.

features again later in his life. She never married and, years later, became a nun at Romsey Abbey, where she educated her sister's 2 daughters, princesses Edith (future wife of King Henry I) and Mary. Her relationship to Waltheof, and to my Robin, is an interesting one, as we shall see in Part II.

The Saxon-Danish gene pool of Waltheof, his father Siward and the House of Bamburgh in general, certainly looks to have produced just the sort of man Robin is alluded to have been in the ballads and elsewhere: physically larger than average, strongly built, good-looking, some education (assuming he experienced early periods of court life), devout, chivalric[108], an engaging personality, a shrewd tactician and a good leader with a strong sense of justice, an aptitude for weaponry skills and forever loyal—to his men and to England. Perhaps these attributes were tinged with the slightly lower-class flavour of the common man and philanthropic influence inherited from his Loxley side: rough edges and the ruthless, fearless streak of the yeoman outlaw of the earliest ballads, plus a knowledge of the greenwood. His targets were always wealthy travellers, in particular men of the church, nobles and sheriffs, all of whom had become rapacious landlords.

Robin's formative years would have been the same as many Anglo-Saxon yeoman class—high festivity in the hall and forest, and skills with the bow and hunting. The hunting was not the ritualistic sport indulged in by Norman noblemen but the simple action of those seeking food in defiance of oppressively strict game/Forest Laws.[109] His skills with a bow and arrow were, of course, legendary. In Child Ballad 139: *Robin's Progress to Nottingham,* the 15-year-old Robin goes to dine, drink ale and enter an archery contest with 15 of the king's foresters in the presence of the sheriff. He makes a wager with them that

---

[108] Chivalry, or the chivalric code, is an informal and varying code of conduct that developed in early medieval Europe, particularly Francia, and was associated with the Christian institution of knighthood. If Robin and his father did observe and absorb court life they would have witnessed this conduct among the Norman elite—a moral system which combined a warrior ethos, knightly piety, and courtly manners, all combining to establish a notion of honour and nobility.

[109] Before his father's death in 1076, Robin probably had legitimate right to hunt on his father's Hallam lands of Loxley and Rivelin Chases. Afterwards, his stepmother, Judith, sublet the estates to the great Norman baron Roger de Busli, based at nearby Blyth/Tickhill castle, and Robin's hunting rights were no doubt curtailed.

he can shoot a deer from 550 yards (500 metres), but when he does, they refuse to pay. All hell breaks loose and Robin kills every one of the foresters.[110]

If indeed Waltheof had a son out of wedlock, then at the age of 15 (c.1074) this son fits perfectly with the ballad's story: He would have claimed the 'rights of manhood' under Danish custom, as his father had done. He would have received 'the arms of a man', after which he would be considered his own master, obliged to provide for himself and expected to live by *'the spoils of the chase and the foray'*. This upbringing certainly would have given Robin the skills needed to survive, or indeed thrive, as an outlaw. However, it is now 1075 and things are about to go very wrong for his father, Waltheof.

---

[110] Without doubt the numbers in the story were exaggerated by the later balladeers to extol the skills of Robin. Modern experiments with a hugely muscular and skilled bowman, using bows of vast pull-weights have rarely achieved a distance exceeding 350 yards, 240 yards being more normal and specific target accuracy totally disappears at such lengths, so maybe these somewhat unlikely distances were originally in 'feet' and took on 'fisherman' enhanced length latterly!

Chapter 5
Treachery and Downfall

"William, who reddened steel and cut through the icy sea from the south, has indeed betrayed the doughty Waltheof under a truce; truly the slaying of men will be long ceasing in England, [but] no more glorious lord than was my gallant chief shall die."
(Extract of 11th century Skaldic poem *Valpjosflokkr* by Thorkell Skallasson, Waltheof's Icelandic 'skald' or courtly poet)[111]

In c.1071, before Robin came of age, when around 12 or 13, his father, Waltheof, married the king's niece, Judith de Lens (a political union undoubtedly arranged by King William), who, at 17/18 was only about 5 years older than her bastard stepson. The couple had 2 daughters, Maud (c.1072, a medieval variant of Matilda) and Adelisa (c.1074, more commonly known as Alice). About a year after the birth of Alice, Waltheof was implicated in an attempted coup to bring down the king; this time not by English rebels but by the Conqueror's own men. His demise is worthy of detail as it triggered a subsequent domino effect of crucial events, shaping my Robin into the credible outlaw of legend.

From 1066, 3 men effectively ruled England as Joint Justiciars, owing to William being in Normandy for much of his early reign. This trio were: Bishop Odo of Bayeux—William's extremely unpleasant and immoral maternal half-brother (he was also Earl of Kent and the man thought responsible for commissioning the Bayeux Tapestry[112]); and 2 more slightly distant cousins,

---

[111] *Skaldic Verse and Anglo-Saxon History*, Alistair Campbell: Dorothea Coke Memorial Lecture in Northern Studies delivered at UCL, 1970 (H.K. Lewis for the College, London, 1971)

[112] The tapestry is actually an embroidery and was most likely produced by English female embroiderers in Canterbury, Kent.

Richard FitzGilbert of Clare and Tonbridge; and William FitzOsbern—both being the king's closest friends (and the sons of 2 of his guardians when he was a child—both of whom were murdered when protecting the young Duke). FitzOsbern was his right-hand man, trusted advisor and great castle builder (made 1st Earl of Hereford post-Conquest). In the king's absence, they all ruthlessly seized land, built castles[113] and raised taxes. As the Anglo-Saxon Chronicle grimly recorded... *"The peasants were sorely burdened, the unhappy people of the country, with forced labour on the castles...and when the castles were made they filled them with devils and wicked men."*

William FitzOsborn was killed soon after Hastings, in 1071, at the Battle of Cassel in Flanders. His eldest son, William II de Breteuil, inherited his father's Normandy estates, becoming Keeper of the King's Treasury in Winchester and will reappear later in Part II of our story.

Meanwhile, FitzOsborn's younger son, Roger de Breteuil, born in Hereford, became 2nd Earl of Hereford and inherited FitzOsbern's English estates and the vast castle network he had constructed, including Hereford itself and subsequently those of Carisbrook, Chepstow,[114] Berkeley, Monmouth and Shrewsbury as well those in the Welsh Marches like Wigmore and Clifford.

Roger is described by chronicler William of Malmesbury, as '*a youth of hateful perfidy*'; in other words, deceitful and untrustworthy. The letters of Lanfranc, Archbishop of Canterbury, complain of his violence and rebellious tendencies, for which the writer eventually excommunicated him. In 1075, Roger arranged the marriage of his sister, Emma, to his friend, the Anglo-Breton baron Ralph de Gael, 1st Earl of Norfolk. Ralph was half English being also born in England c.1040, thus about the same age as Waltheof. The 2 men knew each other well, as Ralph held the earldom (of Norfolk) adjacent to that of Waltheof's (of Huntingdon/Northampton).

Waltheof (35) and Judith (now 21), attended the lavish bride-ale in Exning, Suffolk (but then in Cambridgeshire).[115] Although the events that unfolded at this

---

[113] By the time of Domesday in 1087, after 21 years of occupation, the Normans had already constructed 86 motte and bailey castles.

[114] Chepstow Castle is the oldest surviving post-Roman stone fortification in Britain.

[115] A 'bride-ale' is a wedding feast. Although the Anglo-Saxon chronicle places the event at Norwich (probably because Ralph was Earl of Norfolk), John of Worcester (d.c.1140) specifically says it was in the village of Exning, 50 miles to the south-west, just 15 miles from Cambridge.

wedding were reported by several sources, including *The Anglo-Saxon Chronicle*, we have no idea if the teenage Robin was there, but we do know that, during the festivities, Waltheof became involved in a conspiracy that had been plotted for some time by Roger and the groom, Ralph. Disputing the 'Bastard' William the Conqueror's legitimate right to the throne, they had become increasingly unhappy with the continual encroachments of the sheriffs on their traditional rights and planned a *coup d'état*. Possibly with, or maybe without, the connivance of Waltheof, they devised a plan to overthrow the king and divide England into 3 great feudal Duchies: with Wessex destined for Roger; Mercia for Ralph; and Northumbria for Waltheof (as the only one of the 3 with any chance of containing the wild north). Between them, as Earls of Northumbria, Huntingdon, Northampton and Norfolk, Ralph and Waltheof ruled practically the whole of what had been the Danelaw[116]. Some historians even suggest they were going to promote Waltheof as the next King of England. Prior to this moment though, Waltheof had been held in respect by the church and was highly favoured and trusted by the king, there being no indication that he felt in the least dissatisfied with his current position until this sudden and fatal implication with the 2 troublesome earls.

This plan became known later as 'The Revolt of the Earls at the Bride-ale of Norwich'. Despite Archbishop Lanfranc's low opinions of Roger, he recorded that, in this particular instance, the main traitor was more likely the groom, Ralph de Gael, and that Roger had been '*led astray by the counsel of evil men*'.

According to the chronicler Florence of Worcester '*...they compelled Earl Waltheof, who had been entrapped by their wiles, to join them in the plot*'.[117], but it seems Waltheof was only temporarily led astray. In the cold light of day, perhaps after any alcohol-fuelled enthusiasm wore off, he changed his mind and

---

[116] The Danelaw was the part of England in which the laws of the Danes held sway and dominated those of the Anglo-Saxons from a.d.878, but which came to an end in a.d.954. The areas that constituted the Danelaw lie in northern and eastern England, long occupied by Danes and other Norsemen, roughly comprising everything east of a line drawn between London and Chester.

[117] *Chronicon ex chronicis* is a worldwide history which begins with the creation and ends in 1140 attributed to two monks, Florence (d.1118) and John of Worcester (d.c.1140))

refused to take part. However, as he now had knowledge of the planned treachery, he was made to swear a '*terrible oath*' of secrecy.[118]

The most accepted version of what happened next is that the rather politically inept Waltheof became panicked, even scared, and did not keep the oath. Instead, he sought the advice of the one man he trusted—Archbishop Lanfranc. Sometimes described as Waltheof's patron, Lanfranc was an Italian brought over to Canterbury by King William after Archbishop Stigand was deposed in 1070, much to the disgust of Bishop Odo who loathed Lanfranc intensely, even more than he hated Waltheof, and feuded with him regularly[119]. Lanfranc was Abbot of St Etienne in Caen back in 1067, precisely when Waltheof and others were being held as VIP hostages in Normandy at Caen Castle and they very likely became friends during those months of confinement. Lanfranc's advice to Waltheof was to go immediately to Normandy and reveal the whole plan to King William, which, according to practically all accounts, he duly did. William received him kindly and showed no signs that he regarded Waltheof as seriously implicated, apparently promising him forgiveness. Yet on his return to England, Waltheof found himself immediately arrested by Odo, one must presume, on William's orders.

The uprising failed miserably. Soon after Waltheof's arrest, the Anglo-Saxon but pro-Norman Bishop of Worcester, Wulfstan, raised a huge army and crushed the forces of the would-be rebels. Roger escaped but was later captured, his lands forfeited and he was imprisoned for 12 years until the amnesty given to all political prisoners on the death of William the Conqueror in 1087. Ralph escaped back to Brittany, primarily to seek aid from the Danes. His new bride Emma heroically defended their castle at Norwich in his absence and withstood a siege for 3 months. The Danish fleet arrived too late to lift the siege and Emma then also had to escape to Normandy. Ralph and Emma lost all their English lands as

---

[118] "*coniuratione terribili,*" *Historia Ecclesiastica*, IV: ii, 261–2, Orderic Vitalis. Orderic writing some 45 years after the event considered Waltheof a hero, a good and loyal vassal and 'saintly' and although guilty by omission rather than commission, it was his enemies at court who had pushed through the demands for his execution.

[119] At precisely this moment there was an acrimonious court case called '*The trial of Penenden Heath*' which involved a dispute and enquiry between Odo, Bishop of Bayeux, half-brother of the Conqueror and Archbishop Lanfranc and others into the activities of Odo, who had allegedly defrauded the Church (and possibly the Crown) of lands, during his tenure as Earl of Kent.

a consequence and both died some years later in the Holy Land, when travelling on the First Crusade c.1097, with William the Conqueror's eldest son, Robert Curthose, Duke of Normandy.

As for Waltheof, the king who initially accepted his protestations of innocence, for a reason we do not know, when Waltheof returned to England had him arrested and charged with treason. Orderic and others propose that it was his wife Judith who betrayed him to William and had him arrested. As their marriage was most definitely an arranged political alliance, not a love-match, this betrayal was possible (some conclude 'probable').

Others suggest that Waltheof was caught up in the bitter ongoing feud between Waltheof's friend, Archbishop Lanfranc, and Bishop Odo of Bayeux, because his execution was organised (though not finally sanctioned) in the king's absence by a powerful group led by Odo, who clearly detested both Lanfranc and Waltheof. It must be pointed out that Odo was also Judith's half-uncle (he being a half-brother of the Conqueror) and either wielded a lot of power over her, or on behalf of her.

The general view, however, is that King William must have approved the death penalty himself, given the importance of Waltheof. It is suggested that he had some regrets latterly, having succumbed to the pressures of his half-brother Odo and perhaps others who had reason to get rid of the powerful Anglo-Danish Earl of Northumbria, as the Normans could not hope to control or govern this northern region. While Waltheof lived, the area was closed to Norman ambition only becoming ripe for conquest and redistribution of lands after his death in 1976. Certainly after the execution, William's reign set on a downward spiral and he came to see the event as the trigger for his decline.

Either way, the vast majority of academics conclude that Waltheof was totally innocent of the charge that would claim his life. Most of those in contemporary times believed the same. He was held prisoner at Winchester for nearly a year where he was a model of good behaviour, a 'heros'.[120] He was recorded as spending his captivity as a penitent, fasting and praying daily. Lanfranc lobbied on his behalf for clemency and there was a strong groundswell of support in favour of leniency. His situation must have been debated vigorously in the following months, with English and Normans taking opposite sides, although there was a widespread expectation that he would be spared given the

---

[120] Orderic II, 320–21. *'praefatus heros'*. This has been translated as *'brave earl'* but could also suggest *'hero'* or simply *'a good man'*.

intervention of the Archbishop of Canterbury. No nobleman had been executed by William despite many rebellions and many attempts to overthrow him in the 10 years since Hastings. However, this particular Earl proved to be the exception. Waltheof was tried under English law (undoubtedly a show trial, officiated by Normans and swayed by Odo), for which the penalty for treason was death, whereas the 2 main co-conspirators were tried under Norman law, for which the penalty was life imprisonment.

On 31st May 1076, after giving away his fine clothing to the poor, Waltheof was led up St Giles Hill, Winchester and beheaded—the last member of his family of the House of Bamburgh to ever rule over Northumbria. As he had become a hero to many, the sentence was carried out very early in the morning before crowds could gather, cause a disturbance or even mount a rescue. What happened next was described as 'obscure' in one reference and most accounts vary. It is said that his body was flung, 'unceremoniously, into a ditch by the royal officers present at his execution and hastily covered with fresh turf'. However it was later recovered soon after, presumably by loyal Saxon locals, then taken by nuns to be buried at Romsey Abbey, 12 miles away. Romsey had a long history (back to 907) of Royal Saxon foundation and patronage. The febrile atmosphere in Winchester nourished the idea that Waltheof was a martyr, even a saint. There are accounts that in the last few moments of his life, as Waltheof recited the Lord's Prayer, the blade fell and as his severed head hit the ground, it was heard by all present to clearly utter the words 'and deliver us from evil'...[121]

About 2 weeks after Waltheof's execution, his wife Judith—perhaps feeling some contrition for her part in Waltheof's downfall (maybe expecting a prison sentence for Waltheof, not execution)—wrote to her uncle, King William, and was afforded him a proper and decent burial.[122] With the assistance of Ulfketyl, the Abbot of Croyland, his body was recovered from Romsey and reburied at Croyland Abbey near Peterborough, in the chapterhouse.[123] Prior to this long journey of several days over some 170 miles[124], in order to preserve the corpse

---

[121] Historia Ecclesiastica, II: Orderic Vitalis, pp.320–21

[122] Ibid, pp. 322–23 and 344–47,

[123] Croyland was an Anglo-Saxon foundation from the 8th century which later adopted the Benedictine rule. Hereward the Wake had been a tenant of the Abbey.

[124] In medieval times, speed and distance travelled depended on weather, terrain and road conditions, how much baggage you were carrying, and how much of a hurry you were

the nuns of Romsey would have removed the entrails of poor Waltheof, his *'intestina'*, and treated his body with spices to embalm it, no doubt sewing his head back on. When Waltheof was thus disinterred a couple of weeks later for transfer to Croyland, Orderic reported that his body was, *`integrum cum recenti cruore acsi tunc idem uir obisset erat'* (incorrupt with blood as fresh as if he had just died),[125] all of which only added to Waltheof's sanctity and miraculous nature. For persons of high noble rank, embalming was not unusual at this time, following which the separate burial of heart and body was also not uncommon, with the growing notion of courtly love and ideas about the heart as the seat of the soul, affections, courage and conscience of man. It would seem that the Romsey nuns then preserved that of Waltheof, which became the object of a shrine at the abbey. It seems entirely plausible that a number of the aristocratic Saxon nuns may well have been widows of thegns who had fought and died alongside Waltheof at Fulford, Stamford Bridge and York. They would have revered the heroic, pious Earl Waltheof and relished the chance to create a reliquary for him. 'The Anglo-Saxon Chronicle' for 1075 reported that:

'Earl Waltheof went overseas [to Normandy, to visit the king] and accused himself and asked for pardon and offered treasure', adding that *'the king made light of it, let him off lightly, until he came to England and then had him arrested'.*

This passage seems to contain the germ of the opinion, soon to become widespread, that William had betrayed Waltheof, and that his execution was little more than judicial murder. It was this conviction of the earl's innocence which gave rise to his veneration as a saint and martyr.

It was standard practice at the time for the lands of a traitor to be seized and returned to the Crown, so suspicions of Judith's betrayal of her husband have

---

in—varying as much as from 12 to 60 miles a day. In rainy weather most baggage trains with bullock carts might cover up to 15 miles at best whereas a lone rider in sunshine could achieve around 25–30. Specialist couriers who also rode at night and had changes of horse could even reach 55–60. Details from *'Mistress, Maids and Men: Baronial Life in the Thirteenth Century'*, Margaret Wade Labarge, Phoenix, 2003. (pp. 156–7) and *'Power and Profit: The Merchant in Medieval Europe'*, Peter Spufford, Thames and Hudson, 2002. (p.200)

[125] This exact same procedure was followed after the execution of Charles I.

been hardened by the fact that King William not only gave her all the lands of her deceased husband, but even increased her holdings to 193 manors, covering 11 counties in the Midlands and East Anglia and according to *Domesday,* making her the richest woman and most powerful female landholder in all England by 1086. However, at some point, around this time, the king then tried to force Judith to remarry, to a recently arrived French nobleman called Simon de Senlis,[126] but she refused him, using his 'lameness' as a reason, as seemingly he had some form of gammy leg, perhaps a 'club foot'. This may very well have been a good excuse, as it Is further suggested that with Waltheof's continued absence on church and castle-building business, she was having an affair with another man, an affair that may well have predated Waltheof's betrayal (this will be investigated further in Part II). Simon is described in the Anglo-Saxon Chronicle as 'a brave knight, but lame and ill-formed'.[127] A furious King William temporarily stripped her of most of her lands and later (c.1088) and after the Domesday survey and after he had died, the new monarch, William II, Rufus, made Simon the [1st] Earl of Northampton along with its lands[128] and revenues, previously a good portion of Waltheof's earldom of Huntingdon. At the same time, in a somewhat bizarre turn of events, Simon, presumably with the approval of Rufus, the new king (who had a soft spot for heroic soldiers), then wed Judith's eldest daughter, the 18-year-old Maud, in c.1089/90 instead of her mother!; a marriage that has significant impact upon Robin's story in Part II of our saga...

---

[126] Although historical facts are sparse, It is believed Simon and his elder brother, Guarnerius le Ryche (William the Rich), both came over to England after the Conquest from their home in Senlis, near Paris in the Île-de-France, that part of France ruled directly by the French monarch. On the death of their father, Simon's brother returned to France to claim the paternal inheritance but Simon stayed to ply his trade as a soldier of fortune. (From *A History of the County of Northamptonshire*—'The Priory of St Andrew', published by VCH, London, 1906, Vol. 2, p.102).

[127] *L'Histoire de la conquête de l'Angleterre par les Normands (The History of The Norman Conquest of England),* A. Thierry, 1825, vol. 1, p.286.

[128] This transfer of property to Simon must have been post Domesday (1086), as Northampton is still shown as being held by William the Conqueror at that time. Simon is not recorded anywhere in the Domesday Book such that if earlier, he must have been landless or maybe arrived in England after Domesday, but before the Conqueror died— sometime between autumn of 1086 and summer 1087.

According to Dugdale[129], a consequence of William the Conqueror's earlier wrath and English fury, was that Judith was scorned by the Normans and forced to temporarily flee with her young daughters to the fens around Ely in Cambridgeshire, where the Saxons *'refused her shelter with bitter hatred'*. The monks of Croyland, on the edge of the fens, recorded in their chronicle (believed written by Ingulf, a monk there, prior to his being later appointed abbot in 1087) a visit made by Judith, *'a wicked jezebel'*[130], to her husband's tomb after she heard that it was responsible for miracles. She is reported as having been frightened by the news and to appease his soul she went there and offered a pall—a silken covering—for her husband's tomb. According to author, Charles Kingsley, who used the old abbey records to describe the scene in his historical novel *Hereward the Wake, the Last of the English*:

"Judith, habited in widow's weeds, approached the tomb, and laid on it, as a peace-offering to the manes of the dead, a splendid pall of silk and gold. A fierce blast came howling off the fen, screeched through the minster towers, swept along the dark aisles; and then, so say the chroniclers, caught up the pall from off the tomb, and hurled it far away into a corner. 'A miracle', cried all the monks at once; and honestly enough, like true Englishmen as they were. 'The Holy heart refuses the gift, Countess', said old Ulfketyl in a voice of awe. Judith covered her face with her hands, turned away trembling, and walked out, while all looked upon her as a thing accursed. Of her subsequent life, her folly, her wantonness, her disgrace, her poverty, her wanderings, her wretched death, let others tell. But these Normans believed that the curse of heaven was upon her from that day. And the best of them believed likewise that Waltheof's murder was the reason that William, her uncle, prospered no more in life."[131]

Following a disastrous fire at Croyland in 1091, Waltheof's body was moved again, from the burnt-out chapterhouse to a prominent place near the church altar. During this transfer, his coffin was opened and his 15-year-old corpse was found

---

[129] *Monasticon Anglicanum: A history of Abbeys and other Monasteries*, William Dugdale. Published by James Bohn, London, 1846.

[130] A stinging indictment by chronicler Ingulf, given he was previously a monk of St Wandrille, at Fontanelle in Normandy, an Abbey generously endowed by Judith.

[131] *Hereward the Wake, Last of the English*, The Reverend Charles Kingsley, 1866, Macmillan & Co, pp.329–330. A 'pall' is a cloth spread over a tomb or coffin.

to be uncorrupted and intact—the head rejoined to the trunk with only a fine crimson line showing where it had been cut off. This was perceived as a miracle[132] (though one suspects that the earlier good embalming and needlework of the Romsey nuns were more likely the reason!) and after being publicised by the monks of Croyland, the story began to draw pilgrims who brought welcome financial donations with them.

Stepping backwards, imagine if Waltheof's illegitimate and only son Robin, about 18 years old, had visited his father in prison at Winchester over the months of his confinement, was even present for his execution and perhaps helped out with the rapid internment of his body at Romsey Abbey. Maybe he even assisted the nuns in recovering the corpse and severed head, transporting them to the nunnery and helped establish the shrine—if so, a truly traumatising experience for a young son. Regardless of whether he was there or not, surely with the controversial execution of his heroic and innocent father, the first seeds of vengeance had now been sown. The ballads tell us that, prior to being an outlaw, Robin had been employed in the king's service—in our case as a royal forester, perhaps aided by his stepmother to ensure the charismatic son of near-sainted Waltheof was kept out of trouble and did not, himself, become the focus of support for future rebellion. Was he in fact given a 'pardon' by the Conqueror, in 1076, for any implied involvement in his father's 'treason', prior to his later outlawry in 1080 and then 22 years in the greenwood as detailed in *The Gest* and explored in the next chapter?

Certainly, echoing Waltheof's life, Robin's father was now dead, and his natural mother and her family likely deceased. In addition, his young half-sisters were to be hidden away in a Bedfordshire Priory school by his treacherous Norman stepmother who, for the rest of her life, always avoided the attentions of the chroniclers' quill. Little wonder the bastard son has been hard to find.

---

[132] 'Incorruptibility' is a Roman Catholic belief that divine intervention allows some human bodies (specifically saints) to completely or partially avoid the normal process of decomposition after death as a sign of their holiness. Embalmed bodies were not recognized as incorruptibles.

Chapter 6
The Making of...an Outlawed
Noble or Noble Outlaw?

Writing nearly 200 years after the Norman Conquest and the traumatic years that followed it, 13th century historian Mathew Paris explained how noble outlawry came to be:

> "*The English nobility and gentry were driven out from their possessions. Ashamed to beg, ignorant of how to dig, they and their sons and brothers took refuge in the woods. They robbed and they raided rapaciously but only when they were lacking in game or other victuals.*"[133]

Two surviving contemporary monastic chronicles of the period, those of Abingdon and Evesham, also both speak of plots and claims of '*men hiding in the woods plundering and attacking those who came their way*', and of '*outlaws and robbers who hid in the woods and damaged many people*'. Deposed thegns and people like Eadric 'the Wild' around Hereford and Shrewsbury (who joined forces with King Bleddyn of Gwynedd and King Rhiwallon of Powys) fought an open resistance against the invaders, raising rabble armies and harassing the Normans at every opportunity. Collectively these men were known as '*tilvatid*'—living in tents—or more commonly '*silvatici*'—men of the woods or 'green men'—for which the Normans branded them 'outlaws', or outside of the law. Susan Reyolds notes, when referencing the northern regions in the decade following the Conquest and the failed York rebellions of 1068–69:

---

[133] *Historia Anglorum*, c,1250, Matthew Paris, British Library, Royal MS 14 C VII, fols. 8v-156v.

'If it is true…that the silvatici were for some years a widespread and well-known phenomenon, that might help to explain aspects of later outlaw stories that have puzzled historians. Few outlaws in other countries have apparently left so powerful a legend as Robin Hood…The most famous outlaws of the greenwood before him were probably the Old English nobility on their way down and out'.[134]

I suggest that these outlaws of the greenwood were not *before* Robin, as quoted above, but *contemporary* to him as a youth, in that first decade after the conquest. The *silvatici* surely are the basis in history for the original 'Merrie Men' of the legend, men led by Earl Waltheof and other resistance leaders like Hereward, from 1066–1072, of whom my Robin would have been directly influenced during his formative teenage years.

However, in the earliest renderings of the legend, our hero is a yeoman. It is only later that he is depicted in many sources as a noble. Historians and fans through the ages have picked the heritage that goes with their theory and dismissed the other. Can we clear up this conundrum once and for all?

As a good yeoman, Robin appears in the very first stanza of *The Gest* (and Little John is also defined as such in the third stanza):

> *Lythe and listin gentilmen*
> *That be of frebore blode*
> *I shall you tel of a gode yeoman*
> *His name was Robyn Hode*

One of the earliest sources for the word yeoman is a 12th-century text on Forest Law[135], which stated that yeoman foresters were drawn from '*mediocribus hominibus*'—the class of 'middling sort of men' who the English called '*laessthegenes*' (lesser thegns). However, the Danes of the East Midlands and Yorkshire also called them '*yongermen*'[136] or 'yeomen'. In this sense, the yeomen of England were a sort of free peasantry, owning some land and a title

---

[134] '*Eadric Silvaticus and the English Resistance*', Susan Reynolds, *Bulletin of the Institute of Historical Research*, no.54, 1981, p.105.

[135] *Pseudo-Cnut de Foresta (c.1154–89)*

[136] *In Search of England, Journeys into the English Past,* Michael Wood, Penguin Books, 2001.

derived from the old Danelaw[137] lands, primarily lands of the East Midlands, Yorkshire and Northumbria, from where, as far as we can tell, the tales originated. This fits perfectly with our young Robin of Anglo-Danish Viking stock, yet common Saxon upbringing.

From the later medieval period, a yeoman was a small landholder or farmer, or a freeman under the rank of knight, gentleman or squire—somewhere between the upper crust of peasantry and the lower ranks of gentry. In Chaucer's 14th century Canterbury Tales, the yeoman's social standing is further defined. The yeoman in his 'Canon's Yeoman's Tale' is a servant to a cleric and in the General Prologue the Knight is accompanied by a yeoman who '*knew the forest just as he knew his home…this was a hunter indeed*'. This yeoman has a bow and arrows as well as a coat and hood of forest green, just like the yeoman in 'The Friar's Tale', who is a bailiff of the forest.

However, the definition of yeoman was also a title given to those in the service of the king or nobility (as in 'Yeoman of the Guard' at the Tower of London). A royal post was held at some point by Robin, as his being in '*the King's service*' is mentioned in a number of the ballads although his precise role is never specified. In our Robin's case (and probably Little John as well), this was most likely as a royal forester or 'yeoman huntsman', in the same vein as his Loxley family heritage, working under William Peveril (Peverel in *Domesday*), the Sheriff of Nottinghamshire, Derbyshire and Bailiff of the Royal Manors of the Peak[138]. It is just possible that after his father's execution in 1076, after his royal pardon, the king (along with Judith) gave Robin some right of title to Waltheof's lands in Hallamshire, taking in the Loxley area in an attempt to pacify him. If so, he would have been a yeoman both in job title and in land (then stripped 4 years later when, as we shall see, being outlawed in 1080 and the tenancy given by Judith to local Norman baron, Roger de Busli).

As an interesting adjunct, Ms Stredder tells us (admittedly without reference or evidence provided) that the Saxon retainers of the Senlis family adopted the emblem (see below) of: "…*a tree with a bird on a bough, shadowing a huntsman*

---

[137] Danelaw was the historic name given to the Eastern part of England in which the laws of the Danes dominated those of the Anglo-Saxons.

[138] This proposition is closely allied to the tale in *The Gest* where Little John wins an archery contest and is then briefly employed by the impressed Sheriff of Nottingham. John is obviously a fine huntsman and forester, skills much in demand by Peveril to manage his vast Royal Forest of the Peak.

with bow and arrows in his hand, blowing a horn. On the other side of the tree, there is a stag 'current'[139], pursued by 2 dogs."

8. Borough of Huntingdon Municipal Seal
(this version in silver is from 1628)
Courtesy of Huntingdonshire Borough Council

If you recall, Simon Senlis was the 'lame' French husband of Waltheof's daughter Maud, initially refused by her mother Judith. Yet the man depicted here is surely not of French heritage as he is sporting a typically Saxon hairstyle. Could these loyal Saxons have instead pictured Maud's half-brother Robin: the proud outlaw, yeoman archer, hunter and woodsman? Furthermore, in 1205, the Borough of Huntingdon bought its charter from King John and assumed the identical depiction for their municipal seal that continues to this day. Could the Huntingdon Borough folk have been paying quiet homage to their local 'dispossessed Earl'?

With time and more literature, Robin moved up in the world. In the late 14th century, John of Fordun implied Robin was a disinherited nobleman. By 1542,

---

[139] The heraldic term for 'running at full speed'.

John Leland, Henry VIII's chief antiquarian, referred to him in his *Collectanea* as *'nobilis'*, a nobleman and genuine historical figure, but regrettably without giving any grounds for his assertions. In the mid-1500s, 2 respected writers—historian John Major and chronicler Richard Grafton—describe him as of 'noble parentage'.

So, by 1599—over 200 years after John of Fordun's reference (c.1380)—when Elizabethan playwright Anthony Munday wrote 2 plays on Robin Hood being *'the dispossessed and outlawed Earl of Huntingdon'*, he was hardly being original in depicting the character as nobility. This dampens claims that suggesting such was merely a figment of Munday's imagination and an 'engineered' gentrification to please his middle class audience, as it seems Munday was not original but incorporating common knowledge at the time into his plays. More important, though, is the specific earldom.

We already know much about our Robin's noble heritage. Indeed, he may have believed he had some legitimate claim to his father's title as Earl of Huntingdon. Upon the execution of his father, Robin may have cheekily taken the title upon himself as Waltheof's only son. If he did, then his unauthorised use of it was to last for just 4 years until his being outlawed in 1080 and William awarded the title to Robin's young half-sister Maud in the form of 'Countess of Huntingdon' which she held **suo jure** ("in her own right") and her 2 husbands (Simon Senlis then Prince David of Scotland) only later held **'jure uxoris'** ("by right of (his) wife"). Nine of Waltheof's descendants by his daughter Maud (the offspring of her 2 marriages to Simon and David) held the Earldom of Huntingdon for almost 150 years, from around 1090 when Simon married Maud, through to 1237 when her childless great-grandson, John of Scotland, died. Professor Stephen Knight points out that Munday was a close friend of John Stow, a great archivist and historian who would have known about this link and perhaps told Munday about it. Furthermore, our Robin very much fits with the folklore legend that he had a connection to the Royal House of Scotland.

To quote medieval historian and author Thor Ewing:

"Scholars have got so used to saying that Robin was never Earl of Huntingdon that nobody bothers to question it. The scholars like to say that the link with Huntingdon was invented in about 1600 by a playwright called Anthony Munday. But really, that argument just doesn't stand up. There's every reason

to think Robin Hood was known as Earl of Huntingdon at least fifty years before [the play], *and it probably goes right back to the start of the legend.* "[140]

From the meagre recorded history of the 11th century, the best known noble outlaw was undoubtedly the royal thegn, Hereward 'the Wake' ('the Ever-Watchful'). As his life is inextricably linked with Waltheof's and Robin's, it should be mentioned here. Hereward's feats—set around East Anglia—are sung in the 12th century Latin text *Gesta Herewardii* of Ely Abbey, which tells of his strength, skill in archery, life in the greenwood, quarrels with the Norman abbots and even his being pardoned by the king and betrayed by a woman. In legend, he is often described as the son of Leofric, Earl of Mercia and Lady Godiva, but there is no evidence for such. In fact, historian Peter Rex recently and effectively disproved such, sending this idea into the archives of myth and legend.[141]

Rex's research and thorough analysis of Hereward's true lineage produces a plausible and well-argued conclusion that he was actually the grandson of a wealthy Anglo-Danish magnate. It is inevitable that he knew Waltheof, as his noble Anglo-Danish East Anglian neighbour, and more than likely met and had an influence on the young Robin. Those early 12th century texts from Ely Abbey imply that Earl Waltheof was, for a while, an ally of this local hero. Given that both had landholdings in the area and close connections to both Peterborough and Croyland Abbeys, this is entirely probable. Furthermore, Hereward fought with the Anglian brothers Edwin and Morcar in 1071, who Waltheof had also fought alongside in the earlier northern rebellions a year or 2 before. As a fellow descendant of Anglo-Scandinavian nobility, it seems quite possible that Hereward also became a rebel outlaw ostensibly for the Saxon cause.[142]

---

[140] Extract from article in The National, 23/11/20, re. Thor Ewing's book *The Original Robin Hood: Traditional ballads and plays, including all medieval sources,* Welkin Books, 2020.

[141] *Hereward: The Last Englishman*, Peter Rex, The History Press Ltd. 2005.

[142] The Anglo-Norman chronicler Geoffrey Gaimar, in his poetic *Estoire des Engleis* (*History of the English People,* c.1140), says that Hereward lived for some time as an outlaw in the Fens. He was on the verge of making peace with William when he was set upon and killed by a group of Norman knights. No one seems to know if this is true, but as historian Maurice Keen observed— '*Hereward is the lineal ancestor of later English outlaws*'. (*The Outlaws of Medieval Legend* , M. Keen, Routledge, 1961, p.38).

Unlike Robin Hood, whose tales are unrecorded in written or printed form until the 15th century, Hereward is a fully recognised historical figure in contemporary texts, with stories evolving into a body of ballad hero-lore less than 50 years after his death. As leader of a rebel army in those early post-conquest years, he was worthy of chronicling in the same way that Waltheof and the other earls were. In contrast, by 1080, nearly 15 years after Hastings, the much smaller forest band of Robin Hood was no rebel army and not a serious threat to the Norman yoke. They were simply a free-living group of dispossessed thegns and disaffected renegade Yorkshire highwaymen and kidnappers, in a vast region of virtually ungovernable forest, not noteworthy enough for the official records, only for ribald tavern songs and minstrel tales to evolve with their exploits, the manner of which that so appealed to the common people.

However, Hereward and Robin have often become intermingled over time. The *De Gestis Herewardi Saxonis,* written (in Latin) by an anonymous monk from Ely Abbey in the early 12th century (under the abbacy of Richard de Clare), even contains a tale of Hereward meeting a potter, swapping clothes and borrowing his wares, all as a disguise to get close to his enemy. This is identical to the early ballad of *Robin Hood and the Potter*—it seems almost all medieval outlaws disguised themselves as 'potters' at one time or another! What seems quite extraordinary is that by the 13th century, the legendary status of the very 'real' outlaw hero Hereward, had dwindled and had been usurped by that of Robin Hood, a person whom many now argue never existed.

Much later, in 1568 during the reign of Elizabeth I, the scholar Richard Grafton one time printer to both Henry VIII and Edward VI, wrote a chronicle about the history of England which contained comment on the legend of Robin Hood. In it, he made reference to Robin being a lord, to Exchequer Records of having had his lands confiscated (Hallamshire in 1080?), to his rash generosity and so becoming a noble outlaw. He also notes his heritage and skills:

"In an olde and auncient Pamphlet, I finde this written of the sayd Robert Hood. This man (sayth he) discended of a nobel parentage: or rather beyng of a base stocke and linage, was for his manhoode and chivalry advanced to the noble dignité of an Erle. Excellyng principally in archery, or shootyng, his manly courage agreeyng thereunto."[143]

---

[143] *'Chronicle at Large',* Richard Grafton (dedicated to William Cecil), 1568, pp. 84–85.

Regrettably he makes no notation as to the source of either this mysterious pamphlet or the Exchequer Records (which he said provided proof of a large official royal reward offered for his capture, 'dead or alive', and one would not imagine, given his position, that he made this up), and regrettably none have ever been found. However this intriguing mixture of noble parentage and 'base stock' is still an important 450-year-old solution to the conundrum of Robin's lineage. All this, including the significant archery skills, fits perfectly with our Robin.

Robin's yeoman status, an expert woodsman and bowman with seemingly strong links to the common man; plus connections to higher society, a 'fringe' nobleman, a man once of land and title acting courteously in the treatment of captured victims—have consistently lead to the question: was he of base or noble stock—a noble outlaw or outlawed noble? Because of my proposed Robin's mixed parentage ('*obliquo sanguine*') of nobility and village girl, we surely now have a much more satisfying answer: He was both, and as Dobson and Taylor said, '*Robin Hood possesses many of the knightly virtues and much of his behaviour can be interpreted as that of a courtly hero transferred to a lower social plane*'[144]—and it was perhaps this unique combination that gave him the authority and respect to lead his band, yet at the same time be a friend to commoners and be 'one of us'—a status that would help develop the legend in the populace.

As for Robin's actual outlawry (which I have already stated commenced in 1080), we must return to his kin. In Anglo-Saxon society, family formed the core of a man's friends, the people who fought beside him in times of trouble, provided hostages[145], helped pay his fines and sought justice in the event of wrongful death. Vengeance for the slain, or 'blood feud'—taking retribution for murdered family members—was the most important aspect, especially for those of Danish/Viking heritage.[146] In his teenage years of the early 1070s, when living

---

[144] *Rhymes of Robyn Hood,* R.B. Dobson and J. Taylor, Pittsburgh, 1976, p.32

[145] Unlike the modern interpretation where they are forcibly taken, in medieval times hostages were given in warfare and diplomacy, as a guarantee to secure transactions. Invariably they would be high status, the king would look after them and they would cost a small fortune to get released. In principle, their lives would be taken in the event of a broken agreement, but while violation of agreements was common, execution of hostages was not.

[146] This was true of the Saxons as well, as in early medieval England, offences such as homicide were mostly dealt with through a system of feud and financial compensation

with his father, Robin would have come under the influence of Waltheof's Icelandic 'Skald', his courtly poet Thorkell Skallasson. Thorkell would undoubtedly have recited to the young boy the epic saga of Beowulf ('saga' is Old Norse meaning '*history what is said*' i.e. oral tradition), a blend of fictional, legendary and historic elements and also those poems about the heroes of the 3 major Icelandic outlaw and feud tales (the Grettis, Gísla and Harðar sagas), all well-known historical figures who lived in the second half of the 10th century.[147] These Icelandic heroes are all outlawed as a result of killing men in feuds of various kinds and like Robin, their outlawry did not result from unprovoked crimes and they are outlawed in their absence. Iceland being pagan at this time, none of these outlaws, unlike Robin, shows much devotion to either Christ or the Virgin Mary, but Grettis, is at least devoted to King (later Saint) Olaf of Norway, much admired by Robin's grandfather, Siward, who founded St Olave's Church in York in his name (later becoming St Mary's Abbey).

The many similarities between these Icelandic outlaws and those of early medieval England, both in incident and story-motif, have been keenly observed by a number of historians, who firmly believe there is a common ancestry in old Norse outlaw tradition between Icelandic and English outlaws.[148]

This feud mentality and its significance cannot be underestimated and was likely the tipping point that then led to Robin being declared an outlaw 'in absentia'—just as in the Icelandic outlaw sagas; something that is never explained in the ballads and for which an answer has often been sought. Before he had reached the age of 22, Robin would have borne witness to 2 of the most renowned and documented blood feuds of the era.

---

whereby family and friends of both offenders and victims settled matters largely on their own, without royal or legal intervention.

[147] A poet was one of the most respected persons in Norse society, Thorkell would surely also have related the great exciting sagas and poems of famous Viking 'berserkers' and 'wolfskins'. Following Waltheof's death, Thorkell returned to Iceland and his master was remembered there in Thorkell's poetry for some 300 years until the 14th century. Robin would have been well aware of his father's 'skald' and the existence of his own Anglo-Saxon 'poor man's version', like the wandering minstrel Alan-a-Dale who joins the band, does seem a likely fit and the likely composer of the original 'word-of-mouth' ballads that passed down through the decades.

[148] *The Relation and Development of English and Icelandic Outlaw Traditions*. Joost de Lange, Haarlem, 1935 also *Outlaws in Medieval England and Iceland*, Anthony Faulkes, The Viking Society, 2009, pp.136–148

The first of these was described earlier and involved Waltheof, in the winter of 1073/4, avenging the murder of his grandfather, Earl Ealdred in 1038 and that of his great-grandfather, Earl Uchtred, back in 1016, the touchpaper which started the whole feud off. Noted by the late medieval historian Sir Frank Stenton as '*the most remarkable private feud in English history*'[149], it would have deeply ingrained in the young Robin the Saxon-Danish tenet of 'feud and revenge', so prevalent a feature of the Nordic sagas.

However, it is the second feud that ties in with the many strands of the legend that suggest Robin's outlawry was brought about by his involvement in the revenge killing of a close relative's murderer—giving us an almost precise date as to when his outlawry commenced.

In 1071, following the defeat of the northern rebels at York, a new Bishop of Durham called William Walcher[150] (Walker) was appointed by King William. He was on exceptionally good terms with Waltheof, who was not only qualified ecclesiastically to sit with the clergy when the bishop held synods, but was also given a licence by the Conqueror to build Walcher a castle at Durham as protection against both the Scots and perpetually rebellious Northumbrians. During this period Waltheof presents himself as an interested, generous, humble patron of the church and seems to have been the benefactor to a larger number of churches than most of his contemporaries.

Six years later in 1076, following Waltheof's execution, Walcher was allowed to buy Waltheof's Northumbrian Earldom, it is said for the vast sum of £400—so becoming the first of the great 'Prince-Bishops' (in fact he became the first and only 'Earl-Bishop' of Northumbria) who held both civil and ecclesiastical power in their regions with the right to raise an army, mint their own coins, and levy taxes. As a virtually autonomous ruler, he reaped the revenue from his territory, but also had to remain mindful of his role of protecting England's northern frontier from the marauding Scots. No doubt upon his friend's personal recommendation, Walcher had earlier appointed Waltheof's trusted uncle, the highborn thegn Ligulf of Lumley (from Chester-Le-Street and married to Waltheof's aunt Aldgytha—Appendix 2.1), as one of his favoured

---

[149] *Anglo-Saxon England* (3rd ed.), Frank Stenton, Oxford University Press, 1971, p.390
[150] A priest and a secular clerk from Liège in Lothringia.

advisers, whose presence in the bishop's council provided an ongoing link with the local aristocracy, to theoretically help keep the peace.[151]

Following another Scottish incursion during 1079, which Walcher was either unable or unwilling to defend against effectively, the Scots plundered Northumberland for about 3 weeks unopposed, before returning home with slaves and booty. Ligulf was angered by Walcher's poor leadership, publicly criticised him and his men at the episcopal council and their relationship collapsed. Ligulf evidently upheld the rights of the people against the oppression of the bishop's officers, who were jealous of the favour shown him by their lord, Walcher. Specifically the 2 oppressive and powerful henchmen were—Gilbert (Walcher's kinsman, to whom was delegated administration of the earldom) and Leobwine (his chaplain, responsible for the bishop's private affairs). Leobwine, the chaplain, especially hated Ligulf, and even insulted him in the bishop's presence. On this occasion, Ligulf was provoked to give him a fierce answer and Leobwine left the meeting in wild anger begging Gilbert to get rid of his enemy.[152]

Consequently, and foolishly, probably without Walther's blessing, Gilbert and Leobwine then attacked Ligulf's hall in the middle of the night, slaughtering the nobleman and most of his household, though not his wife. The Northumbrians were naturally enraged at the murder of one of their leaders. This included kinsmen leader Eadwulf Rus who had continued to represent the House of Bamburgh and Northumbrian interests[153] with the Normans post-Conquest and had been very close to Waltheof. They were related, as second cousins, both being great-grandsons of Earl Uchtred, although the younger Rus was descended from Uchtred and his second wife Sigen (see family tree Appendix 2.1). There was a real threat of northern rebellion yet again. The bishop claimed, probably correctly, that he had no part in the killings and in an attempt to calm the situation, offered to banish his kinsman Gilbert, submit his case to the

---

[151] Ligulf had been a close friend of Waltheof, who had arranged for his cousin, Ligulf's son Morcar, to be educated by the monks at the revived community at Jarrow monastery. (*Durham Episcopal Charters*—Offler, 1071–1152, pp.4–6)

[152] Detail from *Dictionary of National Biography, 1885–1900*, Vol. 59, '*Walcher*', by W. Hunt.

[153] *Saints' Cults in the Celtic World*, eds. Boardman, Davies and Williamson, 2009. p,53.

ecclesiastical judgement of the Pope and make Ligulf's widow a compensatory payment by loaning her land at Thorngate and Wingate for her lifetime.

Walcher, accompanied by at least 100 retainers for safety, including Gilbert and Leobwine, travelled the 16 miles north from his castle in Durham having agreed to meet Ligulf's remaining family and kinsmen at Gateshead church in order to resolve the situation. There, Eadwulf Rus (who had raised a sizeable force of kinsmen which I believe included Robin), presented him with a petition of wrongs committed and various demands, which Walcher refused even to consider unless the Northumbrians stumped up the enormous sum of £400.[154] A brief discussion among the Northumbrians ensued who then went crazy, with Eadulf shouting '*Short counsel is good. Slay ye the bishop!*'[155] and the mob then attacked the Norman party as a matter of honour—clearly their intent from the very beginning. Walcher and his men sought refuge in the nearby Gateshead church but the Northumbrians set fire to it on 14th May 1080. Most died in the blaze. When Walcher and the remnants of his party were forced out by the flames, they were all slaughtered. The mob subsequently descended on Durham causing further mayhem and killing other supporters of the bishop. In retribution, the Norman response was swift, decisive and harsh. King William yet again sent his vicious half-brother, Odo of Bayeux, with an army to harry the Northumbrian countryside for the second time in 10 years. The devastation was so complete that, 6 years later, when the *Domesday Book* was compiled, large areas of the north of England were excluded from the survey being classified as 'waste' with zero value.

Odo also forced many of the surviving Northumbrian nobility into exile with large numbers joining the Varangian Guard, the elite troops of the Byzantine Emperor centred on Constantinople, which had become a popular point of exile for many noble Saxons in the years following the Battle of Hastings. Symeon, the renowned monk and chronicler of Durham Priory, although not condoning the behaviour of Walcher's men, recorded in his annals that:

---

[154] This was maybe one million pounds or more today and significantly, exactly the same amount he had been made to pay Rufus to buy the Earldom after Waltheof's execution!
[155] *Chronica Majora,* Matthew Paris, c.1250.

"...all those persons, whom the murder of the bishop had made objects of detestation both to God and man, either died by some kind of violent death, or, abandoning their homes and property, wandered in exile in foreign lands." [156]

There is every possibility that Robin—22 years old and grandnephew of the murdered Ligulf—was one of the raiding party of kinsmen raised up by his 'uncle' Eadulf Rus, who he probably knew well.[157] To Robin it must have seemed like an Icelandic feud saga, as told by Skald Thorkell when he was a child, being played out in real life. He would not have missed this 'honourable' opportunity to gain retribution for the death of his great uncle, but perhaps also he sought the chance to depose the mercenary Walcher who had assumed his father's powers as Earl in Northumbria after his execution. After the massacre of the bishop and his men, having escaped the clutches of a subsequent witch-hunt by Odo—the man most likely behind Waltheof's demise—Robin would have been among those outlawed 'in absentia' and hunted down, but escaping 150 miles south to the forests of Barnsdale. Every detail of this fits with the outlaw of legend.

In addition to this key blood-feud reprisal, which forced many of his friends and kin into exile and himself into outlawry, by 1080 several other events and circumstances had already shaped Robin's character into one which perfectly echoes that of our famous hero. In summary:

1. His noble father was a heroic national rebel from the northern ruling House of Bamburgh. Robin would have witnessed, first-hand, this violent yet futile English resistance in his formative teenage years.
2. He would have been taught swordsmanship and horsemanship by his warrior father, who had '*burnt a hundred Normans*' at York. Waltheof's

---

[156] Translated from the Latin by Rev. Stevenson in *The Church historians of England*, 1855, p. 699

[157] It is very likely Robin knew his great-uncle Ligulf and uncle Eadulf if, as a teenager, he had accompanied his father in the early 1070's, when Waltheof was sitting on the Durham synods with Bishop Walcher and building the castle there.

exploits of beheading many Normans with his long Viking battle-axe were recorded in sagas[158] remembered for years afterwards.

3. His father was betrayed by his Norman stepmother and/or Norman bishop Odo and executed by a Norman king.

4. With the execution of his father and his own descent into outlawry, he lost lands and any faint chance of ever holding the title Earl of Huntingdon. In folklore, this title is said to have been claimed by Robin Hood. He would have likely seen these as his birthright as the oldest child and only son of Waltheof. Even the outside chance of the simple Lordship of Hallam manor (incorporating the aula and Loxley) had now slipped away from him into the hands of the great local baron, Roger de Busli.

5. His mother and Loxley family, of yeoman status, were probably killed in the Harrowings of 1070 and 1080 or died of starvation or disease (no doubt along with many friends).

6. Loxley and Hallam, his village and home, were likely destroyed and laid waste. In 1086, Hallamshire only had 15% of its pre-Conquest value.

7. Virtually all the Saxon lands belonging to his friends and family (apart from his treacherous stepmother) were taken by the king and given to the Norman elite families like de Busli.

8. Norman aristocrats replaced Saxons at all levels of society and installed bishops, abbots, feudal lords and sheriffs to extract money from the local populace through swingeing rents and constant heavy taxation.

9. The feudal system and the imposition of the hated Forest Laws weighed heavily on the defeated, crushed and subjugated English people.

10. He was exposed to a ready source of disgruntled, displaced and disinherited thegns, yeomen and peasants in the environs of Loxley, who would have had good cause to join his band.

The above would not only have created a deep hatred of the Normans, nobles and churchmen, but also the skills to seek effective revenge, sending young Robin on his own personal crusade over the next 20 years of his life. He also seems, not unnaturally, to have inherited the genetic physicality of his father as

---

[158] Waltheof's courtly poet, or 'Skald', wrote that he 'was as brave as Odin' and congratulated him on having 'furnished the wolves of England a repast of Norman carcasses'.

well as his other attributes like leadership skills, engaging personality and religiosity.

But for now, as a newly made outlaw, in order to avoid wandering in '*exile in foreign lands*', he hides up in Barnsdale forest, situated along the main north-south route from London to York and Durham, some 20 miles from Loxley. To survive, he and similar dispossessed friends, yet again these highly skilled '*silvatici*' and '*tilvadid*', would rob those Norman nobles and churchmen and plunder the venison of Barnsdale and neighbouring forests in Sherwood and the Peak district, all of which were controlled by the heavily restrictive new Norman Forest Laws (though Barnsdale was not a royal forest), adding yet more fuel to the fire. Their honed forest and martial skills enabled them to run rings around the Norman sheriffs and their men and evade capture. But they were outlawed[159] and in those times that meant their property had been confiscated and any man could slay them with impunity. It was said of them that they '*bore the wolf's head*'—'caput lupinum' and were to be treated as wolves by those within the law, as animals to be hunted, but the resulting bond of brotherhood and loyalty between them was unbreakable.

---

[159] Women could not be 'outlawed' but were designated as '*waifs*', which amounted to much the same thing.

Chapter 7
Forest Life and Friends

Having now addressed the *'who'* and *'when'* elements of the legend, it is just left to look at the *'where'*, another, often contentious part of the story, that has come in for much research, dispute, polarised opinions and, dare I say, petty squabbling. Without doubt, if asked, most people would associate Robin Hood with Sherwood Forest and Nottingham. This is a clear consequence of the later ballads and more particularly, the modern interpretations of the last hundred years in book and film, as in reality Nottingham hardly receives a mention in *The Gest* and early ballads and Sherwood Forest received no mention at all in either *The Gest* or the 1086 Domesday Book. It is quite clear from the early sources that the bulk of the action takes place in and around the district of Barnsdale in South Yorkshire (see footnote 28).

As the esteemed Professor Holt was keen to observe: *'the nearer Robin gets to Nottingham, the less authentic he becomes'*. (Robin Hood, 1989, p.75)— clearly not a quote the good burghers of that city are anxious to publicise!

However, as mentioned earlier, the Nottinghamshire v Yorkshire debate remains hotly contested and the focus of entrenched regionalism, which Professor Holt most pithily described as: *'pseudo-history expressing local patriotism'* (Robin Hood, 1989, p.199), though I suspect it is more the economic benefits of Robin Hood tourism, rather than patriotism, that has entrepreneurs and the civic authorities in Nottingham clinging so tightly to the exclusive connection, however tenuous.

Although the *'Bernesdale'* of *The Gest* strongly alludes to the one in Yorkshire, there is a second Barnsdale Wood—about 30 miles south of Nottingham Castle and part of what was the Royal Forest of Rutland—which has been proffered by some as an alternative hideout for Robin and his Merry Men. A number of Judith de Lens' Rutland manors were adjacent to this Barnsdale forest area. Some, like Exton, were held previously by Waltheof in his Huntingdon Earldom pre-Conquest and, collectively with Judith's manors, became part of the estates of future Earls of Huntingdon. There are a few other interesting points that work in favour of this southerly proposal which is actually some 20 miles closer to Nottingham Castle than the Yorkshire Barnsdale. As I have said, it was part of a royal forest and hunting ground (which the Yorkshire Barnsdale was not) although little of such still survives. Secondly, Ermine Street—the Great North Road (A1) from London to York oft-used by highwaymen—runs right alongside it. Thirdly, it is only about 25 miles from Croyland Abbey—the final resting place of Waltheof—and the same distance from Sawtry—probable residence of Judith de Lens after 1076. There was even a 'Robin Hood's Cave' in Barnsdale Wood, part of Exton parish (one or the manors of Waltheof, inherited by wife Judith as part of the Earldom of Huntingdon), which local legend states was a refuge for Robin and his gang, although it now lies deep beneath the depths of Rutland Water, a large reservoir created in 1976.

As intriguing as all this seems, it is quite likely for naught. A number of researchers discovered that the Rutland Barnsdale was in fact called Bernard's Hill as early as 1201. It only became known (as in first recorded) as Barnsdale in 1579, long after the construct of the ballads. So it would appear that the Yorkshire Barnsdale, containing, as it does, many Robin Hood landmarks, was much more likely as the place for most of the action.

Taking refuge in the forests or 'greenwood', Robin would have possessed all the skills and experience—forestry, hunting, archery and family heritage—needed to survive alone. Sherwood, neighbouring Barnsdale and even 30 miles further north to Plumpton Park near Harrogate, were perfect locales for outlaw operations and hideaways. This 80-mile stretch was effectively one enormous tract of wild forest and scrubland bisected by the Great North Road and peppered with Norman castles (14 of them by the year 1100—see map Appendix 6). It is even said that the hunting grounds of Loxley Chase formed part of the northern reaches of Sherwood Forest in medieval times. This possibility of the whole area being connected is borne out by a record from March, 1194 that tells of King Richard I rousing a hart while hunting in Sherwood, Nottinghamshire and pursuing it, unsuccessfully, all the way to Barnsdale, Yorkshire.[160] Sherwood

---

[160] From John Manwood's *A Treatise and Discourse of the Lawes of the Forrest* (Wight and Norton, 1598). This singular record of King Richard I once being in Sherwood Forest

Forest and Nottingham barely get a mention in the original *Gest*, whereas Barnsdale in Yorkshire is closely identified as the area of action. The later popularity of the Nottingham setting only really started after the publication of the plays by Munday in 1587–88 and the later 17th century ballads. It is Yorkshire, particularly the West Riding of South Yorkshire, where evidence of identification leads us, and where the tales are given their most detailed and exact locale. In particular, as we know, Barnsdale and '*Robin of Barnsdale*' are repeatedly featured, though the precise area covered by 'Barnsdale' is debateable, some claiming it is a large tract of land between Doncaster and Pontefract, including Wentbridge, while others suggest a more confined area surrounding what is today called Barnsdale Bar taking in villages like Elmsall, Hampole, Skelbrooke and Campsall. The Barnsdale area was part forested and part open heathland and, unlike Sherwood, was not a royal forest. Whatever the specifics, Robin's area of operations were most likely spread along a 50+ mile stretch of what is today the A1 and A614 roads from Nottingham to Doncaster, incorporating, in the 11th century, both Sherwood and Barnsdale in one continuous swathe, perhaps even stretching a further 30 miles south to the other Barnsdale Forest in Rutland and even 40 miles further north to Plumpton Park near Harrogate.[161] In fact, the much vaunted tourist trap of the 'Major Oak'[162] in Sherwood Forest is virtually equidistant from Sheffield, Doncaster and Nottingham!

It was a land rife with potential enemies, but also full of rich pickings. Those monied enough to have horses and pack animals—government officials, tax collectors, high clerics and Norman nobles and merchants—were primary targets. Estimates suggest that a small group with good horses could move as

---

and Barnsdale, is actually the only tangible connection ever found between the 'Lionheart' and the legend of Robin Hood! Richard had come to Nottingham to suppress the final support for his brother Prince John, as the castle was the last to hold out for John's cause.

[161] Plumpton is mentioned once in *The Gest* (line 1427) and also in the 17th century Ballad of *Robin Hood's Fishing*. There is Plumpton Park near Knaresborough and also Plumpton Wood in Lancashire, part of Inglewood Forest near Carlisle and opinion is divided on which is being referred to.

[162] This large ancient tree, according to legend, provided shelter for Robin and his men to hide in the trunk. Given that even 800 years ago it was barely past being an acorn or a sapling at best, this is clearly a very tall story of what was a very short tree.

much as 30 miles in a single day. On the other hand, a larger group that included sturdier pack animals, laden carts or travellers on foot might make only half that distance at best. This does not include rest days, bad weather, difficult or muddy paths, natural obstacles like rivers (Holy Roman Emperor, Frederick I, drowned this way in 1190!), or illness, accident and injury to both human and beast, such that a journey through 'Robin Hood country' might take up to 4 days, longer if pack mules or 'sumpter' horses were used and oxen pulled the carts. To forest men who knew the land intimately, there was ample opportunity for an ambush. With honed archery and martial skills, those ambushes would have proved fruitful. [For more details on the bows, they would have used, bowmanship and archery tournaments, see Appendix 8]

Given the British penchant for talking about the weather, I think it is worth a quick aside. Somewhat surprisingly, the ballads never mention rain, thunderstorms, floods, fog, mist or mud, let alone more severe winter elements like snow, ice, frost, hail, gales and sub-zero temperatures. Instead, all the action occurs during balmy spring and bucolic summer days filled with birdsong and a warm westerly zephyr, which—as people living in South Yorkshire (and Britain in general) can attest—is not the normal state of affairs! It must be said that this setting is common to almost all medieval ballads, not just those specific to Robin Hood. In the summer, the Merry Men would have been somewhat nomadic to avoid detection, constantly moving (albeit to previous) locations to set up temporary camps, with homes made out of branches covered with hide and clothing in hemp, coarse linen, wool (perhaps even in Lincoln Green[163]) and leather, all camouflaged perfectly within their woodland or marshland settings. The ballads regularly detail the Merry Men's lavish dining—feasts of Norman venison, breads, cheeses, fruits and endless supplies of alcohol—no doubt such was strictly seasonal, but included in the storytelling for aspirational appeal to the poor and hungry masses...here were equal, relatable men with ample provisions and laden tables, at the expense of their oppressors. Winter would be a different story—potential targets few and far between, travel nigh on impossible given the state of the cart tracks and bridleways, and forest life hard to survive.

---

[163] The dyers of Lincoln, known for colouring wool with woad (*Isatis tinctoria*) to give it a strong blue shade, created the eponymous *'Lincoln Green'* by overdyeing this blue wool with yellow weld (*Reseda luteola*) or dyers' broom, *Genista tinctoria,* resulting in the colour that has become inextricably linked to the 'Merry Men'.

The Anglo-Saxon Chronicle mentions several instances of severe inclement weather in the late 11th century, as well as numerous failed harvests and cattle disease leading to starvation, events which do not seem to have impinged sufficiently on the lives of our intrepid forest band to require balladic mention. Throughout medieval times in Northern Europe, with a few exceptions, military campaigns were only fought during the summer months, with troops withdrawing to winter quarters until the spring as cleaning weapons, caring for animals and cooking food took on new levels of difficulty. (Heavy rain fell just before 2 of the most famous battles in English history, Agincourt (October 1415) and Waterloo (June 1815), a phenomenon that was a hugely significant factor in both English victories.) Sustaining a disparate group of a hundred or more men, plus presumably some women and children, in a wild forest environment in northern England for several hard winter months would have been extremely challenging in the 11th century.

There would be only 2 plausible options for survival, both delivering the 4 key elements of shelter, warmth, fresh water and food sources in reasonable quantities, not only to stay alive but also to stay alert, efficient and sane for perhaps the 2 most important requirements, decent sleep and good morale. Without these basics, the onset of hyperthermia was likely. The first is that they set up a larger, more permanent facility in winter and caves were one possibility, either natural ones that are prevalent in the area, like Creswell Crags near Worksop and also ancient man-made examples at Annesley[164] and at Rainworth, both in what was once Sherwood Forest—'Robin Hood Caves' as they are called. They would provide shelter, streams abounded nearby and fires could be lit (so long as dry wood was available), but food would have been tricky. The forest would have been open to foraging for edibles such as mushrooms, nuts, berries and roots (also wild honey—for eating but also used for making mead and

---

[164] In 1086, Annesley Manor was held by Ralf FitzHubert, later the Deputy Sheriff/Governor of Nottingham castle. The caves are only 6 miles from the somewhat remote village of Blidworth, which local legend suggests was the homestead of Will Scarlet and where he is buried. It was held by Thomas of Bayeux, the Archbishop of York, had only 5 village families in 1086 but also a mill, so maybe was supplying bread to the holed up outlaws in winter if they were friends or family of Scarlet.

candles[165]), but little or nothing was available in quantity during the winter and many, if not more, calories would be expended in the gathering as gained in the eating. Obviously they could still poach deer, wild boar, rabbits and various wildfowl, but such a protein-heavy diet leads to medical issues without other key ingredients—bread, in particular, but also vegetables, eggs, milk and cheese. They would have had to import such and other stocks (beer and wine would be high on the list) from friendly sources in surrounding villages, as well as the vital services of blacksmiths, bowyers, fletchers, tailors, shoemakers and so forth. Even though money was most likely not an issue, these supplies would have been difficult to secure with regularity as locals struggled to feed their own, let alone another 100.

The second possibility is that they disbanded during winter and returned to the homes of friends and families. This solution, one might think, would have been fraught with danger—as 'wanted' men with rewards/bounties offered for their capture, the chance of betrayal was high and also extremely dangerous, as to feed, shelter or communicate with an outlaw was a most serious crime. However, in line with contemporary military strategy, perhaps the sheriff, his men, the nobles and their retainers also holed up for the duration—a time of unwritten truce when everyone took a breath and tried to stay warm and dry. The only writer to make these observations was antiquary Joseph Ritson who, in 1795, wrote:

It has been conjectured, however, that, in the winter season, our hero and his companions severally quartered themselves in villages or country-houses more or less remote, with persons of whose fidelity they were assured. It is not improbable, at the same time, that they might have tolerably comfortable habitations erected in the woods.[166]

There is a rare 15th century poem, "*The Nut Brown Maid,*" that more faithfully describes the life of an outlaw forced to seek refuge in the woods: brambles, snow, hail, rain; no soft bed; for a roof, the leaves alone:

---

[165] In early medieval times the husbandry of bees was a specialist craft almost exclusively held by the religious houses, such that Friar Tuck was very likely to have the expertise in collecting honey, candle making and mead production.

[166] *ROBIN HOOD, a Col-lec-tion of all the An-cient Poems, Songs and Bal-lads, now ex-tant.* J. Ritson (Nimmo, London, 1885 edition), p.16.

'The snow, the frost, the rain,
The cold, the heat; for dry or wet,
We must lodge on the plain;
And, us above, no other roof
But a brake bush or twain" (lines 172–176)

In truth though there is nothing in the written records or the ballads themselves, regarding all these vital logistical issues, to give us even an inkling as to what actually happened, so this remains a matter of some intrigue.

While modern interpretations suggest that Robin collected his Merry Men one by one, *The Gest* and other early ballads depict them as a well-established group, implying they had been outlawed for a considerable time, maybe at the same time. Most famous of all, of course, was Robin's steadfast lieutenant Little John, who appears in all 6 of the original tales and, as many suggest, was perhaps already the de facto head of this motley group. The chroniclers portrayed Waltheof as a charismatic, charming and chivalric leader, so perhaps Robin's legendary ability to draw people around him was as much to do with his genetics providing strong interpersonal as well as martial skills. Without doubt being the son, albeit illegitimate, of the late Earl of Northumbria would have given Robin a definite cachet. Maybe it also explains why it was said of him and his men:

'So courteous outlaws as they were otherwise never to be found'.[167]

Arguably, this is a reason for their lasting fame over other, more thuggish, outlaw bands. Inarguably, no book about Robin would be complete without some discussion of his Merry Men and other key associates from legend, now considered in a late 11th century context.

The Disparate Band

As we know from legend, ballad, book, film and practically every source available, he was *not* alone in the forests but with his 'Merry Men'. *'Merrie man'* is an archaic, generic term for any follower or companion of an outlaw, knight or similar (not to be confused with *merryman*, a post-Conquest Norman addition

---

[167] *Little Gest of Robin Hood,* 1st fytte, 2nd stanza. lines 7–8.

for a jester, joker or mischievous person, although the mischievous nature of this outlaw band cannot be ignored). '*Merrie*' may have its roots in the Anglo-Saxon word *mæra* meaning famous, illustrious, great or mighty, though the other Old English meaning of merrie is 'bountiful', a possible later reflection on their perceived generosity to the needy. In the early ballads, there were between 20 and 140 ('*7 score*'—rising to 200 in some later tales) of these outlawed yeomen, of which only Much the Miller's son, William Scathelock (Will Scarlet) and Little John are mentioned by name. Alan-a-Dale, Friar Tuck and others, like Gilbert Whitehand, appeared later and became fully attached to the legend. Was this group composed, in part, by the '*silvatici*' who had inhabited the woods of Robin's childhood and with whom he had lived some 10 years earlier in Hallam? The dispossessed thegns, their housecarls and other Saxon locals stripped of their lands, along with ragtag survivors of the harryings, certainly had cause and circumstance. In 1080, when Robin fled back to home from Durham, it seems quite possible that he would propose leadership (or be put forward as leader) of an already hardened local fugitive band who he knew well and they knew of him and his famous late father. Notably *The Gest* refers to the men being at Robin's disposal which would rather indicate that they were all outlawed together and the Bishop Walcher debacle at Gateshead was very likely the trigger.

Much the Miller's Son

In *The Gest*, fierce young fighter Much (variously Muche, Muche, Mutch) helps to capture Sir Richard at the Lee—another major character of the early ballads and a man who has compelling connections to our Robin (more details below). Much's name is most likely a contraction of the Middle English 'Muchel'/'Mochel' meaning great (also a nickname for 'big man' in Northumberland). As a miller, he would have been more affluent than most commoners, as well as useful to the hungry band. In the early tales, Much is strong, opinionated and an aggressive, formidable fighter, often accompanying Little John on adventures. A key figure in the brutal ballad of *Robin Hood and the Monk*, Much helps to rescue a captured Robin and kills a young page boy to stop him talking to the authorities about their murder of the eponymous monk. In later tales, he is younger, softer and known as Midge or Nick, but we know little more about this son of a miller. If he was based on a real person, we are not provided with a surname and his given name originates from the later language of the ballads (1150–1500), making him impossible to trace.

Will 'Scarlet'

Similarly vague is the relationship between Robin and William Scathelock. All derivations of his outlaw name—Scarlock, Scadlock, Shacklock etc—mean 'smash lock', i.e. a thief. While he is consistently described in the early ballads as a 'kinsman' of Robin, cousin, nephew and half-brother are all proffered though when they first meet, appear to be strangers to each other. In our case, it would make sense that he was maybe a son of Robin's birth mother by a different, later, Anglo-Saxon father; that is, a half-brother, but without the noble Bamburgh bloodline. Another suggestion is that Robin's mother had a daughter later (being a half-sister to Robin) and Will was her son, hence his much younger nephew.

According to the early tales, Will also took part in the capture of Sir Richard and later insisted that the debt-ridden knight be given a decent pair of boots. In one of the oldest of the Child Ballads—*Robin's Death*—fearing for his kinsman's life who is about to go and seek medical help, Will urges Robin to take a bodyguard on his journey, which the hero scorns (to his detriment). Whereas the other outlaws are depicted as middle-aged, Will is young, also hot-headed and the most skilled swordsman of the group (sometimes using 2 swords at a time). He is often portrayed as a bit of a dandy and seen wearing red fabrics, no doubt a reflection of his outlaw name. According to local tradition, Will was killed after a battle with the sheriff's men and is said to be buried in the churchyard of St Mary, Blidworth, Nottinghamshire, where an unmarked grave near the iron gates is generally attributed to the outlaw.

What is particularly interesting, however, is their first meeting, described in the ballad *Robin Hood and the Newly Revived*[168]. A finely dressed young man is discovered by Robin shooting deer in Sherwood and introduces himself as '*Young Gamwell*' (only once he joins the Merry Men, does Robin give Will the name Scathelock/Scarlet). The name Gamwell is derived from the Norse byname Gamall meaning 'Old' which was used in northern England (mainly Yorkshire) during the Middle Ages. This name is recorded in *Domesday* in only a handful

---

[168] Child Ballad 128—the origin story for Will Scarlet, date unknown but probably 17th century, long after the first tales.

of direct entries as Gamal or Gamal Son of [another name]. Significantly, Gamal, Son of Barth was Lord of various manors all in Yorkshire, the largest and most concentrated of which were around Cudworth, 15 miles north of Loxley past Barnsley. Was this Gamal, in fact, real-life Will Scarlet's father (whose son was also named Gamel)? If so, it is highly likely that he knew his neighbour Waltheof and also Robin's mother. According to the same ballad, Will/Young Gamwell killed his father's steward and fled their estate to seek out his kinsman Robin. This version of Will claims to have been born and bred in Maxfield. In *Domesday*, although there is one very large Nottingham estate in Mansfield (possibly an alternative spelling) owned by King William, I have found no place existing with this specific name, or any closer derivation, so sadly we cannot trace his origin further.

Little John (Aka John Little, Reynold Greenleaf, and John Naylor)

Little John is depicted in many of the tales as equally skilled as Robin with a bow and the most skilled with a quarterstaff, in addition to being brave, intelligent, ferocious and forever loyal to his leader. In *The Gest*, stanza 149, he tells the sheriff he was born in Holderness (in the East Riding of Yorkshire) and that men call him Reynold Greenleaf, but this was maybe to deceive the sheriff as to his real identity. In Child Ballad 125—*Robin Hood and Little John*—Robin meets his right-hand man when he is about 20, which would have been c.1078 according to our timeline. In the ballads, John is said to have worked for the Sheriff of Nottingham[169]—perhaps both he and Robin were foresters for Sheriff William Peveril after Waltheof's execution, the time most likely when Robin briefly became a yeoman for the Crown, in the king's employ. Indeed, John's current village, Hathersage (although *The Gest* sites his birthplace as Holderness[170]), is a mere 6 miles from Peveril's castle at Castleton and 10 miles

---

[169] While working for the Sheriff, Little John uses the alias Reynold Greenleaf. However, in *The Gest* this character appears separately as one of the Merry Men and it is thought the name might just be rhyming slang for 'thief', as in the modern cockney 'tealeaf'.

[170] Many of the manors of Holderness were, in 1066, under the lordship of Earl Morcar, fellow rebel of Waltheof and Gospatric. Following the Conquest and final defeat of the rebels in 1070, almost the whole area was given to a Flemish companion of King William called Drogo de la Beuvrière. William Rufus later gave all these Holderness manors to

south-west of Robin's Loxley. Their first encounter is famous—fighting on stepping stones over the river with wooden staffs. If one were to speculate where it took place, fair guesses would be what today are known as Packhorse Bridge (image 9), Mill Bridge, Malin Bridge or The Cascades, all crossings over the river Rivelin. All these today are on the Rivelin Nature Trail, right between Hathersage and Loxley in what was Hallam. (see Appendix 1, map pins,1, 3, 9, 14). It certainly would not have been in the photogenic falls at Aysgarth in North Yorkshire on the river Ure, as selected by Hollywood for the depiction in Robin Hood, 'Prince of Thieves' with Kevin Costner.

Little John's Grave in Hathersage churchyard
© Photo: Author's own

Despite a lack of proof of his existence, according to local folklore, Little John is said to be buried in the churchyard of St Michael's and All Angels, Hathersage. A grave owned by the Naylor family (see above image) marks the spot. (Naylor, or its variations, are sometimes given as John's surname.) Purported artefacts like his bow, some arrows, a helmet, chainmail and even his

---

his aunt, Adelaide and her third husband Odo, Count of both Aumale and Champagne (respectively the mother and stepfather of Judith de Lens).

thighbone[171] were recorded. Sadly, these artefacts have been lost to time so cannot now be forensically dated.

As an aside, his alleged 79-inch (2 metre) bow was on display at St Michael's in 1652 until the disrepair of the church in the mid-18th century caused it to be moved for safekeeping—to Cannon Hall, Barnsley from 1729–1951.

9. Packhorse Bridge crossing the River Rivelin in Rivelin Country Park
Use of © photo courtesy of Neil Theasby licenced for reuse under ShareAlike 2.0 Generic (CC BY-SA 2.0)

The photograph below (image 10), taken during the interwar period, shows a tapered, straight, very long weapon that would presumably fit well with a large man like John. However, when last observed hanging in the Hall's ballroom below the minstrel's gallery in 1951, the bow was apparently a thick and heavy

---

[171]This was exhumed in 1784 and considered that of an exceptionally large man—nearly 7ft—however, it is also said that the person who fastened two animal bones together in order to make the fake bone later admitted to it! Others claim the grave is of a local, John Naylor, who was in fact a very small man!

recurved type; one end broken and the other end tipped with horn. This fits better with J.W. Walker's description a few years beforehand:

"I have examined the bow which is made of spliced yew, about 6 feet in length, though the ends where the horn tips were attached are broken off. It required a power of 160 pounds to draw to its full extent. Carved on the bow is the date 1715 and the name of Col. Naylor, who in that year strung the bow and shot a stag with it. It has never been strung since."[172]

10. A photo said to be of 'Little John's bow' held by archaeologist, H.C. Haldane in the grounds of Cannon Hall, near Barnsley, Yorkshire.

However, this is more likely the bow which now hangs in the Cawthorne Victoria Jubilee Museum, not the one that was hanging below the Cannon Hall minstrel gallery, in the early 1950s.

Photo from an early postcard now out of copyright and in the Public domain

[172] J.W. Walker, *Yorkshire Archaeological Journal*, vol. 36 (1944), pp. 44–45.

So long and tapered, or strong and horn-tipped, or simply a couple of tourist traps? Certainly a surviving wooden artefact (in this case a bow) for at least 7 maybe 9 centuries, would be quite unique and a suspiciously rare survivor, apart from a handful of examples recovered from the mud of swamps, lakes and the seabed where lack of oxygen has enabled preservation. In fact, until bows 5 centuries old were recovered in the 1980s from the wreck of Henry VIII's flagship, the Mary Rose, that sank in 1545 in Portsmouth harbour, virtually no complete examples of bows of this era or earlier are known to have survived. Whatever the case, the last owner of this one, Mrs Elizabeth Frazer of Cannon Hall, died in the late 1960s and apparently it was her intention to donate Little John's bow to the Wakefield Museum but, instead, her son took it to his house in Scotland. There it supposedly remained until Mr Frazer's death in 2004 when it went missing such that today, the whereabouts of the longbow are unknown. (see Appendix 8 for more on archery).

Friar Tuck

The name *Tuck* has as many spelling variations as that of Hood (Tock, Took, Toke, Tuk, Tuke, etc.) and is understood to have Norse/Viking origins. The name *Toka*, which appears in *Domesday*, is believed to be the earliest rendition of the name. The first 'family' record of *Tucke* was found later in the Tax Rolls for Norfolk in 1202. If the 11th century, time frame is to be believed then Tuck cannot have been a 'friar' in the true sense of the word, as those particular monks belong to specific Orders, the first of which were Augustinians[173] from around 1103, so almost possible but just on the cusp. Their friars originated after the older Canons Regular who lived within the community. Secondly came the Carmelites, not founded until c.1155 and even later, the Dominicans, founded in 1216 and arriving in England in 1221. These were mendicant orders, a new 12th century form of religious life which sought to bring the religious ideals of monastic life into an urban setting. Legend tells us though that Tuck was either connected to Fountains Abbey, Ripon (Cistercian monks) or St Mary's Abbey, York (Benedictine monks). However, since Fountains was not founded until 1132, too late for our hero, then St Mary's is my clear preference. Furthermore, St Mary's has close connections to my Robin—being originally founded c.1050

---

[173] Perhaps the first priory was at Worksop, founded by William de Lovetot in 1104, 20 miles from Loxley.

as St Olave's by his grandfather Siward and refounded in 1088 as St Mary's—it is the abbey directly involved in the main tale of the original *Gest* and Sir Richard at the Lee.

It seems likely that the title of 'friar' is a corruption of the Norman words *frère* and the Latin *frater* (both of which mean brother), which was widely used in the Latin New Testament to refer to members of the Christian community and might simply have been an appellation used by a chaplain. A monastic 'brother' committed himself to follow Christ in a consecrated life in the church, usually through the vows of poverty, celibacy and obedience. He would be a layman (non-ordained), usually living in a religious community and working in a ministry that suited his talents and gifts. As such, he might also be a doctor, teacher, engineer, cook, lawyer and so on, trying to live his faith by being a 'brother' to others.

The popularity of the character Friar Tuck emerged from the medieval May Games as the 'Abbot of Unreason' (often the Scottish version of the 'Lord of Misrule' in clerical garb). *Frère Tuke* is only mentioned in literature for the first time in a late Robin Hood play from c.1475, usually referred to as *Robyn Hod and the Shryff off Notyngham* (a 21-line dramatic fragment written on one side of a single sheet of paper, now housed in Trinity College Library, Cambridge). The Friar's appearance in this play implies that he was already part of the legend around the time when the earliest copies of the Robin Hood ballads were being made. By 1560, he featured in a May Games play, which tells a story similar to *Robin Hood and the Curtal Friar* (possibly dating to the 15th century).

Later depicted in the May Games (see Appendix 10) as the Morris dancing partner of Marian and somewhat lascivious (often with Marian!). Usually comedic, overweight and rather too fond of his food and drink, actual references to him in surviving literature are, ironically, very thin on the ground. However, in the *Curtal Friar* tale, Robin—boasting of his wrestling skills—is told that Tuck is the best wrestler in the area, not the slothful glutton we have come to know. Robin takes him on in a bout and loses. Tuck has an undisclosed grievance with the authorities, perhaps resulting from the avaricious antics of the Abbot of St Mary's (detailed later in this chapter) and, at Robin's invitation (having been waylaid in the forest?), he leaves the abbey and joins his band.

The surviving list of incumbent chaplains at St Mary's only dates back to 1389, so we do not know if a Tuck was in service there earlier c.1090, however it is much more likely that this was not his actual name but a name adopted once he left the community. In 1416, a writ during the reign of Henry V records a commission to arrest a bandit and *'forest poacher living by the king's venison'* (in Lindfield, Sussex, just 7 miles from Fletching, where the reader may recall was where the surname *Robynhood* was first recorded in 1296). This outlaw—a chaplain called Richard Stafford—had assumed the name *Frère Tuck*. According to Tudor historian John Stow, the chaplain appears again as *Tuck* in a writ the following year. This strongly suggests that the name was adopted by religious outlaws for many centuries, similar to the secular Robin/Hood pseudonyms.

From the ballads, we know that Robin held mass at frequent intervals in the forest glades, often twice a day, both with and without guests. This fits with Robin's likely upbringing and his father, repeatedly chronicled as a devout man. It is highly plausible that his band included a friendly disaffected cleric to perform the daily eucharists. More than that, I suspect the champion wrestler became Robin's personal chaplain. Hereward the Wake—the well-documented Anglo-Saxon thegn and leader of local resistance to the Norman Conquest in the 1070s—also had a chaplain. As told in the 12th century *Gesta Herewardi*, Hugo the Breton, as well as being Hereward's priest, was also a trained man-at-arms. It seems highly likely that Tuck, or whatever his real name was, fulfilled precisely the same role for Robin within the band of Merry Men from around 1088–1100.

Maid Marian

Along with Friar Tuck, Maid Marian is a recurring character in modern Robin Hood stories, both entering the folklore literature at about the same time (c.1475 and c.1500 respectively) and featuring, along with Robin, Tuck and Little John in the Morris dances of the popular May Games festivals from the late 14th - 17th centuries[174], indeed the impression we get is that Marian had no

---

[174] Robin Hood games were even being played in Sussex, Worcestershire and Somerset in the mid-1200s and the French had their own pastoral play called *Le Jeu de Robin et Marion*, which they performed in their May Games in 1283. The first surviving reference to a 'Robin Hood' play in England is for 1426, when the city of Exeter paid 20d (1 shilling and 8 pence, or just 8p decimal today but equivalent to about £700) for the privilege of a performance and there are numerous later 15th century examples of play games from all over England (particularly the South West) and Scotland thereafter, though oddly, none in northern England itself. Although Robin Hood plays were

connection to Robin prior to her introduction in the May Games. However this assumption or interpretation may well be wrong and there is every chance that the lost stories, rhymes and ballads could have included both of them in previous centuries, though the post-Restoration (after 1660) ballad 'Robin Hood and Maid Marian' (Child Ballad 150, c.17th century) is the only one in which Maid Marian, "a bonny fine maid of a noble degree," plays a significant part.

The title 'Maid/Maiden' means 'virgin' and the name Marian literally means 'of Mary' (for example, a shrine dedicated to the Virgin Mary is called a 'Marian shrine'). Given Robin's devotion to the Virgin Mary, evident in the early ballads, it seems entirely credible that it was he who came up with this alias for her.

The beautiful and virtuous Maid Marian—the renowned 'love interest' of Robin—is almost as vital to the modern retelling of the Robin Hood story as the Sheriff of Nottingham. In most versions, she is depicted as highborn, the daughter of a Norman nobleman, a lord, or even the ward or niece of the king. So, it may come as some surprise, for many, to discover that the original *Gest* gave Robin no female companion (save his spiritual connection to the Virgin Mary), and that Marian is only intermittently and elusively mentioned in the earliest tales.[175] It certainly would be somewhat incongruous for such a high class lady to be mixing in a rough tough forest setting with hardened outlaws and with such a pious boyfriend. Interestingly, Robin's religiosity and devotion to the Virgin Mary is a key element of the early ballads and a part of his story that is totally ignored, or avoided, in all modern interpretations, to pander to today's mostly agnostic, secular audience. In fact, stanza 10 of the 1st fytte of *The Gest* implies that Robin, far from chasing Marian around the old oak tree, had maybe taken a vow of chastity.

> *"Robyn loved Oure der Lady;*
> *For dout of dydly synne,*
> *Wolde he neuer do compani harme*
> *That any woman was in."*

---

performed at festivities for well over two centuries, it seems none of their content has survived. See Appendix 10 for more.

[175] Women, apart from the Virgin Mary, and indeed children and families, barely get a mention in the original *Gest*. The wife of Sir Richard at the Lee pops up briefly, and the sheriff's wife, with whom Robin flirts, has a small role in *Robin Hood and the Potter*. The only one of note that features prominently in the original *Gest* is the evil Prioress of Kirklees, a widow maybe in some way related to Robin, who 'bleeds' him to death.

As a notable aside, modern historians Professor Stephen Knight and Tony Scupham-Bilton even suggest that our hero may have been gay and that the ballads have clear homoerotic undertones. The latter proposed that Sir John Clanvowe, a late 14th century knight and poet, was the original writer of *The Gest*. Clanvowe was in a long-term relationship with Sir William Neville and subtly influenced Robin's sexuality based on his own. In the late 1990s, Hood expert Knight found plenty of suggestive gay imagery, with the greenwood being a symbol of virility and references aplenty to arrows, quivers and swords. He argued that one of the political undertones of the tale was that Robin had effectively been exiled from 'straight' society and his resistance to authority was, in fact, opposition to the then-damning views on homosexuality. Since the 'then-damning' time period (and hence society's views) are not clear, this is arguable. In any case, a late 14th century date for a literary creation of Robin, given his name appears in the records for up to 2 centuries prior, somewhat destroys this theory. Their proposition—whether viable observation, invention of a gay scribe or a 'controversial' means to guarantee book sales—remains one for lively debate. As Professor Barrie Dobson points out, homosexuality in the medieval period was not necessarily as repressed as one might think. For example, it was observed by the contemporary archbishop that William Rufus, who never married nor had children (very unusual for monarchs of the time who needed queens for alliance, wealth and heirs), filled his Court with young men who wore their hair as long as women and *'minced about with girlish steps'*[176] and charges of sodomy were widespread among his courtiers.[177]

On the subject of repression, many commentators accept that many earlier oral tales probably included a Marian, or variant Matilda, but the 15th century was a time of unprecedented sexual discrimination and she may have been deliberately omitted when the first ballads were written down. The role of women in literature in the 1400s was reduced to a bare minimum and where possible, excluded altogether, although by the 16th century the situation had improved somewhat.

---

[176] '*Eadmeri Historia novorum in Anglia*'. Rolls Series 81. 1884.

[177] The act of sodomy was not criminalised in England until the Buggery Act of 1533, which made it an offence punishable by hanging, remaining a capital offence until 1861 though the last executions were in 1835. Prior to 1533 such offences had been dealt with by the ecclesiastical courts. The buggery laws were not finally repealed until 1967.

The earliest surviving example we have in literature comes in 1508 when she was referenced, along with Robin, in a series of poems by Alexander Barclay, collectively known as *The Ship of Follies*:

> *"Yet would I gladly hear some merry fytte*
> *Of Maid Marian, or else of Robin Hood."*[178]

This suggests that Marian was an established character in the tales (fyttes) of earlier poems, but sadly for us, none of them have survived.

By 1599, Munday's version of Marian[179] is relentlessly pursued by the lecherous King John and eventually poisoned by him at Dunmow Priory. His plot summary includes a name-change from Matilda to Marian when she enters the greenwood and joins the outlaw band:

> *"On his deathbed, Robin makes Prince John swear to treat Marion honourably and not to love her beyond the bounds of chastity. **Marian reverts to her original name of Matilda.** The King dies and is succeeded by John... obsessed with Matilda...he attempts to woo [her]. When she refuses, John's alternative plan comes into effect: she is given poison and drinks it."*

In their 1995 book[180], Phillips and Keatman state that:

> *"A tradition that Marian's real name was Matilda could well have survived until Munday's time, although the identity of the historical figures behind the legend had long been forgotten."*

However, there is clear evidence that Munday lifted his story from real and identifiable historical people and events, and Marian, it seems, is no exception. While there are a handful of recorded Marians and Matildas who could be

---

[178] *Rymes of Robyn Hood: An Introduction to the English Outlaw*, R.B. Dobson, and J. Taylor, Heinemann, 1976, p.41.

[179] The full title of this play is the somewhat lengthy '*The Downfall of Robert, Earl of Huntingdon, afterwards called Robin Hood of merry Sherwood: with his love to chaste Matilda, the Lord FitzWater's daughter, afterwards his fair Maid Marian*'.

[180] *Robin Hood: The Man behind the Myth*, Graham Phillips and Martin Keatman, 1995, Michael O'Mara.

identified as the actual lady behind the legendary maid, the one who fits with my theory, as well as with literature, is a genuine probability.

11.The alabaster effigy of Matilda Fitzwalter (Maid Marian?) in Priory Church, Little Dunmow, Essex

As we know, the eldest daughter of Waltheof and Judith (half-sister to Robin and great-niece to King William I) was Maud, sometimes called Matilda (c.1072–1131). Descended from a daughter of this Maud (and her first husband Simon de Senlis I), was a great-great-grandson, Robert Fitzwalter (d.1235). Robert was feudal baron of Little Dunmow in Essex and became a key figure in the baronial opposition to King John, leading to the signing of the Great 'Magna' Charter in 1215 and him even being described as the first champion of English liberty. According to Robert's own statement of the reasons behind this conflict, the king had attempted to seduce his beautiful eldest daughter, Matilda, sometimes called Maud (c.1195–1213). In the *Chronicle of Dunmow*,[181] this

---

[181] '*The Chronicle of Dunmow*' was a medieval text partially reproduced in John Stow's *Chronicles of England*, 1580. The fragment in Stow's work offers a somewhat fanciful account of the 13th century, including a sympathetic portrayal of Robert FitzWalter.

Matilda—referred to as *Mawde*—rejects the immoral advances of King John whereupon she is murdered at Dunmow Priory by a poisoned bracelet, which, in turn, drives FitzWalter to take up the part of a constitutional leader.

Obviously, the account of this unfortunate maid inspired both Munday's play and also Michael Drayton's 1594 poem *Matilda, the faire and chaste daughter of the Lord Robert Fitzwalter*. So widely was the story believed, that an alabaster effigy to the doomed Matilda Fitzwalter on a grey altar tomb in Priory Church, Little Dunmow (see fig. 11 above), is considered by many[182] to this day to be the true Maid Marian.

While Robin's descendant via his half-sister seems very much to fit, this Matilda's timeline is obviously too late to be his 'maid' and, according to what we know about her, she died shortly after her 17th birthday—too brief a life, perhaps, to become the lady of the legend. However, it is very possible that Munday and others used a known writer's trick—popular from ancient balladeers to modern authors—of taking real people from the past and placing them in different times to fit with their plots: disinherited earls, doomed maids, lecherous kings and murder plots—all mixed with stories that were already lying in the shadows of oral tradition.

So, was the original Marian, in fact, the ancestral namesake of the young murdered Matilda/Maud—Robin's aristocratic half-sister Maud/Matilda 'FitzWaltheof', alive some 65 years before? Again, it is worth noting that the depiction of Marian as his lover/wife only came later with their connection in the May Games and then leapt upon by gleemen, troubadours, 17th century playwrights and 20th /21st century film scriptwriters[183]—all keen to interpret her as a romantic figure for the greater appeal of their audience. In the earliest ballads Robin and the outlaw band have no mention of wives or families, the only

---

[182] Examples include Fitzwalter descendant and genealogist Stephen Robert Kuta in his 2005 post *The legendary story of Maid Marian; 1195–1213*, referencing The *Chronicle of Dunmow* and *The Graphic and historical illustrator* by E W Brayley, 1831.

[183] Even Nottingham City Council, who have placed a plaque on the outside of Nottingham Castle depicting the totally made up event of King Richard the Lionheart marrying Robin Hood and Maid Marian! This fictional wedding is also claimed by the St Mary's churches of both Edwinstowe and Campsall. Only the latter was extant in the late 11th century, being founded at that time and is the only St Mary's in Barnsdale where Robin claims to have founded a chapel to Mary Magdalene. (**'A Gest of Robin Hood', stanza 440**). Further details on this matter are included in Appendix 11.

feminine interest being Robin's devotion to the Virgin Mary. It is easy to speculate, but there is a good chance that our Robin and his young sister formed a close familial bond. Apart from a fatherless childhood where Maud may have looked up to her devout, chivalrous and skilful older brother (so much like their father), there was also a two-year period (1088–90) between leaving Elstow Abbey aged 16 and marrying Simon, when the blossoming, bright maid might just have occasionally melted into the greenwood to visit her outlaw sibling. Then 10 years later, as we shall see in Part II, when she needed to call on the services of the finest archer in the land to save England—she knew where he was and how he would respond—he was her brother—they were both the children of their father…

And finally…Sir Richard at the Lee

Of all the early tales, one in particular has been praised for its balanced narrative and vivid, evocative dialogue. It is arguably the most famous one—the very first tale in the original *Gest* and forms a substantive part of the whole ballad. Significantly, it does not revolve around Robin helping a poor peasant or a widow, but an impoverished knight of unknown lineage. More poignantly, it demonstrates how real events of the late 11th century can fit quite readily with the legend. This long-standing tale centres on St Mary's Abbey in York, where the phenomenon of men 'play-acting' Robin Hood was latterly recorded in the church's *Anominalle Chronicle* in the 1390s.

In *The Gest* tale, Robin, camped out in the woods of Barnsdale forest, refuses to dine without company, so instructs Little John, William Scarlet and Much the Miller's son to:

> *"Walke up to the Saylis*
> *And so to Watlinge strete*
> *And wayte after some unknown guest*
> *Up chance ye may them meet."*

Researchers get excited by this tale because it contains real places that can be identified today, namely Barnsdale, Saylis[184] and Watling Street. These can

---

[184] Originally a hill, generally identified as Sayles Plantation at the northern end of Barnsdale, on the southern side of the Went Valley, five hundred yards east of

be found on and around the Great North Road running from London to York. The more famous Watling Street—mostly found on today's A2 and A5 roads— runs nowhere near either Nottingham or Yorkshire. However, this ancient street name was also attributed to sections of a number of other paved Roman roads in England and indeed this is precisely what the thoroughfare in Barnsdale was known as, though after 7 centuries of neglect it would have been in various stages of disrepair, decay and overgrowth having deteriorated into a cart track. It would have junctioned with the old A1 at Barnsdale Bar, a place with the nearby landmarks of Robin Hood's Well and Robin Hood's Stone. Furthermore, it cuts through Skelbrooke Park—the location of another ballad robbery[185] and near where the road splits at Hampole and the left fork (now A638) runs up to Wakefield. It looks to have been a good lookout point and both a fertile ambush spot for Robin and a place well-known to the ballad writer, thus providing a strong vote in favour of South Yorkshire as the centre of Merry Men operations.

Wentbridge, which would provide a good lookout point. However, another Sayles in New Close Lane, four miles south, between Campsall and Skelbrook and just south of Barnsdale Bar (as identified by Victorian historian Richard Holmes in the—*Yorkshire Archaeological and Topographical Journal, vol XII, part XLV (1892), pp.42–47*), now seems a more likely location.

[185] *Robin Hood and the Bishop of Hereford*, Child Ballad 144a.

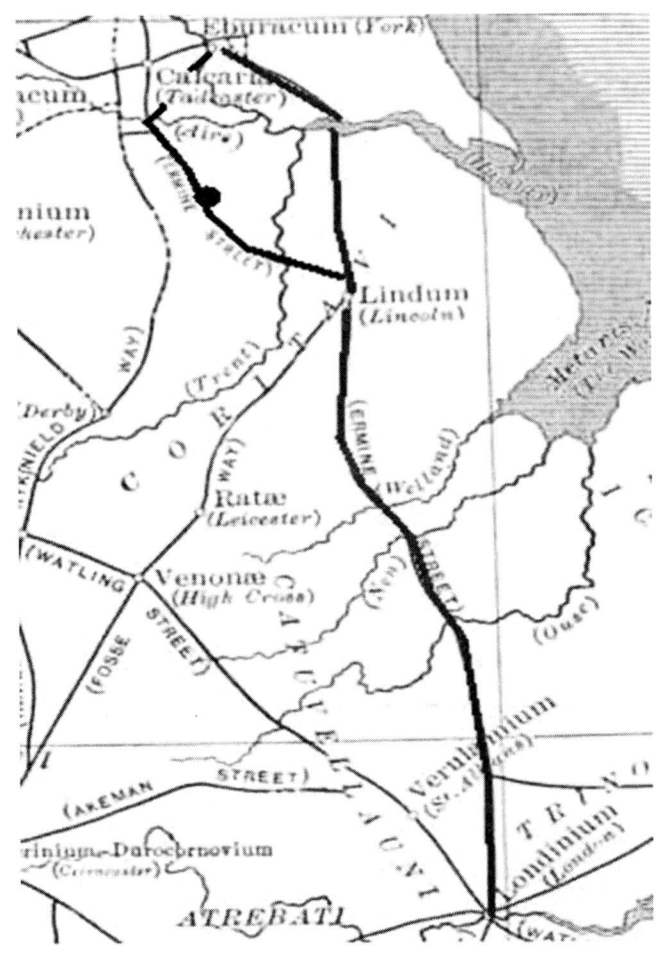

**Map showing the Roman route of Ermine St (Gt. North Rd.)
and the alternative westerly route between Lincoln and York passing via Blyth
Castle, Doncaster and Barnsdale Forest as Watling Street, which avoided crossing
the Humber estuary**

In the time of my Robin, the tenant-in-chief of almost all the manors in this area was the great baron, Ilbert de Lacy, Lord of Pontefract, who was also a close friend of the Sheriff of Nottinghamshire and Derbyshire, William Peveril. Back to the story, Little John asks who should they capture to join them for lunch[186], to which Robin replies:

> "*These Bishops and these Archbishops,*
> *Ye shall them bete and bynde; (beat and bind)*
> *The hye sherif of Notyingham,*[187]
> *Hym holde ye in your mynde.*"
> (Lines 57–60, Stanza 15, *The Gest of Robin Hood*)

However, they were not to molest '*husbandmen* (small farmers) *who till with the plough*' or yeomen, knight or squire '*that would be a good fellow*'. This direction, on how to behave in a chivalric manner, is reminiscent of King Arthur teaching his Round Table knights their duties and emphasises the moral character of Robin and also foretells the error of the Merry Men. They don't find any bishops or sheriffs on the road but hijack a somewhat sorry looking and dishevelled knight with the rather odd title of '*Sir Richard at the Lee*'. He is probably not too scared at this encounter as he declares that he has heard of Robin (suggesting he is perhaps quite local) and that '*he is a good yeoman, of whom I have heard much good*'. True to form, they take him back to their camp for a mass and a fine lunch, for which Robin then demands 'payment'. The knight says he is unable to do so and a search of his possessions proves he is truthful: he has only 10 shillings. He tells them that he is attempting to save his 20-year-old son, who had accidentally (*with blunted lance*) slain a Lancastrian knight[188] and his squire in a joust[189], almost certainly at the tournament ground of Roger

---

[186] Robin (and Friar Tuck) would undoubtedly have been under the influence of the Benedictine Order in which 'hospitality' is a spiritual obligation, hence Robin's perpetual hijacking of travellers for a lavish meal and Mass—the outlaw twist being he would make people pay handsomely afterwards!

[187] It is interesting to note that although they are in Yorkshire, their main concern is the Sheriff of Nottingham, suggesting this man may have had wider control over Yorkshire as well. This will be discussed in chapter 9.

[188] It is likely he was a knight paying homage to Robert de Lacy, who, after 1093, as well as his Pontefract estates also held the lands of the Forest of Bowland and built Clitheroe castle in Lancashire.

[189] In this era, tournaments generally consisted solely of the 'Mêlée', where knights fought in groups, not 'one on one' jousting with lances, though the historical record is unclear. These tournaments, of anything up to 100 participants, were very aggressive and

de Busli adjacent to Blyth Castle and Priory (see later footnote 231). Sir Richard had spent all of his money on bail and legal costs to defend his son or, probably more specifically, to buy his freedom by paying off officialdom. As a result, he has been forced to mortgage his entire estate to the Abbey of St Mary's for £400 (very approximately, this is around £1million in today's money—but as with the names of kings, the later balladeers may well have changed the specific amount to suit their audience). Interestingly, this one action gives further weight to the earlier suggested timeline, since such a financial process was only legal up until the Statute of Mortmain (*de viris religiosis*) of 1279, which then *'forbade alienation of feudal estates to the church or churchmen, by gift, sale or mortgage'*. Subsequent to this date, such a transaction would have required royal licence or dispensation—a process clearly absent from the tale—making the placement of Robin post 1279, in the time of Edward II in 1323, even harder to support.

Robin asks Sir Richard what he will do if he fails to raise the money and loses his home and Sir Richard replies that he will leave immediately to visit *'Calvary, where Christ died'*, rather obliquely suggesting a pilgrimage to Jerusalem or perhaps joining the crusade[190]. So, Robin lends Sir Richard the required £400 and provides him with a new horse, provisions and even Little John as a temporary squire and sends them on their way to York. The avaricious Abbot of St Mary's is apparently gloating—Sir Richard has failed to make the required repayment within a year of the mortgage loan and there is just one day to go before the knight's entire estate will be defaulted and belong to the abbey. We know that the first Abbot of St Mary's was Stephen de Whitby (d.1112) who came from Lastingham Abbey, where he and other monks had taken refuge for a few years, having previously been pushed out of Whitby Abbey, not only by 'brigands and pirates' but also by the powerful local baron (and major benefactor), William de Percy, following disagreements and in order to install his own brother, Serlo de Percy, as the new prior.

---

people were often injured or killed. The fact that the squire was killed as well certainly does suggest this was during a mêlée, rather than in the 'lists' of a jousting tiltyard.

[190] He would not, though, have used the term 'crusade', as this term was not first coined for another century, in the 1210's. In fact the Latin word used was 'crucesignatus', or 'one marked by the cross' and the actual English words 'crusade' and 'crusader' did not appear until around 1700, over 400 years after the final 9th crusade in 1271.

Connecting our Robin to the tale in *The Gest*, the *Anglo-Saxon Chronicle* records that St Mary's was previously St Olave's Church, founded c.1050 by Robin's grandfather, Earl Siward, who was also buried there.[191] In 1088, St Olave's Church was abandoned and refounded as St Mary's Abbey on adjacent land, granted by Breton northern magnate Alan Rufus 'the Red', Lord of Richmond, and the new King, William II (William Rufus—no relation to Alan!). Alan recruited Stephen de Whitby as its first abbot, so they may well have been good friends and equally corrupt and rapacious. Stephen is mentioned in a monastic recording as having governed St Mary's with prudence for 24 years, although the prejudice or otherwise of that author is unknown.[192] However, in *Domesday*, he is recorded as one of the city of York's most prominent landowners, like many abbots of such houses, so he would definitely have been rich and ambitious, and quite possibly a ruthless landlord. The suggestion from *The Gest* that the abbot was more interested in things temporal rather than spiritual seems to fit incredibly well with this real-life clergyman.

Devout as Robin was raised, one can imagine his disgust at the desecration of this sacred family spot where lay his grandfather and his hatred of corrupt French nobles and greedy clergy, friends of William Rufus who were now despoiling and mismanaging the place[193]. For so many reasons, the perfect target for Robin Hood. It is also apparent from the ballad verse that the abbot is very friendly and in cahoots with the corrupt 'High Justice of England', whose services he has retained '*with cloth and fee*', (and who is present when Sir Richard returns to make the payment) something that is both interesting and significant.[194]

---

[191] Siward's burial is the only instance of a non-royal 'lay' burial inside a church in pre-Norman England—and evidence of his importance in Anglo-Saxon-Danish society. St Olave is the patron saint of Denmark.

[192] *Monasticon Anglicanum: A history of Abbeys and other Monasteries, Vol.3*, William Dugdale. Published by James Bohn, London, 1846. MS. bibl. Body. NE. A.3. 20. See Num. LXXI.

[193] As St Mary's was not really up and running before 1090, then the incidents of *The Gest* with Sir Richard must have occurred during the last decade of the 11th century, probably around 1096/7.

[194] *The Gest* of Robyn Hode, line 371 of the second Fytte, '*The justyce of Englonde'*. Francis Child inserts **'hye'** before 'justice'; the expanded title is also found in some other early texts, The Durham See had become vacant in January 1096 with the death of the

The abbot and the hy selerer (high cellarer[195])
Sterte forthe full bolde,
The hye justyce of Englonde
The abbot there dyde holde. (stanza 94 of *The Gest*)

Although as with almost everyone in *The Gest*, he is not identified by name, it seems very likely that this was Ranulph Flambard, the Chief Justiciar of King William Rufus (essentially the head civil servant/Chancellor, tax collector and agent of Rufus's worst financial oppressions) famed for his wit and quick tongue but also his astute but greedy money grabbing policies on behalf of the king, especially from religious houses.[196] He had also been custodian of the vacant See of Durham since early 1096, from where he was extracting the incomes for King Rufus. He was held in such high esteem by Rufus that he was also designated as the 'king's chaplain'. The simple fact that the Norman kings regarded St Mary's as a royal foundation means his joint role as avaricious co-conspirator with the abbot in the land grab from Sir Richard seems totally plausible.

Robin's loathing of the clergy is referenced in several ballads and it is not their religion at issue so much as their irreligiosity and overreaching greed as landlords, for the church estates were only second in size to those of the king (some even had the right to mint their own coinage). So understandably in this tale, Robin is most sympathetic to Sir Richard's plight. In brief, Robin gives him the money required to repay and thus retain his property, secures his son's release and saves the day. Initially Sir Richard toys with the abbot, pretending he is broke and does not have the money—but then, in a grand gesture, produces the gold

---

incumbent, William de St-Calais. Ranulf Flambard was granted the Bishopric by Rufus in 1099.

[195] The role of the cellarer was to be in charge of provisions and basically run the physical side of the monastery, being the most important official in the community after the abbot.

[196] Chronicler John of Worcester (See John of Worcester, 3, p. 92–95) places a large share of the blame on Ranulph for the evils perpetrated by Rufus. Ranulph was the son of a lowly parish priest from Bayeux raised up by Rufus, who Johnn claimed that acting on the king's wishes, he saw to it that no justice was done and that ecclesiastical dignities like abbacies and bishoprics were habitually sold. St Mary's Abbey in York also benefited from further exceptional royal privileges for land purchase and became the wealthiest church establishment in northern England, later acting as the 'Northern Bank' for the Crown.

and throws the money down in front of the abbot, who, needless to say, is dumbstruck, having clearly expected to take possession of the estate. Sir Richard then returns home to his wife, telling her of how they have been saved from ruin by the generous intervention of a certain Robin Hood.

Later, in the fourth fytte of *The Gest*, 2 monks who work for the Abbot of St Marys (one being the High Cellarer from Sir Richard's earlier meeting) are on their way to London to take proceedings against the knight and are travelling south through Barnsdale with 8 packhorses and a 52-man armed guard when they are captured by the Merry Men. The monks then are rude and lie about how much money they have, so the outlaws take all their money—an enormous £800, which was twice the debt owed.[197] When, a year later, Sir Richard reappears with a hundred retainers, he has now saved up the £400 and comes to repay the gang. Robin not only tells him he does not need it but even gives him their £400 excess. In return, Sir Richard, as suggested by his wife, presents the outlaws with a hundred bows and peacock feathered arrows (perhaps giving us an indication of the number of Merry Men) and promises to help them in the future.

So who was this Richard at the Lee and does he have any basis in reality? Unsurprisingly, as with all characters in *The Gest* (and many political or satirical pieces), his real name was likely changed. He could be a blend of several real people and/or characters or he could be fictitious—no-one knows for sure though numerous suggestions have been made. Most modern-era experts are decided upon Sir Richard being a conflation of at least 2 different stories from 2 different dates, melded together latterly by uneducated minstrels. This goes a long way to explaining many of the rather confusing elements in the tale. It also justifies a timeframe that includes events nearly 20 years apart. However, Sir Richard's mention of the Crusade suggests a date of around 1096, which fits with a number of other timed elements, as I discuss in more detail at the end of this section.

While we are venturing into the realm of speculation, we can at least start with the vague geographical facts. In *The Gest*, Richard is described as the 'Lord of Verysdale'—a place that no-one can locate today with any certainty. Many researchers suggest Lee in Wyresdale (in the Forest of Bowland), Lancashire.

---

[197] The timing of this event makes it likely the monks armed retinue was guarding the tax revenues from Durham and York in the north being taken south to the Royal Treasury in Winchester, having been raised by Rufus to pay his brother Robert Curthose for mortgaging the Duchy of Normandy to fund his Crusade in 1097, which also ties in with the comment of Sir Richard about his possible pilgrimage to Calvary.

However, understandably, not everyone is convinced by this as it is so far away from the known geography of the tale: some 110 miles from Nottingham (also 70 miles from Peveril Castle in Castleton, the home of William Peveril who was recorded as Sheriff of Nottinghamshire and Derbyshire after the Conquest[198]).

On the subject of location, we have an important clue. Later in *The Gest*, Little John is badly injured (an arrow in the knee) during a skirmish following being lured into an archery contest for a gold and silver arrow set up by the Sheriff of Nottingham, which Robin has won (a staple scene of nearly every Robin Hood movie and TV show). The outlaws are subsequently pursued by the sheriff's men, so they escape to the safety of their knight friend's home, described as:

> "...a fayre castell
> A lytell within the wode;
> Double-dyched it was about,
> And walled, by the rode.
> And there dwelled that gentyll knyght,
> Syr Rychard at the Lee."

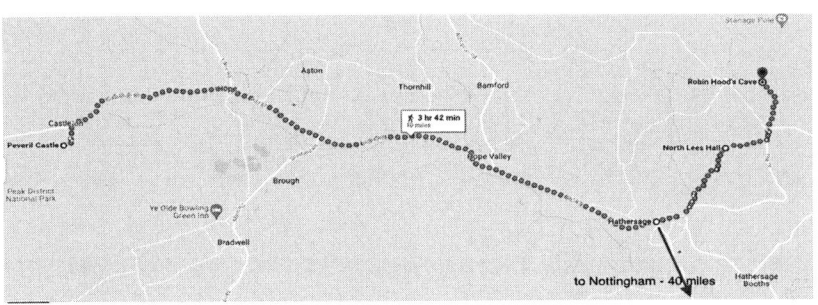

Peveril Castle to North Lees Hall, via Hathersage (8mls) then to
Robin Hood's Cave (9mls)

Sir Richard's castle must have been within practical distance for Robin to physically carry a very large incapacitated John on his back despite taking frequent rests (as described in *The Gest*), from the sheriff's castle and the tournament back to Sir Richard's home. Of course, it depends on which sheriff.

---

[198] *The History of the Norman Conquest of England:* (1871), vol. iv. p.200. E.A. Freeman, noted from the writings of Orderic Vitalis.

My proposed period for when Robin was an outlaw—1080–1100—covers 20 years, during which several people managed this 'territory' on behalf of the king (more on possible suspects in the next chapter), but we can still assume 2 things: 'A little' way inside the greenwood is surely not 70 miles away at Wyresdale in Lancashire! Furthermore, it would be physically impossible for any man to carry his friend 70 miles over wild terrain with no chance to rest (they were being chased). Further evidence lies in stanzas 331–332 of *The Gest*, when later in the story the sheriff stumbles across Sir Richard, when the latter is out hunting with hawks '*by the riverside*' and captures him, taking him to Nottingham,[199] which quite clearly implies that their respective residences are relatively close to each other—and not in Lancashire.

So based on geography and my timeline, let us assume the High Sheriff was William Peveril. Is there a more likely home for this gentle knight that lies closer to Peveril Castle, the ruins of which still exist to this day? My preferred spot is a place today called **North Lees Hall** in the Peak District, just 2 miles to the north of Hathersage, Little John's village, and, perhaps more importantly, although 40 miles from Nottingham Castle, is, depending on your route, **only 7–8 miles from Peveril's fortress at Castleton (and just 30 miles west of Roger de Busli's tournament ground)**. The River Derwent flows down the Hope Valley nearby through Hathersage village, just a mile from the Hall, and was no doubt the riverside locale for the hawking hunt above, since a journey from Peveril Castle towards Nottingham Castle would pass right by this point. (see map above)

North Lees is not listed separately in *Domesday*, neither is anyone named Richard in this area and there are no 'Sirs' in the records, only 'Lords', 'Earls' and the King but I suspect these events are a decade after the time of the survey and things have changed. If there was a real man behind the legend (many experts suggest more than one knight/tale were blended), then he most likely had a different name and title. It is worth noting that there were around 10,000 Normans in England at this time, only 1,400 of which are named as property owners in Domesday. Many of the remainder were knights and vassals listed as

---

[199] The Sheriff has Sir Richard imprisoned in Nottingham castle but on the appeal of his wife, Robin and 140 'merry men' storm the castle, release him and kill the Sheriff (deputy Sheriff/Castellan—Ralf FitzHubert?). 'Hawking' was a form of hunting with birds of prey, in which women regularly participated perhaps because parks were places where both men and women could mingle beyond the usual constraints of courtly life, often being the scene of affairs and lovers' trysts.

sub-tenants of lords/tenants-in chief. As for the property itself, North Lees could very well have been the residence of one of these men in service to his feudal lord, as a 'mesne tenant'. As this incident in *The Gest* obviously happened sometime after Richard's first encounter with the Merry Men in c.1096, then he may well have built it sometime after the 1086 Domesday survey.[200] There are no ruins as the current Elizabethan hall[201] dates from some 500 years after my timeframe/people, but the placename may have existed well before this, as a Romano-British settlement is recorded here from 1306[202] (in fact, as a cultivated site, we have evidence going back to the Bronze age). It is certainly surrounded by woodland to this day and located in a defendable position on top of a hill where a fortified dwelling might have once stood[203]. It would have been of earth and timber construction but, as with many similar structures of the period[204],

---

[200] It is estimated that by the mid-12th century 6,500 knights had been enfeoffed on the great noble baronies. *The Feudal Kingdom of England: 1042–1216*, Frank Barlow, Routledge, 2014. p.93. It is even possible Sir Richard had been enfeoffed with Hathersage manor by FitzHubert post Domesday, c.1090–95.

[201] The lonely romanticism of the hall and its erstwhile occupants, the Eyre family, attracted many writers—most famously Charlotte Bronte who visited Hathersage in 1845 to visit her friend Ellen Nussey, daughter of the local vicar. Through this visit it became immortalised as Thornfield Hall in *Jane Eyre*, where Mrs Rochester jumped from the roof to her death.

[202] *The Peak District Barrow Survey (8 volumes)*, J. Barnatt, 1989, Peak Park Joint Planning Board Archaeological Archive, Bakewell.

[203] North Lees castle was most likely not a true castle but a Norman 'ringwork' fortification of a type built and occupied from the late Anglo-Saxon period to the 12th century—essentially a motte and bailey construction but without the motte. This thus comprised a small defended area containing buildings which was surrounded or partly surrounded by a substantial ditch and a bank surmounted by a timber palisade. Ringworks acted as strongholds for military operations and defended aristocratic manorial settlements. In reality then, Richard's home would not have been a 'castle' (requiring royal authority and a licence to build) but was probably just a high status but plain moated *fortified manor house*. I do not believe the actual ballad description should be taken too literally.

[204] To date, about 500–600 Norman castles and fortified manor houses have been identified, which leaves the homes of a very large number of these 1,800 men as 'disappeared'. Large baronial landlords parcelled out portions of their estates into knight's fees, and bestowed on men like Sir Richard, a high status family who had maybe accompanied them from Normandy into England, with the obligation, as 'Vassals', for

nothing remains today and any surviving archaeology is likely now lost beneath later constructions.

12a. Hood Brook running down from Stanage Edge, passed North Lees Hall, to Hathersage, where it flows into the River Derwent

Clearly, the name 'Lees' is suggestive[205]—it being in plural form does not detract when we remember how variable spelling was in those days. If North Lees was indeed the knight's home, it is surrounded by some intriguing namesakes. It is no more than half a mile from the renowned geological feature in the east-facing scarp of Stanage Edge known as 'Robin Hood's Cave'. In long-standing local lore, this is thought to have been a lair or hiding place for Robin and the first ever place to have the name of Robin Hood attached to it, so perhaps holds more weight than later epithets. Looking to the south, from high up on Stanage Edge near the safety of the cave, one can see 'Hood Valley' with 'Hood Brook' meandering just a couple of hundred yards (180 metres) past North Lees

---

supplying, in cases of emergency, military service and a certain number of mounted soldiers, in proportion to their estates.

[205] Locations with the name 'Lees' are in abundance in the region, A 'Lee' or 'Ley' is an archaic word for a field, meadow or clearing.

Hall down to Hathersage where it flows into the River Derwent in Hope Valley, likely site of Sir Richard's hawking party mentioned above.

12b. Robin Hood's Cave on Stanage Edge
Photos 12a and 12b with kind permission of derbyshire-peakdistrict.co.uk and Stephen Horncastle—ShareAlike 2.0 Generic (CC BY-SA 2.0)

It also seems to work well with legend details. Later in *The Gest*, Little John is 'loaned' to Sir Richard for a year, which is somewhat convenient given that his family lived so close by, just 2 miles away in Hathersage. But perhaps more poignant is our very first meeting of Sir Richard. According to one version of *The Gest*, he was travelling south when he was hijacked by the Merry Men as he was intending to eat lunch at either Doncaster or Blyth (8 and 16 miles south respectively from the Saylis). In another version, he was on his way north to St Mary's Abbey, York. Regardless of the version or direction, Richard was detailed as journeying on Watling Street—the Barnsdale section of the Great North Road/Ermine Street—when he was intercepted at the Saylis near

Barnsdale Bar. This makes a home at North Lees entirely consistent with either the start or end of his journey—not in Lancashire.

This brings us to the timeline—with one particular remark by Sir Richard providing some guidance. In the first fytte, he says that if he is indeed ruined, he will journey overseas:

> "*And see where Christe was quyke and dede.*
> *On the mount of Calveré.*"

The First Crusade was envisioned as a religious pilgrimage to take back Jerusalem from the 'infidel' and no knight could consider his journey complete unless he had prayed at the Holy Sepulchre (the traditional site of Mount Calvary), so this seems to fit logically, both in description and date. The First Crusade commenced recruitment in July 1095 and left France for the Holy Land, in a fairly disorganised state, from August 1096 onwards. This would make Richard's first encounter with the Merry Men most likely between autumn 1095 and the spring or early summer of 1096 and the repayment to St Mary's Abbey at the same time in 1096/7. This would also tie in with Rufus's tough money raising programme, with Flambard, to pay his brother Robert, who was mortgaging his Normandy Duchy to him to fund his crusading ambitions.

It has also been suggested that the dishevelled state of the knight implies that he might have recently returned from campaign. This may have well been either the 1095 northern rebellion of Roger de Mowbray, Earl of Northumbria, and others, in their attempt to supplant William Rufus with Stephen de Aumale or just possibly the successful 1097 expedition into Scotland on behalf of Rufus[206], to remove Donald Bane and install his nephew Edgar (son of the late Malcolm Canmore III) as King of Scotland and vassal of the English king. Under the feudal system, Sir Richard would have been obliged to provide military service to his overlord, Ralph FitzHubert, loyal supporter of Rufus the King and the king's half-brother, High Sheriff Peveril.

One final point that also works with the timeline of our Robin is the prosperity of the outlaw band. Various references in *The Gest* imply that they were already well-established by the time they met Sir Richard. Assuming the

---

[206] This hard fought, but successful, campaign was led by the Saxon prince, Edgar Ætheling. Donald Bane was finally captured in 1099 and blinded, dying shortly thereafter, no doubt as a consequence.

band came together in 1080 and met the knight in 1096, 16 years of collective spoils would likely have been large enough not only to assist him with immediate payment of his debt (of around £1 million in today's terms) but also mean that they could afford to turn down its repayment latterly.

Ultimately, as with any commentator on this subject, the identification of those close to Robin is speculation. While I believe that there is a strong case for my theories about his companions and how they fit into the timeline of what we know, both from documented history and storytelling, you must draw your own conclusions. However, on the subject of experienced plunderers, we now turn to one of the most famous aspects of the Robin Hood and Merry Men legend.

Chapter 8
The Poor Man's Hero

The Norman invaders were, simply put, multi-millionaires abusing an already poor populace (though England was relatively prosperous in medieval European terms) by means of a new feudal system—broadly a way of structuring society around relationships that were derived from the holding of land in exchange for service or labour. Under the feudal system a serf (or villein—a peasant farmer/crofter) could not permanently leave his holding or his village without his lord's permission. Neither could the serf marry, change his occupation, or dispose of his property without his lord's permission. The Normans systematically imposed onerous taxation, tithes and fines on the defeated Saxons and took precious holy artefacts from their churches. If Robin Hood was able to return at least some of the property to its rightful owners as revenge for his father's death and a myriad of other motives, this could well explain the crux of the legend of 'robbing' from the rich and giving back to the poor. In fact, this famed generosity looks to have been embellished much later, in the 17th century, particularly with Martin Parker's ballad *A True Tale of Robin Hood* (Child Ballad 154—from 1632) and as with this extract from a slightly earlier poem by Thames waterman John Taylor, from 1622.

> *...Robin Hood with Little John agreed*
> *To rob the rich men and the poore to feed.*[207]

However, what is clear from the early ballads and surviving stories is that they actually contain very little to warrant such a reputation and the general plight of the medieval peasantry does not seem to be Robin's primary concern.

---

[207] *Outlaw Heroes in Myth and History*, Graham Seal, Anthem Press, 2011.

In fact, matters like oppressive taxes and church tithes on the feudal class receive no mention at all in the ballads. The tales certainly include robberies and abductions, plus disguises, escapes, combat, killings, contests and cunning plans, but not returning the spoils of such to the peasant class. This was something which Professor Holt rather eloquently described as a '*posthumous cosmetic*' and was very probably garnered from his reputation for collecting money and charitable works gained in the later May Games of the 15th and 16th centuries (see Appendix 10). In fact, the first explicit statement to the effect that Robin Hood habitually robbed from the rich to give to the poor can be found in *Annales of England* (1592), a chronicle written by late 16th century historian and antiquarian, John Stow, about a century after the publication of *The Gest*. Stow says that Robin Hood and Little John were '*renowned theeves*' known for '*dispoyling and robbing the rich*', and concluded with John Major's statement that he was '*the most humane and Prince of all Robbers*'.[208]

There are only 3 brief, slightly oblique, mentions of philanthropy in *The Gest* and although the idea that Robin steals from the rich and gives to the poor is not fully articulated, it is clear that he and his outlaws do not rob people indiscriminately.

Firstly where Robin declares:

> "*Of my good he shall have some,*
> *if he be a pore man*"
> (stanza 210)

Then towards the end of his life gives away all his money and declares…

> "Alas!" then sayd good Robyn,
> "My wealth is went away."
> (stanza 436)

Finally, following Robin's death, *The Gest* writer tells us in the very last 2 lines which are somewhat oblique and open to interpretation…

---

[208] *Robin Hood, a Mythic Biography,* Stephen Knight (Cornell UP, 2003), p.48.

For he was a good outlawe,

he did poor men much good

(stanza 456).

We also have his generosity towards the impoverished Sir Richard, although he is gentry and also to 'The Potter', a more middle class tradesman. So quite how generous Robin and his men were with the oppressed Saxon villeins is open to conjecture. Despite helping out a starving widow by rescuing her 3 sons who are to be hanged for poaching deer (Robin Hood and the Widow's Three Sons— Child Ballad 140) the act is more chivalric than charitable. None of the ballads provide specific detail of this famous trait. In fact, we are presented with a life more on the lines of 'steal from anybody and keep for himself'. The only observation that warrants this reputation is that there is equally no evidence of a lavish lifestyle apart from good meals. Just how this direct lack of evidence resulted in such a legendary benevolent nature is unclear; my own view on this is that both his father, Waltheof and his sister, Maud, acquired lasting reputations for their kindness and generosity to those on the margins of society and I am sure there is every reason to believe that Robin, as a consequence of his upbringing and influence of his sister, distributed a good proportion of their outlaw gains to the destitute of the villages in Hallam and Barnsdale, which would only have added to their legacy (and security).

What we do have, with my Robin, is motive. Post-conquest, the new 'Murdrum law' inarguably, would have had an impact on him and his kinsmen. This punitive legal measure was the Conqueror's effort to reduce the number of rebellions and revenge killings resulting in noble Norman deaths that continued after 1066. According to the law, if a Norman was murdered on the king's lands, the local Lord had to produce the culprit within 5 days or pay a huge fine (46 marks of silver—around £30—maybe £50,000+ at current value), levied on the local population wherever the body was discovered (based on the 'Hundred' or 'Wapentake'—official subdivisions of the county). Murdrum law was perhaps second only to the Forest Laws as a symbol of Saxon oppression. The rules did not apply to the murders of Englishmen, to the extent that if no-one knew the identity of the victim, and it could not be proved that they were English, then he was deigned to be a Norman and the fine applied! It took nearly another 250 years—under Edward III in 1340, when it was deemed impossible to distinguish between a Norman and an Englishman—for this law to be abolished by statute.

In reality, through intermarriage, such a 'mixing of blood' would have only taken around 100–150 years.

Every time that Robin shot a retainer or soldier of a local baron or sheriff (more than likely in a royal forest/on the king's lands), it would result in a heavy fine. Giving the money he stole to the locals, for them to pay these fines, may well have earned his reputation as the poor man's hero. In addition, where Robin differed from the violent 'hit-and-run' tactics of his contemporaries and later outlaws, if the ballads are to be taken at face value, is that he often invited potential targets to dine with him (albeit at the point of a sword), attend mass and then relieve them of their purses with a cheeky smile before sending them on their way.

This is a good moment to mention that one of Robin's more famous exploits involved robbing the Bishop of Hereford and making him dance a jig, as told in Child Ballad 144, *Robin Hood and the Bishop of Hereford*.

> *Some they will talk of bold Robin Hood,*
> *And some of barons bold,*
> *But I'll tell you how he served the Bishop of Hereford,*
> *When he robbed him of his gold.*
> *As it befell in merry Barnsdale,*
> *And under the greenwood tree,*
> *The Bishop of Hereford was to come by,*
> *With all his company.*

The work is related to Child Ballad 143, *Robin Hood and the bishop*, which dates from a similar period (1670s) and features an unidentified bishop ending in a nearly identical way. Both are variants of the episode in the much older *Gest* in which Robin robs the 2 St Mary's monks of £800.

In our late 11th century time frame, the most likely candidate is 'Gerard', Bishop of Hereford 1096–1100. Medieval chronicler William of Malmesbury recorded Gerard as not only into devil worship but *'lewd and lustful'* and charged him with *'immorality, avarice and the practice of magic'*.[209]

---

[209] *Oxford Dictionary of National Biography*, Burton 'Gerard' entry, 2004.

13. The 'Proud Bishop of Hereford' from *Bold Robin Hood and His Outlaw Band: Their Famous Exploits in Sherwood Forest*, Louis Rhead, 1912
Image in the Public Domain out of copyright

Furthermore, historian Frank Barlow records the words of contemporary chronicler Hugh of Flavigny, who describes Gerard as having led:

"…a depraved life ever since childhood and completely unfitted for episcopal office."[210]

---

[210] *William Rufus*, Frank Barlow, 1983, Berkeley: University of California Press. If this was not bad enough, Gerard's brother, Peter, confessed to having been impregnated by

…and who planned to make all his friends, vassals and servants communicants of the devil! Sounds like the perfect target for Robin Hood and not the best CV for a bishop!

Bishop Gerard's lineage is unclear but he is said to have been the nephew of Walkelin, Bishop of Winchester (d.1098) and records suggest that he was part of the cathedral clergy at Rouen. Well-educated, he then became a royal clerk under William the Conqueror and later his son, William Rufus, serving as Chancellor from 1085 to 1092 before becoming Bishop of Hereford in 1093. Both William Rufus and Henry I used him as an ambassador to Rome. He looks to have assisted at King Henry's coronation, even becoming one of his senior advisors for the first few years of his reign and was later appointed Archbishop of York by Henry (a position he held from December 1100 until his death in 1108).

As Bishop of Hereford, Gerard would have been a most suitable target for the outlaws had he ventured through Barnsdale: a Norman lackey extracting wealth from the English populace and the church to fund Rufus's ongoing wars in France. Between 1096–1100, there is every chance that he would be required to take substantial donations/tithes/funds from Hereford Cathedral up to York or Durham—the ballad says £300 (£100 in another version). Tradition suggests that the ambush in the ballad takes place by an immense oak tree in Skelbrooke Park[211] where their route would have crossed the Great North Road—with local features like Robin Hood's Well, Robin Hood's Chair and Robin Hood's Stone nearby. This site is now known as Bishop's Tree Root, situated just a few miles south of Wentbridge, right in the middle of Barnsdale.

Although keen to relieve a corrupt clergyman or sheriff of their gold, the overall tenor of the stories is that Robin was not driven by money. Law-abiding citizens in the 13th century were already taking the Robin Hood name for themselves on the basis that it was associated with principles of generosity, valour, chivalry, patriotism and so forth, rather than negatives such as murder, anarchy and material greed.

A common thread throughout the legend is Robin's pursuit of liberty and freedom for all, which surely was an expression of the balladeers' views on the political oppression of the time and after. Interestingly, in that tale mentioned

---

a man and died of the monstrous growth. Denied a Christian burial, he was interred outside the cemetery, like an ass. p.409.

[211] William Camden's, Britannia, 1587.

earlier, called *Robin Hood and the Widow's Three Sons,*[212] Robin saves a trio of young men (in different versions it varies between 3 sons, squires, brothers or even 3 of Robin's own men) from being hanged for stealing the king's deer. However, it wasn't until 1217, with the *Charter of the Forest* (Carta de Foresta)[213]—a companion document to the revised *Magna Carta*—that many elements of the Norman Forest Law (created by the Conqueror and extended and abused by his various heirs including Rufus) were redressed and the rights of access to the royal forest for free men were re-established. However, the overall relaxation of many previous restrictions under the Forest Laws made a fundamental improvement to the lives of simple rural folk. Specifically, Clause 10 of the *Forest Charter* repealed the death penalty for killing deer and abolished mutilation as a lesser punishment.

'*No-one shall henceforth lose life or limb because of our venison, but if anyone has been arrested and convicted of taking venison he shall be fined heavily if he has the means; and if he has not the means, he shall lie in our prison for a year and a day; and if after a year and a day he can find pledges he may leave prison; but if not, he shall abjure the realm of England*'. (Clause 10, *Forest Charter*, 1217)

Since this ballad's dire events of planned hangings are obviously prior to this specific reduction in severity of punishment (now just fines, imprisonment and banishment into exile), then surely any case for a Robin Hood after 1217 is seriously weakened.

Eleanor Stredder's suggestion was that a 'heritage' of freedom-fighting within the family led to an unidentified grandson of Waltheof becoming Robin Hood during the time of King John and King Richard. It is more likely, however, that the influence of the lives and beliefs of Robin and his half-sister Maud, stemming from Waltheof, led their descendants to assume the mantle of fighters for national and natural justice. This, perhaps, is the core of the concept of Robin robbing the rich and giving to the poor—it is not money but power and rights that inexorably, over centuries of political evolution, gradually transferred from the privileged few to the common man, and that Robin and his kin started the

---

[212] Featured in the *Percy Folio* and *Child Ballads*, along with many other versions.

[213] This was during the on-going Baron's War when England was under the Regency government of the new boy-king, Henry III. The charter was originally sealed by the young king (aged 10), acting under the regency of England's greatest ever knight, William Marshal, 1st Earl of Pembroke.

process in motion. In reality, it was only as his stories were retold—countless times, in cheap publications called 'broadside ballads' and 19th -century 'penny dreadfuls'—that Robin Hood became the champion of the downtrodden and adversary of corruption that he is known for today.

Chapter 9
The Nemeses

"The Saxon is not like us Normans. His manners are not so polite.
But he never means anything serious till he talks about justice and right.
When he stands like an ox in the furrow, with his sullen set eyes on your
own, and grumbles, 'This isn't fair dealing', my son, leave the Saxon alone."
~ From the poem *Saxon and Norman* by Rudyard Kipling—verse 2

Corrupt Norman barons, vengeful abbots, a despotic King, the evil sheriff, an assassin and a wicked 'cousin'…we are all too familiar with the arch-enemies of Robin and his men, yet none are identified by name in any of the surviving ballads (with the sole exception of Guy of Gisborne). Again, it makes sense to look at the geography of Robin's general adventures at the time when I propose he was most likely operating as an outlaw—from 1080–1100, during the last 7 years of William the Conqueror's reign and the 13 year-rule of his son William Rufus. We should examine the contemporary local Normans who would have impinged on his life—those who controlled the areas of Barnsdale and Sherwood Forests and the 'settlement' centres of Nottingham, Tickhill, Doncaster, Pontefract, Wakefield, Hallam and the adjacent Peak District.

Before that, it is important to understand the state of Britain post-Conquest. Our peek into this distant past would not be possible without the extraordinary historical legacy of that remarkable 1085/86 economic survey of England embodied into *Great* and *Little Domesday* Books.[214] It is worth mentioning that some large wealthy urban and royal centres like London (the walled square mile),

---

[214] The Domesday Book encompasses two independent works (originally, in two physical volumes): '*Little Domesday*', covering Norfolk, Suffolk, and Essex, and '*Great Domesday*', covering much of the remainder of England—The original surviving manuscripts are now held in The National Archives at Kew, London.

Bristol, Winchester and Tamworth were completely omitted from the records. We are not entirely sure why, but possibly because *Domesday* was essentially a land survey, so urban and royal areas were of little agricultural worth. By and large, artisans, shopkeepers and craftsmen like blacksmiths, potters, tanners, bakers, brewers, and stonemasons as well as shepherds, coastal fishermen, charcoal-makers, ropemakers, bowyers, fletchers and those involved in mining are unrecorded, or get scant mention, as were nuns, monks and people in castles. It does, however, record the details of a remarkable total of 13,418 places (and 6000 mills, 45 castles, 60 religious houses, 48 vineyards[215] and several mints are also noted).

In addition, County Durham and Northumberland do not appear because King William did not fully control these areas, and places such as Cumbria and Westmoreland were excluded since they were part of Scotland at the time. Even so, *Domesday* gives us many valuable facts:

- In 1086, the population of Britain was about 1.5–2 million at most (today 60+million) of which maybe 10% were slaves.[216] Recorded individuals in Domesday number 268,984 though these are only householders—as wives, children, old people etc. were not recorded. Some 40% of this total are listed as 'villani' in Latin.[217]
- Due to the Harrowings (when 100,000+ died), starvation and disease, South Yorkshire supported just 3 people per square mile, compared with

---

[215] These vineyards, often newly-planted (as far north as Ely in Cambridgeshire), catered for the tastes of the new rulers. But this attempt to establish a significant English wine industry was to prove short-lived. English wine was of poor quality, and from the 1150s fine imported wines from Bordeaux and La Rochelle put the English vineyards out of business. Due to climate change and new grape varieties, excellent white wine is now produced in England as far north as Yorkshire!

[216] The commonest sort of slave in later Anglo-Saxon times, by far, was the penal slave, a person enslaved as a criminal penalty for crimes committed. In hard times, the poorer agricultural class sometimes found their only hope of sustenance was in voluntarily submitting to slavery, and sold themselves and their families to survive. By 1100 though, under Norman rule, slavery was virtually abolished.

[217] 'A Villain'—a peasant personally bound to his lord, to whom he paid dues and services, sometimes commuted to rents, in return for his land.

a remarkable 856 today (for example, Sheffield manor consisted of 3 ploughlands and had a population of zero!).

- Only 125,000 of the entire population lived in an 'urban' environment. About 8.3% compared to today's 83%!

- Twenty years after the Battle of Hastings, the populace now included a mere 10,000 Normans, of which, excluding the king, just 11 men controlled a *quarter of the country* via a network of castles, giving out land in exchange for dues and military service.

- By 1086—when every man, field, wood, cottage, plough, mill, pig and chicken had been tallied up—75% of the value/GDP of the whole country's wealth (essentially land, livestock and labour) was in the hands of fewer than 200 men and roughly 100 religious establishments. Overall, the whole was owned and managed by just 1,400 'tenants-in-chief' holding land directly from the king and who virtually all came from Normandy, though many had small manorial holdings. The breakdown of ownership was as follows:

- 54% to baronial vassals (including those 11 men who 'owned' 25% of the entire country);

- 25% to religious houses;

- 17% directly held by the king (although he was freeholder of the whole kingdom);

- Just 4% to a few original Saxon thegns from pre-1066 (of which only 3 were significant—***Thorkill of Warwick, Coleswain of Lincoln and Gospatric FitzArnketil of Yorkshire***) who had managed to keep in favour with their conquerors, in exchange for a few scraps as 'sub-tenants'.[218]

---

[218] Of particular interest, to me, is Gospatric (not the Earl), but the son of Arnketil/Arkyle), a grandson of Ecgfrida (Waltheof's great-grandmother), the ex-wife of Earl Uchtred after she re-married (Kilvert). He is the antecedent of the 'Staveley' family name being the grandfather of the first person recorded to hold this name and from whom I descend, one Swain 'de Staveley', being granted the Lordship there by King Stephen in 1135. Gospatric was one of only three English thegns to still be significant tenants-in-chief at Domesday being associated with 115 places in Yorkshire before the Conquest and 62 after the Conquest—of which *42 were still held as tenant-in-chief*—one being 'Staveley', nr. Boroughbridge. In 1068, as a young man, he was briefly given by his father as one of the hostages during after the rebel abdication at York to the Conqueror

Through the unique record of *Domesday*, we know precisely who—in 1086, at the height of Robin's activities—controlled Barnsdale, Hallamshire and the surrounding areas where 3 counties conjoin: South Yorkshire, North Nottinghamshire and East Derbyshire. This enormous swathe of mostly forested land and heathland, running 60 miles from Pontefract to Nottingham, was effectively ruled by the 2 sheriffs (Derbyshire and Nottinghamshire were combined, plus Yorkshire), who managed their own manors plus those manorial estates directly held by the king (also legal jurisdiction over everybody). There were a few random local manors owned by barons who had large holdings elsewhere (e.g. Walter d'Aincourt, William de Percy and Earl Aubrey de Coucy) but essentially just 4 powerful Norman barons controlled the whole region, in particular the Wapentake of Strafforth—Robin Hood country:

Ilbert de Lacy (son Robert after 1090) Robert de Mortain (son William after 1090) William de Warrenne (son William after 1088) and Roger de Busli (and after his death in 1098, Robert de Bellême)

Incredibly, between them, these 4 men held the lordships and managed nearly 2,200 manors throughout England, the vast majority of which were in Yorkshire. William de Warenne, for example, was estimated to have a personal wealth, in current values, of £60 billion (which today would make him the 10th richest person in the world).[219] That said, the Conqueror was shrewd; he split up the large and dangerous regional earldoms of late Anglo-Saxon England, such as Wessex, so that even with his most trusted lieutenants he diluted the geography of their holdings to different districts to prevent 'kingdom-building' and future threats. For example, de Lacy's main holdings were divided between Pontefract in Yorkshire and Clitheroe in Lancashire, while de Warenne and de Mortain both had significant landholdings in Sussex, in addition to their Yorkshire estates.

It is also worth mentioning that in the 20 years between the Conquest and *Domesday*, the northern lands became comparable with the Wild West; settlements, animals and crops decimated after the Harrowing (reported losses of 100–150,000 people and 80,000 oxen in Yorkshire and North Riding alone), plus large tracts of barren moors, resulted in a wasteland of little value. With a

---

who appeared with an army. Arkyle, had been a lead rebel but then submitted to the king who was given the keys to the city. Father and son probably survived by being associated, by blood and insurrection, with Waltheof, who was so favoured latterly by the Conqueror—*from Yorkshire volume of Philimore series on the Domesday Book, 1976.*
[219] Forbes real-time Rich List, as at 24/4/2021

strong history of independence and separate political identity to the rest of the country, Northumbria (Northumberland—*Bernicia* and Yorkshire—*Deira*) was practically ungovernable and rife with outlaws. When sheriffs moved around, they did so with a large armed retinue. A 1990 study into Robert de Mortain by the academic Dr Brian Golding concluded that his hold over his northern estates, as with de Lacy and the others, was likely no more than nominal.[220] It was only through the deaths or exile of the original Saxon/Anglo-Scandinavian landowners (whether natural, in battle, or the Harrowings of 1070 and 1080) and the reallocation of their estates into Norman ownership, plus substantial Norman castle-building (post-*Domesday*), that a wholesale takeover and subjugation of the North was finally accomplished, 2 decades or more after the Battle of Hastings and right into the middle and final periods of Robin's outlawry.

It is hard for us to imagine what life was like for these conquering barons nearly 1000 years ago, but I was taken by this totally depressing depiction by historian Frank Barlow...

The life of the new aristocracy was not greatly different from that of the old. There was the same lack of privacy in hall or castle, the press of servants and retainers, The stifling promiscuity that drove the rare individual into a hermitage or on a solitary path. There was, perhaps, an even greater disdain for agriculture and a greater love for war and its substitutes—the chase, hawking and military training and sport. The physical ideal was still the coarse athletic figure; courage and fidelity remained the spiritual ideals. The haunting spectre continued to be the tedium which assails isolated communities of limited intellectual interest, and for which there is no remedy but fresh outbursts of physical activity. It was a restless, drunken and emotional society, gorged after 1066 with unaccustomed wealth.[221]

So what do we know about this powerful quartet and their offspring? And how did they impact in restless, drunken style on the undoubtedly less tedious life of Robin Hood?

---

[220] 'Robert of Mortain', Golding, Brian, *Anglo-Norman Studies XIII: Proceedings of the Battle Conference 1990* (Boydell Press, 1991)

[221] *The Feudal Kingdom of England: 1042–1216*, Frank Barlow, Routledge, 2014. pp.94–5.

Ilbert de Lacy (d. c1090) and his son Robert: Pontefract (and Barnsdale)

Ilbert fought at Hastings with his brother Walter (d.1085). For his services in battle, he received the Honour of Pontefract, where he built a huge castle in the town plus 4 smaller ones in the villages of Kippax, Whitwood, Saxton and Armley, all slightly north of Pontefract (see Appendix 6), making him as wealthy as the billionaires of today. Of the 249 manors he held, 189 were in Yorkshire and included almost all of the manors within the district known as Barnsdale itself...Ilbert was one of King William's key commanders during the Harrowing of the North and, as such, Robin would have had particular hatred for the man who was not only obscenely rich at the expense of the original English landowners, but also likely wiped out his home village of Loxley and the surrounding district of Hallamshire, probably causing the death or exile of many of his family and his father's friends.

When he died in 1090, early in the reign of William Rufus, Ilbert was succeeded by his eldest son, Robert. At that time, another great magnate over in Lancashire, Roger the Poitevin, sublet Blackburnshire and the Forest of Bowland, north of the River Ribble, to this Robert de Lacy who, as part of his military power base there, constructed Clitheroe Castle.[222] In the early years of the reign of Henry I after 1100, Robert de Lacy initially supported Robert Curthose and consequently was stripped of his lands and exiled. However, he made peace with Henry and appears to have taken a leading role in maintaining royal authority in the north of England but came badly unstuck again in around 1114 by offending the king, though the reasons are mysteriously unclear, that resulted in Robert and his son (also called Ilbert) being banished by King Henry and forfeiting their English estates for the second time. Robert died in exile c.1130 but will appear later in this chapter with the episode of Guy of Gisborne.

Robert de Mortain (d.1090) and his son William: Barnsdale Forest

The chronicler William of Malmesbury described Robert, in his *Gesta Regum Anglorum*, as a man of *'stupid and dull disposition'* (*crassi et hebetis*

---

[222] Clitheroe castle is just 7 miles from Gisburn, purported home of Guy of Gisborne, one of Robin's famous nemesis, and who will appear later in our story. All these lands, including the Lordship of Bowland, became known as the Honour of Clitheroe and were subsequently incorporated into the royal Duchy of Lancaster.

ingenii). He was a full brother of the powerful Bishop Odo de Bayeux and thus also half-brother of William the Conqueror. He held a staggering 797 manors in nineteen counties at the time of *Domesday*, which made him the richest man in England after the king (numerous of his manors in the North Riding of Yorkshire had originally been held by Waltheof back in 1066). He was barely present in person in Yorkshire as he sublet these estates to his 2 key 'lieutenants' and supporters, Nigel Fossard[223] and Richard Surdeval. From childhood, Robert's son William, harboured a bitter dislike for his cousin Prince Henry[224] and was described as 'incorrigibly turbulent'.[225] Significantly, like Odo and the King, **Robert was also an uncle of Judith de Lens,** who I believe was Robin's stepmother. Such family connections would not have gone unnoticed by our outlaw.

William de Warenne (d.1088) and his son William II (Earls of Surrey): Wakefield, Conisbrough and the Rape of Lewes

William was one of the few proven companions of William the Conqueror known to have fought at the Battle of Hastings. At the *Domesday* survey, he held extensive lands in 13 counties (tenant-in-chief or lord of some 537 manors), including the Rape of Lewes in Sussex (now East Sussex) and the Manor of Conisbrough, as well as many others between Sheffield and Doncaster His wealth has been estimated at around £60 billion in current value, making him '*rich beyond the dreams of avarice*'[226]. The Warennes built castles at

---

[223] Nigel built a motte-and-bailey castle of his own at Hangthwaite, Castle Hills, located just south-east of Adwick-le-Street, off the A1 Great North Road (Ermine Street) on the A638, though only the remains of the motte and ditches survive today (Appendix 1, map pin 16)

[224] Among the reasons for intensely disliking Henry I, almost certainly included his mother's family, specifically his uncles Robert of Bellême, Hugh de Montgomery, Arnulf de Montgomery, and Roger the Poitevin who were all devout enemies of Henry. They had all been dispossessed of their English holdings and exiled from England shortly after Henry became king. See: 'Roger de Montgomery and His Sons (1067–1102)', *Transactions of the Royal Historical Society*, J. F. A. Mason, 5th series vol. 13 (1963), pp. 1–28.

[225] *The Warenne (Hyde) Chronicle*. Edited and translated by Van Houts and Love. Oxford Medieval Texts. OUP. 2013.

[226] *The Gamester*, Act ii, Sc. 2, Edward Moore, 1753.

Conisbrough[227] near Doncaster—just 3 miles from de Busli's smaller fortification at Mexborough—and later another at Sandal (nr. Wakefield) in 1107. (Appendix 6, map pins 3, 12)

William de Warenne fought against Hereward the Wake in 1071, for whom he is said to have had a special hatred as allegedly Hereward killed his brother Frederic. He was also a key character, as Justiciar, during the king's absence in Normandy, in suppressing the Earls' Revolt of 1075. Again, this would have given Robin motive, as such action ultimately led to Waltheof's execution.

Following the Conqueror's death in 1087, de Warenne was loyal to the new king, William Rufus. In early 1088, he became 1st Earl of Surrey, a title created for him which was held for only a few months before he was mortally wounded at the six-week siege of Pevensey Castle during the uprising led by Rufus's elder brother Robert Curthose, along with Robert de Mortain. At the time of his death on 24th June 1088, de Warenne was the third or fourth richest man in England. His inheriting son (yet another William), William de Warenne, 2nd Earl of Surrey, will feature later in our story in Part II.

Roger de Busli I and Robert de Bellême: Sheffield, Blyth and Tickill

Roger de Busli was born c.1038 (slightly before Waltheof). Nobody knows for certain who Roger was, or if he was at the Battle of Hastings. Orderic Vitalis records that he was a cousin of Robert de Bellême, not a 'first' cousin, but quite which type is not explained. Some historians suggest Roger was probably connected in some way with the Conqueror's wife, Queen Matilda, maybe through his own wife, Muriel, but in fact so little is known about him that he has been described by some as: *'famous in Domesday but nowhere else'*[228], being the largest landowner in Nottinghamshire at that time.

---

[227] The later stone castle, built on the same grounds c.1170–80, was featured in Sir Walter Scott's celebrated 1819 novel *Ivanhoe*, as the thinly-veiled 'Coningsburgh'.

[228] Domesday Book Online—http://www.domesdaybook.co.uk/landowners.html.

14. Continuation of extract from *Domesday* with 'Rog de'—evidence of de Busli's control over what had been Waltheof's lands.
Courtesy of opendomesday.org—Anna Powell-Smith, Professor John Palmer and George Slater

What we do know from the survey is that de Busli certainly had the king's favour—with William giving him enormous estates—some 382 manors in Nottinghamshire, Derbyshire and South Yorkshire—that had previously belonged to a variety of Anglo-Saxons, including Edwin, Earl of Mercia, the brother of Morcar, Earl of Northumbria in 1066. Historian E. A. Freeman recorded of de Busli that '*He had supplanted 2 earls in their special homes; he sat by the hearth of Edwin and by the hearth of Waltheof*'.[229] This seems to be a direct allusion to the fact he had taken over the respective aula residences (found in Domesday) of both Waltheof's at Hallam and Edwin's at Laughton-en-le-Morthen. He was tenant-in-chief or lord of much of the land around Sheffield, including Ecclesfield, Tinsley, Wadsley, Norton and Dore, and also held the 3 Lordships of Hallam, Attercliffe and Sheffield as Tenant of Countess Judith—these were amongst the many manors she had inherited from her late husband Waltheof following his execution.

---

[229] *The Reign of William Rufus and the Accession of Henry the First*, E. A. Freeman, Clarendon Press, 1882, Vol. 2. p.159.

The King also granted de Busli (and the other great barons and abbeys) strong judicial powers over their estates including the power of *'infangthief'* (the right to execute thieves apprehended on their own land), which effectively amounted to him being police, judge and jury in order to keep law and order in the region. Although de Busli was not technically the sheriff, his authority would have made outlaws and poachers want to avoid him at all cost.

De Busli built his main castle at Blyth(e), later known as Tickhill. Today this is only a small town but in the 11th century it was an important place. To keep a stranglehold over the local populace, he also erected 3 further motte-and-Bailey castles at Kimberworth, Mexborough and Laughton-en-le-Morthen (Appendix 6, map pins 11,12,13), some of the many manors making up the great 'Honour of Tickhill'. These are all sited between Sheffield and Doncaster. Kimberworth[230] and its castle is just 7 miles from Loxley (Appendix 6, map pin 5). It looks like this castle was either granted, managed or sublet to Roger's younger brother, Arnold, who may well have lived there and overseen its iron smelting production (an important part of the weapon-making process). In 1088, Roger and his wife Muriel founded the small Blyth Priory (granting it the tithes of their Laughton-en-le-Morthen manor) as a Benedictine daughter house of the abbey of La Trinité-du-Mont near Rouen of which they were already generous benefactors.[231]

---

[230] Kimberworth castle was a timber motte and bailey construction and never rebuilt in stone. The de Busli family held the castle until the mid-13th century, eventually moving to a moated manor house nearby. Earthworks survive for all three of de Busli's castles and are scheduled monuments. Laughton-en-le-Morthen is particularly important for being one of the best-preserved examples of its class in Yorkshire. (see Appendix 6)

[231] It has been suggested that Blyth priory was established by de Busli with a view to its brethren ministering to those wounded in the jousts and performing the last rites to such as died. In fact it was not until more than a century after Blyth's foundation that the nearby tournament field was first mentioned, being one of only five licensed by Richard I, becoming one of the most famous in England. However, It is quite probable that as Norman knights were so fond of jousting, there were already knightly contests here in de Busli's lifetime and this was in fact the location of the fateful joust in *The Gest* involving the 20yr old son of Sir Richard at the Lee as their suggested castle is only 25 miles away. The jousting area has recently been re-discovered by archaeologists, in a field known locally as *Terminings (tourneyings) Meadow*, on a tract of land between Blyth and Styrrup midway between the Priory site and the castle. Sir Richard was clearly familiar with the place, since when originally intercepted by the outlaws near *'the Saylis'*

15. Hand-coloured plate of an engraving by George Vertue, from *Vetusta Monumenta (1737)*—depicting Tickhill Castle as it appeared in the sixteenth century.

Image in the Public Domain

Roger de Busli I died c.1098–99 but his son, Roger II, the younger, did not inherit his vast estates. Instead, the bulk if not all of his properties were purchased by a powerful ally of King Rufus. Robert de Bellême (c.1056–after 1130) has been cited as the most evil and cruel man of his generation, living a life diametrically opposite to that of Robin, with the chronicler Orderic Vitalis calling him, "*Grasping and cruel, an implacable persecutor of the church of God and the poor...unequalled for his iniquity in the whole Christian era.*" When Robert's father died in 1194, his younger brother Hugh inherited the English lands and titles, while he inherited his father's Norman properties, which included a good part of central and southern Normandy. He became a successful and loyal military commander for William Rufus during his campaigns in Maine and the Vexin during 1096–7.

---

on Watling Street, he tells them (last lines of Gest stanza 28) "*my purpose was to have dined today at **Blyth** or Doncaster.*"

In 1098, brother Hugh died and Robert thus also inherited their father's English properties, including the vast Rape of Arundel and the Earldom of Shrewsbury. Roger de Busli died at approximately the same time (followed swiftly after by both his brother Arnold and Arnold's son John) such that it is possible that his son (Roger II) retained tenancy of Judith's manors of Hallamshire, Sheffield and Attercliffe (being separate from the 'Honour of Tickhill'), as well as the Busli castle at Kimberworth which had been Arnold's residence, being just 7 miles from Loxley. Bellême was clearly in greater favour with William Rufus as upon Roger de Busli I's death, Bellême not only received his huge 'Honour of Tickhill' estates (more importantly, paying Rufus the vast sum of £3,000 for the privilege), but he also obtained the Countship of Ponthieu in late 1100, all of which combined made him the wealthiest magnate in both England and Normandy at that date.[232]

Roger de Busli II, the younger, and Kimberworth castle will both make a dramatic appearance later in Robin's life, and death, in Part II.

Judith de Lens (*c.*1054–1103)

Last, but certainly not least, we need to consider Judith; the niece of William the Conqueror and the lady proposed as Robin's stepmother who married Waltheof in 1070/1. The close links between the nobility of the Norman Duchy and the English crown is exemplified by the fact that Judith held 14 manors in Lincolnshire, as tenant-in-chief from King Edward the Confessor, prior to the Norman invasion in 1066, though it is unlikely she had ever visited them. Although opinion is mixed over whether Judith was treacherous or not in the downfall and execution of her husband, the leaning is towards the fact that she did show greater loyalty to her uncles, the Conqueror and Odo, but came to regret the dreadful outcome, which may have not been what she had fully expected.

After Waltheof's execution Judith was allowed (or was it *rewarded*?) by a politically astute King William, to inherit most of Waltheof's estates, which encompassed his Hallamshire holdings around Sheffield (which she then sublet to Roger de Busli I) as well as substantial manorial holdings in the Midlands and

---

[232] He acquired this Countship in Picardy '*jure uxoris*' (a Latin phrase meaning 'by right of (his) wife') when his wife 'Agnes of Ponthieu' (c. 1080–aft. 1105) became the ruling Countess of Ponthieu from 1100 when she inherited from her father, Guy I of Ponthieu, who died in October 1100.

East Anglia to the south. Although *Domesday* evidence is scant for Yorkshire, it seems that Waltheof's estates north of Hallam and most of those in Cambridgeshire reverted to the Crown and not to Judith. Despite that, in the *Domesday* records of 1086 she held, either as tenant-in-chief or lord, some 315 manors, mostly in Northamptonshire, Lincolnshire, Leicestershire, Rutland, Bedfordshire and Cambridgeshire. She also held a few very large ones that are today in north London, but were then rural village communities 7 miles from the city, such as Tottenham, Edmonton and Walthamstow. Most of these had been the property of Waltheof, and just these 3 together were worth around £125 per annum in 1086 (at least £250,000+ today or more), which along with the remainder would have made her extremely wealthy. In fact, her holdings, covering eleven counties, made her the richest woman in Domesday England.

In about 1078, just a year or 2 after her husband was executed, Judith founded Elstow Abbey in Bedfordshire for Benedictine nuns, which owing to her status was a 'royal' foundation, that she endowed with the income from her nearby manors of Elstow, Wilshampstead and a part of Maulden. Both historians and tradition say that this act was as penance, atonement and reparation for her treachery to her husband. After his death, she vacated Huntingdon castle and lived in Sawtry, a further 9 miles up Ermine Street, the old Roman road to York, and some twenty-five miles from Elstow. This would have been with her 2 young daughters, Maud (Matilda) and Adelisa (Alice) who were only about 4 and 2 years old at the time of their father's death, and were now maybe 6 and 4. It was sometime later (after the Domesday survey of 1087, maybe around 1098 though the precise date is unknown) that she also established the much smaller Ecclesfield Priory, 4 miles from Loxley, in Hallamshire, within the confines of a manor of Roger de Busli and 7 miles from his castle at Kimberworth (on the outskirts of modern-day Sheffield—Appendix 1, map pin 4). This eventually became a satellite or what was called an 'alien' house of a big Benedictine abbey, maybe Elstow originally and later of St Wandrille in Normandy, to which she (and the subsequent lords of the manor, the de Lovetots) were generous benefactors. We shall take a much closer look at the murky history of this establishment in Part II, as this small religious house takes centre stage in our later story.

In 1087, after the shambles of her refusing her second enforced marriage, this time to Simon de Senlis, no-one seems to know what really happened next except that it is believed she was, at least temporarily, deprived of her estates and ran off with her 2 daughters to hide in the Fens of Ely. It has been suggested by some that she perhaps fled back to her family territory in Lens, Normandy. Her children, Robin's half-sisters, were then about thirteen and fifteen and most likely, once things quietened down, she slunk back home to Sawtry and returned the children to her Elstow Abbey, not as novice nuns but to complete their education, as these establishments were as much schools for children of the nobility as religious centres. It seems Judith lived a quiet life for the next 10 years or so as nothing of her life is recorded anywhere, which, for the richest woman in the land, is somewhat strange.

Her taking the veil at this time, and maybe even becoming the abbess, might go a long way to explaining her quite surprising disappearance given her former status with her uncles, the king, William, and Count Odo, as well as William Rufus, the next king and his brothers, her first cousins. Regrettably though the names of abbesses prior to 1180 have not survived in the records. The Croyland Abbey Chronicle records her at this time as follows…'At length, however, this wretched woman confessed her wickedness and showed extreme penitence for the nefarious destruction of her husband; and so remained unmarried to the end, being from that time an object of suspicion to all and deservedly despised'.[233]

What is certain is that no record does exist showing her as ever having remarried after Waltheof's death—and as a nun, she could not—and her death and place of burial are also unrecorded. As probably the wealthiest woman in England and of such high royal status, this is somewhat unusual and the probable reasons for these omissions will be explored in the later dramatic chapter regarding Robin's demise. One would have expected for her to have been buried at Elstow Abbey, the religious house of her own foundation, the common practice among notable religious benefactors, though there is no record of this[234].

---

[233] *Ingulf's Chronicle of the Abbey of Croyland* trans. Henry T. Riley (1854), p.146

[234] One chronicler suggested that Judith's betrayal of her husband in 1076 was prompted by the fact she had been pushed unwillingly into the marriage and was now conducting an affair with a (Norman) third party. Her husband being a Saxon, could well have been held against her by her contemporaries, making her somewhat of a pariah in social circles. Norman men and Saxon wives was fine, the reverse was rare and not so accepted. A case could easily be made out for this lover to have been Roger de Busli II, as in 1087 she refused to enter her second arranged marriage to newly arrived knight, Simon de Senlis, giving his gammy leg as the rather weak excuse. Certainly, following Waltheof's death, most of his lands that she inherited in south Yorkshire, she sublet to Roger de

During the reign of William Rufus, there were long periods of instability and rebellion by the barons and between the royal brothers. Following his death in the autumn of 1100, Rufus's youngest brother Henry assumed the English throne. However, all Barnsdale landowners—the sons of the original vanquishers—de Lacy, de Warenne, de Mortain and latterly (as de Busli had just died) de Bellême—all sided with Rufus' elder brother Robert Curthose (Duke of Normandy) in the upcoming power struggle upon his triumphant return from the First Crusade. Some even harboured personal hatred of the young Henry. Their fathers' power and wealth had stemmed from the Conqueror so now they looked to support a King of Normandy under whom England would continue to be a subjugated territory. Conversely, Henry saw himself much more as the king of England, whose territories also included the Duchy of Normandy and parts of France.

It does not take much to understand why Robin would have been loyal to Henry. Furthermore, he would have been more than happy to see these heirs dispossessed of stolen Saxon lands and made to pay for all that their fathers had done to his kinsmen. Although rich and powerful Norman magnates capable of raising small armies would have been significant in Robin's life, of far greater impact was the role of the sheriff. So, as intriguing as these wicked barons of Barnsdale are, no serious study can be completed without in-depth discussion of the most notorious adversary of all.

Sheriffs

In the 11th and 12th centuries, except for the royal court, the *'Curia Regis'*, the most significant institution at the king's disposal was the 'Shrievalty'. With origins in the 10th century, the office of 'sheriff' was the oldest secular appointment under the Crown, but vastly empowered by William the Conqueror when Norman aristocracy were appointed to the roles. The Anglo-Saxon word 'sheriff' comes from an amalgamation of 'shire' and 'reeve'. A shire was the archaic equivalent of a county and a reeve was an official position that began in Saxon times, authorised to hold court and try local civil and criminal matters.

Busli I, the father. In founding Elstow Abbey and becoming the first prioress, it ended her chances of remarriage to the man she may be truly loved, but remained his lover for her whole life, the tragic consequences of which we shall explore in Part II.

After the Conquest, reeves were appointed for every shire, and therefore 'Shire Reeve' morphed to become 'Sheriff'.

They were the king's arms of government, via local bailiffs, for tax collection. They were managers of the king's lands in their area, plus the private estates bestowed upon them by the Crown. They were the local judges, via the Shire Court and the Hundred Court and it was plain that the sheriff, not the local earl, had charge of public justice and maintenance of the peace. They were the peace-makers, which included enforcement of the new Forest Laws on 'vert and venison'. Sentences for outlawry and Forest Law violations were pronounced by the sheriff and, other than death, punishments included a ghastly menu of amputation, blinding and the favourite, castration. If you did not agree with a decision or action of the sheriff, the only appeal was to the king himself, which was fruitless. In these early Norman times, apart from the most exceptional cases, the sheriff was the justice of England.

It was a system that ensured the Conqueror's strength and control over the land[235]. As long as they honoured their key roles, sheriffs enjoyed enormous freedom, combining the prestige of a local magnate and the status of a trusted official. They could skim substantial profits off all enterprises under their jurisdiction (they managed the king's own land in their region) and were able, via their subordinate reeves, to manipulate tax collection to their advantage. They systematically stripped Saxon churches and monasteries of their wealth and possessions. The abbeys of Worcester, Ely, Pershore and many other Anglo-Saxon ecclesiastical establishments suffered heavily at their hands.

Periods of tenure of the office were not fixed and personal claims to the king's friendship or gratitude did much to lengthen the term. Indeed, many leading sheriffs held the position for life with some even assuming hereditary status and some survived right up to the reign of Henry I (most significantly with William Rufus and Henry's illegitimate half-brother, William Peveril, as we shall soon see).

If it is accepted that the approximate 22-year span of Robin's outlawry detailed in *The Gest* is roughly correct (which I propose was from 1080–1102), then it is inevitable that he interacted with more than one sheriff (as indeed in the

---

[235] This Crown-led control only began to change in the reign of Henry II (1154–89), when the first identifiable system of what we now know as the Civil Service was instituted by his Chancellor, Thomas Becket.

main legend several sheriffs die). For the purposes of my research in the later 11th century, numerous sheriffs were in control of key areas of Hood territory.

It is surely not without significance that the years in which I propose that Robin grew up and was then outlawed (1080–1100) fit perfectly within the timeframe when the sheriffs' power—and abuse of it—was at its greatest height in English history (1068–1100).

If one accepts that the earliest references to Robin Hood from the 13th century are valid, then this throws up an interesting conundrum: the specific title and post of 'Sheriff of Nottingham'—as in the town itself, rather than the shire county— was not created until 1449 by Henry VI. However, there were much earlier 'High' sheriffs of whole counties/shires/shrievalties established by the Normans. From 1068–1566, this included the position of 'High Sheriff of Nottinghamshire, Derbyshire and the Royal Forests of the Peak' (post-1566, this was split into 2 posts, one for each of the 2 shires). Additionally, a Sheriff of Yorkshire is documented at least a century before any common placement of the legend. Given the enormous significance of the sheriff in the stories, it pays for us to look at these positions in both Yorkshire and Nottinghamshire during the second half of the 11th century.

Finally, it should be noted that there were also the new Norman posts of castellans (castle governors, usually called 'Constables' in the case of royal castles), who were effectively assistant or deputy sheriffs in the larger fortified settlements held by the king like Nottingham, Norwich and Colchester and also those built by the great barons with the king's permission (e.g. Conisbrough, Chepstow, Bolsover, Skipton, Shrewsbury etc.) especially if the baron himself was not resident there. They were usually military men and also powerful landowners, lords and tenants-in-chief who held similar judicial and financial authority to the sheriff being responsible for the royal castles, its urban population and the control of royal forests under the 'Forest Laws'. While not strictly sheriffs (more like urban deputies), the castellans' reign over certain areas cannot be underestimated as they would have done much of the real work like seizing outlaw property and collecting taxes but never get mentioned in the records or ballads. As balladeers may well have updated or simplified terminology of all such men to 'Sheriff' for the easier understanding of contemporary audiences, this makes our field of research in the late 11th century a rather wide one.

However, this clear distinction between the proud sheriff of the city of Nottingham and the overall County High Sheriff is actually made in Stanzas 317–8 of *The Gest* itself, where during the escapade with Sir Richard at the Lee, the city deputy sheriff, the castellan, goes to ask the High Sheriff for help—as it says…

317

Lythe and lysten, gentylmen,

And herkyn to your songe,

Howe the proude **shyref of Notyngham** (How the proud Sheriff of Nottingham)

And men of armys stronge

318

Full fast **came to the hye shyref** (came very fast to the High Sheriff)

The contré up to route (to raise up the countryside—i.e. mount a posse!)

And they besette (beseiged) the knyghtes castell,

The walles all aboute. (all around the walls)

In the 6th Fytte of The Gest, this 'proud' Nottingham sheriff, who has captured Sir Richard (maybe Ralph FitzHubert—see below, or an unknown person), is shot by Robin with an arrow and before he can get up, Robin cuts his head off but insists he will obtain a pardon from the king.

'Sheriff' of Nottingham(shire), Derbyshire and the Royal Forests of the Peak.

While geography and times are debated, one aspect of the Robin Hood legend has evolved with certainty: the most famed nemesis of our hero is the evil Sheriff of Nottingham. He is depicted as an oath-breaker, a coward, a fool and a drunkard. He embodies all the malign elements of corrupt power as a repressive agent of the Crown. He appears frequently and dies several times in the ballad tales, yet is never called by name in any of them. In fact, the search for the sheriff has been almost as thorough and elusive as that of our outlaw. Let us look now at the 5 main contenders covering the bulk of Robin's life[236]:

---

[236]*English Sheriffs to 1154,* Judith Green, Public Records Handbook No. 24 (London: HMSO, 1990)

1. 1068–1069: *William Peveril I*
2. 1069–1080: *Hugh FitzBaldric* (also High Sheriff of Yorkshire 1069–1086)
3. 1080–1087: *Hugh de Port* (also High Sheriff of Hampshire 1070–1096)
4. 1087–1100: No Sheriff recorded. Castellan/castle governor—*Ralph FitzHubert* from c.1095–c.1098—*William Peveril I* likely still in overall charge of the County throughout the whole period.
5. Dec 1100–1105?: *Richard FitzGotse (King Henry's 'new man')*

(1) William Peveril (High Sheriff 1068–9 and Nottinghamshire 'Overseer' from c.1068–c.1115)

After the Battle of Hastings and his coronation, King William returned to Normandy in 1067 and left the management of England to his half-brother Bishop Odo. Among the many knights and barons who had fought with him at Hastings and to whom he granted extensive powers and land, was a particular favourite—and thought by many to most likely be an illegitimate son of the Conqueror—the young William Peveril—to whom he was exceedingly generous.

According to *Domesday* records, William Peveril (spelt 'Peverel' in the survey) was appointed either tenant-in-chief or lord of some 162 manors, collectively forming the Honour of Peveril, principally in Nottinghamshire and to the south (Derbyshire and Northamptonshire). Importantly, in 1068, he was also the very first holder of the specific position of *'High Sheriff of Nottinghamshire, Derbyshire and the Royal Forests of the Peak'*, at only c.24 years of age. By his mid-40s in 1086, with a huge castle in the Peak District just 12 miles from Hallam, he was, significantly, the most powerful local 'sheriff'. Peveril was also responsible for building Nottingham Castle for the king, construction of which started in 1068. He remained in charge of the castle for his lifetime, though appointed governors or 'castellans' in his name—effectively deputy sheriffs.

The records, such as they are, show that Peveril only held the position of sheriff himself for the first year or so from 1068–69, when our Robin was just a 10-year-old boy. However, while others are subsequently recorded as sheriffs, castellans/constables (castle governors) or generally in charge of various local areas during the same period, including minions, or under-sheriffs of Peveril himself (who were either killed or sacked), William Peveril seems to have had overarching authority for Nottinghamshire for nearly 40 years.

It is believed that William Peveril was born c.1044 to a Saxon mother[237] referred to as Maud, purportedly a noble and beautiful Saxon girl, being the daughter of an Anglo-Saxon nobleman called Ingelric[238], the mistress of Duke William, as she was at the time (some historians suggesting she was even married to Ranulph Peveril at this time). The Conqueror is generally accepted to have fathered him around 17 years of age—just like young Waltheof had with Robin. Although not supported by the historical record, the illegitimate William Peveril is said to have been told to take the surname of his Norman stepfather Ranulf Peveril, as part of the agreement to Peveril's marriage to his mother (Ranulph, a dedicated supported of Duke William, received 75 manors in Suffolk after the Norman Conquest). Maud is understood to have been in Edward the Confessor's 'train' or court, so she likely met with young Duke William 'the Bastard' and later Ranulph Peveril, her future husband, at this time in Normandy.

---

[237] Many Saxon nobility travelled to Normandy during the Danish invasions of the early 11th century, and some Norman aristocracy already held lands in England pre-Conquest under grants from Edward the Confessor. Edward (whose mother, Emma of Normandy was also William the Conqueror's great aunt making them second cousins—she being the sister of William's grandfather, Richard II 'the Good') was in Normandy c.1016-1041—the period prior to his accession, having sought refuge there after Viking invaders overthrew his father King Aethelred in 1016.

[238] There are numerous unqualified citations (e.g. Dugdale's quotation of Robert Glover, Somerset herald, c.1680) which propose that Ingelric was an Essex nobleman, an Earl even, and maybe an illegitimate son of King Aethelred 'the Unready'. Maud is also referred to as 'Ingelrica', the feminised version of her father's name. Maud/Ingelrica, the wife of Ranulph Peverel, is said to have founded a college of secular canons dedicated to St Mary Magdalen, and to have spent the remainder of her days there until her death c.1100. In the reign of Henry I, her son William Peverel converted the foundation into the Benedictine Priory of Hatfield Peverel, subordinated to the abbey of St Alban in Hertfordshire.

16. The ruins of Peveril Castle in Castleton today
Attribution: Wikipedia, Creative Commons, 2.0 Generic (CC BY 2.0)

Soon after Hastings, around 1068–70, William Peveril was charged, by his father, with building Peveril Castle at Castleton in the Peak District of Derbyshire, 15 miles west of Robin's hamlet of Loxley (see Appendix 1, pin 3 and Appendix 6, pin 4) and just 6 miles from Little John's Hathersage (a small village with just 8 householders and 2 smallholders recorded in 1086).[239] Prior to the construction of the castle, the village of Castleton was known as Peak's Arse!

---

[239] In a bizarre coincidence, a very dim and distant ancestor of mine, Sir Ralph Staveley (1362-c.1420), was a loyal Lancastrian and steward to Henry Bolingbroke, later King Henry IV. In the early 15th c., as reward for his services, he received a Duchy of Lancaster grant from Henry IV, of estates previously owned by John of Gaunt, Henry's father. It seems that Peveril castle could very well have constituted part of Sir Ralph's Duchy grant, as quoting from his biography (*History of Parliament—The Commons 1386–1421*. 1992 Roskell, Clark and Rawcliffe), it clearly states '*His* (Ralph Staveley's) *authority in the High Peak was greatly strengthened in the following September (1403), when King Henry bestowed upon him the offices of steward, bailiff and master forester there, as well as the constableship of the castle* (Peveril) *which stood at the centre of this wealthy and important duchy of Lancaster lordship'.*—3 Sept. 1403–15 Feb. 1420.
It appears that in Ralph's later years (or maybe after his death c.1420?), the castle had become too old fashioned for a residence and obsolete in terms of defence, being partly dismantled. Its decline continued over the centuries and today its atmospheric remains are cared for by English Heritage.

Peveril chose his castle's location wisely as '*no site could be better protected by nature*'[240]—in one of the wildest and most inaccessible recesses of the Peak. Built on the brink of a threatening precipice overhanging a yawning chasm known as 'The Devil's Cavern', it was surrounded not only by extensive silver and lead mines, but also by some of the best hunting grounds in the whole of England. Unusually, from the very beginning, the castle was built in local stone not of wood, as most early Norman castles were.

In fact, the hunting was so good that the Conqueror created the 'Royal Forest of the Peak' which covered 180 square miles from Longdale to the Wye Valley. He made Peveril his Bailiff of the 'Royal Manors of the Peak', which included Bakewell, Tideswell, Buxton, Chapel-En-Le-Frith, Castleton, Brough, Hope, Hayfield, Glossop and north over the Dark Peak into the Yorkshire Dales, with Edale Cross at its centre. Whenever the Conqueror was in the north of his kingdom, he hunted in this royal forest with his trusted 'bastard' son.

From Castleton, Sheriff Peveril's area of jurisdiction covered not only Peveril Castle but also Nottingham and Bolsover Castles (Appendix 6, map pins 2 and 14), the former a royal castle, built by King William himself but the custody of which was passed to Peveril and the latter being of Peveril's own construction. Initially these would have been of the motte-and-Bailey variety (earth and timber) but soon rebuilt in stone, which must have had an awesome effect on the populace who had never before witnessed such fearsome structures. Although the real seat of power was at Peveril Castle, the forest connected the entire jurisdiction. With these 3 enormous fortifications combined with his numerous smaller castles like Codnor and Aslockton, Peveril and the barons had an iron grip over the whole area, from whence they placed intolerable taxes and feudal dues upon the Saxon inhabitants.

Peveril looks to have inherited his father's shrewdness and played a clever game, using his position as the Conqueror's 'favourite' to keep a low profile yet advance his power and wealth. For 40-odd years, following a favourable marriage, he kept under the radar in his Castleton stronghold, endeavouring to keep, at least nominally, control over this fractious northern region although the impossibly popular outlaw, Robin Hood, would have been a permanent running sore in his jurisdiction. He appears to have displayed commendable family loyalty to all 3 kings—his father and half-brothers Rufus and Henry. Unlike his

---

[240] *The Growth of the English Country House*, Alfred Gotch (Batsford, 1909), p.14.

neighbours the de Warennes, de Lacys and others, he is not recorded in any of the numerous rebellions over that period, nor is he mentioned in any of the military campaigns in France, Scotland, Wales and Normandy.

He does appear from time to time as a witness to 9 writs and charters involving land grants to religious houses[241] but seemingly only when the royal household was in his area, probably hunting. Hollister lists him as one of 10 leading lay curiales of William II[242] (his half-brother,), so rather more of an administrator. Even the difficult, almost ungovernable zone over which he presided was primarily managed by Norman subordinates who struggled to contain the outlaws including, perhaps, Robin Hood for over 20 years. Peveril's strategy of delegation paid off—he is thought to have died of old age, c.1114, at a respectable 70.

We are told in *The Gest* that Robin and the sheriff knew each other, which in the case of Peveril would be entirely plausible, as Waltheof—just 3–4 years older and a landed nobleman neighbour (his Hallamshire lands and chases adjoining those of Peveril to the west) with strong links to the king—would undoubtedly have been known to him. When Peveril was recorded in *Domesday* in 1086, Robin would have been c.28 (his father dead for a decade) and already an outlaw for 6 years, but the lawman's authority stretched back much further to 1068. So Robin's entire cognisant life, teenage years, outlaw activities and stomping ground would have paralleled that of his local, powerful, half-Norman, half-Saxon *bête noire*, who knew of him well and was also best mates with Roger de Busli I, now the custodian of his father's lands of Hallamshire as the tenant of his treacherous stepmother, Judith. In 1114, after Peveril died, his son William

---

[241] A particular favourite was Lenton Priory, 1.5 miles from Nottingham castle founded by Peveril c.1105 'for the souls of the Conqueror, his Queen Matilda and William II Rufus' (seemingly he still had a soft spot for his irreligious late half-brother!). Lenton was also the location for the 'Peveril Court', held right up until 1321, though a version of the court continued until abolished by the County Courts Act 1849. It was a Court of Pleas for the recovery of small debts and damages of trespass with jurisdiction over 127 towns and villages around the shire, further demonstrating the indisputable power and influence of the Peveril dynasty in the region.

[242] *Magnates and Curiales in Early Norman England*, C W Hollister, Viator, 1977, p.76

Peveril the Younger, assumed the almost hereditary role of sheriff (with a short break from 1125–9), until 1153.[243]

(2) Hugh FitzBaldric (High Sheriff of Nottinghamshire, 1069–1080, also High Sheriff of Yorkshire 1069–1086)

FitzBaldric looks to have been a close companion of William Peveril and friend/neighbour of Ilbert de Lacy (Baron of Pontefract and Lord of Bowland), but his origins are frankly uncertain. It is not known which Norman family he came from, or if indeed he was Norman at all. It has been stated in some sources that he was a mercenary German archer in the service of William the Conqueror. However, he seems to have been granted earlier lands very near Rouen in Normandy as, before 1067, he *'witnessed a charter of Gerald, granting the Nuns of St Amand in Rouen, the church of his fief of Roumare'*.[244]

FitzBaldric appears to have held the key Nottinghamshire position for over 10 years from 1069 to 1080, as well as being made High Sheriff of Yorkshire

---

[243] Harking back to the earliest literary reference to Robin in 'Piers Plowman' (see chapter 1), Sloth the priest refers to his knowledge of rhymes of Robin Hood and also the Earl of Chester. There is no reason to conclude that these rhymes were in any way connected or that they were even contemporaneous with each other. The most likely candidate for the Earl is Ran(d)ulf II de Gernon, 4th Earl of Chester, a man who had fame as an outlaw that persisted until the 14th century. In 1153 he was invited to the castle of William Peverel the Younger, under the pretence of discussing a peaceful solution to their quarrels, as this was during the 'Anarchy' and Peverel supported King Stephen while Randulf supported Empress Matilda. Whilst at the meeting William tried to poison Ranulf, and three of his men who had drunk the wine died immediately, while Ranulf suffered agonising pain and also died a few months later. As a result of the treachery of supporting Stephen and the killing of Randulf, after Henry II's succession a year later, Peverel was stripped of his lands and exiled. There was also a suggestion that Randolf's wife, Maud, and Peverel were having an affair and she assisted in the poisoning of her husband, though she never remarried. The rhymes, probably bawdy, were likely about these scandalous incidents. Ranulph's father, Ranulf le Meschin, 3rd Earl of Chester (1070–1129), who also had some claim on the popular imagination, has likewise been suggested as the Earl of the rhymes and would have been contemporary with Robin.

[244] *Histoire de l'abbaye de St Amand de Rouen*, Pommeraye, Jean-Francis (Lallemant, 1662)

and possibly High Sheriff of Lincolnshire, suggesting that he was very good friends with both William Peveril and the Conqueror. Like many others, he fell into trouble some years later by supporting Robert Curthose, Duke of Normandy and eldest son of the Conqueror against William Rufus in the rebellion of 1088. Presumably, he lost his lands and position as nothing more is heard of him after 1089. He may have died, been killed or exiled at this time.

I detail his Yorkshire tenure subsequently.

(3) Hugh de Port (Possible Sheriff of Nottinghamshire, 1080–1087)

Around 1080, the year when I suggest Robin became outlawed, the position may have been taken up by a man called Hugh de Port, believed to have been a vassal of Odo of Bayeux who fought at Hastings. This is when matters become somewhat murky. In the chronicle *Monasticon i. 301*, Hugh is recorded as High Sheriff of Nottinghamshire and Derbyshire from 1081 to 1087. He seems more definitely to have been High Sheriff of Hampshire from 1070 until at least *Domesday* but probably up to his death in 1096, a total of over 25 years[245] (succeeded as Sheriff of Hampshire by his son Henry de Port in c.1101–05, appointed by the new king, Henry I). He held large estates (55 lordships) in that county but, according to *Domesday*, nothing at all in Nottinghamshire or Yorkshire, which is odd. The compilers of *Victoria County History* suggest his holding of the Nottingham office seems unlikely, as evidence is flimsy. However, it was not unknown for a man to hold multiple, or at least dual, sheriff posts. Hugh may have held the Nottingham position as a subordinate appointment from Peveril and then put a minion in charge at Nottingham in his absence—someone like Ralph FitzHubert. Perhaps the antics of Robin and his men were just too much for any official and no-one significant wanted to take the job and be made a fool of…or be killed.

---

[245] *Cokayne's Complete Peerage,* 2nd Edition, Vol. XI, 1949, pp. 316–317

(4) ??? (Sheriff of Nottinghamshire, 1087–1100)/Ralph FitzHubert de Ryes (Constable of Nottingham Castle, c.1095–c.1098)

For 13 years, from 1087–1100, we have not just murkiness but darkness, as there are no surviving records for who was the Sheriff of Nottinghamshire[246]. Coincidentally these 13 years are also the precise regnal years of King William Rufus. The most likely conclusion is that Peveril was the man still in overall charge and Robin Hood was causing mayhem. Furthermore, if you add the 7 disputed years of De Port's tenure, this brings us to the precise time—20 years—that my Robin was an outlaw.

However, we do have a recorded castellan. The Peveril family, no doubt assisted by William's status as illegitimate son of the king, also seem to have become hereditary holders of the High Sheriff position, appointing castellans at both Nottingham and Bolsover when they were busy suppressing uprisings, or ruling other shires. One of the appointees, Ralph FitzHubert de Rie (Ryes, Ryche), is worth a mention.

This significant Norman, undoubtedly known to Waltheof, and latterly Robin and his men, held 62 manors in Derbyshire and Nottinghamshire at *Domesday* (including Lordship of 3 merchants households in Nottingham town, held directly from the king). He is also recorded as holding 2 Lordships in 1086: Lord of Mosborough, today a suburb of Sheffield and Lord of Crich, a village in Derbyshire between Alfreton and Matlock. Crich is virtually midway on a direct route between Peveril and Nottingham Castles (about 45 miles apart/a 2-day ride), which one suspects is not a coincidence.

Ralph's brother, Eudo 'Dapifer', was the powerful and loyal royal steward to all 3 Norman kings, Williams I and II and Henry I.[247] At around the time that Eudo founded Colchester Abbey in 1095, brother Ralph was noted as the

---

[246] *English Sheriffs to 1154*, Judith Green, Public Records Handbook No. 24 (London: HMSO, 1990)

[247] Ralph and Eudo had two other brothers and they were all sons of Hubert of Ryes, who is legendarily known (mentioned by the writer Wace in his *Roman de Rou,* p.13ff), as the loyal vassal who gave sanctuary to Duke William of Normandy prior to his flight from Valognes during a revolt in 1047. (*William the Conqueror,* David C Douglas, Yale, 1999, p. 48 and fn. 8)

Castellan of Nottingham Castle[248] with even a suggestion that he held this post as far back as 1086.[249]

He was described by the great 17th century medieval historian and scholar William Dugdale as '*a fierce man and a great plunderer*'. Here was a character 'robbing' impoverished local kinsmen and peasants within the law—the diametric opposite of Robin and his men, taking from the rich as outlaws. Such traits would make him the perfect enemy.

In addition, Ralph is likely not only to have been known to, but to have personally affected Robin's band. He was the Lord of Little John's village of Hathersage and, if my theory about North Lees Hall is correct, he would also have come across Sir Richard whose property was on his manor (thus Richard was probably a vassal knight paying homage to his landlord, Ralph).

17. Map showing the 39 manors held by Ralf FitzHubert (out of his 62 countrywide), concentrated in the area between Sheffield and Nottingham in 1086, including that of Hathersage, the home village of Little John

---

[248] '...*cui commissa est custodia castelli et comitatus Notingeham*', taken from *The Chronicle of St John's Abbey, Colchester: British Library, Cotton MS Nero D viii, ff 22–5*. This manuscript is well-known, its credibility having been the subject of considerable and sometimes bitter debate.

[249] '*The Barons of Criche*', Waters, Edmond Chester, The Academy (Correspondence), London (May 30, 1885): pp. 385–386.

One final twist: the 17th century antiquarian Robert Thoroton gives FitzHubert's death as 1098.[250] This date seems to fit well with the killing of the sheriff (by Little John) in Child Ballad 118, in relation to my timeline, as we shall see in discussion of another adversary—Guy of Gisborne—later.

(5) Richard FitzGotse (High Sheriff of Nottinghamshire, 1100–1107)

Although there are no surviving personal records or origins for Richard FitzGotse, he is chronicled as holder of this post from December 1100–1107, as he was still being addressed as sheriff in writs of 1107[251]. It seems he was the first man fully appointed by Henry I as High Sheriff of Nottinghamshire and Derbyshire, following on from William Peveril and I believe, as we shall see, that Robin had effectively ceased his outlaw activities by this time. Understandably, Henry I was keen to have his own 'new' men in these powerful positions. If Peveril had lost his power by then, Richard may well have been appointed after the position reverted direct to Peveril, following the death of the previous incumbent who, according to my timeline with ballad references, was killed by Little John at the conclusion of the Guy of Gisborne debacle and was probably Ralph FitzHubert.

Sheriff of Yorkshire

As the records for Nottinghamshire are sparse and the bulk of Robin's activities were likely in South Yorkshire, it is only sensible to see if we have more luck with this adjoining shire. The first holder after the Conquest was a Saxon continuation, Gamal, son of Osbern but he was quickly replaced by the great Norman baron, William Malet (though he may have had an English mother as he held 6 manors from Edward the Confessor, prior to 1066). He was one of the fifteen 'proven' companions of the Conqueror at the Battle of Hastings, where it is said he fought ferociously and heroically, but after just a brief tenure

---

[250] *History of Nottinghamshire,* Dr Robert Thoroton, 1677, republished with additions by John Throsby, 1797, Vol I, p.85.
[251] *An Outline Itinerary of Henry I,* William Farrer, reprinted from *English Historical Review Vol. XXXIV,* 1919

of a year[252] or so was removed and given the sheriff's post for Norfolk and Suffolk, along with the vast 256 manors of the Honour of Eye, all having been stripped from their Saxon owner, Eadric of Laxfield.

So, following Malet's departure, we have 5 possible suspects who cover Robin's period of outlawry, namely:

1. 1070–1086: *Hugh FitzBaldric*
2. 1086–1088: *Erneis de Burun*
3. 1088–1093: *Ralph Paganell (or Paynel)*
4. 1093–1095: *Geoffrey Baynard*
5. 1095–1100: *'H'*

After 1100, possibly very briefly, Bertram II de Verdon, followed by Osbert of Lincoln until 1115 (who also Sheriff of Lincolnshire)

(1) Hugh FitzBaldric (High Sheriff of Yorkshire, 1069–1086/High Sheriff of Nottinghamshire, 1069–1080)

After the Fall of York and the crushing of rebels in the Northern uprising during the winter of 1069–70, Hugh FitzBaldric is recorded as holding the High Sheriff of Yorkshire post for more than fifteen years, from late 1069 to c.1086,[253] (as well as High Sheriff of Nottinghamshire and Derbyshire to 1080). As such, he was probably the first Sheriff who Robin came across in his teenage years when his father was alive. He would also have been the likely incumbent official for the whole of the Barnsdale area for the first 6 years of Robin's outlaw activities and was most likely the sheriff who outlawed Robin in 1080, over the murder of Bishop Walcher.

That said, the lack of control exercised over 'wild' Yorkshire during FitzBaldric's rule was noted. As Peter Rex writes of this time, using the

---

[252] This culminated in the sacking of York by Earls Gospatric and Morcar, Edgar Ætheling and Waltheof along with other rebels like Arkle and Siward Barn, supported by a large Danish force in the autumn of 1069 (3000 Normans were massacred). William Malet, his wife and two children were spared.

[253]*The Office of Sheriff in the Early Norman Period,* W.A Morris, *English Historical Review Vol. XXXIII*, April 1918, pp. 145–175.

contemporary source material *Gesta Normannorum Ducum* (c.1071) of Norman monkish chronicler William of Jumièges:

"Trouble never really came to an end. The benefactors of Selby, only 10 miles from York, were harassed by outlaws, and Hugh FitzBaldric, the sheriff, needed a small army as escort whenever he travelled because of the continued hostility of the English. The monks of Whitby were to complain of trouble from outlaws as late as the reign of William Rufus and 'brigandage' remained a problem as disinherited thegns became outlaws."[254]

During FitzBaldric's tenure, and preceding Robin's outlawry by a decade, another robber called Swein (or Swain—about the same age as Waltheof) is chronicled in this same South Yorkshire area and no doubt others were around as well. Swein has even been proposed by some as the real Robin Hood. Certainly, he could have been an influence on the young boy Robin, possibly, as a disinherited English thegne, even known to him during his *silvatici* period and the later northern rebellion in 1069–70 and Harrowing that followed. According to William of Jumièges, Swein led a gang of outlaws who raided Selby Abbey and 'ruined the peace' of Abbot Benedict[255], Sheriff FitzBaldric and the de Lacy family. This Swein or Swain was the 'son of Siccga and noted as a mysterious and *cursed villain* [who] *constantly prowled around Yorkshire's woods with his band* and amassed huge wealth through '*raiding and piratical theft*'. Pre-dating Kevin Costner's sobriquet by nearly 1,000 years, he was described in the 11th century *Coucher Book of Selby Abbey* as '*The Prince of Thieves*'![256] There are a number of landowners called Swein recorded in *Domesday* in 1066, particularly in Yorkshire, although none specifically called 'son of Sic(c)ga' or 'Sigge'. As

[254] *English Resistance,* Peter Rex, Amberley Publishing, 2014, p115. In fact, military entourages for bishops and abbots were not novel at this time and many new 'Norman' appointments made in 1070 were military and ecclesiastical.

[255] Selby Abbey was the first monastery in the North to be built post-Conquest and local tradition suggests that the town is the birthplace, in late 1068/early 1069, of Henry I. The Abbey was founded in late 1069/early 1070 by Benedict of Auxerre who used funds from local landowners/nobility Hugh FitzBaldric and Ilbert de Lacy. From 1095–1123, the second Abbot was Hugh de Lacy, the younger son of Ilbert and brother of Robert, Lord of Pontefract.

[256] The title of a novel also used by Alexander Dumas in his '*Prince des Voleurs*' (1872)

he cannot be precisely identified, frustratingly his fate remains unknown. However, Judith Green, in her booklet *English sheriffs to 1154*, indicates that Hugh FitzBaldric, as Sheriff of Yorkshire and Nottinghamshire, was responsible for bringing Swein to justice[257]. Whatever the case, with his old Norse name, it seems entirely plausible that Swein was one of the many dispossessed Yorkshire Danish/Saxon thegns and thus well-known to Waltheof. As Selby Abbey is only 15 miles north of Barnsdale, it is also more than likely that these original 'Prince of Thieves' exploits of abbot-robbing and sheriff-baiting later became conflated with those of Robin.

(2) Erneis de Burun (High Sheriff of Yorkshire, 1086–1088)

Erneis de Burun probably fought at Hastings, becoming a man of moderate social status as tenant-in-chief of 65 manors in North Yorkshire and Lincolnshire.[258] He held the position for less than 2 years and stayed loyal to the crown in the rebellion of 1088, recovering Durham Castle for the king with Ivo Taillebois. He seems to have given up or lost his job and afterwards went into obscurity. During his brief tenure he famously lent 100 marks to Abbot Benedict, co-founder of Selby Abbey, who left the grisly, but the abbey's most revered, religious relic of St Germain's finger as collateral. Erneis's reverence towards the shrivelled digit was supposedly rewarded by the recovery of his son, Hugh, from epilepsy! He did re-emerge in 1102 to back the wrong horse, Robert Curthose, in his struggle for the crown against his brother, King Henry and as a result had all his lands confiscated which were given to Robert de Romille, a supporter of Henry, who had built Skipton Castle c.1090.

---

[257] *English Sheriffs to 1154*, Judith Green, Public Record Office, Handbook no.24, 1990, HMSO pp. 67/ 89

[258] Interestingly, these included most (11) of those 14 manors originally held by Countess Judith, prior to 1066, but which had clearly been surrendered to the crown, possibly following her marriage to Waltheof or maybe after refusal to marry Simon de Senlis. They were all in a cluster in the Wapentake of Wraggoe, Lincs., just 10–15 miles to the north-east of Lincoln.

(3) Ralph Paganell (High Sheriff of Yorkshire, 1088–1093)

Ralph Paganell (sometimes Paynel) was one of great landowners in Barnsdale, with many manors inherited—via his marriage to Matilda Surdeval—upon his father-in law's death in 1087. Matilda's father was Richard Surdeval, the important South Yorkshire sub-tenant of Count Robert de Mortain (half-brother of the Conqueror and thus Uncle of Judith de Lens and Rufus). He was the first sheriff under the new King Rufus. Not only sheriff over Barnsdale, but also a large private landowner, making him a prime target for Robin's activities.

Ralph Paganell's tenure as sheriff ended in 1093, possibly with his death, but as the manner of his demise was unrecorded and the *DNB* gives it vaguely as 'before 1124', it may well have been later and just old age. There has also been a suggestion that Ralph may have died in 1098 but this is also unsourced. Whatever his fate, he seems to just disappear, maybe returning to Normandy, but he was succeeded in 1093 by an interesting character.

(4) Geoffrey Baynard (High Sheriff of Yorkshire, 1093–1095)

Geoffrey was likely the landless younger brother of the East Anglian tenant-in-chief, Ralph Baynard, and was certainly a newcomer to Yorkshire. This Rufus policy of using 'new men', closely allied to the royal court for these northern appointments was later perpetuated by his brother Henry. Often described as 'The King's Champion', was the appointment of Baynard an attempt by King Rufus, and his half-brother Peveril, to unearth the most damaging and elusive outlaw, Hood?

Little or nothing seems to have been recorded of Baynard's time in office until 1095 when he defended against a second rebellion by the Norman barons who made an ill-fated attempt to replace Rufus with Stephen of Aumale (Judith's half-brother!) as King of England. One of the leading rebels, William II, Count de Eu, was tried, found guilty and sentenced to 'trial by combat' which he lost, then being blinded and castrated, dying shortly after as a consequence! His opponent was the champion, Geoffrey Baynard, who had left his sheriff's office just prior to this event after which, subsequent details of the incumbent sheriff, just like in Nottinghamshire, become deliciously vague precisely when more solid facts about the Robin Hood legend are needed.

(5) 'Sheriff H' (1095–1100)

The next sheriff, who lasted until just after the accession of King Henry I, is only ever recorded, in a few tantalising fragments and somewhat oddly, as just '*H. Vicecomes*' (the French equivalent of sheriff). These documents include a charter of William Rufus, issued at Pont de L'Arche after 1096, and addressed to '*Thomas (of Bayeux) the Archbishop of York,* **H. the sheriff,** *and the barons of Yorkshire*'.

Despite my numerous initial enquiries to various establishments and institutions, no-one seemed to know who this mysterious 'H' may have been with certainty. However, it is now generally accepted that he was a man known as Herbert of Winchester, thought to be the illegitimate son of Count Herbert II of Maine. If that is the case, we know a fair amount about him as he was brought up apparently under Duke William's tutelage and made a career for himself in the royal administration in England. Despite holding a small amount of land in Hampshire (mostly as a tenant of Hugh de Port), Herbert was clearly a Yorkshire-based baron, where his children were born and where he held significant estates, mostly as a sub-tenant of the Archbishop of York who had made them over to Herbert in return for financial support at a difficult time.[259]

Under King Rufus, he held the senior position of Chamberlain of the Winchester Treasury (2nd in command after the Treasurer to Rufus, William de Breteuil). After 1100, he held this office combined with that of Treasurer itself for Henry I, following Breteuil's demise for supporting Curthose over Henry. However, chronicler Abbot Suger of St Denis later named '*H. the Chamberlain*' as the attempted assassin of Henry I in 1118. He further noted that the would-be assassin had been close to the king and received great rewards from him. Chronicler William of Malmesbury also does not name the assassin, but says that he had custody of the Royal Treasury, which seems pretty conclusive proof that Herbert was the same man; obviously he had become one of the disaffected barons later in Henry's reign. Suger added that the king only had him blinded and castrated, which the abbot considered to be mild compared with the hanging that he deserved, though he did die anyway a year or 2 later.

American historian Warren Hollister first made the connection between 'H. the Chamberlain' and Herbert, noting that there was only one Chamberlain in

---

[259] *St William of York*, Christopher Norton, York Medieval Press, 2006

King Henry I's reign whose name began with 'H'. It is entirely plausible that this 'H' was chamberlain, failed assassin and the earlier Sheriff of York from 1095–1100 and all being Herbert of Winchester.

During the 20-odd years of Robin's outlawry in my late 11th century timeline, the precise names of both the Yorkshire and 'Nottingham' sheriffs are not clearly recorded. While intact 950 year old documents featuring England's very first High sheriffs are naturally hard to come by, the presence of Robin and his men in the area during this lawless times and district may also have had some relevance to this. Regardless, the absence of real detail would go a long way to explain why the sheriff(s) in the many stories of the ballad writers over the later decades are never named.

One thing we do know is that several sheriffs and castellans came and went between 1080–1100—perhaps in part due to outlaw activities and the authorities failure to tackle such, and perhaps in part due to their own ill-chosen rebellions. While FitzBaldric had powers in both Yorkshire and Nottinghamshire in the early part of Robin's 'reign', the only man who was a consistent local force throughout this whole time period was William Peveril (plus his lackies). Peveril had overall jurisdiction over the whole of Robin's operating area and, playing a shrewd game, appointed Norman subordinates to do the dirty work in these practically ungovernable and dangerous northern lands, allowing him to survive to a very respectable 70 years of age. For these reasons, and all those set out above, **I believe that he, William Peveril I, illegitimate son of the Conqueror and half-brother to both kings, Rufus and Henry, is the most likely candidate for the original 'Sheriff of Nottingham' around whom the stories of him being Robin Hood's prime enemy were built.**

On the subject of the sheriff's death, there is, of course, one other famous 'named' adversary from legend who could have crossed paths and swords with our Robin, in which both the adversary and the sheriff perish. Let us conclude with him now.

'Sir' Guy of Gisborne

This key 'baddie' and perennial villain, features prominently in one of the original ballads and in almost all TV and cinematic renderings. In some early texts, he is also described as a yeoman, but in what is considered the very earliest, *Ballad of Robin Hood and Guy of Gisborne* (Child Ballad 118 and from the Percy

Folio) and many later versions, he is portrayed as 'Sir Guy'. Modern interpretations make him a friend of the sheriff (often second-in-command and sometimes portrayed as related), usually depicted dressed in black horsehide or leather, perhaps acting as a form of protective armour, clearly a hired 'hitman' and a generally nasty piece of work. In modern reworkings, he also becomes a determined romantic rival to Robin Hood for Maid Marian's love. His origins and identity have been the subject of much speculation and discussion, but of course none in a late 11th century setting, until now.

A brief summary of the story from the original ballad runs as follows: Early on, when Robin is absent, Little John finds out 2 'merrie men' have been killed and Will Scarlet is on the run: following a skirmish with the sheriff, Little John is taken prisoner when his bow breaks. Soon after, Robin Hood meets a stranger in the greenwood of Barnsdale (stanza 46, line 181).[260] This man is dressed from head to foot in leather made from a horse's hide and claims to be looking for Robin Hood so he can join his band. Robin doesn't immediately tell him who he is, but proposes an archery contest. The stranger shoots well, but Robin's archery skills are superior. The stranger is impressed, remarking that he 'must be better than Robin Hood himself'. The stranger wants to know his opponent's name. Robin refuses to oblige until the man gives his own name.

> *'I dwell by dale and downe', quoth hee,*
> *'And Robin to take I'me sworne;*
> *And when I am called by my right name*
> *I am Guy of good Gisborne'*.[261]

He turns out to be a bounty hunter and an assassin hired by the sheriff[262], and tells the outlaw of his target. Then, our man announces that he is Robin Hood of

---

[260] The setting for the action is Barnsdale and confirms the often confused geography of the Robin Hood tales, for in the antepenultimate stanza 57, line 225, the Sheriff and his men run from Little John '*towards his house in Nottingham*', this, at fifty odd away miles would have required him to run a double marathon to get home!

[261] *Reliques of Ancient English Poetry*, Dr Thomas Percy, 1885—vol. i. p. 81

[262] It is interesting to note that although action takes place in Barnsdale (line 181), Yorkshire, it is the Sheriff of Nottingham that is the outlaw's major enemy. This would be easily explained by Robin constantly crossing County boundaries and William Peveril, being at the heart of the plot, with overall jurisdiction of two shires

Barnsdale, '*a fellow thou has long sought*', suggesting he is aware that Guy is on a mission to kill him.

The 2 men draw their swords and begin to fight and Gisborne is clearly no slouch with the blade as the fight lasts for 2 hours. Eventually, Guy wounds Robin on his left side, but Robin retaliates with a backhanded stroke, killing his opponent. He then cuts off Guy's head, sticks it on his bow and disfigures the face with an Irish knife to make it unrecognisable. This level of violence does not sit happily with many people's image of Robin Hood, but perhaps was closer to reality. To deceive the sheriff he then switches identity by donning Guy's leather clothes and possessions and sets off for Barnsdale to find his men, where, on approach, he blows Guy's horn to signify 'success' to the sheriff. In his new disguise, he dupes the sheriff (but not Little John who recognises his voice) and says he does not want gold but his reward should be to execute Little John. The sheriff thinks he is mad but agrees. Robin, getting close to John, just cuts his bonds with his 'Irish knife' and rescues him. Robin then gives Guy's bow to Little John who proceeds to shoot the sheriff in the back, right through to the heart. All pretty grisly stuff.

(Derbyshire/Nottinghamshire and Yorkshire). Also, Roger de Busli strategically built his castle at Tickhill 'directly on the border (of both counties) as a matter of deliberate policy' to create ambiguity and claim rights in each. *'Yorkshire's southern boundary'*, *Northern History 37*, David Hey, (2000), p.43.

18. Robin Hood and Guy of Gisborne fighting—by artist Walter Crane Image from *Robin Hood and the Men of the Greenwood* by H. Gilbert, 1912.
Public domain image out of copyright

Does this tale have any basis in reality? Again, let us start with geography. The village of Gisburn[263] (now in Lancashire) is just 7 miles from Clitheroe, and

---

[263] Most historians agree with Child who says that, "Gisburn is in the West Riding of Yorkshire, on the borders of Lancashire, seven miles from Clitheroe" (*The English and Scottish Popular Ballads (*Houghton and Mifflin, 1888/89) Vol. III, p.91), but Bellamy suggests, less convincingly, that Guy is connected with the village of 'Guisborough in the North Riding (known in the middle ages as Giseburne' (*Robin Hood: an historical enquiry,* John Bellamy, Indiana Univ. Press, 1985, pp. 34–35). At Domesday, a large

proposed by many as Guy's hometown. Historically, and in the late 11th century, Gisburn was not only right on the edge of the Forest of Bowland[264] but also part of the West Riding of Yorkshire, with its own motte-and-Bailey fortification, Castle Haugh, still partly visible in ruins today. As far as I am aware, no-one has ever uncovered a historical 'Guy' personage there or anywhere else and I am not about to change that. However, I would like to propose some real people and documented events that seem to fit with this character of legend.

One of the 11 great Norman 'barons' who owned a quarter of England post-Conquest was Roger de Poitou (often called Roger 'the Poitevin'), brother of the formidable Robert de Bellême. A key part of de Poitou's Lancashire estates, acquired following his support of King Rufus' successful invasion and annexation of Cumbria in 1092, was the great Honour of Clitheroe. He was also appointed as the 1st Lord of Bowland in the same area; an honour he received in 1093 after the removal of Dolphin of Carlisle, the Northumbrian magnate who was the ruling agent of King Malcolm of Scotland at the time and son of Gospatric, the erstwhile Earl of Northumberland and relative of Waltheof (see Appendix 2.1). Almost immediately, Roger sublet these estates to his Yorkshire vassal, Robert de Lacy, son of Ilbert de Lacy, the 1st Baron of Pontefract, who had died that same year.[265] Significantly, Gisburn village and church were also under de Poitou's lordship (who had built Castle Haugh there, on the banks of the River Ribble, c.1080), about 60 miles or a 2–3 day ride from Barnsdale, along a well-worn medieval road which never left the 'de Lacy' estates.

One explanation for the events in the *Ballad of Robin Hood and Guy of Gisborne* is that de Poitou and de Lacy, along with their local 'sheriff' (Peveril) and probably de Busli as well, hired a skilled vassal knight to kill long-time problem outlaw and local enemy of the rich, Robin Hood. 'Sir Guy' (with his knight's title[266]) would have fitted the bill as a highly-experienced swordsman

---

part of the manor of Guisborough was held by Count Robert de Mortain, who held much of Barnsdale, being half-brother of the Conqueror. It is 80 miles north of Barnsdale.

[264] The designation 'Forest of Bowland', is used in its traditional sense of 'a royal hunting ground', as in the 'New Forest' and 'Sherwood Forest'. Rather than being covered by trees, much of the land is actually heather moorland and blanket bog.

[265] Robert de Lacy then set about the building of Clitheroe Castle.

[266] The Coronation Charter of Henry I (1100) speaks of those holding knight-service as *militibus qui per loricam terras suas deserviunt* ('soldiers who serve [or are subject to] their lands by means of armour').

and was very likely a bailiff of the Forest of Bowland (hence his archery skills) working for de Lacy. We are told—from the surviving fragment of a play from c.1475 (the same one mentioned earlier in the chapter about Friar Tuck)—that the knight expects to get a fee of £40 in gold from the sheriff for this job[267]. In reality, a plotted killing by a bounty hunter of an outlaw, a 'wolf's head' (versus a royal or high nobleman) would not have been recorded, but might have been relatively commonplace in the violent and crime-rife setting of 11th century Yorkshire.

So, as we know, according to the ballad, in retaliation for this threat upon his leader's life, following his rescue, Little John kills the sheriff in a somewhat uncourteous style by shooting him in the back![268] However, Sheriff William Peveril, who was a very close associate of de Poitou and de Lacy, does not fit, as he lived until c.1115 (dying, we believe, of old age). Conversely, the mysterious Ralph FitzHubert (brother of the royally favoured steward, Eudo Dapifer)—with a death date recorded by antiquarian Robert Thoroton as 1098— is a possible contender. He was most likely Peveril's lackey as Castellan of Nottingham Castle in 1098—could he have succumbed to John's arrow? Events in the ballad are, of course, undated but intriguingly this suspect and other sheriffs of the period, either disappear or are unrecorded at this time. What is interesting here, as has been noted before, is the location of the duel in Barnsdale. As we know, it is in Yorkshire, outside of the jurisdiction of the sheriff of the ballad (Nottinghamshire). This may well be explained by the wide area of Robin's outlaw activities, the fact that barons like de Busli and de Lacy had extensive manorial holdings in both counties and William Peveril's overall control of both counties. For all we know, Sheriff 'H'—Herbert, was away in Winchester on treasury business for Rufus at the time and simply not available, leaving his 'locum', FitzHubert, in charge.

---

[267] This detail comes from the play *Robin Hood and the Sheriff* (c.1475), of which only 21 lines survive. It overlaps part of the story in the ballad of *Robin Hood and Guy of Gisborne*, opening abruptly with an arrangement between the sheriff and the knight who promises to capture Robin in return for '*golde and a fee*'. (Holt, 1989, p.33). This bounty might be worth around £80–100k in today's money.

[268] This killing of the Sheriff by Little John and that of the Nottingham Sheriff by Robin in *The Gest* both seem likely in the final years of the 11th century and may account for the sparse record of the incumbents at this time.

William Peveril may or may not have been the sheriff of legend who commissioned Guy's killing of Robin and whose subordinate ended up being killed by Little John, but he would have been the most prominent and dangerous adversary to our Robin—his true rival 'Sheriff of Nottingham' of the legend for more than twenty years. The last few years of the 11th century were dramatic times indeed. By 1100, Robin, now nudging 42 and 20 of those years as a forest outlaw, must surely have begun to feel tired of this life and been considering an exit strategy. He would have seen the crushing of the northern rebellion in 1095 as well as the more recent 1097 Lothian campaign against the Scots led for Rufus by Edgar Atheling. It would appear that the episodes of both Sir Richard at the Lee and his own near-death encounter with Guy of Gisborne also occurred around this time and with the Nottingham castellan and the hired assassin both dead, the sheriff and great barons remain out for his blood. The First Crusade proper was under way (the initial People's Crusade was a total fiasco, though English involvement in that 1st Crusade was pretty minimal). Taxes were still cripplingly high due to Rufus's clawing back the huge sums paid to his brother Robert Curthose for the Normandy Duchy, plus the cost of his subsequent incessant campaigning in the counties of Maine and the Vexin on the Normandy/France borders.

The latest news is that the king was mounting a huge invasion force in Southampton, at vast expense, aiming to land in Normandy and planned to secure further French territory at the start of the new century. On top of all this, the much loved Archbishop Anselm of Canterbury, a monk and scholar generally recognised as the keenest philosophical and theological mind of his time, had been forced into voluntary exile by the ungodly king. If this was all not enough, it seems that God was clearly annoyed! The weather was extreme, harvests had failed and animal disease was rife—the country was in a mess and assassins were closing in. All in all, time for a change?

Then one day, through their clandestine channels, Robin no doubt received a message from his sister Maud, Maid Marian, the Countess of Huntingdon and wife of Earl Simon de Senlis since 1090. Would he come to Northampton Castle and meet with her; she has a proposition to put to him—one that will settle a family feud but primarily will save England, start it on a new path of righteousness, peace, prosperity and kingship—all in all, an offer that he will find it hard to refuse? Robin is intrigued and having a great love and admiration for his sister whom he totally trusts, despite the fact she moves in the high society of Norman royal court circles, sets off to Northampton, little realising that he is about to extend his trip, right down to the New Forest in Hampshire and change the course, not only of his own life, but of English history…

Part II
The Death of a King

19. Symbolic depiction of William 'Rufus' II being shot by an arrow in the forest, sitting on what is presumably an artistic impression of his hunting lodge.
Royal MS 20 A II, f. 6r, British Library c.1307–c.1327. Public domain image

Introduction

The premature death of a nation's monarch, or equivalent leader, is an incredibly significant event. Everyone alive at the time remembers where they were when JFK was shot in Dallas or when Diana, Princess of Wales, met her end in a Parisian underpass. It was even more poignant centuries ago when the king or queen was Divine Ruler Absolute and their absence meant a country could quickly descend into anarchy. Coupled with no formal rules of succession, if their death was sudden and/or mysterious, the consequences were particularly dramatic.[269]

It is somewhat ironic that William II, 'the Red King' or, more commonly, William Rufus—who ruled England for 13 years through a fascinating period of history—is now only remembered for the last second of his life. He met his end on an early summer's evening, in the bucolic surroundings of Hampshire's New Forest (today a National Park), when an arrow embedded deeply into his chest. Consequently, the only contemporary character that might be recalled from hazy history lessons is not one of the famous figures of the age, but a French knight called Walter Tyrell…the man generally thought to have fired that fatal shot on Thursday, 2nd August 1100.

Rufus's sudden demise is perhaps not held so vividly in the public imagination as others, but it is one of the more gruesome events of British history, comparable to the murders of the Princes in the Tower[270] or the

---

[269] A total of 17 English and Scottish monarchs have been murdered, assassinated or executed away from the battlefield. Untimely royal deaths were relatively frequent in medieval England, for example, Edward II, Henry VI and the 'Princes in the Tower' (12-year-old Edward and his 9-year-old brother Richard, Duke of York).

[270] In a curious coincidence, four centuries later, Sir James Tyrrell, a distant descendant of Walter, allegedly confessed to the murder of the young Princes on behalf of Richard

executions of Anne Boleyn and Charles I. The most intriguing element is the mystery that surrounds it. Considering that it occurred over 900 years ago, it is quite remarkable that the day's details were fairly well, although disparately, recorded. So we have the possibility to hold it up to the light and examine it in ways that we cannot with the vast majority of medieval deaths.

While many accounts provide elaborate descriptions, the most respected of all, and the earliest—written just a few months after the event—was the *Anglo-Saxon Chronicle*, which simply notes that on the morning after Lammas Day (Aug 1st):

...King William [was] shot in hunting, by an arrow from his own men and afterwards brought to Winchester, and buried in the cathedral.

Interestingly, this specifies neither accident nor deliberation. Victorian historian E.A. Freeman interpreted such vagueness as suggesting treason without directly declaring it.[271] Certainly, if we take the most academic and respected translations of its Middle English[272] text, we might raise an eyebrow at the scribe's use of '*men*' rather than '*man*': If Rufus's death lay not just at the hands of one individual, surely it becomes questionable.

Words may, of course, be open to interpretation, but blanks can be much more revealing. The *Anglo-Saxon Chronicle* clearly demonstrates that no suspect, or suspects, were named at the time. This did not come until some quarter of a century later, in the works of 2 Anglo-Norman monks and noted chroniclers—William of Malmesbury (c.1125) and Orderic Vitalis (c.1127)—who record Tyrell as the accidental killer.[273] If accidental, why did Tyrell

---

III, before his execution for treason in 1502. He appears briefly in Shakespeare's eponymous play of c.1593.

[271] *William Rufus*, E.A. Freeman, Oxford Clarendon Press, 1882. p.325

[272] The original language of the *Chronicle*, from approximately 890 ad, was Anglo-Saxon Old English, but by the time of Rufus's death, the monks who compiled it essentially used Middle English. Reverend James Ingram's version from 1823, is the most respected translation. The two modern academic full translations of the *Chronicle*—Project Gutenberg, the world's first digital library, and The Avalon Project of Yale Law School—both use Ingram's interpretation.

[273] *Gesta Regum Anglorum,* William of Malmesbury, c.1125 and *Historia Ecclesiastica,* Orderic Vitalis, Book X, Chapter xiv, c.1127

immediately flee? And if accidental, why wasn't he mentioned in 1100? Tyrell would have likely been known to the *Chronicle*'s scribe(s) at the time, as he was significant to Rufus. Peter of Blois described '*Tirel*' (one of numerous alternate spellings) as: '*...a very powerful baron. The king received him with the most lavish hospitality, and honoured him with a seat at his table*'.[274]

Here we have another conflict: As a Frenchman, a '*foreigner*'[275] and noted 'guest' of Rufus, Tyrell hardly fits with the *Chronicle*'s description as one of the king's '*own men*'.

Given the enormous significance of the event, the *Chronicle*'s omission of both name(s) and detail is curious. While most of its entries are simple and short, it is known, and valued, for being factual. So, absence of the most crucial facts in this case are worth lingering on. Perhaps the monkish scribe was the only accurate reporter of a witness-free event, wishing for more clarity but failing to find it.[276] Perhaps he had wise reasons to leave out details—you would have to be brave or foolish to point fingers that might lead upwards to the new king or the church. Perhaps the omission was a request from higher authorities. Or perhaps it was simply the dismissiveness of an irreverent man by a reverent one. Afterall, while Rufus is acknowledged by more recent historians for his military skills, administration, courage and generosity, the verdict on his morality was, and is, uniformly negative. As historian A. L. Poole sums up:

"*From the moral standpoint he was probably the worst king that has occupied the throne of England.*"[277]

Whatever the chronicler's motive, it is revealing that—in the exact same entry—after a mere 10-word summary of Rufus's death, he goes on to thoroughly criticise him in some 200 words.

---

[274] *Chronicle of the Abbey of Croyland (with the Continuation of Peter of Blois c.1135 and anonymous writers),* trans. Henry T. Riley (London: Henry G. Bohn, 1854), p. 229.

[275] Geoffrey Gaimar—L'Estoire des Engleis—History of the English People—c.1136–1140

[276] For example, the author places Rufus's death in the morning, whereas later chroniclers universally state it occurred in the late afternoon.

[277] *Domesday Book to Magna Carta, 1087–1216,* A. L. Poole, 2nd Ed. Oxford, 1955, pp.98–99.

'...*harsh and severe...through the counsels of evil men...forever tyring this nation with unjust contributions...hated by almost all his people and abhorrent to God*'.

With so much to say about his life and reign, it seems incongruous to be so brief about his premature end.

Yet, despite all the questions it raises, we must rely on this one short, near-contemporary record as our foundation. We have no official or Crown records, or none that have survived, and there were—as far as we know—no accounts from the hunting party or any other witnesses, no attempt at resuscitation, no pursuit of a culprit, no examination of the body, no interviews, no statements, no arrests and no trial. Of course, we must take into account the post-Conquest mentality towards death. The role of Coroner was not formally established until nearly a century later in 1194, the medical world was unequipped for proper investigation and any inquest into sudden, violent or unnatural deaths was usually for the purposes of collecting Murdrum fines—but does a total lack of action by everyone present and everyone powerful seem a fitting response to the startling end of the Divine Ruler of All?

In 1997, the death of Diana, Princess of Wales, involved hundreds of actions: Intense police investigations, more than one autopsy, interviews and arrests, blanket media coverage for months and an inquest exceeding £12.5 million. Naturally, one cannot compare such efforts with the resources available 900 years prior, but the fact that absolutely no effort was made when Rufus fell, strikes many modern thinkers as suspicious.

Despite their differences in approach, the conclusion of officialdom in both modern and medieval cases was effectively the same: To paraphrase—'No plot to murder, just an accident, an act of God, now let's move on'. But to be human is to be curious, ergo we are not so good at moving on. Academic and public conclusions often go against official ones, with alternative theories on the deaths of Diana, Rufus and many others still abounding to this day. For example, in 1964, the Warren Commission that investigated President Kennedy's assassination concluded that Lee Harvey Oswald had acted entirely alone.[278] However, the most recent poll of 2013 noted that 61% of Americans remain

---

[278] At the time, JFK's younger brother, Robert Kennedy (the attorney general) described the Warren Report as '*a shoddy piece of craftsmanship*'.

unconvinced as to its findings and suspect some kind of conspiracy and cover-up.[279]

There are 3 possible reasons for such levels of doubt. First, regardless of the amount of information provided, people are drawn to conspiracy and controversy. Tabloids and tell-all books have been making a living off such, practically since the invention of the printing press. Now, with internet forums and social media, sudden deaths are put under the microscope, suspicion is magnified, distrust of once-omnipotent institutions is at an all-time high and alternative ideas, more often termed 'conspiracy theories' can be global/viral within minutes. The second reason is psychological—that we cannot accept sad truths, we need a mystery when it comes to the premature death of a popular figure (Marilyn Monroe, Elvis, Bruce Lee, James Dean, John Lennon, Jimi Hendrix and Kurt Cobain, to name but a few). As late Professor Warren Hollister, renowned Anglo-Norman historian and Henry I biographer, asked in his much-referenced article supporting the Rufus accident theory:

"Are we tempted to look for some hint of human calculation such as we would not seek in the reportedly accidental deaths of lesser men?"[280]

Perhaps we are indeed starstruck or seeking scandal. Or perhaps we are simply searching for something concrete when the 'facts' we are presented with are too sparse, fragile or conflicting, and the benefiting parties are nonchalant at best. This leads us to the third explanation, which—in Rufus's case—some academics and many history buffs prefer. Perhaps, just perhaps, the cynics are right and the official version of events is not what actually happened.

Whatever one's stance on such, certainly the new powers in 1100 did not question the conclusions, despite them seemingly being questionable. According to every 'report' from 1125 onwards, the only 2 people present at the death scene were Tyrell and the King, who had separated from the rest of the hunting party. This is the one significant detail that does not waver between writers. However, as Rufus died and Tyrell is understood to have fled to France and never been

---

[279] This US Gallup poll marked the 50th anniversary of the assassination. Such public sentiment was reflected in the well-rated Oliver Stone films, *JFK* (1991) and recent *JFK Revisited* (2021).

[280] '*The Strange Death of William Rufus*', an article by Prof. Warren Hollister in *Speculum—A Journal of Medieval Studies*, Vol. 48, No. 4, October 1973, p.637.

interviewed, the origin of any source material is not just mysterious, but suspicious. With no first-hand witnesses yet reams of 'first-hand' details, we are left with 3 possibilities: The chroniclers interviewed the same fabricators, or shared the same collective imagination—both of which seem impossible given the period over which their accounts were written—or, more likely, Tyrell and the king were not quite as alone as stated.

This brings us to the timing of the records. After the brief *Anglo-Saxon Chronicle* entry, there was a gap of 25–75+ years between the events of 2nd August and any accounts of them.[281] As far as we know, there is *not one* record of Rufus's death in the 25 years that followed it—all English, Latin and French writers, monks, poets and diarists were either silent on the matter or their works have not survived. The English ecclesiastics Eadmer[282] and Orderic Vitalis[283] were the only 2 scribes to write about it who were adults in 1100, and their chronicles were written several decades later (although one assumes they made diary entries and notes along the way). The most quoted version of events, and probably the first to be published, came from William of Malmesbury with his renowned *Gesta Regum Anglorum* (*Deeds of the English kings*, completed 1125). Modern historians agree that he was a reliable recorder (with Barlow's caveat that both he and Orderic had '*a weakness for the sensational*'[284]). However, he was just 5 years old in 1100. Basing his work purely on the recollections of contemporary or later men, one wonders to what extent his and subsequent reports lost their accuracy and integrity.

Consequently, we have numerous accounts using second or third-hand information, or simply writer-invention. While essentially the same limited

---

[281] The invention of the printing press and widespread use of paper was nearly four centuries away, so these were singular handwritten manuscripts, on vellum, and not in wide circulation.

[282] Eadmer's two major works, referenced throughout, are:

(1) *Vita S. Anselmi* (The Life of St Anselm), c.1124

Ed./Trans. R.W. Southern, T. Nelson, OUP, Oxford, 1972.

(2) *Historia novorum in Anglia* (Recent History in England), c.1093–late 1120s.

Ed. M. Rule, Rolls Series 81. 1884. Trans. by G. Bosanquet, 1964.

Eadmer was 25 years old in 1100.

[283] *Historia Ecclesiastica, Books viii-xii,* Orderic Vitalis, written c.1127–30 and covering the years 1092–1119.

Orderic was 40 years old in 1100.

[284] *Rufus*, Frank Barlow, Yale University Press, 2000 (1st ed. pub. 1983), p.430.

sources would have been used by the scribes, no 2 versions are precisely the same and, in many cases, vary considerably—like a 12th century version of Chinese Whispers. These range from the king shooting at and wounding a deer, or missing it completely, or aiming to shoot but breaking his bowstring; shouting out to Tyrell to shoot at it; Tyrell shooting the deer with or without royal prompts; Tyrell shooting at a second target, with his arrow glancing off an oak tree, a wild boar, a stag's flank or antler (of a hind or a hart), or off nothing; Tyrell with the sun in his eyes shooting blindly, or shooting while caught up in his cloak; the king being shot in the heart, the lung, the back, the forehead and elsewhere; the king attempting to pull the arrow out, or snapping off the shaft and falling forward onto it, thus accelerating his death; the king crying out for redemption, groaning, saying nothing at all; Tyrell fleeing alone; Tyrell fleeing with help…and so they go on. There was even an account, some 90 years later, accusing another knight. With such wide-ranging, overlapping and conflicting details, the same question rings loudest: Who was supposed to have witnessed any of these versions when, of the only 2 allegedly present, the king was dead and Tyrell disappeared to the continent without a word?

Some 40 years later, chronicler and romantic versifier Geoffrey Gaimar declared with uncharacteristic plainness in his *L'Estoire des Engleis*: *'We do not know who shot the king'*. Echoing the *Chronicle*'s brevity, this seems to be the most logical conclusion: No-one saw, thus no-one knew. Taken together, these 2 accounts certainly cast doubt over Tyrell as a suspect. As such, they also cast doubt over the credibility of the scribes who named him—suggesting that their notes were retrospectively altered once they knew Tyrell had fled. However, the majority stance was convenient for all in the upper echelons who wished to move even higher—name the man who acts guiltily and cannot be questioned. Perhaps that is all it was—collective relief at the demise of an unpopular ruler and creative writing for the sake of quashing potentially dangerous rumours. But could it also imply some kind of cover-up? Or indeed that Tyrell was just a scapegoat—willing or otherwise?

The assassination theory is not universally accepted and opinion remains divided, however a sizeable handful of modern scholars, including Emma Mason—recently retired as Senior Lecturer in Medieval History at Birkbeck College, London, and author of a substantial and authoritative biography of Rufus—now believe it to be both credible and compelling, being masterminded by the French king.[285] If indeed it was an assassination, its masterstroke was that it could be written off as an unfortunate accident or 'act of God'—a conclusion immediately supported by Rufus's younger brother and future king, Henry. But why would Henry be satisfied with such weak or vague explanations of his sibling's shocking death? Did he, in fact, have reason(s) to see his brother killed—a treacherous and reputation-shattering act? He was a member of the hunting party that day, along with his key supporters, and seized the throne within hours. Did he envisage riding into the forest as a prince and leaving as King?

Over the next few chapters the aim is to re-examine old evidence and follow new clues regarding the suspicious death of King William II, 'Rufus' and equally importantly, to answer the key question—**why is any of this relevant to a book about Robin Hood?**

To answer such, we need to go back a little further in time to the father of these royal brothers, and his controversial deathbed bequests when trying to make provision for his succession.

---

[285] *William II: Rufus, the Red King*, Emma Mason, Tempus, 2005.

Chapter 1
A New King

20. William the Conqueror's Tomb at Abbaye-aux-Hommes, Caen, in Normandy
Due to desecration in both the 16th and 18th centuries, a single surviving thigh bone is
all that lies beneath the marble slab
Public domain photo by Supercarwaar, Licence CC BY-SA 4.0

On the 9th September 1087, William the Conqueror died, aged 59, at the priory
of Saint Gervais, Rouen. His condition had been worsening for some 5 weeks
prior, following an injury sustained while attempting to capture Mantes[286], when
a piece of flaming timber fell in front of his horse causing it to suddenly rear up

---

[286] A fortified town in the small county of Vexin, between Normandy and the royal Île-
de-France. Mantes was constantly in dispute between the Norman Dukes and French
crown and, in 1077, it had been seized and annexed by King Philip I; King William was
on a retaliatory raid at the time.

and his obese stomach to rupture on the pommel of his saddle. He had 4 sons and 5 or 6 daughters with his wife Queen Matilda (niece of Henry I of France, d.1083). His second son Richard had died some 25 years earlier, c.1074, when in his late teens/early 20s, uncannily also in a hunting accident in the New Forest.[287]

His 3 surviving sons were eldest **Robert 'Curthose'** (a moniker teasingly given to him by the Conqueror from the Norman French *'Court heuse'* or 'Short stockings', due to his little legs). About 4 years his junior was **William 'Rufus'** (from the Latin for 'Red',[288] there is no record of the nickname being used during his lifetime, but it is used throughout this book to avoid confusion with his father). Finally, some 12 years younger than Rufus and 16 years younger than Curthose, was **Henry 'Beauclerc'** (a tag given by later medieval writers and Anglo-Norman for 'Fine scholar',) denoting his good education, probably, like Waltheof, originally intended for a career in the church).

Orderic Vitalis noted that there had been rivalry between the trio since youth. The first much-quoted instance occurred in 1077, probably at Caen castle, when the 2 younger boys played a prank on Curthose, then about 25 years old. Rufus (21) and Henry (8 or 9) threw the contents of a full chamber pot onto the heads of Curthose and his companions, who were playing dice in the courtyard below. With indignity suffered, Curthose's friends urged him to start a brawl with his brothers, only interrupted by the arrival of the king. When the Conqueror failed to punish his younger sons, disgruntled Curthose and his cohort of knights dashed off and attempted to seize another of his father's castles at Rouen a few days later. The rebellion failed and they fled, plundering and causing mayhem en route, to take refuge with Curthose's uncle (his mother's brother), Count of Flanders. This was to be the first of many conflicts between Curthose, his father and his brothers.

---

[287] The precise circumstances are hazy but most reports suggest that Richard hit his head on an overhanging branch when at the gallop.

[288] The sobriquet 'Rufus' was coined some years after his death by the Anglo-Norman chronicler Orderic Vitalis, probably in regards to his complexion or maybe temper, but not his hair as often thought. He was likely blonde, as Malmesbury described him, *"Well set; his complexion florid, his hair yellow, of open countenance; different coloured eyes; of astonishing strength though not very tall, and his belly rather projecting."* It is recorded that during his lifetime Rufus was actually known as William 'Longsword'. (De Miraculis Sancti Eadmund)

21. The 3 brothers: William Rufus, Robert Curthose, Henry Beauclerc
(L and R: British Library MS Cotton. Middle: *Chronicle of Matthew Paris*
(1236–1259)). WikiCommons public domain licence

There are many records of Curthose's fractious relationship with his father
and he was usually in exile as a result, often residing with his uncle, Count Robert
I, whose sister, Matilda, had married William back in 1051 when he was Duke
of Normandy. In 1080, things came to a head when Curthose plundered the
Vexin, which brought King William and King Philip I of France together as allies
in order to stop him. That same year, with the help of Queen Matilda, father and
son made peace, although it was not to last. After Matilda's death in 1083,
Curthose seems to have left court and spent several years travelling throughout
Flanders, France and Germany, siring several illegitimate children as he went.

Upon the Conqueror's death in 1087, animosities between the brothers
deepened. In fact, the division of the king's power and assets caused fraternal
turmoil and political instability that was to last beyond their respective lifetimes.
While the king lay dying, Curthose, then aged about 35 (who, being estranged,
had not seen or spoken with his father for some years), was some 80 miles away
in the County of Ponthieu, Picardy, now allied in revolt with the king of France
against his father. William, perhaps feeling obliged under the rule of
primogeniture[289], bequeathed him only the original family lands of the Duchy of
Normandy, along with its Dukedom. His second (and favourite) son William
Rufus, then about 31, was granted his new kingdom and the Crown of England.

---

[289] The right of succession belonging to the firstborn child—usually male line.

From his clear deathbed instructions, William had probably intended to make Rufus his heir for some time, effectively penalising his rebellious firstborn.

Although the rule of primogeniture was not generally accepted in 11th century England, as eldest son and natural heir to the Crown, it must have stung Curthose that Rufus was made King of England. Kings ruled with the Divine Right of God, Dukes did not. Despite that, the power of the Norman Dukedom and its influence and prestige was, in truth, greater than the new, recently conquered kingdom of England.

Meanwhile, 19-year-old Henry was even worse off—inheriting £5,000 of silver but no estates in a world where land was everything. Historians are undecided as to the king's reasoning for this, but it is solely the consequences that are of import here. Although he was young, Henry had solid grounds for resentment. After all, he was the only one of the 3 brothers born in the new kingdom (probably in Selby, Yorkshire[290]), thus the one true 'English' prince born 'in the purple'.[291] In the eyes of many, himself included, this increased his legitimacy to both property and the Crown. Indeed, Vitalis wrote that the Conqueror had declared to Henry as a boy:

"You, in your own time, will have all the dominions I have acquired and be greater than both your brothers in wealth and power."

If this is true—which is questionable as it was written retrospectively once Henry held the Crown and in conflict with the old King's last commands—it was certainly prophetic.

What is known is the brothers' initial reactions to their respective legacies. Rufus, who was in attendance with Henry at Saint Gervais priory when his father died, did 2 things to secure his claim to the throne. He rushed to England and took possession of the Royal Treasury at Winchester, then had himself crowned as soon as he could. His coronation was conducted by Archbishop Lanfranc at Westminster Abbey on 26th September 1087, barely a fortnight after his father's death.

---

[290] *Monasticon Anglicanum*, W. Dugdale, 1693, vol.3, p.485.

[291] This is the literal translation of the ancient Greek and later Medieval Latin *porphyrogenitus*, used in Byzantine times. It could only be claimed by the first offspring to be born **after** the King's accession to the throne. In this case, both Curthose and Rufus were born pre-1066.

A few months' later, in 1088, landless Henry tried to make up for his father's deficit by using a large chunk of his inheritance (£3,000 of the £5,000) to buy the Avranchin and Côtentin peninsula districts of Normandy (today, the Cherbourg Peninsula) from brother Curthose and to call himself Count of the Côtentin. In fact, his power and landholding encompassed a third of Normandy. Curthose was happy to oblige Henry, as he needed cash to mount his planned invasion of England against their brother, the new King.

Both contemporary scribes and later historians acknowledge that King William II, Rufus, was a good military leader, consummate tactician and enthusiastic campaigner who, at a time when Norman lords had a propensity for uprisings and rebellions, understood the importance of army loyalty, rewarding them generously and only exceptionally using force to keep them in line. In Court, he was known for his short fuse, blasphemous language and quick-witted, sarcastic humour among friends and commanders.

22: Depiction of William II. Artist unknown,
but seduced by the idea that 'Rufus' equated to red hair

Edward Alleyn collection of royal portraits, 1618–20, Dulwich Picture Gallery.
Public domain

As King, he was certainly not a church-goer. He did, however, profit greatly from clerical vacancies, leaving senior positions unfilled and taking the incomes.[292] Aided by his sharp-witted, influential and morally questionable first minister Ranulph 'Flambard'[293] (a Norman clergyman of humble origins who had served his father), this money not only funded his lavish lifestyle but also paid for mercenaries for his border campaigns against the Welsh, Scots and French. As most writers were monks whose fellow brethren suffered under his rapacious rule, they painted a picture of a crass, blasphemous king whose most recorded characteristics were excessive greed, time spent hunting, a love of rich cuisine, probable alcoholism and a preference for young male companions. On this latter point, much has been written. There is no solid evidence that Rufus was gay, but he neither married nor had children, even illegitimate ones (his younger brother Henry had about 23!), which was highly unusual for a medieval monarch. While the 12th century Welsh *Chronicle of the Princes* (*Brut Y Tywysogion*) detailed Rufus's habitual use of concubines, the main scribes of the day—Malmesbury, Eadmer, Orderic, Henry of Huntingdon—seemed keen to taint him with suggestions of sodomy,[294] describing his Court thus:

"flowing hair and extravagant dress...shoes with curved points; the model for young men was to rival women in delicacy of person, to mince their gait, to walk with loose gesture, and half-naked. Enervated and effeminate, they unwillingly remained what nature had made them; the assailers of others' chastity, the prodigal of their own."[295]

---

[292] At the time of his death, Rufus was sucking out the revenues from the empty See of Canterbury, four vacant bishoprics including Winchester, and at least 11 abbeys, including Ely.

[293] Flambard was a nickname, meaning 'torch-bearer', 'incendiary' or 'devouring flame'; probably on account of his fieriness or political influence. In 1099, he was made Bishop of Durham by Rufus, a post that had been vacant for the previous three years.

[294] The chroniclers' inferences have been taken as fact by many. However, there are no records of him having either mistresses or specific male favourites. As such, he could have been impotent, asexual or perhaps took a vow of celibacy. The most likely conclusion is that he was bisexual, possibly infertile, and on balance preferred the company of young men in his bedchamber.

[295] *Gesta Regum Anglorum*, William of Malmesbury, c.1125. Trans. by J A Giles, 1847. p.386

This negative sentiment extended beyond the chroniclers. In 1088, just a year after Rufus's accession, came the first of 2 major baronial rebellions during his reign. A number of the most powerful Norman earls, counts and bishops who owned land in both Normandy and England had been ruffled by the new division of power between Rufus and Curthose. When Curthose planned to usurp his brother as England's ruler, several noblemen joined forces. This included 2 of the late Conqueror's half-brothers—Bishop Odo of Bayeux (who was also Earl of Kent), and Robert de Mortain—plus Robert de Mowbray, Richard FitzGilbert de Clare and his son Gilbert de Clare. Remarkably, the indolent Curthose failed to arrive from Normandy in time to take part in his own uprising, not helped by bad weather, and after just a few weeks of hostilities, the rebels were easily defeated (Curthose thereby wasting the £3000 from brother Henry, then trying to renege on the transaction and reappropriate the territory of Western Normandy by force). Odo, previously the richest man in England, was stripped of his holdings and banished to Normandy for life, while his nephew Robert Curthose was allowed to stay in England and keep his estates in Normandy, on the proviso that he recognise Rufus as king and set aside his claim to the throne.

Rufus was greatly assisted in his victory by 2 men: Bishop Wulfstan of Worcester, the only English-born bishop left in power after the Conquest; and Lanfranc, the Archbishop of Canterbury who had overseen his coronation. Both rallied support (money and men) based on all sorts of wild promises made by the king, including unlimited bribery plus slackening of the hated Forest Laws which, being Rufus, he later reneged on.

Some 7 years later, in 1095, undaunted by their earlier failure, a second baronial uprising began. Essentially a northern-based revolt and not very well supported, it consisted of several of the rebels from 1088 including ringleader Robert de Mowbray plus Gilbert de Clare, and many others such as Roger de Lacy and William, Count de Eu (an Anglo-Norman aristocrat and son-in-law of Roger de Busli).

Their plan was a *coup d'état* to murder Rufus and install Stephen of Aumale on the throne. Stephen was Rufus's cousin (son of his aunt Adelaide and her third husband, Odo of Champagne). Stephen was thus also the half-brother and only sibling of Judith de Lens, Waltheof's widow (she being Adelaide's daughter by her second husband, Count Lambert de Lens). How different both her life and English history would have been if this rebellion had succeeded and her half-brother had become king. Instead, Rufus conducted a lightning campaign, outflanking the rebels at Newcastle-upon-Tyne and capturing their stronghold at Morpeth. The uprising collapsed with the surrender of Bamburgh castle, at which point Judith, now about 41, seems to have melted away into obscurity, at least for a while.

Due to the significance of the de Clare family in both these rebellions and in the events that were about to unfold, it is worth lingering on them for a moment. Richard FitzGilbert de Clare (b. pre-1035–c.1091) was a second cousin of William the Conqueror as they were both great-grandsons of Richard I of Normandy, 'the Fearless' (932–996), by the Danish-descended Gunnora, his second wife (see family tree below).

Going back just one generation, Richard de Clare's father, Gilbert[296], Count de Brionne and d'Eu, was a first cousin to William the Conqueror's father, Duke Robert I (d.1035). Gilbert had been tutor to the young Duke William (aged 8— later the Conqueror) and became one of his early guardians when the boy's father died.[297] The formidable Bec Abbey, arguably the most significant institution in this story, was built upon Gilbert's donated lands and with his financial support. However, in 1040, Gilbert was murdered by Norman baronial rebels in a failed plot to kill the then 12-year-old William the 'Bastard', who they refused to accept as their leader.

In 1066, Gilbert's son, Richard FitzGilbert de Clare, joined William in the Norman Conquest of England and was subsequently rewarded with a very generous 224 manorial holdings, split between areas around Tonbridge in Kent and Clare in Suffolk, plus the right to build a castle at each and use the title of Earl of Clare.[298] Richard certainly did not start as a rebel, as a loyal supporter of

---

[296] Apparently Gilbert had the nickname of 'Crispin' because his unruly hair stood up like the branches of a pine tree. From *Gilbert Crispin, Abbot of Westminster*, J. A. Robinson, University Press, 1911.

[297] William's only uncle, Richard III, and his grandfather, Richard II, were also both already deceased when his own father, Robert, died in 1035. His other guardians, along with Gilbert de Brionne, were Alan III of Brittany and Osbern the Steward (whose son William FitzOsbern became the Conqueror's great friend). Like Gilbert, both Osbern and Alan were also murdered c.1040 – throat cut and poisoned respectively- while protecting the young duke. (see genealogy chart below)

[298] Some modern historians consider this title self-styled. According to *The Norman Conquest: A New Introduction,* R. Huscroft (Routledge, 2013), William the Conqueror only ever had a maximum of seven earls during his reign and just four at the time of *Domesday.*

the Conqueror he had played a major part in suppressing The Revolt of the Earls in 1075. Along with William's other family relations who had joined him in the Conquest, such as his half-brother Robert de Mortain, Richard de Clare became one of the richest and most powerful men in the country, and most trusted by the king. He was one of only 3 Joint Justiciars who ruled England while the Conqueror was in absentia in Normandy for much of the time post-1066. The other 2 were William's half-brother, Bishop Odo[299] (Robert de Mortain's full brother), and his second cousin, right-hand man and trusted advisor, William FitzOsbern, 1st Earl of Hereford.

Richard de Clare had 5 sons with his wife Rohese (née Giffard): Roger, the eldest, then Gilbert (named after his grandfather), Robert, Walter and Richard. They also had 2 surviving daughters: Rohese (named after her mother), who married Eudo Dapifer, the loyal royal steward to all 3 Norman kings; and Adeliza (Alice), who married her half-cousin—a French knight named Walter Tyrell…

Lineage of Richard FitzGilbert de Clare

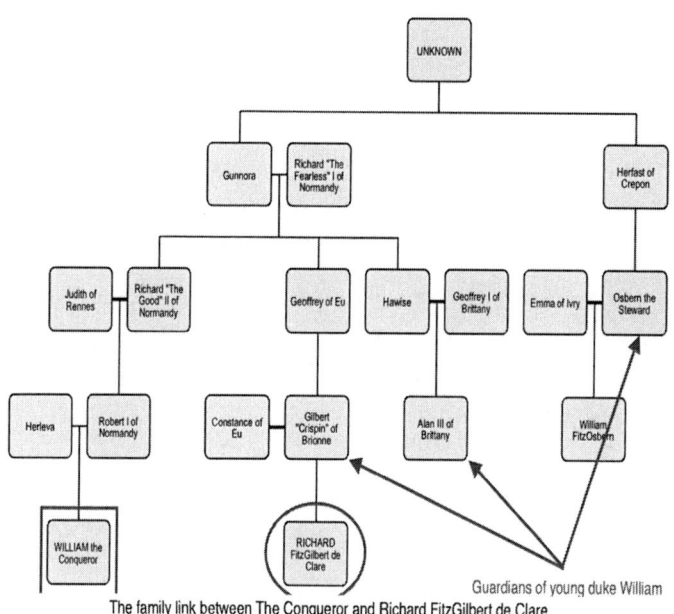

Guardians of young duke William
The family link between The Conqueror and Richard FitzGilbert de Clare.
Both were second cousins via their shared great-grandfather, Richard I of Normandy

---

[299] Odo of Bayeux and Robert de Mortain were sons of William the Conqueror's mother, Herleva, and his step-father, Herluin de Conteville.

Richard was faithful to his King, not, as it turned out, to the Crown. In 1088, following the death of the Conqueror, he became one of the main protagonists in the first baronial uprising against King William Rufus. After a two-day siege at Tonbridge Castle, he surrendered and was duly punished, with his castle and the town of Tonbridge being burnt to the ground. As religious houses occasionally acted as secure prisons for high-status captives, Richard was 'involuntarily retired' to the monastery of St Neots that he had earlier refounded with his wife. He died there, a broken man, 3 years later in 1091. His second son, Gilbert, would have been about 21 at the time and although he was part of the 1088 rebellion (wounded and captured at the Tonbridge siege[300]), was pardoned by Rufus. This was possibly due to his age and/or their close family history, but clemency (both a Rufus and Norman trait) was widely shown to many of the rebels.

In the later Northern Barons' rebellion of 1095 led by Robert de Mowbray, Gilbert's name appears again as an insurgent and traitor. However, as the retaliatory royal army led by Rufus approached the frontiers of de Mowbray's territories, duplicitous Gilbert (now 28), who was accompanying the royal party, made a U-turn. He confessed to Rufus that he was privy to a plot (to which he had sworn a solemn oath of secrecy), to assassinate the king by cutting his throat in the wood they were about to pass through. He went further, supplying the names of the traitors, who were subsequently defeated by Rufus after sieges at Newcastle and Bamburgh castles, the latter being surrendered by de Mowbray's wife after Rufus threatened to blind her captive husband.

Chronicler Eadmer gave his reasoning for Gilbert's change of heart:

"The man who, as the king approached the wood fraught with death, fell at his feet and implored him to avoid it, was Gilbert of Tonbridge [and Clare], a son of Anselm's friend, Richard FitzGilbert [de Clare]. May it not have been the memory of lessons of manly faith, of high-souled honour, and of Christian truth taught him while he was yet a boy in his father's castle at Tonbridge by the saintly Abbot of le Bec [Anselm] that prompted this interposition? Who shall say? It is, in any case, worthy of note that the man to repent of the treachery, to save his accomplices from the guilt of blood, and to reassert in himself the character of Christian knight, was the son of Anselm's earliest benefactor among the barons of England."[301]

---

[300] Detail from *John of Worcester iii, 52*

[301] *The Life and Times of St Anselm*, Martin Rule, Wipf & Stock, 2016, Vol.2, p101.

As faith-centred as Eadmer's view is, it was more likely that Gilbert acted as such in the interests of self-preservation and also to convince the conspirators that their best course of action was to seek reconciliation with Rufus as the revolt looked doomed. Following his confession,[302] Gilbert escaped royal retribution and was pardoned a second time, but maybe he was never to fully regain the trust of Rufus, perhaps rightfully so.

Now back to the royal brothers. In February 1091, between the 2 rebellions, Rufus led an expedition to Normandy, persuading Curthose into signing the Treaty of Caen.[303] Significantly, this was a pact to cease their rivalry and join forces in order to suppress young Henry, who had commenced a rebellious campaign in the Côtentin peninsula of Normandy. Even more significantly, the Treaty included the agreement that if either Rufus or Curthose should die without legitimate heirs, the other would take over the whole Kingdom of England and the Duchy of Normandy, as their father had. With this, Henry was effectively excluded from the chance of kingship. One can only imagine his reaction. Furthermore, with both brothers physically now against him, he was forced to take sanctuary in the Norman monastery of Mont St Michel. In April, Rufus and Curthose accepted his plea for surrender and it is likely he went into exile for the next couple of years in the Vexin, a small province of the French Crown, bordering Normandy to the northwest of Paris.

There is a slight possibility that he stayed with Walter Tyrell at this time, as the brother-in-law and cousin of his close friends, the Clare brothers. Tyrell was castellan of Pontoise Castle and surrounding territory, one of the key Vexin fortifications of French King Philip. Certainly, Prince Louis, who had been granted control of the Vexin by his father and the responsibility for defending it (along with Mantes, Chaumont and Pontoise castles) would have known Walter Tyrell well.

Then in 1095, at around the same time as the northern rebellion, came Pope Urban II's famous sermon in the Cathedral at the Council of Clermont in the Auvergne (then part of the Duchy of Aquitaine), to about 300 clerics, announcing his call-to-arms for Christians 'to recover Jerusalem from the Infidel'.

---

[302] According to Orderic's *Ecclesiastical History*, Vol IV, p. 280–281, Gilbert offered a '*deditio*', a medieval act of ritualised submission and request for mercy performed before a monarch.

[303] Interchangeably called the Treaty of Rouen.

23. Pope Urban II preaching to the Council in Clermont Cathedral, 1095.
Miniature by Jean Colombe (c.1474) in the Bibliothèque Nationale from Sébastien
Mamerot's, *Les Passages d'outremer*
Public Domain Image from Wikipedia

Urban declared that anyone who answered his call would be promised remission of sins and a guaranteed place in heaven. The following year, Robert Curthose ventured on this First (Great) Crusade (following the total debacle of the People's Crusade a few months earlier). To raise the large sums of money needed to fund such an expedition, he made the dramatic decision to mortgage his Norman Duchy to brother Rufus for 10,000 marks (a bargain for such, but a great deal of money all the same).[304] On his departure to the Holy Lands, Curthose reaffirmed the earlier agreement made between himself and Rufus in the Treaty of Caen, effectively ostracising Henry even further from any chance

---

[304] 10,000 marks (a mark was worth ⅔ of a pound—160 old pence/67p decimal) was purportedly a quarter of Rufus' annual income and about 10% of England's annual GDP at the time.

of the crown. In order to pay Curthose for the Duchy, Rufus imposed punitive taxes on the English people, the church and the nobility.[305] In his older brother's absence, he took over Normandy and expanded its borders, clearly hoping to keep it long-term, probably expecting his brother to perish in the Holy Land.

With Curthose off to the Crusade, Henry was now granted freedom and seemingly restored to favour with Rufus, helping him with Scottish and Welsh border revolts. Again with Henry's support, Rufus spent the next 2 and a half years campaigning across the Channel in the counties of Maine and the Vexin[306] in efforts to expand his empire, as well as to quash further uprisings along the home borders. So secure had these borders become by 1099, that King Edgar of Scotland (elder brother of Princess Edith, who became Henry's wife the following year) bore King William Rufus's sword before him at the Whitsun crown-wearing ceremony, held in the recently completed great Westminster Hall in London.[307]

Rufus's strategies thus brought relative peace to England and success in Maine. However, in autumn 1098, things finally ground to a halt in the Vexin campaign. It was defended by the young Prince Louis and the fortified towns of Mantes, Pontoise and Chaumont proved impregnable to the Norman advance. As we know, the French castellan of Pontoise Castle, the last stronghold before Paris, was none other than Sir Walter Tyrell, the man history has inextricably linked to the death of William Rufus.

---

[305] The huge financial pressure put on the Anglo-Norman nobility by Rufus was a major factor leading to their inability to take part in the crusade themselves. Virtually no English soldiers or Anglo-Norman knights went on the First Crusade, apart from the few assisting Robert Curthose, who led his own contingent to the Middle East. It is said Walkelin, Bishop of Winchester, died of a heart attack brought on by receiving a demand from Rufus for £200 whilst conducting Mass on Christmas Day, 1098 (detail from *Domesday, Book of Judgement,* Sally Harvey, OUP, 2014, p.47.)

[306] Rufus laid formal claim to the three fortified Vexin towns of Chaumont, Mantes and Pontoise.

[307] Rufus complained that the new Hall was '*not big enough by half*', despite being the largest in Europe. It is the only surviving element of the original Norman Palace of Westminster. This is the same building where Queen Elizabeth II lay in state prior to her funeral in September 2022.

24. Robert Curthose at the siege of Antioch (1097) while on crusade by J.J. Dassy, 1850

Image: Courtesy of Encyclopaedia Britannica in the public domain

In the spring of 1099, both sides seemed exhausted by the continual campaigning and stalemate, so Rufus declared a truce with the French king and returned to England for some recovery time and to celebrate his 2 great building projects of Westminster Hall and the new walls around the Tower of London. Somewhat oddly, Walter Tyrell came with him. There is a possibility that Walter might have been captured,[308] though as Pontoise castle was never taken by Rufus, this seems unlikely. So, whether he willingly changed his allegiance or was

---

[308] While English captives were quickly released with ransoms paid, Prince Louis had little money, so French captives could often only obtain freedom by swearing an oath of loyalty to Rufus and fighting for him, on the English side.

headhunted and 'bought' by Rufus[309], we do not know for sure. His defection may well have been engineered by the de Clares—later events would certainly suggest this. What is clear is that Walter was a good soldier, an attribute much-admired by Rufus, and according to numerous accounts they subsequently became close companions.

By autumn of 1099, Rufus received surprising news of the July capture of Jerusalem by the Crusaders, meaning the heroic return of brother Curthose could be expected in 1100. Preparations were made for a large French invasion force, with a vast fleet assembled and fitted out in Southampton during the summer of 1100. Orderic suggests that, upon Curthose's return via France, Rufus was planning to attack him with this force, thus keeping him from entering his pawned inheritance of Normandy.[310]

25. A 12ᵗʰ century fresco in the Chapelle Sainte-Radegonde (built around the tomb of a 6th century religious hermit) depicting a Royal Hunting Party, likely Henry II (1133–1189) and his wife Eleanor of Aquitaine.
Photo by Chinpa: Reproduced under licence Creative Commons-ShareAlike
CC B-Y 4.0

---

[309] One 16ᵗʰ century chronicler later declared of Tyrell that Rufus—'*had retained* (him) *in service with a large stipend'. Chronicles of England Scotland and Ireland'*, Raphael Holinshed, c.1577, Vol.2.

[310] Orderic Vitalis 5, book X, Ch. 13, iv. 80, p. 280.

An unusual lull then occurred in the life of Rufus and his Court—at least in the records for 1099/1100.[311] Warring had temporarily ceased and the Court drifted in between Gloucester, Winchester and London for the various lavish festivities of Christmas, Easter and Whitsun, featuring flamboyant 'crown-wearing' ceremonies for the king. Up to this point, Rufus seems to have lived a charmed life. As late as 1099, during the siege of Mayet in Maine, a knight standing next to him was hit by a rock fired from the ramparts and had his brains dashed out. However, the king's luck was about to run out.

To counteract years of warfare, keen huntsman Rufus would have no doubt looked forward to a more peaceful summer in 1100 and indulging in his favourite sport with a return to his vast royal hunting grounds of the New Forest, staying at Malwood Lodge near Minstead village. This six-week period was known as the 'fat season' or 'grease-time', when hunting the great red stags was permitted. It ran for 6 weeks from 1st August—'Lammas day' (the Feast of St Peter's Chains)—to 14th September (the feast of the Exaltation of the Holy Cross).

This brings us up to that fateful day on 2nd August 1100, the second day of the fat season. The wild arrow in question did not, as one might expect in a bow-related hunting accident, embed in a thigh, arm or back, allowing survival or perhaps death by septicaemia some days later. Instead, according to the vast majority of reports, it found its way directly into the chest and, more precisely, the vital organs (lung) of the king, killing him in an instant. The odds of this happening by accident, in the wide open, 3 dimensional space of a forest, seem most unlikely, especially when we take into account the chroniclers' reports that the suspect bowman, Walter Tyrell, was an excellent archer. Effectively, he was a professional soldier and skilled mature huntsman, so the idea of him firing an impetuous or careless deadly shot, with the king in his line of fire, stretches the bounds of credulity.

In fact, several pertinent elements (and equally poignant omissions) suggest foul play. Tyrell not only repeatedly protested his innocence, but he denied even shooting the arrow or being near to the king. We know this from conversations

---

[311] The exception was an extraordinary episode in June 1099 when Rufus, while hunting in the New Forest, received news that Count Elias of Maine had retaken Le Mans. In true impetuous style, he immediately set off for the coast, crossed to Normandy despite a dangerous storm, assembled troops, rode on to Le Mans in Maine province and recovered it.

in later life between Tyrell and his friend, the renowned French chronicler (lifelong friend and biographer of King Louis VI), Abbot Suger of St Denis:

"It was laid to the charge of a certain noble, Walter Tirel, that he had shot the king with an arrow; but I have often heard him, when he had nothing to fear nor to hope, solemnly swear that on the day in question he was not in the part of the forest where the king was hunting, nor ever saw him in the forest at all." [312]

If Tyrell is to be believed—and it is certainly a reasonable stance with all that solemn swearing and nothing to gain from it—then who might have drawn the fatal arrow, and why?

Even if one prefers the argument that Rufus's premature end was a freak accident, can the geography, ready availability of the necessary people to sign paperwork and conduct formalities, and what Henry benefited from it, also be explained away by coincidence?

---

[312] *Life of Louis VI 'Le Gros'*, Abbot Suger, c.1140. Under Suger, the Abbey of St Denis became the principal religious sanctuary of French Royalty, where the Kings were both crowned and interred.

Chapter 2
A Possible Plot

Within the realms of modern police detection, for any unnatural death they look first at those closest to the victim who have the most to gain…and with good reason. More often than not, it is a family member, even if they are not the ones to get their hands dirty themselves. The priority is to build a profile of the deceased and, if applicable, to look at potential enemies and their alibis. Therefore, it is logical to approach this 11th century case in the same way, starting with the facts.

Fact 1: From practically all contemporary accounts, we have a victim who was wholly unpopular with his subjects, with the church, with the French monarchy, with many of his own nobles (apart from those close courtiers he lavished favours upon) and arguably with both of his brothers.

As Henry of Huntingdon so scathingly wrote, long after the event c.1135:

"The king [William Rufus] *was rightly cut off in the midst of his injustice. For he was savage beyond all men; and by the advice of evil counsellors, and such he always chose, he was false to his subjects, and worse to himself; he ruined his neighbours by extortions, and his own people by continual levies for his armies, and endless fines and exactions. England could not breathe under the burdens laid upon it. For the king's minions seised on and subvert\ 11ed everything so that they even committed the most violent adulteries with impunity. Whatever wickedness existed before was now brought to the highest pitch; whatever had no existence before, sprung up in these times…In short, whatever was pleasing to God was displeasing to this king and his minions; nor did he practise his infamous debauchery in secret, but openly in the light of day."*[313]

---

[313] *The Chronicle of Henry of Huntingdon: The History of England, From the Invasion of Julius Cæsar to the Accession of Henry II,* Ed. Trans. T. Forrester, 1853, p.239.

Fact 2: Until the day in question, to quote historian and journalist Charles Spencer, 9th Earl of Althorp, *"Henry seemed destined to be nothing more than a footnote to their [his brothers'] life stories—until his chance came, and he seized it."* In fact, by early summer 1100, with his 2 brothers very much alive and well, it seemed likely that he would soon lose the only landed possessions he had left, on the Cherbourg Peninsula in Normandy. To quote historian and broadcaster Dan Snow:

"As the fourth son of William the Conqueror, he was an obscure figure destined to be a well-bred non-entity. Yet he became a titan of European history in the first 35 years of the 12th century."[314]

On 2nd August 1100, Henry gained everything he had long been deprived of, and most likely coveted. Ostensibly, Henry had been friendly and helpful to brother Rufus since 1094 right up to 1100. Henry had used his military skills for his own benefit, but generally both elder brothers had treated him with disdain. They manipulated him, stole the lands that he had either been endowed with or bought for himself, and even kept him prisoner. Just one of those things would provide enough motive for a modern police investigation.

Fact 3: According to all surviving records, Henry was very intelligent. He was definitely capable of devising an intricate plan and also possessed the unscrupulous and ruthless character to carry it off—Hollister notes that he once threw a man off a tower to his death.[315] Furthermore, every contemporary account shows that this day gave him the unique opportunity to enact such a plan. And finally, he had 'the means', including, crucially and one feels by design, plenty of loyal friends and potentially willing associates around him; before, during and after the 2nd August—a close relative happy to take the blame and more particularly, a very secretive and able assassin…

Without a 900-year-old parchment inked with credible, definitive evidence, the crime of regicide is never going to be proven absolute. On the basis that 'accidents do happen', many historians take what we know on face value and conclude it was a bowman's tragic error. However, others, such as A.L. Poole[316],

---

[314] *BBC History Magazine*, 'The White Ship disaster'. December 2020. p.38.

[315] *Henry I*, Warren Hollister, Yale University Press, 2001 p.73.

[316] *From Domesday Book to Magna Carta, 1087–1216*, A. L. Poole. 1955, 2nd Ed. Oxford.

F.M.L. Parker[317], W.L. Warren[318] and Emma Mason[319] lean towards the likelihood of a conspiracy, Henry-driven or otherwise, and even the somewhat ambivalent renowned medievalist Professor Christopher Brooke concludes, *"If Rufus's death in August 1100 was an accident, Henry I was an exceptionally lucky man."[320]*

I readily admit that my own proposition is based on—as you shall soon see— a single piece of paper, wrapped in a thick blanket of associations that was unearthed during my research. I also do not deny that I worked backwards from this discovery. However, it was a methodical journey, with supporting evidence found along the way and a case strengthened by intricate circumstances, geography and genealogical relationships of late 11th century England. Make of it all what you will.

Let us start with the latter of the 3 key facts: Character. Although there are many aspects of the royal brothers that scribes and historians cannot agree on, there seems to be one of universal accord: Prince Henry was by far the most cerebral, shrewd, devious and ruthless of the trio, with chronicler Henry of Huntingdon later recording:

"The king was a man of greatest guile (summe simultatis) and inscrutable mentality (mentis inscrutabilis)." [321]

Following Robert's departure to the Holy Land in 1096 on crusade, Henry seemingly became quite close to Rufus, successfully campaigning with him from 1097 to early 1099 in Maine and the Vexin. He had sided with one brother or another over the years but it is quite obvious, perhaps understandably given their history, that he did not really have a liking for either of them. His trusted royal counsellor Robert Bloet, Bishop of Lincoln (who had also served both his brother and father), later said:

---

[317] *The Forest Laws and the Death of William Rufus.* English Historical Review, xxvii, F. M. L. Parker, 1912)

[318] *William Rufus's Death*, History Today, W.L. Warren, Jan. 1959

[319] *William II: Rufus, the Red King*, Emma Mason, Tempus, 2005

[320] *The Saxon and Norman Kings*, Christopher Brooke, B.T. Batsford Ltd. 1963.

[321] *Historia Anglorum*, c. 1129, Henry of Huntingdon, vii. p.26.

"Henry never spoke well of a man, with but at the same time meaning to ruin him." [322]

Essentially, if you thought Henry to be your friend, this was the time to be most wary of him. This personality trait might simply have created an unpleasant and untrustworthy individual, but it would also fit with someone planning fratricide, regicide, seizure of the Crown of England and later life imprisonment of one's remaining brother. There may even have been some skewed sense of honour behind it. As Christopher Brooke suggested, just the fact that Henry was the only son born in the purple *'made the murder of Rufus not an act of treachery, but the removal of a blaspheming usurper'.*[323] Indeed, Henry played on his unique legitimacy to the throne, particularly to the bishops, after his coronation.

Into the mix of duplicitous prince, unpopular king, fraternal rivalry and prior conflicts with their father, we should add the contemporary setting, namely the Conquest, the massacre at York (where it is said Waltheof killed 50 Normans), the Harrowings, the Earls' Revolt, the campaigns at home and in Normandy… this was a time of constant rebellions, uprisings, back-stabbings, mutilations, murders, imprisonments, banishments, changing allegiances, plots and trial by combat. Is it such a leap to assume Henry followed both country and family history?

In addition to motive and mentality, Henry also had opportunity. On 2nd August 1100, his eldest brother, Robert Curthose, was most likely halfway between southern Italy and Normandy, perhaps only just a week or 2 away. There he had recently married Sybilla of Conversano from Apulia who contemporary writers described as a beautiful, intelligent and very wealthy Italian-Norman princess (he had spent the last few months there, as the lauded guest of her father, Geoffrey, Count of Conversano and Lord of Brindisi). As Rufus fell dead to the ground, Henry was, critically, not just the only brother in the forest, but in England.

Furthermore, we have the perfect location. Conveniently, or by design, the site was only 20 miles from the Palace of Winchester where Henry headed

---

[322] *De Contemptu Mundi*, Vol. viii of *Historia Anglorum (The History of the English People)* by Henry of Huntingdon (c.1130–35), Bloet's biographer. Text and Translation: ed. D. E. Greenway (OUP, 1996).

[323] *The Saxon and Norman Kings*, Christopher Brooke, B.T. Batsford Ltd. 1963. p.78

immediately to take control of the Royal Treasury and have himself crowned in London at Westminster Abbey, just 3 days later.

Perhaps most significantly, Henry abandoned Rufus's body in the process, leaving no instruction to retrieve it (a peasant found the bloodied corpse later by chance), nor stopping for prayer or a moment to collect himself due to shock or grief. As Charles Spencer put it, *"Henry left his brother to stiffen in death."*[324]

This was not only the king, this was his brother. While taking the Crown swiftly was vital to ensure England's political stability, even an unloved sibling's death would justify a moment of pause had it been unexpected. By any account, such action—or inaction—paints a picture beyond ambition and into suspicion.

This all leads us to a provocative question: Did Henry, in fact, use this one-off time and place not just to his advantage, but also with premeditation? If we step a little further into such a theory, to commit regicide without besmirching his reputation would require careful planning and an intricate, multi-strand plot. Being an intellect, that was something Henry could plausibly carry off (with a little help from his friends).

However, using 21st century detection, we examine the prerequisites of a 12th century assassination to see if it is anything more than merely plausible. To do such, I invite you to step back before 2nd August and enter the mind of a much darker Henry and a contemporary checklist…

1. Timing

Even sceptic Hollister concedes that the king's death occurred in the nick of time. His suggestion that it would have been better for Henry if Rufus had been killed during the French campaigning of 1097–99 seems obvious. Of course, it would have been more convenient had Rufus (and indeed Curthose) died in battle or naturally. However fate had not worked that way: Rufus was 44, fit and likely to reign for another 20+ years.[325] If Henry wanted the Crown, this was perhaps

---

[324] Article in The Catholic Herald *'Henry the First: The man who was never meant to be king'* by Charles Spencer, August 5th 2020.

[325] Although infant mortality and death in childbirth were very high, if a man reached 21 and didn't die by accident or violence, he could be expected to live almost as long as men today—an average of 62–70 years. Those in the higher echelons of society had even better odds with better housing, diet, some medical care and lives free of the daily agrarian grind. A few contemporary examples are: Henry I (67), Robert Curthose (83),

his last opportunity. Rufus and Curthose had made each, the other's heir, to the exclusion of their youngest brother Henry who had no hope that Rufus would nominate him; his only chance of the throne was to seise it by force when eldest brother Robert Curthose was in no position to intervene.

Allied to this, many powerful barons with vast estates in both Normandy and England believed Robert had a far stronger claim to the throne than Henry and, as a newly-wed, may soon produce an heir. Remarkably the Duke had survived battles, wounds, disease and famine in the Holy Land and was on his way back from Jerusalem, soon to approach the borders of Normandy[326]. If he had arrived even just 3 weeks earlier, Henry would most likely never have been king. Therefore, any plan would need to be enacted prior to: Robert's return to Normandy, expected in September, and Rufus's imminent departure back to the continent at the head of his large invasion fleet.

There is particular significance in the first of these points. The death of the king combined with the absence of the elder brother would have led to anarchy if Henry had not 'stepped in' since with the monarch's demise, the 'King's Law' or 'King's Peace' was suspended until a successor had been crowned and during this interregnum there was no power available to preserve order[327]. This fact alone could provide justification for his actions. His ability to win support from the barons in assuming the Crown would come from their desperation for national stability, despite the fact that a number of them favoured Curthose (supporting him in later rebellions). Was it luck or good planning that the death occurred late in the day and in a remote location such that the news could be contained for a further day or so, as events unfolded?

One also gets the feeling that the death occurred at Lammastide quite by the design of the plotters; if not, then we can chalk up yet another factor of extraordinarily convenient coincidence. Lammas was originally one of the 4 ancient Celtic pagan festivals of the seasons. Then called *Lughnasadh*, it was a

---

Ranulph Flambard (68), David I of Scotland (69), Alexios I, King of Byzantium (70), and Archbishops of Canterbury—Lanfranc (c.79–84) and Anselm (76).

[326] Barely 20% of those who set out in 1096 made it all the way to take Jerusalem in July 1099.

[327] It is recorded in the *Anglo Saxon Chronicle* under the date of I135, that on the death of Henry I. *"there was tribulation soon in the land, for every man that could, forthwith robbed another."* Extract from 'The King's Peace in the Middle Ages', F. Pollock, Nov 1899, *Harvard Law Review*, Vol. 13, No. 3, p.185.

harvest festival that ran from sunset August 1st until sunset August 2nd, thanking the Grain God, Lugh, for the benefit of the years' harvest. Then adopted by the Christian church, it revolves around bread being made from flour of the first grain harvested for that year and used for the bread of mass at a communion service of thanksgiving—Lammas being a corruption of 'Loaf Mass'. The pagan and satanic links that still held, were to do with death, human sacrifice and rebirth, although the actual Christian and pagan origins of this somewhat ignored festival are gloriously blurred and disputed. Many believed the death of William, precisely as the sun was going down on August 2nd, was brought about by God (through a little human intervention), that having made a wasteland of his kingdom, gorged himself on the fruits of the labours of the populace, he was killed as a Lammas sacrifice, like the Green, Corn or Wicker Man of Celtic pagan festivals, who has to die in order to bring new life, and a rebirth next year, to the earth, to the land, to the people…to the nation. What mattered to the believers was that the Red King's death had happened in the right place and the right time for the ritual fertility magic to work. Maybe the original plan was for the 'hit' to occur on Lammas Day itself, August 1st, but for a myriad of reasons they had to postpone it for 24hrs. Notwithstanding, the timing for the regicidal plotters could not have been better—to suggest the king's death was God's will, being part of some ancient sacrificial fertility rite, was perfect cover for their scheme.

2. Location

The killing had to occur in an isolated, remote spot where the assassin could be concealed and the king would be as alone as he ever was, such that any witnesses were limited to the smallest number possible, preferably none. It also had to be somewhere that the royal party was known to regularly frequent, so it would require little/no persuasion nor arousal of suspicion. Additionally, it needed to be certain (no chance for interruptions or last-minute changes by the impulsive Rufus) and accessible—enabling the setup with the assassin to be pre-arranged.

Lastly, it had to be not more than a couple of days' journey away from 2 key places: Winchester for the state treasury and for 2 cathedrals with friendly bishops, Winchester, to bury Rufus; and Westminster in London, with friendly bishops, Maurice and Gerard, to crown the new King. The New Forest deer park was perfectly placed and both Henry and his close friend Gilbert de Clare, would be very familiar with this location from previous hunts and knew it was the ideal spot.

3. Appearance

The very fact that hunting was considered a high-risk activity, with various severe injuries and deaths recorded, provided the perfect cover. The boys' elder brother Richard had been killed in a hunting accident several years before and their nephew (Curthose's illegitimate son), also named Richard, met the same fate just a few months earlier in May. This, too, could be waved off as another tragedy, or perhaps even a family curse but was certainly good 'grist to the mill' for promoting an accident. Conversely, an impromptu or crude assassination, any obvious signs that it was murder not a mistake, and mayhem would have ensued. Rufus's death had to be made to look like an accident. No hint of suspicion could fall on the new King as fratricide was considered a deeply ungodly act and particularly heinous crime—if even a whisper of such had taken hold in the country, Henry's rule would have been undermined from the outset.

4. Certainty

Death had to be assured: one arrow, one life. If the king survived, naturally the consequences would be disastrous.[328] Although the alleged site of death—where the Rufus Stone now sits—is an open clearing (apart from the odd tree, there were no obstacles to obscure the sightline or deflect the arrows), it would take a bowman of considerable skill (and nerve, given the target) to factor in the undulations of the land, shadows of the setting sun, precise draw for the right trajectory, angle, wind speed, and so forth. A top 'marksman' (familiar with shooting at humans) would be needed to 100% guarantee the result.

5. Friends

The entire hunting party had to be capable of providing an alibi for Henry. Such may have been given unwittingly and innocently as no-one is recorded as

---

[328] The terrible consequences for the plotters in the failed bomb plot by Von Stauffenberg to kill Hitler in July 1945 are clear evidence of what can happen in such circumstances— more than 200 senior personnel and 4,980 people in total, were executed subsequently.

a witness to the actual death. However, it is surely not a coincidence that the party was almost totally composed of loyal family members and a handful of trustworthy friends of the prince who, even if they did suspect foul play, could maintain secrecy from before the event to their graves. With the promise of restoration of bishops, better sheriffs, a revised foreign policy, perhaps money, property and court positions, any supporters (or indeed suspects) would have received varying benefits for their complicity.

6. Enemies

Of all the known members of the hunting party, conveniently the major barons who notionally supported Robert Curthose (and disliked Henry) were absent. Many of these potential antagonists were the very men whose large estates and castles were at the geographic centre of Robin's activities in and around Barnsdale for the last twenty years. With the imminent triumphant return of Duke Robert, many had travelled to the continent and to their Norman estates to await his arrival, where a heightened sense of excitement was building. Those loyal to Robert would hope that he ascended to the throne and thus lighten the burdens imposed upon the Duchy by Rufus. Hence the likes of mega-barons Robert de Lacy, William Count de Mortain, William de Warenne and Robert de Bellême[329] (plus his brothers Arnulf de Montgomery and Roger de Poitou) were not recorded as present that day. If indeed it was premeditated, the timing—and ergo, the names on the hunting party guest list—must surely be counted.

7. The assassin

Obviously, for all the reasons already mentioned, Henry could not carry out the deed himself. The archer had to be capable of remaining unseen before and during his work, disappearing completely afterwards and forever keeping his secret. Ideally he would have some close association to Henry's entourage. Even

---

[329] In 1094 Robert had inherited the family lands in Normandy on his father's death. His younger brother Hugh of Montgomery, inherited the English lands and titles, becoming 2nd Earl of Shrewsbury. 1098 saw the death of brother Hugh with no heir, at which Robert then inherited the English properties as well, making him the wealthiest magnate in both England and Normandy and to become a thorn in King Henry's side until captured and imprisoned by him for life in 1112.

more ideally, he would have a personal agenda for carrying out such—a familial grudge or other strong motive—thus ensuring total confidentiality and anonymity.

In this very period of time—100 years earlier than any previous placement—fulfilling all the above criteria, already operating outside of the law, debatably the country's finest bowman and seemingly impossible to catch…enter our old friend, number one outlaw and half-brother of the Countess Maud Senlis—Robin Hood.

8. The scapegoat

Assuming we have not lost every key contemporary account that recorded Tyrell or another, no-one was named at the time. However, certain figures of authority and influence would not be convinced by an anonymous conclusion, so a potential scapegoat from the hunting party would be needed. Whether volunteering their name out of loyalty to Henry or some other motive, or framed, this scapegoat would ideally not live in England (nor be English or Norman), be able to make a speedy getaway to avoid being questioned, have no major financial assets to confiscate, nor close blood relatives to persecute if things turned sour. So, poor old Frenchman Sir Walter Tyrell, new close friend of the king, plus brother-in-law to the de Clares (and, as I discovered, also a blood relative—see next chapter)—would be the perfect choice.

9. The aftermath

The following days would require a number of people loyal to Henry—both temporal and spiritual—to be in the near vicinity. Equally importantly, we know that the Curthose-favouring noblemen were mostly absent from Winchester when Henry seized the treasury and was proclaimed King.[330] Furthermore, many of the great barons had become independent from the royal court, lending weight to R G Southern's observation that with Curthose approaching—"*the country was ready for a revolution.*"[331] As such, it is unlikely there were enough

---

[330] Their signatures are missing from all key documents, including the Coronation Charter.

[331] *Medieval Humanism*. R. W. Southern, Harper and Row, New York, 1970, p.231. Henry would have been well aware of this and judiciously factored a number of clauses

influencers in situ to constitute a quorum of the Witan (Royal Council). The hereditary right to the Crown was not clear-cut in those days, and being in the right place at the right time provided the advantage. All Henry needed was a nucleus of supporters so that the majority assembled would all declare, in a robust proclamation signifying the continuity of sovereignty and avoidance of an interregnum: "The King is dead! Long live the King!"

Meanwhile, it would not have been difficult for Henry to gain the support of the church. It had suffered so much under Rufus who had even refused to acknowledge the new Pope, Paschal II (Urban having died a year earlier). Anselm, the universally well-regarded, self-exiled Archbishop of Canterbury— and close friend to many in Henry's entourage—could be brought back into favour with the Crown, and vice versa. Henry sorely needed Anselm's support to establish himself firmly as England's new king and for his planned marriage. Plus, if Anselm remained in France he might, even against his will, come under the control of brother Robert and even be forced to obtain papal support for an invasion of England, in precisely the same manner their father had done back in 1066.

---

into his Coronation Charter to benefit the barons, which threw cold water on the flames of revolt. However like modern manifestos, in reality it promised more than it delivered.

Chapter 3
Henry's Inner Circle

With the prerequisites seemingly all in place, let us spend a little time on Henry's years beyond the chamber pot incident, his influences and his key trusted supporters. The 3 main chroniclers to describe the events of his life were William of Malmesbury, Orderic Vitalis and Henry of Huntingdon. Although each held bias, incorporating considerable social and moral commentary into their accounts and using a range of literary devices and inspirations from previous works, we can still extract a fairly detailed picture of the future King.

William of Malmesbury recorded (*Gesta Regum Anglorum*) "*He was of middle stature, greater than the small, but exceeded by the very tall; his hair was black and set back upon the forehead; his eyes mildly bright; his chest brawny; his body fleshy.*" also adding that '*he was sociable and witty, temperate in eating and drinking, casual and informal in speech. He slept soundly and had a most regrettable tendency to snore*'.

Other notable chroniclers I draw from (writing either at the time or in the decades soon after) include Eadmer, John of Worester, Abbot Suger, Geoffery Gaimar, Master Wace and Peter of Blois. In addition, there are a number of surviving royal acts, itineraries, charters, writs and letters that help us to confirm times, places, events and people.

Growing up, it is believed that Henry was close to his younger sister Adela, who was close to him in age (also born post-Conquest), but he was unlikely to have seen much of his brothers, being many years their junior. We have sparse documentation of his early years, but as the youngest royal son, he would likely have been groomed for a career in the church, probably under the tutelage of his father's Chancellor, Bishop Osmund at Salisbury Cathedral. He read Latin and Greek and spoke Norman French. Crucially though, Henry also spoke English, which his brothers did not. Both William of Malmesbury and Orderic Vitalis recorded that, also unlike his brothers (and father), Henry was '*literate and, indeed, well-educated in the liberal arts*'.[332]

While Henry was effectively passed over in the Conqueror's Will, Hollister states:

"*It is reasonable to suppose that Queen Matilda* [of Flanders] *had a special fondness for her young son who bore her uncle's royal name.*"[333]

When she died back in 1083—four years before her husband—the queen left her son, then young teenage Henry, estates in Gloucestershire and Buckinghamshire worth in excess of £300 a year (perhaps £600k+ today). However, he was not yet 'of age' and chronicler Orderic notes that he never took possession of the properties as they were later seized by his older brother—the first of many instances where he was taken advantage of by one or both of them.[334] Experiencing fraternal abuse over the subsequent years, plus left no land or property by his father, it seems fairly inevitable that the clever, determined and scheming Henry—with arguably the most legitimate claim to the throne of England—felt hard done by and wished to take the Crown for himself.

In addition, Henry was, by all accounts, a rather serious character (though highly promiscuous!), who showed enduring support for the church and some semblance of duty towards the English, speaking their language and eventually going on to make reforms, secure general peace over his lands, have 2 long-term marriages to popular, pious wives and father at least 22, mostly illegitimate, children.[335] This was in stark contrast to the recorded follies, abandonment of

---

[332] *Henry I (The English Monarchs Series)*, C. Warren Hollister, Yale University Press, 2003, pp. 34–5. Hollister suggests that Osmund was in part responsible for his education; Henry was consistently in the bishop's company during his formative teenage years, c.1080–1086.

[333] Ibid. p.40. Her uncle was King Henry I of France.1008–1060.

[334] According to Orderic, in 1088, after the Conqueror's death, Henry journeyed to England to ask Rufus to grant him custody of his mother's lands left to him in her will, but Rufus instead granted them to his great friend Robert Fitzhaimo, son of the sheriff of Kent, as reward for his support in the recent unsuccessful Barons revolt against him.

[335] In addition to his two legitimate children from first wife Edith (William and Matilda), Henry is believed to have had as many as 20–24 illegitimate offspring by various mistresses both before and after his marriage. One lover was the great beauty of the age, the Welsh Princess Nest, who gave birth to his son Henry FitzRoy in 1103. Henry did

bishoprics and dubious bachelor status of his French-speaking brother Rufus, which surely grated on young Henry. As William of Malmesbury noted on the *'troops of pathics and droves of harlots'* who followed Rufus's court:

> "*...It was said with justice, by a wise man, that England would be fortunate if Henry could reign, because he abhorred obscenity from his youth.*"

Little wonder Henry gained loyal support in some quarters. I count 10 key figures close to and trusted by him who may well have assisted him with his New Forest plans. Most of them were either on the hunt or at the hunting lodge that day. Of course, with early medieval history we have paucity of information working against us. There are a few scraps about the lives of these people, but we cannot truly peer into their characters, or be sure of the motives behind their actions. In a world where 50-year-old men married 12-year-old girls, where slavery, executions, blindings and trial-by-combat were commonplace, where feudal servitude, disease, famine, prophesies, hermits, witchcraft, constant warring, death from childbirth or even septicaemia from a tooth abscess, plus the overbearing power of the church and fear of God, Heaven, Hell and Purgatory were all just part of daily life. Unlike the more secular times we live in today, there was almost universal, unconditional and total belief in Christianity, such that trying to place ourselves into the mind-set of an 11th century person is extremely difficult. However, these 10 people held a number of direct links and family connections that have not been discussed in detail before. It is only circumstantial evidence, but from 10 torches you get a strong light. I am convinced that they add up to something, well, convincing.

1. Gilbert de Clare

Gilbert had already twice rebelled against Rufus, the second time specifically involving the king's planned murder. From all we know of him, it is not too much of a step to believe that he would have been involved in a third much more intricate and successful plot against the king some 5 years later, especially with his close family connections to both Bec Abbey and Anselm. With his father's

---

not dally with harlots and his sexual conquests were always highborn Norman and English, often married, women. Many of the bastard sons were educated by Henry's confidante Robert Bloet, Bishop-Baron of Lincoln.

punishment and eventual death at the hands of Rufus c.1090, it fits that Gilbert was Henry's key collaborator and planner, if not the instigator.[336] Importantly, he is recorded as being on the hunt that day, along with his brother Roger. How he managed to stay in favour with Rufus is remarkable—one can only imagine that the king believed in the phrase, *"Keep your friends close and your enemies closer,"* especially those from such powerful families. However, to attempt rebellion and regicide a third time, surely with unpardonable consequences if it failed, Gilbert would have needed to devise and/or only been convinced by a secure, well-laid plan. Such would require the involvement of his close family members and trusted associates.

2. Roger de Clare

Of Gilbert's 4 brothers, he seems to have been closest to the eldest, Roger, who never married or had children. Roger had inherited the family lands and title of Bienfaite and Orbec in Normandy after their father's death in 1090 (while Gilbert gained those in England at Tonbridge in Kent and Clare in Suffolk). William of Malmesbury concluded that Tyrell had assistance with his escape, noting that *'some helped his flight'*. I strongly suspect that this came from Roger de Clare, who does not appear on any document in the subsequent days, but was on the hunt with Gilbert and Rufus that day and seems to just disappear. He was well placed to help and had the key role in spiriting Tyrell away to Normandy and their castle at Orbec near Bec Abbey.

3. Richard de Clare

Younger brother Richard had been a monk at Bec Abbey since 1080 and may very well have conveyed the news of Rufus' demise from Roger and Tyrell to Archbishop Anselm, whom he knew well, some 300 miles to the south where he resided in exile. In fact, the close association between all these figures to Bec Abbey, plus their friendship with Anselm, are 2 key elements that prove to be the very centre of my theory, so I ask that you keep both in mind as they are discussed throughout.

---

[336] Gilbert and Prince Henry were about the same age, Gilbert born c.1065 and Henry c.1068 and in their mid-30's in 1100 and having known each other since childhood.

4. William Giffard

Brother of the de Clare siblings' mother Rohese, their uncle William Giffard was Rufus's Lord Chancellor. His father, Walter Giffard, was one of the 15 documented 'proven' companions of William the Conqueror at the Battle of Hastings.[337] William Giffard was nominally a cleric, as he was Dean of Rouen and a close friend of Archbishop Anselm. Although not thought to be on the hunt itself, he was probably in the general hunting party at the lodge (or just 20 miles away at Winchester Castle) as his signature appears on key documents such as the Coronation Charter (also called the Charter of Liberties) and the letter recalling Anselm from exile, both signed and sent out just 2 or 3 days later. He was also immediately appointed by Henry to the vacant position of Bishop of Winchester and is believed to have been responsible for the burial of Rufus on Friday the 3rd August. He stayed on as Henry's Lord Chancellor for a few months until his replacement, Roger of Salisbury, was fully up to speed. He is described in the Winchester annals as a man of patience, piety, and gentleness which together suggest he must have found working for Rufus very difficult indeed.

Giffard's brother-in-law was Richard FitzGilbert de Clare (sister Rohese's late husband and father of the de Clare boys). A close companion and distant cousin of the Conqueror, Richard had fought at Hastings with Walter Giffard, and he was richly rewarded as a result. As mentioned earlier, he suffered greatly at the hands of Rufus in the 1087 rebellion and died in 1091, locked away in St Neots Priory (a satellite of Bec Abbey refounded by himself and his wife in 1081). As such, William Giffard, his sister and the whole de Clare family had good reason to support Rufus's demise.

5. and 6. Simon de Senlis and his wife Maud

As discussed in Part I but crucial here too, Maud was second cousin to the 3 royal brothers. Her mother, Judith de Lens, was their first cousin (daughter of the Conqueror's sister Adelaide (Adeliza)).

Following a likely shared education with her sister Alice at Elstow Abbey, Maud married Simon in c.1090 when about 18 years old. Although there is no

---

[337] *Gesta Guillelmi II Ducis Normannorum* (The Deeds of William II, Duke of the Normans), William of Poitiers, published c.1071–1077.

suggestion that she was ever Henry's lover, given his charisma and outrageous track record in collecting mistresses (married or otherwise), there was always a chance, especially as a young, bright and beautiful woman with an ageing husband. They were close enough in age (she was about 4 years his junior), family and rank that she would certainly have been well-acquainted with him at the royal court. Furthermore, as a similarly convent-educated aristocrat, it is inevitable that Maud was also a friend of Henry's future wife, the young Anglo-Scottish Princess Edith (later re-named Queen Matilda, aged about 20 in 1100) who is thought to have attended the royal court for a few years once she left Romsey and Wilton Abbeys. Edith had a number of siblings—among them was the then King of Scotland, Edgar, and also Prince David. The latter took Maud as his wife some years later (after Simon Senlis died c.1112), and became his Scottish queen later still, in 1124, when David inherited the Crown.

With her father, Waltheof, mercilessly executed by the Conqueror, his irreligious son on the throne, and his younger, English-speaking son likely to restore many of the ideals and figures she missed (including Archbishop Anselm), the devout Maud had strong feudal, political, religious and personal reasons to be involved…she could also prove very useful in what, or rather who, she could bring to the party.

As for husband Simon, he had come to England from France (not Normandy) after the Conquest (maybe not even until the late 1080s as he receives no mention in Domesday) as a 'soldier of fortune' and was eventually, as we know, well-rewarded by Rufus with assets previously held by Waltheof (and Judith), namely the earldom and lands of Northampton. The Conqueror had, of course, originally intended him to be the new husband of his niece, Waltheof's widow, Judith de Lens (Maud's mother) but had been rejected with her excuse of his 'lameness'. Simon must, unquestionably, have had the finest pedigree, perhaps, I venture, some royal French blood in his veins; as to be offered the king's niece in marriage has all the look of a political union organised by William to maintain smooth relations with the French Crown. He was certainly mightily furious with Judith when it did not take place. Simon does not appear in *Domesday*, so no earlier than 1088/89, he was finally granted (by the new King Rufus) a prised English Earldom, Northampton estates plus the hand of Maud (Rufus's 2nd cousin) in marriage, all implying he was of the highest social standing.

So, although late to the party and initially one of the Conqueror's men, Simon evidently remained in royal favour with Rufus after the Conqueror's death, very probably helping him quell the 1088 barons rebellion, being granted the Earldom of Northampton and the hand of 19yr old Countess Maud, c.1090, as reward for his support. He fought on the side of Rufus in Maine and the Vexin in 1098, when he was taken prisoner by the forces of 18-year-old Prince Louis, son of King Philip of France.[338] Highly regarded by Rufus, Simon was ransomed or exchanged for important French prisoners captured by the Normans, as was quite commonplace at that time, as capturing important prisoners was far better than killing them. By the following year, he was free and back in England though described by Sir William Palgrave as now *'lame, decrepit, yet still active'*. [339]

As Rufus's trusted advisor, brave soldier and much-admired military commander, Simon would naturally have been wary of any plot, but this one, exceptionally, he may have been influenced by his formidable wife Maud and close friends. Furthermore, his inherent loyalty to the Conqueror passed only by default to his son Rufus. The new King, with wild intentions of enlarging his empire, likely did not sit well with the older, wiser Simon, but in such politically precarious times, he would have had little choice but to follow him. While probably quite happy to fight against territories like Maine, Anjou and Poitou, his close family connections at Senlis to the French monarchy likely made his recent military involvement for Rufus in the royal lands of the Vexin feel very uncomfortable. On a personal level, by 1100, Simon and Maud had 3 young children and he had been able to spend time with his family for the previous year or so since peace had prevailed following the end of the Vexin campaign and his release as a prisoner. He was no spring chicken and Rufus was about to drag him off to the continent again for a new campaign in France of indeterminate length and danger. Simon's enthusiasm for further conflict, particularly against the French monarch (his country/king of heritage), can surely be questioned. We know that the hereditary family estate at Senlis, where his elder brother Garner resided, was in the Île-de-France, close to Paris and in that part of the country directly controlled by King Philip and where the French monarchs hunted.[340]

---

[338] *William Rufus*, E.A. Freeman, vol ii. Oxford Clarendon Press, 1882. p,190

[339] *The History of Normandy and England, Vol.4 , 'Accession of Henry Beauclerc',* Sir Francis Palgrave, Macmillan, 1864, p.691. (Palgrave was Deputy Keeper of Her Majesty's Public Records')

[340] Simon de Senlis's father was Landri de Senlis, Lord of Ermonville and Chantilly, two forests, between which lies the town of Senlis, situated on the river Nonette about 25 miles north of Paris in the Île-de-France. The monarchs of the early French dynasties

If the planned invasion was cancelled, he could instead stay at his castle in Northampton with his young family, build his monastery, expand the town and plan his pilgrimage to Jerusalem (all of which, following Henry's accession, it is recorded he later undertook). It could be said that, like Walter Tyrell, he maybe retrospectively had some scruple of conscience and expiated his share in the murder with a trip of redemption to the Holy Land, a penitential pilgrimage, seeking salvation, forgiveness of sins and a route to heaven.

If the assumption is correct, that Simon was malcontent or at least malleable, he would have had regular opportunity to meet with young Prince Louis during the 1098–9 Vexin campaign during his subsequent months of 'imprisonment' (more likely as a comfortable captive of the French court). Perhaps there, the early outlines of a plot were hatched that would equally serve the French monarchy. Certainly, Simon was at the very heart of the English government, witnessing charters on a regular basis, and had every chance to recruit potential supporters to the cause of Henry. Like Giffard, it seems that Simon was also either at the hunting lodge or Winchester Castle on 2nd August, but is not mentioned specifically as attending the hunt itself.

7. Eudo Dapifer[341] (sometimes Eudo FitzHubert)

Senior steward and Officer of State to Rufus, plus brother-in-law of the de Clares (being married to their sister Rohese), Eudo certainly had influence. As chief steward (probably in his mid-fifties), he was undoubtedly at the lodge that day to support Rufus in his official business when not hunting (the most senior steward, elderly Haimo Dapifer was very ill at this time, probably with cancer, dying just a month or 2 later). Of all the Norman administrators and landowners, Eudo stands out, not only as an astute and sagacious politician, but also as one of the very few Norman barons who endeared himself to his English vassals (unlike his unpleasant brother, Ralph FitzHubert, erstwhile Castellan of Nottingham Castle). A known favourite of Prince Henry, a great benefactor of

---

lived in Senlis, attracted by the proximity for hunting in the two forests. Simon's family was undoubtedly close, possibly blood related, to the French royal Capetian dynasty as the town of Senlis itself is where the royal house was first established in 987.

[341] Eudo's unofficial surname stems from his position as a steward or server which, in Latin, is 'dapifer'. The 'Dapifer' was considered the key officer of the royal household being the king's chief administrator and executive officer.

Bec Abbey and, significantly, particularly close to Archbishop Anselm,[342] he was certainly quick to support the new King—signing Henry's Coronation Charter, just 3 days later and received enormous largesse as a result of his loyal support.

8. Walter Tyrell III

There are 5 scribes we know of who later referred to Walter Tyrell as the man who shot the arrow that killed the king, accidentally or otherwise. They were—in approximate date order—William of Malmesbury (*Gesta Regum Anglorum*, c.1125), Orderic Vitalis (*Historia Ecclesiastica*, c.1127–30), Henry of Huntingdon (*Historia Anglorum*, 1135–54), Geoffrey Gaimar (*L'Estoire des Engleis*—History of the English People—c.1136–1140) and Master Wace (1160–75). The last on the list was an Anglo-Norman poet who featured Tyrell in his epic, detailing the history of the Dukes of Normandy, *La Roman de Rou* (The Romance of Rollo), which was commissioned by Henry II. However, it is well accepted by modern historians that medieval writers referencing earlier English history relied heavily on copying the efforts of their previous counterparts, with an early chronicler naming Tyrell subsequently being just copied and repeated. As such, just how much these scribes had copied one another or was truly original research done by them, e.g. interviewing surviving witnesses and checking facts, is questionable as their sources are never given.

Walter Tyrell III (born c.1060) was the brother-in-law to the de Clare boys, being married to their sister Alice (Adeliza). A French knight, his family name derived from Tirel on the banks of the Seine in the Vexin,[343] although his own family home was in Picardy (a vassal state of the Kingdom of France), 70 miles to the north, where he was Lord of Poix. (As part of the marriage dowry of Alice Clare, her father, Richard, gave Walter the Lordship of his valuable manor of Langham in Essex that Walter held for his entire life—see later footnote 509). Various genealogy sources demonstrate that the Tyrell lineage stretched back to the noble families of Normandy, while the full family history shows that they

---

[342] *Magnates and Curiales*, W. Hollister, Viator. Vol. 8, University of California Press. 1977.

[343] Today this place is called Triel-sur-Seine, 4 miles from Meulan, 7 miles from Achères, 12 miles from Pontoise and just 25 miles from Paris.

were of Norman, French and English extraction, with some references even suggesting Walter was born in England.

Significant to our story, according to numerous genealogical resources, Walter's mother, Ann, was a daughter of Gilbert, Count of Brionne—precursor to the de Clare family name. Equally significantly, the de Clare siblings' father, Richard de Clare, was a son of the same Gilbert (but from a different mother, as Gilbert married twice) thus being Ann's half-sister. Sharing the same grandfather, Walter Tyrell and the de Clare siblings were therefore half-cousins (as well as being brothers-in-law) and Walter's mother would have been half-aunt to the de Clare children. So, to answer the question that might reasonably be asked—How come this English noblewoman, Alice de Clare, is married to (or even knew) the French Castellan of Pontoise castle?—she was his half-first cousin! Strangely, given its importance, this glaring omission of the direct blood link between the Tyrells and the de Clares is not mentioned (or observed?) by Freeman, Hollister, Barlow, Mason, Grinnell-Milne or any other significant historian in their analyses of Rufus's death.[344]

On his father's side, Walter's great-grandfather was Fulk Tyrell, who became the Seigneur of Guernanville and Dean of Evreux. Walter's grandfather, Fulk's son Walter I (one of 8 sons, died c.1080), is understood to have been married to a Saxon lady called Olga and his own father, Walter II, predeceased his grandfather, dying around 1069 when his son, Walter III, was only about 9. Little is known of either of Walter I or II, but Walter I is believed to have fought bravely at Hastings (maybe with his son) and it is even suggested he is depicted on the Bayeux Tapestry, but which exact figure is unknown. No doubt Walter I was well rewarded, but given both he and his son died prior to the *Domesday* survey, they do not appear within and young Walter III, who was maybe back in France and a minor, clearly did not inherit any English family estates, which must have reverted to the crown or been redistributed. However, through his 3 x great-grandfather, on his mother's side, Robert I (and maybe even links on his paternal side)—the family does appear to have had genetic connections with the royalty in question.[345]

---

[344] See Appendices 9 and 9a for the full Giffard/Clare/Tyrell/Brionne family tree details and their bloodline link to William the Conqueror himself.

[345] Walter I and Robert I's relationship is recorded in *The Charter of the Primal Church of Rouen,* 1030. This extract taken from '*Further genealogical notes on the Tyrrell-*

Walter Tyrell III was noted as a good friend of Rufus. What is more likely is that with his Clare connections, he was 'bought' by Rufus, either defecting his loyalty from France to England with the promise of riches or seemingly switching sides in order to protect his own interests, as noted by historian David Crouch he was:

"...seemingly one of those French border knights who abandoned King Philip for Rufus during the campaign of 1098."[346]

Whether this defection was before or after the Vexin truce of 1099 is unknown. However, historian Emma Mason makes a strong case that Tyrell defected willingly in order to act as a double agent, in cahoots with his cousin and brother-in-law Gilbert de Clare, as an agent of Prince Henry.[347] Mason believes that, together with the French monarchy, a plan was devised to infiltrate Walter into the court of Rufus and provide intelligence back to Paris. Indeed, the possible involvement of Prince Louis (on behalf of his father King Philip) and the French connections of many of the plotters is worth further note, to be considered in the next chapter.

His family home in Poix was in Picardy not Normandy, (at the time part of the Kingdom of France being ruled by King Philip, as the Countship of Amiens that encompassed Picardy was vacant—the Count being on the 1st Crusade), where significantly Tyrell was recorded as a friend of Anselm[348] and hosted a visit from the Archbishop c.1094/5.[349] However, it seems they spent most time at his other property in Achères in the Vexin (also part of France) and in the castle accommodation in Pontoise, where Walter was the castle governor, the

---

Terrell family of Virginia and its English and Norman progenitors'. Edwin H. Terrell, 2nd. edition with Addenda and Corrigenda, San Antonio, Texas, 1909, p.11.

[346] *The Normans*, D Crouch, 2007, p.154.

[347] *William II, Rufus, the Red King*, Emma Mason, 2005, ch.8.

[348] *Vita Anselmi*, Eadmer: Ed. Paris, 1721, p.6.

[349] *Anselm—a Biography*, J M Rigg, Methuen, 1896, p.41. Tyrell put on a banquet but there was a shortage of fish. Anselm assured his host that more fish was on the way and a short while later two men appeared carrying a large, freshly-caught sturgeon.

castellan,[350] working under Prince Louis and, due to Norman incursions, his presence was almost constantly required.

In addition to having a Saxon grandmother and an Anglo-Norman wife of a powerful dynasty, Walter III was a Lord, not only of Poix but also of Achères, just fifteen miles north-west of Paris. As castellan of Pontoise castle, just 7 miles north of Achères, significantly Walter and his family had the hereditary right to land and a key position within the French court in the capital of the Vexin province. With fingers in so many pies, he would have been a vital asset to Rufus's court and military plans, indeed, a great 'coup' to convert him to the Norman side. According to Orderic, at the time of his death, the king considered Tyrell '*his constant companion*'. If Mason and others are to be believed, Walter had played his part well.

9. and 10. Robert and Henry Beaumont

And finally, in the royal party at the lodge, but not on the hunt, were the 2 mature Beaumont brothers. By 1100, Robert Beaumont, Count of Meulan (55, later 1st Earl of Leicester and sometimes called Robert de Meulan) and his brother, Henry Beaumont (52, 1st Earl of Warwick and later, Lord of Gower) were 2 of the most senior and trusted statesmen to the Crown. Although they were unlikely to be party to the specifics of any advanced scheming, given their actions at the time and thereafter, it seems very likely that they had been brought into the fold.

Robert was one of the last survivors of the Conquest generation having fought bravely as a young man, and one of 15 proven companions of the Conqueror at the Battle of Hastings more than thirty years earlier. He impressed contemporary peers with his unbroken prosperity under successive kings, by his steady advance in wealth and power '*while those around him were being ruined*',[351] and, above all, by his unerring astuteness. '*A cold and crafty statesman... the Achitophel of his time*', scribed Henry of Huntingdon, "*Sapientissimus omnium hinc usque in Jerusalem*" [the wisest man from here to Jerusalem] and, "*Persuader of peace, dissuader of strife... as though the oracle of God had been consulted,*" declared William of Malmesbury. These were

---

[350] Once widowed, Alice Tyrell later became a nun and died at the Priory of Conflans in 1139, a daughter house of Bec Abbey, just three miles from both Achères and Pontoise.
[351] *Ecclesiastical History*, Orderic Vitalis, Book xi, Volume vi.

impressive plaudits and although described as loyal to his king, Rufus's vacillations, treatment of the church and general lifestyle conduct may have shaken Robert's loyalty. Or perhaps he was merely loyal to whomever was in power or favour...In 1112, he made a grant of lands to Bec Abbey[352] '*for the souls of the Conqueror and his wife Matilda, Henry I, his wife (also) Matilda and children, plus his own parents, wife, children, brother Henry and family*'. Pointedly, any reference to honouring the late King William Rufus's soul was glaringly omitted.

In the aftermath of Rufus's death, Robert's younger brother, Henry, proved a key figure when there was division among the barons who had gathered at the door of the treasury in Winchester to secure Crown money and choose a successor. It was mainly owing to his advice and impassioned speech that Henry was selected. In the year following Henry's coronation, many of the most powerful barons who had large estates in Normandy (and were absent on the day of the hunt), were openly or secretly disloyal, supporting the attempt of Robert Curthose, now Duke of Normandy again, to gain the Crown of England. The Beaumont brothers, the new King's foremost advisors, were among the few that remained faithful to him.

It is worth noting that, ostensibly, some of this list of 10 (those who held high positions in Court) would be loyal to Rufus...but not everything is always as it seems. For a moment, let us exclude Maud, whose sole task may have been to recruit the country's best bowman, and Richard de Clare, who resided as a monk in Normandy far from the action. Of the remaining 8, 5 were well over 50, leaving just Gilbert, his brother Roger and Walter Tyrell in their mid- to late-30s. Additionally, 6 were married with children (all except Walter Giffard and brother Roger). As senior government advisors and religious men (Giffard was a Dean), who founded Benedictine houses, supported Bec Abbey and were loyal to the exiled Archbishop Anselm, I am convinced that none of the 8 would have happily rubbed shoulders with the young, half-naked, long haired effete of Rufus's court or associated with the troupe of pathics, catamites and harlots surrounding them. Undoubtedly, the conduct of the king and his entourage, plus the lavish royal expenditure, would have been met with disapproval or disguised disgust.

---

[352] This was for the foundation of Chisenbury Priory in Wiltshire, a cell of Bec Abbey, of which nothing now remains.

In a period of frequent revolt, one can see how the scheming duo of the youngest royal brother and the twice-rebellious Gilbert may have presented a very convincing argument for the dispatch of Rufus and the crowning of Henry. This group of potential plotters had close ties by blood and marriage and much to gain…their friend Anselm returned to Canterbury, the European invasion cancelled, bishops and abbots re-appointed, and power-hungry local sheriffs removed (often as big a bugbear to the barons as to the villeins)—let alone promises of further lands, titles and positions of power. It would have been as easy to sell as any act of treason could ever be.

11. The fatal addition?

For all this to truly make sense, there must have been another person in the shadows, debatably the only one who could turn the plot into reality. At least on the surface of things, my Robin Hood was the perfect choice to carry out this infamous deed. Of course, no-one has connected the dots before because no other study places the legendary outlaw in this time frame or this specific geography. Before we get to the physical evidence, let's look at the possible incentives and motives for Robin:

(1)   Familial motivations

As I have already theorised, Maud (now aged 27/8), Countess of Huntingdon and wife of Rufus's advisor and militarist Simon Senlis, was Robin's half-sister. The killing of Rufus would have provided Robin with the opportunity to settle their family feud and avenge their father's death by beheading, in true Anglo-Danish blood-feud style. On that note, one might think that both siblings would have wanted Henry dead as much as Rufus, but feuds were complicated. For example, during their father's 1074 massacre of the sons and grandsons of Carl, a favoured few were spared.[353] Henry possessed much more agreeable characteristics and a positive vision for their country and countrymen. He was also preferable to Robert Curthose (see next entry below)

---

[353] Although 1100 is now 24 years after the death of Waltheof, which may seem a long time, it should be remembered that Waltheof's massacre, finally ending his family feud in 1074, was 36 years after the murder of his grandfather Ealdred in 1038 and 58 years after the feud started with the murder of his great-grandfather, Uchtred, in 1016.

(2)   Personal motivations

Robin was undoubtedly aware that the 4 oppressive baronial powers dominating his homestead of Loxley and the English peasants of Barnsdale and environs—namely de Mortain, de Bellême, de Lacy and Warenne—would support Robert Curthose as, to a man, they loathed Henry, such that there was a mutuality of detestation between him and Robin for this quartet. They would be quashed should Henry assume the crown.

Additionally, he and his 'merry' men would likely receive a full royal pardon for all previous crimes. In 1100, Robin would have been in his early 40s, no doubt worn out after 20 years of outlawry and living wild. If betterment could be achieved with one well-aimed arrow, and he and his men could retire as 'freemen' and yeomen of substance, this offer would be hard to turn down.

(3)   Financial motivations

There was every chance that Robin would be provided with cash or a pension for his fatal bow skills, perhaps even land with the Lordship of Hallam. He could use the money to help the loyal poor of Barnsdale and those of Waltheof's hereditary estates, including his maternal village of Loxley, that were now in the hands of his stepmother Judith and her tenant Roger de Busli II. While of very little worth to Judith and/or Maud,[354] gaining Hallam would have had significant familial value to Robin and mean that justice had been served.

(4)   Patriotic motivations

Henry planned to clear out the corrupt shrieval government, reduce the crippling levels of taxation (guaranteed if the planned invasion of France was

---

[354] Judith, Maud and Simon between them had very lucrative estates, those near London such as Walthamstow, Edmonton and Tottenham, were together worth over £100 pa and hence they were able to be generous sponsors of Elstow Abbey and other monastic foundations. Meanwhile, Hallam, despite comprising several hamlets, would have been only around £2 pa.

cancelled), soften the Forest Laws and that of Murdrum, plus return to the laws of Edward the Confessor, subject only to amendments made by the Conqueror.[355]

(5) Political/National motivations

In 1100, Henry was set to marry Anglo-Scottish Princess Edith (later name changed to Matilda), the daughter of King Malcolm III of Scotland and Margaret of Wessex and great-granddaughter of Edmund Ironside. If Henry were King, their marriage would restore the original royal Saxon bloodline, the House of Wessex, to the English Crown, currently usurped by that of a Norman. Their union would also strengthen the bonds between the kingdoms of England and Scotland. Even more remarkable, if Suthen, wife of King Duncan I of Scotland, had indeed been the sister of Siward the Great (as most modern academics suggest), then she would have been both Edith's grandmother and Robin's great-aunt! (see Part I, chapter 4 and Appendices 2.1 and 2.2). To be precise this would make Princess Edith and Robin second cousins and she will soon be Queen of England![356]

Here was a unique chance to make a real difference, rather than just highway robbery—to remove an ungodly, uncouth, money-grabbing king, with a famous disdain for the local English culture and bring an end to an unjust 13-year reign. In his stead, the nation would see the crowning of a fairer King with a unifying wife as his queen—a royal blood relative no less—and the re-establishment of the church in England under the reputable and popular Archbishop Anselm, a man whose devout love and worship of the Virgin Mary, emphasising virtue, especially virginity, and intent upon achieving salvation, even exceeded that of Robin's.

Any combination of these would have created a tempting package for Robin. If my theory is correct, there would be little difficulty persuading him to make the journey down to Hampshire that summer, the same journey, I am convinced, he had made a quarter of century earlier when his father was imprisoned for months in Winchester Castle, before being led out to his execution.

---

[355] In reality, when it came to matters of taxation and the Forest Laws, Henry was not that much better than his brother—like leaders from time immemorial, promising more than ever delivered.

[356] This also made Edith's father, Malcolm III Canmore, King of Scotland from 1058 to 1093, Robin's first cousin, once removed.

Connected by Henry's second cousin—Robin's half-sister Maud—the nation's most formidable archer, ambusher and notoriously elusive outlaw, would be the perfect assassin and not a word would pass his lips.

Chapter 4
The Other Suspects

Rather like an Agatha Christie novel, there are many possible suspects who had motive for killing Rufus—ranging from a disgruntled and displaced New Forest peasant/poacher to a random disaffected noble or royal forester with a grudge and even an assassin 'at *the request of Archbishop Anselm and the persuasion of a fanatical monk*'.[357] It is easy to get lost in a sea of accusations and scenarios, but we should try to brush away the smoke and mirrors and see what is left.[358] Although the above declaration is somewhat fanciful, it does demonstrate an almost contemporary view that the church was under suspicion. The French monarchy has also been thrown into the spotlight recently by Dr Emma Mason[359], with salient arguments. Certainly, both institutions would have benefited greatly from a change of kingship. Hundreds of miles away in France, there is little practical reason to suggest that the exiled Anselm or King Philip

---

[357] *History and Antiquities of the County of Essex,* Philip Morant, 1768, Printed for T. Osborne [etc.], London, Vol.1, p.208. In his book, Morant explains that this unnamed monk was 'an assertion of Alain de Lille c.1120–1202, renowned French theologian, writer and poet, better known as le Docteur Universel, who lived not long after the event and who argued that sodomy was one of the most serious sins, since it called forth the Wrath of God' and was perhaps the first chronicler to actually state that, in his opinion, the death of Rufus was caused by treachery.

[358] Theories abound to this day of conspiracies involving a whole raft of suspects in the death of John F. Kennedy—they include the CIA/FBI, or rogue elements thereof, the Mafia, the military/industrial complex, Cuba and Castro, Russia and the KGB, the Vatican and even Lyndon Johnson, Kennedy's vice-president who succeeded him. Many suggest Lee Harvey Oswald was set up as a 'patsy' and had to be eliminated as soon as possible afterwards—which he was.

[359] *William II, Rufus, the Red King,* Emma Mason, Tempus 2005.

(or his son Prince Louis) had actual blood on their hands, but their involvement should be questioned.

It is most likely that the tight-knit cabal detailed earlier were the only ones who knew what was going to unfold that summer's evening. However, Henry would have used his shrewd political judgement, guided by Giffard, Gilbert and Roger de Clare, plus the very experienced Beaumonts, to anticipate how support might develop on his behalf in the event of his brother's 'accidental' death. With many believing that Robert Curthose should and would be King, Henry crucially needed his claim for the throne to be recognised by the English Church, the Pope and the French Crown.

Apart from the close familial and geographic connections between the plotters, there are 2 other threads binding them together that we have already touched upon briefly; namely their long-term friendship with Archbishop Anselm, and their links to the French monarchy. When we weave all these threads together, as we are about to, it looks as though the Prince and plotters— either directly or indirectly—may have already brought these 2 most influential parties into the fold, perhaps best summed up by F. Parker:

"...There are many signs which go to indicate, not merely that William Rufus was slain of malice, but that there existed a powerful and elaborately organised conspiracy to compass his death."[360]

The Church

As upholders of morality and the sanctity of life, on the surface of things, the church would have been the least likely party involved in an assassination, though it must be remembered that at this time it was a body almost as powerful in the temporal sphere as the monarchy. Bishops were quite able to raise armies and even fight in battles! However, we already know, individual clerics (both decent and self-serving) and the institution as a whole, held Rufus in disregard and would have been relieved by his removal. The King's irreligious behaviour, an unexplained sympathy for Jewish people (in a highly antisemitic era[361]), his

---

[360] *The Forest Laws and the Death of William Rufus*, F. H. M. Parker, 1912, *English Historical Review*, Vol. xxvii, p.32.

[361] Rufus seemed to realise that the Jews were most useful to him when as a community they were left unhampered to simply get on with business, generating credit, facilitating

refusal to acknowledge the current Pope, his treatment of senior ecclesiastics and constant financial attacks on respected religious institutions all add up to provide strong motive, even if nothing can be proven. The official reaction of the church to Rufus's untimely death—proclaiming consistently and widely that it was preordained by God—must come with a whiff of suspicion. Did it extend to something deeper and darker? There is a tranche of evidence to suggest that key clergymen were aware of the king's impending demise which, if true, meant they were complicit in its cover-up.[362]

Let us focus for a moment upon the church's most influential figure in this drama. In 1078, Anselm was unanimously elected as Bec's new abbot following the death of its founder, Herluin. Under his direction, Bec became the most respected seat of learning in Europe, with students coming from France, Italy and elsewhere. In 1089 after the death of Lanfranc, the then Archbishop of Canterbury, Rufus refused to fill the position for nearly 4 years, taking all incomes for himself and imposing vicious tax regimes on religious establishments. It was not until his near-fatal illness in 1093 that he hastily appointed the popular and respected Anselm (who stubbornly tried to resist taking the post but under great pressure, failed) in a bid to save himself. This he regretted, as they were at loggerheads thereafter (Barlow described their relationship as a 'black comedy', *William Rufus,* p.301), with Anselm supporting Pope Urban II, who opposed the traditional claim of European monarchs to control ecclesiastical appointments, while Rufus favoured the anti-pope Clement III, who did not. Their hostilities, finding it impossible to work with each other (which bore similarities to the later notorious 12th century feud between Henry

trade and freely building up individual wealth. This created ever greater royal tax bases throughout the kingdom, and a reliable stash of ready-capital resided in the Jewish community whenever needed by the king. Rufus managed to prevent, in England, the massacres of Jews that occurred in Rouen, and across France and the Rhineland, in the bloody frenzy that preceded the departure of the First Crusade in 1096.

[362] If connections to a plot were strong enough, they may even have been guilty of an early form of high treason under the uncodified pre-Norman common laws and erratic feudal court judgements of the period (later codified into the Treason Act of 1351), though 11th century royal justice was usually dispensed somewhat more summarily.

II and Thomas Becket) culminated in Anselm's self-imposed exile in 1097, when Rufus yet again took the incomes of Canterbury for himself.[363]

Among the wilder conspiracy theories, Anselm was a rejected lover of Rufus and had him killed as a result. Barlow is quite certain that Anselm clearly disliked the king's company, in addition to which, in 1100, they had not seen each other for nearly 3 years, so this all seems rather far-fetched. However, many of Anselm's early letters and poems—written to monks, male relatives and others—contained passionate expressions of attachment and affection, typically addressed to *dilecto dilectori* [beloved lover]. These missives have led to debate among academics. Some believe them to be symbols of his homosexuality, some that they stem from a pure spiritual affection and Anselm simply considered that human love and divinity were closely interwoven ideas. Either way, there is wide agreement that Anselm was committed to monastic celibacy.

Moving from assumptions to proof, there are many documented connections between the suspected plotters, Anselm and Bec Abbey. Indeed, the evidence is strong enough to suspect his involvement and other connected religious personnel. Prince Henry, the de Clares, Giffards, Beaumonts, Tyrells, Senlis, Princesses Edith and Mary (and their aunt Christina at Romsey Abbey) were all noted as close friends of Anselm.[364] We even have that record of Walter Tyrell entertaining Anselm at his home in Poix.[365] The day after Rufus was killed, Henry sent a letter to Anselm recalling him to the Archbishopric of Canterbury that had lain vacant since his exile—proof of both his trust in Anselm and his tactics to ensure brother Robert would not purloin the cleric's loyalty for himself.

---

[363] Anselm left England to petition the Pope for his judgement on the situation but unfortunately, he'd picked the worst time to drag Pope Urban II into the English situation. At the time, Pope Urban was preoccupied with his own issues with the anti-Pope, Clement III, so rather than make William into an enemy, Urban actually turned his back on the Archbishop and took William's side resulting in Anselm's continued exile until the death of Rufus, though Urban himself died a year prior, in late July, 1099, just after the capture of Jerusalem, which he may just have known about on his deathbed.

[364] The one exception here was Robert de Beaumont, who, for a period in the 1090's, had a well-known rivalry and hostility to Anselm, brought on while Robert was loyalty acting for Rufus in the on-going dispute in the late 1090s whereby Anselm's vision of a universal Church with its own internal authority, clashed with Rufus' desire for royal control over both church and state. However, they did bury the hatchet prior to Henry's accession,

[365] see footnote 349.

In the letter, Henry made it clear he was prepared to abandon Rufus's policies on the church and pledged to submit himself to the archbishop's counsel and in return Anselm publicly supported Henry against the claims and threatened invasion of his brother Robert Curthose. Anselm wooed wavering barons to the king's cause, emphasising the religious nature of their oaths and duty of loyalty; he also supported the deposition of Ranulf Flambard, the disloyal new bishop of Durham; and he even threatened Duke Robert with excommunication. Anselm was also a close friend of Rohese de Clare (née Giffard), mother of the de Clare siblings who, along with her late husband Richard, had refounded the Benedictine St Neots Priory in 1079 and its first monks had been sent there from Bec Abbey by Anselm, abbot at that time.

Perhaps Anselm's deepest admirer was the future Queen Matilda, then Princess Edith (i.e. prior to her name change after marriage). Her father, Malcolm III Canmore, King of the Scots, and her eldest brother Edward, had both died in their ill-fated struggle with Rufus at the Battle of Alnwick back in 1093. Her mother Margaret, a sick and broken woman, succumbed to grief just 4 days later. Edith's enmity towards Rufus must have been palpable. Conversely, as her confidante and one-time abbot of her favoured Bec Abbey (1079–1093), Edith would have been very keen for Archbishop Anselm's reinstatement at Canterbury. They wrote to each other often (in fact she was one of his most frequent female correspondents) and her love and devotion for him is quite clear in the following extract of a letter (originally in Latin) sent by her in reply to his:

"...I embrace the little parchment sent to me by you as I would my father himself. I cherish it in my bosom: I place it as near my heart as I can. I read over and over again, the words flowing from the sweet fountain of your goodness. My heart broods over them, and I hide the pondered treasures in the very secret place of my heart."[366]

As for the great Bec Abbey itself, pertinent connections stretch beyond Anselm right back to its creation. It was founded in the 1030s upon the patronage of some of the most powerful men in the Conqueror's retinue, including estates donated by Count Gilbert de Brionne, grandfather of the de Clare siblings (on their father's side) and of Walter Tyrell (on his mother's side). In fact, Bec Abbey

---

[366] *Letters of royal and illustrious ladies of Great Britain*; ed. Mary Anne Everett Green (H. Colburn), 1846.

was built on Count Gilbert's land, sited just 3 miles from the town of Brionne. Without exception, all the suggested plotters, and especially the Clares and Giffards, were patrons and generous benefactors of Bec—numerous charters record their donations of land and money. Perhaps unsurprisingly, it was also particularly richly supported by Princess Edith, who was probably already Henry's romantic companion in 1100, with William of Malmesbury recording that *'Henry had long been attached to her'*.

If all this does not weave strong enough threads, we also know that in 1100 the youngest Clare brother, Richard, had been serving as a monk of Bec since 1080. Plus, in the same year, the Abbot of Bec (who had succeeded Anselm in 1093), was Guillaume de Montfort-sur-Risle, a second cousin of the Beaumont brothers (see Appendix 4).[367]

The French Crown

Across the English Channel, we have equally strong connections to our plotters. Interestingly, even with all the intermarriages and blood mixes of that period, Geoffrey Gaimar specifically describes Walter Tyrell as a 'foreigner'.[368] Meanwhile, Simon de Senlis's family estate was on King Philip's hunting grounds in the Île-de-France and he was a one-time 'captive' of Prince Louis during the Vexin campaign of 1098. Heralding from the same area, the lands of the noble de Clermont family were also under the direct rule of the French king and pertinent to our story, Gilbert de Clare had been married to Alice de Clermont, daughter of Hugh I, Count of Clermont-en-Beauvaisis, since c.1088.[369]

---

[367] *'Anselm of Bec and Robert of Meulan'*, Sally M. Vaughn, University of California Press, 1987.

[368] Gaimar was an Anglo-Norman who spoke French and although Walter also spoke French, he may well have had a heavy accent with the Picard dialect—deriving from Picardy and spoken in territories from Paris to the Netherlands, including Walter's home town of Poix in the Countship of Amiens. Given Walter was a brother-in-law and cousin of the Clares and his grand-father and father had very likely fought at Hastings, 'foreigner' seems an odd description for him. Maybe as he was now on the 'French' side and outside the tight 'Norman' orbit was enough.

[369] Gilbert de Clare was married to Alice de Clermont. His father-in-law, Hugh, was Lord of Clermont and Creil, and his mother-in-law, Marguerite, was a daughter of Hildouin

However, with even deeper French/Norman links was the influential statesman and plotter, Robert de Beaumont. Upon the death of his mother in 1081, Robert had inherited the family title and lands in the disputed Vexin, as Count of Meulan, just 12 miles west of Tyrell's castle at Pontoise and manor house at Achères (see all in Fig.26 below). Robert thus found himself awkwardly situated between 3 parties—owing fealty to King Philip of France for his Vexin estates and to King Rufus and Duke Robert Curthose for his large estates in England and Normandy respectively, though one suspects that the dominance of the latter, both being under Rufus in 1100, probably skewed his loyalty towards the English king, for whom he was working!

VEXIN AND PICARDY LINKS

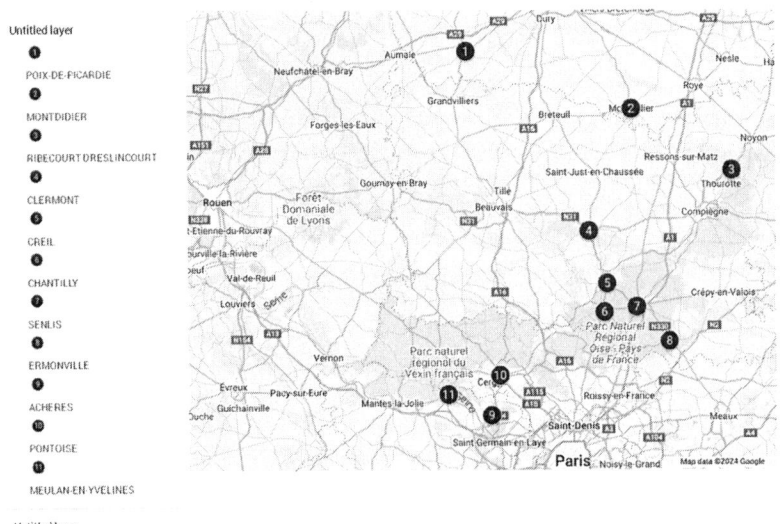

26. The Vexin and Picardy locations connected to the plotters and their families where they either held lordships or had castles
Map data Imagery ©2021 Google, Geobasis-DE/BKG (©2009)

Robert had even sat as a Peer in the French Parliament at Poissy, just 2 miles from Tyrell's Lordship of Achères and on top of all this, he had not long been married to Elizabeth de Vermandois, niece of King Philip I (daughter of Hugh

---

III, Count of Montdidier, 30 miles from Poix in Picardy. Creil is just five miles from Senlis. See map fig.26 above.

'the Great', Philip's younger brother). Poor Elizabeth had been married off to Robert in 1096 aged only 11 (12 was the minimum age permitted by the church, which itself was dreadful), now being 14/15 in 1100, with her father having obtained special papal dispensation for the marriage prior to him leaving on crusade with Robert Curthose.[370]

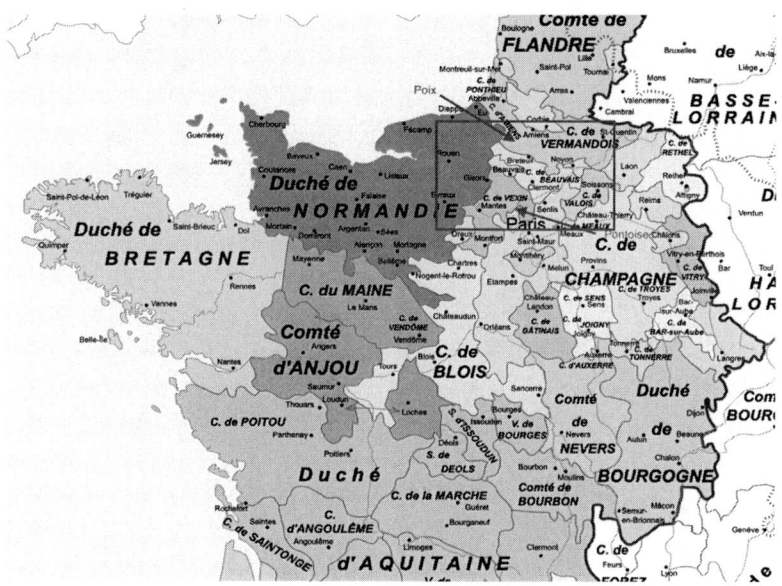

27. Approximate late 11th century boundaries of the various French vassal states, the Duchies (Normandy, Aquitaine, Brittany etc.) and the Countships (Amiens, Maine, Vexin, Anjou etc) also the royal lands around Paris (the Île-de-France) ruled directly by the French Crown itself.
(Rectangle highlights area of previous image 26, showing Poix and Pontoise)
Courtesy of Zigeuner: data from W. R. Shepherd, *The Historical Atlas*, 1911.
Reproduced (cropped and annotated) under Wikimedia Creative Commons Licence,
ShareAlike 3.0 Unported (CC BY-SA 3.0)

---

[370]Bishop Ido of Chartres had tried to prevent this marriage on the grounds of consanguinity i.e. that the two were related within prohibited degrees, but failed, as in April 1096 Elizabeth's father was able to convince Pope Urban to issue a dispensation for the marriage. If the marriage was designed to have Robert Beaumont support the Capetian royal dynasty rather than Rufus, this also failed, but maybe softened his views. The fact their first child was not born until 1102 suggests that, despite her father's haste in arranging Elizabeth's marriage, her husband at least gave the young girl time to mature before taking her to his bed.

By 1100, Robert and his teenage wife, Elizabeth, would certainly have been well placed with connections in both camps to have readily acted as intelligence gatherers. Based in England, they may well have passed information gleaned from Rufus's court and noblemen, via a network of messengers, back to the French royals, specifically to Elizabeth's cousin, Prince Louis, the young teenage heir who had been charged by his father, King Philip, with defending the Vexin.

Leading medieval historian Emma Mason (author of the most recent definitive academic biography of Rufus), believes that it was Rufus's increasingly megalomaniacal designs on territorial expansion that lay behind the assassination, and that King Philip and his son and heir, Prince Louis, were determined to halt him. Philip's throne was at risk—Rufus already had seats of government in Rouen in Normandy and Le Mans in Maine (as well as Westminster). Although the Vexin campaign had stalled the previous year, Philip knew that Rufus, with more money and access to more mercenaries, would return, very possibly with his sights set on the gates of Paris. With a huge fleet being assembled in Southampton to embark on campaigns to neutralise his brother Robert Curthose, acquire Aquitaine[371] by mortgage purchase and Poitou and Anjou by force, Rufus was a genuine threat. As Abbot Suger later wrote, the French realised that there was a huge imbalance between this new English force and any army that they could muster, as Rufus had huge wealth enabling him to buy and retain mercenary knights with great effect as well as to pay ransoms if required.[372] Conversely, if the Red King could be seen off, Henry would most likely be too preoccupied with establishing his new kingdom to wage war on an old ally...for now.

The only person ever named besides Tyrell, as the archer who felled the king, is a somewhat mysterious Ranulf. Ranulf's name appears just once, as Ranulf

---

[371] At this time the Duke of Aquitaine was William IX, called the *Troubadour* who had shown interest, like Robert Curthose, in mortgaging his duchy to Rufus, to help fund the Crusade of 1101, of which he was subsequently one of the leaders. Though his political and military achievements have a certain historical importance, he is actually best known as being the earliest troubadour—whose work survives.

[372] *Life of Louis VI, 'Le Gros'*, Abbot Suger, c.1140. p.8. Rufus's ability to recruit men who also held lands of the French king is also noted in *The Ecclesiastical History of Orderic Vitalis*, Book V, pp. 214–15; 240–41.

d'Aquis, in the chronicle of Gerald of Wales around 1190.[373] Gerald's record was written after all witnesses and contemporary scribes from 1100 would have died—and his source is unknown. Mason's summation was that Tyrell was an agent of the French Crown and his alleged retainer, Ranulf d'Equesnes, was the archer who shot Rufus under Tyrell's direction. Emma Mason describes Walter as a knight '*d'Equesnes*'—a name also mentioned by historian Walter Map[374] in his later work around the same time as Gerald of Wales. Mason believes this word-of-mouth transition of the name could have changed in phonetic transcription from *Aquis* to *Equesnes* and refer to the same man. Ralph has assumed a similar mystique to the much vaunted second 'grassy knoll' assassin of John F. Kennedy.

Mason suspects that the later writers who named Tyrell knew that Ranulf had acted for Walter, but as a nobody, rather than a key figure, he would have been less newsworthy. In fact, no-one seems entirely sure of Ranulf's origins or even his name, which also appears as Ranulph, Raoul and Ralph (being the Latin, French and English versions respectively of his first name) and was recorded into several phonetic versions including Aquis, Equesnes, Equennes and even Aix. The Tyrells had a number of titles, among which they styled themselves '*Sires de Poix et Vicomtes d'Equesnes*'[375] whereas Ranulf was simply 'from Equesnes'. I discovered that there is a village just 3 miles south of Poix, today called Equennes[376], which most likely explains the suffix tagged onto this Ranulf. Given that no contemporary account makes any mention of him, it seems likely that any involvement by him in the affair was unlikely and the lack of any sources

---

[373] *De Principis Instructione Liber*, Gerald of Wales, c.1190, Opera, viii, p.325–26, Ed. G. F. Warner, Rolls Series, London 1891, reprinted 1984.

[374] *De Nugis Curialium—'Courtiers' Trifles' or 'Trinkets of the Court'*, Walter Map, 1181–93.

[375] *Walter Tyrell and his wife*, J. Horace Round, p.360. n.3. In '*Feudal England'*, 1895—new edition, Barnes and Noble, New York, 1964.

[376] From: '*A Genealogical History of the TYRRELLS'*: Biographical Notes p.14. by J.H. Terrell, Twickenham, privately published, 1904, it is recorded that their title was Viscounts of EQUENNES, though renowned medieval genealogist Horace Round states it was EQUESNES. Also '*Further Genealogical Notes on the Tyrrell-Terrell Family of Virginia and its English and Norman-French Progenitors'*, Edwin H. Terrell, San Antonio, TX: privately published, 1909.

for his being mentioned and 'fingered' almost a century later must surely be questioned.

Whether Henry was in negotiation with the French before the death of Rufus is likely to never be known, but there is a strong suspicion he was. To quote Mason:

"No doubt spies were active at William's court, able to keep King Philip and Prince Louis informed of developments."[377]

With no supporting evidence, Mason remains convinced that Tyrell was 'bought' by Rufus. This may be likely, but other possibilities—that he was captured, he voluntarily or in time, defected, he went as part of a plot on the instructions of Gilbert de Clare/Prince Henry—are ignored. There is, however, credibility in her theory that Tyrell was acting as an agent for the French, collecting intelligence on the activities of Rufus's court and his military intentions. I, however, would go further and suggest he was also a key component of the plotters cabal with Prince Henry, Gilbert et al, and his 'defection' was all part of the detailed plan for committing regicide and replacing King William with his younger brother.

Allegiance between the French Crown and new English monarch was demonstrated at Henry's first Royal Christmas. This was held in London in 1100—less than 6 months after his brother's death and less than 18 months after Rufus was at war with the French. It was noted by Orderic Vitalis that Prince Louis, the 20-year-old King Elect, along with a select group of attendants, *'few in number but mature in judgement'*, were honoured guests at Henry's table under the guise of a courtesy visit. As Mason suggests, this visit was more likely a cover for an agenda of discreet discussions over demarcation of interests in northern France and tactics for dealing with Henry's surviving and increasingly threatening brother, Duke Robert Curthose, who remained deeply unhappy about Henry's throne grab in his absence. While any new leader may wish to heal old rifts and discuss potential threats to/strategies for their country, such an intimate meeting, so soon after the downfall of his brother and France's nemesis, does suggest an older alliance between Henry (plus his close advisors, such as the Beaumonts, Clares and Senlis) and the French monarchy.

---

[377] *William II: Rufus, the Red King*, Emma Mason, 2005, p.216

In support of this, despite being blamed for Rufus's death, Walter Tyrell went unpunished by both countries.[378] In England, he retained his Essex manor[379], while across the Channel, he was reinstated as Castellan of Pontoise castle by King Philip, became prominent in the French court, entertained Prince Louis at Pontoise castle in 1102 and was witness to several of Louis's Charters as late as 1107...hardly the acts of a monarchy who considered him to be a defector and traitor—much more the trusted scapegoat.

Mason's overall conclusion seems unconvincing, as the mechanics of carrying out such a staged assassination would have been too difficult, indeed nigh impossible for Tyrell, and his squire alone. To carry out such a plan within the constraints as simple guests on a royal hunting trip, over which they had no control, is extremely unlikely. This surely put far too much reliance on luck and circumstance to successfully engineer, unsupported, such a dramatic assassination and escape.[380] Everything points to a far more complex and wider plot at work. The consequences however, can be agreed by all:

---

[378] There are some references to Henry I officially pardoning Tyrell, but no reliable sources for this claim are evident.

[379] The sizeable manor of Langham, roughly 300 acres (44 households, value £15 p.a.— by comparison, the Essex manor of Chelmsford was valued at £8 and Maldon at £12) was the only one held by Walter Tyrell III, as Lord, at the time of Domesday in 1086 and still in 1100. It was most likely part of the marriage dowry, c.1080, from Walter's wife, Alice de Clare, as the tenant-in-chief in 1086 was his father-in-law, Richard FitzGilbert de Clare (who may well have fought with Walter's father at Hastings). Alice still held the manor as late as 1130 when a widow (Pipe Roll, 1130, Henry I) and it then passed to her son Hugh after her death in 1139. Hugh subsequently sold the manor to fund his expedition on the 2nd Crusade in 1147.

[380] Aborted plans by the Allies in WWII to assassinate Hitler illustrate the difficulties of trying to conduct a long range assassination from the other side of the Channel, even in modern times. Plots included bombing his train, poisoning his drinking water and lastly, Operation Foxley in late 1944. This was to be a sniper attack at Hitler's country retreat, the Berghof, while on his daily walk near the woods and where he was out of sight of sentry posts (not that unlike the Rufus 'hit'). The plan was cancelled due to lack of an insider at the Berghof to provide detailed reliable intelligence as to Hitler's daily routine at the Berghof to give the attack team a reasonable chance of success and also disagreement in British Government as to the overall merits of killing the 'Führer' at this late stage of the war as his terrible deranged decision making was actually helping the allied cause and the possibility of 'martyrdom' existed.

"One minute there are big English forces gathering around the Solent area, then Henry takes the throne, and the invasion is suddenly called off."[381]

[381] '*French agent killed William Rufus*', article by Jonathan Thompson, *The Independent*, 11 December 2005.

Chapter 5
Omens and Portents and Doom—Oh My!

Out of necessity, we rely on the writings of just a handful of chroniclers, mostly monastic Anglo-Normans, to piece together a picture of late 11th century England and, specifically, what happened in the New Forest in August 1100. If we believe that 21st century news providers often fail to provide an objective narrative, those medieval scribes were the original masters of spin, slanting their reports to make one point or another. Even the most reliable recorders would embellish and, alongside historical events, include a whole raft of stories, dreams, visions and prophecies, which could be readily dismissed by modern, cynical eyes. However, it would be churlish to ignore them completely—in those fervently religious times over 900 years ago, snippets of truth were often woven into even the tallest of tales. The fundamental point here is that these 'dreams and visions', by serious holy men, were most likely a way of dressing up the 'knowledge' they had of unfolding events but were clearly unable to state matters openly and give out and out warnings, so they disguised their knowledge in the smoke and mirrors of dreams and visions. The only logical conclusion therefore is that these Benedictine clerics had a foreknowledge of events in the New Forest in August 1100. They knew a plot was afoot and, as we shall see, unlike Rufus, their portents are not to be ignored…

In the years leading up to the summer of 1100, life was particularly tough for English inhabitants, as recorded in the Anglo-Saxon Chronicle. A series of failed harvests due to inclement weather, coupled with livestock disease, had left many folk struggling and starving, and portents of national doom and gloom were everywhere, as vivid chronicler Peter of Blois (c.1130–c.1210) later wrote:

"For there were thunders terrifying the earth, lightnings and thunderbolts most frequent, deluging showers without number, winds of the most astonishing

267

violence, and whirlwinds that shook the towers of churches and levelled them with the ground. On the earth, there were fountains flowing with blood, and mighty earthquakes, while the sea, overflowing its shores, wrought infinite calamities to the maritime places. There were murders and dreadful seditions; the Devil himself was seen bodily appearing in many woods; there was a most shocking famine, and a pestilence so great among men, as well as beasts of burden, that agriculture was almost totally neglected as well as all care of the living, all sepulture of the dead."[382]

All in all a pretty dire picture and one that had driven a number of middling and lower-class people to join Rufus's brother, Duke Robert Curthose, on the First Crusade in the hope of redemption and riches. The most recorded 'supernatural' event took place in May 1100, as the *Anglo-Saxon Chronicle* reported blood bubbling up from a spring at Finchampstead in Berkshire—a phenomenon now likely explained by the sporadic presence of red algae in iron-rich water and which chronicler John of Worcester said went on for 3 weeks prior to the king's death. This had happened on previous occasions at Finchampstead and other locations and was deemed to be a portent of national crisis. When the king heard of this, in usual Rufus style, he sensibly laughed it off.[383]

While many such terrifying happenings and visions were logged, it is thought that there were many more rife in the abbeys and bishoprics at this time—either too many to note, destroyed or lost to time. Certainly, Peter of Blois and the Anglo-Saxon Chronicle monk were not the only doom-mongering scribes. Alongside recording actual events, Orderic Vitalis, William of Malmesbury, Eadmer and Florence of Worcester also told of numerous portents involving Rufus, the Devil, Christ, the mother Church and horrific consequences all round. According to their writings, these visions appeared before various people—from

---

[382] *Rerum Anglicorum Scriptores,* Peter of Blois, Ed. Gale, 1684, I, pp.10–11. The Anglo-Saxon Chronicle for 1099 also recorded 'This year also, on the festival of St Martin (Nov. 11th), the sea-flood sprung up to such a height and did so much harm, as no man remembered that it ever did before'.

[383] *Gesta Regum Anglorum,* 1125, William of Malmesbury. The spring's fame for such occurrences happening at times of national disaster continued throughout the early Middle Ages. It was generally said to have curative powers and was visited by pilgrims. The well was accidentally destroyed in 1872 when deepening of the adjoining ditch collapsed it! (berkshirehistory.com)

regular citizens and lowly monks, to noblemen and top ecclesiastics, including foreign abbots. If, on the 2nd August, Rufus had taken any of these warnings seriously, retreating to bed with his hangover after lunch and having a long nap would have been a far healthier option than venturing into the woods with wild animals and sharp sticks. However, true to form, his invincible attitude and general disregard for his own safety prevailed.

With reasonable cynicism, some modern historians suggest that these gloomy predictions were added retrospectively by the scribes in order to give weight to the fate of an irreligious King, dying due to 'God's will'. The most poignant example of such was the account written by Gerald of Wales, some 90 years after the king's death.[384] Gerald notes that on August 1st, the Prior of Dunstable foresaw Rufus's end by an arrow the following day. In this dream, the Prior sees a beautiful virgin (the church) pleading with God to end the king's blasphemous reign, when suddenly he also sees a man *'Niger et ispidus'* (black and rough)—approach the king and offer some arrows. The Lord Jesus declares that one of these arrows will be his vengeance on Rufus.

To avoid his fate, the Prior was convinced that the king must repent his attacks on the church, so he rose immediately, soon after midnight, and hastened to the New Forest, where he found William preparing to go hunting. Having related his dream, William apparently gave the Prior 40 marks and sent him on his way. However, 2 major factual errors are raised with this story. Firstly, the journey from Dunstable Priory to Malwood hunting lodge is over 100 miles, a journey that would take more like 3 or 4 days, not 13 hours.[385] Secondly, the Augustinian Priory at Dunstable was not even founded until 1132, over 30 years after the event! Gerald's account also provides the unique claim that a Ranulf (not Walter) was the knight supplied with new arrows by Rufus on the day of the hunt, an event which clearly reflects the dream. Given that Gerald scribed his account some 90 years later when all contemporary witnesses were deceased, it is very likely that he confused the story with that of the monk of Gloucester and the presentation of arrows (see both below), so its reliability (as with his inclusion of Ranulph Aquis) has to be questioned.

However, one of the warnings, or interpreted as such latterly, was rather more credible and more accurate than a dream. It was proclaimed from the very

---

[384] *Giraldi Cambriensis Opera*, c.1190, Rolls Series, 1891. Vol. VIII pgs. 324–325.
[385] Allegedly he rose at midnight and arrived in the New Forest at 1pm—just 13 hours later. Freeman, E.A. , *William Rufus* (Oxford Clarendon Press, 1882) p.334.

forum of the pulpit of St Peter's Abbey church, Gloucester—a newly re-consecrated edifice that had been destroyed in the 1088 rebellion and beautifully rebuilt over the last twelve years. The man responsible was its long-standing abbot, Serlo, who had invited Fulchered, the Abbot of Shrewsbury, to address his congregation on 1st August, the Feast of St Peter's Chains (Lammas Day), the day before Rufus died. Orderic Vitalis, whose own family was from Shrewsbury, gave an account of the sermon in which Fulchered denounced the sins which were corroding England's morality, particularly pride, lust and avarice. The abbot then went on to declare, with remarkable precision:

"The revolution is at hand, the rule of the sodomites is at an end; the Lord God is about to appear and punish the enemies of his bride [the church]...For behold, the bow of divine wrath is drawn against the sinners and the arrow swift to wound has been taken from the quiver, soon now it will strike and the wise man will correct his life so as to avoid the blow." [386]

Given that this was the day before Rufus's death[387] and that Gloucester and the hunting lodge in the New Forest are also some 100 miles and 3 or 4 days' ride apart, the king would not have had the opportunity to heed these words to be 'wise' and remedy his lifestyle—warnings were customary prior to excommunication. However, this logistical problem could be overcome if we assume that Serlo knew the contents of Fulchered's sermon a few days in advance of its oration and dispatched a messenger to the king; as Orderic later recounts that Rufus was warned in time by a monkish emissary from Gloucester on the morning of the hunt. Presumably Fulchered was not privy to the exact timing of the arrow's 'strike' either, however the more cynical among us might suspect that he had at least some prior knowledge of events about to unfold, given the remarkable accuracy of his prediction. The question is how?

Perhaps the answer lies in St Peter's itself (now known as Gloucester Cathedral since being refounded by Henry VIII in 1541 during the Reformation) and its chief servant, Abbot Serlo. They were certainly at the heart of the Rufus prophecies, at least those laid down by Orderic. On 15th July—two weeks prior to Fulchered's arrow-themed homily—St Peter's had been host to a grand celebration and service when the newly completed church was dedicated by Serlo. We know from surviving documentation that Serlo had attended Rufus's

---

[386] Orderic Vitalis, v, 286–88.

[387] It is very possible the assassination was actually planned for Lammas Day, the 1st August, but for a variety of reasons was delayed 24 hrs.

Christmas Court in Gloucester at least as far back as 1093 and most recently in 1099, so it is likely that a number of senior Court members, in turn, attended St Peter's reconsecration, certainly including Robert Fitzhaimo[388]—close friend of Rufus, powerful baron and the major benefactor of the new abbey—and possibly, or probably, the Benedictine supporting Clare brothers. However, it is thought that Rufus was not present as he had little interest in matters 'spiritual', so perhaps this was the perfect place, time and guest list for plots and rumours to be shaped.

Just a few days before Fulchered's prophetic sermon, a monk of St Peter's, apparently had a vivid vision of Christ in heaven approached by a radiant virgin who spoke to him. Again, it was recounted by Orderic (and probably later reshaped by Gerald):

"Lord Jesus Christ, the saviour of mankind, for whom you shed your precious blood on the cross, look mercifully we beseech you, on your people who groan under the yoke of William. Avenger of all wickedness, most just of all judges, deliver me, I pray, from William and set me free from his hands for he does all that he can to pollute me and afflict me savagely."

To which Jesus answered:

"Be patient and wait a little while, for before long I will exact from him the full penalty."

The virgin's complaints were taken as symbolic of the Church's complaints against the intolerable, immoral crimes of the King and his Court, and that such, having reached the ears of the Lord, meant the king was about to come to a sticky end.

Before we detail the third St Peter's/Serlo connection, we should mention the most poignant warning of all. It was a dream, or more accurately a nightmare, experienced by Rufus himself the night before his death, as recorded by William of Malmesbury. Rufus, we are told, went to bed after an evening of feasting and

---

[388] In 1100, Fitzhaimo was probably the most powerful baron in England. He had been awarded the Barony of Gloucester by Rufus for his support during the 1088 rebellion, making him even richer. He founded Tewkesbury Abbey in 1092, before contributing greatly to the building of St Peter's.

heavy drinking and dreamt that he was being bled by a surgeon who had opened a vein in his arm. A stream of blood spurted into the sky blocking out the sun, and the devil appeared and said to him, *"I can't wait for tomorrow, because we can finally meet in person!"* Unsurprisingly, he woke suddenly, clearly rattled, calling for the help of the Blessed Virgin, demanding candles be brought into his bedroom and for 'chamberlains' to stay with him for the rest of the night. For some time, he struggled to get back to sleep and was restless thereafter until dawn broke. In addition to the nightmare and too much alcohol, Malmesbury reported that Rufus also had an upset stomach and many of us can painfully confirm how simply excessive alcohol consumption affects the stomach. The general conclusion, both contemporary and modern, is that Rufus simply had a terrible hangover, coupled with being tired from interrupted sleep, hence the hunt was postponed while he recovered, attended to state business and ate a late lunch with his 'friends'...

On the way to the dining room for this repast—with a splitting headache, queasy stomach and frayed nerves—Malmesbury then reports that the king was met by his good friend Robert Fitzhaimo, who informed him that Abbot Serlo had sent a foreign messenger monk who had arrived before dawn and relayed an account of a dream to him. In the monk's dream, the king entered a church looking scornfully round the congregation with his usual haughty and insolent air. He then proceeded to gnaw on the limbs of a crucifix until the figure responded with a kick, knocking the king backwards and causing a flame to be emitted from his mouth to reach the stars. In other words, the king had desecrated the church with his devilish beliefs and was about to get his retribution. Upon receiving the message later, Rufus, despite his delicate state, laughed loudly and said:

"He is a monk and to get money he dreams like a monk. Give him 100 shillings and send him away!"[389]

---

[389] *Gesta Regum Anglorum*, Malmesbury, 1125, ii, 377–8. This may be a nod to Rufus's generosity. as 100 shillings or £5 has a modern equivalent of approx. £10,000. Perhaps he viewed it as a belated gift to St Peter's, Gloucester cathedral, towards its recent rebuild.

In another version, he derisively added:

"How can an intelligent man take seriously the fantasies of a snoring monk? What does he take me for, an Englishman, who puts faith in the dreams of every old woman!"[390]

Some courtiers tried to persuade him to abandon the day's hunting but he ignored them and so later rode off to his death.

With St Peter's playing a seemingly significant role in the prediction of this historical event, one wonders if its long-standing resident abbot was in some way complicit. Perhaps at least he had motive to be—the numerous Christmas visits of the king would have been exorbitantly expensive for the abbey and exposed its monks to the corruption and vices of his Court. No god-fearing abbot could approve of such ungodly lives. Equally, they were used to keeping secrets in confessionals. A plot would be none too different. So did Serlo pick up on a rumour? It is quite possible that Orderic invented everything for dramatic effect (later adapted by Malmesbury and others), but it is equally possible that Serlo knew something. What is likely—stemming from a courtesy between abbots—is that he would be shown the contents of Fulchered's sermon prior to its delivery and thus had ample time to dispatch a messenger or the anxious monk with his similar vision. Or did he, in fact, furnish the details to Fulchered in advance and just invent the monk as a cover for his own very real knowledge? Were these warnings merely attempts to ingratiate himself with the king in the event that he survived[391] or because he had genuine, pious concern for his soul? Sadly we will never know—prophetic letters were routinely destroyed after receipt, and particularly if the king's incredulity and mirth were noted. One thing we do know for sure is that the church, its servants and its scribes constructed a fantastical tableau of smoke and mirrors.

Meanwhile, over in southern France at Lyon, the self-exiled Anselm was residing at Cluny Abbey (the most powerful Benedictine foundation in France),

---

[390] William Rufus, F. Barlow, London, 1983, p.423, based on Orderic Vitalis.

[391] *English Historical Review*, F. H, M. Parker, xxvii, 1912. Parker suggested that Serlo was acting like Themistocles before the battle of Salamis, sending a message to the King that would not compromise the plot, but if it failed, might afford himself protection, promotion even, when the King set about punishing the would-be regicides.

along with his chaplain, chronicler, biographer, secretary and friend, Eadmer.[392] The latter recorded a number of signs and visions from correspondents foretelling the king's death as punishment for his poor treatment of the archbishop. While Eadmer is known to have distorted the narrative of Rufus's reign and included tales that he knew to be unreliable in order to damage the king's reputation and to raise Anselm's, his 'recollections' are still of import as a primary and recognised contemporary source.

A significant example is logged the day before Rufus was killed, on August 1st, when Anselm was in the company of his host and companion, Hugh, the Abbot of Cluny.[393] Eadmer tells us (as does the Warrenne Chronicle) that Hugh claimed he had '*seen in a vision*' that Rufus had died that day, explaining:

"The previous night, the king had been brought before the throne of God, judged and condemned to hell!"

Anselm, with his usual obfuscation, was '*content to trust his words alone and omitted to ask him how he knew this'*. Assuming every other monk and abbot was not a legitimate psychic or receiver of visions in 1100, just how Hugh did know this is mystifying; however he was a deeply respected man known for his piety and the truth of his words (as was Anselm). If his honest reputation was warranted, his 'prediction' was more than a little suspicious. In Anglo-Norman historical writing in general, there is a decided hierarchy in preferred witnesses, with high-status clergymen being considered the most trustworthy authorities; William of Malmesbury considers Eadmer himself to hold enough authority to

---

[392] In fact at this time, as recorded by Eadmer, they were not at Cluny itself, but were moving about the area, having first stayed at the nunnery of Marcigny (Anselm went there to, unsuccessfully, enrol his much younger sister Richeza as a nun, after the recent death of her husband on the crusade), then moving on to the Benedictine monastery of La Chaise-Dieu, about 100 miles to the south in the mountains of the Auvergne, probably to avoid the summer heat.

[393] Hugh (1024–1109) was one of the most powerful leaders of the monastic orders in the Middle Ages. His influence upon Pope Urban II, who had been prior at Cluny under Hugh, made him one of the most influential figures of the late 11th century. He was canonised in 1120 by Pope Callixtus II.

repeat his story almost word for word. Indeed, Eadmer stresses how everybody trusted the abbot and did not ask how he knew.[394]

Eadmer goes on to report that the same day, one of Anselm's clerks, Brother Adam, also had a vision of an angelic young man who appeared to him and declared:

> "*Know for certain that the whole dispute between Archbishop Anselm and King William is at an end and settled.*"

A settlement which quite obviously would be achieved if King Rufus was dead.

The next day, the day of Rufus's death, one of the clerks, having finished singing psalms at matins, was lying down resting with his eyes closed when a note was pressed into his hand on which it was written that King William had died. As his eyes were closed, he did not see who gave him the parchment and when he opened them he saw '*no-one but his companions*'—a miraculous revelation is quite clearly implied by Eadmer.[395] Assuming one doesn't believe in miracles, it would seem there are only 2 possible explanations for these mysterious goings-on: Firstly, that Eadmer simply made them up latterly, to protect both Anselm and Hugh's reputations and uphold their innocence, and published his book after both had died (post-1109) so they could not take issue with the 'facts'. The second theory is the one I favour—that Anselm had prior knowledge of the unfolding plot (probably via messengers from Bec Abbey) which, if successful, meant his imminent return to England. The opportunity to be rid of an irreligious monarch would provide moral justification for laying out some godly intervention in advance, with the help of his friend and colleague Hugh and the pen and parchment of his chronicler. When the official news of Rufus's death did finally arrive by messengers at Cluny, Eadmer reports that Anselm burst into tears. However, this reaction was apparently not because he

---

[394] '*Vita Anselmi*', Eadmer, ii.46, p. 123.

[395] In Malmesbury's retelling (in his *Gesta Regum Anglorum,* p.572–3*)*, the revelation Eadmer ascribes to Hugh, Abbot of Cluny, is described as an 'oraculum', Latin for 'oracle', that is a prediction or divination. This event also features in Gilo of Paris's '*Vita Sancti Hugonis*' *(Vie de Saint Hugues: Abbé de Cluny 1024–1109*, ed. A. L. Huiller (Solesmes, 1888) pp. 588–9.

was upset per se over his death, as there was certainly no love lost between them, but solely because 'the king had died in his present [i.e. sinful] state'.[396]

Reflecting on Eadmer's contributions, we must remember that once back in England, as Anselm's secretary, he was a man at the heart of royal circles, with contemporary access not just to records, but to Henry's closest advisors like Robert de Beaumont and William Giffard, yet at no time does he ever suggest that Tyrell was Rufus's killer. This omission, in contradiction to the more widely-peddled conclusions at the time, could be because i) he knew about the plot and Walter's innocence (being instructed not to mention it), ii) because Tyrell was a generous benefactor to Bec Abbey or iii) Tyrell's close family and friendship ties to many of the plotters and Anselm—or most likely, all 3.

Just to add to all this confusion it was also later reported that on the very day of Rufus's death, Robert, Count of Mortain (the Earl of Cornwall, half-brother of William the Conqueror and Rufus's uncle), had been hunting in the Cornish woods and had suffered a ghastly vision whereby he encountered a large black hairy goat carrying the dead figure of the king on his back, black, naked and wounded in the middle of his breast. The goat apparently spoke to the Earl:

"I bear your king, rather your tyrant, William the Red, to his doom. For I am the evil spirit, I am the avenger of the wickedness with which he raged against the Church of Christ, and I brought about his death, at the bidding of the blessed Alban[397], protomartyr of England, who made his moan to the Lord, because this man sinned beyond measure in the island which he had been the first to hallow."[398].

But we end with the premonition that occurred closest in time to the event (just minutes prior). From the pen of the poetic Norman chronicler, Robert Wace, writing several decades later.[399] This well-known tale was likely included in his epic as a tribute to Henry—the book was commissioned by grandson Henry II

---

[396] *'Vita Anselmi'*, Eadmer, 49, p.126. '…quam illum sicut erat mortuum esse'.

[397] St Albans was one of the 13 abbeys which Rufus had kept vacant to take their revenues.

[398] *William Rufus*, Freeman. p.342, referenced by Roger of Wendover, vol. ii. p.159. (c.1225)

[399] *La Roman de Rou, Robert Wace* (1160–75)—Trans. by Glyn S. Burgess in *'The History of the Norman People'*, Boydell Press, 2004. (lines 10075–10116)

and the tale gave his grandfather the perfect alibi. In it, Henry was not even at the scene but had apparently gone off, with some attendants, to get his broken bowstring mended at a nearby peasant hut. The wizened crone asked who the hunter was and being told by one of the hunting party that it was 'Prince Henry, the brother of the king', she foretold that he would soon be king himself. In truth, the idea that a royal prince out hunting would not have had a bow-bearer or squire with a spare bowstring is somewhat ridiculous, as a broken string would be replaced not mended. In any case, the driven quarry had not even arrived at the hunters' stations yet, so how had he already broken a string? Most likely, it was just a fanciful literary device, but if there is any truth in the prescient knowledge of this old woman, it hints that the local New Forest people had seen or heard something in the days prior to the hunt, indicating an imminent regime change.

Omens aside, hunting was, and still is, considered a dangerous activity. Could it have been accountable for not just Rufus's death but other 'accidental' deaths within the same royal family? Or were other forces at play?

Chapter 6
The Deathly Forest

28. The sun setting (wintertime) over Canterton Glen (from the King's position)
Photo: Author's own

He made deer parks and he established laws therewith,
so that whosoever slew a hart or a hind,
should be deprived of his eyesight.
As he forbade men to kill the harts, so also the boars;
and he loved the tall deer, as if he were their father.
~ The Rime of King William[400]

The Conqueror, like most kings in the Middle Ages and beyond, was passionate about hunting, as were his sons. However, the Normans took it to a whole new level. Anglo-Saxon rulers had created quite modest hunting grounds, like

---

[400] Written upon William the Conqueror's death, this poem was in *The Peterborough Chronicle 1070–1154* forming part of the Anglo Saxon Chronicle for 1087.

Kingswood in the Kentish Weald and Woodstock Chase in Oxfordshire, but William I introduced 2 major changes. Firstly, he vastly extended the area of game reserves ~ with the New Forest in Hampshire being the most 'notorious' along with The Forest of Dean near Gloucester, Windsor Forest near London and also the Royal Forest of the Peak in Derbyshire, mentioned earlier.[401] In 1079, he took nearly 75,000 acres of mostly deserted Hampshire countryside (wasteland comprised of mostly infertile sand and gravel—nearly half the New Forest is not woodland but open heath, grassland and bog) and added a further 15–20,000 acres of cultivated, inhabited land[402] by allegedly forcibly removing some 500 families as a precaution against poaching, demolishing their homes and numerous churches (the numbers of which in a sparsely populated, non-agricultural forest seem very unlikely and are hotly disputed) thereby creating his 'Nova Foresta' or New Forest. There is in fact neither archaeological evidence for this destruction—investigations over the last 2 centuries show no remains of any earlier resident population—nor a single record in *Domesday* or the *Anglo-Saxon Chronicle* telling of such devastation.[403]

The second change by the Conqueror, recorded by all ecclesiastical scribes, were the Forest Laws, created by William and subsequently extended by son Rufus. Universal clerical opinion was that these laws were made and enforced with such ruthlessness that God had reason to wreak vengeance upon the royal family, a view held by William of Malmesbury who agreed with the wrath of God interpretation and stated, '*This was a region which his father, William, with villages abandoned, had reduced for thirty miles and more, to woodland glades and lairs for the wild beasts*'.[404] What is more likely was that this was a deliberate

---

[401] There were some 70 royal forests in 12th century England, a large number of chases, or hunting grounds in the private hands of nobles—perhaps as many as there were royal forests—and a far larger number of enclosed deer parks, held by wealthy lords—the number has been put as high as 3000. Detail from *'Walter of Henley and other Treatises on Estate Management and Accounting'*, D. Oschinsky, ed, Oxford, 1971

[402] In a Domesday entry for the Ringwood Hundred, the land was assessed as 28 hides for taxation purposes in 1066 but in 1086 only six hides are recorded as giving a financial return as the remainder now lay in the forest. (National Archives—World of Domesday—Landscape).

[403] *Domesday Woodland: The Economic History Review*, H. C. Darby, New Series, Vol. 3, No. 1, Published by Wiley on behalf of the Economic History Society (1950), pp. 21–43.

[404] *Gesta Regum Anglorum,* Malmesbury, 1125, Vol. I, iii. p.275.

narrative by a complicit and Rufus-abhorring church, to divert any suspicions away from them. Notes on the destruction of forest homes and parishes were only added by later chroniclers and became the accepted truth for centuries thereafter. Orderic alleged that 60 parishes—including presumably as many churches—were destroyed. Walter Map claimed 36; Henry Knyghton argued 2 possible alternatives—22 and 52.

However, in addition to the absence of archaeological evidence and contemporary documentation, local historians of the last 2 centuries, such as Mudie, Woodward, Wilks, Lockhart and Wise, have all sided against these clerical claims. In the mid-1800s, the Rev. Edward Duke, an original-thinking antiquary, declared:

"It is astonishing in the early ages, how readily a fiction promulgated by one was eagerly seised on and adopted by successive writers until at last it surreptitiously took its place among established truths…To the recorded fact that William I, dispeopled the country for 30 miles round and destroyed 30 churches to make a New Forest I attach very slight faith: but I believe that he afforested merely that which was native woodland; that be rendered then a large tract of country subject to the Forest Laws."[405]

In 1905, the antiquarian Charles Cox wrote:

…stories set on foot by early chroniclers as to William's reckless cruelty in destroying scores of churches and burning out villages for the sake of hunting, can readily be shown to be gross and absurd exaggerations.[406]

Undoubtedly, there is a degree of hyperbole in the chroniclers' accounts; but Domesday Book unmistakeably shows some 30 to 40 villages were without ploughs, peasants or value in 1086, and a further 40 or so partially included within the forest and therefore presumably with reduced resources and populations, so the actuality remains somewhat clouded.

Whatever conclusions one draws on royal destruction of forest communities, 2 facts remain: The Normans were passionate hunters and the Conqueror's laws

---

[405] Quote from 1846 in *The Forest Laws and the Death of William Rufus*, F. H. M. Parker, English Historical Review, xxvii, 1912.

[406] *The Royal Forests of England*, Charles Cox, Methuen & Co. London, 1905, p.305.

were universally hated. Omens, godly punishment and clerical bias aside, it is surely of note that not one but 3 members of William's close family died while hunting in the New Forest, all purportedly in 'accidents'.

As already discussed in brief, the Conqueror's second son Richard died sometime between 1079 and 1081, when it is generally thought that his head hit the overhanging branch of a tree during the chase and was thrown from his horse.[407] In fact, no-one seems really sure what happened, for other accounts say he was gored by a stag or even that he, too, was accidentally shot by a friend. According to William of Malmesbury, writing some 25 years later, Richard's cause of death *'a disorder from a stream of foul air while hunting deer in the New Forest'* or similarly in Camden's Britannia c.1587 (who called the boy Henry!) *'poisoned by a pestilential blast,"* which the 19th century author John Wise rightly concluded was *'surely, at the least, a very unsatisfactory account'*[408]. Given how unpolluted the forest must have been in the 11th century, this does seem a rather dubious conclusion. The grieving King appears to have concluded differently. According to *Domesday* records, he subsequently returned some New Forest lands to their original owners in order to ensure the *'repose of his son's soul'.*[409] Richard's marble tomb is in Winchester Cathedral.

Now we come to the death of another Richard (as if matters are not confused enough, he is also erroneously called Henry in some versions!)—the illegitimate son of Robert Curthose (one rarely, if ever, discovers who the mothers are of such 'bastard' children, who history never records). He met his end in May 1100, in his late teens, only 2 months or so before his uncle Rufus. This event has received little comment from historians but may well hold significance here. Back in 1096, Richard had been too young to accompany his father on crusade so he went to live in Rufus's court, where he grew up much admired. According to the sparse accounts, he was a charismatic young man, handsome, clever, educated, of good morals and brave…the stuff of kings. Orderic suggests that he was of dynastic importance and looked likely to go far in life, describing him as *'an illustrious young prince…worthy and amiable'*. A son of the eldest son and thus a possible threat to other members of his dynasty?

---

[407] *William the Conqueror*, David Bates, Yale University Press. 2016, p. 330.

[408] *The New Forest, its scenery and history.* John R. Wise, Smith, Elder, London, 1867, p.99.

[409] *The New Forest: A Personal View.* C. A. Brebbia, WIT Press, 2014, p.8

The 1091 Treaty of Caen between Rufus and Robert meant that one of them stood to gain everything should the other die without legitimate heirs. Despite the church's views about illegitimate heirs at this time, the nobility were somewhat more relaxed and Richard could have become the focal point for insurrection in the future. One could even make out a case that Rufus organised his nephew's demise. With Curthose on the horizon, returning to claim Normandy, it is believed Rufus had no intention of handing the Duchy back to his brother in return for a few thousand marks. If Curthose took up arms in response, young Richard would have invariably switched to his father's camp in England, making things difficult for Rufus. However, from what we know about Richard, he was extremely well-liked in Court, including by the king, who arguably did not see him as a threat. Rufus would surely have been preoccupied with more direct claimants—namely his older brother and any legitimate male offspring with his new bride.

Conversely, if the death of Rufus was a plot to put Henry on the throne, then the presence of Robert's charismatic son in Court, loyal to his father and uncle Rufus, accepted and well-liked by all, would have been a threat to such plans being enacted in the first place. There were, as time would show, many noblemen with sizeable estates in Normandy who would support Robert (and ergo his progeny) over Henry, for the Crown of England. As a natural strategist, Henry, like that of many monarchs before and after, might have sought to remove all possible heirs from the equation in order to secure his claim.

So, was the untimely death of young Richard just a forerunner to the assassination of Rufus? Just as with the deaths of his 2 uncles, there is no common agreement as to what actually happened (variations of tree branches, stray arrows, stag goring, foul air etc. feature throughout all of them!) and both William of Malmesbury in his *Gesta Regum Anglorum* suggests he was caught round the throat by an overhanging branch of a tree and William Camden made a similar declaration but was probably just regurgitating Malmesbury (Gesta Regum, ii, p.332–3 and Camden's Britannia, 1587, p.115) but since one of the party believed he was guilty of shooting him and fled in fear of his life for sanctuary in a monastery, this seems unlikely.

Indeed, most reports state that Richard, then about 18, died from an arrow accidentally fired by one of his friends while hunting with a band of royal knights. While Richard and his peers were young and likely inexperienced hunters, making the accidental verdict at least superficially probable, his death and the events that followed it were strongly reminiscent of Rufus's. The alleged culprit, who was not named, fled to the sanctuary of the great Cluniac Priory of St Pancras at Lewes[410] for the sanctuary of a church and holy ground where he reportedly became a monk, both as a penance and to avoid persecution from Richard's father and friends. Mason suggests that Richard's death might well have given the plotters the *modus operandi* to kill Rufus. Certainly, the sudden end of this young, popular potential heir, whether by luck, coincidence or connivance, made things a lot easier for Henry. However, I strongly suspect that plans for Rufus had been brewing for some considerable time. Just 2 months or so between these deaths was not enough to devise a complicated plot and bring together all elements required. In any case, Tyrell, who had a crucial part to play, had been in the country for a year or so already so could not have acted as a last-minute inclusion. Above all, if Henry sought to avoid suspicion in Rufus's death, playing any part in an almost carbon copy death a few weeks earlier would have raised more than eyebrows.

---

[410] Lewes was the first Cluniac house in England, founded c.1081 by William de Warenne, 1st Earl of Surrey (one of the great landowners, castle builders around Doncaster and Wakefield), probably in 1081 and one of the largest monastic churches in the country. The final resting place of William de Warenne, his wife, Gundrada, his son William Warenne II and his wife Elizabeth Vermandois. In her lifetime, from her two marriages, Elizabeth had about 13/14 children!

Chapter 7
The Not-so-Deathly Hunt

If one thinks of the hunt that day, in the setting of the first year of the 12th century, images are conjured up of the king and his companions galloping off into the vast New Forest, bows at the ready, horns blaring. They then follow paths deep into the dark woods looking for prey, whereupon, the chroniclers note, the king and Tyrell were somehow 'separated from' the party and seemingly hunted alone together—not something that would happen. The King then shoots at a deer, misses or wounds the animal, shouts at Tyrell to fire and his arrow deflects off— a tree, a deer—and hits the king right in the chest, piercing his lung and killing him stone dead—an apparent total shambles constructed by 2 professional huntsmen, albeit one of them is somewhat inebriated. All in all a most unlikely train of events.

Most artistic representations of Rufus's death are Victorian and heavily romanticised. Almost all show the solitary King being struck while on or near his horse (and falling over onto the arrow), often with a glimpse of Tyrell fleeing in the background, these being the only 2 figures depicted. This unlikely scenario was certainly my long-term imagining, held since school days and still seems to be the common view…but it could not be further removed from reality.

Given how nervous, timid and scared wild deer become around noisy humans, the idea of blaring horns is ridiculous; getting close to a herd on horseback (or with a horse) without startling them would be impossible; Norman nobility in deep forests were not the skilled Mongolian and Seljuk Turkish horse archers on the open steppes of Byzantine Asia and the bow and arrow was never the weapon of war of the chivalric medieval European knight on horseback.[411]

---

[411] There is just one mounted Norman knight shooting a bow depicted on the Bayeux Tapestry.

Shooting a longbow (let alone trying to load a crossbow!) while riding a horse is nigh on impossible, and inaccurate (only very compact composite recurve bows are used—known as horsebows, requiring exceptional skill), thus any use of bow and arrow would be dismounted, not on horseback and require the hunter to get within a suitable shooting range to ensure a kill, not much more than 30 metres away. This would need patience, quiet and great stealth (hence the 'deer-stalking' form of the hunt that was also occasionally undertaken in later medieval times).[412]

29. Death of William Rufus, lithograph by Alphonse de Neuville, 1895
A popular 19th century depiction of the death of Rufus
Public Domain image courtesy of Wikimedia Commons

None of this seems to ring true with the story as normally presented, of small groups of hunters galloping about the forest, loosing off arrows, seemingly willy-nilly.

---

[412] Nowadays stalked deer are commonly shot with a high-powered bow or a rifle. It's not illegal to use a bow for hunting in many countries in the world, but in the UK it is now illegal to hunt any animal (even vermin) with a bow.

Despite its great popularity with both royalty and the nobility, there are no 'surviving' 11th or 12th century treatises on hunting and few pictorial illustrations which inspire confidence in the process. The first, that has survived, is the beautifully illustrated French *'La Livre de Chasse'* (The 'Book of the Hunt') by Gaston Phoebus dated c.1388.[413] The considered view of historians is that although perhaps less elaborate than those depicted within its covers, in essence, the same overall process, procedures, staff and hounds etc. would have prevailed in the late 11th and early 12th centuries. The brief inventory mention of hunting staff and hounds in a surviving handbook from c.1135, *'Establishment of the King's Household' (Constitutio domus regis)*, would seem to confirm this, though no role of 'Chief Huntsman' or 'Master of the Hunt' is mentioned. The overall responsibility for all aspects of the king's sport (horses, hounds, hawks etc) rested with the 'Constable of England' (who in 1100 was Robert de Montfort—but whose primary responsibility was as commander of the royal armies and the Master of the Horse).

In fact, medieval hunting was quite formalised and primarily divided into 2 different and distinct types: The mounted 'Par Force' hunt (full title 'Chasse Par Force de chiens'—'Hunting by strength with hounds') and the driven 'Bow and Stable' hunt (the 'Stable', nothing to do with horses which did not take part, was the collective noun for the whole hunting party, hounds and handlers). The Par Force hunt, although less common, was the most esteemed version of 'the noble hunt' conducted by Norman nobility, with highly ritualistic protocols and social mores. It was the most strenuous form, designed for young, fit and active men, indeed men of an age to go to war. It was effectively considered a form of military training, normally starting at, or before, dawn. Nobility and royalty were able to transfer—from the hunting grounds to the battlefield—such martial skills as horsemanship, weapons management, pursuit, terrain assessment, strategy formation and general bravado, all regarded as the peacetime equivalent of prowess in chivalric wars.

The Par Force hunt was mounted (i.e. on horseback) and an all-day affair, devised primarily for the running down of large red deer—the great pointed stag called a 'hart'—over potentially as much as twenty or thirty miles of woodland and open terrain. In this case, as with fox hunting, the blowing of horns would

---

[413] 20 years later the text was translated (and adapted) into English by Edward of Norwich, 2nd Duke of York, between 1406 and 1413, as *'The Master of Game'* of which 27 manuscripts survive.

take place as a signal from the head huntsman to either his hounds or followers, to indicate what is required, the direction to ride or to denote what is happening. Aided by dogs, the location of a large stag would usually be identified by the chief huntsman and his staff the day before or early in the morning. Although red deer topped the 'hit list', there is extensive evidence that their quarry also included wolves, otters, hares, and other smaller game—in particular, mature male wild boar, extremely dangerous animals, were also considered a very popular alternative target (later becoming the heraldic symbol of King Richard III). For the top echelons of society though, it was really only deer and boar that were suitable quarry with the great stag antlered red deer at the top of the list.

30. Par Force hunting a great stag with hounds from *'Le livre de la chasse'*
[The book of the hunt] **by Gaston Phoebus**
Manuscript parchment, Paris, c.1388, Public Domain image

Hunters would chase a singular prey with hounds to near exhaustion and corner it, forcing it to turn and face its attackers, 'at bay', before the kill. The nearest modern equivalent would be the now-illegal pursuit of fox hunting, albeit with a smaller, more docile prey, but with the specific difference that this was a 'coursing' hunt, i.e. pursuit with hounds by sight and not by scent.[414] It certainly tested the stamina, riding skills and nerve of the participants. It would culminate in the kill by the most important noble or a chosen guest, mostly by sword or spear. After dispatching the creature, a highly ritualised butchering of the carcase would take place and the hounds would be rewarded with a portion of the kill, the entrails, in a ceremony known as the '*curée*'. The aim of the entire endeavour was to take one prized stag/hart, in great spectacle, followed by celebratory feasting.[415] This was very likely the form of hunt chosen by the royal party on their first outing the day before, Lammas Day, the 1st August, which would account for their hangovers the next day. It was undoubtedly the form of hunt in which Rufus's brother Richard and nephew Richard both perished, as described in the last chapter and fatal accidents were not unknown in this most dangerous form of the hunt, through forests and open country at full gallop.

The 'Bow and Stable' hunt, however, was a 'driven' hunt (using beaters) and was the more common form undertaken by the nobility and essentially required prowess with bow and arrow though a commonality of both types of hunt was the presence of specialist handlers of hunting dogs, of a variety of breeds (e.g. Brachet hounds) though mostly rough types of sighthounds were used, like the Irish wolfhound and Scottish deerhound, as well as the smooth elegant courser, the greyhound.

The 'Bow and Stable' was less strenuous, less dangerous and designed for all, including the older and less active (in later times women also participated[416]). Closely resembling the grouse shoots of today, the practices and principles of the driven hunt for large game have fundamentally remained unchanged over the

---

[414] The Hunting Act 2004 was a UK Act of Parliament which banned the hunting of wild mammals with dogs by sight or scent; the Act does not cover the use of dogs in the process of flushing out an unidentified wild mammal (to be shot), nor does it affect drag hunting, where hounds are trained to follow an artificial scent.

[415] A Red deer with 12 points or 'tines' (six per antler) to his antlers is called a Royal stag, while 14 points make an Imperial stag and an animal with 16 points or more is referred to as a Monarch.

[416] One of the earliest recorded sporting prelates was the Abbess of Barking (Essex), who in 1221 was permitted to hunt foxes and hares in Havering Park (*VCH, History of Essex*, 1907b, p.118).

centuries.[417] Beaters on foot with specially-trained hounds would 'line drive' the quarry generally within the confines of a large deer park or 'hay', slowly, with skilful control, to an open glade, the '*Battue*', where the killing took place—by dismounted archers who had waited in silent ambush, ready to shoot. They had a clear aim from their camouflaged stands, fixed along the shooting line. The same locations were used repeatedly, with shooting positions being man-made hides of timber and brushwood (or perhaps just specific trees and bushes, known, from Old French, as *'trysting trees' or 'trysts'*) refreshed by royal foresters in advance of each hunt.[418]—the 'King's Position' would be unchanging and obvious. In fact, as pointed out by Dolly Jørgensen[419], most deer hunting appears to have been undertaken using these enclosures known as deer-folds or hays (also called *haiae* in Latin and *haga* in Anglo-Saxon), into which the deer were driven and held. Such areas, generally making use of landscape features, were enclosed within an artificial barrier, usually a timber fence or 'Pale', or even simple wattle hurdles, up to 3 metres high, maybe a spiny hedge (hawthorn), but a barrier impenetrable to animals. These enclosures (sometimes temporary) were often constructed within a wooded area and it is thought that some were probably just intermittent boundary structures rather than continuous enclosures—thus enabling animals to enter and leave the woodland.

---

[417] Knowledge and practice of Bow and Stable hunting by Robin's outlaw band is clearly implied in *The Gest* and, as an erstwhile royal forester, he would have been totally au fait with practice, procedures and protocols of the day's events. In the 7th fytte of the *Gest*, stanzas 387–8, he even lays on such a hunt for the King (who is disguised as an abbot).

[418] For more on this type of hunt see '*William Rufus*', F. Barlow, London, 1990 (Yale), pp.130–2 also *'Transactions of the Devonshire Association'*, F. Barlow, cxiii, 1981, pp. 7–8 and '*The Master of Game*' the oldest English book on hunting—by Edward Norwich, 2nd Duke of York, c. 1413: (being a later English translation of the Gaston Phoebus book) edited by Wm. A. and F. Baillie-Grohman, foreword by Theodore Roosevelt, Pub: Duffield, 1909. New Ed. Penn Press, P. Back, 2005.

[419] '*The Roots of the English Royal Forest*': Dolly Jørgensen, Anglo-Norman Studies: Proceedings of the Battle Conference XXXII, Edited by C. P. Lewis, Boydell Press, 2009.

31. Hand-split oak deer-fence or 'Pale'
Photo ©—courtesy of Graham Cooper

Della Hooke has also convincingly argued that this Latin term *haiae*, as well as the Anglo-Saxon *haga*, which both appear in Domesday, denote a hunting enclosure, specifically for (fallow) deer.[420] They may have covered from 50–200 acres of both woodland and grassland, but could be significantly smaller or larger and were essentially 'larders for live meat', especially for winter, when otherwise only heavily salted preserved venison would be available. The Domesday Book records 7 such *haga* connected with deer (out of 100 detailed) and 37 other deer parks (9 belonged to the king, 5 were held by bishops or monastic houses and the other 23 were owned by various Norman barons). However there are no specific references to a *haiae* or *haga* in the management of the New Forest, though being the primary royal forest such omission of detail from the survey is perhaps hardly surprising, being deemed unnecessary.[421]

Surviving archaeology suggests that soon after 1100 the new King Henry did indeed create a large deer park, a 'hay', 4 miles south of Malwood Lodge, just

---

[420] '*Medieval Forests and Parks in Southern and Central England*', in European Woods and Forests: Studies in Cultural History; Della Hooke, ed. Charles Watkins, New York, 1998, pp,19–32. and '*The hays of medieval England: A reappraisal*', The Agricultural History Review, Sarah Wager, December 2017, 65(2): pp.167–193.

[421] *Ancient Oaks in the English Landscape.* Farjon, Aljos. Richmond: Royal Botanic Gardens, 2017, p.188.

east of Lyndhurst, encircled by the Park Pale, partial evidence of which still survives as Lyndhurst Old Park.[422] One imagines that the idea of subsequently hunting in the same park and at the same spot in the forest where he had his brother killed did not sit comfortably with Henry, such that he had it abandoned and dismantled soon after, quickly creating a new one elsewhere. The question of whether such an enclosure had actually encompassed all or part of Stricknage Woods, Canterton Glen and Malwood Walk to supply Winchester Castle is so far unanswerable, but by no means unlikely. If it was of a temporary 'wattle fence' nature or similar wooden barrier, as described earlier and taken down, then no archaeological evidence would survive and there would be nothing to see today, 900 years later.

Bow and Stable was the hunt of choice when there was less time and larders to fill. Naturally, they were less theatrical or exciting and carried less status, but they were the best test of archery skills in peacetime for competitive noblemen. Importantly, they could produce abundant results, with dozens of animals killed, usually a large herd of roe or fallow deer[423], with much of the meat salted thereafter and put in barrels.[424]

Significantly, when deer are driven calmly and quietly out of woods, they will generally take to those worn trails (also known as 'game paths' or 'trackways'), formed by regular use across the heathland and open glades, that they take daily when moving between grazing areas and drinking ponds. The fact that deer, in a manner similar to sheep, will pick up and follow these well-worn paths is key to directing the driven herd. Knowing the paths in advance makes it possible to position shooters in a way that increases their opportunity for

---

[422] https://newforestguide.uk/history/new-forest-history/

[423] Red deer and roe deer are the true native species of the New Forest. Large numbers of fallow deer are thought to have been introduced by the Normans, although suggestions have been made that the Romans also brought herds across. These may have died out prior to their re-introduction in the 11th century. Some sources suggest that at its peak the forest contained as many as 10,000 deer. Normal numbers were around 6,000 but today this is managed by culling to approx. 1,500.

[424] In Inglewood (part of the vast Cumberland Forest), King Edward I and his party killed 400 red deer in a day. The 1234 Pipe Roll for Henry III records a payment for killing and salting no less than 235 deer in Cumberland, while in 1251 and 1252, 200 harts and 200 hinds were killed, salted and removed; so that it is clear that they were killed for kitchen use and not just for sport. Detail from *The Forest Laws and the Death of William Rufus*. English Historical Review, F. H. M. Parker, xxvii, pp. 32–35, 1912.

selective shots. One of these trails most likely lay westwards up Canterton Glen to Ocknell Pond, Cadman's Pool and Stoney Cross Common—one of the highest parts of the forest, from where Romsey Abbey may be seen in the far distance.

This now brings us to the huntsmen's accommodation, Malwood Lodge[425], located near Minstead village, where a 12th century Norman church—holding the final resting place of Sir Arthur Conan Doyle in the churchyard—still stands. Named after the 1066 Lord of the Manor of Minstead,[426] one Godric Malf, Malwood Lodge (originally 'Malf's wood') would have been a sizeable wooden establishment (plus other outbuildings) with either a thatch or oak shingle roof— probably not totally dissimilar to Waltheof's earlier aula and looked after by a Forest Keeper (much like Robin's 'Loxley' family role in Hallam), a position and title still in use today (see image 7, in Part 1, chapter 4). Indeed, the 'Keeper's Cottage' of Malwood Walk was situated at Malwood Lodge right up to the 19th century and the structure still survives.[427]

---

[425] Variably called Malwood Castle Lodge, Malwood Keep or Malwood Lodge but not to be confused with Castle Malwood, a few hundred metres to the west. This latter high point was the site of a beacon, only built on with a significant residence in 1802. Although there is a large prehistoric earthwork, no trace of any 11th century archaeology exists, but this location is sometimes erroneously proffered as the Norman hunting lodge in question.

[426] In 1066, Minstead is referred to in the Domesday Book as Mintestede (Mint place) and worth £8, then, as a consequence of being absorbed into the New Forest hunting grounds and subject to Forest Law (which did not preclude the continued holding of private lands within it) by 1087 it was only worth £1 and had just 7 dwellings (4 peasants and 3 slaves). In 1086 the manor was unusually still held as 'Tenants-in-Chief' by the sons of Godric Malf (he no doubt now deceased) and this was very probably because they were charged with care of the hunting lodge and deer park (probably royal foresters) in the King's absence and the manor's reduced value.

[427] The New Forest, C. J. Cornish, Seeley and Co. London, 1894, p.56

32. Dismounted archers at a Bow and Stable hunt from *Le livre de la chasse*
[*The book of the hunt*] by Gaston Phoebus c.1388
Manuscript parchment, 1405–1410, MS M.1044, fols. 100v-101r.
Image in the Public Domain

Lying on a flat plateau of nearly 4 acres atop a hill (just south of today's A31, but then a cart track), the site has sadly been so disturbed over the centuries and built over that nothing exists of it today.[428] The only surviving archaeology is

---

[428] On the site of an earlier large Iron Age double-ditched hillfort, the Lodge's plateau location was later built upon by a large late 19th century mansion, now flats. Being of a wooden construction with lathe and plaster walls, apart possibly from post holes it is unlikely any archaeology of the original Lodge survives underneath. Peripheral staff would have lived 'under canvas' organised by a royal household officer called the Keeper of the Tents. Modern opinion is that like many subsequent hunting lodges built in the New Forest (and other places over the centuries) the absence of confirmed structural remains suggests buildings displaying 'a more ephemeral and perhaps temporary use of the site'. *New Forest Historical Research and Archaeology: who's doing it?* Excavations at the 'Royal Hunting Lodge' at Church Place, Denny Wait: New Forest Knowledge Conference, 2017: NFNPA Archaeology.

earthworks in the form of double ring ditches that surround the plateau from a much earlier iron age hill fort (c.150 BC) that could well have been conveniently re-utilised by the Normans in situating the lodge, as they were often ditched and/or moated.

33. Modern bird's eye view of the hill/plateau (circled), site of a former Iron Age hillfort upon which Malwood Lodge stood (now a 19th century mansion converted into flats)—Rufus was shot half a mile northwest in Stricknage Woods (arrowed), now cut off from the Lodge by the modern A31 (an ancient route) which runs from Wichester to Poole via Ringwood.
Image: ©2021 Google, Getmapping plc, Infoterra Ltd. and Bluesky, Maxar Technologies, Map data

However, in 1100, the Lodge and surrounds provided the king and his entourage (the hunting party plus secretaries, chamberlains, constables, under-marshals etc.) with sleeping quarters, food, wine, entertainment, horses, guards and staff like royal foresters and huntsmen,[429] as well as farriers, stable lads, fletchers, bowyers, falconers and houndsmen (called 'fewterers'—specialist handlers of hunting hounds), plus housekeepers, cooks, cellerers, servants, housemaids and so forth. This might well have been up to 100 people or more, in and around the Lodge.[430] Many household staff, some perhaps locals, would

---

[429] Due to the importance and social exclusivity of hunting, such positions had very high status—'Croc, the huntsman' even witnessing royal writs on occasion. Mason, p.218.
[430] It is hard to say how many of the Winchester Castle staff would have decamped to the hunting lodge but the following details of royal household staff gives some idea of what was involved in serving the royal court.

have arrived some days earlier to prepare everything, with the royal hunting party (maybe 25+), including older statesmen like William Giffard, secretaries and chaplains like William Warelwast, stewards (dapifers) like Haimo and Eudo Dapifer, plus a whole royal court entourage of, butlers, chamberlains, constables, marshals, chaplains and secretaries probably arriving a day or 2 before, in time for the six-week 'fat season' of hunting starting the next day.[431]

On 1st August, the party most likely had a successful Par Force hunt. This was of course Lammas Day, but whether any, some or all of the party attended mass that evening in Minstead Church, to 'take consecrated bread' made from the first harvested grain of the year, is open to question. However it was certainly noted that they enjoyed mighty feasting and revelry that night, following the day's exertions. However, with up to 50–100+ guests and staff in situ, it was the responsibility of the nobles as much as anyone, to keep the larder full and the spits turning, not just at the lodge but also for the ladies and others who had remained at Winchester Castle. On the second day of the royal visit, there would have been a pressing need for sufficient fresh meat stocks, in spite of hangovers and omens.

Given the location of Rufus's death in Stricknage Woods being so close to the Lodge, in addition to the timing—with various chroniclers recording that the hunting party did not leave until late afternoon and the requirement for large quantities of meat, I believe it is without question that Bow and Stable was the form of hunt undertaken on 2nd August. This opinion is further reinforced by the fact, as we shall see, that arrows were handed out prior to the hunt, a vital part of the Bow and Stable but rarely, if ever, used in the Par Force. It began with the

---

The chancellor, the treasurer, stewards in charge of the hall, chamberlains in charge of the 'chambers', stewards under the master butler in charge of the pannetry, the great kitchen, the royal kitchen, the larder, the butlery, wine dispensers, cooks, keeper of the cups, scullions, keeper of the dishes, usher of the spithouse, keeper of the spits, the carter of the great kitchen, the carter of the larder, the fruiterer, the ewerer, chamberlain of the candle. Also, the master of the writing office, various grades of constables and marshals and so on.

Detail from *'The Household of the Norman Kings'* Transactions of the Royal Historical Society, Geoffrey H. White, CUP, Vol. 30 (1948), pp. 127–155.

[431] *"Minstead was held originally on the basis of providing accommodation for the King when he went hunting in the area, but was later converted to a military holding."* The New Forest National Park publication (Forest Central, North and South, Conservation Area Appraisal), Jan. 2008.

noble hunters trotting the half mile or so down to Canterton Glen in Stricknage Wood (which as mentioned earlier may well have been part of a large deer enclosure where the beaters would be preparing to drive the contained deer herd towards the hunting party). They would then dismount in the woods and, with horses attended to, be led quietly through the trees by a forester, along with their bow-bearer and dog-handler, to take up positions at those bends in the glade where the stands or trysts were set up for the archers, alongside the area where the deer were to be driven and killed in Canterton Glen, the *Battue*. This firm belief is backed up by the later records of 3 scribes:

(1) Orderic Vitalis, who describes something quite different from a Par Force:

"...*The King and Walter de Poix (Tyrell)* <u>*posted themselves with a few others*</u> <u>*in one part of the forest,*</u> *and stood with their weapons in their hands eagerly watching for the coming of the game.*"[432] (this runs counter to the claim that Tyrell and the King were totally alone.)

(2) Peter of Blois, who mentions the stands/hides:

"*After the king had pointed out* <u>*to each person their fixed station*</u>..."[433]

(3) Master Wace, who describes the form:

"*For the king, the knights and those who were his archers,* <u>*took up their*</u> <u>*positions*</u> *and stretched their bows just as they saw the hinds coming.*"[434]

Despite these early chroniclers' observations, only Duncan Grinnell-Milne,[435] of modern authors, makes this distinction with any detail (though later endorsed by Frank Barlow[436]), yet it seems both the most logical choice of hunt

---

[432] Orderic Vitalis, Book X, Chapter xiv.

[433] *Ingulf's Chronicle of the Abbey of Croyland with the Continuation of Peter of Blois and other anonymous writers*, Trans. Henry T. Riley, 1854, Henry G. Bohn Publisher, p. 230.

[434] '*The History of the Norman People—Wace's Roman de Rou'*, c.1165, Trans. Glyn S. Burgess, 2004.

[435] *The Killing of William Rufus—An investigation in the New Forest*, Duncan Grinnell-Milne, Pub. David and Charles 1968. (new ed. 1973), p.62.

[436] *Rufus*, Frank Barlow, Yale University Press, 2000 (first pub. 1983), p.425

for the variety of reasons outlined earlier and the most crucial to the non-accidental theory, as we shall see.

For a day that was to end as dramatically as Thursday 2nd August 1100, its morning, by most accounts, was a much quieter affair, save the arrival of one or 2 clerical messengers bearing gloomy warnings, all ignored with bravado by Rufus. The exception comes from chronicler Geoffrey Gaimar (whose account differs markedly from those in other sources) who records that during the lull in proceedings before lunch at Malwood Lodge, a heated conversation took place between Tyrell and Rufus. Quite who supplied this information (a guest hunter, staff member or simply Gaimar's imagination), is not known; likewise, whether the person was present, eavesdropping, had the conversation relayed by a third party or was making it up is also a mystery. Gaimar was a poetic writer (in rhyming French couplets) and translator and it has already been noted that his versions of events are somewhat 'creative', so the account is no doubt embellished as ironically the use of direct speech, such as there is here, is usually an indication that a story contains a good deal of invented material! However, the gist of the discussion apparently revolved around Rufus's extravagant European territorial ambitions and intentions, which, given that his invasion fleet was gathering at Southampton, seems most plausible. It certainly seemed to wind Tyrell up. One part of the discussion was also recorded by William of Malmesbury—the claim by Rufus that he would *'spend this Christmas in Poitiers!'*[437] lending weight not only to his noted military objectives (i.e. the conquest of Poitou province) but also the veracity of the conversation.

From what we can gather, things calmed down and Rufus tucked into a late lunch with his friends. William of Malmesbury also recorded that after his nightmare and recent portents, Rufus *'soothed his cares with more than the usual quantity of wine'.*[438] Perhaps, as he liberally downed his 'hair-of-the-dog' remedy to cure his physical and mental ills, the plotters feigned their alcohol intake, otherwise all would have been well over the limit of any modern-day blood/alcohol test, yet they would need to have their wits about them for the next few hours.

---

[437] *Gesta Regum Anglorum*, William of Malmesbury, 1125, Vol II, p.379

[438] From various reports on his drinking habits, one gets the impression that Rufus was alcohol-dependent.

Crucially significant to our story, and darkly ironic to Rufus's story, Orderic Vitalis then described the preparations for the hunt—Rufus was joking with his attendants while his boots were being laced up and...

"An armourer came in and presented to him [Rufus] 6 arrows. The King immediately took them with great satisfaction, praising the work, and unconscious of what was to happen, kept 4 of them himself and held out the other 2 to Walter Tyrell...saying 'It is only right that the sharpest be given to the man who knows how to shoot the deadliest shots'."[439]

If such an account is to be believed, it tells us 2 important things. Firstly it confirms that Tyrell was the best archer in the hunting party that day. Secondly, as mentioned earlier, it strengthens the argument on the type of hunt they were about to embark upon, as Par Force hunts rarely, if ever, used bows and arrows as this was not a weapon of war ever deployed by the nobility and medieval mounted knights.

The exact details of who was present on the hunt itself are as vague as most other recorded parts of the story. Notwithstanding the exceptions below, no-one can be precisely placed at the 3 locations of the royal group that summer's eve, namely Winchester Castle, Malwood Lodge and Stricknage Woods. Winchester Castle was where most of the women would have remained, arguably Maud Senlis with her 3 young children; Robert de Beaumont's young wife Elizabeth (pregnant with their daughter Isabel); and Gilbert de Clare's wife Adelize, who was also 7 months pregnant at the time with son Gilbert FitzGilbert, one of their 8 children. (Somewhat intriguingly, these 2 unborn children, Isabel and Gilbert, were later to marry—Isabel was also a favoured mistress of King Henry and bore him a daughter!).

---

[439] *The Ecclesiastical history of England and Normandy*, Orderic Vitalis, 1075–1143; Forester, Guizot and Delisle, book X, Chapter XIV, p. 263

**34. The unchanging view over the New Forest from the high point of
Castle Malwood**
Photo: courtesy of Marisa Tomaselli

As we know, several friends of the royal brothers and numerous government officials moved onwards to Malwood. Not all of these men were 'hunting types', due to lack of skill, interest or infirmity or perhaps not of a high enough social standing to be invited on the actual hunt.[440] Some of the other significant figures I have spoken of—signatories to surviving documents just a day or so later (the Coronation Charter and the letter to Anselm) so presumably somewhere nearby, were most likely guests at the Lodge or the Castle—close enough to be included in the general 'party' but not on the hunt itself. The split seems to apply to those

---

[440] A good example is William Warelwast, chief clerk and secretary to Rufus, and afterwards immediately to Henry (he was a witness to the letter recalling Anselm, of 5 August 1100—*William Rufus* Barlow, p. 420). His loyalty and service were rewarded with the Bishopric of Exeter in 1107. Hollister described Warelwast as a '*canny and devoted royal servant*'. *Henry I*, Warren Hollister, Yale University Press, 2000, and it remains unclear quite how aware he was of the plot.

of more mature years—William Giffard, Simon de Senlis, Eudo Dapifer and the de Beaumont brothers. One can only imagine how anxious these 5 possible insurgents must have been, awaiting life-changing news from deep within the forest.

The following 10 men were the only hunt participants specifically named by any chronicler and essentially all of them were military men and no doubt wishing to better each other in archery skills. The list varies between the scribes and no precise list of the king's entourage exists as one imagines none of those present wished to be associated with the tragedy. So while we cannot be absolutely certain how many or who was there, we have mention of:

Rufus
Prince Henry
Gilbert de Clare
Roger de Clare
Robert Fitzhaimo
William de Breteuil
Walter Tyrell
Ranulf d'Equesnes (Tyrell's retainer)
William de Montfichet
Gilbert de l'Aigle

Apart from the attendant staff, it seems quite reasonable to assume that the above 10 men, at most, comprised the full quota of huntsmen that afternoon. If my theory is correct, it was either a masterstroke of social engineering, or a series of coincidences and good fortune, for a situation to occur whereby everyone present was, or could be persuaded to be, a supporter of Prince Henry. Not one of the powerful noblemen who were known to be, and/or later proved to be, loyal to his brother, Robert Curthose, were there, with the singular exception of William de Breteuil, Rufus's Treasurer and eventual supporter of Duke Robert. The only 3 noblemen probably not party to the plot but equally probably on the hunt were Robert Fitzhaimo, William de Montfichet and Gilbert de l'Aigle. However, a brief look at these men is revealing.

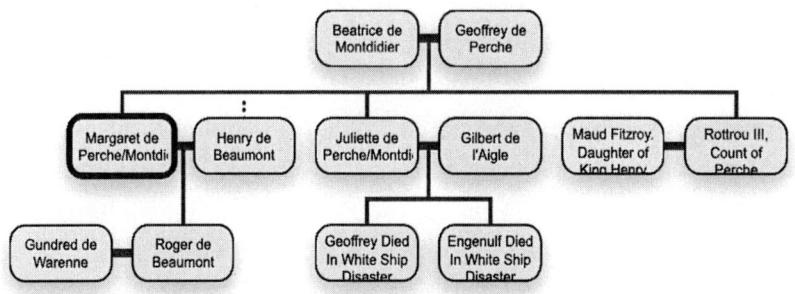

35. The Perche-Montdidier family and its links to Henry Beaumont, Gilbert l'Aigle, William de Warenne, Gilbert de Clare and King Henry.
(Beatrice de Montdidier, daughter of Hildouin III de Montdidier had a sister, Marguerite d.1110, the mother of Gilbert de Clare's wife, Alice de Clermont)
Created using Family Echo—online family tree maker

Although sparsely recorded at the time, William de Montfichet and 27-year-old Gilbert de l'Aigle were close friends of both the royal brothers and the suspected plotters. In fact Montfichet was later to marry Margaret, a daughter of Gilbert de Clare. Meanwhile, Juliette, the wife of Gilbert de l'Aigle, was sister-in-law of Henry de Beaumont (Juliette, and Beaumont's wife, Margaret, were the de Perche/Montdidier sisters—see Fig.34 above). De l'Aigle was particularly close to Henry and subsequently became his Commander-in-Chief.[441] With close family ties, the promise of key courtly positions and possibly some generous cash payments, Henry would have been pretty confident of keeping both 'onside' following the coup.

Arguably, the most interesting hunt member was Robert Fitzhaimo, a kinsman of the Conqueror. Long-time close friend of Rufus (some historians have even suggested, but not proven, lover—like Piers Gaveston then Hugh Despenser were to Edward II), Robert was the son of Haimo Dapifer,[442] senior

---

[441] The two sons of Gilbert and Juliette, namely Geoffrey and Engenulf, were among the 300 who drowned in the Great White Ship disaster. along with King Henry's only son, William, in 1120.

[442] By summer 1100, Haimo was very ill, probably with cancer, and died shortly after the hunt.

Anglo-Norman royal official and steward (and sheriff of Kent) to both the Conqueror and Rufus. Robert had supported Rufus during the 1088 rebellion and been very well rewarded with the immense barony of Gloucester,[443] where he subsequently became the main sponsor for building the new abbey church. After this, he took his forces and subdued the Welsh in Glamorgan, for which Rufus then gave him the hugely powerful barony of Glamorgan based at Cardiff Castle.

According to Gaimar, Fitzhaimo was visibly distraught upon Rufus's death—falling briefly senseless to the ground and crying out that he wished himself dead instead. Whether a sign of genuine grief, good acting or, more likely, pure later literary invention, we will never know, but left with a choice between the surviving brothers, he was quick to side with Henry. In fact, all the nobles had a choice of either waiting maybe a few weeks during a dangerous interregnum until Robert Curthose arrived and a period of great national instability, or siding straightaway with Prince Henry. One could logically argue that, in the flurry of the aftermath, Fitzhaimo would not have had the time to strategize nor the courage to go against the probable new king that all others on the hunt, bar one, were swearing their loyalty to.

36. Rufus's final journey: The entrance up to Malwood Lodge from Minstead. The party would have come down this lane on their way to the hunting glen.
©Photo: Author's own

---

[443] This included those lands of the late queen which she had intended for Henry. See footnote 334.

However, he ultimately proved his trustworthiness—firmly supporting Henry in the subsequent struggles against Curthose and his supporters, negotiating the Treaty of Alton in 1101 which brought temporary peace with Henry's brother, and becoming one of the new King's closest aides. As a keen strategist, Henry probably knew the man well enough to predict his allegiance on 2nd August, but likely kept him away from any plot beforehand. Fitzhaimo had a powerful and formidable group of brothers-in-law (through his marriage to Sybil de Montgomery)—namely Robert de Bellême, Arnulf de Montgomery and Roger the Poitevin—who were definitely not fans of Henry, all being fervent Curthose supporters and military commanders who sided with the elder brother in the ensuing struggle for the Crown.[444]

Fitzhaimo's loyalty was also well rewarded by Henry who made him Count of Corbeil and Lord of Tewkesbury, enabling him to immediately embark on the extensive build of Tewkesbury Abbey. Wace notes that, in 1106: *"Henry granted Robert the wardenship of Caen as a fief, for himself for all time and for his heir. He also gave him other revenues which Robert had asked of him. The king cherished Robert greatly and Robert served him well."* However, a year earlier, in 1105, Fitzhaimo had suffered a serious head injury, received while fighting for Henry at the siege of Falaise and, seemingly slightly brain damaged, died 2 years later in 1107. His eldest daughter Mabel, then a girl of just 7, inherited his honours and vast property holdings, the great feudal barony of Gloucester. In deference to his late friend's loyalty, service and friendship and in order to protect his young daughter, Henry contracted Mabel to be married to his eldest illegitimate son, Robert FitzRoy, who was about 12. Ten years later, in 1117, they were duly wed and Robert was made the 1st Earl of Gloucester.

Now back to the 2nd August. Late in the afternoon, likely somewhere between 5–6pm, Rufus is noted as riding out, slightly inebriated but determined to hunt. Suddenly all those people who had been waiting patiently all day, discreetly out of sight of the royal party awaiting the 'go' signal—a whole entourage of beaters, royal huntsmen, grooms, bow-bearers, fewterers, carters, personal attendants etc., maybe 3 or 4 dozen participants—sprang into action at

---

[444] It was a great irony that not long after Henry took the crown, many of the Normandy nobles, incensed by the profligate and indolent rule of Robert Curthose pushed for the Duchy to be taken under the English Crown, whilst at the same time, numerous senior barons in England who had sworn fealty to Henry were seeking to bring the country under the control of Robert Curthose!

last on the king's whim. Despite Fitzhaimo's reservations, others in the hunting party were also impatient to go and so off they all trotted down the lane into Malwood Walk and Canterton Glen in Stricknage Woods, barely half a mile from their Lodge. This open marshy glen, sloping upwards to the west, would have no doubt been a popular location given its proximity to Malwood Lodge and crossed by deer trails (especially if contained within a deer park). It is surely beyond coincidence or convenience that both the Royal Treasury to the east and an escape route to the west, across the Channel, were only an hour or 2 away.

The delayed order of the day would have given plotters ample time to get instructions to the assassin, while the static nature of the hunt meant he could ready his position…just as the bright summer sun dropped lower in the sky and directly into the eyes of the king and his attendants looking westwards, up the slope of Canterton Glen—where the unseen archer assassin lay in wait…

Chapter 8
The Red King Falls

37. The Rufus Stone
It marks the site near where Rufus fell by the oak tree in Canterton Glen,
Malwood Walk, Stricknage Wood.
©Photo: Author's own

No study on this subject would be complete without a proper discussion of 'the crime scene'. In Norman times, the New Forest extended to some 150,000 acres (around 200+ sq. miles) but is today only around 90,000 acres.[445] It is important to note that the early chroniclers and historians say nothing more precise than 'the New Forest' as the place where Rufus met his end and the more specific details are cobbled together from legend, folklore and hearsay.

---

[445] The loss, now arrested due to National Park status established in 2006, had been due to relentless encroaching development around its perimeter.

The one exception is the somewhat unreliable Gaimar, when writing in his native Anglo-Norman some 35 years after the event, he does, somewhat imprecisely, mention Brockenhurst—the largest named village in the forest with a church and further telling of the actual spot being heavily wooded and near a marsh:

'*Li reis estait le chaser…**vers** Brokehest a archeier*'
[*The king went to hunt…**towards** Brockenhurst to shoot.*]

There are the well-preserved remains of a much later 14th century hunting lodge at Queen Bower (then called Queneboure), 3 miles north of Brockenhurst, however no archaeological evidence of an earlier 11th /12th century lodge has ever been found in this area, which if of a scale as described earlier and possibly ditched and moated would suggest it never existed there. Conversely, Malwood Lodge, originally the site of an iron age fort on a 4 acre plateau and described as a royal hunting residence, is just 7 miles north of Brockenhurst. However, it might readily be described as '*towards*', simply using Brockenhurst as a known central landmark of 10 dwellings (the largest in the forest and 7 miles beyond Malwood Lodge) when travelling down from Winchester into the New Forest. As Grinnell-Milne quite justifiably pointed out, it is also quite possible that Gaimar did not even mean Brockenhurst village at all (and other references of his, like Wakelin, the Bishop of Winchester, being alive in 1100 are totally erroneous). In Anglo-Saxon, '*Bróck*' and '*Hyrst*' meant simply 'badger' and 'wood' i.e. 'Badger's Wood'[446] and less than a mile north-west of the Rufus Stone lies Brook Wood, on the edge of what was later to become Brook Common near the hamlet of Brook.[447] Thus as Milne suggests, anyone at Malwood Lodge being asked where the event took place might well, in the absence of other landmarks, point towards the northwest saying, "*Over there, towards bróc-hyrst*" i.e. towards *Brook/Badgers Wood*. Just an idea and not entirely unconvincing and certainly much else of the detail in Gaimar's account is very questionable and open to different interpretations.

---

[446] *A Concise Anglo-Saxon Dictionary for the use of Students,* John R. Clark Hall, 2nd Ed., Macmillan, 1916.
[447] D. Grinnell-Milne, pp.20–21.

38. Looking southwest up the slope of Canterton Glen with the Rufus Stone and oak tree in the foreground and the South Wood 'shooting line' in the distance.
Photo: courtesy of alanandmatth/www.atlasobscura.com/places/the-rufus-stone

More significantly Malwood Lodge is just half a mile from the killing site firmly established by local history and oral tradition and believed to be accurate by most modern academics.[448] The summation by New Forest historian and naturalist Charles Cornish is also significant when he concluded, following his analysis...

'...*the evidence as to the exact place of the king's death does not depend on history or upon general tradition. It is fixed by a concurrent and very coherent, though independent, set of circumstances'.*[449]

Marked by the Rufus Stone monument, the site lies to the north of Minstead village in an open glade called Canterton Glen in Stricknage Wood. This must surely be our starting point.

Charles II was shown the spot in the late 17th century and the Rufus memorial was first erected in 1745 by Lord Delaware (De La Warr) and is at, or very close to, the site of the king's stand and where the original oak 'trysting' tree once stood, off which, in one version, the arrow supposedly glanced before hitting the king in the chest (a tree propagated from an acorn of that original oak stands

---

[448] For example, the late Robert Hardy (d.2017), actor, author, historian and acknowledged world expert on the history of the medieval English longbow, was always convinced that the Rufus Stone did mark the actual location of what was an assassination.
[449] *The New Forest,* C. J. Cornish. Seeley & Co., London, 1906, Chap. 4, pp 134–141

nearby today). I firmly agree with the reasoning of Freeman, and others, on the matter that:

'The place and circumstance of the death of Rufus were such as could not fail to stamp themselves upon men's minds'.[450]

The original 1745 plinth, topped with a stone ball finial, was so damaged by relic hunters and vandals over the years that in 1841, with the ball removed, it was encased in an inscribed triangular cast-iron cover by the Forest Warden, William Sturgess Bourne, which is what we see today. (Figs.37 and 38 above)

With the assassination of President Kennedy, virtually every fine detail is known—there is even film and photos of the tragic event. As such, the precise time, the location of the limousines, the victims, the security agents and the bystanders can all be accurately determined, along with the actual window in the Texas school book depository where assassin Lee Harvey Oswald was situated and the rifle discovered. Despite all this available data, there still remains much debate and speculation about a possible second gunman on the 'grassy knoll', a 'magic bullet' and so on. With the death of Rufus, we only have the vaguest of notions precisely when it took place and as for the specific locations of the king, Tyrell, other members of the hunt (let alone the assassin) along with the location of specific trees, bushes and the target deer herd, we can only speculate with as much common sense and logic as possible when making our 'best guess' reconstruction of events over 9 centuries after they happened. After all, it is even proposed by some that Canterton Glen was not even the locale! In 2000, an alternate location was popularised when advocated by the now-late New Forest historian Arthur Lloyd, who picked up on the lost settlement of Th(o)rougham, in his booklet on the subject.[451]

---

[450] *William Rufus* , Freeman, E.A., Oxford Clarendon Press, 1882, p.335. It should be pointed out that the precise locations of notorious deaths/assassinations like those of Julius Caesar, Gandhi, JFK, John Lennon, Leon Trotsky, Archduke Ferdinand, Martin Luther King, Rasputin, Malcolm X, Abraham Lincoln, Thomas Becket, Louis Mountbatten and the Romanovs are remembered and recorded with memorials and I see no reason to believe that of Rufus, the King, and its dramatic nature, would have been any different and somehow 'lost to time'.

[451] *'The Death of Rufus'*, A. Lloyd, The New Forest Ninth Centenary Trust, 2000.

Lloyd proposed that this village, possibly destroyed and abandoned in the creation of the larger forest, once lay on the west side of the Beaulieu river, just 3 hundred metres from a pebbled beach of the north shore of the Solent, today the site of Park Farm (a dairy farm) on Park Lane. This suggested location, in the Hundred of Boldre, is some 15 miles to the south-east of Minstead being on the extreme southern edge of the National Park. In *Domesday*, it was still recorded as an agricultural area, consisting solely of 17 ploughlands and meadow, devoid of woodland, much as it is today. This place name of Thorougham, for the death of Rufus, was actually first proposed as far back as 1540 by John Leland, the 16th century antiquary and topographer of Henry VIII as: "*The place where it is said Tyrell killed King William Rufus is called Thorougham.*"[452] Although some 450 years after the event, Leland's undocumented source for this information apparently came second hand, from a conversation with a Sir William Berkeley. Berkeley (d.1551 aged 86), was not a historian and not of Berkeley Castle as incorrectly stated by Lloyd), whose family, in the 15th and 16th centuries, variously held the New Forest manors of Bisterne, Ibsley and parts of Minstead. These are all near Ringwood and Fritham, on the north-west side of the great forest—not near Beaulieu, which is on the south-east side some twenty miles away. Quite where Sir William garnered his story from is unknown and quite why Leland (and modern pundits) gave it so much credibility without any evidence, some 450 years later, is a mystery.[453] Leland gave no indication of where this place was, save the comment by Berkeley and its veracity can be questioned on a number of levels, with alternate suggestions by local historians having been made.[454] Perhaps more significantly, the land around Park Farm still

---

[452] '*Itinerary*', John Leland. Edited by Lucy T. Smith, in 6 vols. 1906–1910, Vol.4, p.142

[453] John Leland seems to have been easily seduced by unsubstantiated local folklore, as he fervently believed that King Arthur was a real person and did exist in historical fact. He stated in his *Itinerary* of 1542, despite a total lack of evidence, that Cadbury Castle, an Iron Age hill fort near Yeovil in Somerset, was the location for Camelot—not a view endorsed by current students of the topic.

[454] Another theory is that Thorougham is a corruption of the *Domesday* name Througham (4 ploughlands with no population) that was later confused with 'Truham', in the Rodedic Hundred, and a misreading of the calligraphy—into today's nearby Fritham (a place name not recorded in Domesday), just a mile to the west of the Rufus Stone. This location was accepted (*though is often disputed*) by three renowned 19th century New Forest historians namely, Revd. Gilpin, '*Remarks on Forest Scenery*', 1808, P. Lewis, '*Ancient and Modern State of the New Forest*', 1811 and John Wise, '*The New Forest,*

resembles the more familiar English countryside of open fields and hedgerows, much as it was recorded in *Domesday*—it is without tree cover, marshes or a hill or slope and is not known (now or historically) as deer territory—far removed from the chroniclers' depictions of the site of Rufus's demise.[455]

Conversely, the topography of Canterton Glen fits the various near-contemporary descriptions perfectly, being an open area, heavily wooded on 3 sides, marshy and sloping upwards from east to west. This direction is key—as William of Malmesbury first recorded that the wounded stag ran towards the sun, causing the king *'who ran after it, keeping his gaze fixedly on the quarry, to shield his eyes from the powerful glare of its rays'*.[456] In addition, the local woodcutter/charcoal burner Purkis (Purkess)—immortalised in the inscription on the Rufus Stone—is claimed by legend as the man who, saving Rufus's corpse from 'rook, dog and vermin', took the royal body in his cart the twenty miles to Winchester Cathedral for burial. Although William of Malmesbury does not mention any Purkis, simply 'a few countrymen', Purkis is inextricably linked to the retrieval of Rufus's body.

This is a family name closely linked to the nearby villages of Minstead, Canterton and Fritham—not a site near Beaulieu some 15+ miles away, where Purkis would never have been that late in the day or at all, given how far away it is. 19th century historian of the New Forest, Percival Lewis, wrote that *'lineal descendants of Purkis were said to have been rewarded with an acre or 2 of*

---

its scenery and history', 1863. and also by Horace Round, *The Hampshire Domesday Introduction and Text. VCH of Hampshire and the Isle of Wight*, Vol.1, 1900. At the time of Domesday, Truham, Minstead and Brockenhurst were among many small settlements, all in the 'Rodedic' Hundred—later the 'New Forest' Hundred.—see *'Historical enquiries concerning forests and forest laws with topographical remarks upon the ancient and modern state of New Forest'*. Percival Lewis, London: T Payne, 1811.

[455] In fact Park Farm was originally the site of a monastic grange and chapel, being farmed by monks as part of the Beaulieu Abbey estate founded in the early 13th century under King John which would tend to confirm its unwooded nature and quality arable land. *Historic England: Heritage Category: Listed Building Grade: II. List Entry Number:1156997. Date first listed: 08–Oct-1959: Statutory Address: Park Farmhouse, Park Lane.*

[456] *De Gestis Regnum Anglorum*, Malmesbury, trans. in English Historical Documents, op. cit. pp. 292–3.

ground...near Canterton and Fritham',[457] although he also gives no source to substantiate this claim.

Other commentators suggest that Purkis may have opted for the privilege of collecting wood 'by hook or by crook', of inestimable value to a charcoal burner.[458] Either way, the Purkis family's thatched 'cruk' house apparently survived at Canterton until the end of the 19th century and descendants (now Purkess) still live nearby to this day, all of which would tend to lend support to the Stricknage Wood location for events rather than anywhere near Beaulieu on the opposite side of the forest.

As of 2023, Stricknage Wood is only about 30 acres, but as recently as 1789 it can be identified on maps running to some 150 acres. 700 years earlier, it would have been even more extensive and indistinguishable from that of the surrounding forest.

There is no better in-depth analysis of the hunt and the specifics of the geography, geology, topography and meteorology in Stricknage Wood than that made by Grinnell-Milne in his intriguing, yet somewhat maligned 1968 book *The Killing of William Rufus*.[459] Although he somewhat muddies and weakens his theory by getting carried away by specific trees and bushes, I believe his basic construct of events that day is sound. Perhaps his most vital observation, albeit one that seems banal, is the matter of soil and drainage. While trees in wooded areas have come, gone and come again over the subsequent centuries, due to the unchanging geology of the poor soil of clays with gravel beneath it, Canterton Glen and indeed almost the whole New Forest—with its commons, ponds, marsh, forest and heathland—would have looked remarkably similar in 1100 as it does now.[460] According to a recent BBC Hampshire New Forest History

---

[457] *Ancient and Modern State of the New Forest*, P. Lewis, 1811. pp. 51–61.

[458] As detailed in Part I, chapter 2, this was permission to pull down dead branches for firewood, normally a criminal offence. It is said the Purkis family displayed a wheel from the cart that conveyed the royal corpse, right up to the 18th century. Detail from *The History of Normandy and England: William Rufus. 'Accession of Henry Beauclerc'*, Sir Francis Palgrave, 1864, *Vol.4*, p.687.

[459] '*The Killing of William Rufus—An investigation in the New Forest*', Duncan Grinnell-Milne, Pub. David and Charles, 1968. New Ed. 1973.

[460] I have been to the site numerous times over 60 years and can confirm that my most recent visit presented exactly the same vista as that of six decades earlier. The underlying soil quality of the New Forest is very poor, making it totally ill-suited for agricultural use.

article, "*…in many ways the forest itself has changed little over the centuries. There are areas of ancient woodland which are today almost exactly as they were hundreds of years ago.*"[461]

I, like others before me, have narrowed down this vast area to the lodge, the walk, the woods and the glen ~ an open marshy slope (drier in high summer depending on recent rainfall, as the clay subsoil means it drains poorly) about 40 metres wide that runs roughly east/west. As detailed in the previous chapter, this area was very likely part of a large contained deer park or 'hay'. Malwood Walk is formed by the dense oak and beech trees, matching the descriptions of Gaimar and reinforced as '*the*' place by oral tradition and local history. I have been to this spot numerous times over 60 years and it remains an unchanging, wild and eerily quiet place, naturally silenced by the thick woodland all around.

Now imagine, if you will, the hunters riding up to Canterton Glen, skirting woodland to the north and south in Stricknage Wood, and arriving in the glade. They dismount, horses attended to, and walk westwards through Southwood to their prescribed camouflaged positions on the edge of the 'Battue'—each hunter with attendant bow-bearer and dog-handler in tow. Soon, in the distance, the beaters with their sticks can be heard and the startled deer herd advance, rustling through the undergrowth of the northerly wood…shortly to slowly emerge from the forest cover into the bright early evening sunshine of the open glade, taking up the 'deer trail' to the west, towards the grazing land, ponds and open plains of Stoney Cross, but unknowingly, into the sightline of the awaiting archers with bows bent.

So, far from the remote, empty, densely wooded forest depicted in later images, what we actually have is 9 or 10 hunters on the edge of an open field supported by 30–40 silent, concealed hunting staff and foresters.[462] With Bow and Stable hunting, as well as each participant having a bow-bearer and a dog-

---

[461] www.bbc.co.uk/hampshire/content/articles/2005/03/24/newforest_history_feature.sht ml.

[462] While this may seem like a high figure, using the modern equivalent of the grouse shoot, it is actually a modest estimate though many, like beaters, carters and domestics, would be locals from Minstead and Canterton and not resident at the hunting lodge itself. According to Colin Adamson, retired head keeper of the Duke of Northumberland's Burncastle estate, on a normal grouse day they have 'about 24 beaters, six flankers and three or four pickers-up' and this excludes staff like loaders, minders and those providing lunch, chauffeurs etc—50+ people.

handler, there would be the beaters, groomsmen, carters, servants and so on, in the wooded background. With such numbers, I believe there would have to have been witnesses, as although it is likely that all of the staff were illiterate, most hunting staff were trained to be highly observant, but of course, observing an event you are unaware is about to occur is not so easy, more a matter of luck, as invariably no-one is looking in the right place at the precise time—and the archer assassin is well camouflaged. As far as we know, none of them were ever interviewed, gave a statement or officially commented on the circumstances of the shooting. We have nothing apart from the self-driven confessions/denials of Tyrell. So again, all we can go on are the chroniclers' later entries.

The line of stands would have started from the east, with the king in the prime position—the approximate location of the Rufus Stone. Naturally, he would have been the first to see, and have a chance to shoot at, the driven herd. It was etiquette that a favoured hunter stood at the second stand so if the king missed his shot, the better hunter would secure it and the king could pass the kill off as his own. So to Rufus's left, some 50–60 metres away, I believe that we can place his new good friend and 'best shot', the Frenchman, Walter Tyrell. This substantial gap between each archer was for both safety reasons and hunting protocol—primarily to prevent them from accidentally shooting each other, but also to minimise interference in the target area/range of adjacent archer(s).

39. KING'S POSITION: Looking west, up the slope of Canterton Glen. Tyrell would have been 50–60m beyond this on the Southwood treeline (left above). TYRELL'S POSITION: Looking east towards the Rufus Stone (centre of image). Photo taken from where Tyrell's stand was likely located.
©Photos Author's own

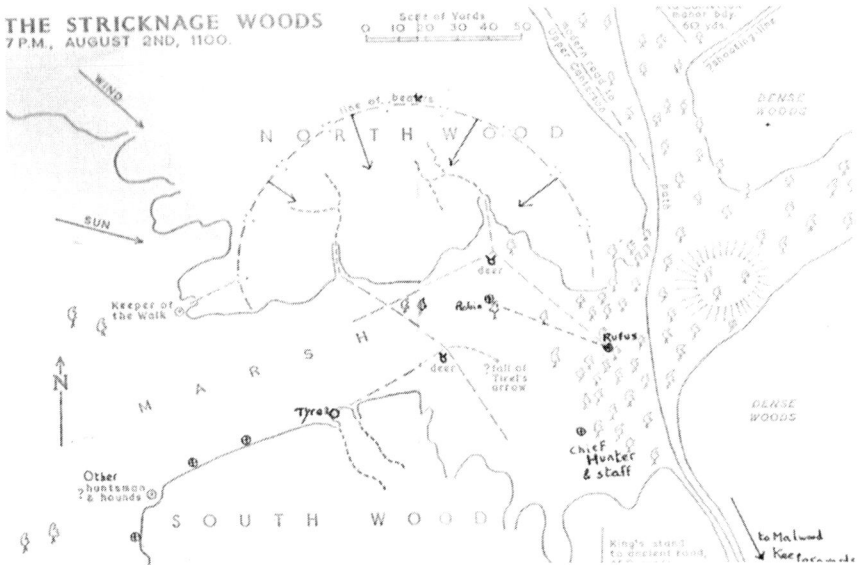

40. The 'Death Zone' showing possible positions of the parties when Rufus dies: Map showing the probable positions of the parties

Author's own markings superimposed on original Grinnell-Milne sketch from
The Killing of William Rufus, 1968, pp.72/3, courtesy of David and Charles publishers.

So beyond Tyrell, we have the remaining firing positions spread out westwards (in much the same vein as a modern grouse shoot), also at 50–60 metre intervals over some 350 metres, where the Southwood tree line curves left and slopes upwards through marshy ground[463] towards the higher ground of Stoney Cross Plain. Due to this unique topography, the other 7–8 archers, behind their trysts, would have been completely out of sight of the king.

Expanding upon this theory, what is particularly auspicious about this hunting format is that the position of the king could be guaranteed on a precise day at a specific time, all predetermined. Rufus's royal stand, by the oak tree 'tryst', would essentially be isolated yet likely adjacent to the stand of his closest companion, Walter Tyrell. Convinced of this more gentle type of hunt, one can interpret what the chroniclers meant by *separate from* the rest of the party, namely that the 2 men were 'apart' from the others, as them being not at the same stand but at their own stands, just about in view of one another (Tyrell may later claim 'just out of sight' and 'in a different part of the forest') and no other bowman.

41. Looking due west (in winter) into the sun from the Rufus Stone, up Canterton Glen with the edge of Northwood to the right, from where the driven herd would have emerged. (The New Forest pony is standing in a spot where a target deer may have been. Similarly, Robin would be hidden in that large oak tree to the right.)
©Photo: Author's own

---

[463] It is quite possible there were fewer stands than hunters, as most e.g. Walter and Ranulph, also the two Clare brothers, most likely paired up and shared the same position together.

Separate, totally stationary and brightly lit by the sun while waiting for the beaters to bring forth prey, Rufus was effectively, and somewhat ironically, a sitting duck himself. Any camouflaged assassin up in a tree would be completely invisible and obscured from his view by the glare of the setting sun. One just has to be persuaded that this was not the *'misaimed arrow of some blundering archer'*[464]—Tyrell was repeatedly noted as an expert shot by his contemporaries—but, in fact, a remarkably ingenious plan. See image 40 above for a rough idea of the locations of the significant figures of that day when Rufus fell.

Despite this detailed analysis and reconstruction of the scene, I will be the first to admit that after more than 900 years much of the precise details have been lost. It is solely based on an intuitive and common sense interpretation of the geography of the area, the type of hunt undertaken and the little details we can glean from the chroniclers reports. At the end of the day, quite precisely where the king's stand was (and adjacent oak tree), which tree was Robin positioned in, what was Tyrell's exact location on the tree line and where did the deer enter the glen etc. can all only be given a 'best guess', along with many other unanswered questions. However, overall I believe the sequence of events as presented represent a more than credible reconstruction of what unfolded that fateful late afternoon.

When explaining away the arrow that struck Rufus, historians like Hollister often surmise that *'hunting accidents were not uncommon'*.[465] I both agree and disagree. In the context of a Par Force hunt, with horses and prey darting about, hedges being jumped, a lethal stray missile from young, impetuous or adrenaline-fuelled hunters would not be impossible to imagine. However, within the much more structured and controlled confines of the Bow and Stable hunt (especially if confined to the limits of a constructed deer enclosure) specifically designed for safety and accuracy, the chances of an accident were practically zero. These were highly skilled, expert archers and intelligent military men—it is rather ridiculous to think that they could find themselves in a situation, indeed in an

---

[464] *The Strange Death of William Rufus*, Warren Hollister, *Speculum—A Journal of Medieval Studies*, Vol. 48, No. 4 (October 1973). P.653. From Tyrell's proposed position at the hunt, even if deliberately aiming to shoot Rufus, the chances of securing a guaranteed 'kill' would be barely more than 20%—this was not an option.

[465] The examples Hollister provides are the much later deaths around half a century later of Miles of Gloucester, 1st Earl of Hereford, 1143 (by arrow on Christmas Eve) and Malcolm de Morville c.1163 (cause unknown)—so not that common.

open glen, with stands set far apart in a line, whereby they fired arrows east and west (i.e. right and left) towards each other instead of north towards the prey. The only people in any danger of being hit were the beaters emerging from the north woods behind the driven target herd and even they are effectively out of range. In the unlikely event of the accidental death of such lowly staff, however experienced, one doubts it would even be registered. At least, there are no existing records of such.

Getting slightly technical for a moment—the trajectory of an arrow shot at a deer's vital organs 30 metres away would never 'carry', at a man's chest height, to a target another 20–30 metres further on, but start to fall to earth. The topography of the land suggests that Walter, unless he moved well forward of his position, would not have had a good view of the king. This backs up Tyrell's later protestations that he was '*in a different part of the wood*' to Rufus. Any arrow loosed from in or near his stand would, at most, not have had the penetrative force to cause death and, at least, fallen to the ground well short of the King's position, particularly if it had glanced off a deer or a tree or, as in one report, both, as an arrow loses virtually all impetus immediately if coming into contact with another solid object and almost immediately tumbles to the ground. Bowhunting deer, even with powerful, modern, sighted, magnesium alloy or carbon fibre compound bows coupled with an expert bowman, is very difficult at ranges beyond 40 metres, especially so with a moving target. The physics-defying claim of instant death from a further distance with much more rudimentary 11th century bows seems just too far-fetched. Yet, what is clear from most accounts is that the impact of the arrow was significant; Rufus could not pull it out himself and it snapped off in his chest, so must have been barbed and deeply embedded. As a keen amateur English longbow archer myself, such required impetus would firmly suggest a shorter and uninterrupted flightpath of 30 metres maximum.

It is worth remembering that it would be another 25 years before anyone mentioned Tyrell's name, by which point most of the people likely involved in the plot were dead.[466] No-one present in the glen or surrounding woods claimed that Tyrell fired the arrow—they would have needed to be within his sight,

---

[466] By 1125, only four of the original 10 plotters were still alive, plus King Henry himself. They were William Giffard—the now elderly Bishop of Winchester; Maud, now Queen consort of Scotland; Roger de Clare, probably retired in Normandy; and Walter Tyrell, retired back in France.

which, as we know from the layout, would have been impossible. As no nobleman saw anything, no name was put forward, until the chronicler William of Malmesbury wrote of Walter's 'accident' because, he surmised—who else could it have been?

If we believe that Tyrell provided no other name but, to his deathbed, vowed he '*did not shoot the king*', and if we take the favoured version of events based on Malmesbury's 1125 account that the king and Tyrell were far enough removed from rest of the party for all other hunt members to be absolved, then we are really left with only one possible conclusion…

The fatal arrow must have been fired by an unseen third party.

With such a large group (hunters plus staff), I am convinced that at least one or 2 of the king's attendants must surely have witnessed the shooting, or more precisely, the immediate aftermath as the arrow struck the king's chest, though not the responsible archer. Although nothing was officially noted, I suspect that word-of-mouth accounts of those few seconds were widely circulated at the time and these are what Malmesbury, Orderic and others picked up on years later, second hand or further diluted. From such, we are told that Rufus either fell forward onto the shaft, snapped it off or pushed it further in, thus hastening his death. We are also told that the first person to arrive on the scene (apart from the king's attendants) was Tyrell, possibly with his retainer Ranulf, who both dashed the 50+ metres from their stand to where the body lay. We know that Rufus had presented Walter with some of his new arrows earlier. This is incredibly significant, as the assassin's arrow would have been markedly different from that of the king's arrow gifted to Walter. Based on my unique theory and research, this 'foreign' arrow would have been instantly distinguishable in 3 ways:

(1) Longer by 2–3 inches (5–7.5cm).

Robin would very likely have inherited the large 'Bamburgh' physique of both his father Waltheof and grandfather Siward. Add to this his famous archery skills and we can conclude that his famed longbow, maybe 2 metres tall, would have had a deep 'draw', thus needing significantly longer-shafted arrows than average. Meanwhile, Rufus—understood to have been stocky and relatively short (with a bit of a paunch)—would have required a smaller bow and shorter arrows. Further, images of archers depicted on the Bayeux Tapestry show us that the standard Norman bow was at least a foot or so (0.5m) shorter than that belonging to the enemy Anglo-Saxon.[467]

(2)   Not new.

The King's/Walter's arrows were newly made for the occasion, ergo pale and with fresh-looking shafts. Even if Robin's were also new (debatable as an outlaw, not local, who had recently travelled a long distance), a shaft made by another fletcher, hewn from a differently aged tree, perhaps even in a different type of wood, would be immediately identifiable.

(3)   Lacking distinctive feathers.

12th century noblemen had exclusive access to peacocks and swans, delicacies eaten at banquets. Their feathers would have been used by royal fletchers—not just for their high quality but also as symbols of prestige. Conversely Robin's fletchings, while good quality, probably would have come from a white goose. Even if the king's feathers weren't so exotic, the odds are they would have been plucked from a completely different type, colour and size of bird.

42. (1) Bronze peacock feathers (2) Arrows fletched with white goose feathers
(3) A broadhead arrow for hunting (and murder!)
42.
1.and 2. Use of ©photos courtesy of Wayne Robinson
3. Use of ©photo courtesy of 'Fraternity of Saint George 1509'.

---

[467] See Appendix 8 on archery.

An additional 4th element is also critical, but not a physical characteristic of the arrow itself. Given Robin's position in the tree some 20–30yds. To the north (see fig. 40), both angles of his incoming arrow, horizontally and vertically, compared to Tyrell's position at ground level, would be quite different such that if anyone was to have seen the shaft embedded in the king's torso. And its angle of entry, then they would quickly realise that the Frenchman was in no way involved. But Walter, required as he was to 'take the blame', at least 'in the moment', needed to make it appear he was the stupid culprit.

With all this in mind, I am convinced that Walter's first task would have been to pick up or snap off this different shaft and feathers and secrete it in his cloak before anyone noticed. Additionally, the removal of the shaft would destroy the evidence of the 'angle of entry' of the arrow into Rufus, as I say, clearly Robin was not in precisely the same line of fire as Walter and shooting from up above. I suspect this 'arrow snaffling' act by Tyrell ultimately led to the long-held legend that Rufus did such himself. Whether or not you share the same suspicion, given the unexpected and incredibly forceful impact of a broadhead-tipped longbow shaft shot from 20–30 metres, deeply piercing his heart or lung, it defies what we know about human biology (even with adrenalin and alcohol added) that Rufus would have had the strength and wherewithal to do such himself.

At this point, it is worth a side-step to Grinnell-Milne's theory. In his 1968 book, he suggested that the Chief Hunter was the agent of the plotters. He goes on to name Ranulf de Aix ~ Gerald of Wales's c.1190 suspect and Mason's modern revamp (as Tyrell's aide, not as chief hunter—if we accept Ranulf d'Equesnes as a variant spelling). However, this conclusion is flawed. Despite his title, the Chief Hunter was responsible for organising the hunt, not actually hunting with the royal party. Not being in a shooting position, he likely did not have archery equipment readily to hand. Furthermore, Grinnell-Milne places him approximately 30 metres behind (south of) the king's stand—see fig.40. Various accounts claim that Rufus was looking westwards and shielding his eyes from the setting sun—if true, this is a key point, both in terms of a manoeuvre by the king beyond the remit of any planning/prediction and in terms of who now potentially had the best shot. From the Chief Hunter's southerly position, the sightline to the king would have been side-on…an impossible angle for a direct hit to the chest.

43. Robin shooting from up a tree
As depicted on the new Robin Hood 2021 1oz Gold Bullion Coin
© Image reproduced by courtesy of the Royal Mint

Conversely, for the best archer in England, concealed in a tree just 20–30 metres away to the west, between Rufus, face on and the bright sun behind, we have an easy, perhaps perfect target. The Royal Toxophilite Society states that even an averagely 'good' bowman can repeatedly hit a 15cm/six-inch diameter circle from a range of 25–35 metres.[468] As an averagely good bowman myself, I can confirm this regular hit rate to be true.

From everything we know or can reasonably assume about that day, about hunting protocols and about the physics of archery, I believe that the following was the order of events:

The beaters drove the deer herd from the tree cover of Northwood into the open glen towards the king (then up the slope on the 'deer trail' past Tyrell, then onto the others along the southern tree line and even further on to Stoney Cross

---

[468] *The Killing of William Rufus—An investigation in the New Forest*, Duncan Grinnell-Milne, Pub. David and Charles 1968. New Ed. 1973. p107.

Plain, the route of Tyrell's flight just minutes later). As the deer appeared into the glen, 3 arrows then fired in quick succession, almost simultaneously: First from the slightly inebriated King, either missing or, as recorded by William of Malmesbury, wounding the animal, which then ran on westwards towards the sun. The King turns westward himself to face the slope, the wounded animal and the sun, shouting at Tyrell—*"Draw, draw your bow, for the devil's sake and stretch out the arrow, or you will be sorry!"* (*Trahe, trahe arcum ex parte diaboli et extende sagittam, alias te poenitebit*).[469]

If a wounded animal was getting away, a fewterer would have immediately released the dogs from their leashes, confirming the record by Peter of Blois that *'hounds were hunting a stag up a hill'*.[470] Second came the decoy shaft from Tyrell, maybe glancing off the animal but falling someway short of Rufus. Finally, Robin's shot, from a relatively short range and camouflaged position in a tree, finding the centre of the king's heart/lung. It would have been a matter of seconds between these 3 arrows and death. Put together in this way, the disparate descriptions from the various chroniclers present a credible and compelling picture of that early evening in Canterton Glen.

Furthermore, if we assume that Robin was at least in approximately the same line of fire to the Westward as Tyrell, as would be the intelligent choice for such an experienced archer and outlaw, any observer would understandably believe it must have come from the Frenchman, including the archer attendant to the king, being distracted by the glaring sun, the shouting king, the wounded deer and yelping hounds. To him, while perhaps baffled by the distance the arrow travelled, it could not have been anyone else, since all the others were out of sight and far away. Of course, the king's favourite would never have done this deliberately…

---

[469] Although written some 250 yrs. later, this was recorded in *Knighton's Chronicon, col.1337;* Henry Knighton (died c. 1396), was an Augustinian canon in Leicester and an ecclesiastical historian who wrote a history of England from the Norman conquest until 1396, thought to be the year he died. His source for this outburst, variously translated, is unknown and probably made up.

[470] *Rerum Anglicorum Scriptores,* Peter of Blois c.1170s, Vol. 1, Eds. Fulman and Gale, 1684. Hounds were generally released in pairs or threes and were vitally important to ensure a 'kill', as rarely was the first strike by an arrow accurate enough to be fatal, resulting in the wounded animal continuing to run onwards.

On that note, I keep returning to the same question: If it had been an accident, if it had indeed been a freak physics-defying arrow or Tyrell's carelessness, or if he had witnessed another member of staff innocently making the same mistake, then what reason did he—by all accounts a sincere and religious man—have to commit perjury on his deathbed following a pilgrimage to Jerusalem to redeem his soul? Surely, with Henry happily on the throne and all chroniclers declaring that Rufus's dramatic end had been God's will, Tyrell would admit that he, or another official attendee that day, had been a divine instrument in the death of an unpopular King.

**44. View eastward to the Rufus Stone/King's position from the
base of the tree where Robin may have been located**
©Photo: Author's own

Instead, we have numerous accounts declaring that he repeatedly protested his innocence. With that, and the fact that he was the only nobleman with even a vague sight of the king and his attendees, we are left with one logical conclusion: Tyrell was innocent of the crime, but guilty of knowing, and perhaps abetting with, the truth—a truth so explosive that he could never reveal it—the arrow had been shot by a third-party assassin. In its stead, an 'accident' was the perfect cover for the perfect murder—regicide.

So, with the corpse of Rufus left lying on the grass with just the stub of a broken off shaft protruding, his chest covered in blood and going cold by the minute, Walter made his getaway with, I believe, the considerable planning and support of his relatives, the Clare brothers.

Chapter 9
The Next Hours

45. Purkis taking the body of Rufus to Winchester on his cart
Illustration from *Danes, Saxons and Normans* by J.G. Edgar, 1863, freely reproduced
under the terms of the Project Gutenberg Licence

According to chroniclers Orderic and Malmesbury, both of whom had a certain
tendency for the dramatic, Rufus's body was *'like a wild boar stuck with*

spears[471]. The idea of Rufus being a human pincushion, à la St Sebastian, does seem somewhat sensationalist given that the accepted death was by a singular arrow! This is a perfect example of the difficulties we have in getting to the truth of the matter in the hours of dusk and beyond. The chroniclers' descriptions of events immediately following the king's death, when all the other members of the hunt discover the 'tragedy', all get very differing treatments. In some versions, perhaps the best known, poor old Rufus is abandoned on the ground where he fell, leaving Purkis, a local peasant charcoal burner (no doubt a supplier to the blacksmiths, household and kitchens at Malwood Lodge[472]), to discover him an hour or 2 later, presumably on his way home after tending his charcoal kilns. In the interim, Tyrell escapes while the local nobles flee—either to their properties should civil unrest break out or to accompany Henry back to the royal palace at Winchester.

Then we have the contrasting poetic depiction by Gaimar. Although an important source, we need, though, to be a little wary of Gaimar's account as he was not a monk but a lay historian and poet whose patron was Constance, wife of Ralph FitzGilbert, a Lincolnshire landowner. Constance's grandfather had been one of 4 under-marshals in the Rufus royal household, who was very probably at the hunting lodge the day Rufus was killed and thus a likely first-hand witness to the day's events, which he surely must have related to his son and granddaughter in later years. It is thought that Gaimar, writing somewhat fancifully decades later, was something of a PR agent for the nobility and wrote his account (under Constance's direction) to improve on the perceived poor conduct of the nobles following Rufus's death, focusing, as it does, firmly on the theme of loyalty, not desertion.

Gaimar claimed the king survived for a few minutes, long enough to cry out 4 times and beg to be given the 'host', consecrated Holy Communion bread. With no time to carry him to Minstead Church for the last rites and some Lammas loaf, his loyal adherents do what they can, giving him a handful of grass and flowers to eat in place of breaking bread. They then surround the corpse, weeping, beating their breasts, declaring that, "*they will never again have such a wonderful Lord*" and other such platitudes. Lovingly, they create a funeral bier[473] out of tree

---

[471] *Gesta Regum Anglorum*, Malmesbury, 5:292, 2: p.378.

[472] At this time, charcoal was vital, being the only fuel hot enough to smelt iron for items like horseshoes, arrow heads, spears, swords etc.

[473] Moveable frame upon which a body or coffin is carried.

branches and leather straps from the horses and de l'Aigle and Fitzhaimo cover the king in all manner of luxurious materials ripped from their cloaks. Removing Purkis totally from the process, they then take the body in procession to Winchester. This version not only is fanciful but illogical, given there would have been nearby carts brought for the transportation of the deer carcases back to Malwood Lodge or Winchester Castle. In any case, the lodge at Malwood was itself just 5 minutes' ride away, where numerous suitable forms of transport, along with copious fabrics, could have been readily deployed.

More reliably, the majority of reports note that Purkis, with or without some lowly royal servants, and possibly upon instruction from the Constable of Malwood Lodge (Robert de Montfort), later put the king's body on his humble cart and took it to Winchester Cathedral. Since this is a journey of some 20 miles (one he would know well, often going to the city to both sell his charcoal and deliver such to the castle and abbey), it must have taken at least 4–5 hours along the rough track, now the A3090 and in part still known locally as the King's Road or Lane.[474] With dusk turning to night, Purkis and his sorrowful load, slowly stiffening as 'rigour mortis' set in, probably did not reach the cathedral precincts until around 11pm to midnight, maybe later.

In addition to the fanciful *'wild boar stuck with spears'* description, according to William of Malmesbury, the king's blood *'watered the earth the whole way'*. We are told by the majority of chroniclers that Rufus lay dead in the forest for a good hour or 2 before being recovered. However, if Malmesbury is to be believed and the 'body' was in fact dripping blood on the journey, a basic understanding of human biology and forensics tells us that his heart was still functioning as only living bodies bleed and, if true, means that poor old Rufus was still alive at the start and died of blood loss (exsanguination) along the way. I doubt this version, as a body with a single fatal entry wound, plugged by an arrow shaft and left on the ground for an hour or 2, would not result in such drawn-out gore for several hours over 20 miles. More likely, Malmesbury's graphic description was a symbolic embellishment—given that Purkis probably made the journey alone (or maybe with a lowly royal servant), such detail can only have come from him or the writer's imagination. Perhaps Malmesbury chose to depict 'bleeding out'—traditionally a form of capital punishment—as criticism of Rufus, perhaps because blood-letting was a popular medieval

---

[474] *The New Forest, its scenery and history.* John R. Wise, Smith, Elder, London, 1867, p. 97.

method of salvation (letting out the bad blood to leave only the good), or more likely it was a literary device consistent with the contemporary belief that the blood of a divine sacrifice must fall upon the ground in order to fertilise it.[475] The general consensus however, backed up by the accounts of chroniclers like Orderic Vitalis and Peter of Blois, is that Rufus died instantly. If not, it would take the assassination theory beyond reasonable doubt, highlighting the disregard of all for the king's condition: To not ascertain if he was still alive, to not attempt to save him or seek medical help, or at least to bring a cleric from the lodge or nearby church to give him, the king, his last rites and absolution seems outrageous—unless, of course, he was stone dead…

Gaimar goes on to say that, upon arrival in Winchester Cathedral, *"Bishop Walkelin held vigil over the body that night."* As Bishop Walkelin had died 2 years earlier in 1098, one must yet again question the veracity of Gaimar's account! In fact, there was no bishop residing in Winchester at this time— Walkelin had not been replaced, allowing Rufus to filter all the cathedral revenues into his own coffers to help fund his Maine and Vexin campaigning.

At the same time as the king's last journey, Walter dashed to the coast with his squire, Ranulf. As suggested by William of Malmesbury, he probably had help, *'with one party conniving at his flight'* and although the chronicler names no names, I propose that the 'party' was Roger de Clare, who was key to this escape plan and accompanied them. Later rumours, accurate or not, suggest that Rufus's 'familiars' were later seeking to tear him [Walter] apart[476] but presumably had no idea where he had gone. To make a successful getaway, horses, attendants and a safe sea passage must have been organised in advance. The route of their journey to the continent is not recorded by any chronicler, although local history and legend firmly maps out a path, including a departure from Poole Harbour, then an expanding maritime and fishing centre. A route south-west, directly opposite to that taken by Henry, was required, establishing greater distance between them with every mile ridden.

Two well-known watery folklore tales accompany Tyrell's flight. The first occurred at Ocknell Pond, just a mile or so west of the Rufus Stone. The water was said to turn red on the August 2nd anniversary each year, in memory of Walter stopping there to wash his hands of the monarch's blood (consistent with

---

[475] *Medieval Blood,* Bettina Bildhauer (Cardiff, 2006), pp. 63–4.
[476] *The Strange Death of William Rufus,* Warren Hollister, *Speculum—A Journal of Medieval Studies,* Vol. 48, No. 4 (October 1973). p.652.

him having got them covered in blood while retrieving the snapped off arrow shaft). While unprovable, as there is no evidence of this 'blood' occurrence today, it seems suspiciously 'miraculous' and highly unlikely. However, it was surprisingly 'confirmed' in an official 1951 Forestry Commission Guide to the New Forest, perhaps to boost the local tourist trade![477]

Halfway to Poole, Walter, Ranulf and Roger would have needed to cross the River Avon and most likely at the shallowest point, a crossing by the tiny hamlet of Avon, midway between Ringwood and Christchurch at a place still known to this day as 'Tyrell's Ford'.

46. Tyrell's Ford, the shallow crossing of the River Avon, today made easier by a small bridge to the north.
Image courtesy of: Imagery©2021 Google, Getmapping plc, Infoterra Ltd. And Bluesky, Maxar Technologies, Map data©2021

The second tale takes place here. It is said that, prior to crossing, they had their steads' horseshoes reversed by the local blacksmith in order to confuse their pursuers. Bizarrely, it was reported as late as the 1860s that the blacksmith's descendants (or Lord of the Manor) were still paying an annual fine of £3–10s

---

[477] *'The New Forest in History'*, Forestry Commission Guide, M. G. Davis, 1951, p.7. If the water had turned red at some point, this could be explained by the sporadic presence of a red algae which occurs in hot weather. This is similar to Finchampstead spring detailed in the *Anglo-Saxon Chronicle*, see Part II, chapter 5, but its appearance is totally random.

to the Crown (c. £250 at today's value) for what their predecessor had done to assist the escape![478] While the party may well have stopped to re-shoe or repair loose shoes, the idea of the Smithy putting them on backwards is totally impractical and apocryphal. Quite how the poor blacksmith was supposed to have been aware of what had taken place earlier some 15 miles away is unclear. Furthermore, there is no evidence that anyone was chasing after them anyway and the whole story has the whiff of a myth.

However the one useful commonality of these tales is that they provide specific locations. Placing Rufus's death in the woods near Minstead, then following the popular narrative of Tyrell's escape route, via Ocknell Pond onto the 'convenient' ancient routes of what are now the A31 towards Ringwood, then down (B3347) to Tyrell's Ford and (B3073/3068) to Poole Harbour, all of which fit the geography precisely, as opposed to any alternative 'Thorougham/Park Farm' location near Beaulieu river. This latter locale does not work as the site of the king's demise for the reasons highlighted earlier and also, if it was 20 miles away, near Beaulieu, surely either of the nearby harbours on the Solent (Hythe and Eling Creek) or Lepe, near the mouth of the Beaulieu River, all only 7–9 miles ride from Park Farm, rather than the 30+ miles from Thorougham to Poole, would have been the clear obvious choices for a rapid cross Channel departure. It is worth pointing out that Southampton would also have been closer, but it was full of Rufus's invasion fleet and obviously best avoided.

Once at Poole, they would catch a boat, no doubt pre-arranged by Roger, and probably on the first tide early the following morning.[479] It makes sense that they would have sailed to the adjacent ports of either Honfleur or Harfleur in Normandy, where horses would have taken them the last 30 miles to Bec Abbey. They could then have retired to rest, initially at the abbey then maybe at Robert

---

[478] 'The New Forest, its scenery and history'. John R. Wise, Smith, Elder, London, 1867, p.127.

[479] Given Roger de Clare and Robert de Beaumont's large property holdings in Normandy and their proximity to Bec Abbey, this cross-Channel sea passage from Poole was no doubt one they both made quite frequently over the years as a recognised departure point and would undoubtedly, with their huge wealth, have had local contacts to organise the trips back and forth on both sides of the Channel. They may even have had their own boat. Roger de Clare had his own castle and estates, just 25 miles south west of Bec Abbey at Orbec/Bienfaite.

de Beaumont's castle at Brionne[480] (just 3 miles from Bec) and more likely at Roger de Clare's own castle at Orbec, just 25 miles away to the south-west.

Roger and Walter thus brought the dramatic news of Rufus's death that they delivered to the Abbot of Bec and to the third Clare brother, monk Richard, for onward delivery to everyone's favourite cleric, the self-exiled Archbishop Anselm in southern France. We are told it was delivered within a week to Anselm at the Chaise-Dieu monastery (see footnote 392) by 2 swiftly travelling monks, one of Canterbury and one of Bec, who was surely Richard de Clare, as Richard then accompanied Anselm back to England by the 15th September and joined the king at Salisbury; all of which was remarkably, almost impossibly, fast.[481]

The official letter from Henry, requesting his return, was understood to have been delivered to Cluny Abbey near Lyon shortly after Rufus died (some 325 miles south-east of Bec Abbey). It was mentioned earlier that, conveniently, the Abbot of Bec at this time was a second cousin of the Beaumont brothers, Guillaume Beaumont de Montfort-sur-Risle (d.1124). He had been Anselm's successor in 1093 and was the son of Henry and Robert de Beaumont's cousin Aubrée[482] and husband Turstin de Montfort-sur-Risle (see Appendix 4). So Guillaume was yet another trusted family ally and no doubt well briefed by the Clares regarding the whole scheme. He would undoubtedly have been very keen to re-establish his great friend Anselm back at Canterbury and delighted to be told that Rufus had met a sticky end as planned. Significantly, King Henry

---

[480] In somewhat complex circumstances involving Duke Robert Curthose and William de Breteuil, c.1090 the Beaumonts acquired the castle and Lordship of Brionne in exchange for Ivry Castle (on the borders of Normandy and the Vexin). Ironically, Brionne was the castle and title originally held by Walter Tyrell's maternal grandfather and the Clare siblings paternal grandfather, Gilbert de Brionne, back in 1040 and was where Walter's mother was born and grew up. See appendix 9.

[481] They were also accompanied by Anselm's nephew, the son of his only, much younger, sister, Richeza. He was, confusingly, also called Anselm and looks to have made a career riding on the coattails of his famous uncle. He had been with his uncle at Cluny since 1098 and lived in Canterbury until his uncle died in 1109, then becoming firstly abbot of St Sabas in Rome, then papal legate to England in 1115, and lastly abbot of Bury St Edmunds in 1121 to his death in 1146. He had briefly been elected Bishop of London in 1136 and enthroned in 1137, however, his election was quashed by Pope Innocent II in 1138.

[482] 'Anselm of Bec and Robert of Meulan—The Innocence of the Dove and the Wisdom of the Serpent', Sally M. Vaughn, University of California Press, 1987.

personally visited Abbot Guillaume on his deathbed at Bec in 1124, so clearly a close relationship existed between the 2 men. Two other close associations are also worth noting, firstly, Montfort-sur-Risle, near Rouen, is one family seat of the de Montfort family (and one of just 3 hereditary Constableships of the Norman period[483]), much intermarried with the Beaumonts (Appendix 4.0 tree) and secondly, before his Bec appointment, Guillaume had previously been the Prior of Notre-Dame de Poissy, just 2 miles from Achères in the Vexin, where Walter Tyrell held the Lordship, and just 9 miles from the Beaumonts family seat at Meulan, so undoubtedly well-known to both of them.

Back in Winchester and within hours of his death, Rufus's body was now lying in the cathedral awaiting burial and it would have been Henry's new bishop elect, the plotter William Giffard, assisted by the Prior, Godfrey of Cambrai, who arranged its speedy and rather undignified, even unchristian, burial within the cathedral the following day (Friday 3rd August). Bells which would ring even for paupers and prostitutes were silent, no alms distributed, no prayers or masses for the good of his soul and Godfrey, a stern moralist and renowned poet, composed no historical epigram about Rufus' death, all together suggesting little show of grief. The only mourners were said to be those who lamented their likely loss of income like, mercenaries, scroungers and harlots, adherents to Rufus that Orderic called 'suis parasitis'—his parasites.[484] Orderic stated harshly in his chronicle '...The doctors and prelates of the church, considering his squalid life and dreadful death, ventured to pass judgement, declaring that he was virtually past redemption and unworthy of absolution by the church, since as long as he lived they had never been able to turn him from his vices to salvation'.

We shall never know if the rapid burial at a location under Giffard's personal control (below the tower[485]) guarded day and night by his own retainers, was to make sure the body was never examined by supporters of Duke Robert of Normandy, who was only a few weeks away on his return from the Crusade. They may have wished to cast doubt on the story of the conveniently fatal arrow,

---

[483] Hereditary Constable of England to both Rufus and Henry was Robert de Montfort (d.c.1111) and almost certainly at Malwood Lodge when Rufus died, being one of the eleven signatories to Henry's Coronation Charter. He must have defected later to Robert Curthose, as he was accused of treason in 1107 and had all his lands confiscated.

[484] Orderic Vitalis 5, book X, Ch. 15, iv. 86, p. 288.

[485] The tower collapsed seven years later, something ascribed to Rufus's wickedness though actually it was just badly built.

hitting an overhead branch or glancing off a tree trunk or flank of a deer and striking Rufus right in the heart or lung, or whether he was shot from a distance or different direction and so forth. His body never lay in state where all could see the death wound—the origin of the custom continued to this day.

47. Henry confronted by William de Breteuil at the Winchester treasury, from James William Edmund Doyle's *A Chronicle of England*, 1864
Image courtesy of Public Domain licence from Wikimedia Commons

Matters were moving fast but, rather than chaotically, took on the look of a well-oiled machine smoothly running to plan. Soon after arriving at Winchester, Henry and his friends, in a somewhat undignified rush, endeavour to secure the great treasury. However, at the door they find none other than fellow hunting party member William de Breteuil[486], Rufus's 'Treasurer' (and abbot of

---

[486] William, along with his elder brother Roger, were the brothers of Emma, who had married Ralph de Gael back in 1075 in the 'Brideale of Norwich', the event which led to the downfall and execution of Waltheof in the 'Revolt of the Earls' covered in detail in Part I, Chapter 5.

Breteuil), who, clearly suspecting trouble, has beaten them to it with his sword drawn[487] (see image 47 above).

Just maybe, he was the only witness to events in the forest who had his suspicions about the circumstances of the king's death. In any event, he had made a mad dash back to Winchester from Malwood Lodge in order to protect the nation's cash and stood there defiantly, if somewhat out of breath. As most of his own inherited estates were in Normandy, he is known to have been a supporter of Robert Curthose (one of the very few there on the day) and would have wanted to prevent any usurper gaining access to the national treasure. He stood firm at the door making an impassioned plea—*"You and I,"* he said to Henry, *"ought to remember the faith we have pledged to your brother, Duke Robert; he has received our oath of homage and, absent or present, he has a right to this money."*[488]

The Prince did not agree and the argument escalated with Henry also drawing his own sword and with de Breteuil still resolutely maintaining that Robert was the lawful sovereign of England, Henry, threatening death to anyone who opposed him, moved forward supported by a number of the barons from the hunt alongside and declared he would permit no further *'frivolous delay'*.[489]

It is understood from Orderic that *'through the intervention of friends and prudent counsellors'* matters were settled.[490] In particular, the Beaumont brothers stepped up to the mark, with the younger Henry de Beaumont, 1st Earl of Warwick (and close friend of Prince Henry) by disposition a quiet and retiring man normally overshadowed by his elder brother, calming things down with an eloquent speech, probably composed earlier—'just in case'. It was his big moment in the plan and he no doubt pointed out that the succession agreement between Rufus and Robert that they signed up to in the 1991 Treaty of Caen, had not been agreed with Henry, who was thus not bound by its terms and in any case, in the event of a lengthy interregnum the country could dissolve into anarchy to the detriment of all. He might also have mentioned that early reports

---

[487] Historian E. A. Freeman conjectures that the order of events may have been reversed and that Henry was in fact declared King 'prior' to seizing the treasury. *'The Reign of William Rufus'*, 1882, Clarendon Press, Vol. II, p.681.

[488] *The Cabinet History of England*.........Charles Macfarlane, pub. Charles Knight, 1845, vol. 2, chap. 2, p.134.

[489] Orderic Vitalis, iv. 87 f.

[490] Orderic Vitalis, x. Ch. Xiv.

suggested that Robert had already been declared King of Jerusalem by the Crusaders and would never leave the Holy Land for an ordinary kingdom (Robert had actually been offered the position but turned it down). In the face of this, the solitary and outnumbered figure of William de Breteuil (who was probably more persuaded by the likelihood of physical injury rather than the rhetoric, as his swordsmanship skills, as an abbot in his fifties, were probably not up to much!) backed down, moved aside and let Henry into the treasure house.

Henry then distributed funds (greased the palms) to a number of those in attendance to ensure their 'loyalty', such that the emergency meeting of the truncated 'rump' Witan (council of nobles) that convened early next morning, officially sanctions Henry's actions, quickly agreeing to him as King. Following robust cheers and shouts of that rather chilling phrase, "The King is dead, long live the King!" (though no doubt in Norman French!), the whole court upsticks, skipping the funeral and leaves Winchester for London and the Coronation as soon as possible. This though is not before Henry performed one royal act of great importance to his cause and skilfully chosen as a declaration of principles—he appointed fellow plotter William Giffard as bishop elect of Winchester, though also retained him as his Chancellor for the next few months as well, prior to appointing the great Roger of Salisbury in his stead.[491]

---

[491] Roger was a bright young priest from Caen who had greatly impressed Henry when giving a brief sermon and who was then remarkably plucked from obscurity by the King, to be his Chancellor (creator of the first Exchequer), Justiciar of all England, the King's regent and later became Bishop of Salisbury.

Chapter 10
The Next Days

Imagine, if you will, that it is now Sunday August 12th 1100 and Henry has been crowned King for a week, the coronation having taken place on Sunday 5th August, just 3 days—72 hours—after the death of Rufus. Relaxing after the frantic and stressful activity of the last 2 weeks, he is secreted in a private chamber at either Westminster Palace or Windsor Castle along with Gilbert de Clare, William Giffard, Eudo Dapifer, the 2 de Beaumont brothers (Robert and Henry) and Simon de Senlis, with goblets of wine primed for a debriefing session—one might even hope that Mrs Senlis, the young Countess Maud, was also invited into this secretive male enclave! (An enclave that very probably also included a certain 50-year-old called Robert Malet, whose significant inclusion I shall shortly explain.)

A review of the original plan of the plot and the precisely detailed scheme for the assassination, show that so far, absolutely all elements of the enterprise, despite the odd rocky moment, have been perfectly executed—along with Rufus by Robin! The treasury was secure, the crown was on Henry's head, Tyrell was safely back on the continent, Ranulph Flambard was being arrested, Anselm was coming home, the Coronation Charter of Liberties was winging its way around the country, his fiancé was choosing her wedding dress and nobody was crying foul, but blaming (or thanking) God for Rufus's demise. One might say 'the perfect murder' and as Hollister observed…

'Not the slightest breath of scandal ever touched Henry I from any contemporary or near-contemporary writer'.[492]

---

[492] *The Strange Death of William Rufus*, Warren Hollister, *Speculum—A Journal of Medieval Studies*, Vol. 48, No. 4 (October 1973). p.653. The absence of suggestion of

On top of that, the actual assassin, Robin Hood, had melted away into the greenwood, unseen, unheard and unknown. The whole complex charade they had created around willing scapegoat Tyrell, his 'shameful accident' and subsequent 'terrified' flight, had been swallowed hook line and sinker with the true modus operandi totally unsuspected, or if it was, people were keeping quiet, being happy with the outcome. However, with Princess Edith still to marry and with heroic brother Robert Curthose appearing over the horizon, plus any number of unhappy nobles, it is by no means yet a done deal. Henry still needed to widen the base for his support and to emphasise his legitimacy both with the aristocracy and the church, but despite this they must have been pretty pleased with progress of the plan so far.

Consider for one moment that Rufus took nearly 3 weeks to organise his own coronation and Henry's grandson, Henry II, took 3 months. In more modern times a lapse of up to 18 months is not unknown. Henry's though, was done and dusted within just 3 days and for the first 2 they were travelling, at some speed on horseback, the seventy miles back from Winchester to Westminster. They had a brief night-stop, probably at Windsor Castle (after the gruelling first leg of 47 miles), to snatch a few hours' sleep and more fresh horses before finally pushing on to Westminster (another 23 miles). Incredibly, by 5pm on Sunday the 5th August, just 72 hours after Rufus fell to the ground dead, Henry was in London being crowned King of England at Westminster Abbey and vast swathes of the kingdom would still have been totally unaware of the change of kingship.[493] One would have to think that this breathtaking operation would have been a virtual impossibility without a considerable degree of pre-planning. In fact, the whole

---

conspiracy seems to convince Hollister as to the accidental nature of the event whereas it could just as well point to him also being hoodwinked and a brilliantly conceived and executed 'cover-up' of a regicide—precisely as the plotters intended at the start. I have always felt that the very fact Hollister headlined his article as the '*strange*' death of William Rufus, rather than the '*accidental*' death of William Rufus, displayed a subliminal element to his theory whereby even he possibly thought other elements were at play. An accident is not strange—but a convoluted assassination plot is.

[493] This was so fast that it seems very unlikely the ladies, children, elder statesmen and many others of the court (comprising a vast royal baggage train, household staff and officials), would have had sufficient time to make the journey back from Winchester for the ceremony, which one imagines was short on extravagant ceremonials, quite sparsely attended and a somewhat minimalistic affair requiring just a crown, a throne, some holy oil, a complicit Bishop and witnesses.

rolled out process, the burial, the draughting of precise letters to Anselm and other prelates, the taking of the treasury, the proclamation as 'King', the journey to London and the coronation by complicit and readily available archbishop and bishop, complete with the detailed 'King's Coronation Charter', all suggest a drill-like precision to cover the first few days that can only denote an absence of surprise at the initial triggering event down in Stricknage Wood.

To secure his precarious hold on the throne, the Coronation Charter of Liberties declaring that Henry had been crowned, putting into writing his coronation promises and announcing his intention to correct the wrongs of his brother, was drawn up, signed, witnessed, sealed and circulated to every shire. This document enshrined in writing the traditional promises Henry had made at his coronation—to keep the peace, forbid all iniquities, and to maintain justice and mercy—alongside further concessions to his barons and pledges to redress specific complaints. This key charter was regarded by many as atonement for the past abuses of his predecessor and brother, along with garnering support from the baronial class, to whom, in truth, most of the charter contents applied and benefited. It restored a number of elements to their previous status under Edward the Confessor and covered various issues including specifying a number of rights to the church, landowners, heirs and even widows. In retrospect is often viewed as an early blueprint or 'first draft' for the more famous Magna Carta, more than a century later. The speed of its preparation, its importance and fine detail, does lead one to suspect that this document was pre-prepared in the knowledge that it would be needed at short notice. It certainly does not have the appearance of something cobbled together in forty-eight hours by tired men while on horseback dashing between Winchester and London but in fact quite the contrary, being full of subtly contrived nuances and a masterpiece of political spin[494]. This was all a cunning manoeuvre to strengthen his shaky support in the days and weeks after the coronation, as initially Henry would need significant military support from his nobles and sheriffs in the likely event of a rapid invasion by brother Robert.

---

[494] I refer the reader to *'The Character and Antecedents of the Charter of Liberties of Henry I '*, Author: Henry L. Cannon. Source: *The American Historical Review,* October 1909, Vol. 15, No. 1 (October 1909), Pub. OUP, pp.37–46 on behalf of the American Historical Association and also, *'The Coronation Charter of 1100: a postponement of decision'*. Henry B. Teunis, Journal of Medieval History, 4:2, 1978, pp.135–144.

48. The Coronation Charter of Henry I in a 13th-century copy made for
Canterbury Cathedral Priory
(London, Lambeth Palace, MS 1212, ff. 97v-98r)

One specific pledge in the charter was laid out in the wording of article number 9, being: *'I pardon all murders which were incurred before the day on which I was crowned',* and the Murdrum compensation system reverted to that which had been in place during the reign of the Confessor. So, he forgives all murders prior to his accession which meant Robin is pardoned for regicide as well as the deaths of all the other Normans, including the sheriff in *The Gest,* that he and his men have dispatched over the last twenty years. A pardon, which as *The Gest* suggests, he is not hoping for, but expecting. Such pardons from the sovereign, expressing his will, were issued as letters 'patent' and sealed with the king's great seal pendant. Sadly, like the many other records of this early period referred to in Chapter 3, the earliest patent rolls of Chancery only survive from the reign of King John onwards, some hundred years later, such that any documented ancient royal 'pardon' to a 'Robert de Loxley', a 'Robert FitzWaltheof' or even a 'Robertus Hode' or similar, from the early 12th century will, regrettably, never come to light.

Another signatory of the Coronation Charter was Gerard, the Bishop of Hereford (the depraved character once robbed by Robin Hood in Barnsdale—

Child Ballad 144, see Part I, chapter 8), who is also rumoured to have been either in the hunting party itself, though given his advanced age (and likely lack of archery skills), probably just a house guest at Malwood Lodge or Winchester Castle. The general historical view is that due to Archbishop Anselm's absence in France, Henry was crowned by Maurice, Bishop of London, assisted by Gerard. However, the medieval chronicler and courtier to Henry II, Walter Map, writing in the 1170s, states that in the absence of Anselm, who theoretically should have officiated[495], it was Gerard who crowned Henry in return for the promise of the first vacant archbishopric.[496] This he duly acquired as he became Archbishop of York just a few months later in the November, just a week after Henry's marriage to Matilda, following the death of the incumbent for the last thirty years, Thomas of Bayeux, who had been gravely ill for some time. Gerard, despite his many personal frailties, was clearly a very clever man and a survivor, becoming a senior advisor to Henry for the first 4 years of his reign.

As we know, when that fateful arrow flew, Archbishop Anselm was still over 600 miles away in voluntary exile in southern France, but was very quickly returned at Henry's invitation after Rufus' death, arriving in Dover on the 23rd September 1100 and joining Henry's court at Salisbury soon after when Eadmer recorded the whole county was rejoicing, expecting the abuses of the church to be corrected. Their own friction regarding the ongoing struggles between state and church and the ordination of bishops (the Investiture Controversy), rumbled on for some years before being settled in the Concordat of London in 1107. Whether Anselm, via his friendship of Tyrell and the Beaumonts or directly with Henry, was aware of the planned assassination is a matter for conjecture, one which historians have argued at length and was discussed in some detail earlier in Part II, chapter 5. You may recall that according to Anselm's secretary and biographer, Eadmer, the first note received by the archbishop, telling of Rufus' demise, was delivered to him in France **on the day it occurred** which, if true, would certainly implicate him and suggest a planned rather than accidental death

---

[495] In the absence of Anselm, it really should have been Thomas of Bayeux, the Archbishop of York to officiate but he was a long way away in York and very unwell, nearing his death (which occurred on Nov.18th). Thomas was initially angry at the slight, until it was explained to him that the King had worried over the chance of disorder in the kingdom if there was a delay. To mollify him, Thomas was allowed to crown the King publicly at a church council held soon after the coronation.

[496] *De Nugis Curialium* V. vi, Camden Society 1850. Pgs. 222–223.

(the approximate travel time for a letter from Winchester to Lyon would be nearly 2 weeks at best, depending on the weather and if specialised messengers were used). Henry's official letter[497] requesting that Anselm return to England as soon as possible, did in fact arrive 2 weeks later at Cluny Abbey and advised him not to travel through Normandy (where Curthose supporters might kidnap him) but leave from Wissant in Flanders (betwixt Calais and Boulogne), a port held by Eustace III, Count of Boulogne, a great friend of Henry's and also an heroic Crusader[498] very recently returned from the Holy Land and soon (1102) to marry Henry's future sister-in-law, the other Romsey educated princess, Mary of Scotland, younger sister of Edith/Matilda. Henry promised Anselm that *'my barons will meet you at Dover with money to receive you'* and the archbishop was duly back in Canterbury 6 weeks later, which was very quick indeed.

Just 10 days after his coronation, King Henry immediately ousted Rufus's number one henchman, Ranulph Flambard, from the Bishopric of Durham (a position he had only obtained from Rufus within the last year), had him charged with embezzlement and imprisoned in the Tower of London. He then famously escaped[499] and fled to France, where 6 months later he incited and supported Robert Curthose in his effort to take the crown in his failed rebellion against brother Henry in July 1101. Although pardoned in the Treaty of Alton[500] which

---

[497] The letter, signed by Henry, was witnessed by Bishop Gerard of Hereford, new Bishop William Giffard, brothers Robert and Henry de Beaumont, the royal clerk/chaplain William Warelwast and trusted royal steward Haimo Dapifer (Robert Fitzhaimo's father who was very ill and died soon after).

[498] As well as Eustace, his brothers, Godfrey of Bouillon and Baldwin of Bouillon also went on the crusade and both became Kings of Jerusalem. Eustace himself was offered but declined the title.

[499] After six months in prison, Flambard hatched a plan for his escape. He proposed to throw a party for his guards and requested that several barrels of wine be provided for the occasion. Within one of these barrels was a length of rope. The wine was plentiful and very soon they became intoxicated, enabling Flambard to make his escape out of the window, down the rope and onto a waiting boat in the Thames. From here he travelled to Normandy. Ranulph Flambard was probably the first state prisoner ever confined to the Tower, and also the first to escape from it!

[500] Under the terms of the treaty (sometimes called 'of Winchester'), Robert was seemingly duped by the more astute Henry (and his chief negotiator, Robert Fitzhaimo), into recognising Henry's title to the English crown in return for an annuity of 3000

resulted from that rebellion and restored to his Bishopric, he in fact stayed in Normandy with Robert for another 5 years until Henry finally defeated his brother at the Battle of Tinchebrai on 28th September 1106 (exactly 40 years to the day after his father's arrival in England in 1066), to rule over the joint kingdom of England and Normandy for almost another 30 years. This final defeat not only deprived Robert of his lands and Dukedom but also his freedom, as ruthless Henry locked his brother away for 28 years, firstly in Devizes then Cardiff Castle[501], there to die in 1134 at the ripe old age of 83, just a year before Henry. Flambard at last made his peace with Henry, withdrawing from political and public life in his old age, save for his position as the tolerably respectable Bishop of Durham.

It seems likely that the whole intricate 3 part plan of a) the 'death' of Rufus on the 2nd August, b) the rapid coronation of Henry on the 5th August, and c) his planned November wedding[502] to the beautiful bright 20-year-old Princess Edith of the Saxon House of Wessex, was one that Robin's sister, Maud, included him in. Edith was, as the Anglo-Saxon Chronicle specifically records, as being '*of the right royal race of England*'.[503] I suspect though that Robin was only present

---

marks. The payments ceased in 1103 when Robert, visiting England to intercede on behalf of his friend, the outlawed William de Warenne, was forced to give them up.

[501] Robert Curthose's final gaoler (more an open prison) was his nephew, Robert Fitzroy, Earl of Gloucester, a favourite illegitimate son of King Henry, who had married Mabel, daughter of Robert Fitzhaimo in 1117, and who now held Cardiff castle, built by his late father-in-law.

[502] The wedding was delayed three months for an investigation to take place due to concerns Edith may have taken 'vows' as a nun during her time at Romsey and Wilton Abbeys, which if true meant the marriage could not take place. This will be discussed further in chapter 12.

[503] Henry would have been drawn to the fact that his bride's late mother, Queen Margaret of Scotland, was the great-granddaughter of King Edmund Ironside. In the first year of his reign it is suggested, in a brief passage in William of Malmesbury's Gesta regum Anglorum (1: 716–17), that Edith-Matilda's Anglo-Saxon blood, whilst popular with the English, was not universally seen as a good thing with the Normans, breeding dissent against Henry in the court and being openly mocked:
'*Robert Curthose reached Normandy; on hearing which, nearly all the English nobles threw over the homage they had pledged to the king. All either sent secretly for Robert offering to make him king, or openly insulted their own lord, calling him Godric and his consort Godgifu (Godiva)*'.

for a) since as the secret assassin (and famous outlaw) he was no doubt 'persona non grata' in the public and royal forums! In any event, Henry's marriage to the beautiful Edith of the House of Wessex, and her elevation to the throne, coupled with the expulsion of his brother's minions, did at least lead to the hearts of the English people being filled with momentary joy.

Although Robin would not perhaps have realised the future great implications on English history of his arrow shot that day, he very likely believed it would result in greater freedoms and less oppression for the English people and this was his main motivation along with the king's marriage to Edith and the restoration of Archbishop Anselm. At the core of the Robin Hood legend is always the Sheriff of Nottingham, agent of the king, representing bad justice in a corrupt position of royal authority and his antithesis, Robin, a naturally just man, deprived of justice and true freedom, maintaining an independent spirit and protesting against social injustice. If part of the deal for his killing Rufus was a promised revision and clear-out of these corrupt officials, not just in Nottinghamshire and Yorkshire but countrywide it would surely have formed part of his motivation to take it on. To a greater rather than lesser extent, Henry was at least true to his word in this regard.

After some 35 years of severe Norman oppression, it would certainly have been the pinnacle of Robin's life to complete his family feud and obtain revenge for the death of his father by the killing of the catamite and ungodly son of the man whom he felt responsible for his father's death and probably other family members as well. Given he had, as a youth, seen his father finally conclude a bloody family feud that had lasted almost 60 years, I am quite convinced he would have had little compunction and no qualms in similarly following his lead. Granted he is helping another son take the throne but at least this one was born in England, spoke English, was firmly heterosexual, god-fearing and perhaps most important of all, would, by marriage, help restore the royal line of Anglo-Saxon Kings of the House of Wessex and the laws of Edward the Confessor into

---

This slur (said to have been coined by William de Warenne) was the 'Jack and Jill' or maybe the 'Wayne and Sharon' of the period and was despite Edith changing her Saxon name to the Norman, 'Matilda', Henry's marriage to an Anglo-Scottish princess, allied to his own birth in England and speaking the English language! Edith's good queenship eventually silenced detractors of her Englishness and she became a great favourite of all the English and Anglo-Norman peoples, known as 'Good Queen Maude', being a significant influence over her husband, the king.

the reigning and future monarchy of England and also significantly improve relations between the Scottish and English crowns. In truth, Robin was probably somewhat seduced by this idea and like many of the English, when it happened, conceived the futile hope of witnessing the return of the old Saxon times, when the granddaughter of the Saxon kings should wear the crown. On top of all this though, Robin would gain a royal pardon for all these acts, and more besides for the people of England, in the 'promises' to be made in the forthcoming Coronation Charter of Henry 1st, just a few days later. Things were never going to be perfect but this resulting situation was a great deal better than the 'status quo'.

It seems likely Robin had already been ensconced in the woods near Romsey Abbey during July, checking out Stricknage Woods and Malwood Walk in good time to prepare for the 'hit' and maybe spending a few days in the Romsey Abbey gatehouse guest accommodation. As we know, Robin had a lifelong issue with the corrupt Norman run monastic houses but if there was just one religious establishment which would have appealed, then this was it. Clearly his appearance at this long-time Saxon-founded house run by upper-class Saxon nuns, educating royal and other highbred Saxon girls and where his father's body had been brought and cared for following its execution, now the site of a shrine containing his heart, seems an intriguingly potent mix of elements that cannot be ignored.[504]

Following his successfully completed 'task' on August 2nd, Robin just melted away into the deeply forested area of the New Forest just to the east, to Pipers Copse and Bignall Wood where his horse was tethered. As all hell broke loose at the hunting lodge, he laid up, quiet and unseen on that warm summer night and early next morning rode the 8 or 9 miles to Romsey Abbey to seek refuge there with his old friend, nun Princess Christina, with whom he had no doubt made an earlier arrangement for sanctuary—not as an assassin but just in case his true identity was ever revealed.[505] Since 1097 Christina had been the aunt of

---

[504] Prior to 1066, monastic houses of original Saxon foundation were few and far between, around fifty, but an intriguing number of them feature in this tale of Robin Hood. St, Olave's in York (founded by Siward but refounded by the Normans as St Mary's and which appears more than once in the ballads), Croyland, Ely, Glastonbury, Durham, Jarrow, Wilton, Romsey, Peterborough and St Neots are all examples.

[505] I believe we can be quite sure Robin did not disclose the main reason for his being in Romsey. Apart from the required secrecy, he would have been well aware of Christina's

the King of Scotland, as her nephew Edgar (Edith's brother, now 26) had finally taken the crown in that year. Within a week or 2, the new King Henry was asking Edgar for the hand of his sister Edith in marriage, which was duly given, though as we shall see, Christina herself was not so keen on this match with her one-time protégé and niece.[506]

Some people no doubt did suspect that Henry and the Clare family had a hand in the death of William Rufus but kept quiet, as it was almost universally accepted that it was an accident and the 'will of God' for all his ills (a belief which suited Henry well). Whatever the truth of the matter, the Clare family and their connections obtained considerable 'benefit' from the death of William Rufus, which could well be construed as reward from the new King Henry. We shall explore this 'benefit' further in the next chapter as it is a key element of the plot theory.

The de Clares had gained revenge against Rufus for the imprisonment and premature death of their family head, Richard FitzGilbert de Clare, the husband of Rohese (William Giffard's sister) and father of Gilbert, Roger, Robert, Richard, Rohese (wife of Eudo Dapifer) and Adelize (wife of Walter Tyrell— Richard FitzGilbert also being Walter's *half*-uncle). I have often pondered on just how much pressure sisters Rohese and Adelize might have brought to bear on their respective husbands (encouraged by brother Gilbert), to take an active part in the plot, with their desire to seek vengeance on Rufus for the suffering of their parents—probably more than one might imagine.

Hollister makes a couple of quite erroneous, or rash, assumptions in his analysis of the conspiracy theory in the death of Rufus and it is quite clear from

---

brother, Edgar the Ætheling, being a close friend and military supporter of Robert Curthose, right up to his final defeat by Henry at Tinchebrai in 1106 and any leak of information or hint of a plot would have been devastating. Even so, Christina probably blamed and hated Rufus, not just his shameful lifestyle but believing him responsible for the untimely death of her sister Margaret after she died of a broken heart following her husband and son being killed at the Battle of Alnwick in 1093

[506] Henry knew King Edgar quite well, as Rufus had agreed to pay him forty to sixty shillings per day maintenance when in attendance at the English court, which he had done from time to time. and in 1099 King Edgar even 'bore Rufus's sword before him' (*Anglo-Saxon Chronicle*) at the crown-wearing in the new Great Hall that Rufus had built at Westminster, perhaps his most memorable surviving monument to posterity.

later research[507], subsequent to his article of 1973, that many of his conclusions are flawed. Firstly, he wrote—*'there is nothing to suggest that prior to the shooting, Henry had any relationship whatsoever with the Clares, the Giffards or Walter Tyrell'*.

This odd statement can be questioned on a number of levels. Henry and Gilbert (and Walter) were virtually the same age and had both grown up in court circles together for over thirty years and would have been teenage hunt companions. Gilbert's father and William the Conqueror were, after all, close friends, both were great-grandsons of Richard I, 'The Fearless', of Normandy and Gilbert had undoubtedly fought well at Hastings with the Conqueror (probably also with Walter Tyrell's father and grandfather), rewarded as he was, with 176 lordships and the rights to build both Clare and Tonbridge castles. Gilbert, we know, had rebelled twice against Henry's brother, Rufus, even party to a plot to kill him 5 years earlier in 1095, but was seemingly now back in favour, though suspicions as to his loyalty must have lingered. The very fact they were on this exclusive royal hunt together, with another Clare brother, implies close ties between them. Similarly William Giffard, older than Henry, had been at the very centre of government for years and in 1100 was the Chancellor of England, and would have been in close contact with Henry at this time, particularly over the last 3 years during the Maine and Vexin campaigns. In addition to the foregoing, they were also all major benefactors of Bec Abbey and friendly with Archbishop Anselm. What cannot be disputed is that both families were to receive considerable largesse from Henry after his accession, hardly the action expected in the distant relationship suggested by Hollister.

Of Henry's relationship with Walter Tyrell we can only speculate, though clearly he was on excellent terms with his relatives. It was hardly relevant to the plot that Henry knew Walter, though given the reportedly ongoing close friendship (real or pretend) between Rufus and Walter, he must have done, but it was probably better for the plot that he did not get too close. Gilbert obviously vouched for him as his brother-in-law/cousin and he had been a guest at the court of Rufus for a year or so, such that there must have been close interaction at court between all of them, especially at the great royal court get-togethers of Christmas, Easter and Whitsun and their previous hunting parties at the 3 great royal castles—Gloucester (the Forest of Dean), Windsor (Windsor Forest) and

---

[507] In particular *'Royal Service and Reward: The Clare Family and the Crown, 1066–1154'*, *Anglo Norman Studies,* vol. XI, Jennifer Ward. Boydell and Brewer, 1987.

Winchester (the New Forest). I am quite convinced that this friendly French relative of the Clare's, who had inveigled his way into a position of trust and friendship with Rufus over the previous months, would have become well acquainted with Prince Henry, in particular if this was all part of the wider planned regicide. Of Henry's closeness to the Beaumont brothers and Simon de Senlis throughout the preceding years, as key courtiers and recent campaigning, there can be no question. One feels sure that at court his wandering eye settled on his first cousin (once removed) the young and beautiful Countess Maud, wife of the ageing Simon de Senlis (Appendices 4, 5 and 6 show all these familial links).

Hollister's second rather odd and, dare I say, somewhat naïve summation, is the following: *"Moreover, there has long been serious doubt that Tyrell actually fired the arrow, and if he did not, the Clare-Giffard hypothesis collapses at its base."* Surely quite the opposite is true, ignoring completely, as it does, the concept of a third-party assassin under their direction. If Walter was a willing 'patsy' and simply the 'fall guy and distraction' then this was a brilliant element of the plan. The likely fact that he did indeed <u>not</u> shoot the arrow, but was aware of and complicit with the actual marksman (even though he most likely never ever met or even saw Robin), seems to pass Hollister by. One imagines the closely guarded secrets of the identity of the assassin and Robin's familial link to the Countess Maud were only shared among the very smallest handful of people on a 'need to know' basis, to include Henry and Gilbert.

Importantly, there is a later account that Tyrell was indeed not the marksman in question. The senior French cleric, statesman and renowned chronicler, Abbot Suger, was a friend of Tyrell in later life and although thought to have maybe sheltered him in his French exile was not yet either 'senior' or 'renown', being only 19 years old in 1100. He was many years away from being an abbot, but then simply an oblate priest at the Priory of Saint-Denis, near Paris where he had been entered by his parents when aged 10. Most significantly, also at the Priory in 1100 was Prince Louis (heir to the throne of France), also 19, who had reason to loathe Rufus whom he had been fighting in the Vexin to a bitter stalemate for the last 2 years. It was at Saint-Denis that Suger first befriended Prince Louis (later becoming his confidante and biographer[508]), even later serving as Regent

---

[508] Abbot Suger (1081–1151) is also renowned as being instrumental in the development of the Gothic style of architecture, which originated under his supervision with the rebuilding of the Abbey church of Basilique Saint-Denis in Paris, the burial site of the

of France from 1147–1149 to his son, King Louis VII, while the king was on the second Crusade (with Hugh Tyrell, Walter's son)[509]. This Priory—just 14 miles from both Pontoise castle and Walter's home in Achères, was safely in territory firmly under the protection of the French monarchy and was quite possibly where Walter laid low for a while after returning from Bec and his exertions. He would, of course, have carried the news of Rufus's death but more importantly, as part of his reward for taking part, relate to King Philip and Prince Louis that Henry was calling off the planned invasion and seeking peaceful terms with the French Crown. An invitation for Prince Louis to join King Henry for Christmas festivities in London was to arrive shortly thereafter (and seated at the banquet between Anselm and the King), most likely delivered by plotter Robert de Beaumont whom King Henry had dispatched to the continent soon after his coronation to conduct foreign affairs with the French Crown.[510]

In his writings, Suger later recorded that Walter, after his return to France, *became a prominent member of the Capetian* (French) *court,*[511] so very likely met up with Robert de Beaumont during his visit soon after. Quite clearly Walter was never going to be openly rewarded by the King of England but he was not pursued, his English relatives were not punished, his Langham manor was not forfeit and I strongly suspect he was well rewarded by the King of France, the details of which would never become public knowledge! As previously noted, Suger wrote some years later that Walter always solemnly swore his innocence in the matter of shooting the arrow, even when the charge against him was reduced to purely one of it being 'accidental'. This claim was supported by the

---

Kings of France and dedicated in June 1144. Using the lancet, a pointed arch, it resulted in graceful buildings with thinner walls and more light.

[509] Walter Tyrell III is often stated as having later gone on crusade, but more likely died on what was a pilgrimage to Jerusalem or on his way back c.1136 (as asserted by Barlow from Orderic Vitalis, v, p.294), though Tyrell genealogists suggest he made it home to die in his castle at Poix. However, his son Hugh did go on the 2nd Crusade in 1147 with King Louis VII, which he funded by selling the Langham family manor, and his grandson, also called Hugh, went on the 3rd Crusade in 1189 being present at the siege of Acre.

[510] *Anselm of Bec and Robert of Meulan—The Innocence of the Dove and the Wisdom of the Serpent'*, Sally M. Vaughn, University of California Press, 1987. p,225

[511] Suger, *Vie de Louis VI le Gros*, Waquet, H. (ed. and tr.), Belles Lettres, 1929 and 1964, p. 12.

later 12th century Anglo-Norman chronicler John of Salisbury, c.1115–1170, who went even further when he rewrote Eadmer's book on the life of Anselm[512].

When describing the death of Rufus, he used the Latin word *'caede'*, which directly translates as 'murder'. John confirmed that Tyrell repeatedly proclaimed his innocence, even on his deathbed while invoking God's judgement for his eternal soul said that *'The King himself had loosed the fatal arrow'*. It is unclear from this (and without doubt John was not at Tyrell's deathbed to record his last words) if by *King* he was implying Rufus or Henry, though it really maybe only makes sense if he meant the latter as the former would suggest a form of self-inflicted suicide (and has been interpreted as such by some—being a Lammas sacrifice!)[513] I am however very dubious as to this much quoted translation which I feel sure is erroneous. The actual Latin chronicle reads **'Qui ipsium regem jaculum quo interemptus est misisse'**, that I understand more literally translates as **'Who sent the arrow by which the king himself was slain?'** which to me has an entirely different meaning and simply questions who might have loosed the arrow.

John went on to declare that Tyrell said *'whoever shot the arrow will never be known'* which perhaps suggests he might know, but is not telling. One could interpret his statements as pointing the finger at Henry as being behind the plot but a specific assassin actually fired the arrow (the truth), but no-one knows who that was—unlikely, but maybe Robin's true identity was kept secret even from him. One thing is certain—solemn oaths at death's door in god-fearing times must be regarded as more reliable evidence than most (even if the 2 statements are somewhat contradictory). As Orderic Vitalis observed: *"Much weight is doubtless due to this solemn denial."*

It seems Walter died in 1136 aged around 70, a year after King Henry (d.1135 aged c.68) and as such he just may have felt, on his deathbed, less encumbered by his oath of silence now that the king was deceased and that he was able to nudge a finger of guilt in the direction of Henry. However, we must remember that Walter probably died when returning from pilgrimage to Jerusalem, so quite who it was who heard/recorded these deathbed statements is completely unknown and their accuracy and authenticity must be in doubt.

---

[512] *'Vita Sancti Anselmi and Vita Sancti Thomae'*, John of Salisbury ed. I. Biffi, in *'Anselmo e Becket, due vite'* (Milan, 1990) and other editions.

[513] See Appendix 10 for more on this.

The suggestion that Rufus managed to shoot himself in the heart (surely impossible), clearly does not make sense. Apart from this, Walter's consistent and solemn declaration is most likely true—he did not shoot the deadly arrow himself that day. This is backed up by the French and English Crowns' generous treatment of him subsequently. Furthermore, if my theory is correct, we can interpret from Tyrell's choice of deathbed words that he knew who did, being party to the plan, but while refusing to lie, he would never reveal the assassin's identity.

The man who let fly that fateful arrow struck the first blow in the battle for the freedoms and justice, not just of British democracy, but democracy worldwide. Many years later in 1215, the Magna Carta, signed by King John under duress from the barons, has become the most well-known document in the struggle for civil liberties, however its earlier forebear—the Coronation Charter of Henry I—signed voluntarily in 1100, should not be overlooked. Large portions of Henry's Charter were a withdrawal of practices that were politically corrosive and of questionable legality. Various feudal dues, instead of being arbitrary and *ad hoc*, were reduced to reasonable limits. While many of the promises in the charter could not be enforced and Henry chose to ignore others, it was at least the start of that long inexorable journey over the centuries towards parliamentary democracy and something better for the people of England.

Chapter 11
The Next Years—and the 'Clare Benefit'

Henry's rule over England did not have an easy start: brother Robert, although probably exhausted from his 3 years of crusading, came under the influence of the fiery Flambard and took up the fight against Henry. This dragged on for 5 years and clearly the issue would only be settled by war. Its denouement was the epochal Battle of Tinchebrai in 1106. When Henry finally defeated his brother, taking the greatest prize of all—as his father had once foretold—overall kingship of England and Normandy—and all sibling rivals now deceased or locked away.[514]

---

[514] In 1102, Robert had a legitimate son, William Clito, with his new wife. With support from Norman nobles and the French King Louis VI, Clito proved a constant source of rebellion against Henry for a decade from 1118. His threat strengthened upon the drowning of Henry's sole legitimate son in the Great White Ship disaster in 1120 and only ended with his death from a gangrenous wound in 1128, caused in a scuffle at the siege of Aalst, Belgium.

49. Coronation of Henry I
British Library MS Cotton Claudius A. III f. 19r (12ᵗʰ century)
Public domain image courtesy of Wikimedia Commons Licence

Following Henry's rapid accession to the throne in 1100, all of those being suggested to have been involved in the plot (and numerous close relatives), received considerable perks from the new king, either soon after or over time. Historians have pondered and pontificated at length on the significance of what has become known as 'The Clare Benefit', that is the gifting of position and wealth to that extended family by Henry, for their suspected help in him taking the crown through conspiracy and regicide. Of the 10 plotters I have highlighted, 6 of them are of the Clare family group—the 3 Clare brothers, Gilbert, Roger and Richard (plus their other 2 brothers who benefited as well), the Clare uncle, William Giffard and their 2 brothers-in-law, Eudo Dapifer and Walter Tyrell (who was also a cousin). This leaves just the 2 Beaumont brothers, Robert and Henry and Maud and Simon Senlis apart. What is more, in the years after, the offspring of the Beaumonts, Senlis and Clares became widely intermarried as well (Appendices 2.1 and 4).

As such, the tag of 'Clare' to the benefit is slightly narrow, as these 'others', as we shall see, not only gained considerably but their descendants determinedly intermarried within the Clare and Senlis dynasties, something not even considered by Hollister. Although there can be no argument that patronage to all of them (Tyrell apart, for obvious reasons, though his sole English property was left untouched, only to be sold by his grandson nearly a century later) increased during Henry's reign, Warren Hollister's proposition in his treatise that the 'Benefit' was not sufficient, or of a scale, to imply that this family, over and above others, received overt favouritism towards them from the new king, can surely been demonstrated as untrue.

It is true that Henry was famed, as Orderic described metaphorically, for 'raising men up from the dust'[515], believing more in the power of meritocracy rather than simply aristocracy and amply displayed in numerous of his new appointees of sheriffs. He bestowed all sorts of such advantages on his 'new men', many of whom were not from the great landed families, though he judiciously looked after them as well, becoming a master at melding patronage, wealth, justice and peace. However, I think Hollister has perhaps missed a key angle in this analysis. The people concerned in the plot were, by any standard, extremely wealthy individuals, the multi-millionaires and Sunday Times Rich List of their day. The Beaumonts, Clares, Giffards, Maud/Senlis, and others like Eudo Dapifer that I suggest were involved, already had vast estates, incomes and titles. The sagacious Robert de Beaumont, already one of the most powerful men of the realm, though not the richest, is swiftly elevated, in the first year of Henry's reign[516], to be 1st Earl of Leicester, becoming his closest and most astute baronial advisor, the eventual witness to a remarkable 112 charters and writs and sorely missed by Henry after his death in 1118. Robert's Domesday holdings were quite modest compared to other magnates, it was only after Henry's accession that his wealth exploded, raising him to the summit of the aristocratic order. In 1102, he acquired the vast Grandesmil estates and further manors in Leicestershire, Northamptonshire and Dorset from the royal demesne. Plus he obtained all those lands of Aubrey, Earl of Northumberland in Leicestershire and Northamptonshire, forfeit before 1086 and later, the estates of William de Mortain in Northamptonshire and Sussex, forfeited to the crown in 1104. This surely truly is 'benefit'.

---

[515] Quotation from the *Ecclesiastical History* of Orderic Vitalis, XI.2.

[516] In fact the date of his appointment cannot be distinctly ascertained. Some historians believe it was not made until 1107, after the Battle of Tinchebrai in 1106, following his successful command of the army against Robert Curthose when aged c.60.

Robert, with his close French links and well placed as husband of the French king's niece, may even have been active in the French court on behalf of Henry soon after his coronation, arranging for the Christmas visit to London by Prince Louis. In 1106, his younger brother, Henry de Beaumont (whose impassioned speech at the treasury door in Winchester had so helped King Henry), acquired the Lordship of Gower in south Wales as a favour from the king for his loyalty, and built the great castle at Swansea the following year.

Is it not a little simplistic to believe that people in the late 11th century would only become embroiled in such a scheme solely for pecuniary gain? Despite the fact that the 'Benefit', such as it was, can be deemed more than generous (and not solely for the Clares), is it not possible, probable even, that there were other, nobler motives at work, or simply those of revenge? Admittedly this was an early period of English Kingship and it would take a long time for the power of the monarchy to be reduced and wider freedoms restored to the populace, but the legacy of these families due to the death of Rufus is surely significant.

Perhaps the key character to consider in all this is the man being placed at the head of the plot for Henry, Gilbert de Clare; he who had rebelled twice before against Rufus and even been implicated in a previous regicidal assassination plot. Gilbert's motives whether they were noble, familial revenge, family advancement or a combination thereof, will always be unclear, but it seems unlikely his own personal financial advantage was number one on his list of motives, for as I say, he was already fabulously wealthy.

In 1101 after the threat of invasion by Duke Robert subsided following the Treaty of Alton, there was a large baronial gathering in the September at Windsor castle (a great Council meeting with associated hunting and lavish banqueting) at which virtually every member of the Clare family, bar one, was in attendance.[517]

The first 2 plotters to receive direct reward from King Henry were the 2 ecclesiastics, uncle of the Clare siblings, William Giffard, and youngest Clare brother, Bec monk Richard (who likely brought the exiled Anselm the news in southern France and returned with him to Canterbury[518]). This was primarily due

---

[517] The only Clare brother not mentioned as one of the witnesses and assumed to be absent was Robert de Clare.

[518] As was often the case of younger sons of the nobility, Richard had lived a life for the church and had been a young monk at Bec Abbey in Normandy as far back as 1080. He would have known Anselm very well, as he was the Abbott there from 1078–93 when

to the fact that these high positions came with large church estates/incomes already attached to them whereas dishing our lands to the others was more difficult, as by 1100, 35 years after Hastings, all the country's estates had already been allocated to the new Norman aristocracy who had accompanied the Conqueror. The only way Henry could obtain more property for distribution was either through forfeiture due to treason and rebellion[519], surrendering some of his own royal demesne lands or by acquiring further territory through invasion, particularly in Wales. So, as mentioned earlier, William Giffard was immediately made bishop elect of lucrative Winchester[520] just hours after Rufus fell to the ground, and a month or so later, Richard de Clare was given the Abbacy of Ely, an equally rich post that had been left vacant for 7 years since the death of the last abbot in 1093, with the incomes of the abbey, as with those of Winchester, having been seized by Ranulph Flambard on behalf of Rufus. The immediacy of Giffard's appointment, plus the instant return to England of Richard de Clare with Anselm, both reek of decisions made by Henry prior to Rufus dying rather than spontaneous occurrences—all part of the plan.

Somewhat ironically, by late 1102 both Richard and Walter (and favoured Anselm) had rather fallen out with Henry over the seemingly endless struggle between church and crown over ecclesiastical appointments—the investiture of bishops—and went into exile.[521] At the Council of Westminster, in 1102, Henry had tried to strip Richard of his appointment (which one feels had been part of

---

Richard first arrived and they were together there for some thirteen years. In 1100, some twenty years later, Richard. now in his late thirties, was still just a simple monk at Bec.

[519] Henry clawed back huge estates from those many barons that supported his brother Robert Curthose in the next few years and were exiled with their lands forfeited.

[520] Note that Malmesbury tells us that the Winchester bishopric was violently forced upon Giffard by Henry, and that he accepted it with the greatest reluctance (*Gesta Pontificum Anglorum,* William of Malmesbury, p.110). But if the alternate charge that he purchased the Winchester see from Henry for a large sum of money, as implied in Matthew Paris's word 'remuneratus', is to be accepted as historical, this reluctance was entirely feigned, and a smokescreen to hide the real nature of the transaction which was of course, as a most lucrative and impressive appointment given as a 'benefit' for his support in the plot. (*Historia Anglorum,* Matthew Paris, vol. ii. p.181).

[521] Just like later Thomas Becket, when these men are given senior church appointments they tended to side with the Church Establishment, not the Crown, in matters. When Henry failed to co-operate with his archbishop, Anselm seems obliquely to have threatened to support Curthose against him. *Anselm of Bec.* Sally N. Vaughn, 1987, p.298

the deal with Henry forged by his brother Gilbert de Clare back in 1100) and demanded 'the surrender of his staff and ring'.[522] Richard refused and set out to Rome with his old friend Anselm (plus Anselm's confidante and secretary Eadmer) and his uncle, William Giffard, along with Henry's own representative, his papal envoy or 'nuncio'—the royal secretary and chaplain, William Warelwast (who had very likely been at the hunting lodge on the day of the Rufus shooting). Richard had the Pope secure his position in 1103 and Henry is clearly not too angry at the outcomes, as on the return of Richard in 1104 and Anselm in 1105, they are all soon reinstated to their previous positions and Warelwast is upgraded from a chaplain to become Bishop of Exeter![523] Countess Adela, King Henry's sister and friend of Anselm, is understood to have smoothed the path of reconciliation between them all. I also strongly suggest that his bright young queen, Matilda (Edith as was), close friend and confidant of Anselm (with whom she was corresponding frequently at this time, begging him to return from exile[524]), was another peacemaker and persuaded Henry in this regard, as she is well recognised as having been an important intercessor between Anselm and Henry.

All Richard's energy after his return from Rome was devoted to the building of the great cathedral in Ely (which was finally elevated by the Pope from an Abbacy to a Bishopric and Holy See in 1108) and to preparing for the transfer of the remains of St Etheldreda and the 3 sainted abbesses, from their tombs in the

---

[522] In Richard's case there was also a worrying groundswell of hostile opinion among the nobles about the degree of favouritism and patronage being granted to the Clare and Giffard families from which he derived. These reports would certainly seem to run counter to the view of Hollister, who suggested that the 'benefits' given to the Clares were not out of proportion to those of anyone else.
Detail from 'Houses of Benedictine monks: Abbey and cathedral priory of Ely', in *A History of the County of Cambridge and the Isle of Ely:* Volume 2, ed. L F Salzman (London, 1948), pp.199–210. Also *'Concilia'*, vol. 1, p. 382, Wilkins (1737); and 12th c. *'Liber Eliensis'*, p.287.

[523] As previously secretary to Rufus and believed present on the hunting party at Malwood Lodge, perhaps there were reasons of secrecy and loyalty, as well as competence, that Warelwast was also rewarded so generously by Henry.

[524] *Sancti Anselmi Cantuariensis Archiepiscopi, Opera Omnia,* ed. F.S. Schmitt (Edinburgh: T. Nelson, 1946–63), epistles 317 and 320; translation and annotation from *The Letters of Saint Anselm of Canterbury,* trans. Walter Fröhlich, Cistercian Studies (Kalamazoo: Cistercian Publications, 1990–94)

old Saxon abbey to shrines behind the high altar of the new cathedral. [525] This was finally accomplished on the 17th October 1106, a year before Richard's somewhat premature death. [526]

In 1101 after the threat of invasion by Duke Robert subsided following the Treaty of Alton, there was a large baronial gathering in the September at Windsor castle (a great Council meeting with associated hunting and lavish banqueting) at which virtually every member of the Clare family, bar one, was in attendance. [527]

During those early years of Henry's reign, he kept a core of loyal advisors around him and it is the 2 quite elderly plotting Beaumont brothers (Robert and Henry) along with co-plotters, the 2 elder Clare brothers, Gilbert and Roger plus their uncle Bishop William Giffard, younger brother Robert and cousin Robert Malet, all of whom were particularly close to the king and in constant attendance of Henry at court, attesting charters and writs. Also included is Robert Fitzhaimo (who helped Henry negotiate the Treaty of Alton), whose loyalty is unquestioned but his involvement as a plotter maybe can be. It is significant that in these early years Roger and Gilbert de Clare often witnessed charters with only this small group of barons and officials, which can only be taken as an indication of the strong relationship these 2 brothers and Malet had with the king (in fact the unmarried Roger became the more prominent, probably due to his land holdings and influence in Normandy on behalf of Henry, which was initially the more pressing issue with his brother Robert Curthose).

It was mentioned in the last chapter that one of the people probably quaffing wine with the new king, just a week or 2 after the coronation, was this Robert Malet character, who suddenly pops up from nowhere. Aside from the favours dished out to the Clare brothers and sisters, he is perhaps the most intriguing and significant beneficiary of the 'Benefit'. Robert was born c.1050—and died

---

[525] This appears to have been allowed in the midst of a Norman-French hierarchy (but maybe with Maud and Edith's influence), being an unexpectedly enthusiastic development of the cult of these pre-Norman saints and benefactors, but no doubt a means keenly used by Richard whereby a religious establishment could develop its status as a cult centre and compete with rival houses for pilgrims, money, and benefactors.

[526] The nature of his death, aged c.46, is unrecorded but presumably illness—some of his elder siblings were to live for another 25 years or more.

[527] The only Clare brother not mentioned as one of the witnesses and assumed to be absent was Robert de Clare.

c.1130—(though some unvalidated sources claim he was killed at the Battle of Tinchebrai in 1106) and was one of the key witnesses and signatories to Henry's Coronation Charter of Liberties issued on Sunday 5th August 1100, just 72 hours after Rufus slumped to the ground.

It is this Robert Malet who provides perhaps one of the most damning pieces of evidence to support a Clare led plot to remove Rufus. Previously, like his father William Malet (see Part 1, chapter 9, 'sheriffs of Yorkshire'), under the Conqueror Robert had been High Sheriff of both Norfolk and Suffolk and had inherited, aged just 21, the vast barony of the Honour of Eye (256 manors, 13th largest in the country) on his father's premature death in 1071 fighting Hereward the Wake. However, Robert had later fallen out with Rufus sometime between 1087–94, probably for supporting Rufus's brother, Robert Curthose, and been banished back to his castle in Le Havre, Normandy, forfeiting his English lands. Then, just 3 days after the death of Rufus, he is suddenly back in London for the Coronation, witnessing the Charter of Liberties, restored to his Sheriffdoms, other lands and high office by King Henry, of whom he became a close adviser and first Lord Great Chamberlain.

Given the normal slowness of communications and travel in 1100, this just has to suggest a degree of foreknowledge, pre-planning and that he was very likely already on his way from Normandy, much like Anselm, as Rufus fell to the ground, maybe even bringing the boat over to Poole Harbour, enabling Walter Tyrell's escape with Roger de Clare and himself to quickly travel onwards to London. Even more revealing, Robert's mother was Elisée (Hesilia) de Brionne (who had married the great baron William Malet, erstwhile Sheriff of Yorkshire back in 1068/9), an aunt of the de Clare siblings, as Elisée was a sister of their late father, Richard FitzGilbert de Clare, who had been cruelly incarcerated in St Neots Priory by Rufus after the 1087 rebellion, to die there shortly thereafter c.1090. One imagines that Robert was furious with Rufus for the treatment of his uncle Richard which must have caused great upset to his mother (See Malet's link to the Clares in the family tree Appendix 9).[528]

So, Robert Malet was part of the family, a first cousin of the Clare plotters and no doubt totally 'au fait' with the scheme, hence his foreknowledge and yet

---

[528] Robert Malet and Walter Tyrell were thus also quite closely related as cousins, given they were both grandsons of Gilbert 'Crispin' de Brionne (but had different grandmothers), the great original benefactor of Bec Abbey. See Appendix 9.

another of that dynasty quick to benefit greatly from Rufus's death.[529] His hereditary Normandy estate and castle, his 'caput', were in Graville-Sainte-Honorine, now a suburb of Le Havre and just 2 miles from Harfleur harbour. Whether he sailed over to Poole in advance to meet up with his escaping cousins Walter Tyrell and Roger de Clare or met them off the boat at either Honfleur or Harfleur and then took the same ship directly back to England, leaving them to continue their journey to Bec Abbey just 40 miles away, is open to conjecture. Either way, to be in London by Sunday 5th August and witnessing the Coronation Charter, just 72 hours after Rufus died, he must have been in on the plan and was clearly highly favoured by King Henry. It is this sort of incriminating detail that Hollister (and others), either ignores or misses in his treatise supporting 'accidental death'.

There is no denying that throughout their history the Clare family had an insatiable desire for land and wealth[530] and by being instrumental in bringing Henry onto the throne, even if Gilbert was not looking after no.1, he was able to have the new king endow others of his extended Clare family with wealth, land and position, who in return gave their support to his kingship. Indeed, in addition to cousin Malet, it is the 2 other younger Clare brothers, Walter and Robert, who while not seeming to have been overtly involved in the plot or regicide, were first to receive the largesse of land and position from the king when he was able.[531] Although neither of them were down in the New Forest that memorable day, as a tight-knit fraternal group, I do suspect they were all well aware of the

---

[529] Following his return he did in fact have a brief falling out with Henry in the 1101 revolt (he had been a former Curthose supporter and sided with that group of rebels including Walter Giffard, Ivo de Grandmesnil, Robert de Lacy (Robin's bête noire), William de Warenne and Robert de Bellesme in their failed insurrection) and was stripped of his lands—but this quickly passed and clearly favoured by the King (and a relative of the Clares), paid a large fine and had his estates and positions restored (as did Warenne), remaining a close adviser to King Henry. (Orderic Vitalis, Vol. iv, p.161)

[530] It was noted in the *Brut* that King Henry made a statement saying Gilbert often pestered him for land, though primarily this seems to have been for the benefit of his sons and brothers. *'Brut y Tywysogyon'*, Ed. T. Jones, Red Book of Hergest Version, Board of Celtic Studies, Univ. Of Wales, History and Law Series, xvii, 1955, pp.70–1.

[531] Gilbert himself wisely kept a low profile for the first year or so; although at court he did not appear as a charter witness until December 1101 and sensibly kept his head well down to avoid any possible association with the demise of Rufus. The evidence of his hand on documents escalated greatly latterly.

unfolding plot. Brother Robert was immediately given the senior post of steward to the king, a position he held right up to Henry's death in 1135 such that he, Gilbert and Roger were all at the king's side in those early years. But Robert had to wait a few years for his grant of the large feudal Barony of Dunmow (in Essex) and that of Baynard's Castle, in London, when forfeited by William Baynard '*by misfortune and felony*'[532] and for supporting Robert Curthose against Henry. In about 1114, when in his early fifties, Robert married Maud de Senlis, some 28+ years his junior, the 22yr. old daughter of co-plotters Countess Maud and the late Simon Senlis I, the widowed Countess by then being newly remarried herself, to Prince David of Scotland.

Next, despite no evidence of his direct involvement in the plot, King Henry granted the fourth Clare brother, Walter, the great Lordship of Nether, in Gwent, Wales, along with the castle of Striguil (Chepstow) in the southern Marches. These were territories previously held by Willliam de Eu but had been forfeited by him to the crown as a consequence of his involvement in the failed barons rebellion of 1095. Although surviving evidence of Walter's life is sparse, he was clearly a favourite of King Henry, witnessing 12 royal charters and although some historians think he was unmarried, other sources have him marrying Isabella, c.1122, a daughter of Ralph III de Tosny and Alice, the younger daughter of Waltheof, sister of Countess Maud (and half-sister of Robin). Later in life, in 1131, he founded the great Cistercian Tintern Abbey, 6 miles north of Chepstow. However, he did not have any children and after his death the Countship of Striguil and his castle at Chepstow, passed to the Clare descendants of his elder brother, Gilbert.

This new distribution of wealth by the king to these younger Clare brothers has somewhat perplexed modern historians but surely the answer is clear. Gilbert, with his huge baronies of Tonbridge in Kent and Clare in Suffolk and Roger with the large ancestral family estates of Bienfaite and Orbec in Normandy were well provided for, but both are now in a position to help their 'landless' younger brothers, Robert and Walter plus cousins, who were not so well established. Not that Gilbert himself was ignored though; in 1110 he was granted the lordship of Ceredigion (and Cardigan castle) in south-western Wales, and taking a lower profile at court, immediately embarked upon an intensive campaign, on behalf of Henry, to subjugate the area until his death c.1115–17. A

---

[532] '*A History of the County of Essex: Volume 2, Houses of Austin canons: Priory of Little Dunmow*', Victoria County History, 1907, pp. 150–154.

key beneficiary was Gilbert's daughter Adelize (Alice), as Henry sanctioned her marriage to Aubrey de Vere II, who became one of Henry's key 'new men'. He served as one of the king's chamberlains and Justiciar under Henry, also appointing him as Sheriff of London and Essex and co-sheriff, with Richard Basset (one of Henry's 'new men'), of no less than eleven other counties (*Pipe Roll*, Henry I, *1130*), bringing vast wealth to Aubrey and his 'Clare' wife, daughter of the king's late close friend, Gilbert, the man who helped bring him the crown—the 'kingmaker'.

Gilbert's eldest son Richard (d.1136—killed in an ambush in Wales), is thought, though unconfirmed, to have been made 1st Earl of Hertford by King Henry and his second son, Gilbert FitzGilbert de Clare (c.1100–1148), who became 1st Earl of Pembroke and Count of Striguil, was just about to be born when Rufus fell to the ground. But when grown up was also well looked after by King Henry, as he married none other than Isabel de Beaumont, daughter of the great but now deceased Robert de Beaumont, 1st Earl of Leicester (one of the plotters, but d.1117) and his young French wife, Elizabeth de Vermandois.

He later became nicknamed 'Strongbow', either due to his strength, prowess and promotion of the longbow or a mistranslation of 'Striguil' (though this nickname of 'Strongbow' is much more readily associated with his son, Richard). He was high in the favour of Henry I,[533] most likely because his wife Isabel was one of Henry's favourite mistresses and bore him an illegitimate daughter! This younger Gilbert de Clare was really the only son who was to achieve any great prominence, being the founder of the great cadet branch of the family, better known for their opposition to the Crown than for loyal service, playing an important part in the civil war of King Stephen's reign and in the Norman conquest of Ireland. The Lords of Clare itself, are best known for their participation in the baronial opposition both before and after Magna Carta and for their activities during the Barons' Wars from 1258 to 1267.

The final 2 plotters who must be afforded some attention are Eudo Dapifer and Simon Senlis.

---

[533] When his uncle Roger (the plotter who helped Walter Tyrell escape to France) died without heirs in 1131, Gilbert junior was granted all the Clare family estates in Normandy at Orbec and Bienfaite by King Henry I.

Eudo, was the steward or 'dapifer' to Rufus, a position of high governmental office and a job he had held under the Conqueror as well[534]. As we know, Eudo's wife from 1088 was the de Clare brothers' other sister, Rohese, thus he was connected by marriage to Tyrell as a fellow brother-in-law of the Clares (see Appendix 5). He was very likely in the hunting party at Malwood Keep, but not actually on the hunt himself, and 3 days later back in London he too was one of the witnesses to Henry's Coronation Charter. He continued in the position under Henry, of whom he was obviously a great favourite and for his service he acquired yet more lands and several manors. Eudo was seemingly a much admired 'good man' and in 1101, soon after his succession, King Henry granted Eudo the town of Colchester, partly bestowed on him at the request of the English townsmen, who had petitioned *'that they might have this famous Eudo to govern among them,"* adding that, *"he eased the oppressed, restrained the insolent, and pleased all, being a great prince in all his doings and dealings."*[535]

Eudo and Rohese's daughter, Margaret, had married William de Mandeville, Constable of the Tower of London, but William had a third of his lands confiscated as a punishment by King Henry for letting Bishop Flambard escape the Tower in 1101. It is not really known whether Mandeville was incompetent or complicit in Flambard's escape but all these forfeited lands were given to his father-in-law Eudo, whose property portfolio and wealth just seemed to grow and grow.[536]

The last person, and plotter, to mention is Earl Simon de Senlis, husband of Robin's sister Maud. After the regicidal event (which maybe his wife somewhat pushed him into, as he was doing quite well under Rufus), he possibly had a conscience problem over his involvement in the plot (which frankly was minimal apart from supporting Henry), as sometime later (he was still witnessing writs at court, though low profile, in 1109[537]), despite his advancing years, he left Maud and the children behind in England, and went on a pilgrimage to the Holy Land in 1110. Although a great military man, one suspects that politics and

---

[534] The other steward to Rufus (also sheriff of Kent) and previously to the Conqueror, was Haimo Dapifer, d.1100, the father of Robert Fitzhaimo.

[535] *Battle Abbey Roll*, Cleveland, 1889, vol 3. p.74.

[536] William and Margaret's son, Geoffrey de Mandeville would recover the seized estates and the constableship during the reign of King Stephen.

[537] *'Outline Itinerary of King Henry I'*, ed. William Farrer, Reprinted from the English Historical Review, Vol. XXXIV, July-Oct 1919.

statesmanship were not really the forte of ageing Simon and apart from witnessing Henry's Coronation Charter and a few subsequent writs, was quite happy, after all the drama, to have taken a back seat during the first decade of the new century, back at his Northampton Castle with his family and plan his penitential trip to Jerusalem. If nothing else though, Simon was a survivor as amazingly, given his age and the trials and tribulations of visiting Jerusalem (and his famously gammy leg!), he returned from the Holy Land in one piece after about 15 months. This is evidenced by him being a witness, in summer 1111, to a royal writ at Bishop's Waltham Palace in Hampshire (a grant of Henry I to Bath Abbey on 8th August 1111), a residence of the Bishop of Winchester (still fellow plotter William Giffard). This was made as the king was awaiting a favourable crossing to Normandy with the queen and Simon may very well have gone with them, as he died in France in 1112, being buried at the priory of La Charité-sur-Loire[538].

Soon after, in 1113, King Henry arranged the significant marriage of his widow, the Countess Maud, to Prince David of Scotland a marriage sanctioned by Henry which Judith Green described as '*both generous and risky*'[539]. David was of course Henry's brother-in-law and had been prominent at the English court ever since Henry had taken the throne and married his elder sister Edith (now called Queen Matilda) back in 1100. It is claimed the queen persuaded Henry to allow this match in order that something be done for her brother, who received the Earldoms of Northampton and Huntingdon as a result, though only as custodian for Simon II, who was not yet of age (the young son from Countess Maud's first marriage, to Simon I de Senlis).

---

[538] This documented chain of events conflicts with the VCH version (*A History of the County of Northamptonshire— 'The Priory of St Andrew'*, Vol. 2, p.102) which states he died during his return from the Holy Land. The priory of La Charité, 150 miles south of Paris, was very new, having only been consecrated by Pope Pascal in 1107. From the 11th century, paupers and pilgrims seeking charity from the abbey monks gave rise to the name of this important fortified crossing point on the Loire south of Paris. Its long stone bridge—the oldest along the river—became a symbol for travellers. The powerful Benedictine abbey of La Charité-sur-Loire was the 'eldest daughter-house of Cluny', on the Santiago de Compostela pilgrim way and it founded fifty filials across Europe. One of these filials, a cell, was the Priory of St Andrew in Northampton, founded between 1093 and 1100 by Simon and Maud.

[539] '*David I and Henry I'*, *The Scottish Historical Review*, Judith Green, Vol. LXXV, No. 199, Part 1 (April 1996), p.6 of 19.

For a moment, let us consider just some of the many quite extraordinary intermarriages between these families. The Isabel de Beaumont above, who married Gilbert de Clare's son, had an elder brother, Robert de Beaumont, the 2nd Earl of Leicester, whose daughter (also called Isabel) married none other than Simon de Senlis II just mentioned above, son of Countess Maud and Simon de Senlis I. If this were not enough, Maud and Simon's own daughter, also called Maud, married Robert de Clare, the Lord of Dunmow detailed earlier, King Henry's trusted steward and younger brother to Maud's plotting friends, Gilbert and Roger de Clare. (all these links are shown in Appendices 2.1 and 4)

It should be noted that Maud and Robert de Clare are the ancestors of the Barons FitzWalter and that they had 2 most interesting grandchildren. One, called Maud FitzWalter b.1157 (making her the great-great-granddaughter of Judith de Lens and Waltheof) married William de Lovetot, the grandson of an earlier William de Lovetot who built Sheffield castle and held the Lordships of Hallam and Sheffield Manors, granted him by Henry I back in 1103, thus bringing them back into the possession of the descendants of Waltheof, who had held them prior to the Conquest a century earlier.[540] I believe that this younger William de Lovetot may very well have been a great-grandson of Judith de Lens and her lover, Roger de Busli II (see text and possible lineage in Appendix 7 and also Appendix 2.1).

The other was a grandson, called Robert Fitzwalter, a great champion of English liberty around whom a considerable amount of legend and romance has gathered, which again, is just maybe how that name became associated with Robin Hood and more particularly Marian throughout the ages. This Robert Fitzwalter was perhaps the key baron in the later revolt against King John in 1215 and was one of the 25 signatories to Magna Carta whose daughter Maud was supposedly poisoned by a rejected King John, contributing to the Maid Marian legend. (see Part I, chapter 7)

This all appears to be an extraordinarily determined effort to keep the cabal of the Beaumont, Clare and Maud/Senlis families closely intertwined, protecting the 'great family secret' that continued with grandsons and granddaughters and

---

[540] The Tenancy-in-chief of Hallam must have remained with Countess Maud though (as heiress to Judith) as control of the Hallam Manor was acquired by Prince David of Scotland, by 'right of his wife' on becoming Earl of Huntingdon on their marriage in 1114, arranged by King Henry.

(from *Conquest, Anarchy and Lordship*, Paul Dalton, 1994, CUP, p.96+fn. 69)

was surely a very deliberate process that cannot be ignored. All these interrelationships are much clearer with a brief study of Appendices 4 and 5.

What also simply cannot be ignored is the extraordinary legacy of Waltheof's grandchildren and great-grandchildren for the pursuit of freedom for the people, primarily through those of his daughter Maud but also her sister Alice. To quote Ms Stredder from her 1887 article (Part I, footnote 71) regarding their significant legacy…

'…they were thus allied with conqueror and conquered alike. A union from which the true Old English spirit arose. In every effort for the restoration of the liberties of the land, we find one or other of their names'.

In trying to peer into the minds of these people, from a distance of 900 years, it is not easy to interpret the true motives behind their actions. If as I suggest, the Countess Maud was complicit in the plot then her motives must truly have been more honourable, laudable and altruistic than monetary gain and this surely is particularly the case with regard to not only her, to whom I have already made reference earlier but also to the Clares and Beaumonts. A remarkable sixteen of the twenty-five signatories, or sureties, to Magna Carta, a century later, were direct descendants, or connected by marriage, of these few conspirators[541]. (See Appendices 4 and 5).

What is more, from the consistent intermarriage between the Beaumonts and de Montforts (the town of Montfort is less than 20 miles from the Robert de Beaumont's seat at Meulan), came the renowned Simon V de Montfort of the 1260s (Robert de Beaumont was his great-great-great-grandfather) and who is often recognised as the progenitor of parliamentary democracy following his famed revolt against Henry III (Appendix 4). If you go back to that fateful week in 1100, of the eleven signatories to King Henry's famed Coronation Charter in 1100, it included both Beaumont brothers, Robert and Henry, William Giffard, Simon de Senlis, Eudo Dapifer and Robert de Montfort. A further signatory was Robert Fitzhaimo, whose direct involvement in the plot can be questioned, with Gilbert de Clare himself probably wisely keeping a very low profile early on.

---

[541] Henry de Bohun, Geoffrey de Mandeville, William de Lanvallei, William d'Aubigny, Robert FitzWalter, Robert de Vere, Geoffrey de Say, John de Lacy, John FitzRobert, Roger le Bigod, William de Huntingfield, Hugh le Bigod, Richard de Clare, Gilbert de Clare, William Marshall II, Saer de Quincy and Richard Montfichet.

Just how much of this desired reform for a better kingdom, protection for the church, improved laws, extension of freedoms and the abolition of the perceived abuses of Rufus, lay behind their involvement to remove the Red King and install Henry will never be known but I suspect was much more a set of motives than any promise of more money and titles. For example, Henry immediately '*purged the court of the effeminates, restoring the use of lamps at night which had been given up in his brother's time*'.[542]

Although the reality was, of course, that Henry pretty much ignored much of the content on his accession leading to continued unrest. In truth, he frequently turned out to be more ruthless than Rufus as well as there being evidence of him as being a cold-blooded murderer.[543] He did though manage to reign England for over thirty years of peace and on his death the Anglo-Saxon Chronicle of 1135 did at least describe Henry as the '*rex pacifus*' and Geoffrey of Monmouth, in his 1136 'Historia Regum Britanniae', as the '*The Lion of Justice*', with modern historian Dan Snow tagging him—'*a titan of European history*'.

Henry's reign is noted for his opportunistic political skills, the aforementioned improvements in the machinery of government (getting rid of rapacious sheriffs included[544]) and creation of the Exchequer, improving the justice system, integrating the divided Anglo-Saxons and Normans within his kingdom, reuniting the dominions of his father and the peaceful integration of Scotland due to his marriage. He certainly favoured negotiation over confrontation and this view is believed to have been driven by his chief advisor, friend and plotter, the wise old Robert de Beaumont. Despite all of Henry's

---

[542] *Gesta Regum Anglorum*, William of Malmesbury, vol. 1. p.715

[543] In late 1090 Conan Pilatus, a powerful burgher in Rouen, had rebelled against Robert Curthose. Henry arrived in Rouen to help his brother and took Conan prisoner. Henry was angry that Conan had turned against his feudal lord (Robert) and had him taken to the top of Rouen Castle and then, despite Conan's offers to pay a huge ransom, threw him off the top of the castle to his death. (*Henry I*, C. W. Hollister, Yale University Press. (2003). p.73)

[544] Specifically, Henry removed the great magnates, replacing them with his 'new men' who owed everything to his favour and were often officials in the royal household, thereby creating a much more centralised system under his control. However, removing some of the great feudal families and their effective hereditary positions was more difficult.

foibles of which he had a few, Orderic Vitalis was certainly impressed by his reign and was particularly complimentary when writing in later years…

'*From the onset of his reign, he wisely conciliated all groups, and enticed them into his fellowship with royal generosity. He honoured his great men generously, supported them with wealth and honours and thus won their fidelity with his soothing policies. He favoured his common subjects with just laws and protected them by his authority from unfair exactions and robbery. The sublime prince thus stood out among all the lords and monarchs of the west and merited the favour of everyone, churchmen and laymen alike, who rejoiced at being governed with reason*'.[545]

So, Rufus is dead, Robin has fulfilled his part of the plan, his father's death is avenged, a royal pardon for him and his men is agreed, Archbishop Anselm is coming home, the worst of the sheriffs and Barons in Yorkshire, Nottinghamshire and elsewhere are to be weeded out, with the invasion of France cancelled taxes will fall and in the forthcoming marriage of the new king to the beautiful Saxon/Scottish princess, the 'English' royal House of Wessex will be re-established to produce heirs to the throne. Little wonder the populace were rejoicing.

So, let us ponder for one moment on that arrow that flew from the bow of Robin Hood into the chest of the King of England—killing him stone dead. The great Victorian historian E. A. Freeman summarised the significant effect of this archer's action and what it meant with his death…'*But, however we judge the man* (Rufus)*, there is but one judgement to be passed on his reign—The arrow, by whomsoever shot, set England free from oppression such as she never felt before or after at the hand of a single man*'.[546]

Perhaps then it was only appropriate that the legendary icon of English freedoms, and hero of the populace, Robin Hood, should have let fly that deadly shaft.

So what does he do next…?

---

[545] '*Historia Ecclesiastica*', Orderic Vitalis, ed. A. Le Prévost. Pub. Paris 1838–55. Book IV, p.92.

[546] *William Rufus,* Freeman, E.A. , Oxford Clarendon Press, 1882, p.337.

Chapter 12
The Nun, the Princess, the Son,
the Shrine and the Letter...

From the evidence I am about to disclose, what Robin does next is to retreat to the relatively safe confines of that great Saxon foundation for nuns at nearby Romsey Abbey. This is just 9 miles from the Rufus Stone and from around September 1100, he began to worship there at his father's shrine—a shrine he very likely helped establish nearly twenty-five years earlier following Waltheof's horrific execution on Giles Hill, Winchester, just twelve miles away to the east.

As such, this would be an appropriate point to say a little more regarding the abbey and specifically the Romsey nun (and erstwhile abbess), Princess Christina[547], plus one or 2 other related characters that impact our story. We need to very briefly go back in time, about eighty years, to the early part of the 11th century. In 1016, following the successful Danish invasion of England by Cnut, Edward and Edmund, the 2 very young children of the defeated, now dead King Edmund Ironside, were spirited away to the royal court of Sweden.[548] Following further moves, to Ukraine and Poland, they finally ended up in Hungary where they lived in exile, in the custody of Henry III, the Holy Roman Emperor.

---

[547] It is recorded in the *'Menologium Benedictinum'* by Bucelinus (Feldkirch, 1655) that Christina was later venerated as a saint but modern records do not appear to endorse this. Certainly her mother, Queen Margaret of Scotland, was definitely made a saint in 1250, being Scotland's only royal saint.

[548] 1016 is the same year that Cnut was complicit in the massacre, at his court, of Earl Uchtred and his companions (Robin's great-great-grandfather) by Thurbrand the Hold, which started the great family blood feud concluded in 1074 by Waltheof, Uchtred's great-grandson. See Part I, chapter 4.

Moving forward forty years, to 1056, the ageing English king, Edward the Confessor[549], on hearing that his now grown-up nephew, Edward 'the Exile', was still alive (brother Edmund having died some years earlier *c.*1050), he sent for him with the intention of making him his heir to the English throne. The 42-year-old Edward arrived back in England in 1057[550] with his wife, Agatha[551] and their 3 children, Edgar the Ætheling (the Prince), and Princesses Margaret and Christina. Many people think he was murdered, maybe by the Godwinsons, who had aspirations of their own where the Crown was concerned[552], but whether by malice or fate, just days after his arrival on English soil and before he had even met the king, Edward 'the Exile' was dead.

His 3 children were aged around 6 to 12, though their birthdates are not known precisely nor the order in which they were born, but usually taken as between c.1045–1050 with the eldest being Margaret then Christina and Edgar. The boy, young Edgar the Ætheling, was nominated as heir apparent but was too young to count for much, being eventually, in 1066, to be swept aside by Earl Harold Godwinson, Edward the Confessor's brother-in-law. On the death of King Edward in early January that year, it left the throne of England to be disputed by 3 men, all of whom could claim some degree of legitimacy to the title—his brother-in-law, Earl Harold Godwinson, who claimed that on his deathbed the Confessor had 'commended the kingdom to Harold's 'protection'; Harald 'Hardrada' Sigurdsson, the King of Norway (supported by Godwinson's exiled brother, Tostig) who claimed the right of succession from the previous king of Norway, Magnus, which had been granted by Harthacnut, King of England 1040–42 (aka Cnut III); and lastly Duke William of Normandy, whose blood claim was in fact the strongest, being a second cousin of Edward the Confessor. William swore that Edward the Confessor had earlier promised him

---

[549] The 'Confessor' was the half-brother of Edmund Ironside, being the son of Æthelred the Unready by his second wife, Emma of Normandy.

[550] This is precisely the same year I believe young Waltheof and his Loxley maiden are conceiving their son, Robin/Robert, in their 'roll-in-the-hay in the aula stables at Hallam.

[551] Agatha's antecedents are famously unclear and the subject of much speculation. Noble links to Hungary, Germany, Bulgaria, Russia, Poland and Sweden have all been suggested, but none proven.

[552] Harold Godwinson (later King Harold) was then the Earl of Wessex, arguably the most powerful man in England after the king, and his sister was married to King Edward the Confessor.

the crown as far back as 1051 and that Harold Godwinson had sworn in 1064 to uphold William's right to succeed to the throne (as believed to be depicted on the Bayeux Tapestry). It was thus all these different claims which ultimately led to the Norman Conquest of England.

Following the triumph of Duke William of Normandy in his famous victory at Hastings (thus becoming known as William '*The Conqueror*'), he became the 'last man standing'. With the death at Hastings, whether by arrow in the eye or otherwise, of King Harold Godwinson (preceded 3 weeks earlier by the deaths of both his brother Tostig and Harold Hardrada at the Battle of Stamford Bridge in Yorkshire), the attempted English resistance against their Norman invaders over the next 4 years, adopted Prince Edgar Ætheling (now aged perhaps 20/21) as their figurehead, as he represented the true male line of succession of the Anglo-Saxon Royal House of Wessex. For most of this time, he, his 2 sisters and their mother, resided in Scotland under the protection of King Malcolm III Canmore. This situation was consolidated when, in 1070, King Malcolm concluded his significant marriage to Edgar's elder sister, the Princess Margaret. The 3 siblings, Edgar, Margaret and Christine, may well have been in close contact with Waltheof during this period and possibly with Robin as well, if, as suggested, Waltheof took his young, 10-year-old illegitimate son north with him in late 1068, to the safety of the Scottish Court, for him to emerge after the defeat of the rebels at York in the winter of 1069/70; all followed by his submission to the Conqueror and the terrible Harrowing of the North. The defeat at York was effectively the end of major hostilities by the rebels, save the flickering revolt of Hereward the Wake in the Anglian fens, to be finally extinguished in 1072.

For the next fifteen years, it would seem that Christina probably resided in the Scottish household of her brother Edgar Ætheling, but, sadly for her, no suitors came calling and no marriage was arranged. The year was now 1085 and her brother had a falling-out with King William and left his court and the country, because, as the Anglo-Saxon Chronicle put it, '*he did not have much honour from him*'. This falling-out was no doubt partly due to Edgar's deepening friendship with the king's troublesome eldest son, Robert Curthose, who was similarly peripatetic in Europe during this period. Edgar secured the king's permission to emigrate, with a retinue of 200 knights, to seek his fortune in the expanding Norman colonies of Apulia and Sicily in southern Italy; the Conqueror though would be dead within eighteen months.

Christina was left with few options so now, in 1086 aged about thirty-eight with both parents deceased, her sister queen consort of Scotland and her brother overseas, she clearly gave up all hope of marriage and a family, becoming a nun at the renowned Saxon-founded Romsey Abbey in Hampshire, between the New Forest and Winchester. It is probable she was appointed abbess at this time[553] and charged with the education of her 2 young nieces, Edith and Mary, the princess daughters of her sister, Queen Margaret and King Malcolm.[554] She may also have been drawn there in the knowledge that a part of the visceral remains of the 'martyred' and semi-sainted Waltheof, very probably his heart, was interred there within a shrine created following his execution, a decade earlier back in 1076.

In addition to her brother leaving the country, the key factor that really influenced her decision to take the veil was that her sister's 2 young daughters, Edith about 6 and Mary, 4, needed to be educated and Romsey, as a safe sheltered environment, was a great centre of learning, especially for the daughters of the English nobility.[555] Along with its neighbouring abbey at Wilton, near Salisbury, Romsey had been founded in 907 by their direct ancestor King Edward the Elder, for his daughter, Princess Aelflaed, a nun at Wilton who became the first Abbess of Romsey.[556] We know from *Domesday* that the Conqueror had generously (or

---

[553] *Victoria County History of Hampshire,* vol 2, 1903, p.126.

[554] If Waltheof's aunt Suthen, sister of Siward, had indeed married King Duncan I, as many believe, then this would mean Robin, Edith and Mary were all second cousins. See footnote 356.

[555] In due course, *c.*1113, the youngest brother of the girls, Prince David, would eventually marry Robin's half-sister, the widowed Countess Maud, eldest daughter of Waltheof and Judith, becoming the Earl of Huntingdon. David became one of the greatest Kings of Scotland from 1124–53 often quoted as 'the king who founded modern Scotland). Somewhat unusually for the times, on their marriage Maud was aged about 40 and David just 29. Despite her age they had at least one son, Henry of Scotland and maybe two daughters (Claricia and Hodierna). Henry and his half-brother, Simon de Senlis II, were at loggerheads for years over the Earldom of Huntingdon.

[556] It should be pointed out that following the Dissolution in 1538, the only surviving structure today is the beautiful Abbey church (now the parish church of Romsey)— However, even this was built circa 1120 to 1140 AD (though not fully complete until 1230), on the old Anglo-Saxon foundation, by Henry of Blois, Bishop of Winchester, the younger brother of King Stephen. None of the structures of pre-1100 are still extant (save

for political reasons) granted Christina 4 sizeable manors in Warwickshire and Oxfordshire, worth £58 *per annum* in total, that would have provided very well for her and her fellow nuns in the cloisters to live comfortably and perform many charitable works, being the equivalent of around £100,000 or more today, though comparisons are irksome. (Welcome extra income though, as the 7 manors held by the abbey itself at Domesday, in Hampshire and Wiltshire, only generated £119. 10s, thus boosting its income by 50%)

It is apparent that the sole reason the girls' parents, Malcolm and Margaret, wished them to be at Romsey was as monastic 'oblates', for their education and preparation for marriage and not to enter the novitiate, despite the fact that their aunt Christina might have hoped otherwise. As William of Malmesbury intriguingly recorded *'Matilda (Edith), queen of Henry I, was educated at Romsey and Wilton, where she studied letters as well as the more feminine ploys'.*[557] Christina though seems to have been a formidable woman and stern disciplinarian, less like one of the nuns from *The Sound of Music* and more like those from *The Magdalene Sisters*! Edith's own words when giving her later statement to Archbishop Anselm, as recorded by his biographer and secretary Eadmer, make clear her views both on her strict aunt Christina and also those of *not* wishing to be a nun.

"When I was quite a young girl and went in fear of the rod of my aunt Christina, whom you knew quite well. She, to preserve me from the lust of the Normans which was rampant and ready at that time to assault any woman's honour, used to put a little black hood on my head, and, when I threw it off, she would often make me smart with a good slapping and most horrible scolding, as well as treating me as in disgrace. That hood I did indeed wear in her presence, chafing at it and fearful; but as soon as I was able to escape from her sight, I tore it off and threw it on the ground and trampled on it, and in that way, though foolishly, I used to vent my rage and the hatred of it which boiled up in me."[558]

---

two Anglo-Saxon roods/crosses—one internal and one external) such that sadly there is no archaeological evidence of Waltheof's shrine to be seen.

[557] *Gesta Regum Anglorum*, Malmesbury (Rolls Ser.), p.493.

[558] Eadmer's *'History of Recent Events in England' (Historia Novorum in Anglia)*, Geoffrey Bosanquet, trans., foreword by R W Southern (London, 1964), pp.127–128.

By early 1093, Edith, by all accounts now a bright, well-educated, attractive and blossoming 13-year-old, was already being courted by 3 significant men of the realm. The first to turn up was the great Count Alan Rufus, 1st Lord of Richmond in Yorkshire. Known as 'Alan the Red', he was a Breton who had fought for the Conqueror at Hastings and had sought the king's permission to marry Edith (this is the same Alan who, with King Rufus, had refounded St Mary's Abbey in York back in 1088—see Part I, chap. 7). In current times, this might be thought a somewhat unsavoury and questionable alliance given her pubescent state and their forty year age difference! It was though not an uncommon practice at that time among the nobility, where such political 'unions' were frequent.[559] and with the recent loss of Cumbria to the Scots, such a union would have been of great advantage to him. However Edith, clearly a young lady of independent spirit, wisely gave Alan short shrift and a polite refusal, sending him on his way.[560]

The next suitor at the abbey was a very different proposition, being none other than the young (maybe late 20s) 2nd Earl of Surrey, William de Warenne, who held the manor of Wakefield and many others around Barnsdale, where Robin was operating. William was dashing, handsome and one of the richest men in England. However, despite his more obvious attractions, certainly compared to Count Alan, she refused him as well (in any event, the royal consent Warenne sought for the marriage was refused by Rufus) and this rebuttal stayed with Warenne as a grudge he bore against Prince Henry, who was to marry Edith 7

---

[559] As we know, in 1096 Robert de Beaumont, also aged about 56, married 11-year-old Elizabeth Vermandois, niece of the King of France, to draw him into the French royal house. In 1114, Edith's own daughter (with Henry I), Matilda was to marry (in a political union) Henry V, the Holy Roman Emperor when she was only 11 and he was 27! After he died of cancer, she married Geoffrey of Anjou when she was 25 and he was just 13! Unusual times.

[560] Not wanting to go home empty handed, Alan then rode the 20 miles over to Wilton Abbey to try his luck there. He scooped up (abducted?) Gunnhild (27), the slightly more appropriately aged younger daughter of the late King Harold (Godwinson), who abandoned her nun's habit and eloped with him back to Yorkshire! The young lady was clearly too much for Alan after her closeted life, as he died suddenly just weeks later and she immediately took up with his inheriting younger brother, Alan the Black. Archbishop Anselm wrote her several harsh letters urging her to return to Wilton and her religious vocation, but to no avail—the convent girl had escaped! Alan died in 1098 and her own fate is unknown.

years later.[561] In fact, Wace recorded in his **Roman de Rou,** that Henry and Warenne had already fallen out at an earlier age, and the latter used to tease the Prince when they were young, calling him 'stag foot' due to his obsessive love of hunting and Henry's claim that he could tell the number of points or 'tines', on a stag's antlers by examining the beast's hoofprint (see footnote 415). Warenne first supported Robert Curthose in his rebellion against Henry in 1101, but finally overcoming his resentment with Henry, sensibly switched allegiance soon after and assisted Henry in the final defeat of Curthose in 1106, eventually becoming a close friend, military leader and advisor to the king.

The third man to arrive at Romsey, in that August of 1093, as reported by the French abbot and chronicler Hermann of Tournai[562], was none other than the King of England himself! William Rufus was no doubt intrigued by this procession of suitors to see this entrancing young Anglo-Scottish princess but may also have been concerned at the potentially dangerous political consequences with Scotland of a royal marriage between her and Count Alan (or, indeed, Warenne) and was trying to intervene. He had, a few months earlier, recovered from a life-threatening illness and maybe with church and courtly pressure being applied, the need for a son and heir had become all too apparent to him in his near-death moments when it is thought that the new archbishop, Anselm, suggested or even tried to impose marriage on Rufus in his hour of need.

Hermann declared as his source, an anonymous abbess, but undoubtedly Christina, '*who had received the daughter of the king of Scotland, not to be instructed as a 'religious' but simply to be educated*'. When the girl was about

---

[561] '*The Taming of a Turbulent Earl: Henry I and William of Warenne*', Warren Hollister, *Historical Reflections.* (1976) Vol. 3, p. 87.

William de Warenne, 2nd Earl of Surrey, was apparently determined to marry into royalty. Although he failed with Princess Edith, he did finally achieve his goal some 25 years later, in 1118, by allegedly having an affair and eloping with Elizabeth Vermandois (niece of the King of France), now 33 and the wife of plotter, Robert de Beaumont, who was then in his 70's and at death's door. They subsequently had five children of which the two daughters, one Ada, married Henry of Scotland, 3rd Earl of Huntingdon, son of Countess Maud and King David of Scotland and the other, Gundred, married Roger de Beaumont, the son of her ex brother-in-law, Henry de Beaumont and Margaret (Montdidier). See appendices 2.1, 2,2, 4.0 and fig. 35.

[562] *Restauratio sancti Martini Tornacensis (Restoration of the Monastery of Saint Martin of Tournai)*, Hermann of Tournai, Edited and translated by Lynn H Nelson, Catholic University America Press, 1996.

thirteen, the abbess was informed that King William Rufus had arrived with his retinue of knights at the gates to visit her and demanded entry to pray.[563] Hermann reported the abbess' alleged words:

"I was very upset by the news, for I was afraid that the king, who was young and wild and always wanted to do immediately whatever came into his head, might, when he saw how beautiful she was, indecently assault her, especially since he had arrived so unexpectedly and unheralded. Therefore with her agreement I put a veil on her head, so that when the king might see her, he would be deterred from an unlawful embrace."

The ruse succeeded; King William, after admiring 'the roses and other flowering shrubs' in the cloisters and spying on the girls from behind the bushes, saw her in the veil and was either not smitten with her beauty or convinced by the abbess' trickery that the girl was a professed nun and thus 'unavailable' as a consequence, so departed forthwith to hold court at Gloucester.[564] The story of the abbess' anxiety and suspicions, her tact and the evident pleasure she displayed over her success is delightful, if the tale is true. However, the author Hermann says he had it from Archbishop Anselm himself who was well-known to both Edith and Christina. 'It may be', writes E. A. Freeman with a touch of irony and amusement:

"...that the abbess did not know the secrets of the Red King's Court, and reckoned him among ordinary instead of extraordinary sinners. This is, as far as

---

[563] Rufus is recorded as staying at Winchester at this time in 1093 on his way down from Windsor to Gloucester to meet King Malcolm. It was during the desperation of his illness that he had appointed Anselm to the vacant position of Archbishop of Canterbury. When Rufus actually fell ill he was at the palatial hunting lodge/deer park at the royal manor of Alveston, between Bristol and Gloucester, of which no archaeological evidence survives.

[564] Rufus' reticence to push his luck with Edith may also have stemmed from the knowledge that his late mother, Matilda of Flanders, had stood as Edith's godmother at her christening back in 1080. At the baptismal font baby Edith pulled off Queen Matilda's headdress, which was seen as an omen that the infant would be Queen one day, which of course she was—not Rufus's queen though, but his brother Henry. In addition, Rufus's elder brother, Robert Curthose, was Edith's godfather so he must have been wary.

I know, the only time in history or legend in which William Rufus is brought into connection with any woman. Such a tale must be taken for what it is worth, but the picture of William Rufus contemplating either maidens or roses at least puts him in a light in which we do not meet him elsewhere."
(*The Reign of William Rufus,* 1882, Vol II, Chap. 5, p.33)

It seems Rufus let slip the fact of Edith's veil wearing to her father during his visit, who was apoplectic, as less than a week later King Malcolm left the Gloucester court and arrived to visit his daughters and sister-in-law at Romsey—when he saw the veil on Edith's head, he grabbed it off in a fury, threw it to the ground and trampled on it, furious with his sister-in-law, Christina, saying '*he would rather see her as Earl Alan's wife than locked up in a monastery!*'[565]

Although the historical record is not at all clear, historians seem to agree that it was most likely either at this point that Malcolm took the girls away with him, back to Scotland or they fled in the middle of the night a few weeks later. Some historians believe that Malcolm was still holding out for the marriage of Edith to Count Alan, which would have been of great advantage to him and detrimental to Rufus. Hermann's story, and Eadmer's, clearly relate to the same 'veil' incident, which took place in the summer of 1093, the year in which Kings Malcolm and Rufus had a violent falling-out during the former's visit to the English Court at Gloucester. Malcolm had come south, at the request of Rufus, in an attempt to finally resolve a number of territorial disputes, particularly that of Carlisle[566], but due to Rufus's intransigence, resulted in his return to Scotland in high dudgeon. It is plain from the Peterborough Chronicle that Rufus was in the wrong, and true to form had refused to do something for Malcolm which he had earlier promised to do.

---

[565] *The Collected Historical Works of Sir Francis Palgrave, K.H.*, Vol. 4, CUP, 1921, p.196.

[566] Perhaps Rufus' greatest achievement had been his expedition into Cumbria in 1092, restoring the historic border between England and Scotland. He removed the northern ruler, Dolphin (son of Earl Gospatric and like Waltheof, a great-grandson of Earl Uchtred); built the castle at Carlisle; appointed a Sheriff; put the area under the Bishopric of Durham and imported English settlers. Dolphin's sister, Uchtreda, was the wife of Duncan II, who became King of Scotland the following year, 1093, on the death of his father Malcolm Canmore II int the Battle of Alnwick, but was murdered by the usurper, his uncle Donald III (Donalbane), just seven months later. See Appendices 2.1, 2.2

Some 3 months later, in mid-November, Malcolm, in a fit of pique, led a final, rash and ill-advised incursion into northern England which turned into a tragic train of events. It led to his defeat and indeed, his death in battle, at Alnwick, when his eldest son and heir Edward was also killed[567]. Next, Malcolm's poor queen, Margaret (Christina's sister), died in Edinburgh Castle just 4 days later, it is said from a broken heart[568], having first entrusted her 2 young daughters welfare to her confessor, Turgot, Prior of Durham[569].

All sources agree that Christina was a nun, not necessarily Abbess at Romsey (apart from the perpetually reliable *Victoria County History*, which says that she was, though precisely 'when' in not determined) but it seems likely this was the case, though the abbesses of this period are not recorded. In fact, the religious house from which Edith was removed by her father was said to be the nearby sister abbey at Wilton, some 20 miles away. It would seem that with the departure of her 2 nieces, Christina likely resigned her position as abbess, remaining in situ at Romsey as a simple nun thereafter.

---

[567] The man responsible for these deaths was Rufus's local man, Robert de Mowbray, Earl of Northumbria and Rufus was furious since it was not a scenario he favoured. Mowbray was, two years later, to lead the barons' later failed revolt against Rufus, in 1095.

[568] From the writings of Prior Turgot it is clear Margaret had been very ill for some months with something akin to stomach or ovarian cancer, but their deaths were clearly the final straw for her. Turgot was a Lincolnshire cleric who had fled to safety in Scotland from England in 1069, later to return to Durham Cathedral c.1071 after the rebel defeat and went into the service of Bishop Walcher—no doubt arranged by Waltheof.

[569] The whereabouts of the two princesses, Edith and Mary, during their teenage years between 1093 and 1100 is somewhat of an enigma to historians. It is thought unlikely they were in the Scottish court of their usurper uncle Donalbane after late 1093/94 and it is suggested they came under the protection of the English monarchy, i.e. Rufus, along with their sibling brothers. Edith seems so well educated (beyond her age of 13 when leaving Romsey Abbey) that she and her sister very likely received further instruction somewhere or by someone, during their teenage years and were probably attached to the Norman/English court as Edith clearly later became close to Prince Henry. The sisters may have returned to Scotland when their elder brother, Edgar, became king of Scotland in 1097. Between 1100 and 1107, Turgot subsequently wrote the biography of Queen Margaret of Scotland, at the request of daughter, Edith, then wife of King Henry I of England (and now called Queen Matilda). Margaret was made a saint in 1250 by Pope Innocent IV.

In 1094, after the death of both of Edith's parents, she and her sister were now in the care of Turgot, the Archdeacon and Prior of Durham. Archbishop Anselm then wrote to Osmund, Bishop of Salisbury, in whose diocese Wilton lay, ordering him to persuade or compel Edith to return to her vocation, though it is unclear if this happened.[570] It was to Wilton too, according to Eadmer, that envoys were sent in 1100 to enquire into the truth of Edith's statement to Anselm, and obtain depositions, that she had not been a novitiate, just a schoolgirl and where they were told 'nothing which was inconsistent with the account given'.

It has nevertheless been concluded that Hermann's unnamed and unlocated abbess was Christina herself, something Frank Barlow is quite adamant about.[571] Indeed, it is on the strength of Hermann's testimony that she is included among the abbesses of Romsey though as stated earlier, I am sure (as is Barlow, *William Rufus*. p.310, fn.207) that she likely resigned from this titular role in 1093 when Edith and Mary returned to Scotland though there are unconfirmed reports that she moved to Wilton and, by no means certainly, became abbess there. Hermann's abbess, however, seems a more complacent creature than the savage figure in Edith's own account. This may simply mean that we are hearing the same story from 2 different viewpoints: what appears tyrannical to a young girl (especially in retrospect), may seem perfectly reasonable to her guardian (especially after a few years have passed).

Alternatively, Hermann's informant may have been neither Christina nor anyone at Romsey, but the Abbess of Wilton, whose nuns supported Edith's account of events in the enquiry of September 1100, to establish that she had not been a nun and was thus 'cleared' to marry King Henry. Perhaps the obvious solution is the correct one, though not universally accepted: William of Malmesbury stated that Matilda was reared partly at Romsey and partly at Wilton. Did she, perhaps, move from the stern governance of her aunt at Romsey, to pursue her studies in a more congenial atmosphere at Wilton? Wilton and Romsey Abbeys are just 20 miles apart (less than a day's ride) and it seems there

---

[570] A recent book suggests Edith and her sister did in fact return to Wilton Abbey, not Romsey after her father died, c,1093 (thus avoiding her strict aunt Christina) and remained there until her marriage in 1100. *The Writings of Medieval Women: An Anthology*, Marcelle Thiebaux, Author, Ed. and Trans, Taylor and Francis, 2019. Although her 'closeness' to Prince Henry suggests she left the monastic confines some time prior to this.

[571] *'William Rufus'*, F. Barlow, Yale Univ. Press, 2000, p.311

was a close relationship between the 2 Benedictine establishments, with an interchange of personnel. Endeavouring to untangle the precise nitty gritty of such events after such a long passage of time with such little record is always going to prove difficult and just maybe the chroniclers, writing some decades after these events, were as confused, or unsure as we are, about the specific nunneries involved at the time.

All we know of Christina after this is that, according to William of Malmesbury, '*she grew old as a nun at Romsey*' (Gesta regum, II § 228). As such, given her deposition to the conclave in late 1100, Christina very likely did play a part in the last glimpse that we have of our eleventh-century story in Romsey, and interacted with Robin Hood at his father's shrine at the start of the new century. Here she was, in here early fifties, harbouring the son of the great Earl Waltheof, a son whom she had met as a twelve year old boy, thirty years before back in Scotland, but now a renowned outlaw and camped out in the woods near the abbey, worshipping his sainted late father with Princess Christina. This would be something the church authorities, and no doubt the government, were clearly very unhappy about...after all, it was a Saxon shrine to an heroic executed traitor to the Norman cause, a traitor now on the edge of sainthood—and his son was an emerging English legend. This needed to be stopped.

As we know, in 1076, 10 years prior to Christina's arrival at Romsey Abbey, Waltheof was beheaded on St Giles's Hill for his involvement in the 'Revolt of the Earls' the previous year. He was then briefly interred and embalmed at the abbey prior to his 'removal' a few weeks later, by wife Judith and Abbot Ulfketyl, to Croyland Abbey[572] near Peterborough, for burial soon after in the chapterhouse there. A shrine to Waltheof was then created at Romsey Abbey, containing his heart.

Some twenty-five years later (probably in early 1101 and at Christina and Robin's request, not long after Robin's arrival), the Abbess at Romsey, Athelits, wrote to Archbishop Anselm requesting permission to officially venerate Waltheof as a saint at his shrine. It is clear that the archbishop refused such permission but that the instructions given by him had been wilfully ignored by

---

[572] '*Abbot Ulfketl began to build a new church, and received much help from Waltheof, then earl of Northampton and Huntingdon, afterwards earl of Northumbria. He gave the vill. of Barnack, noted for its quarries*'. From '*A History of the County of Lincoln*' Vol. II, published by Victoria County History, London, 1906. pp. 105–118.

the nuns. News of this flagrant disregard of his diktat had obviously filtered back to Canterbury as a year later it resulted in a strongly worded second letter from Archbishop Anselm to the abbess and her community, forbidding, **'on pain of excommunication'**, the continued veneration of a certain 'dead man' and ordering the expulsion from the abbey's grounds of **a man claiming to be the son of the deceased**[573] and who was promoting a saint's cult of his father. Anselm's words imply that the son was camping out in the woods near the abbey, close to his father's shrine: *'decumbit ad tumbam ipsius et ibi moratur'* [**'he dosses down at the tomb of the man himself and loiters about there'**]. Anselm commanded that this man be expelled from the township of Romsey and be given no further assistance in dwelling there. There is a veiled, and not to be ignored, suggestion that the nuns were both 'assisting' the man and that he was providing monetary support to them, as shown in the following 1102 letter from Archbishop Anselm to the Abbess of Romsey, Athelits:

Anselm Archbishop, to his dearest daughters, the lady Abbess Athelits and the nuns serving Christ under her, greeting and blessing. Did I not love you greatly, I would not rebuke you strongly because, after you yourselves sent your messenger to me and requested our advice on what you should do about the dead man whom certain people wished to have as a saint, you did not stand by our advice but in addition showed yourselves disobedient to our command. ***Therefore, I order and command you that if you do not wish to be suspended from divine office, you take away from the dead man, from now on, all honour of the kind due to a saint and do not make any offering to him, nor accept any made, for your benefit. You should drive away from the village his son who lies (dosses down) at his tomb and loiters there, and take from him any possibility of his remaining there any longer. Farewell.***

---

[573] **We know from the surviving King's itinerary that he, along with the Beaumont brothers, Robert Fitzhaimo and others, were down in Winchester Castle at Easter, April 13th, 1102,** such that with local Romsey Bishop William Giffard no doubt in attendance, Robin's antics and Anselm's correspondence may well have been a hot topic of court conversation. Is this the moment when King Henry, Bishop Giffard and Gilbert de Clare meet with Robin, officially enact his pardon, grant him his fathers' historic Lordship of Hallam and send him home well rewarded, but out of the way?

Anselm's letter reveals 2 things, firstly that Robin's presence was clearly a very real issue, now involving the Archbishop of Canterbury himself and was so serious that it could lead to the abbess being dismissed and excommunicated[574]; and secondly that Athelits had already sought permission for the offending cult around this revered figure who people wished to be canonised and continued to promote, or at least allow it for several more months, when that permission was refused. There may well have been older nuns at Romsey, possibly Athelits herself (and certainly Romsey residents), who remember the dramatic circumstances of the build-up and execution, with this 'son', then just 18, likely accompanying his famous father's torso and head to Romsey, for embalming, twenty-six years earlier back in 1076. Within one generation, the story of Earl Waltheof had passed into the sphere of hagiography and romance (see Orderic Vitalis II: pp 312–322, 346–348) and undoubtedly this cult was later promulgated by Christina (who was clearly a big supporter of Waltheof's memory), now a senior and respected figure in the Romsey hierarchy and well-known to Anselm.

---

[574] If this 'worshipper' was simply some fanatical and dedicated Anglo-Saxon peasant, then the involvement of the Archbishop is surely most unlikely.

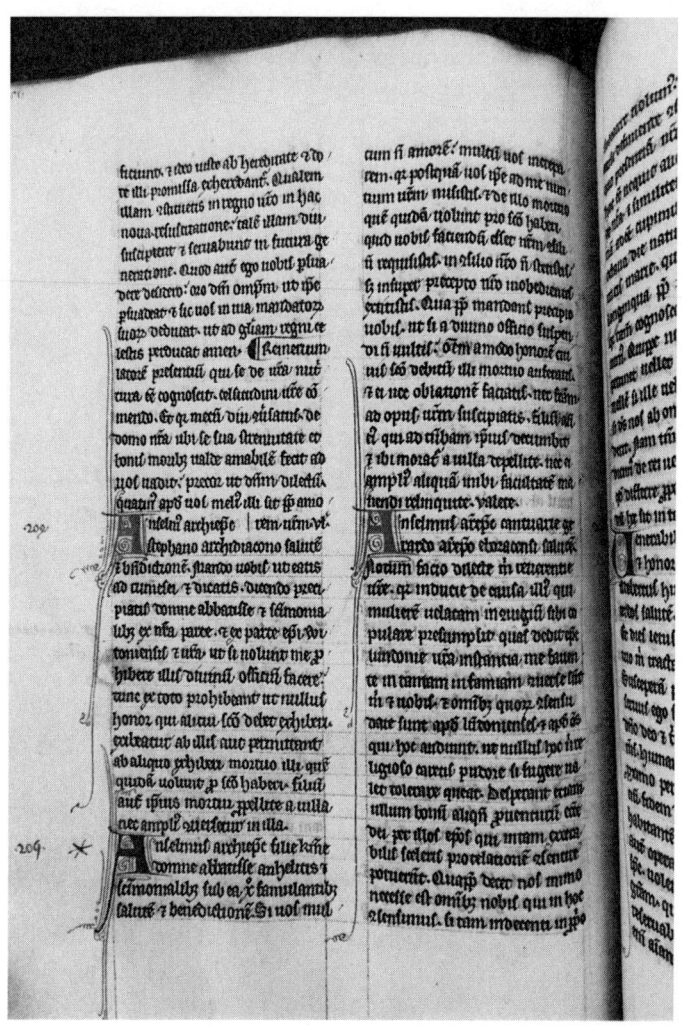

50. *Letter from Anselm to Athletis, Abbess of Romsey in 1102,* transcribed in the early 12th century. **British Library: Cotton MS Claudius A XI (folio 100v)**
Image courtesy of British Library

The abbess' request for authorisation might well have been declined by Anselm in his surefire knowledge of the upcoming new decree of the Council of London, which he chaired later that same year, at Michaelmas 1102, that was to declare *'deceased persons were not to be venerated without the permission of the diocesan bishop'*. In fact, it is believed by many historians that this 'canon' was specifically drawn up by the church (indeed, by Anselm himself) to prevent Waltheof's sanctification, both at Romsey and Croyland Abbeys.

The presence of Robin at this shrine, supported by Christina and Athelits, was no doubt proving an embarrassment to the authorities in Winchester, where the bishop, Walter Giffard, had very likely been turning a blind eye to this veneration for eighteen months or so, being perfectly aware who this man in the woods was, both of them having been party to the infamous regicide nearly 2 years earlier which resulted in Giffard's now elevated status to the Bishopric and expanding power of the Clares. It is apparent that Christina's own 'connections' to Anselm were of no avail as, at the same time as he wrote to Athelits, Anselm dispatched another letter, this one to Stephen, the Archdeacon of Winchester (thus avoiding Giffard's direct involvement), commanding him to go to Romsey and put a stop to the cult *'in his own name and that of his bishop* [Giffard]*, as well as of Anselm himself'*. He certainly seemed pretty determined to halt any further veneration of the martyred late great Waltheof, even threatening excommunication of the sisters from the church.

It has been supposed that the 'dead man' *must* be Earl Waltheof and given he was a convicted Saxon traitor, no wonder the 'authorities' were going to put a stop to a stirring in public pressure to have him made a saint.[575] To quote Ann Williams (perhaps the leading Anglo-Saxon/Norman historian of the last fifty years):

'The name of the dead man is never mentioned in these letters, as though memory of him was being obliterated, but he has been identified as Waltheof. This identification is generally accepted'[576] p.185

---

[575] Waltheof became venerated as a saint (though never officially canonised) and his grandson by Maud and Simon de Senlis (also named Waltheof after his 'traitorous' grandfather and a nephew of Robin), became the second abbot of Melrose in 1148 until his death in 1159, and later achieved full sainthood as St Waltheof of Melrose. After the death of Simon in 1113, Maud married Prince David (latterly King of Scotland and brother-in-law of King Henry I), whose own mother, Queen Margaret of Scotland, also became elevated to sainthood in 1250. Robin was also closely linked to Archbishop Anselm, canonised in 1163. This close association of Robin with four 'saints' seems quite remarkable, most with Scottish genetic connections and is not perhaps without significance for us in consideration of the legend and its strong Scottish links.

[576] *'The English and Their Legacy, 900–1200': Essays in Honour of Ann Williams— Invoking Earl Waltheof* (Ed. D. Roffe, 2012), p.185–86.

Also from 'Epistolae, Columbia University, Medieval Women's Latin Letters':

'Archbishop Anselm reprimands the abbess and her nuns for asking his advice and then disobeying him by continuing to worship the Anglo-Saxon Earl Waltheof, who had been executed for treason, as a martyr and saint'.

But equally important and vital to our story…

'Yet Waltheof possibly fathered an otherwise unrecorded son…he may well have fathered a son by 1066'. *Ann Williams, p.186*

If so, the son must have been a pre-marital offspring prior to the Conquest, since the earl had only the 2 daughters, Maud and Alice, by his wife Judith in the early 1070s. This is the illegitimate son I say was born c.1058 to the 2 teenagers, Waltheof and the Loxley girl, when he was living in the Hallam aula; the child who, in 1080, had grown up to become the outlaw Robin Hood.

Although there is no firm indication that Waltheof was ever buried at Romsey, the fact that the archbishop talks of a *'tomb'* certainly suggests otherwise, or at least that some part of him, probably his heart, was preserved and became the object of a shrine as suggested back in chapter 4. In the first few years of the 12th century, there were still aristocratic English women among the nuns and though they might have had varying opinions of Waltheof as an individual, would have welcomed the opportunity to display discrete resistance to Norman rule, which had so dramatically reduced the state and status of their own kinfolk.

The point was also well made recently by historian Elizabeth Tyler who wrote…

*'Anselm's acute awareness of the capacity for these nunneries (Shaftesbury, Nunnaminster, Romsey and Wilton) to act as repositories of Anglo-Saxon loyalties and cultural memory is evident when he rebukes the nuns of Romsey for venerating as a saint, Waltheof, the Anglo-Saxon rebel executed on the order of William the Conqueror, **and for sheltering his son within their foundation'.**[577]*

---

[577] *'Edith Becomes Matilda'* from 'England in Europe: English Royal Women and Literary Patronage, c.1000–c.1150', Elizabeth Tyler, University of Toronto Press, 2017.

Imagine just how much more worrying this would have been for the authorities if it was not just the memory of the heroic martyred Waltheof that was festering at Romsey but also its promotion by the presence of his 'English' son. If word got out that he was the renowned outlaw Robin Hood, around whom stories, ballads and myths were already forming as a totemic symbol of English freedom—it might have all the makings of a potential new revolt against Norman rule and had to be snuffed out.

51. A surviving 12th century example of a preserved heart reliquary, encased in a wooden container and metal cage.

© Image courtesy of www.reliquarian.com

If this proposal is accepted, and that Robin Hood is indeed the illegitimate son of Waltheof, then this one vital single authenticated record is, I believe, the only piece of documentary evidence from over 900 years ago that mentions the physical man of the legend, and at a specific time and place, that has ever been found, albeit he is not named in person. Having disposed of Rufus, assured of a royal pardon, he settled down in the grounds of the abbey, close to his father's shrine, where he remained for the next eighteen months, worshipping (sometimes with Athelits, Christina and other nuns), until evicted in the late spring, early summer of 1102. This perfectly and logically explains why, some twenty-five years after his father's death, he is now found in Hampshire, over 200 miles from Loxley and Barnsdale in Yorkshire, when he could much more readily have worshipped at his father's actual tomb at Croyland Abbey, just 90 miles from Loxley, which did indeed also become a place of pilgrimage and veneration. It was, though, a cult that did not specifically focus on English feeling against the Normans, but 'a local observance in which both English and Normans shared'.[578]

Much of the material in this chapter is drawn from 2 academic papers in the last few years: one written by Ann Williams,[579] English medievalist, historian, author and erstwhile Research Fellow at the University of East Anglia; and the other by medieval historian Dr Joanna Huntington[580] of the University of Lincoln. The following key extract from Ann Williams reads:

"If Athelits' 'dead man' was indeed Waltheof (and it is difficult to think of another candidate), then it is possible that her house was too close to the centre of royal authority in Winchester to be allowed to venerate a man officially regarded as a traitor, and one, moreover, whose death had become a matter of reproach to the founder of the Norman line. Romsey, as a royal abbey, was a suitable place for the burial of a royal prince who died untimely, and for the honourable retirement of a royal princess who had become surplus to requirements. But the very fact that it had been founded, endowed, and protected by successive kings carried counter-obligations; it was no place for dangerous cults with political overtones hostile to the incumbent king. Croyland, tucked away in the Fens, might be left to go its own way; Romsey, on the doorstep of the royal palace at Winchester, was expected to toe the party-line."

---

[578] *The English and the Norman Conquest*, Ann Williams, Boydell Press, 2000, p.146.
[579] *The Speaking Cross, the Persecuted Princess, and the Murdered Earl: the early history of Romsey Abbey*, Ann Williams, Anglo-Saxon 1, 2007, pp.221–238.
[580] *The Taming of the Laity: Writing Waltheof and Rebellion in the Twelfth Century*, Dr Joanna Huntington. Proceedings of the Battle Conference (Boydell and Brewer, 2009)

Athelits' failure to obey the original refusal suggests that the cult of the 'dead man' was already well established by Christina at the abbey (and Robin may well have been financially supporting it for nearly eighteen months following the death of William Rufus). This seems to have been true of Waltheof's cult elsewhere and the financial benefits of visiting pilgrims was important income to these religious houses. In 1119, the monks of Croyland told Orderic Vitalis that, when their house was rebuilt in 1092 after a disastrous fire, Waltheof's body was discovered 'incorrupt' in the ruined chapterhouse, with only a thin red line around the neck to show that his head had once been severed from his body. Indeed, veneration of Waltheof may predate the death of Archbishop Lanfranc in 1089, for John of Worcester reported that Lanfranc, who was convinced of Waltheof's innocence, used to say that *'he would be pleased to enjoy, at the end of life, the blessed repose of the earl'*.[581]

Despite these indications, it was not until the beginning of the second decade of the twelfth century that miracles began to be reported at Waltheof's tomb at Croyland Abbey: the first, according to Orderic, took place in the third year of the rule of Abbot Geoffrey (c.1112). After this, the veneration of Waltheof spread rapidly; it was enthusiastically reported by John of Worcester who wrote that, *'it is to be believed that he is worshipped with the saints in heaven'*.[582] William of Malmesbury also recorded the cult at Croyland, although he was more dubious about it:

"*Our own times have found someone to consecrate there as a martyr, on the grounds that the report pronounces that he was put to death when he was innocent; I hope that report and the truth are not in conflict.*"

It is easy to see why Waltheof's cult should be promoted at Croyland[583], for he had been Earl of the East Midlands since 1065, back in Edward the

---

[581] *The Chronicle of John of Worcester: The Annals from 1067 to 1140 with The Gloucester Interpolations and The Continuation to 1141*. McGurk, P. (ed. and trans.). Vol 3. OMT. Oxford, 1998.

[582] Ibid.

[583] One assumes the Church edict of 1102, created by Archbishop Anselm at the Winchester Church Council, forbidding by 'canon' the veneration of deceased persons, without the Bishop's permission, was still in force in 1112, which suggests Bishop/Baron Bloet of Lincoln (which covered Croyland), King Henry's friend, must, given the

Confessor's day, and was a notable benefactor of the abbey and other religious houses of the region, like Peterborough abbey. The cult's popularity in the second and third decades of the twelfth century may be connected with the second marriage of Waltheof's widowed daughter, Maud/Matilda, to Prince David of Scotland, which also took place in 1112. David thereby succeeded not only to the substantial Earl of Huntingdon estates of Waltheof and his widow Judith (which has passed to Maud), but also to the Earldom of Northampton previously held by Maud's late husband, Simon de Senlis—holding all these lands and titles *Jure uxoris* (a Latin phrase meaning 'by right of his wife'). The cult remained a local affair however, and Waltheof never found a place in the pantheon of English saints, although his sanctity was remembered in Iceland up to the fourteenth century.[584]

So, as said at the beginning of this investigation, there is this one tantalising authoritative record of an illegitimate son of Waltheof in the Archbishop of Canterbury's correspondence of 1101 and 1102, centred on Romsey Abbey, only months after the death of Rufus and just 10 miles away from today's commemorative 'Rufus Stone' in the New Forest, where an ageing Saxon princess nun in her fifties—Christina, Aunt of both the current King of Scotland and Queen of England—was ensconced. In addition, she would have met Waltheof and quite possibly his young son, back in the Scottish court during that turbulent period in 1069–70.

The marriage of Edith to King Henry in 1100 united the Norman line to the Anglo-Saxon royal line of the House of Wessex and also allied England and Scotland, with Henry himself, in some sense, becoming an Anglo-Saxon king and legitimising his dynasty. Indeed a unification of Norman, Saxon and Scottish royal houses would be uniquely satisfied. Christina may have been a strict disciplinarian but the product of her labours was clearly outstanding. At the time of her marriage to King Henry, Edith (20) was seemingly very beautiful, finely educated and extremely devout. There is clear evidence that she was genuinely attracted to Henry and that these feelings were reciprocated. In the 19th century, anthologist and poet Sir Francis Palgrave observed…

---

passage of time, have sanctioned this activity as Anselm was now deceased and the see of Canterbury vacant.

[584]For example, according to the early thirteenth century saga *Fagrskinna,* Waltheof— albeit misremembered as a son of Godwin!—was treacherously killed by William's knights, and posthumously cured many people.

'She was very beautiful. She inherited her mother's talent, her mother's warm affections, sweetness, patience, piety, and had profited by all the cultivation, both intellectual and moral, that Margaret had bestowed'.[585]

The much earlier writings of a 12th century chronicler glowingly reported her as a significant influence on the life of Henry and the country...

"For as long as she lived, she was the glory of monks, the honour of clergymen, the refuge of the poor, the consolation of the wretched and the fortress of safety to all taking refuge with her, insofar as it was permitted. It is agreed that by her merits King Henry ruled and the kingdom of the Norman-English grew in manifold ways. In fact enemies of that king worshipped her with much reverence and guarded most carefully against offending her."[586]

Marbod, the Bishop of Rennes (and something of a poet, often including somewhat erotic love lyrics!), in addition to saying Edith had 'fluent, honeyed speech', wrote of her in a manner that bears an uncanny resemblance to the headline making photo of Princess Diana taken in 1980 in that accidental see-through Laura Ashley white skirt moment, when backlit by the sun:

It causes pleasure to see the queen whom no woman
Equals in beauty of body or face
Hiding her body, nevertheless, with a veil of loose clothing
She alone, with a new modesty, wishes to conceal herself
But what gleams with its own light cannot be hidden
As the sun, penetrating the clouds, hurls his rays.

Edith was a quite remarkable lady with both English and Scottish royal blood and hence Robin would also have held her in the highest regard. The very thought that she, his second cousin, would become Queen of England and progenitor of

[585] *The Collected Historical Works of Sir Francis Palgrave, K.H.*, Vol. 4, CUP, 1921, p.366,

[586] *The Warenne (Hyde) Chronicle.*(c,1180) Edited and translated by Elisabeth Van Houts and Rosalind Love. Oxford Medieval Texts. OUP. 2013. p.49. A Latin chronicle concerning the history of Normandy and England around the time of the Norman Conquest from 1035–1121 commissioned by descendants of the Warenne family.

all future monarchs, as a result of his intervention, would have thrilled him—and we must always remember that his half-sister Maud, who put him up to the task, was herself, in time, to marry Edith's brother David and become Queen of Scotland bringing the bloodline of their own father to the future Scottish monarchy. Perhaps now, all those initial very early references to Robin Hood being made by Scottish historians can be more readily understood.

However, back to Robin and the fateful year of 1102. After some eighteen months, he is now forbidden to worship at his father's shrine any longer and is turfed out of Romsey. He abandons his camp in the woods and following, no doubt, a final prayer session at Waltheof's shrine, he bids Christina farewell, for it is time to go home, back north, to Yorkshire, to Hallam, to Loxley...[587]

---

[587] One might readily speculate that on Robin's return journey, in May 1102, he called in at the Senlis castle, in Northampton, to visit his sister Maud and his young nephews and niece, telling her of his ejection from their father's shrine, his promised royal pardon and thanking her for her influence with King Henry on being finally granted Lordship of their father's old Hallam Manor. This also maybe just prior to the famous episode when, as depicted in *The Gest,* he met up with King Henry, first in the forest, then Nottingham (Henry was on his way to lay siege to Blyth Castle) where Robin, his men and Sir Richard at the Lee are all officially pardoned. (*7th fytte of The Gest*)

Chapter 13

The Death of Robin: A Treacherous Nun and Red Roger

Sir Roger of Doncaster,
By the prioress he lay,
And there they betrayed good Robin Hood,
Through their false play.

Christ have mercy on his soul
That died on the Rode[588]
For he was a good outlaw
And did poor men much good
(The final 2 stanzas, 455 and 456, of *The Gest of Robin Hood*)

Scattered throughout the 456 verses of *The Gest* are what could be considered a few precious 'facts', where specific references to people and places can be found that might make locating Robin, in terms of a particular timeframe and geography, seemingly possible. None are pointed to more than the much discussed 'comely King Edward' and also 'Barnsdale', both covered at some length in Part I.

Such facts are naturally leapt upon in order to justify a possible era or location for Robin's activities. The flip side to this is that all commentators and academics are agreed that the writers of the ballads and the troubadours who acted them out as entertainment over the centuries, were totally inclined to mix and match tales, update them to appeal to contemporary audiences and even purloin, embellish and invent new material. This is in precisely the same vein as writers of Robin Hood novels, TV series and screenplays of the modern era (just

---

[588] Rode or Rood is a Saxon word meaning 'Cross'.

as with the recent, popular 'Sherlock' TV series starring Benedict Cumberbatch, set not in smoggy Victorian London but in the contemporary period of 2010). The unfortunate consequence of all this is that it is really not possible to take as gospel any 'fact' found within the original texts, which themselves were only written down after decades, centuries even, of mangled word of mouth transmission by numerous different storytellers, with these rare surviving texts thought to represent only a fraction of the original oral tradition.

52. The Passing of Robin Hood. Painting by N. C. Wyeth, 1917
Image in the Public Domain

One of these well-known 'facts' centres around the location and perpetrators of Robin's eventual death and is one of several 'Holy Grail' mysteries of the

Robin Hood legend, namely—where was the site of his demise and his grave, who killed him and why? It is that part of the legend omitted from virtually all film and TV renderings, with the notable exception of the 1976 Columbia Pictures strange 'suicide poisoning' portrayal in the loss-making 'Robin and Marian' starring Sean Connery and Audrey Hepburn. Several suggestions in answering these questions have been proffered over the years, most famously the location of Kirklees Priory, mentioned in the final part of *The Gest*, a place not only somewhat removed from Robin's usual locale, but his death is brought about by a betrayal instigated by 2 individuals who seem to have absolutely nothing to do with what has gone on before. Indeed, this short end tale of somewhat incongruous melancholy (just 24 stanzas ending with no.456—not even 100 lines and presumably at one time a standalone ballad), seems somewhat uncomfortably 'tacked on' at the end of *The Gest* and was very likely added by the/a compiler later. In the earlier stanzas 413–4 (7th fytte) that proceed the death tale there is, following all the stirring tales and adventures, a suitably happy 'Hollywood style' ending when, in the forest, Robin and the Merry Men (a somewhat precise 143!) go down on one knee in front of the king, are pardoned, pay homage and thank him, all offering to go into the king's service.[589] Likewise, a little later in Nottingham, Sir Richard at the Lee is also pardoned, bends the knee and the king restores his lands—stanza 432 (8th fytte). But then suddenly, in the middle of this final fytte, we launch abruptly into the denouement and depressingly tragic death of our hero.

---

[589] This scene (fig. 53 below) is another staple in most film and TV renderings—often including the marriage of Robin and Marian! If *The Gest* is taken literally, Robin must have returned to Barnsdale prior to the King's arrival in Nottingham for as told, the King and five of his knights disguise themselves as monks, leave the city for the forest, and have themselves deliberately captured by Robin. It seems likely that Henry would have met up at the castle with his illegitimate half-brother, William Peveril, at this time. The king is seeking out Robin personally over the death of the Nottingham Sheriff (Peveril's man), the rescue of Sir Richard and the recent decimation of the deer population in the royal forest. Robin and the king have an archery contest, the king reveals himself and they become reconciled, leading to their pardon. The King also intended to strip Sir Richard at the Lee (almost now one of the Merry Men) of his lands and give them to someone else—but a wise old knight (Simon de Senlis?) tells the King that Robin would kill anyone taking Sir Richard's lands and it would effectively be a death warrant for them.

53. The King pardons Robin and his Merry Men:
A scene often used in modern film and tv conclusions;
sometimes coupled to a 'happy ever after' marriage between Robin and Marian
Image out of copyright and in the public domain

Appearing in a number of versions of the legend, the Cistercian Priory of
Kirklees at Mirfield, near Brighouse in Calderdale, some 30 miles north-west of
both Loxley and Barnsdale, is the purported site of Robin's death and burial.
However, this location does not fit at all with the proposed hypothesis as Kirklees
Priory was not even founded until the reign of Henry II, c.1155—some 50+ years
too late for a death scene in 1103! Not only does it not appear to have any
connection to Robin, its location, just 4 miles north of Huddersfield, between
Dewsbury and Halifax, seems too removed from Robin's normal zone of activity

or suggested place of repose in 1102, which was much more likely to have been back in his original home territory of the Loxley/Bradfield area of Hallamshire or, just perhaps, Barnsdale. Either journey is some 25+ miles, which even on horseback is a good day's ride and would seem an unnecessarily long one to make when ill[590] but Kirklees has clung to this part of the legend from a reference in the eighth fytte of *The Gest* (stanza 451–2)…where we are introduced to the wicked prioress and her lover, Sir Roger of Doncaster.

> *Yet he was beguiled, indeed,*
> *Through a wicked woman's sin—*
> **The prioress of Kirksley**
> *That near was of his kin.*

> *For the love of a knyght,*
> *Syr Roger of Donkesly* (Doncaster)
> *That was her owne speciall* (lover)
> *Full evyll mote they thee!* (in evil they met together)

Its notoriety has been assisted by both the 19th century writings of renowned antiquarian Joseph Hunter[591] and also what is now generally agreed by all to be a totally spurious grave (of unknown age) located within the (now private) grounds of the old nunnery site (today a farm), with its 17th century Robin Hood inscription on an undatable epitaph stone.[592] Later 18th century ballads tell of how

---

[590] For those people promoting Sherwood Forest as Robin's haunt, this is some 60 miles from Kirklees Priory, at least two or three days travel distance which, for a sick man, makes it even less likely.

[591] *The Great Hero of the Ancient Minstrelsy of England, Robin Hood; his Period, real Character, etc., investigated and perhaps ascertained.* Joseph Hunter (1852). Hunter was determined to support his theory of Robin being the porter from the time of Edward II. (see chapter 2). He proposed a prioress at Kirklees from c.1345 called Elizabeth de Stainton as being the betrayer and tried to convince people of some familial link through a marriage of a Robertus Hood of Wakefield. All evidence suggests that the legend of Robin Hood was established at least 100+ years earlier and that Hunter's assumptions cannot be substantiated by hard facts.

[592] Following the Dissolution, the church and priory buildings were demolished and the stone used to build Low Hall now known as Old Farm. All that now remains of Kirklees Priory are the long double aisled barn, parts of Old Farm House and the famous priory

the site of the grave is where Robin's final arrow landed, shot through the priory gatehouse window from his deathbed (see Fig. 52). Since this gravestone is over 600 metres away and even a healthy man with a really powerful longbow can barely achieve 225–300 metres at the very most, let alone a wounded man, short of blood and at death's door, this romanticised version of events only adds to the dubiousness of the claim.[593] If the 'arrow story' is myth, then 600 metres from Robin's deathbed does seem an unnecessarily long distance away to move his body and site his grave. Maybe all is not as it seems…

The first mention of Kirklees Priory outside of the ballads was in 1540 by the poet and antiquary John Leland who wrote of the grave and 'the noble outlaw'—this some 2 decades prior to even the birth of the playwright, Anthony Munday. The Priory came into the possession of the Armitage family in the 16th century, following the Dissolution of the Monasteries, and in the late 18th century Sir Samuel Armitage undertook an archaeological dig to a depth of 6ft under the gravestone, with its totally inconsistent pseudo-archaic Chaucerian Middle English inscription, and its death date for Robin of 1247.[594] Not only were no human remains found but the subsoil appeared undisturbed, further supporting the fictitious nature of this location.[595] The 1569 chronicle of Richard Grafton

---

gatehouse. The 'grave' is on private property which has led to constant acrimonious disputes over the last 50 years between the landowners and Robin Hood aficionados.

[593] In *'On The Outlaw Trail Again!', Chapter 'Kirklees—A Grave Mistake?'*. (Holmes Publishing, 2004) — the author, Richard Rutherford-Moore, used reconstructive experimental field archaeology to show that 60–80 metres was the most likely distance travelled by Robin's final arrow — not the impossible 600 metres required for the Kirklees grave.

[594] 'Hear Underneath dis laitl stean Laz Robert Earl of Huntingtun Ne'er arcir ver az hie sa geud An pipl Kauld im robin heud Sick utlawz az hi an iz men Vil england nivr si agen Obiit 24 Kal Dekembris 1247'

This epitaph was apparently found by renown antiquarian Ralph Thoresby, d.1725, among the papers of Thomas Gale, dean of York (1697–1702). This text bears a strong similarity to the 1630 ballad *A True Tale of Robin Hood (Child ballad 154)* by Martin Parker from which it may have been taken, although the death date he gives is 1198.

[595] *Robin Hood, a Mythic Biography,* Stephen Knight (Cornell UP, 2003), p.88, and, *The Outlaws of Medieval Legend,* Maurice Keen (Routledge, 1961), p.181. A further modern investigation was also conducted with the aid of Ground Penetrating Radar, by the TV programme 'Expedition Unknown' in 2015—it was found that there were no indications of ground disturbance or skeletal remains to indicate a burial.

changes the narrative by proposing that it was the prioress, clearly having not committed suicide but still alive, who determined the site of the grave, not Robin or Little John, though Grafton's declaration that it was, '*by the highway side*'. is not the location of the grave as we know it. Grafton's description, and a later sketch by historian Nathanial Johnston in 1665, both describe a very different undated stone, engraved with a long cross 'fleury' and 3 names[596], that of 'Robard Hude' as well as of a 'William Goldburgh' and an undefined 'Thomas', whoever they were.

54. Robin Hood's spurious gravestone (now missing) as drawn by Nathaniel Johnston in 1665
Public domain image from *A Topographical Dictionary of England,*
Samuel Lewis, compiler.
7th Edition (London, 1848). vol.2. p.700.

---

[596] This style is not unique as there are numerous surviving cross slab grave covers from the 12th through to the 15th century. This slab apparently bore the inscription, *"Here lie robard Hude Willm Goldburgh Thoms,"* and interestingly, looks remarkably like the equally distracting unmarked grave slab of uncertain origins, carved with a sword, in St Nicholas' churchyard, Loxley, Warwickshire—with a later inscription for a Constance Cove Jones (the owners of Loxley Hall in the late nineteenth century) (see part I, chapter 2). It is unclear if this is a copy of the original stone or if the stone has been moved, but skulduggery is not far away I feel. Such shenanigans are explored in more detail by Philips and Keatman, *Robin Hood*, 1995, pp.138–142.

The somewhat random nature of the name carving (later recorded by antiquarian Ralph Thoresby in 1715 as having eroded away and become virtually illegible) might suggest it, or perhaps just the *Hude* element, was added at a later date or was on a reused slab. This earlier stone's validity, fate and current location are all unknown. Armitage concluded that the later and current 18th century memorial that can be seen today had been '*brought from some other place, and by vulgar tradition ascribed to Robin Hood*'.[597]—in essence, a hoax or at best, a 'folly'—a Robin Hood version of the 'Piltdown Man'…without the bones!

However, as is being strongly suggested (and first referenced back in Part I, chapter 9, when discussing Judith de Lens), there is an outstanding, though perhaps controversial, contender for an alternative monastic site, perfectly fitting into the character, geography, history, people, circumstances and timeframe of 1102/3, namely **Ecclesfield Priory**.[598] Ecclesfield village itself was mentioned for the first time in the *Domesday Book* of 1086 when it was recorded as *Eclesfelt* and *Eclesfeld* and contained more than 2,000 acres of woodland. As no Foundation Charter for the Priory survives (if indeed there ever was one) the precise date for its foundation is not certain, but if evidence given before Parliament in 1386 by the then Prior is to be believed, then the priory was definitely founded around 300 years beforehand, in the late eleventh century. Informed guesswork based on later evidence and that it receives no mention in *Domesday*, suggests it was founded sometime between 1087 and 1102, probably not long after the death of Roger de Busli I in 1098, by Judith de Lens and Roger's son, Roger II, as the de Buslis still held Ecclesfield manor at this time.

Apart from its location (just 4.5 miles from both Loxley and the de Busli castle at Kimberworth) and its founders, who we will come to in more detail shortly, the most revealing feature is the toponymy of the 2 place names, Kirklees

---

[597] *Sepulchral Monuments in Great Britain, applied to illustrate the history of families, manners, habits and arts at the different periods from the Norman Conquest to the Seventeenth Century*. Richard Gough and Thomas Payne, Vol 1. 1786, Vol 2. 1799—(p. back Hansebooks, 2016).

[598] There is a degree of irony and coincidence here, in that Joseph Hunter (see footnote 313) antiquarian, archivist, and author of the important local history, *Hallamshire* (1819), also keen advocate of Kirklees for the site of Robin's grave, just happens to be buried himself in St Mary's churchyard, Ecclesfield, right next to the priory (plot 3, grave 1125).

and Ecclesfield, which are both geographic portmanteaus or 'blends'. The name Kirklees derives from 'kirk'—(Northern Middle English) meaning 'church'—and 'lees', Old English Saxon for fields or clearings in the forest (just like the 'ley' of my own surname, Stave*ley* and the North *Lees* mentioned in Part I mean 'field(s)'). The derivation of Ecclesfield is a combination of '*ecclesia*' (from the Latin and originally '*ekklesia*', Greek), meaning a Christian 'church', and 'field', which is a generic suffix deriving from the Old English '*feld*', meaning a forest clearing, now come to mean a 'field', though originally a much larger area.[599] So, Kirklees and Ecclesfield, while at first glance appearing different, do both mean exactly the same—churchfield(s)[600]—or more loosely, church in the field(s), that is the land owned by and surrounding the church, such that it is not hard to see how the 2 may well have become confused and conflated over the centuries of storytelling.

Even more likely, nearly 3 centuries later, a balladeer or storyteller simply updated the tale by changing the name from Ecclesfield to Kirklees when the former was dying on its feet and finally no longer extant following the general expulsion of alien monks (*c.*1386). Being so small and somewhat obscure anyway, it was probably unknown to most audiences and for storytelling and entertainment purposes in the 15th/16th centuries (when Robin Hood Days and the May Games were at their height of popularity), the much more substantial, extant and renowned Kirklees, not a million miles away, effectively having the same name and surviving until the Reformation of 1539, fitted the bill just fine for the purpose of entertaining storytelling. One suspects that it was around this time or later that the spurious grave of Robin Hood 'appeared' at Kirklees, to back up the story.

We know from *Domesday* that Waltheof's widow, Judith, had already endowed the great Benedictine Monastery of St Wandrille at Fontanelle in Normandy with income from her inherited estates in Northamptonshire (she had given the abbey 3 hides at Boughton manor with the king's consent, worth £2pa) and was financially committed to her large foundation of Elstow Abbey in Bedfordshire from as early as 1078, to whom she had gifted the income from 4

---

[599] *History of the Parish of Ecclesfield*, by Rev. J. Eastwood, London, Bell and Daldy, 1862

[600] There are two lines in the 'A' Percy Folio version of *The Gest* which actually read: '*Till I have been to merry **Churchlees**, my vein for blood to let*' (spoken by Robin) and also '*And to burn up all **Churchlee**' (spoken by Little John)*

of her manors. Seemingly this later small monastic house was established by her in the de Busli manor of Ecclesfield (today absorbed as a suburb of northern Sheffield) along with the lord of that manor, who by late 1098 was not only the son of her long-time tenant (Roger de Busli I, then recently deceased) in adjacent Hallamshire but I firmly suspect also her long-time lover, his son, Roger de Busli II, 'the younger'. It seems that together they founded the priory at this time, on his land and with her money, though it is unclear (as no foundation charter survives or perhaps ever existed), indeed unlikely, that it was, as yet, attached to a large mother house but may initially have just been quite independent or maybe a small Benedictine satellite cell of her Elstow foundation.

Following the Norman invasion of 1066, the wealthy new Norman landowners founded numerous monastic houses in an almost competitive fashion in their efforts to buy their way into heaven.[601] In a number of cases, these were ostensibly founded as 'monasteries in miniature'—daughters of some large Norman abbey. Benefactors, in this case Judith and Roger de Busli II, were maybe anxious to establish just such an establishment and endowed it with land and income.[602] However, although these 'cells' or 'alien priories' as they became known were normally dependent on a large mother house in Normandy, this may not have been the case here. These small communities were of 2 types, those controlled quite directly from the mother house who appointed a prior and whose monks or nuns, often sent over from the continent, chiefly acted as stewards of their English possessions returning income to the mother house in France and secondly, those of a much more autonomous nature which had the occupants appointed by themselves—("...*absolute in themselves*" as Eastwood describes them[603]) and directly controlling their own income.

---

[601] Post the conquest, the Norman elite founded hundreds of monastic houses over the next 150 years numbering over 1000 by 1215. All these establishments came literally crashing down during the Reformation of Henry VIII in 1537. At that date, in total, Yorkshire alone contained 35 abbeys and priories, 19 friaries, two major monastic hospitals and 21 nunneries. Just before the Dissolution, these foundations accommodated well over a thousand monks, canons, friars and nuns.

[602] Later Charters show that the Priory had two large monastic farms (called Granges) nearby, both on originally de Busli, later de Lovetot land—Prior Royd Grange to the west and Woolley Grange to the east.

[603] *History of the Parish of Ecclesfield*, Rev. J. Eastwood, London, Bell and Daldy, 1862, p.81.

It is quite clear that Ecclesfield was originally of this latter variety. I will go even further and suggest that this early foundation by Judith was in fact more likely to have been a nunnery and probably housed 2 or 3 nuns, possibly brought up from her large Elstow Abbey in Bedfordshire near to where she lived (which took decades and huge funds to complete) but had already been in existence for some twenty years. The records, such as there are, suggest that the Priory was not donated to the Abbey of St Wandrille until the late 1130s[604], as the first mention of the Priory being attached to St Wandrilles is 1141 (from a confirmation charter of its possessions by Pope Innocent II). It most likely changed from nuns to monks at this time.[605]

It was generally the intention of the mother abbey, in this case St Wandrille, that these cells would grow and eventually become independent. As no foundation charter survives it is unclear precisely what the arrangements were but it seems that St Wandrille did not actually send a community of monks to Ecclesfield much before 1161 when this is first mentioned[606] and before that they were left well alone. In most instances and for numerous reasons, the interests of the mother house, the diversion of benefactions to new orders or in this case, the downward spiral of Judith, many, if not all, of these 'alien' establishments had arrested development, stagnated and like some failed species in the evolutionary process, finally died out.

So, just how could this concept of the final episode of Robin's life being at Ecclesfield Priory have come to pass…? Let me paint a picture.

The suggestion is that in the spring/early summer of 1102, after Athelits, the Abbess of Romsey, received that letter from Archbishop Anselm, followed by a visit from Stephen the Archdeacon of Winchester Cathedral (and maybe Bishop

---

[604] This was done by William de Lovetot, now Lord of the Manor. The Lovetots originally came from the small town of Lovetot in Normandy, just 6 miles from St Wandrille's Abbey, of which they were also generous early benefactors.

[605] At Elstow Abbey, from at least from the 13th century, and maybe even from the outset, there were a few lay brothers attached to the house, but it is not clear what was their exact status—probably managing the farms (granges) owned by the abbey. 'Houses of Benedictine nuns: The abbey of Elstow', in *VCH, A History of the County of Bedford: Volume 1 (London, 1904), pp. 353–358.*

[606] Agreement between Abbot Roger and Richard de Lovetot about various assets and forestry rights, reproduced by Yves Poncelet. *'Les possessions Anglaises de L'Abbaye de Saint-Wandrille',* Annales de Normandie, 1987, op. cit. Appendix C. p.141.

Giffard himself), all pressing her to remove Robin from the shrine; as a courteous, devout man and obedient to Anselm (and not wishing for Athelits and Christina to be in deep water), Robin duly obliged and left Romsey, returning home, the 250 miles north to Loxley in Hallamshire, South Yorkshire.[607] The reconciliation between Robin and the king at the end of *The Gest* is of particular significance, where he makes peace with the monarch and was likely given a retainer as a royal forester or huntsman and even the Lordship of Hallam, the latter having been stripped earlier from Judith and de Busli. As highlighted earlier, this may possibly have already happened back in Hampshire when King Henry was just 10 miles away from Romsey at Winchester Castle for Easter 1102 (see footnote 573), precisely when Robin is being evicted.

This may very well have been the carrot used by Henry and Gilbert de Clare (suggested by sister Maud?) to lure Robin away from his devotions at Waltheof's shrine at Romsey and entice him back home to Yorkshire—to take back the Hallam family lands of his father. This certainly strikes a chord as a likely outcome between Henry and Robin after the death of Rufus and fulfils that long held element of the legend that he eventually receives his rightful inheritance, though his illegitimacy, his outlawry and the perceived treachery of Waltheof, meant Robin was never going to receive the great earldoms once held by his father. Of one thing we can be certain, the storytellers and balladeers of Robin Hood were never going to be privy to the 'great secret' of the regicide, the real reason behind this reconciliation and royal pardon such that they would have to invent their own narrative to tell the tale. However, just as in real life, the royal pardon and the death of Robin, as depicted in *The Gest,* follow closely together.

Robin's new life back home, as a free and pardoned man, was brief and not to last, just a few months maybe, as we find an increasingly saintly Robin having,

---

[607] We know from the surviving 'King's Itinerary' that at precisely this moment, in late June of 1102, King Henry himself joined Bishop Robert Bloet of Lincoln, who he had despatched to lay siege to Blyth (Tickhill) castle, finally defeating the rebellious Robert de Bellême, who had been granted it by Rufus after the death of Roger de Busli I three years earlier. Bellême was also a year into the unlicensed construction of Bridgnorth Castle in Shropshire which had infuriated Henry. Blyth/Tickhill castle is situated on the main road, 40 mls. north of Nottingham and just 15 miles south of Barnsdale and with King Henry's appearance, a Yorkshireman no less, the Blyth garrison quickly surrendered to the King's forces, 'and gave homage'. Henry then took the castle back into royal ownership. (E. A. Freeman, *William Rufus*, pp.431–432)

as *The Gest* tells, lost almost all his wealth through his generosity, seeming ready for his eventual martyrdom and the final scene.[608] As implied towards the end of *The Gest*, he started off in high society but soon returned to the greenwood, not as a base for banditry but as a place for penitence in the eventide of his life. It is really the only place, and the woodland people, that he has ever loved and known intimately. Thus he returned to the forest '*barefote and wolwarde*' that is, '*without shoes and with wool next to his skin*' *i.e.* with a sheepskin turned inwards [stanza 442 of *The Gest*]—seemingly an eremitic life of fasting and without sleep, obeying a vow.

In *The Gest*, the urban life of the court and gentry is contrasted with that of the forest and Robin, at heart a simple man, not only unable to handle the hustle and bustle of the former but unhappy about his elevated status, chooses the latter and pining for his old life, retreats to what he knows best—the peace of the forest. As a royal forester, he asks the king (or more likely his agent—Peveril, as Keeper of the Royal Forest of the Peak, and Sherwood?) for a 7 day 'leave of absence' to honour Mary Magdalene; this is granted and he dissolves into the greenwood—never to return.

---

[608] One might easily imagine that any wealth acquired from the king as a result of his escapade in the New Forest would readily have been spread around by Robin, among the poor and needy families in the parishes of Hallam and Barnsdale districts who had helped him so steadfastly over the last 20 years, particularly his Merry Men.

**55. The wicked Prioress greets Robin at the Priory door,
when he gives her £20 in gold for his treatment and lodgings**
Public Domain image by artist Walter Crane c.1914
Creative Commons Attribution-Share Alike Licence 3.0

There are several ballads that then tell the tale of Robin's death that follows and true to form with Robin Hood (as with Rufus!), none of them agree on the details. In *A True Tale of Robin Hood* (Child Ballad 154—from 1632), a 'faithless friar' is said to have killed Robin Hood, and in *Robin Hood and the Valiant Knight* (Child Ballad 153), it is a monk who does the dirty deed. These are both later ballads and it is really the 2 earlier stories that contain the longest-lasting traditions of Robin Hood's death. There is the short story of the 'wicked' prioress in *The Gest (*Child Ballad 117), a version in which Little John does **not** feature and which clearly states the prioress was simply 'near' to Robin in kinship, but of a status that is not specifically defined.

The second well-known, longer and even earlier, ballad of his death (Child Ballad 120a), the one that does include Little John, is found in the famous Percy Folio[609], which also says that it was Robin's *cousin*, the wanton Prioress of Kirklees (apparently being the daughter of his aunt), who killed Robin Hood by bleeding him to death, assisted by her lover, 'Red' Roger, a cleric and a knight.

In Martin Parker's quite late and fanciful version (*The True Tale of Robin Hood*, 1632, Child Ballad 154, stanzas 90–105) mentioned above, it is the 'faithless friar' who bleeds Robin and the prioress who buries him, right by the roadside with a headstone, such that all who passed by might see his fate. We are told she hated Robin yet respected his memory and thought it would be a terrible pity if his fame died with him—she certainly got her wish there! Robin's relationship to this woman is thus not at all clear and sometimes only stated that she was 'near his kin' or 'of his kin' and a widow. It should be pointed out that the term 'cousin' is often used in medieval times to denote a number of forms of close relationship (and indeed by modern family genealogists for pretty much anyone on your 'tree' who is not a direct descendant), and definitely not just that defined form by which we more commonly use it today.

Judith, the wicked stepmother, fits the bill perfectly, perhaps providing the best explanation of 2 conundrums—the first, of them both being 'near' related, of his 'kin' and loosely 'a cousin', as his stepmother is clearly a relative, but not by blood. It seems more than likely that the original storytellers and later balladeers had no real idea of the actual relationship between Robin and the prioress, just dim and distant echoes that there was a familial link and which 'cousin' or even just 'of his kin', served to describe. It also neatly solves the second question of how our 'English' Robin, a simple Saxon yeoman and an outlaw, could possibly have had a relative as a prioress, a position only attainable by ladies of the very highest social order and unless an ancient Saxon-founded house (which neither Ecclesfield or Kirklees were) would be of highborn Norman extraction—which Judith, of course, was. The concept of a Saxon yeoman having a highborn, religious, female, Norman 'near kin' in 1100 would

---

[609] *'The Death of Robin Hood', Percy Folio, The English and Scottish Popular Ballads—* Francis Child—Ballad 120a. (1883). The original is held in the British Library and just twenty-seven stanzas survive from the complete work that is thought to have originally contained over fifty.

have been unheard of...apart from our noble outlaw/outlawed noble, Robin Hood, with the heritage of the Anglo-Danish earls of the House of Bamburgh.[610] We can only speculate, and wildly at that, at what Robin's personal relationship with this Norman woman might have been. She, just a teenage girl of seventeen or eighteen who had become his stepmother nearly thirty years earlier at the time of her marriage to Waltheof in 1071, when Robin was only about twelve or thirteen; through to being mother of his 2 closest surviving blood relatives, his half-sisters, Maud and Alice. Then the period of her perceived treachery leading to his father's death 5 years later; subsequently fleeing to the fens of Ely, being tagged a 'jezebel' by the monks of Croyland and now in a somewhat dubious relationship with one of his nemesis, Roger de Busli II (maybe even her lover when still married to Waltheof) who undoubtedly wished Robin much ill will.

Through her lifetime links as founder of Elstow Abbey, even as abbess or prioress (for it had both) and a noble lady, she would have acquired good medical knowledge for the times (religious houses doubled as hospitals/hospices). Robin, it seems, had gone to be bled[611] for his health as, for an unspecified reason, he is feeling most unwell and as such he sought skilled medical assistance from the nuns at her little priory, which had probably only been open about 4 years at most. An old handwritten notation in the Sloane Manuscript suggests Robin left for the Priory because he can't keep his food and drink down and '*he felt distempered with cold and with great pain in his limbs, his blood being corrupted*' (something like gastroenteritis, influenza or perhaps even sepsis). In the Percy Folio version of the tale, we are told that soon after leaving on their journey to the priory, when crossing a river[612] Robin and Little John meet an old

---

[610] There are several examples of aristocratic Norman/Saxon intermarriages, even prior to the Battle of Hastings, but these were always between a Norman male and a Saxon female.

[611] Blood-letting was a common but disastrous medieval practice also known as 'venipuncture' or 'phlebotomy', that continued for centuries, being the withdrawal of an amount of blood from a patient to prevent or cure illness and disease but also to restore the balance between the four humours, which corresponded with the bodily substances of phlegm, blood, yellow bile and black bile. Oddly, for a quack' practice, 'The Lancet', the leading British medical journal, is named after the instrument used for opening up the vein.

[612] If travelling the 4.5 miles from Loxley to Ecclesfield Priory, after 1.5 miles they would have had to cross the River Don at Wadsley Bridge.

crone who is lamenting Robin's fate, foretelling of a bad outcome to the visit, claiming that she and the other women are weeping for Robin's body *'that this day must be let bloode'*…and although she tries to prevent their progress she is ignored.[613]

Tomorrow I to Kirkley go
to skilfully have blood let.
I cannot drink or eat my meat
for it makes me most unwell.

Till I have been to merry Church Lees
my vein for blood to let.
Then said Will Scarlet 'I won't let you go,
for bad Red Roger lives close to the route.
He loves so to fight he won't let you pass,
without a good guard, a challenge he'll make.
To gain my consent, fifty bowmen take,
for you my good friend my love knows no end'.

Once arriving at the priory, to add insult to injury, Robin gives the prioress £20 in gold for his treatment and aftercare, with, as the Gest tells, Robin firmly believing this woman will do him no harm (see Fig. 55 above). The ancient Percy Folio document from which we get the ballad about his death has been damaged which frustratingly includes the key part outlining the prioress' motives for what she was about to do. Some scholars even suspect that up to half of the original text of the tale may be missing. However, it does describe how this nun set the *'blood irons'* on Robin and started draining his blood, betraying Robin to her lover, Roger of Doncaster, who tries to arrest Robin. In the ensuing duel, the now weakened Robin kills Roger but receives a mortal wound himself, just managing a weak blow on his horn to summon faithful Little John who had accompanied him. *"Bury me where my arrow falls"* (see image 56 below) are traditionally

---

[613] The old woman lamenting at the river (*'banning'* is the word used in the ballad) is a motif of Celtic origin which appears in chivalric romances of the middle ages. She may be connected to the Irish banshee (*bean sidhe*); a female spectre whose wailing heralds the imminent death of whoever hears it, though caution should be taken in drawing such conclusions.

Robin Hood's last words to Little John. In some more embellished 18th century versions, John assists Robin to sit up and fire one last arrow from his deathbed through the window and where it lands is to be his final resting place which was probably not, as one comedic writer has suggested, owing to Robin's weakened state, on top of the wardrobe! In fact, a shot of some 60–80 metres (see footnote 593) would very likely have landed, appropriately, in the corner of the large graveyard of the adjacent St Mary's church near the road, which seems the most likely actual location of Robin's grave (see Fig. 59 below). Although more likely just creative storytelling, if in fact true, this well-known (now popular and oft illustrated) part of the tale further strengthens the belief in Robin's Danish heritage, as the last surviving lines of the ballad give his dying instructions to Little John-

'Set my bright sword at my head
My arrows at my feet
Lay my yew bow by my side'

This uncannily mirrors those dying words of his grandfather, Siward the Great, as to die ready for battle, with a weapon in their hands, was the ardent wish of every freeborn Dane and undoubtedly etched into his psyche from his father's upbringing in his teenage years (see Part I, Fig.5). What is clear is that in no version does he make any reference whatsoever in his final moments to a wife, children or lover.[614]

---

[614] The matter of Robin's questionable marriage to Marian or A N Other, rumbles on in folklore. Further notes and details on this matter are in Appendix 11.

ROBIN HOOD SHOOTS HIS LAST ARROW

56. Robin, helped by trusty Little John, shoots his last arrow—
to be buried where it falls

Free use of image courtesy of the terms of the Project Gutenberg Licence

In the Percy Folio ballad, Little John wants to burn the priory down…[615]

"For Christ's love, give leave to me,
To set a fire within this hall,
And to burn up all Churchlee."

---

[615] The oldest stone structure at Ecclesfield that survives today is of 14th century origin and is built over the footprint of the original 11th century priory building, undoubtedly a two storey cruck house design with a thatched roof made of very combustible materials which again reinforces an early date for the action.

(Child Ballad 120a, stanza 492, lines 121–123)

He also wants to kill the prioress, but Robin, who never condones force against women, forbids him. He particularly, and significantly, mentions not harming 'widows' as '*God would blame me*', and his stepmother Judith is of course, the widow of his father, Waltheof. In other versions, the prioress then takes her own life, which seems a likely outcome. It is thus on the word of Little John alone that this tale of *The Gest* must be based, as seemingly he is the only survivor of the bloodbath (unless other Priory nuns were present, which seems unlikely), who then buries his friend's body nearby where the arrow fell. The ballad tells us that Robin Hood was killed by the prioress who was in charge of the priory, some twenty-two years after he had left the king's service. In my hypothesis, this would be in 1102/3 following his being outlawed in 1080/81 after the debacle with the killing of Walcher, Bishop of Durham, when previously having been in the king's service as a royal forester for 2 or 3 years or so under Peveril, from maybe 1077–79, following his father's execution in 1076.

Just how culpable Judith was, in the downfall of her husband, is something that has been widely discussed by historians, though never answered and probably never will be. The general consensus going back to *The Anglo-Saxon Chronicle*, right up to most recent opinions, suggests her duplicity and treachery in his arrest and execution, no doubt manipulated by her unpleasant uncle, Odo of Bayeux.[616] It would seem at the time she was widely despised due to the undoing of her husband, but then again, there are some conflicting accounts that suggest she lived quite peacefully at her manor of Sawtry,[617] during the first decade after her husband's execution, apart from her temporary self-exile into the fens to avoid her forced marriage to Simon de Senlis. Local Sawtry historian Harry Milford wrote (though his sources are unclear):

---

[616] The Earl of Kent and maternal half-brother of the Conqueror who detested Waltheof.

[617] The Parish of *Sawtry Judith* still exists and was in Huntingdonshire, but is now in Cambridgeshire and lies precisely midway between Elstow and Croyland Abbeys, 25 miles from each. In about 1147–8, Judith's grandson, Simon de Senlis II (son of Maud and Simon I—see appendix 2.1), founded Sawtry Abbey which stood on the eastern edge of the parish. It was an independent foundation for Cistercian monks, who came from Warden Abbey in Bedfordshire, but the buildings were entirely destroyed in the Dissolution of the Monasteries in 1536.

During her life in Sawtry, Countess Judith was popular and loved by the local people because she cared for the sick and poor, some even called her 'Saint Judith', which is how the names of St Judith's Lane and St Judith's Field originated, and although she owned land throughout the country, she chose to live in Sawtry.[618]

It would seem that maybe for 10 years or more, while her daughters were being educated by the nuns at Elstow, feelings of guilt and contrition set in about the execution of her husband (indeed, tradition states that it was these feelings that led to her original foundation of Elstow), and she lived a quiet, even virtuous and penitential, life, probably serving some time as the abbess or prioress. After nearly fifteen years, around 1089/90, still only aged about thirty-seven and with her 2 girls now grown up (Maud is eighteen and about to marry ageing Simon de Senlis, he of the 'gammy leg'), she now finds herself under the influence of her lover, Red Roger II, son of Roger de Busli I, the long-time tenant of her late husband's Yorkshire manors of Hallam, Sheffield and Attercliffe and her life has changed[619]. Although the concept of a nun with a lover—a monk or priest even— seems somewhat odd to us today, such 'licentiousness', or 'incontinence' as it was phrased then, was quite commonplace and often tolerated, though in the case of Judith and Roger it is unclear to what extent either of them had taken holy orders. Many clerics, even bishops, were married or had what was called euphemistically—a 'housekeeper', or that the chronicler Gerald of Wales called a '*hearth-girl (focaria)—who kindled his fires but extinguished his virtue*'! But to quote Christopher Brooke, erstwhile Professor of Ecclesiastical History at Cambridge University.

---

[618] *A Glimpse Into Sawtry's Past*, Harry Milford, (Caresco, 1998)

[619] Readers will recall the rather weak excuse given by Judith for her refusal to her arranged marriage to Simon de Senlis due to him being 'lame of leg'. It has been suggested that her betrayal of husband Waltheof was really because she wanted rid of him, as she was having an affair. There seems every likelihood that if true, then Roger de Busli II, was the object of her desires (in 1076 he was c.19yrs. and she c.23yrs) a relationship that never led to marriage but that then continued for over 25 years, leading to her 'jezebel' status given by the monks of Crowland—a biblical term for a morally unrestrained woman, lecherous wife, whore and harlot who betrays family members.

'...*clerical marriage was sufficiently common to be safe and even respectable*'

and '...*hereditary benefices flourished between the Conquest and the Anarchy*'.[620]

Misconduct, manifested in the form of waywardness and temptation is widely reported throughout the religious houses (particularly mixed sex establishments) with pregnant abbesses and nuns being well-documented. Elstow, as with many monastic establishments, even acquired a bad reputation over later years with the nuns constantly drifting towards a secular rather than religious lifestyle and that 'the spiritual life of the convent was marred by worldliness from first to last'.[621]

It is perhaps a point to note that in the later Confirmation Charter for Elstow Abbey of Henry I, granted about 1126, among the names of the then current benefactors, like Nicholas and Richard Basset and Nigel de Stafford, was the **Countess Maud** (Robin's half-sister, whose 'alma mater' I believe it was, and is now the Queen Consort of King David of Scotland). The property then held by the abbey was considerable and scattered across twelve counties, which gives some idea of the spread of its wealth and property holdings. The surviving list of abbesses (earliest 1222) serves to show that the daughters of baronial families were frequently received at Elstow and the later names are those of the neighbouring gentry. I remain firm in my belief that Maud and her sister Alice (despite the latter's benefaction being absent, though she was now married to Ralph III de Tosny and probably living in Normandy) were educated here and that their mother Judith, as well as the founder of the abbey, was probably the one-time abbess (or at least the prioress) as well, though regrettably no records of this early period survive.

Others, particularly the play by Munday (so hardly historical truth but drawing on the oral tales), state that it was a monk who murdered Robin Hood (my preference is for a joint effort between a knight—now perhaps a corrupt self-appointed 'hereditary' parish priest and a dissolute nun) and the likely candidate who perfectly fits this rather odd hybrid 'knight/monk/cleric' is the

---

[620] 1066–1138. *Gregorian Reform in Action: Clerical Marriage in England, 1050–1200*, C. N. L. Brooke, *The Cambridge Historical Journal*, Vol. 12, No. 1 (1956), CUP, p.18.

[621] 'Houses of Benedictine nuns: The abbey of Elstow', in *A History of the County of Bedford: Volume 1*, VCH (London, 1904), pp. 353–358.

younger 'Red Roger' de Busli II, her lover of many years. It seems very likely that both Judith and Roger II had been closely involved in the failed 1095 barons rebellion of Roger de Mowbray against Rufus and subsequent debacle. Not only was Roger's sister, Beatrice, married to one of chief conspirators, William de Eu[622] (who came to a sticky end as a result), but the aim of the rebels was to place the king's cousin, Stephen of Aumale, on the throne, who was none other than the half-brother of Judith![623] She had been deprived of properties once before (by the Conqueror c.1087) as a result of her refusal to marry Simon de Senlis and although these were restored (probably by Rufus c.1089) it may well be that now her remaining holdings were stripped from her by Rufus this second time (1095), given she and Roger must have given at least their tacit and probably overt support to the uprising.

Roger de Busli II's father (the great baron, Roger I) had died in 1098, about 4 years or so before I suggest Robin died. His son, Roger II, is said to have died a few years after his father in about 1102 and had no offspring of his own. *Roger de Busli, the founder of Blyth Abbey, died in 1098; he left a son who died without issue in 1102.*[624] After de Busli senior died, his brother Arnold (sometimes *Ernald, Ernulf or Arnaldus*) succeeded him[625], albeit briefly. It is evident that

---

[622] The personal details of William de Eu are very sketchy. Most sources seem to agree he was twice married, to Beatrice (sister of Roger de Busli II) and also to Helisende d'Avranches (sister of Hugh d'Avranches, Earl of Chester). He also had a son and heir, Henry I, Count of Eu. However no dates are attributable to any of these events such that we cannot be sure which wife came first, their fate or indeed, which one was the mother of Henry. Consequently we cannot be sure who was his wife at the time of his death in 1095. having lost in 'trial by battle'—a judicial duel—being blinded and castrated and dying as a result. In some accounts Beatrice is the sister of Roger de Busli I, making her the aunt of Roger II but with the dates and ages this seems unlikely.

[623] Stephen was the son of William the Conqueror's sister, Adelaide (Judith de Lens' mother), by her third husband Odo de Champagne. It is interesting to note that after the widowed Countess Maud married David of Scotland c.1114, her two teenage sons by first husband Earl Simon, namely Simon II and Waltheof III were sent to France and brought up by Maud's uncle, Stephen of Aumale, this half-brother of the now deceased Judith. *The Life of Waldef and its Author, Jocelin of Furness,* by George McFadden, The Innes Review, Aug 2010, vol. 6, No.1: pp. 5–13

[624] *Victoria County History of Nottingham,* 1910, Volume 2, pp. 83–88.

[625] According to *Domesday,* in 1086, Arnold was Lord of just one small manor, part of East/West Leake, 10 miles south of Nottingham, which he held from his seemingly

none of the vast estates of the great de Busli barony (known as the 'Honour of Tickhill'), were passed either to brother Arnold or his own son Roger II, as the Crown, i.e. Rufus, took them back and then granted them to the evil and power mad Robert de Bellême, 3rd Earl of Shrewsbury, making him the most powerful subject in the kingdom.[626] Orderic states that Bellême claimed a 'right' over the Tickhill estates as he was purportedly kin of Roger de Busli I, being a cousin.[627] One would have thought brother Arnold's claim was stronger but whatever Arnold's rights, or the familial claim of Bellême, Rufus typically followed the money and hence de Bellême, who was then charged a huge sum of money by Rufus to acquire the Honour, becoming the only estates he ever held in England (from just 1098–1102).

Apparently just bullied out of the way by powerful Bellême, Arnold seems to have inherited little, apart from a few rented scraps not held from the king, like the small manor of Leake, south of Nottingham, that he had been previously subletting from his brother Roger and maybe also that of Maltby, 4 miles west of Tickhill. I suspect Roger II took over Kimberworth manor (living in its motte and Bailey castle and benefiting from the lucrative ironworks) and just a few miles away, Ecclesfield manor. It is my contention that Roger II, 'the younger', then founded the Priory at Ecclesfield with his lover, Judith, and donated some land to support it, thus ring-fencing it from further forfeiture and keeping control of the assets within the de Busli family from his nearby castle at Kimberworth.

---

ungenerous brother Roger I, the Tenant-in-Chief. Value to Lord in 1066, £2. Value to Lord in 1086, £0.5.

[626] In addition to Robert's inheritance (following the death of his father in 1094), of the Montgomery-Belleme lands straddling the southern Norman March, in 1098 Robert had paid a relief of £3,000 to Rufus for his father's English earldom of Shrewsbury. His marriage to Agnes, daughter and heir of Guy, count of Ponthieu, had brought Robert even further lands on the northeastern frontier of Normandy.

[627] '*The Ecclesiastical History of England and Normandy*', Orderic Vitalis, Book X, chapter VII. It is thought de Busli was somehow connected to Roger de Montgomery by blood or marriage (Montgomery himself being related to the Conqueror) but it is not clear if Robert de Bellême and Roger de Busli were first cousins.

Roger de Busli's castle at Kimberworth probably looked something like this.

keep

motte

bailey

The ground still slopes away very steeply to the gardens below. All the area in the photograph would have been in the bailey of the castle with the drawbridge entrance somewhere behind the large building.

57. The view today from the top of the Motte—Kimberworth Castle
Use of © images courtesy of Kimberworth Village Trail—by Peter Machan

At the close of the 11th century, the de Busli family looks to have suffered a series of family bereavements. Following the death of Roger I in 1098, his brother Arnold looks to have died shortly after, whose meagre estates passed to his son John (sometimes Jordan) who also seems to have shrugged off his mortal coil almost immediately, as in the *Victoria County History*[628] it says that John, *'being weary of the world, entered his uncle's priory (Blyth) as a monk'*, which was common practice and usually a medieval euphemism for 'end of life care'. So, by late 1099, Roger II finds his uncle Arnold deceased and his cousin John seemingly now also dead, the assets of that side of the family, such as they were, came to John's son, Richard, as after John died, on the day of his burial, *Richard laid his father's grant upon the altar and confirmed it by attaching his own seal.*[629]

Richard (who died c.1179, and the great-nephew of Roger de Busli I) must have been very young[630] in 1102, perhaps in his early teens and lived a very long life (90?), but he did inherit John's properties and maybe the assets of Roger II as well. He certainly prospered, as 45 years later, in 1147, he co-founded with Richard FitzTurgis, the great Cistercian Roche Abbey in the lands of his donated Maltby manor near Tickhill. However, back in 1099 Roger II was the only surviving male heir on his side of the family line of the 2 de Busli brothers and the manor of Kimberworth (along with its castle[631] and the valuable iron-ore smelting works) only 4 miles from Ecclesfield Priory, now belonged to him.

The motive of the nun and Roger, the ballad says, is Robin's opposition to the corruption in the church which, given their shenanigans at Ecclesfield, certainly must have touched a nerve with them. Also, in the Percy Folio ballad, it says Roger stabs Robin, while he's weak, in revenge for Robin having inherited his land and title, which if Robin had indeed been given the Lordship of Hallam manor (that included Loxley village) by King Henry, as his reward for the regicide and as a sweetener for leaving Waltheof's shrine at Romsey, it makes

---

[628] 'House of Benedictine monks: The priory of Blyth', in VCH, *A History of the County of Nottingham: Volume 2*, ed. William Page (London, 1910), pp. 83–88

[629] Ibid. details from *Harleian. MS. 3759, fol. 105.*

[630] There is some suggestion that a de Busli 'minor', no doubt the child Richard, had, on the death of his father John in 1099, been made the ward of relative, Robert de Bellême, by Rufus, as part of the deal for Bellême, acquiring the 'Honour of Tickhill'. Any such arrangement would have ceased when Roger was stripped of his lands and titles when banished from England, by King Henry, after his surrender in 1102. However no evidence for this wardship has ever been provided and whilst the acquisition is mentioned by Orderic Vitalis, the wardship is not.

[631] Kimberworth castle was a timber motte and bailey construction and never rebuilt in stone. The de Busli family held the castle until the mid-13th century, eventually moving to a moated manor house nearby.

for a most intriguing set of circumstances that would appear to match the whole scenario well.[632] The proximity of the de Busli castle at Kimberworth, a stone's throw from Ecclesfield Priory (4 miles—map pins 4 and 5, Appendix 1), would well explain Will Scarlet's concern for his master's safety and if we look at the words of the ballad, the combination of the priory at Ecclesfield and its founders; its proximity to Loxley (5 miles); the stepmother Judith (a corrupt prioress, a widow and 'cousin' of his kin); a bad Red Roger living nearby, who is a 'knight' and maybe a pseudo priest or corrupt and 'faithless monk' and lover of the prioress (and possibly deprived of the Lordship of the Hallam lands just given to Robin); but all put together are surely a most compelling mix of elements and persuasive set of circumstances to explain Robin's death as portrayed in the various versions of the legend—which Kirklees comes nowhere near by comparison...

The joint deaths of Judith aged c.49 and that of Roger (as recorded in the VCH) in late 1102 or very early 1103 also fit the hypothesis well. Judith's younger daughter by Waltheof, Alice (sister of 'plotter' Countess Maud), is also well looked after by King Henry (part of the 'benefit' for Maud?), who arranges her marriage to his great loyal friend, Ralph III de Tosny, at that time and along with her sister Maud, Alice inherits her share of the estates of their mother, like the hugely lucrative ex-Waltheof manors near London, of Walthamstow, Edmonton and Tottenham, collectively worth the enormous sum of around £100pa in 1087.[633] Not only that, but in this same year when Judith, Roger and Robin die, a new baron from Huntingdonshire, William de Lovetot, is granted by King Henry, not only large chunks of the previous de Busli estates of the Honour of Tickhill[634] but also the lordship of Hallam (plus Sheffield and

---

[632] What a delicious irony it would be if, in that in the summer of 1102, as a consequence and vindication of the assassination of Rufus, the now pardoned famous ex-outlaw Robin Hood is probably granted the Lordship of Hallam, once held by his father whilst two of the formerly greatest barons in the land and scourges of Barnsdale, William de Warenne and Robert de Bellême, have now both been outlawed and banished by the new King, being stripped of lands and titles!

[633] *The Environs of London: Volume 4, 'Tottenham' and 'Walthamstow'*, Daniel Lysons, Originally published by T Cadell and W Davies, London, 1796.

[634] He also received a number of the de Mortain manors in Yorkshire that had recently been forfeited by William de Mortain, who had fled to Normandy to continue his ill-

Attercliffe), the long-time Judith/de Busli manors (once held by Waltheof) and quite possibly now held, albeit briefly, by the deceased Robin. These are all clear signs that Judith (49), 'Red' Roger de Busli II and poor old Robin (43) are all now dead and the manors are vacant—and coincidence or not, exactly at this time and all at the same time…the jigsaw seems to be coming together.

Roger's father, Roger I, had originally built, and was based, at Blyth Castle just 7 miles from the sizeable settlement of Doncaster[635] and as such, both he and his son could very well have acquired the nicknames of 'Red Roger of Doncaster' if, as with William Rufus, they both possibly had hereditary red hair, ruddy complexions, hot tempers or combinations thereof. Blyth Castle (mentioned more than once in *The Gest*) only became known as Tickhill Castle later (Appendix 1, map pin 10). De Busli had built the original motte-and-Bailey castle on 'Tica's Hill', a sandstone hill 7 miles south of present-day Doncaster and 20 miles east of Loxley. The location of this castle was to give its name to a new settlement—'Tickhill'—after which the later improved stone castle took its name. It must not go unmentioned that *The Gest* specifically refers to the castle as 'Blyth' (first fytte, line 108), which is precisely what it was called in the eleventh century and in the time of Henry I, *not* 'Tickhill', a name that was only used later. This is significant in that if, as some proponents would suggest, the ballads relate to the later periods of the thirteenth century and beyond, why did the ballad writers not call it Tickhill Castle, but instead used its original eleventh-century name? Orderic Vitalis called Blyth, *Blida*, it is also referenced as such in the Pipe Rolls of 1130 and in a charter of Henry I confirming the tithes of Laughton to the monks of Blyth, speaks of 'Castellum de Blyda'; such that it would seem this was the name used in the oldest oral tradition. If this had not arisen until the 13th century or later, then why did the balladeers not call it Tickhill, which the castle and its tournament ground were widely known as by

---

fated support of Robert Curthose to remove Henry's crown. From childhood, William, Count of Mortain, had harboured a bitter dislike for his cousin, now King Henry.

[635] At *Domesday*, the Tenant-in-Chief of Doncaster was Count Robert de Mortain, whose undertenant was Nigel Fossard. Shortly after *Domesday*, in 1088, Robert rebelled, with others, against King William II 'Rufus' (his nephew), and lost, being banished and having all his estates forfeited (dying c.1091–5), many passing directly to Fossard as tenant-in-chief, in particular a large feudal barony whose *caput* was at Mulgrave, near Whitby, where he built a large castle. It seems likely that Doncaster passed to Roger de Busli I at this time, though he looks to have retained Fossard as his under-tenant.

that time? Answer—because the oral tales of Robin Hood had started right back in the last years of the 11th and early years of the 12th centuries.

Another key question that might be asked is—why is the death of Judith unrecorded? To be fair, the birth and death dates of even the most important people (and mostly men) are often absent from the records of this era but given she was, after all, the niece of the Conqueror; cousin of 2 Kings and the Duke of Normandy; widow of renowned Earl Waltheof; the most important (and wealthiest) woman in the *Domesday Book,* just 15 years prior; co-founder of both Elstow Abbey and Ecclesfield Priory (and probably the abbess/prioress of both at one time); and mother of a daughter married to a leading noble at court, Earl Simon, then her death and burial might surely have been expected to be at least mentioned, if not recorded somewhere. Her virtual absence from the record for the last 25 years appears to confirm a life in the shadows since the execution of her husband back in 1076, being a 'jezebel' and 'persona non grata' in all social circles.

It seems more than likely that the events detailed above—their links to the 1095 rebellion, the bloodbath at Ecclesfield, the murder of Robin, her possible suicide, the dead lover, indeed, the whole dreadful debacle—are *precisely* why nothing was recorded, as the chroniclers and ecclesiastics would most certainly have not put quill pen to parchment to record such scandalous goings-on in this seedy religious outpost regarding a lady of royal pedigree (first cousin of the king no less), guilty or otherwise. Suicide was widely felt to be too terrible to talk about, with greater stigma the higher up the social scale you were. It was a mortal sin against God and brought shame upon your family. Hence her death does not appear in any record, as she would have been denied a Christian burial by a priest in consecrated ground and all her property would have reverted to the king and/or her daughters—the founder of Elstow Abbey was never going to find her resting place behind the high altar.

It is sobering to think that if the barons revolt of 1095 had been a success, then Judith's half-brother, Stephen of Aumale, would have become King of England and one imagines her fortunes would have changed significantly along with the history of England! But, to quote the words of Charles Kingsley, when describing Judith in his 1866 historical novel *Hereward*: '*Of her subsequent life, her folly, her wantonness, her disgrace, her poverty, her wanderings, her wretched death, let others tell*'. Does this not seem an uncannily apt description to fit the life and death of the woman being proposed? A further and most poignant quote comes from the highly respected Victoria County History: *"The priory of Ecclesfield seems to have had a shadowy existence. There was probably at no time a cell there in the stricter meaning of the word, and apparently the connection with St Wandrille was severed in the time of Edward III."* [636]

Since Ecclesfield is being promoted here as the much more likely locale for Robin's deathbed rather than Kirklees (and his resting place somewhere in its environs), then a more in-depth look at the history of Ecclesfield Priory may place a few more shreds of 'factual' flesh on the somewhat bare bones of this tale and so further justify an already heady mix of circumstance. The reader will find further such details in Appendix 7.

There are, regrettably and frustratingly, so many unanswered questions that due to no recorded history will likely forever remain unanswered. Were Judith or Roger ever a 'nun', 'monk' or 'priest' in the true sense? Following their change of fortunes and reduced circumstances for the reasons outlined earlier, maybe clinging onto Hallam, Kimberworth and the Ecclesfield revenues (which would have been from lands donated by Judith and Roger upon its foundation and the iron works), these providing some sort of financial security, did they assume 'lay' roles, as a form of cover. Indeed, were there actually any monks/nuns at all attached to Ecclesfield in the period 1102/3 or was it more just a lovers retreat? Even if there had been, a cell of this size is unlikely to have supported more than 2 or 3. To suggest how Judith and Roger may have spiritually and morally declined, there is the following quote, describing these alien houses. They certainly sound the perfect setting for the somewhat dissolute lifestyle being suggested for Judith and Roger and the location for the tragic demise of our hero, Robin Hood:

"Natural as was the process by which these small houses came into being, their appearance must be pronounced one of the most unfortunate by-products of the Conquest in England; save for a few of the larger priories, they served no religious purpose whatsoever, and were a source of weakness to the house that owned them. **In the course of time they became the most considerable of all the elements of spiritual decay in the monastic life of the country.**"[637]

---

[636] *Victoria County History, A History of the County of York:* Volume 3, London, 1974. pp. 387–91.

[637] *The Monastic Order in England* , David Knowles, CUP, 1940/1963/2004.

**58. THE PRIORY CHAPEL THE PRIORY TODAY (chapel to the right)
and part of a private house**
Image (l) in Public domain and (r) © photo courtesy of Nicola Pleasants-the Starfleet
Blogger

In addition to all this rather salacious innuendo regarding goings-on at the Priory, there are also a surprising number of Robin Hood-related place names that attach themselves to this area. First, barely a couple of miles or so from Ecclesfield Priory and 4 from Kimberworth castle, on the B6086 near Harley, are the remains of an ancient wooded area known to this day as *Hood Hill*. Second, there was a place called *Robin Hood's Bower and Moss*, understood to be four miles north of Sheffield. Although the precise site of this placename is apparently lost, it was recorded in 1637 as '*Robin Hood's Bower, Bower Wood*', near Ecclesfield and may well be the same location as Hood Hill. Third, there is a *Robin Hood Well* in Low Hall Wood, just 2 miles to the north-west of Ecclesfield and it appears as '*Robin Hood's Well*' in 1773.

59. The location of Ecclesfield Priory (circled) and St Mary's church
An arrow, shot by Robin, circa 70m from the upper floor of the Priory with the
help of Little John, would land, fittingly, in the corner of the churchyard near the
road junction.
After 900+ years, the precise location of his grave would have been lost to time.
Imagery ©2021 Getmapping plc, Infoterra Ltd. and Bluesky, Maxar Technologies,
The Geoinformation Group, Map data

Bordering Ecclesfield are still sizeable remnants of ancient woodland (e.g. Wheata Wood, Prior Royd, Birkin Royd and Greno Wood), some of this once attached to the Priory and is essentially unchanged since the eleventh century. Today they form part of Sheffield Heritage Woodland and is mostly public amenity land, managed for wildlife and visitors, remaining an evocative legacy of the 'greenwood' of Robin Hood.

60. Photo taken from the corner of St Mary's churchyard where Robin may be buried, with a view of the Priory beyond the church between the trees, 70m away in the distance.
©author's own

So, is this in fact the location of Robin's demise, and not Kirklees, where Robin was to die thirty-five years after the Norman Conquest in late 1102/early 1103 aged forty-four?[638] Granted this is somewhat controversial, but food for thought and not so unlikely given the seeming lack of proper recording of what we suspect may have been real events. What is key is that the priory was effectively closed down and its connection with St Wandrilles severed, following a long period of decline, during the final year of the reign of Edward III (1377). As such, the writers of the ballads, minstrels and tellers of tales in the late 14th century and thereafter, may very well have substituted another 'Church Field(s)' in the area of South Yorkshire, so that the audience could relate to a real and known place with a similar derivative name.

---

[638] As Loxley had no church, then (and still today) residents from there are buried in the large Ecclesfield churchyard, such that it was very likely the resting place of Robin's mother and other family members.

Just imagine if Robin and his men really had given these Normans the run-around for more than twenty years and lived to tell the tales—that surely would have been the stuff of legend and perfect material for the balladeers and storytellers to entertain the masses. After Robin's death in 1102/3, matters really did improve for the English populace under the auspices of Henry I, who ruled right up until 1135, producing a royal bloodline now linked directly back to the Anglo-Saxon kings of Wessex. In addition, we read that one of Henry I's initial actions was to throw out a whole group of rapacious sheriffs for exceeding their authority and instead using itinerant 'circuit' officials in the judiciary to kerb abuses of power at the local and regional level; just what Robin would have hoped and prayed for after all his efforts. It had taken a generation, but the terrible effects of 1066 were beginning to dissipate at last and Robin Hood (and his sister Maud—Maid Marian) had been a fundamental part of starting this process off.

Chapter 14
Conclusions

"Sometimes legends make reality, and become more useful than the facts."
(*Midnight's Children*, Salman Rushdie)

When I first held up my feeble lantern and entered this dark rabbit hole of investigation, the words of Winston Churchill came to mind...

"History with its flickering lamp stumbles along the trail of the past, trying to reconstruct its scenes, to revive its echoes, and kindle with pale gleams the passion of former days."[639]

The overall purpose of this book, therefore, has been to establish, with passion, in a readable and entertaining manner, the identity of the real Robin Hood and also the 'whys, whos and hows' of the death of King William Rufus (and Robin), and how those objectives are interconnected. Aside from that, my intention was also to correct some modern misconceptions about Robin Hood perpetuated by film and TV. In many of the early texts, Robin is a yeoman, not a true nobleman, more betwixt and between; he is from South Yorkshire, not Sherwood Forest in Nottinghamshire; he does not have a girlfriend or marry a lady named Marian; he does not 'rob from the rich to give to the poor' and there are no Moors or Saracens[640] among the Merry Men. In fact, it is suspected that at times Robin was, despite his chivalric attitude to women and devotion to the

---

[639] Churchill in his November 1940 panegyric to Neville Chamberlain.

[640] This now popular idea only began less than fifty years ago with the 1984–86 television series *Robin of Sherwood*, which included the character Nasir (Mark Ryan) and later developed as Azeem (Morgan Freeman) in *Robin Hood, Prince of Thieves.* 1991.

Virgin Mary, impetuous, hot-tempered, a poor loser, a highway robber, a murderer even, and far more violent and rough than later ballads depict him.

There is not a shred of evidence from the surviving ballads to support the notion that he was ever a Crusader or lived in the times of either King Richard I, 'the Lionheart' or his brother King John.[641] I do sometimes muse though on the intricate relationship between the 3 royal Norman brothers, Robert (Curthose), William (Rufus) and Henry (Beauclerc). The writers and the film-makers from later centuries have clearly seen fit, more often than not, to depict the setting for Robin in the late 12th century period of brotherly enmity between Prince John and King Richard, despite the fact many serious historians favour the later era of Edward I or II. Just maybe this royal fraternal infighting did form part of the Robin Hood story but was in reality from a somewhat earlier period of history (in fact around 100 years) and it was not John but William Rufus who was the 'baddie' king and Mr Niceguy was in fact Prince Henry, not Richard the Lionheart.

From Douglas Fairbanks (1922) and Errol Flynn (1938) through to Kevin Costner (1991), Russell Crowe (2010) and Taron Egerton (2018), not to mention the Robin Hood TV series of the 1950s, 1980s and 2000s, all have consistently placed the setting of Robin Hood in the time of Prince John and/or King Richard I, which the public has now come to accept as a given 'truth'. This, though, is with no evidence of historical foundation whatsoever, solely the unsubstantiated claims of some medieval historians, like 16th century John Major and the 19th century legacy of Sir Walter Scott's novel, Ivanhoe. As Nazi propaganda minister Joseph Goebbels once famously said—"*if you repeat a lie often enough it becomes the truth.*"

When writers say that Robin Hood attempted to remedy some of the injustices committed under King John, they are just reciting a Hollywood fantasy and pretending that it is history As we have seen, the only king ever mentioned in the old original tales is an 'Edward', and even the weight put on this singular reference by the balladeers is questionable for, as we know, numerous other kings' names then appear in later ballads. Although there is no historical connection between Robin Hood and King John or between Robin Hood and King Richard, Hollywood has repeatedly linked those 3 figures in various ways. John was not believed to be as bad as history has made him out to be (though

---

[641] Notes on Robin Hood's tangential connections to the Crusades are given in Appendix 12.

some think worse!) and his brother Richard, while a great warrior (though he never recovered Jerusalem), was a dreadful king, father and husband, who bled the country dry with his crusading costs, spoke solely French (not the mellifluous Scottish lilt of Sean Connery!) and only ever lived in England for 6 months!

Regrettably, for those people wishing to correct these misnomers when telling the tale and its almost total modern reliance on the Sheriff of Nottingham, Sherwood Forest, Prince John and a crusading King Richard, they may find their work cut out. These inclusions are only matched by the total exclusion of Robin's Christian faith, devotion to the Virgin Mary and the taking mass at least twice a day, none of which sit happily with the modern audience. To try now to shift the action to Doncaster, Barnsdale and South Yorkshire in a completely different time frame, excluding the Crusades (and Marian!) and bring in religion, is nigh on impossible. Rightly or wrongly (and I believe wrongly), these, and other, elements of the legend have now become so entrenched into the minds of people and are such intrinsic parts of the Robin Hood story, that Hollywood et al, will continue to defer to popular opinion rather than, God forbid, to the truth.

The whole basis for the legend of Robin Hood is contained within the corpus of the 37 ballads collated by James Child in the 19th century plus the 21 discovered in the 1670 Forresters Manuscript in 1993 as detailed in Part I, chapter 1. These 58 ballad tales (some being better duplicates of earlier versions) make up all the stories of Robin Hood and nowhere within these tales is there any mention of Kings Richard and John, the Crusades, or ever any suggestion he took part in a major insurrection or rebellion against a king (or for the king) à la Hereward the Wake or William Wallace—just generally courteous abduction and highway robbery. Yet candidates continue to be proposed for the real man, generally connected to either the uprising of Simon de Montfort in the mid 1260s against Henry III or the Barons War against Edward II in 1323 led by the Marcher Lords, Roger Mortimer and Humphrey de Bohun. What is more, the activities of Robin are said to have covered a period of 22 years, whereas these civil war incidents are over and done with after just a year or so.

If this detail was not enough for these candidates (and others) to be readily dismissed, we must recall the point strongly made by Professor Holt—that it is quite apparent from the written records, sparse as they are, that criminals (and others) were happily taking the sobriquet of Robin Hood (or its variations) in homage to this popular outlaw, many decades before these later events and characters played out.

It is also apparent from the early Robin Hood ballads that our hero is not one of the downtrodden serfs and villeins of the feudal system. He does not appear as a by-product of those agrarian social struggles of the 13th and 14th centuries leading to the Peasants Revolt of 1381 (struggles that began right back to 1066). Instead, they speak of a far more upper-class yeoman, perhaps fighting partly for the discontented peasantry against the landlords, but more often in a battle with corrupt churchmen and government officials—the 'shrieval administration' as Holt coined it—the sheriff, being the king's power base at a local level, his principal financial agent and a past master at extortion—as discussed in Part I, chapter 9. This would seem to be the perfect fit and plausible consequence of the origins, upbringing and early life of our Robin. The early ballads occasionally hint at the ruthless nature of Robin and his gang. In *Robin Hood and the Monk* (*c.*1450), the earliest surviving poem, outlawed Robin is spotted by a monk while praying at a church in Nottingham. The monk reports Robin to the sheriff, who captures our hero. Later, the monk is executed by Little John for informing on Robin, and Much the Miller's son casually kills a little boy, who witnesses the act, to stop him giving evidence of the murder. It is difficult to imagine Hollywood scriptwriters having Kevin Costner, or one of Russell Crowe's Merry Men, killing an innocent child to stop him ratting on Robin to the sheriff.

When, as a young man, driven into the greenwood as an outlaw back in 1080, the saga tales of Beowulf and famed Icelandic outlaws were still ringing in his ears. They displayed some of the most Anglo-Saxon-Danish values, including bravery, truth, honour, loyalty, duty, hospitality and perseverance, all of which he now embodied into his somewhat 'chivalric' lifestyle and that of his band of followers, all leading to their legendary status, far surpassing that of the usual criminal gang.

The best summation is that Robin, the illegitimate son of an Anglo-Danish noble (Earl of both Northumbria and Huntingdon), was a low-level guerrilla fighter in the second half of the eleventh century, possibly called a terrorist today, but in truth just a devout gentleman highwayman. Or more precisely a 'libertarian rebel', who for the reasons laid out in this treatise, lived an outlaw life for twenty odd years from c.1080–1100 with a thuggish gang in the forests of South Yorkshire/North Nottinghamshire and East Derbyshire. Here they proved to be a running sore under the skins of the all-conquering new ruling Norman class and their generally corrupt officials, a beacon of light piercing this black cloud which must have permanently hung over the heads of the defeated English people in those early decades after 1066.

His reputation with the oppressed populace, who needed a hero, built on this, as his personality, martial skills, ability to avoid capture (or always escape or be rescued) and live a free life eating royal venison, clearly struck a chord with the common people that began as hero worship and turned into legend. In addition, I have tried to show, through the strong circumstantial evidence of real events, places and people of the period, how Robin came to be born, outlawed and pardoned; who Maid Marian may really have been; and the likely events leading up to his untimely death. I have frequently referenced the most well-known and longest ballad, *The Gest of Robin Hood* (Child, 117) throughout this work. An overall study of the numerous clues in this set of tales—*The Gest*—(Sir Richard at the Lee, St Mary's Abbey, The Bishop of Hereford, the death of the Sheriff, Robin's death at the Priory, Sir Roger of Doncaster etc. (and the other ballad encounters with Guy of Gisborne and extended death tale), combined with a good dollop of common sense and logic, suggests it is a compilation of separate ballads and pretty much represents the goings-on and events in the final 7 years or so of Robin's life, from about 1096 to 1102/3, and clear reasoning has been given when appraising the various tales. Even the rather tacked on nature of Robin's pardon and death in the final fytte (being 22 years after being outlawed in 1080) could well represent his 2 year absence from Yorkshire (in Hampshire, summer 1100 to summer 1102), for reasons the balladeers would never know.

By his death, in early 1103, times were slowly changing. It was now nearly 4 decades since the Norman victory at Hastings and English-speaking King Henry I had taken the throne; levels of hatred were diminishing. Slowly the English and Normans were coming together through the necessity of living side by side as well as, like the new king, through intermarriage. With many of the rank and file Normans being men of small worth, they had little option but to mix in with their English neighbours (and marry them), leaving their noble masters to carry on the illusion of being truly French. But even they, with their children raised by English nursemaids and their English reeves and stewards managing their estates, became first Anglo-Norman and then over time, to all intents and purposes, English.

As regards Part Two of this treatise—was Robin Hood a key part of a plot to assassinate the king—William Rufus—recruited by his Anglo-Norman sister, Maud, who moved in the highest echelons of court life? Stated like that, as a cold, simple proposition, it sounds unlikely, fanciful even. In 1895, a renowned historian and genealogist of the medieval period, called Horace Round, pointed out some of the family links between the Clare, Giffard and Tyrell families and first suggested that perhaps it was more a conspiracy than an accident that brought about the death of William Rufus, particularly in the light of the favours subsequently received by the Clares[642].

The very earliest comment, from the Anglo-Saxon Chronicle stated that Rufus was killed 'by an arrow from his own men' and not as often reported 'from **one** of his own men'. This tiny three-letter word omission suggests, to me at least, something much more conspiratorial by the writer. In addition, Tyrell, a Frenchman, a guest and 'foreigner' at court, can quite justifiably **not** be described as 'one of Rufus's men' further suggesting not he, but A N Other, was culpable in the king's death. This idea spread among historians in the 20th century until Hollister, in his much referenced 1973 treatise, did his best to nonsense the idea of a plot though I have tried to show, firmly yet politely, that many of his arguments hang by threads and ignore other, significant, contrary elements and more recent research, which put together, quite readily display the stronger possibility of a plot rather than an accident.

Historians remain divided and some, like Emma Mason, have changed their mind from accident to murder over the years. Hollister's 'accidental' view was heartily supported by medieval historian David Crouch in 2007, whose somewhat naïve conclusion was, that '*Rufus died because he played with sharp weapons*'[643]. Some might consider the perfect murder is when the culprit is never interviewed, never arrested and thus gets away with the crime. However, it is my opinion that the absolutely perfect murder is where the intended victim dies and no-one ever suspects that a murder has even been committed—it was just an accident. It certainly has been a long running mystery and how apposite it is, that buried in the graveyard of nearby All Saints church, Minstead, not half a mile from the commemorative Rufus Stone, is none other than Sir Arthur Conan Doyle, the creator of Sherlock Holmes, who would surely have solved the mystery!

---

[642] These facts were pointed out by J. H. Round (*Feudal England*, 1895, p.472) and also F. H. M. Parker (*The Forest Laws and the Death of William Rufus*. English Historical Review, xxvii, 1912, pp. 32–35).

[643] *The Normans: The History of a Dynasty,* David Crouch, Hambledon Continuum, 2007, p.155.

If you peruse the website for Winchester Cathedral under the 'History' tab, it tells you of Rufus being buried there and that his bones are preserved, among other royals, in the mortuary chests displayed there. These have been the subject of a recent and ongoing forensic osteo-archaeological investigation as they were all vandalised and mixed up by Cromwell's soldiers in the 17th century during the English Civil War.[644] However with regard to his death, the website summation, with no reference at all to Walter Tyrell, is uncannily like that of the Anglo-Saxon Chronicle, being *'He was killed by the arrow of an unknown bowman while hunting'*. If one accepts the very strong possibility, as laid out in Part One of this work, that Robin Hood, the famous outlaw and archer was, indeed, the illegitimate son of Earl Waltheof and half-brother of the Countess Maud, then suddenly what seems unlikely, suddenly seems all too possible. Here we have the man, the iconic outlaw, the expert archer and close family member to one of the plotters, appearing at Romsey Abbey just a few miles from the murder scene at precisely the moment when Rufus dies; this being the one confirmed fact that could have been used in a court of law. Circumstantial maybe; highly coincidental certainly; suspicious definitely. His overall motive, means and opportunity have already been laid out in detail and are convincing, such that the *'unknown bowman'* suddenly takes on a very real persona.

Despite all this, it has to be admitted that no further 'facts', other than those of strong circumstance—'trout in the milk' as Thoreau would say—as to his involvement in the regicide of the king that can be proven or would stand up in a court of law and despite the great amount of that circumstantial evidence piled up against Henry, a Scottish verdict of 'not-proven'[645] seems likely, though if all the evidence suggesting premeditation had come to light, a jury (if such had existed!) might well have thought otherwise.

---

[644] The publication of isotopic data from the Winchester Mortuary Chests is expected soon. So far, more than 1,300 human bones for at least 23 partial skeletons have been reconstructed which are thought to contain the remains of Rufus as well as Egbert, Canute and other Anglo-Saxon royals, as well as some Winchester Bishops— significantly more than the 15 individuals the chests were thought to contain.

[645] In Scottish law there are three verdicts in criminal law, *Guilty, Not Guilty and Not-proven*. The last of which provides the accused with the same result as Not Guilty but leaves the impression that the jury thinks they are guilty but that the Crown has been unable to prove it conclusively or beyond reasonable doubt!

It would seem that what we are faced with here is indeed 'The perfect murder' and they all got away with it. The proposition of Robin's involvement is certainly original and not a little intriguing. Certainly, by removing Rufus and replacing him with Henry, thus obtaining a full pardon, Robin's retirement from the outlaw life could not have been better timed. The mixed motives of the other plotters can be questioned. To me they range from personal vendetta, defence of the church, reinstatement of Anselm and undoubtedly some personal gain and advancement. However I believe that, together, they all viewed the removal of Rufus as a quite altruistic, noble project and a vital thing for England and its people and indeed, this was key to their being able to recruit the services of the People's Champion—Robin Hood and carry the support of Anselm, the Archbishop of Canterbury and his prelates. Their success was not immediate though and the hour was not yet at hand for England's deliverance; as was stated in Parliament in Charles I's time—*"Things must become worse before they can mend"* and England had, therefore, to live under the tyranny of Kings Stephen and John for more than a century longer. Eventually though, 'good' was at length accomplished, as out of all the woes and wretchedness came the Bill of Rights (Magna Carta, 1215), the Charta de Foresta (the Forest Charter, 1216) and the later efforts of Simon de Montfort in the 2nd Barons War in 1267.[646]

On the death of King Henry in 1135, the Anglo-Saxon Chronicle gave him a somewhat different epitaph from that of his brother Rufus, and noted rather sinisterly:

'*...the land immediately grew dark, because every man, who could, immediately robbed another'. The king (*Henry) *had ensured that '**in his time no man dared to do wrong against another; he made peace for man and beast; no man dared say anything but good to whoever carried their load of gold and silver'.*[647]

So Henry's reputation as a good monarch was established and 2 centuries later we find the 14th century chronicler Henry Knighton seeing fit to add to the

---

[646] Simon de Montfort, 6th Earl of Leicester (the great-great-grandson of plotter Robert de Beaumont—see Appendix 4) is known as one of the '*fathers of representative government*', being later described by Napoleon as 'one of the greatest Englishmen'.

[647] Anglo-Saxon Chronicle, p. 262 (D-version); Thorpe, Anglo-Saxon Chronicle 1, Translation by Swanton. p. 381.

Chronicon's account of Henry I's death with—*"a virtuous man, good and true towards God and the people."*[648]

As far as Robin's involvement is concerned, his key assist in the removal of Rufus and replacement by Henry must have resulted in a high degree of satisfaction as one by one, many of the great nobles (with those few notable exceptions like the Clares and Beaumonts), the very sons of the men who had achieved the conquest of England (and many being those who had a stranglehold on Robin's people of South Yorkshire) were themselves driven out of the land as traitors and outlaws with their estates or 'honours' being redistributed among Henry's 'new men'.

There is no escaping the hard fact that trying to unravel the 'true history' of a thousand years ago is not easy, given even the history of fifty years ago can prove elusive, debateable and hazy. We only have to listen to the phrasing of the many leading historians, archaeologists and experts on the numerous TV history programmes when discussing their interpretations of the distant past or the artefacts dug up from ancient history: 'it is possible'; 'we suspect'; 'it is quite likely'; 'we now believe'; 'it seems that'; 'our interpretation is'; 'it would appear' and so on, are in constant use. I fully confess that some of these have appeared within the pages of this book and make no apologies for it, as there is little or no chance that sufficient irrefutable evidence, such that would stand up in a court of law, or fully convince the readers of a book such as this, will ever surface to settle these matters conclusively. In writing about these events from a thousand years ago, I have tried to combine a forensic eye with a colourful imagination and the honesty to admit where the line lies between knowledge and speculation.

To quote from the author and historian Ian Mortimer:

All contentious history—academic and scholarly research as well as amateur sleuthing and popular writing—is built on shaky foundations. This is because all the evidence underpinning it is open to question. Very often one piece of evidence conflicts with another.[649]

---

[648] '*Chronicle of Henry Knighton, Chronicon*', c.1370, edited by Joseph Lumby 'Chronicon: Henrici Knighton' (Rolls Series), 2 vols., London 1889–1895. p.128.
[649] *Notes on the Death of Edward II*, 2008, Ian Mortimer: http://www.ianmortimer.com/EdwardII/death.htm.

Regrettably this is an inescapable truth. Wyntoun, Bower, Major and Grafton, the 4 earliest chroniclers to mention Robin (writing from 1400–1550), all make reference to the popularity of the ballads and by including Robin Hood in their chronicles clearly intended to imply he was a real person and to give him an historical pedigree. However, although they all claim to be describing the man of the ballads, they all diverge in providing a time period. Given the events they are trying to describe occurred 300–450 years earlier, it is hardly surprising as one suspects they had exactly the same amount of information as we have today (and no internet!). As Holt says, even though Robin Hood is essentially fiction, *"From the first he was believed to be a real historical person."*[650] Dobson and Taylor also concluded that, *"the geographical allusions in the early Robin Hood ballads, and especially The Gest, are sufficiently specific to suggest the exploits of a real Barnsdale outlaw lay behind the later Robin Hood saga."*[651]

Although I have gone on at some length, I am quite sure there is much more to be said on the topic and the continual publication of books on the subject is testament to that. I suspect that many readers may dismiss it all as 'tosh', but I see it as a jigsaw in which some pieces fit together perfectly, other pieces can be made to fit if you push them a bit harder, some are damaged and some pieces, as with most jigsaws, are missing entirely. However, the clarity of the resultant picture is left to the judgement of the individual viewer, as I believe that everyone is entitled to their own Robin Hood theory, especially as none of them can be proven absolutely. I freely admit that owing to the absence of any written record it has not been possible to find any solid documentary evidence for a Robin Hood's existence earlier than 1225, nearly 150 years later than my hypothesis, but hopefully the reasons for this have been made clear. I have endeavoured to write a compelling story and throw out some ideas and trails that maybe better scholars than I will follow.

The main reason the contemporary English were so sympathetic to such noted outlaws as Robin Hood, Little John and their companions—indeed, why they became so heralded in common folklore—is that they were driven to become such as a consequence of Norman tyranny, the English loss of land and forest rights to the Crown and powerful noble landlords, swingeing taxes and the corrupt power of the sheriffs, the church and their officials. They maintained

---

[650] *Robin Hood*, J.C. Holt, Thames and Hudson, 1982. p.40
[651] *Rymes of Robyn Hood: An Introduction to the English Outlaw*, Dobson, R.B. and Taylor, J., Heinemann, 1976, p,11

their freedom in the 'greenwoods', when the bullying sheriffs and barons, cosseted in their many castles, had reduced the people effectively to slavery and the corrupt, immoral church hierarchy lived the high life in their abbeys and priories. Hence their exploits told by storytellers and sung by every minstrel, were received with enthusiasm by the working people. However, the 'Norman' and church chroniclers were not about to record their exploits for a myriad of political reasons. They flew beneath the radar but the populace knew them well…but could not read or write, only gather around the storytellers in taverns and market squares to hear the 'saga' tales of Robin and other outlaws. Maybe we should reflect on the observations of the renowned French historian Augustin Thierry.

"History has not understood these outlaws; it has passed them over in silence, or else, adopting the legal acts of the time, it has branded them with names which deprive them of all interest—such as 'rebels', 'robbers', 'banditti'. But let us not be misled by these odious titles. In all countries, subjugated by foreigners, they have been given by the victors, to the brave men who took refuge in the mountains and forests, abandoning the towns and cities to such as were content to live in slavery."[652]

According to his view, 'Jollye Robin' was a representative of his class, the Saxon patriots, who from the forests of the northern counties waged interminable war against their Norman tyrants. Of these Robin was 'the brightest and the last'. However, outlaw robbery and associated misdemeanours are the subject of the tales of *The Gest*, not 'interminable war'. To me, this almost uncanny comparison between the two is startling, not only in content but in precisely matching time frames and surely cannot be ignored as further evidence of the original hero originating from this period of history and the subsequent development of the legend.

My placement of Robin in such an early time frame will undoubtedly be considered somewhat controversial but such readjustment of historical timelines are not unknown. For example, only recently, historian Monica Green has found concrete evidence that the great plague we are familiar with of the mid-14th century was, in fact, already spreading from China to central Asia in the 1200s.

---

[652] *Histoire de la conquête de l'Angleterre par les Normands [History of the Conquest of England by the Normans]*, Thierry, Augustin, 3 volumes (Firmin Didot, 1825)

This discovery pushes the origins of the Black Death back by over a hundred years, meaning that the first wave of the plague was not a decades-long explosion of horror in the 14th century, but a disease that had crept across the continents for over a century until it reached a crisis point.[653] Just maybe Winston Churchill and Steve Jobs were right when they said—*"The further backward you can look the further forward you can see." (W. Churchill)* and *'You can't connect the dots looking forward; you can only connect them looking backwards'. (S. Jobs)*

Those writers who do refer to the possibility of an early Robin often attach a phrase such as 'quite absurd', to such an idea. They then often throw in what they believe to be 'facts' to dismiss it—like 'longbows were not around then'; or 'no Englishman was called Robert or Robin at that time'. In particular I cite the totally erroneous statement of Phillips and Keatman:[654]

'For a peasant-folk to be represented as a longbowman would be meaningless before 1282, as the longbow did not achieve prominence in England until after the battle of Orewin Bridge in 1282...'

They then quote this as 'evidence' to back up their spurious conclusion that Robin was around in the early part of the 14th century, Full details of why this is a totally false conclusion are contained in Appendix 8—Archery, which addresses many of these misnomers which I hope I have been able to correct.

The original tales from the eleventh century would have formed into oral stories as the legend built throughout the twelfth, but were gradually changed by creative storytellers, balladeers and playwrights in the process, then being copied to parchment in the centuries that followed, before finally ending up in print in the late 15th century, novels in the 19th and mangled celluloid by the 20th and 21st! We are indebted as much to them as to the man himself, for the constant development of the legend to suit the audience of the day. This is perhaps why accepting such an early date for the real man is not so easy.

The representation of the Robin Hood we know today results from centuries of change relating to social, economic and ideological pressures. His original folkloric presence in legends, place names, proverbs, Mayday games, plays and,

---

[653] *'The Four Black Deaths'*, The American Historical Review, Monica Green, Vol.125, Issue 5, Dec. 2020. pp.1601–1631.
[654] *'Robin Hood: The Man Behind the Myth'*, G. Phillips and M. Keatman, 1995, pp.57–8.

of course, the spoken word of the ballads, has been overlaid by a variety of narrative treatments that variously gentrify, politicise and romanticise the story and its hero. However, the roots of Robin Hood and the heroic outlaw tradition[655] can be traced to Anglo-Saxon origins, and although many of those shadowy figures of Dark-Ages saga and medieval romance have long since faded from popular memory, the image of Robin Hood, the iconic outlaw hero, lives on around the world in myth, legend and in history.

Military historian, Jim Bradbury, in his excellent book[656] on the history of archery, was keen to observe that the 150 years, covering the whole of the 12th century and more, from around 1070 to 1220, is a 'missing chapter' in the developmental history of the longbow. As a consequence, he points out that many people have suggested that this novel and lethal weapon appeared in the 13th century and that the English longbow was somehow invented in the time of Edward I, as it was he who banned all sports (including football!) except archery on Sundays, to make sure Englishmen practised with the longbow. Bradbury makes it clear that this assumption is patently untrue and that the bow was slowly developing over many decades during this period[657] and, thanks to archaeological findings, today we are aware that such a weapon existed long before the English started to employ it[658]. It immediately struck me how similar this conclusion was to that of the legend of Robin Hood. With the first appearance of felons and outlaws called Hood from around 1225, people have come to believe that this is the earliest period when the original outlaw must have operated, ignoring the real possibility and likelihood that the oral stories, ballads and fireside tales had already been swirling around the illiterate lower social classes for a century or more, it only being in the 13th century that the Hood name began to creep into

---

[655] Many examples like: William Wallace, Dick Turpin, Rob Roy, Butch Cassidy and the Sundance kid, Bonny and Clyde, John Dillinger, Jesse James, Pancho Villa, Ned Kelly, Pretty Boy Floyd etc.

[656] *The Medieval Archer*, Jim Bradbury, The Boydell Press, 1985, p. back 1996.

[657] In fact changes in bow design over time have been minimal. Bows recently recovered from the wreck of the Mary Rose (1545) are essentially identical to those in use during the battle of Crécy (1346), two centuries earlier. See Appendix 8.

[658] It is worth remembering that the Similaun warrior (the famous 'Ötzi the Iceman' who died in 3,200 BC) was found (frozen in the Alps in 1991) with a 182cm long wooden bow, which was very long for a man about 160 cm tall and effectively a longbow.

the written record as both the legend grew, people took his name and such documents, where that was recorded, have survived.

If, as is being suggested, Robin died around early 1103, it does not seem unreasonable that the 'legend' of his activities would have evolved by word of mouth and early ballads over the next century and it is very likely men, notably other 'outlaws' or felons, began to assume his name as an honorific. It is simply that no records for this period survive. It is only when we creep into the early thirteenth century that frugal, surviving records are found and the name begins to appear in ink on parchment, but by then the legend looks to have been well established for over a century, taking on a life of its own and people then used his name for themselves. This surely is the best explanation of all as to why no-one has been able to identify unquestionably a historical character from a later age, who really fits the bill with a life like the 'original' Robin Hood of the ballads and subsequent legend.

I have made frequent reference throughout this book to the seminal work of perhaps the foremost Robin Hood scholar, the late Professor James C. Holt. Holt's book, *Robin Hood*, was first published in 1982, some forty years ago, but is still generally considered the definitive study of the legend, having undergone several re-releases and re-publications. It is a lengthy work as Holt's time span began in the medieval period and ended in the twentieth century. However, he felt the need to address the historicity of Robin Hood in his final chapter.

Holt analysed in great detail most of the existing candidates who might be said to be the original Robin Hood. He focused on one particular candidate, the Robert Hod who was listed as a 'fugitive' in the Pipe Rolls of the York Assizes in 1225, and who appeared again one year later, in 1226, under the nickname 'Hobbehod'. The evidence pertaining to this man, in Holt's opinion, makes him perhaps the most likely candidate for being the original Robin Hood. The nickname that he was given on the Pipe Roll of 1226, *Hobbehod*, may well reflect the emergence of the legend. Old, well-known evidence suddenly looks refreshed. The Scottish historian, John Major, writing in 1521, believed that Robin Hood and Little John were active in 1193–94. The epitaph left on Robin Hood's grave by Thomas Gale in 1702 recorded that Robin died in 1247. If we arrange all these items chronologically, we seem to have the shadowy outline of a biography; Robin active in the 1190s; an outlaw in 1225; dead in 1247—an interval matching his twenty-two years in the Greenwood in *The Gest*; then a figure of legend by 1262 (when the court clerk changed armed robber William le Fevre's name to William Robehod.)

By Holt's own admission, however, this would require a lot of faith: *'there is nothing to prove it, but it is not impossible'*. However, he is quick to shoot down his own proposition on 2 main counts. Firstly, he says that if this Robert Hod of 1225 was the 'real' Robin Hood and committed numerous robberies, kidnappings and murders throughout the country, he would have expected more contemporary documents to mention his name, particularly as this is said to have occurred over a period in excess of twenty years. As William Simeone concluded *If he were an authentic figure, would he not have won enough reputation in his lifetime, at least enough to insure a niche in contemporary records, even if they were kept by men with a religious and political bias?*[659] But not perhaps, if he was from an even earlier era. Secondly, it would also have required a very quick generation of a legend, for this Robert Hod died in 1247, but the alias of Robin Hood, or variations of it, began to appear in Pipe Rolls by 1262; a mere fifteen years (and 200 miles south) for a man to become 'legend' and for other criminals to appropriate his name seems unlikely. The underlying suggestion is that the real man was considerably earlier than this as Holt states in summary: *'the legend must have become a national one by the second half of the thirteenth century'*.

Professional historians, who I suspect have often had a go at trying to find Robin (and failed), are rather sneering of those, often dedicated amateurs, who have continued to search for the real man. Their view is best summed up in the words of Professor Alexander Kaufman: *'the origins of Robin Hood the person and his original context, are perhaps best left to those individuals who wish to search for that which is forever to be a quest'.*[660] Well, perhaps the quest is over but in any event the important caveat, which Holt emphasises, is that to search for a 'real' Robin Hood is to miss the point: *'at the end of the day the identity of Robin Hood matters less than the persistence of his legend'*. It can, he says, be a fruitless endeavour as no-one would ever arrive at a conclusive, satisfactory and unassailable candidate from the fragmentary evidence available. Moreover, Holt concludes by saying that it is the legend that has grown up around the man, which is much more important than any real person could ever be, owing to what the

---

[659] *'The Historic Robin Hood', The Journal of American Folklore*; William E. Simeone, Vol. 66, No. 262 (October-December 1953), pp. 303–308

[660] *'British Outlaws from History and Literature', Essays on Medieval and Early Modern Figures from Robin Hood to Twm Shon Catty,* Kaufman, A. L. , MacFarland, 2011

legend signifies to different audiences throughout the ages: justice, fairness, and an expression of revolt against harsh authority. These are immortal qualities, argues Holt, and cannot, and should not, be pinned down to any one period or any one man. That is the remarkable thing about him: it is a legend that has matured over the centuries to suit the ever-changing audience—from oral tradition to film script. Perhaps more relevantly, poised as he is between upper and lower class, the defining difference between Robin and other outlaws and maybe why his fame has endured, is his demonstration of the many aspects of courtly knight ideology—chivalry. Through his martial prowess, respect of women; religious faith, voluntary daring, quest for unpredictable adventure; solidarity of the group and generosity to the poor, he clearly exhibits the courtly virtues imitating knightly behaviour that are far removed from what would be expected of a ruthless ruffian and murderous outlaw.

Over recent decades, considerable academic effort has been put into dissecting the literary elements of the ballads, particularly their social, economic and political components. The later medieval ballads in particular can be read at one level as affirming, through Robin's reconciliation with the king, the rule of law, the political order and royal authority. Historian A.J. Pollard also argues that they celebrate the violent defence of justice by an outlaw. Not only is Robin portrayed as defying the Crown and rejecting royal authority, he is also depicted as returning to the greenwood, an alternative 'kingdom' with its own utopian social order. Robin can thus be interpreted as *'a social revolutionary envisaging an idealisation of anarchy as an alternative to monarchy'*[661]. The later armed struggles by 'commoners' in the fourteenth and fifteenth centuries, by people that had developed their own political ideology and role in the political world, showed that they believed they had a right to defend the proper order of society and the common good. Pollard cautiously suggests that these later 'rebels' were influenced by the hope of creating a world not unlike the greenwood kingdom to which Robin returned.

There is a quote by Joseph Ritson, from his 19th century book on Robin Hood, where he openly admits, like Holt, that due to the *'silence or loss of contemporary writers'* there was no chance of there being *'an authentic narrative of the life and*

---

[661] *Imagining Robin Hood: The Late Medieval Stories in Historical Context* Pollard, A. J. (Routledge, 2004)

transactions of this extraordinary personage'.[662]*,* our hero. He further concluded that any *'zealous pursuit'* of the subject will indubitably *'fail to satisfy'* in the search for the real man, his life and times. After more than 200 years of endeavour by endless historians, academics, researchers, authors and keen amateur sleuths, the situation is all but the same, save for those few well-documented scraps that have been thrown in the pot. The late Professor Holt would surely have considered this book another 'fruitless endeavour', but hopefully it has not been so and has at least, as Ritson suggested, *'served to amuse'*.

As we have seen, all sorts of random characters have been put forward as the original Robin Hood, ranging from spurious nobles of the late twelfth century, minor felons of the early thirteenth, through to outlawed Crusaders and fully blown rebels against the Crown in the fourteenth. In the cold light of day, one has to feel that none of these really and truly represent the heroic life of either the legend or as depicted in the ballads, and that the 'real man' lies further back in history.

If you want a really outstanding candidate for the original Robin Hood, then for all the reasons set forth in this book, Robert of Locksley, 1058–1103, the illegitimate son of the great thegn, Waltheof II 'Siwardson', Earl of both Northumbria and Huntingdon, was that man…and both died as a consequence of the treachery of the same woman.

This truly is at the heart of the proposition that the illegitimate son of Earl Waltheof, outlawed in 1080, took to the forests of South Yorkshire within the fellowship of his loyal band and under his new alias became the renowned outlaw Robin Hood for the next twenty years. Orderic Vitalis wrote the following about Robin's father, Waltheof, as the Earl languished in Winchester Castle prison awaiting execution back in 1076.

"…he often deplored his offences, recounting them with tears to religious bishops and abbots. There for the space of a year he did penance according to the counsel of the priests, daily chanting in prayer to God, the hundred and fifty psalms of David, which he had learnt in childhood. He was a man of great and elegant physique, exceeding many thousands in his largesse and courage. He was a devoted worshipper of God, a humble auditor of priests and of all

---

[662] "*Robin Hood: A collection of all the Ancient Poems Songs and Ballads now extant, relative to that celebrated Outlaw*", Ritson. J., pub. William Pickering, 1832.

religious, and a kind lover of the Church and the poor. On account of these and many other spiritual gifts in which, in the lay order, he delighted to a remarkable degree, he was dearly loved by his own people and by others who recognised those things that are pleasing to God."[663]

I cannot think of a more fitting and likely tribute to the father of Robin Hood and thus the likely character of his only son being, with him following in the almost sainted footsteps of his revered father, *'a saintly man and lover of all justice'*[664], but outside of the repressive laws of the land, as a champion of the common good; to live a life that became a legend that lives on nearly a thousand years later. The many similarities between Waltheof and Robin Hood are startling and surely cannot be dismissed or ignored. Whether it be the engaging personality, the martial skills, the mantle of leadership, great strength, the pious nature, the concern for, and generosity to, the weak and poor, the upholding of justice—then the case for 'like father, like son' is well made, even down to the fact neither of them were also without their faults. This conclusion is drawn without all the other assembled evidence and seems our hero truly appears to be 'a chip off the old block'; one just feels the two of them were very close during Robin's formative early years in the 1070s and that Robin was greatly influenced by the example and life led by his noble Anglo-Danish father. Having learnt from him, and his mistakes, he was consequently considerably more cunning than his father and I imagine that his half-sisters, Maud and Alice, were quite in awe of him, the dashing much older brother Saxon outlaw who embodied all those great characteristics of their famed 'sainted' father; the father that they never really knew.

Whether your own image of Robin today is as a low-level guerilla fighter, a wronged and disinherited noble, a laid back highwayman or a handsomely athletic Errol Flynn with the jokey one-liners, he is always on the side of the

---

[663] *Historia Ecclesiastica,* Orderic Vitalis, II, p.320–1. See also the *Chronicon de Hyda,* in which Waltheof is desperate to renounce his lay status, p.295: *'being imprisoned he turned fully to the Lord and begged with fasts, tears and assiduous and intense prayers to be allowed to become a monk and to be held in God's service forever'*. His wish was however not fulfilled, p. 20.

[664] *'The Red Book of Thorney',* the *Abbey Cartulary* (Cambridge University, MSS Add. 3020 and 3021)—Compiled from the early fourteenth century, the cartulary as a whole contains transcriptions of material from before the Conquest to 1531.

poor, he corrects injustices, champions freedom and is the enemy of the corrupt and powerful. He has become not just the archetypal gentleman robber, relieving the rich of their ill-gotten gains, but is now a worldwide symbol of resistance to oppression and protector of the defenceless downtrodden from their unruly rulers.

The renowned 19th century folklorist and compiler of ballads, Professor Child, opined on the Robin of *The Gest* with *'yeoman as he is...he has a kind of royal dignity, a princely grace and gentlemanlike refinement of humour...for courtesy and good temper he is a popular Gawain'*.[665] Gawain of course, was popularly portrayed as a formidable, courteous, and compassionate warrior, fiercely loyal to his family. As such he is a friend to young knights—his 'merrie band', a defender of the poor, and as 'the Maidens' Knight', a defender of women as well. However, Child's rather gentle view of a fundamentally harmless Robin, who was indubitably pretty vicious, was probably derived from the depictions of Robin and his men in numerous post-medieval broadsheet ballads where, rather than depicting serious bloody violence, *"the episodes tend to repeat the tableau of good-humoured cudgellings."*[666]

As A J Pollard so well observed (p.157) *Robin Hood, the noble robber, is not a social revolutionary, he seeks restorative justice, the re-establishment of things as they used to be and ought to be. He does not abolish oppression but he does demonstrate that poor men need not be passive, helpless or meek. He is a continual reminder that without justice, as St Augustine observed, "kingdoms are nothing but robbery."*

This surely is the history, not of a man who became an outlaw, but a legend, both of and for 'the people', that has lasted nearly a thousand years and has indeed, over the millennia become bigger than the man himself.

I conclude with a quote being the final paragraph of an article I have unashamedly purloined from a late 19th-century piece by a certain Colonel W.F. Prideaux entitled *'Who was Robin Hood?'*, written 6 months earlier than the previously quoted article by Miss Stredder in the same publication (Notes and Queries, 1886). I choose this for two reasons: firstly because it perfectly summarises my own views; and secondly, perhaps more importantly, it demonstrates how little has changed despite all the assiduous scholarship of those intervening 138 years.

---

[665] *English and Scottish Popular Ballads,* III, 1888, p. 43.

[666] *European Balladry,* William J Entwistle, Oxford/Clarendon Press, 1951. p.235.

The various theories (on the origins of Robin) *have been ably and succinctly summed up, and their respective merits have been weighed in a spirit of judicial calmness by Professor F.J. Child in the introduction to the fifth volume of his English and Scottish Ballads, but final judgement has been deferred. Whether it will ever be delivered I cannot say, but in the meantime I am venturesome enough to offer an hypothesis which, so far as I am aware, has not yet been advanced in aid of the solution to the mystery, and which seems, to my mind, to have a colour of extreme plausibility.*[667]

I leave the reader to decide just how plausible the colour is of the hypothesis I have ventured between the covers of this book and just maybe it is a small victory for 'vulgar empiricism'. I conclude by addressing you, the reader, by echoing the sincere words of Martin Parker in the final verse of his 1631 ballad, 'A True Tale of Robin Hood'.

> *I shall think my labour well*
> *bestowed to purpose good,*
> *that it should be said that I did tell*
> *true tales of Robin Hood*

In my clearly prejudiced opinion, I believe I have finally identified the man behind the original Robin Hood, but given there is still so much of the story we don't really know about, the following words are still ringing, however faintly, in my ears…

"Would the tale be as exciting if we discovered who the man was? We'd lose the mystery, and the mystery is the allure. In the age we live in, you can find out anything quickly. There's something wonderful about there still being things we don't know about. It's tantalising."

Quote c.2020 by John Dower—documentary filmmaker—about US 1971 hijacker D. B. Cooper.

---

[667] *'Who was Robin Hood?'*, Prideaux, Col. W.F., Notes and Queries, 7th series, November 1886. Pp.421–424. The Colonel pushed his much derided theory that Robin was an alias for Fulk FitzWarin.

Appendices

Appendix 1

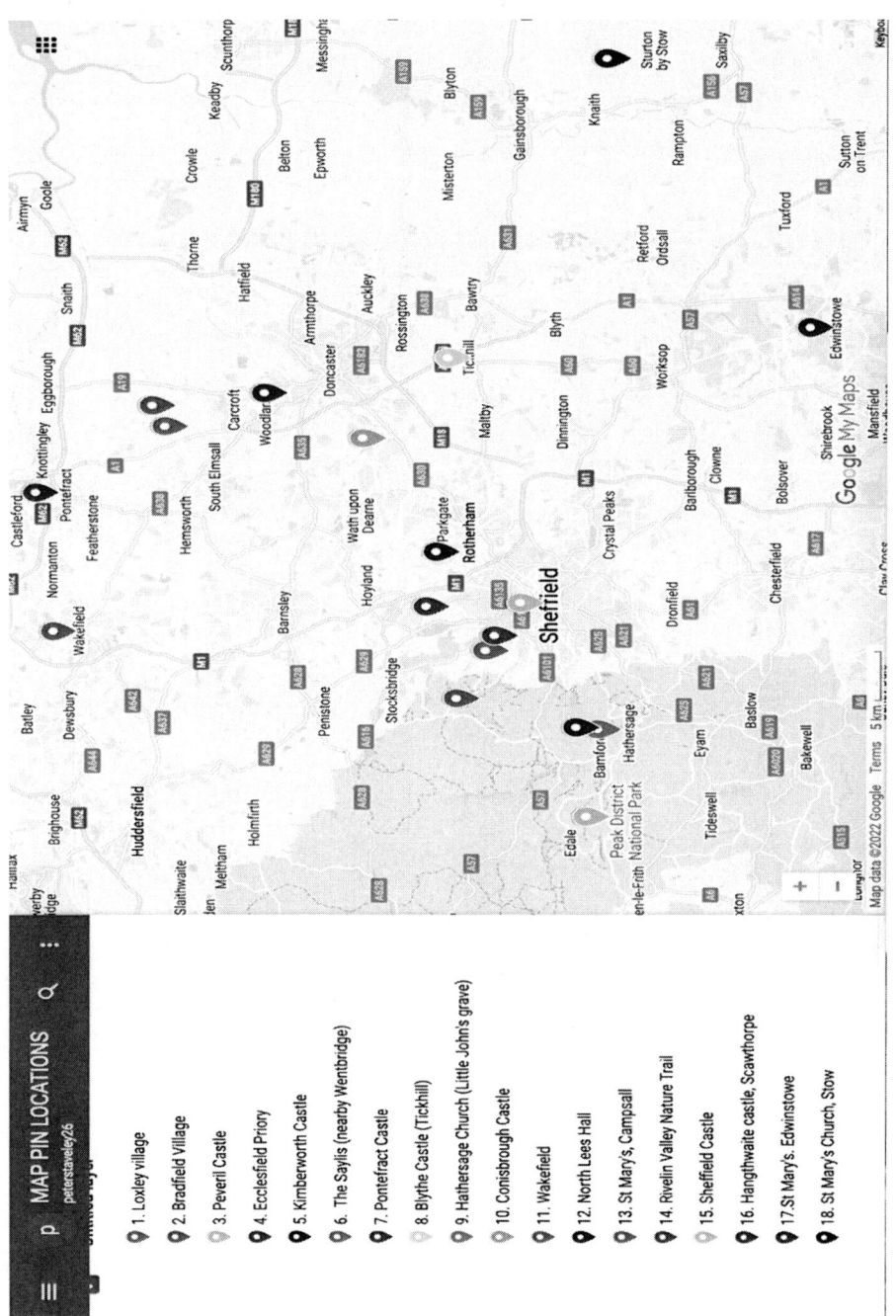

p. **MAP PIN LOCATIONS**
peterstaveley26

1. Loxley village
2. Bradfield Village
3. Peveril Castle
4. Ecclesfield Priory
5. Kimberworth Castle
6. The Saylis (nearby Wentbridge)
7. Pontefract Castle
8. Blythe Castle (Tickhill)
9. Hathersage Church (Little John's grave)
10. Conisbrough Castle
11. Wakefield
12. North Lees Hall
13. St Mary's, Campsall
14. Rivelin Valley Nature Trail
15. Sheffield Castle
16. Hangthwaite castle, Scawthorpe
17. St Mary's, Edwinstowe
18. St Mary's Church, Stow

APPENDIX 2.1 PART 1
Lineage of Robin Hood and the House of Bamburgh

APPENDIX 2.1 PART 2
Lineage of Robin Hood and the House of Bamburgh

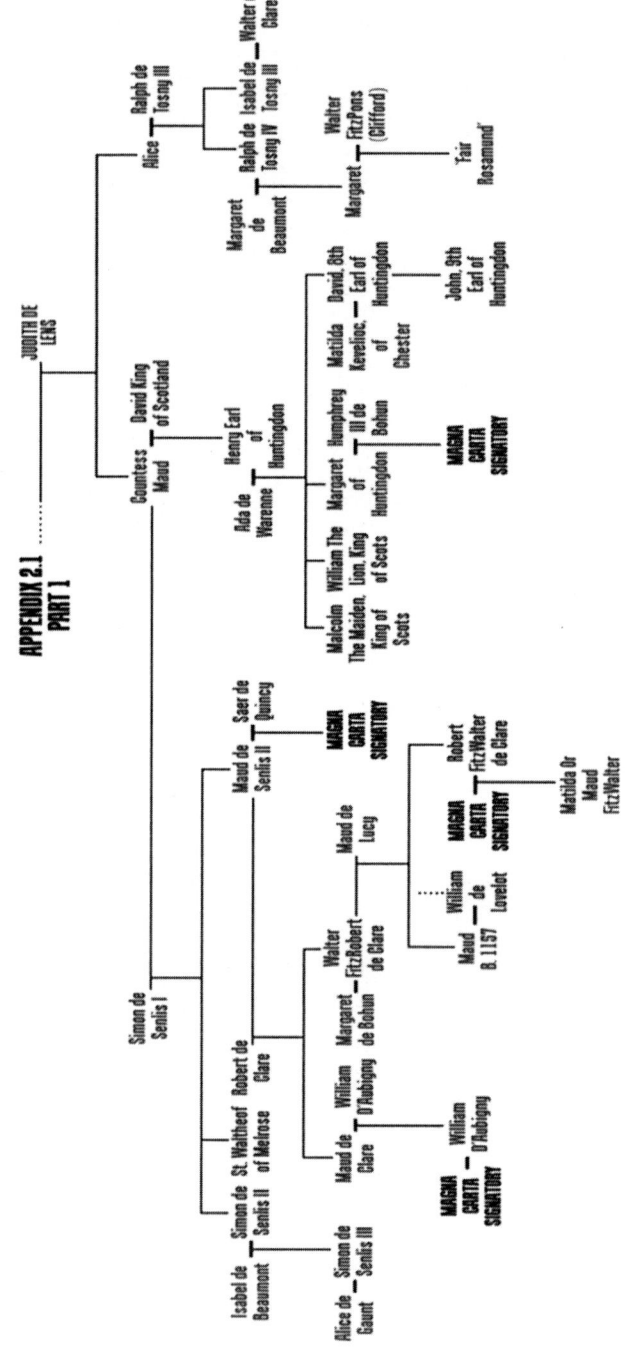

Appendix 2.1 (Part 2)

APPENDIX 2.1 PART 2
Lineage of Robin Hood and the House of Bamburgh

APPENDIX 2.1
PART 1

JUDITH DE LENS

Ralph de Tosny III — Alice

Margaret de Beaumont

Ralph de Tosny IV — Isabel de Tosny III — Walter de Clare

Walter FitzPons (Clifford) — Margaret

'Fair Rosamund'

David King of Scotland

Henry Earl of Huntingdon — Ada de Warenne

Malcolm The Maiden, King of Scots

William The Lion, King of Scots

Margaret of Huntingdon — Humphrey III de Bohun
MAGNA CARTA SIGNATORY

Matilda Keveloic, of Chester — David, 6th Earl of Huntingdon

John, 9th Earl of Huntingdon

Countess Maud

Simon de Senlis I

Maud de Senlis II — Saer de Quincy
MAGNA CARTA SIGNATORY

Walter FitzRobert de Clare — Maud de Lucy

Maud B. 1157 — William de Lovelot

Robert FitzWalter de Clare
MAGNA CARTA SIGNATORY

Matilda Or Maud FitzWalter

Robert de Clare

Margaret de Bohun

William D'Aubigny

Maud de Clare — William D'Aubigny
MAGNA CARTA SIGNATORY

St Waltheof of Melrose

Simon de Senlis II — Isabel de Beaumont

Alice de Gaunt — Simon de Senlis III

450

APPENDIX 2.2
Links to the Scottish Royal Line

King Malcolm II

Bethoc

Donalda — Finlay Glancail

Macbeth King of Scotland — Gruoch — Sille Cinnsington

Lulach Dingman of Macbeth

Macbeth Crinan

Donald III Trathhne

Duncan I King of Scotland — Suthen, sister of Siward?

Margaret of Wessex

King Malcolm III Canmore

Ingeborg Finnsdottter — King Duncan II of Scotland ..... Ulfreda of Northumberland

Mibred King of Cumbria — Ealdgyth

Gaspatric Earl of Northumberland

Ulfreda — King Duncan II of Northumberland / King Duncan II of Scotland

Dolpin of Carlisle — Waltheof Robert of Crowland — Gospatric d.1138

King Alexander of Scotland

King Edgar of Scotland

King David of Scotland — Countess Maud

Simon de Senlis I — Isabel de Simon de Beaumont Senlis II

Henry of Scotland — Ada de Warenne

Malcolm IV King of Scotland

William The Lion King of Scots

Margaret of Huntingdon — Humphrey de Bohun

Matilda Earl of Chester

David 8th Earl of Huntingdon

Mary of Wessex — Eustace Count of Boulogne

Matilda of Boulogne — King Stephen of England

King Henry I of England — Edith/ Matilda

William died on White Ship Sinking

Geoffrey of Anjou — Matilda

King Henry II of England — Eleanor of Aquitaine

MARIA GREEN SHAWSBURY

Appendix 3

<u>Notes on Possible Locations for the Aula of Waltheof</u>

A lord's aula or hall was essentially a domestic residence, only very lightly fortified, and also served as the location for the regional court and also as a hunting lodge. It may well have had a similar appearance to a Viking Longhouse as depicted in fig.60 below. The precise site of the Hallam aula is sadly lost but it seems reasonable, for comparison, to look 15 miles east where a similar aula is recorded. The Domesday Book records that, prior to the Conquest, Earl Edwin of Mercia had an 'aula' or hall in the manor Laughton-en-le-Morthen (Appendix 6, map pin 13). Edwin was a leading noble of Edward the Confessor, but also a leading rebel against the Norman regime after Hastings. Brother-in-law of Harold Godwinson, Edwin, together with his younger brother Morcar (who had been made Earl of Northumbria in 1065, just prior to the Conquest after Tostig was exiled), Waltheof, Earl Gospatric, Arkyle, Edgar Atheling and others, raised an unsuccessful rebellion against William the Conqueror after the Battle of Hastings being finally defeated at York in late 1069.

Dispossessed of his large estates, in 1071 Edwin, being betrayed by one of his own men to the Normans, was ambushed and killed on his way to Scotland. The Laughton manor was one of many then given to Roger de Busli I who built a large motte and Bailey castle there, right on top of the previous site of Earl Edwin's 'aula' and other buildings, which had been surrounded on all sides by a ditched enclosure enhanced with a palisade. This theory was confirmed in 2020 with the Landscapes of Lordship archaeology project, supported by the Castle Studies Trust.[668] It is of note that the community and farms that built up around this hall were very substantial and must have been similar to that of Hallam. It was still worth, in annual value to the lord: £15 in 1086 and a very sizeable £24

---

[668] https://www.castlestudiestrust.org/Laughton-en-le-Morthen.html.

back in 1066, having probably avoided the 'Harrowings' of 1070 and 1080 which Hallam seemingly did not.

So, what are the ideas regarding the location of the Hallam aula.

1. One theory places Waltheof's hall a mile or so east of Stanage Edge, on the steep decline and cliff between Hathersage and Loxley (map pin 2—Appendix 1). The manor house may have been sited at Hallam Head [near Sandygate and a place intriguingly called Burnt Stones, nowadays a built-up suburb of Sheffield near Hallamshire Golf Club]. A whole raft of alternate suggestions, all within the general environs of this area, have been suggested like Redmires Lane, Stumperlowe Hall, Lodgemoor Road and Sandygate, but no archaeological evidence has come to light and much of the district is now submerged under the urban sprawl.

60. Reconstruction of an early 11ᵗʰ century Viking Longhouse at the Viking Centre, Fyrkat, near Hobro, Denmark
Photo courtesy of Malene Thyssen: Creative Commons Attribution-Share Alike 3.0 Unported licence

The village of Hallam was later completely destroyed by the Normans under its first 'Harrying of the North' campaign in 1070 (which in itself must be significant regarding Robin's attitude to the Normans as a young boy of maybe eleven or twelve). This was absolute total destruction and killing with all houses, barns and crops being burnt, all living creatures, men, women, children and livestock being slaughtered in a manner similar to the Nazi invasion of Russia in

1941—a true 'scorched earth' policy designed to snuff out any possible embers of a future uprising. Those not dying by the sword succumbed to famine and disease. It seems likely that the whole area including Locksley, or what was left of it, was maybe 'harrowed' for a second time after the murder of Bishop Walcher and uprising in Durham of 1080, and both events are covered in detail in Part I, chapters 4 and 6. It was the result of this wholesale destruction that gave the area such a reduced value in Domesday in 1086, from twenty years earlier (down 60% from 1066). The precise location of Hallam has only recently been established as probably having been on the banks of the Rivelin, today an outer suburb of Sheffield but of course Sheffield in 1066 was just another tiny manor recorded in Domesday, having just 3 ploughlands and no recorded dwellings or population! The Overlord in 1066 was Waltheof and the sub-tenant was the thane, Swain son of Svavi (of whom sadly nothing is recorded, apart from his 23 landholdings in 1066, with 14 of them in Strafforth, the southernmost Wapentake in the West Riding and later called Strafforth and Tickhill and almost all of them, in 1086, now owned by Roger de Busli. His other manors were in Lincolnshire.

2. A second theory which has only very recently come to light from another recent archaeological dig concerns the remains of a castle at Bolsterstone (about 4 miles north of Bradfield), though opinion is that this was more likely just a fortified manor house, i.e. aula, rather than a true castle. A recent 'dig' has not disproved the existence of an early castle at Bolsterstone but the experts are still far from proving that they have the correct site and that they have features of the correct date. This whole area is called Waldershelf ('*Walder*' is how Waltheof just might have been spelt in old documents and '*Shelf*' is a Norse word for *watchtower*) and Waldershaigh and Walders Low are names of other parts of the village. A Low is a barrow or burial mound and local tradition has it that Walder, the chief, is buried here, though this would not be true were it to be our Waltheof, since he lies in Croyland Abbey near Peterborough and this seems more likely to be a much older burial of an Anglo-Saxon chief from much earlier Anglo-Saxon times prior to the Norman invasion. Waltheof's later Norman successors to the estates of Hallam and wider area, were the de Lovetots, in fact William de Lovetot, was also to be granted a number of the de Busli's lands after the deaths of

Roger de Busli in 1099 and that of his son, Roger II in 1102. Lovetot probably built the first parish church, St Mary's, in Ecclesfield, adjacent to the Priory there, but also founded[669] Worksop Priory in 1103, which seems to have had close links later with Ecclesfield Priory. The Lovetots are known to have had a castle in Sheffield, commenced in 1103, and maybe another somewhere north-east of Sheffield which has never been found and the site at Bolsterstone may well be it (though north-west), set on the site of their Saxon predecessor's original aula.

3. A third theory for the aula's location, supported by Joseph Hunter in his 19th century survey of Hallamshire, argues against the claims put forward for Hallam Head due to the absence of any earthwork, settlement, or convincing documentary evidence and says that the best defensive site was undoubtedly at the confluence of the Sheaf and the Don in Sheffield itself, where the Norman Lord, William de Lovetot, later erected his castle. In the 1920s, there was a plethora of articles, letters and investigations around the castle which became almost obsessive, with most trying to convince people that the aula of Waltheof lay under the castle foundations. Excavations under the Castle Market from 1927–30 revealed the presence of an Anglo-Saxon timber building of at least 3 bays, supported on crucks which some are convinced was the aula of Waltheof though the claims seem more based on a need to establish early Anglo-Saxon origins for Sheffield, a connection to the heroic Earl Waltheof and a sense of civic pride rather than proven archaeology.[670] I am very sceptical and suspect these remains are from a later 12th /13th century date but if they are from an earlier period then they were more likely those of the residence, not of Waltheof, but Swain,

---

[669] William de Lovetot founded the parish churches of St Mary at Handsworth, St Nicholas at High Bradfield and St Mary's at Ecclesfield at the start of the 12th century in addition to Sheffield's own parish church of St Mary. He also built the original wooden Sheffield Castle, which stimulated the growth of the town. Handsworth was one of a number of manors he was granted, once held by Richard Surdeval on behalf of Robert de Mortain.

[670] Sheffield Castle: Archaeology, Archives, Regeneration, 1927–2018: Chapter 3—The Origins of Sheffield Castle, pp.69–104. Moreland, Hadley, Tuck, Rajic, White Rose University Press. 2020.

No mention of a structure at this location in Sheffield manor is given in Domesday, 1086.

the Lord of the Manor prior to the Conquest though no dwelling is recorded in Domesday. The new castle was defended by steep slopes rising from the rivers and by a ditch to the east and the south. Fragments of eleventh-century pottery have been found at the bottom of this ditch but this is hardly conclusive—perhaps some ploughing farmers threw a broken plate or mug in there after their lunch break! Topographical considerations thus enhance the claims of this site but none of this evidence is totally conclusive and does not rule out the existence of a further hunting lodge/aula further to the west as Domesday is specific as to it being in Hallam, whereas Sheffield was a totally separate manor of just a few ploughlands and did not even support any population or dwellings in 1087. This makes it very unlikely as the site location which by Domesday in 1087, would surely have had some structures and inhabitants but receives no mention of either.

4. Fourth and last is a most interesting structure in the village of High Bradfield itself, just 3 and a half miles west of Loxley. The following is an entry from *Hunter's Hallamshire (1819)*: '*The Chapelry of Bradfield is a bleak, high, and mountainous tract of country, lying between the Riveling and the Don, extending north westward to the point, where meet the 3 Counties of Chester, Derby, and York*'. (Some portions of it are among the highest grounds of the English Apennines.) '*Near the church is Bailey Hill, a saxon camp, as fair and perfect as when first constructed, save that the keep is overgrown with bushes*'. The castle site (still visible today, is located behind the church of St Nicholas, off Jane Street. 7 miles west of Sheffield) and appears to have been reconstructed into a motte-and-Bailey type, on a plateau, with a steep slope to the west and low ground to the south and east.

It is thought this was done by the de Furnival family in the 12th century, who had married Matilda de Lovetot of the female line, when the male line expired[671]. On its vulnerable northern side is the steep sided motte,

---

[671] "*Matilda, an heiress of this family of Lovetot, was given in marriage by Richard I. to Gerard de Furnival, of Norman extraction. The succeeding generations which issued from this union between the houses of Lovetot and Furnival shine resplendent like a perfect galaxy of nobility, allying themselves with the powerful families of Warwick, Salisbury, Montague, Neville, Ormond, Stafford, Hastings, Dacre of Gilsland, Rutland, Cavendish, Arundel, Lennox, and finally rising to the restored dukedom of Norfolk, in*

encased by a broad ditch but its southern side has been mutilated to provide access to what is now a very narrow summit. On the southern side of the triangular Bailey is a lofty rampart, encased by a deep ditch, while on the steep western scarp, only a low bank remains of a probable timber palisade. There is no obvious approach to the castle and the earthworks are constructed of heaped stone. Its origins, be they Saxon or of even earlier usage and then probably updated by the Normans, remain obscure.

Apart from around the 80+ larger stone castle structures which took many years to complete, most famously the Tower of London, the conquering Normans relentlessly built over 500 of these timber and earth 'motte-and-Bailey' and 'ringwork' castles throughout England to keep the populace subdued. The development of the Bradfield site from Saxon hall to a later Norman fortification seems very similar in design and process as the use by the Normans of earlier Anglo-Saxon hill forts as the basis for their castles (based on their excellent defensive locations) and was not uncommon, as demonstrated in the example at Laughton-en-le-Morten discussed earlier.

In summary though, the precise location of the original Hallam aula of Waltheof still remains a mystery.

---

the person of Thomas Lord Arundel, in 1664." from *The History and Antiquities of the Parish of Blyth;* Rev John Raine , 1860).

APPENDIX 4.0
The Beaumonts / Senlis / Clare / Tosny / Warenne / Montforts

Aubree de la Haye — Humphrey de Vielles

Dunelma

Thurstan de Montfort-sur-Risle

Aubree — Montfort-sur-Risle

Guillaume - Abbot of Bec

Adeline de Meulan — Roger de Beaumont

Margaret de Perche / Montfichier — Henri de Beaumont

Gondred de Warenne — Roger de Beaumont

Elizabeth Vermandois — Robert de Beaumont 1st Earl of Leicester

Waleran de Beaumont - TWIN

Robert de Beaumont - TWIN 2nd Earl of Leicester

Amice de Montfort

Robert de Beaumont 3rd Earl of Leicester — Petronella de Grandmesnil

Robert de Beaumont 4th Earl of Leicester

Amice de Beaumont — Simon de Montfort

Simon de Montfort 5th Earl of Leicester — Alix de Montgomery

SIMON DE MONTFORT D. 1265

Isabel de Beaumont — Simon de Senlis II

Margaret de Beaumont — Ralph de Tosny IV

Isabel de Beaumont — Mistress of Henry 1st

Gilbert de Clare II

Richard 'Strongbow' de Clare

William de Warenne

Gundred de Warenne — Roger de Beaumont

Ada de Warenne — Henry Earl of Huntingdon

Malcolm. IV King of Scotland

William The Lion. King of Scots

Margaret of Huntingdon — Humphrey de Bohun

MAGNA CARTA SIGNATORY

Appendix 5

APPENDIX 5.0
The Giffards and the Clares

Ermengarde Flaitel — Walter I Giffard

Walter II Giffard

William Giffard

Rohese Giffard — Richard Fitzgilbert de Clare …

Richard Fitzrichard de Clare …

Alice de Clermont — Gilbert de Clare

Robert FitzRichard de Clare — Maud de Senlis II

Richard de Clare

Roger de Clare

Rohese de Clare — Eudo Dapifer de Clare …

Alice de Clare — WALTER TYRELL III MAGNA CARTA SIGNATORY — Isabel de Tosney III

Walter de Clare

Hugh TYRELL Crusader

Alice de Gernon — Richard de Clare

Roger de Clare — Maud de St. Hilary

Rohese de Clare — Gilbert de Gant Earl of Lincoln

Amice FitzWilliam — Alice de Gant — Simon de Senlis III

Richard de Clare MAGNA CARTA SIGNATORY

Gilbert de Clare MAGNA CARTA SIGNATORY

Margaret de Clare — William de Montfichet Beaumont MAGNA CARTA SIGNATORY

Isabel de Clare — Gilbert de Clare

Adeliza de Clare — Aubrey De Vere II

Richard 'Strongbow' de Clare

Robert FitzRichard de Clare — Maud de Senlis II

Maud de Lucy

Walter de Clare — Margaret de Bohun

Maud de Clare — William D'Aubigny …

Maud — William de Lovetot B. 1157

Robert FitzWalter de Clare MAGNA CARTA SIGNATORY

William D'Aubigny MAGNA CARTA SIGNATORY

459

Appendix 6

The Castles Surrounding Barnsdale and Their Owners/Builders— Built Between 1066 and 1100

CASTLES OF BARNSDALE

Untitled layer

1. BARNSDALE DISTRICT
2. Nottingham - the King
3. Conisbrough - Warenne
4. Peveril Castle of the Peak
5. Pontefract Castle - de Lacy
6. Kippax - de Lacy
7. Whitwood - de Lacy
8. Saxton - de Lacy
9. Armley - de Lacy
10. Tickhill - de Busli
11. Kimberworth - de Busli
12. Mexborough - de Busli
13. Laughton en le Morthen - de Busli
14. Bolsover Castle - Peveril
15. Hangthwaite - Mortain/Fossard

61. Remains of Roger de Busli's Laughton-en-le-Morthen motte-and-Bailey castle (map pin 13)

Use of Photo © Mike Nield under licence cc-by-sa/2.0

Appendix 7

Further History of Ecclesfield Priory[672]

There is some evidence that, like some other priories, the earliest origins of the cell at Ecclesfield derive from the donation of a former Saxon minster church and its revenues to a Benedictine abbey. Although there is no surviving pre-Conquest record of a minster community at Ecclesfield, nor any reference to a church or priests in *Domesday*, the name itself meaning 'church in a field' strongly suggests that it had, at least at one time, been an important ecclesiastical centre. The most important indication that there was a Minster at Ecclesfield, therefore, lies in the vast size of its medieval parish and its clearly documented status as an important mother church in the mid-twelfth century, which appears to represent a continuity of its pre-Conquest status.

Before the detachment of Sheffield at some stage between 1376 and the Reformation, the parish of Ecclesfield covered more than 70,000 acres. Its principal chapelry, at Bradfield (where you may recall the De Locksleys were reeves and bailiffs), was first mentioned by name in a late twelfth-century charter

---

[672] Most information in this appendix derives from four primary sources:
1. *History of the Parish of Ecclesfield*, by Rev. J. Eastwood, London, Bell and Daldy, 1862
2. *Ecclesfield Priory—A History,* by Edward Impey (research paper—2001)
3. *Hallamshire. The History and Topography of the Parish of Sheffield in the County of York*: Joseph Hunter, 1819. It is perhaps a remarkable irony that Joseph Hunter, the famous 19th century historian who wrote extensively about Robin Hood and so actively promoted Kirklees Priory as the location for Robin's demise, is actually buried in the graveyard of St Mary's, Ecclesfield, maybe just yards from Robin Hood!
4. *Early Yorkshire Charters,* edited by William Farrer, Cambridge University Press, 2013.
(first published in 13 vols. by the Yorkshire Archaeological Society 1914–1965)

and was referred to in Papal Bulls of 1142 and 1146. There is no available evidence giving the date at which the earlier minster community ceased to exist, but this probably took place around the time of the Conquest and well before the foundation of the priory by Judith and Roger (around 1098–1100), as by the time of *Domesday*, in 1086, we know the entire manor of Ecclesfield was in the hands of tenant-in-chief, Roger de Busli I and no mention is made of any monastic centre or related lands.

As intimated in the main text of Part 2, chapter 13, the cell at Ecclesfield could well have been set up originally as a nunnery and left to its own devices for some decades as it is not until the late 1130s that William de Lovetot (or more likely his wife, Emma) donates the small house to St Wandrille's Abbey in Normandy and there is no evidence that they sent monks to the site before 1161. It seems likely that for a greater part of this time, right up to 1310, the religious community might have been withdrawn to St Wandrille in Normandy. This may have already occurred by 1187, when the priest Jeremiah de Ecclesfield tried to usurp the full rectoral tithes; an attempt which would presumably have been unrealistic had the abbey still maintained effective monks of its own within the parish. Moreover, the terms by which the resulting dispute was settled, which in themselves indicate the weakness of the abbey's authority, made no provision for the support of a community of monks.

Jeremiah evidently had a very strong claim to his position, and despite their reference to him as 'clericus noster' (our priest), there is no evidence that he owed his appointment to St Wandrille. Although nothing can be said of his predecessors, the fact that he seems to have been succeeded in office by his brother and ultimately by his son or grandson, or both, in succession, suggests that Jeremiah and his family enjoyed some sort of hereditary right to the benefice. Such an arrangement would clearly not have been in the best interests of the abbey, nor is it one that they would have been likely to establish by choice. It is therefore possible that Ecclesfield was already served by an established hereditary priesthood when it was granted to St Wandrille in the early twelfth century, and that the right confirmed a long-established practice. Conceivably an arrangement of this sort could have derived from the organisation of a decadent minister, if the priest's revenues had become concentrated in the hands of one man (or woman) and were subsequently claimed by his descendants. A reasonable take on this is that the priory was still firmly in the hands of the decadent and greedy de Busli family and descendants, having been granted the hereditary rights by Judith and Roger in 1101–2 or earlier. Indeed, one of the very earliest documents from 1161, which details forestry agreements[673] between Richard de Lovetot (son of William who had died c.1158[674]) and the priory, reveals that the abbot at that time was called Roger (Yves Poncelet: *Annals of Normandy* p.141). This seems more than plausible when we know for a fact that after Roger de Busli I died in about 1098 and his son Roger II in 1102/3, followed by the exile of Robert de Bellême (and William de Mortain), Henry I took the estates back into royal ownership before then granting them to William de Lovetot in 1103. There is some mystery over how and why de Lovetot, a quite lowly sub-tenant of de Busli, with just 16 manors, received such generous handouts from King Henry I. He seems to have been one of Henry's 'New Men' and it must be assumed he fully supported Henry against the ill-fated efforts of his brother Robert Curthose to remove his crown. William had been 'a man' of de Busli, who was his overlord. He was an Anglo-Norman, who seems to have

---

[673] Smithy Wood lies between Kimberworth and Ecclesfield. It has long been believed that the name Smithy Wood relates to the utilisation of the ironstone seam that lies beneath it and for the charcoal from the trees growing on the site (they would have been coppiced to ensure a sustainable supply) by the monks of Kirkstead Abbey in Lincolnshire. The monastery was, in 1161, granted a large site on nearby Thorpe Common (about a mile to the east) on which to establish a grange (an outlying economic unit, based on iron ore smelting—*Monasticon Anglicanum*. Dugdale, vol. i, p.811) by Richard de Busli, the Norman lord of the manor, with the consent of his wife Emma, on which to establish two furnaces and two forges and the freedom to dig for ore in any part of the manor. About the same date they were also granted several hundred acres in the adjoining parish of Ecclesfield by the lord of the manor of Hallamshire, Richard de Lovetot. It would seem de Lovetot and de Busli were working together on this project and as early as 1161 they clearly had no desire to donate to Ecclesfield Priory which was probably already devoid of monks by this time. There is much later evidence from 1324 that the monks of Ecclesfield maintained a farm/house at Thorpe Hesley—the location of the Kirkstead Abbey Grange—with a sizeable inventory of animals, stock and equipment which would appear to be a legacy of the de Busli foundation. Traces of this building survive to this day as Monks Smithy House, a Grade II Listed Building in Thorpe Hesley—part of Kirkstead Abbey Grange Farm. English Heritage Legacy ID: 335709

[674] William and Emma had a second, younger son, Nigel, to whom William seems to have left his original Barony of Huntingdon. Interestingly, Nigel's grandson Robert de Lovetot, was briefly Sheriff of Nottinghamshire and Derbyshire and Governor of Bolsover castle in 1257 in the time of Henry III.

held a barony in Huntingdonshire (being a close neighbour of Judith de Lens at Sawtry, as their closest adjoining manors were touching, being only 8 miles apart—Wymeswold and Brooksby) comprising seventeen lordships originally held by his father, Roger de Lovetot, in Nottinghamshire, held as a sub-tenant of Roger de Busli I[675], but none as tenant-in-chief himself.

The Lovetots originally came from the small town of Lovetot in Normandy, just 6 miles from St Wandrille's Abbey, of which they were early benefactors. Any remnants of this strand of the de Busli clan were seemingly no more and certainly not on the royal radar for largesse and their lucrative lands and money supply appear to have mostly dried up. By 1103 though, and with Judith and Roger dead, William de Lovetot took over everything. With all this new income, a year later he founded, with his wife Emma, the great Worksop Priory for Austinian canons, 17 miles south-east of Sheffield in one of his new, ex. De Busli, manors.[676] William seems to ignore Ecclesfield entirely, centring all his efforts and cash on his new Sheffield manor (ex. Judith/de Busli) which previously was just a few dwellings and fields and where he now builds a castle and church at the confluence of the rivers Don and Shaef leading to its subsequent expansion from initially just a few straggling huts and smithies forming an irregular street extending from the castle and bridge to the church gate, with a few houses lying towards the town-mill. (It seems the de Busli family did manage to retain their manor and castle at Kimberworth and probably their interest in Ecclesfield).

---

[675] Robert Thoroton *The Antiquities of Nottinghamshire (London 1677)*. From *Monasticon Anglicanum* (William Dugdale) Vol. 2. p. 25.and p. 50.

[676] It was this very year, 1104, that the body of Saint Cuthbert was removed into the cathedral of Durham. Perhaps the great reputation of the Northern saint had spread over England and induced Lovetot to dedicate his church to him.

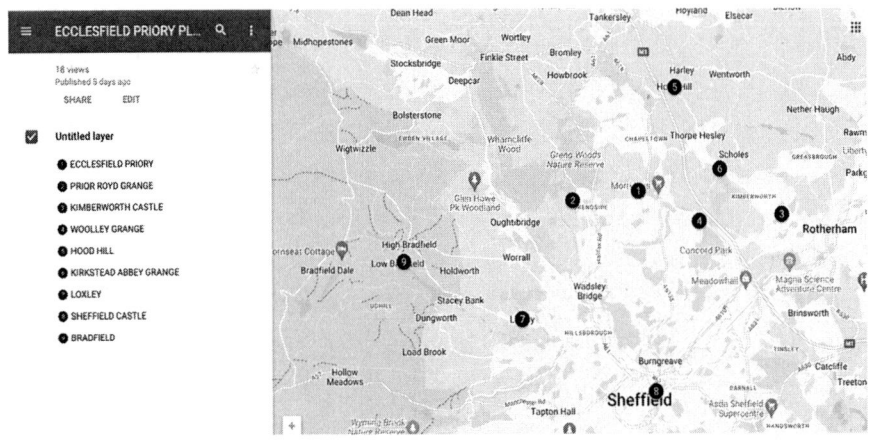

62. Places associated with Ecclesfield Priory
Map data created from Google Maps—Google © 2022

As this is the Appendix, rather than the main text, I am going to allow myself a little logical speculation here. William de Lovetot's wife is only ever recorded as Emma but I believe a strong case can be made for her to be the illegitimate daughter[677] of Judith de Lens and Roger de Busli II, likely born about 1080 (see possible family tree below). In the later 1160 Confirmation Charter of Worksop Priory made by Richard de Lovetot, he details the monks rights to various lands and manors donated by his father, William, but specifically a number made by his mother, Emma, e.g. Rampton, Houghton and Tuxford which were discreet de Busli owned manors—but also Normanton and Car Colston, these having been previously tenanted by her husband William de Lovetot, from the overlord Roger de Busli I. These must have passed to her at some point and perhaps explains why her husband was treated so well by the new king (she being the 'illegitimate' daughter of the king's late cousin, Judith).

---

[677] The chronicler of Croyland Abbey uses the specific word 'jezebel' when describing Judith, which defines as a 'shameless and wicked woman', and perhaps her treachery of her husband, Waltheof, this affair and lovechild with Roger de Busli II are at the heart of it.

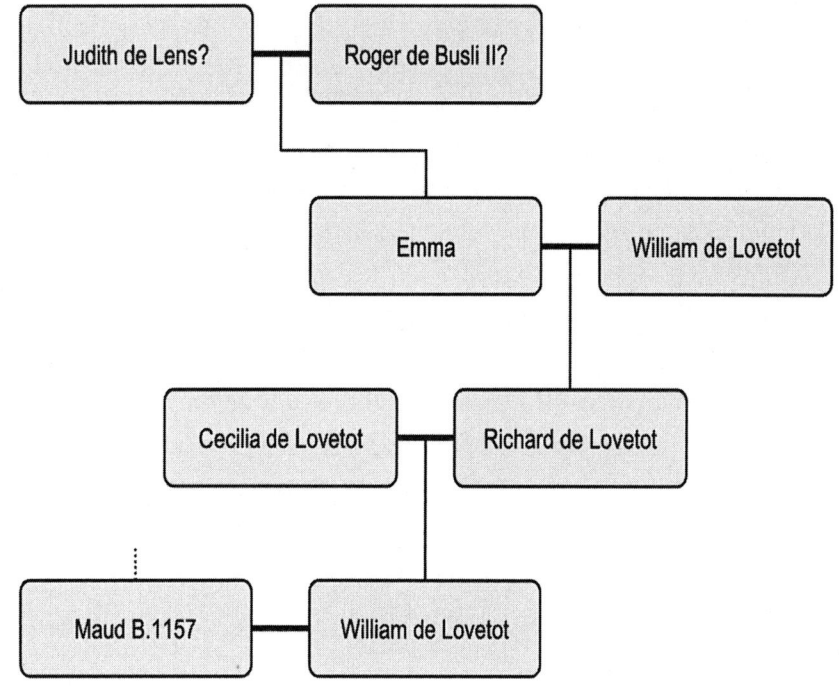

Maud, b.1157, 2 great-granddaughter of Judith and Waltheof via Senlis and Clare descent

See Appendix 2.1

It seems likely that in 1102/3, William de Lovetot was supporting the new King Henry and was likely militarily involved in supporting Bishop Blouet's siege of Bellême at Tickhill/Blyth castle. He could well be described as one of Henry's 'new men'. Did his young wife, Emma (22), let herself become yet another sexual conquest of King Henry; married women were not off his radar? She was, as a daughter of Judith de Lens, Henry's second cousin, albeit illegitimate (and a sort of step-sister of Robin!), and just maybe as a consequence she obtained great favour for her de Lovetot husband in grants of the confiscated lands of Bellême, the Honour of Tickhill, which had previously been those of her grandfather, Roger de Busli I, a stalwart follower of Henry's father, William the Conqueror. Following the deaths of Judith, Roger II and Robin, the couple,

Emma and William de Lovetot, also then acquired Hallam, other manors and rights to build the castle in Sheffield.

I am tempted to go further and propose that at least one more illegitimate offspring may have come from this Judith/Roger partnership and that the Jeremiah mentioned above derived from this line. The parents being unmarried and the children being illegitimate, they would be unable to legally take the de Busli name and almost inevitably, like the 'de Locksley' of Robin/Robert, they attached the suffix of '*de Ecclesfield*' as a surname.

It would make logical sense that any remnants of this family would have clung on to any income source they could find. As they did not inherit the big estates, now forfeit, they would have needed to find an easy living. Being a beneficiary of incomes from Ecclesfield would seem to fit the bill well, and just 4 miles from the relative comfort and safety of their cousin Richard de Busli's manor and castle at Kimberworth. Also, even though they had lost those of Ecclesfield, Hallam and Sheffield to the de Lovetots, their sister had married into that line and they were in fact continuing the Judith de Lens/de Busli bloodline…

Appendix 8

282 Lyth and lysten, gentil men,
And herken what I shall say,
How the proud[e] sheryfe of Notyngham
Dyde crye a full fayre play;
283 That all the best archers of the north
Sholde come upon a day,
And [he] that shoteth all ther best
The game shall bere a way.
(from the fifth fytte of Child Ballad 117: *The Geste of Robyn Hode*)

Robin Hood was 'the greatest archer in all England', with almost supernatural skills, or so the legend would have us believe. In truth though, his famous skills in the arts of being a warrior have left him wanting in almost all of the early ballads, being bested by better men. Little John and others beat him on more than one occasion and Robin does not take this graciously at all; he is almost petulant and receives defeat with bad grace. Despite this, his fame with the longbow (along with taking from the rich and giving to the poor), is surely the one feature of the man that everyone thinks of when his name crops up and as such, a brief look at how this sits with our Robin in an eleventh-century context is necessary. It should be pointed out that the shooting of people with an arrow (much like the famed redistribution of wealth!) is a rarity and only occurs 3 times in the early Robin Hood ballads, 2 occasions being in *Robin Hood and Guy of Gisborne* (Child Ballad 118) and both shot by Little John, killing William of Trent, one of the sheriff's men and the sheriff himself respectively.

Stanza 299 Full many a bow there was bent,
And arrows let they glide;
Many a *kyrtell* (*short tunic*) there was rent (torn),
And hurt many a side.
Stanza 302 Little John was hurt full sore,
With an arrow in his knee,
That he might neither go nor ride;
It was full great pity.

The third occasion is in the 6th fytte (stanzas 347/348) of *The Gest,* when Robin shoots the sheriff and before he can recover, cuts his head off!

It seems archery (or that recorded) is mainly restricted to hunting, tournaments run by the sheriff and displays of skill between the Merry Men, themselves very clearly 'yeomen archers'—foresters and huntsmen. Where death is meted out by Robin or his men, swords are the weapon of choice.

The longbow was rapidly improved and developed in design after the Battle of Hastings, and in essence looks to have been a development of the Welsh bow, which was the true design forerunner of the more famed English longbow. The Welsh bow seems to have been around well before AD 1000, but it is not known if it developed there independently or if it was borrowed from other parts of Europe, but the most informed view is that it probably arrived with the Viking raids of the 10th century based on surviving examples in Scandinavia. The key difference from the Norman bow was that the Welsh drew their longer bow to the face/ear, not the chest, allowing for a) a much longer arrow, b) more power and c) greater accuracy.

**63. Very early image of an English bow, back quiver and hunting dog
extract from the illuminated Old English Hexateuch, c.1040**
Courtesy of British Library Images, Cotton MS Claudius B IV. F.41.v. part.

In every cinematic and TV representation of Robin and his men (including this book cover), they always keep their arrows in a back quiver. However, the general consensus among all the experts in this field is that in combat or while hunting, archers, almost universally, mounted their quiver at their hip, on one's belt. This is certainly borne out by the embroidery of Norman archers on the Bayeaux tapestry (and later medieval images), which also show arrows being held in the left hand and in ground mounted quivers (with just one exception having the more recognisable back quiver), such that maybe personal choice prevailed. I suspect that when simply travelling about, especially in woodland or on horseback, the positioning of the quiver on the back would have proved more accommodating with less chance of fletchings becoming snagged or damaged, as shown in the image above.

Young Robin and his father may well have observed that the longbow was an ideal weapon for guerilla fighters/ambushers and the Welsh used it to fight off attacks from the English before the end of the 11th century in the border campaigns of William Rufus and his father. There is reliable evidence of Welsh archery, 11 years before Hastings, in the account of Ralph 'the Timid', Earl of Hereford (d.1057), on the expedition he led into Wales. When the Saxon horsemen had ridden into the Welsh mountains they were ambushed by archers who shot so accurately and strongly that, according to the Abingdon Chronicle, *'the English people fled, before ever a spear had been thrown, because they were on horseback'*. One estimate from the time puts the English casualties at 5 hundred while the Welsh suffered no losses. Here was a lesson that, if the Saxons had learnt from it, could have changed the outcome of the Battle of Hastings; cavalry are helpless against well-ordered archers; sadly though, only **one** lonely looking Saxon archer appears on the whole Bayeux Tapestry, being depicted without mail or a helmet and it is believed made small, both in size and solo depiction, to represent the meagre number of English archers at the battle whereas the Normans were reckoned to have a thousand.[678]

Only Gerald of Wales[679] emphasises pre-Norman use of the bow on our island and this in Wales. Waltheof and teenage son Robin could well have been exposed to this weapon while involved in skirmishes with Welsh marauders around 1073–4, when completing the building of the motte and Bailey Huntington Castle (also known as, or recorded in historical documents as; Huntingdon; Huntedon; Huntindon; Huntinton[680]) which significantly sits right on the English/Welsh border in south Herefordshire, bordering Gwent, historically the emergent area of Welsh longbow archery. There is a strong possibility that this Huntington Castle project was one Waltheof was personally charged with completing under the aegis of his friend, Roger de Breteuil[681], the

---

[678] In Domesday there is recorded a certain Fulcher 'the Bowman'. This is an old Anglo-Saxon name and he held no places before the Conquest and just 7, all as Tenant-in-Chief, afterwards (all around Exeter in Devon). He may have been a bow maker but more likely a mercenary archer and these lands were the reward for fighting for the Norman invader.

[679] *Itinerarium Kambriae et descriptio Kambriae*, Gerald of Wales, ed. J. F. Dimock, London, 1868, pp.123, 177, 179

[680] Details from **GATEHOUSE**: The comprehensive gazetteer and bibliography of the medieval castles, fortifications and palaces of England, Wales, the Islands.

[681] His father, William FitzOsbern 1st Earl of Hereford, a relative and close counsellor of William the Conqueror, was the great Marcher Lord in South Wales and who built numerous castles including Chepstow and Monmouth.

2nd Earl of Hereford (he of the 'Revolt of the Earls', whose sister was married at the 'Bride-ale of Norwich' a year or so later, in 1075), and hence how it got its name—after Waltheof's title of Earl of Huntingdon. Roger had inherited his title and lands after his father, the first Earl of Hereford, had died in 1071. Waltheof had already built Durham Castle in 1072 for his friend, the then Bishop William Walcher, as defence against the Scots (and restless locals) in the bishop's role (later, after Waltheof's death, as Earl of Northumbria and Prince Bishop) of protecting England's northern frontier such that Waltheof was clearly fully qualified in this form of Norman construction. Waltheof could readily have justified his co-operation with the Normans, as keeping the Scots and in this case the Welsh, subdued, was a firm English policy as well.

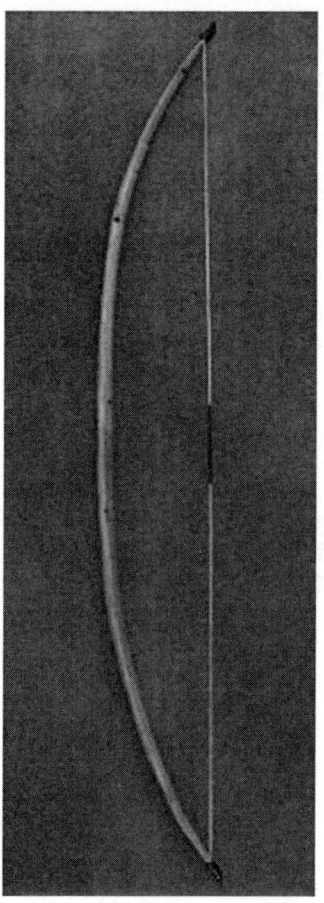

64. Replica early English Longbow made from a single yew stave.
Image in the public domain courtesy of James Cram, Hitchhiker89 at Wikipedia

Apart from the Bayeux Tapestry and other illustrated sources, there are many written references to the bow, the most notable being in the epic Beowulf and also those in a renowned poem 'The Battle of Maldon' (991ad—75 years prior to Hastings—and generally agreed to have been composed very soon after the event). This was when the Anglo-Saxon Earl of Essex, Byrhtnoth, led his thegns, unsuccessfully, against the Viking invaders led by Swein Forkbeard, and it has direct relevance to the Robin Hood of Saxon-Danish heritage of the 11th century.

'And yet no warrior could injure another, except by the flight of a feathered arrow'.

'Bowstrings were busy, shield parried point'.

'The hostage helped them with all his might—his name was Æscferth, the son of Ecglaf; he came from a brave family in Northumbria. He did not flinch in the battle-play but shot his arrows as fast as he could. Sometimes he hit a shield, sometimes he pierced a man, again and again he inflicted wounds for as long as he could hold a bow in his hands'.

The first 2 extracts from the poem tell us that bows were being used, but not who was using them (Saxon or Viking, Highborn or low). The third extract, above, tells us that Æscferth was a hostage and that he 'came from a brave family of sturdy stock in Northumbria'. To be of any use as a hostage he would have to have been fairly highborn, most likely from the House of Bamburgh, so one could argue that the upper ranks did use the bow in war, however we also know he came from Northumbria, an area heavily influenced by the Vikings so he could have just been carrying on the Viking tradition for archery. Amongst the Danes/Vikings, archery was quite widely used by both high and low born and surely an influence on both Waltheof and especially his son, Robert (Robin).

The inclusion of expert archery in the stories has often been used as a vehicle to point to a later rather than earlier date for Robin, but as J.C. Holt (1989) says, 'this has not proved convincing', even Waltz[682] concedes that the earliest dating must be from 1066. Despite its effectiveness, the bow was generally scorned by the gentry in the 11th and 12th centuries as a weapon of war, though used early on for hunting. The chivalric skills of sword, lance and horsemanship prevailed—in battle the bow was for use by yeoman, peasants and mercenaries.

---

[682] *The Gest of Robyn Hode: A Critical and Textual Commentary,* Waltz, Robert, (History. E-Books, 2013)

As early as 1120, bows were banned in Flanders in an effort to keep the peace and, in 1139 at the second Lateran Council, they forbade the hiring of bowmen (and crossbowmen) against other Christians![683]

Medieval military historian, Jim Bradbury, points out that the word 'longbow' does not appear in any of the early ballads, and further develops this point regarding differentiation. There is no given definition of a 'longbow', which is more a derivative of the stature of the archer than anything else, and the prefix 'long' was simply used to distinguish it from the crossbow or the shortbow proper. He produces a wide range of evidence regarding the use of bows of some considerable length in the eleventh century, and concludes that the average bow at that time was around 5 feet long, and this extended to 6 feet in the following 3 centuries. Near Kirby Moorside (on the Yorkshire Moors), one finds St Gregory's Minster, a church rebuilt in about 1060 by Orm (Waltheof's uncle) whose son Gamel was murdered by Tostig in 1064. On one of the surviving 11th century Anglo-Danish tomb markers (thought to be of a huntsman and today known as the 'archer stone') is a carving of a bow (with arm) that is very clearly a large English-style longbow which is proof enough of these large weapons being in use during the 11th century, probably prior to the Conquest.

---

[683] *The Medieval Archer* , Jim Bradbury, The Boydell Press, 1985, p. back 1996.

65. St Gregory's Minster 11th century 'archer stone' tomb marker
© photo courtesy of Lionel Wall (greatenglishchurches.co.uk)

There is also surviving graffiti on a wall of Colchester castle of a figure wielding a longbow which while hard to date has been suggested as being Norman, from the early 12th century, when the castle was being hugely extended by the then owner, Eudo Dapifer.

Everyone associates the longbow with the Hundred Years War, which started in the 1330s, but as Bradbury asks 'how long had that weapon been in existence prior?' He concludes that this is as difficult a question to answer as the dating of the time of Robin Hood, or with as much certainty. His summation is that the bow of the Hundred Years War was not fundamentally different from that of the previous 2 centuries. There is no need, he says, to seek for the invention of a new weapon, and there is certainly no evidence that a truly new weapon had been developed.

What is true is that the social standing, status, popularity and romance of the yeoman archer grew over the centuries of the medieval period. This characteristic of Robin Hood certainly weaves its way into the later ballads of the sixteenth and seventeenth centuries, since the heroics of the common archer at the victories at Crécy and Agincourt had now raised the yeoman archer into a new higher social status, and become the ideal personification of a folk hero for the common people.

66. Carved image of a longbow archer on a wall of Colchester Castle dated to Norman times.

Image from *The Medieval Archer* by Jim Bradbury, courtesy of Boydell Press

As I said, it would seem quite possible, probable even, that the great warrior Waltheof and his teenage 'woodsman' and 'bastard' son had picked up on the great effectiveness of the Welsh weapon, recognising its awesome power and accuracy, and which in design, form, and performance was significantly superior to any Norman or Saxon equivalent for 'stand-off killing'. From such observations, coupled with exposure and experience against the Welsh, they may well have been fundamental in the design and development of the English equivalent (1072–75), particularly as it could be used with greater effect for hunting and competitions, as well as warfare.

Was this why Robin, having already absorbed the military skills learnt from his father (particularly swordsmanship), the guerrilla tactics of the '*silvatici*', allied to the 'forester' and hunting heritage of his mother's Locksley family, became so proficient in the use of the bow...maybe even the greatest archer in England? What is sure is that within just forty years, contemporary sources confirm, for the first time, the devastating use of English archers in the Battle of the Standard at Northallerton in 1138, during the early part of the 'The Anarchy' Civil War, when they decimated the charging Scottish line of King David's forces that were then routed by King Stephen.

A number of the long-standing legends of Robin Hood, as in the Geste and like *Robin and the Golden Arrow* (Child Ballad 152), revolve around archery contests. The winner of these would receive a silver or golden arrow as a prize— or a beautiful noble girl for a wife! This is often depicted as the hand of the king's niece in marriage, perhaps being a later confusion over the marriage of Robin's father, Waltheof, to the king's niece. Most often the girl put up as a 'prise' is also depicted as the daughter or 'ward' of the sheriff. Robin knew, of course, that if he attended the contest he would be captured and so he went to the competition disguised, where he competed and won. Owing to their disguise (which, somewhat unconvincingly, seem to be coloured shirts instead of Lincoln green!), the sheriff does not recognise them and is only advised he was duped by letter, delivered attached to an arrow fired by Little John into the town. In other versions, the sheriff knows Robin will attend incognito and, at the moment of Robin's triumph, has him arrested. Robin's men soon come to the rescue. The night before Robin is due to be hanged for high treason against the Crown, his band of Merry Men sneak past the dungeon guards and spirit him away.

As stated from the outset, it is not the intention to try to dissect all these tales in the context of my chosen timeframe, but only to mention something, an event, that appears not to have been closely observed before. In White's 1857 *Directory of Derbyshire* (pp. 526–536) I came across (and latterly in various other publications) a description of how a splendid tournament was held at Peveril Castle in the time of the first of the Peverils (though no precise date is given).

The circumstances of this occasion somewhat mirror the stories of the legend and although no direct link to Robin Hood, no-one seems to have mentioned it previously.

67. Later depiction of a 14th century tournament mêlée when plate armour was used.
In the 11th-13th centuries, only a padded tunic and chainmail would have offered protection.
Public domain image from *'Le Livre des Tournois'*, René d'Anjou, Bibliotheque Nationale, Paris, MS 2693, ff62.2v-63 (c.1460)

The Norman Lord notionally in charge of the Welsh Marches, and childhood friend of William the Conqueror, was Roger de Montgomery (1030–94, who married Mabel de Bellême), who looks to have been granted Whittington Castle (near Oswestry, Shropshire in the Welsh Marches) by William Peveril, who is generally credited with its original construction. It seems Montgomery and Peveril then gave the original castle to William's half-brother, Pain Peveril, who then built a new castle on the site and became Lord of Whittington. The genealogy of the Peverils is, unsurprisingly, somewhat unclear. In most versions

Pain Peveril[684] is, indeed, said to be the younger half-brother of William Peveril (Local High Sheriff and owner of Peveril Castle, location of the tournament in Castleton, Derbyshire). Both the boys were sons of their mother Maud but Pain's father was her husband, Ranulph Peveril[685]. Pain Peveril, Lord of Whittington, had 2 daughters, one of whom, named Mellet (or Miletta or Matilda)[686], was no less distinguished by a martial spirit than her father, and she declared that she was resolved to marry no-one but a Knight of great prowess. To this end, her father, to satisfy her wishes, invited all the eligible young men—who were inclined to enter the lists, to meet at Peveril's Place, in the Peak, and *'there decide their pretensions by the use of arms, declaring at the same time, that whoever vanquished his competitors should receive his daughter, along with his castle at Whittington'*—quite a prize! Following an 'It's a Knockout' type competition, Guarine de Metz, a descendant of the house of Lorraine, and an ancestor of the Lords FitzWarreine, vanquished all opponents, who included a son of the King of Scotland[687] and a Baron Burgoyne, and thus obtained the prises for which he fought—young Mellet and a castle.

In this version of the tale, Mellet is Pain Peveril's daughter (the commonly accepted version and that she is to be the heiress of her father) and he gives Whittington Castle as a dowry to the successful champion and son-in-law to be. The form of this tournament might be debated, as one-on-one jousting did not feature in tournaments this early, but took the form of a general mêlée with dozens, even hundreds, of knights over a large arena or rural area—not the best way to determine a singular winner unless it was 'last man standing', à la a

---

[684] Pain Peverel went on Crusade in 1096 and was the standard bearer for Robert Curthose. Upon his return he evidently found favour with the new King, Henry I (his half-uncle), being granted the barony of Brunne (today Bourn) in Cambridgeshire, as much a reward for his loyalty to the royal family as for his crusading exploits. These estates look to have been among those forfeited by Robert Picot (son of the late Sheriff of Cambridgeshire) for siding with Robert Curthose against King Henry in 1101.

[685] Ranulph, a supporter of the Conqueror, was very probably at the Battle of Hastings, or certainly provided men and materials and was thus rewarded by the new King with manorial rights in 75 places mostly in Suffolk, Norfolk and Essex.

[686] Mellet is said to have been younger and more beautiful than her elder sister, Hawise, and 'a bit of a handful'!. Unreliable genealogy gives her birth as c.1075, which does however work well for the tournament being in 1093 when she is 18.

[687] If, as I believe this was Malcolm Canmore III, he had 9 sons such that it is unclear to whom this refers but probably either Prince Edgar or Edmund.

demolition Derby! Although blunted lances and swords were used, blows to the throat or groyne, for example, could prove fatal. The 13th century French romance, the *Castellan of Coucy*, although a work of fiction, captures the dangers of jousting in the following passage:

The next day the joust continued [until] only 3 knights were left, the others all being wounded...At the first pass the Castellan knocked down his adversary's helmet into the dust, and blood ran from his mouth and nose...On the third try both men were disarmed and fell unconscious to the ground. Valets, sergeants and squires laid them on their shields, and carried them from the field...but it was only, thank God, a passing unconsciousness, neither man was dead. (Gies, 182)

One version suggests a mêlée was held on day 1 and then the top dozen 'surviving' competitors went through to a Knockout tournament on Day 2 and this particular 'competition' was seemingly held inside the castle walls, in the Bailey. It may well have featured specific competitions of the martial arts (fights with sword, mace, axe for example) maybe jousting and even including archery but we are unfortunately spared the details. The competitors seem to have come from countrywide, even France, Normandy, Burgundy and Brittany.

The champion of this remarkable medieval bash is understood to have been Guarine (Guy) Warreine de Metz[688], described in the *G.E.C. Complete Peerage* as 'a shadowy or mystical figure' but, as history records, did indeed marry Peveril's daughter, Mellet. It would appear that Guarine was helping Roger de Montgomery defend the Welsh Marches at this time and there would look to be a familial link between them. Although no date is specified precisely it can be calculated roughly by the birth and wedding dates of Guarine and Mellet, suggesting they were both born about 1075 and that the tournament took place maybe around 1093–4, a period of constant Welsh raids on the border.

This random little tale has 2 most interesting connections to our story though not, I believe, any possibility of Robin having taken part! The first is regarding the great-grandson of Guarine Warreine de Metz. He was called Fulk de Warreine, born about 85 years later in 1175; the name Fulk was used by almost

---

[688] Guarine is recorded in some places as being Sheriff of Shropshire and chief counsellor to the great Earl of Shrewsbury, Roger de Montgomery d.1096, father of both Robert de Bellême and Roger the Poitevin.

all the male descendants of this family for generations (which makes individual identification tricky sometimes!). He lived in the latter part of the twelfth century and is often mooted, as a result of being recorded in medieval French romance, as having provided the basis for a number of the Robin Hood legends and stories, which show a surprising number of parallels and hence are worthy of some further investigation.

The traditional story of Fulk's life survives in a French prose 'ancestral romance', extant in a miscellaneous manuscript containing English, French and Latin texts, which is based on a lost verse romance. A sixteenth-century summary of a Middle-English version has also been preserved. According to the tale, as a young boy Fulk was sent to the Court of King Henry II, where he grew up with Henry's son, the future King John, of whom he was an exact contemporary. John, who seems to have had a short fuse and a long memory, became his enemy after a childhood quarrel when, as I understand it, John, probably a bad loser, broke a chessboard over Fulk's head who retaliated by kicking John in the stomach. However when John went crying to his father, it was John who was beaten for complaining and being a bad loser. As an adult, Fulk rebelled against his childhood friend, now King John (1199–1216) from 1200 to 1203, mainly over a dispute concerning his familial right to the Whittington Castle, 'won' (along with his great-grandmother!) by his great-grandfather over a century earlier at the Peveril tournament. He was stripped of his family's holdings by King John and took to the woods, having been declared an outlaw. This enmity was not helped by the fact Fulk's father had been a loyal supporter and highly regarded friend of John's elder brother, the late King Richard I, the Lionheart. The story may combine aspects of the lives of the 2 Fulk FitzWarins, father and son, who lived in the late twelfth and early thirteenth centuries.

The story relates his life as an outlaw and his struggle to regain his patrimony from the king. It is written in Anglo-Norman and survives in a miscellany of some sixty works in Latin, French and English, dated c.1325–40. The prose romance is based on a thirteenth-century poetic version, now lost, and another version in Middle English is similarly lost. The first third of the ancestral romance traces the history of the FitzWarin family from the Norman Conquest to the late twelfth century, and recounts the opportunistic marriages of Fulk's great-grandfather, Warin de Metz (to Mellet after the tournament), and that of his father, Fulk le Brun, to 2 propertied heiresses, resulting in their lordship over

Whittington and Ludlow. As the first part ends, the family loses control of both properties.

The last two-thirds of the romance covers the career of Fulk FitzWarin III, who after a four-year period (1200–1203) of rebellion and outlawry in the time of King John finally wins back his lands (including Whittington Castle) and titles. Of interest here is the outlaw narrative, consisting of the now familiar elements. After an argument with King John, who refuses to return his lands and titles, Fulk renounces his homage and leaves the court. When fifteen of the king's knights pursue Fulk and order him to return, he responds by killing fourteen, leaving one alive to report the incident—not unlike a story in the ballad *Robin's Progress to Nottingham* (Chapter 3).

Fleeing to Brittany, Fulk is outlawed and stripped of his remaining lands. Returning to England, he hides in the forests, assembles a group of loyal knights, and plays a deadly game of Hide and Seek with the king's agents. Like other documented outlaws such as Hereward the Wake and Eustace Monk, Fulk and his second-in-command, John de Rampaigne, don various disguises—as a monk, a merchant, a collier—to avoid detection and to gather information.

Three scenes in particular remind us of Robin Hood: like Little John in the *Geste*, Fulk's sidekick (also called John!) waylays a caravan of merchants travelling through the forest and delivers them into Fulk's hands; in another episode, King John, like the sheriff in the *Geste*, is tricked into the forest, where he is captured and later released after swearing an oath; and finally, Fulk's brother William, after being severely wounded, begs his brother to kill him, as Little John begs Robin in the *Geste*. There are significant differences between Fulk FitzWarin and Robin Hood, but the core of the outlaw narrative is substantially the same.

Although the careers of those like Eustace and Fulk, particularly the resistance to King John, sound familiar to film-goers, these features were added to the original Robin Hood story. The hero of the early ballads, and indeed many of the later texts, was never dated in the time of King John. That timeframe, of around 1193–94, was first suggested by John Major in a history of Britain published in 1521, but does not appear to be backed up by any evidence or proof, and seems to have been part of a general movement towards making Robin more respectable. If, like Fulk, he opposed a bad king as a dispossessed lord, then his resistance was, in a real sense, in support of the existing structures of authority—

very different from the guerrilla tactics against Forest Laws and sheriff's rule, which are found elsewhere in the medieval texts.

A summation of all this is that the original great-grandfather of Fulk, namely Guarine de Metz, either knew Robin himself or certainly, by 1093, was totally immersed in contemporary tales after thirteen years of Robin's exploits (particularly in William Peveril's territory), which would have unfolded during his lifetime and been on everyone's lips, if not on parchment. Would he not have passed down all the stories and legends to his son and indeed, grandson? He knew Robin Hood after all and this fact and the tales would impress any child as the legend was already spreading throughout the land via the minstrels attached to the large baronial families, who travelled between properties in different parts of the country. Consequently, I believe these stories have become intertwined with the Warreine's own family storytelling and that of the poets and troubadours maybe, and most likely copied by the outlawed great-grandson a century later.

If, as suggested, this tournament took place in about 1093, Robin's young sister, Maud 20, had only been married for about 3 years to the fifty-something Simon de Senlis. Was this the same tournament of legend, where archers were brought to the castle supposedly for a competition to find the greatest bowman of all, with the prise of the beautiful Mellet (then 18) and a castle thrown in, when it was really a trick to catch Robin? One suspects not, but whatever the answer, if as suggested, this all occurred around 1093, Robin would have been about 35 years old and at the height of his powers.

Appendix 9

APPENDIX 9
Walter Tyrell and the Clares - half first cousins

Richard I Duke of Normandy

Geoffrey Count of Eu

Gilbert 2nd Count of Brionne And Eu

Constance of Eu

Ann de Brionne

Alice de Clare — WALTER TYRELL III

Walter Tyrell II

Richard III Duke of Normandy

Robert I Duke of Normandy

Gunnora d'Avnou?

Elisie de Brionne — William Malet

Robert Malet

Richard de Clare

Rohese Giffard

Roger de Clare

Maud de Senlis I — de Clare

Robert de Clare

Richard de Clare

Rohese de Clare

Eudo Dapifer

Margaret — William de Mandeville

Geoffrey de Mandeville 1st Earl of Essex

Duplicate: Alice du Clare

Gilbert de Clare

Alice de Claremont

Margaret de Clare — William de Montfichet

Alice de Clare

Aubrey de Vere II

Rohese de Vere — Geoffrey de Mandeville 1st Earl of Essex

Isabel de Beaumont — Gilbert de Clare

485

Appendix 9a

Walter Tyrell and the Clares Half-First Cousins

Genealogy for pre-conquest England and France, is shaky to say the least, but over the centuries antiquarians, genealogists and historians have done their level best, using all the various archival records, to stitch together the familial connections of all the leading players. This was, of course, long before records of births, marriages and deaths became standard practice and such evidence that there is, comes from the scant surviving official pedigrees, writs, charters, monastic foundations, wills, chronicles, legal and court records etc. much content of which is in itself, readily accepted as being somewhat untrustworthy. Many of these early 'family trees' are strewn with errors but have gradually been amended over time by more assiduous researchers[689] such that I give it my best shot!

What crops up (and the primary source for such claims cannot be identified) is the possibility that Walter Tyrell was not just a brother-in-law to the Clares but also a first cousin (half, to be precise). It is proposed in a variety of sources that he and the Clare siblings shared the same grandfather, Gilbert 'Crispin' de Brionne, but had different grandmothers (as Gilbert married twice) although it must be admitted that like a great deal of 11th century genealogy, the Crispin line is notoriously convoluted and uncertain. Walter's mother is understood to have been Ann de Brionne, who had married Walter's father, Walter Tyrell II—Ann being the daughter of Gilbert (2nd Count of Brionne and 2nd Count of Eu, d.1040), by his second wife, Constance d'Eu.

---

[689] A good example of this are the early notations that Walter Tyrell's wife, Alice, was a Giffard and seemingly confusing her with her mother, Rohese, the sister of Walter Giffard. This is now widely corrected although you will still find this persistent error on some genealogy websites.

It was a knight called Herluin (c.996–1078) at the court of Count Gilbert who subsequently became a Benedictine monk and founded Bec Abbey in 1034 becoming its first abbot. Herluin is often referred to as Saint Herluin but was not canonised. Brionne is just 3 miles from Bec Abbey.

The father of the Clare brothers though, was Richard FitzGilbert de Clare, a son by Gilbert's first wife, who was probably Gunnora d'Aunou, making Richard a half-brother of Tyrell's mother, Anne, who in turn was thus an aunt (half) of the Clare boys and their sister Alice, Walter's wife. (all is a good deal clearer with a brief study of the family tree—Appendix 9/9a). This certainly goes some way to explain how the marriage of Walter and Alice (half-cousins) may have come to pass and more relevantly, his direct involvement in the regicide of Rufus with the Clares was more than just a brother-in-law.

Resources:

A Genealogical History of the Tyrrells, Sometime of the French Vexin, Poix in Picardy, by John Henry Terrell (privately published. 1904).

Further Genealogical Notes on the Tyrrell-Terrell Family of Virginia and its English and Norman-French Progenitors. By Edwin H. Terrell (privately published, 1909).

'Walter Tirel and his wife'—Feudal England: Historical studies on the eleventh and twelfth centuries, by J.H. Round, first published 1895, third impression 1909.

Foundation for Medieval Genealogy: https://fmg.ac/

Appendix 10

Robin Hood, May Games and Celtic Folklore
But how many merry moones be in the yeare?
There are thirteen, I say;
The midsummer moone is the merryest of all,
Next to the merry month of May.
(*Robin Hood and the Curtal Friar,* Child Ballad 123, 1st stanza,
Percy Folio version)

One of the more widely held views as to the origins of Robin Hood is that he never existed at all and is solely a figure of mythical legend and Celtic and/or Saxon folklore. Poet Robert Graves, in his *English and Scottish Ballads* (Heinemann, London, 1957), used the stanza at the top of this page to support his argument for pagan survivals in the Robin Hood legend, and for the popular survival of a supposedly pagan thirteen-month calendar.[690] As such, it would seem churlish not to give these views some due attention and consideration. At present, there is little or no scholarly support that the tales or genesis of the Robin Hood legend stemmed from folklore, fairies or other mythological origins. However, many people still believe, as in Lord Raglan's *The Hero: A Study in Tradition, Myth and Drama* (Methuen, 1935) and Lewis Spence's *The Supernatural Character of Robin Hood* (Hibbert Journal 40:280, 1941), that he evolved out of the myriad of pagan and fertility figures of the forest, like the Green Man, Robin Goodfellow, Puck, John Barleycorn, Robin of the Wood, Jack-in-the-Green and the Garland King. During the medieval era of the

---

[690] The thirteenth or 'blue moon' is a phenomenon that occurs because full moons take place every 29.53 days—which means the lunar 'year' of 12 cycles lasts just over 354 days. This, of course, means the lunar year comes in almost 11 days shorter than the time it takes the Earth to orbit the sun, resulting in some years having 'extra' full moons. They occur about every two or three years.

fourteenth and fifteenth centuries, most of these became associated with either the May Day or Whitsun springtime festivals and/or the late summer festivities of the first harvest at Lammastide at the beginning of August. Perhaps the key figure is that of the Green Man, a face which is made of, spouting or completely surrounded by, leaves and often symbolises British folklore. It has many variations, branches or vines may sprout from the mouth, nostrils, or other parts of the face. It is a symbol of rebirth and a motif carved into many English churches, and it is he who morphed easily into the character of Robin Hood at this time and many academics feel that the traditions of the Green Man and the Wild Man influenced the growth of the Robin Hood legend.

Back as far as the 16th century, this 'mythological theory' was promulgated by Reginald Scot (*The Discoverie of Witchcraft*: *Treatise upon the Nature and Substance of Spirits and Devils,* 1584), who identified Robin with the Teutonic elf 'Hodekin' and associated him with Robin Goodfellow, as clearly the similarity of names suggested a link. He is perhaps better as Puck, the fairy from Shakespeare's 'A Midsummer Night's Dream', a sprite well-known for playing the trickster role and creating 'misrule'...

This general folklore idea was re-started in 1846 by a Victorian antiquarian called Thomas Wright who argued, in his *Essays on the Literature of the Middle Ages* (1861), that Robin Hood was an imported Saxon myth, a 'spirit of the forest', simply 'Robin of the Wood'. This view was later reinforced in the early twentieth-century entry in the *Dictionary of National Biography* on Robin, written by Sir Sydney Lee, who stated that there was little doubt that the origins of Robin *'belonged to a mythical forest-elf who filled a large space in English and apparently Scottish folklore'*. Also around this time, in the mid-19th century, 2 German philologists, Jacob Grimm and Adalbert Kuhn, weighed in with somewhat convoluted theories. The former pushed the Hodekin theory, suggesting a goblin Robin Hood seemed more plausible than an historic one, and the latter created a totally Germanic concept, based around our hero being a corruption of the mythic Ruprecht Wodan. Such flimsy theories are now accepted by no-one, but the mythical origins of Robin Hood still retain some popularity. The historic Robin Hood is a fiction they say, the origin of the hero is an old religious rite—on the details of the rite there is no agreement, perhaps some sort of deity linked to spring and vegetation, with fertility at its core.

It has long been known that Robin Hood (plus often Maid Marian and Friar Tuck) became inextricably linked in popularity with the May Games during the

14th, 15th and 16th centuries, when in the 1300s the original ballad exploits became transmuted into plays accompanied by Morris dances, athletic events, archery competitions and revelry held on festival days but generally at Whitsuntide (49 days after Easter and now commonly known as the Spring Bank Holiday). Within these festivities, Robin loses his dangerous edge and bears no resemblance to the violent common outlaw portrayed in the early medieval writings. In fact it is likely that without Robin's invasion and domination of the May Games for 3 centuries, his legend would not exist as we now have it. Any vestiges of the religious festival of Pentecost seemed to have dissipated and it even became more commonly known as 'Robin Hood's Day'. Villagers and townsfolk would dress up in outlaw garb and in high party mood (bad behaviour, sexual shenanigans and excessive drinking were key features!) dance around the village or town collecting money for good causes, perhaps the lingering remnant from the last line of the Geste, *he did poor men much good*'. In the spirit of the 'fertility' element, there was usually a play in which Robin takes his May Queen (Marian) into the woods where the 'Abbot of Unreason' (Friar Tuck) would bless their 'coupling'. It is said the numerous resulting illegitimate children born in the following January, following all this frolicking in the woods, were called 'sons of Robin' and are the derivation of the surname 'Robinson'!

The writers mentioned above, and others that followed, have all centred on Robin's involvement in these May Games, pageants, plays, dances and seasonal festivals, based on an assumption that the folklore preceded the ballads (none of these celebrations, to me, suggest any form of 'religious rite' being more pagan in form, linked to fertility rights). The truth though, is that there is no historical evidence for this and Robin is firmly a ballad hero not a hero of ritual drama. There is one fourteenth-century reference, around 1376–79, when an English poet, John Gower, wrote his long poem *Mirour de l'omme*, in French, that has a Robin and Marian participating in rustic festivals.[691] The French Robin and Marian may have become associated with the Robin and Marian of the English May Games, but it is also more likely they developed independently as their romantic version bears no resemblance to the Robin of the ballads.

---

[691] *Mirour de l'Omme* ("the mirror of mankind") is a poem of 29,945 lines by English poet John Gower (c. 1330—October 1408), though written in French, which has a Robin and Marian participating in rustic revelry. Gower's major theme is man's salvation and evidence suggests it was completed before 1380.

Well before Englishmen were enjoying rhymes of Robin Hood, Frenchmen were celebrating May Day—perhaps as a vestige of the Ancient Roman festival Floralia, which honoured the goddess of spring and flowers, specifically licentious and pleasure seeking aimed at the common man, the plebeians, rather than the gentry, the patricians. By the 1200s, French commemorations of May Day had become associated with a character named Robin des Bois (Robin of the Woods). This has led some historians to speculate that Robin Hood originated when the practice of celebrating May Day spread to England, and the name Robin des Bois was translated into Middle English, for the Middle-English word for wood was '*whode*', which perhaps, through some sort of mistaken homophony, was transformed into 'hood'.

One other root suggests the name 'Hood' implies the face is 'covered, hidden' and became a nickname for someone who wore such a head covering. Add to this the forename 'Robin', derived from the French '*robe*', the garment that cloaks the body, thus suggesting the person is concealed, totally hidden from view from head to foot, without a persona, often in disguise and within the essential locus of his concealment, the forest canopy his hood and the foliage his clothes, both provide his primary disguise.

There are also references to a Robin and Marian in the early French pastoral play *Le Jeu de Robin et Marian* written in about 1283, by Adam de la Halle. The shepherdess Marian resists the advances of a knight and remains loyal to her lover Robin, and this story became attached to the May Games in France. However, Robin is not an outlaw or an archer, nor is he involved in any exploits resembling the early Robin Hood ballads, although the connection of the 2 names from such an early date, coincidence or not, is intriguing. Did Munday simply draw on this early source as the idea for a lover for Robin and the name of 'Marian', owing to this early association of the 2 characters or from their later link within the May Games? It is understood that Robin Hood pageants existed separately in early times, but soon Robin Hood, Friar Tuck and Maid Matilda or Marian (as the May Maid) were slowly absorbed into rural folklore and became central characters in the English May Games from the fifteenth to early seventeenth century though their popularity peaked during the Tudor period. In fact the May Games became, during those centuries, as a saint's day for the canonised outlaw!

What comes as a surprise to many is that Marian is no stunning and virtuous Olivia de Havilland character but was usually depicted as a bawdy, promiscuous (often with the priest rather than with Robin!) and somewhat overweight figure of fecundity, a sort of pantomime dame, and as such usually played in drag by a man or boy. It seems that by the Tudor period, she was clearly put in a role to wed Robin who had, by then, become 'the man in green' and the spirit of spring during the fertility celebrations.

In 1607, churchwardens in St Cuthbert's parish church in Wells, Somerset, needed money to repair a bell so they held a 'church ale' with a procession involving not only Robin Hood, but also Noah and his Ark, St George and his dragon, the Sultan of Egypt, Morris dancers and giants. These 'Church-ales', as they were called, were not unlike a mixture of village fête and university rag-day. Combining with the Robin Hood/May Day festivals, they were used to raise money, with the proceeds being distributed by the parish to the poor and needy, thus lending credence to the idea of Robin extracting money from the rich and giving to the poor, which has so attached to his name. Historian David Underdown described how in the mid-fifteenth century the May Games were part of a very rich tradition of religious plays, civic processions and pageantry: '*In Cornwall and other counties miracle plays still flourished, and even the small Somerset village of Croscombe could promote an annual cycle of plays and revels, complete with Robin Hood and folk heroes*'.[692]

However, the May Games also embodied a potential undermining of traditional authority with Robin depicted as 'the Lord of Misrule' (a character dating far back to the pagan Roman December festival of *Saturnalia),* and further, it created the conditions for unlicenced sexual behaviour and generally a time of ruckus, drinking, gambling, and overeating. The Scottish historian, John Major, wrote in 1551 that the May celebrations were, '*kept in a tavern, not a church, in such intemperance of eating and drinking as is the enemy of chastity, in dances and lewd songs that are equally her foe*'. In fact in Scotland, in the first half of the 16th century, the May Games with Robin Hood and related plays (particularly with the Abbot of Misrule) became so incredibly popular that by 1555 official hostility rose up to suppress the celebrations. Probably motivated by fear of religious dissension, Scottish authorities attempted to curtail, then

----

[692] '*Revel, Riot, and Rebellion: Popular Politics and Culture in England, 1603–1660*', David Underdown,(Oxford University Press, 1985). It is interesting to note that the numerous surviving histories of Robin Hood games and plays etc. occur in places like Cornwall, Somerset, Norfolk and Scotland—but seemingly never in Yorkshire or Nottinghamshire.

suppress, the Robin Hood revels where he seems to have presided over a variety of '*danssis, farsiis, playis, and gamis*', in which neither the Morris dances, nor Maid Marian and Tuck, played a part. By, decree it became illegal in Scotland to 'chose or impersonate Robin Hood'. Heavy penalties provided that anyone attempting such an office would be 'banished from the realm', and anyone 'choosing people for these impersonations' would be imprisoned for 5 years!

A few years earlier, back in England in 1549, Bishop Hugh Latimer, in a sermon to Edward VI, griped about poor congregations during a visit he made to a town in the 1530s where the church stood almost empty on a Sunday (it must have been Whitsun) because, he was told, '*it is Robyn Hoode's day. The parishe are gone abroad to gather for Robyn Hoode*'. Latimer stated (obliquely suggesting a real rather than fictitious person behind the Robin Hood character):

"*It is no laughing matter…it is a weeping matter, a heavy matter, under the pretence of gathering for Robin Hood, a traitor and a thief, to put out a preacher, to have his office less esteemed, to prefer Robin Hood to the ministration of God's word, and all this hath come of unpreaching prelates. This realm hath be ill provided for, that it hath had such corrupt judgements in it, to prefer Robin Hood to God's word.*"[693]

Reference was made in Part I, chapter one, on the likely loss of much of the pre-reformation material about Robin Hood, a point that needs to be reinforced here. As we know, the May Games and the Robin Hood plays were so popular in Scotland that they were effectively banned by 1555, yet the only surviving play prior to this date is the fragmentary (21 lines) *Robyn Hod and the Shryff off Notyngham*. This apparently dates to around 1475 and circumstantial evidence suggests it was probably performed at the household of Sir John Paston[694] and

---

[693] *Life in Shakespeare's England'*, ed. J. D. Wilson (Cambridge, 1925) p.25

[694] Sir John Paston (before 1442—1479), was a Norfolk landowner. A number of his letters survive among the family correspondence known as the *Paston Letters*, a rich source of historical information on the lives of the English gentry of the period 1422–1509. In one letter he conveys the news to his brother that one of his servants, William Woode, has 'goon in to Bernysdale'—that is, departed without his permission to Robin Hood's haunt in the West Riding of Yorkshire. John laments his leaving because he has not only lost a good servant (the horse-keeper) but seemingly more importantly, a family-sponsored actor in the plays of 'Seynt Jorge' and 'Robynhod and the shryff of

appears to tell a version of the story of Robin Hood and Guy of Gisborne, also featuring the first literary appearance of Friar Tuck. After this, we have to wait until 1560 when the printer William Copland appended 2 plays to his edition of the *Mery Geste of Robyn Hoode*. Copland described the 2 plays on the title page of this edition, as '*a newe playe for to be played in Maye games very plesaunte and full of pastyme*'. He actually published them as one play, without a break in the text, but in reality are 2 separate works: the first is based on a version of the ballad *Robin Hood and the Curtal Friar*; and the second was derived from the opening stanzas of the ballad *Robin Hood and the Potter*.

These plays all seem to contain a lot of mock combat, Robin fights the potter, the friar and the knight (known as Guy of Gisborne in the ballad). There is sword play, battles with the quarterstaff and archery contests. The only conclusion that can be drawn from this is that quite clearly there were numerous other plays based around the oral traditions about Robin Hood being performed at the Games in the 15th and early 16th centuries and they just have not survived. What they contained regarding further stories and evidence of the date of Robin and the appearance of other characters we shall, sadly, never know, but clearly there was a great deal more material in the public domain that we shall never see.

Notyngham' who had acted these out for the last three years at the appropriate times of the year. It has been argued convincingly by Dr John Marshall, senior research fellow at Bristol University, that John Paston was the patron of the play if not the composer.

68. May Day Morris dancers with maypole and pipe and taborer.
(Robin, Marion and Tuck characters bottom right)
Public Domain image from Chambers Book of Days, Ed. Robert Chambers, 1864

In Castleton, site of Peveril Castle (the original 11th century home of the Sheriff of Nottinghamshire and Derbyshire), the villagers have celebrated Garland Day on the 29th May for at least 700 years. It is a typically English blend of paganism and early Christianity. It is also known as, or has become absorbed into, the later Oak Apple Day, which was once celebrated widely throughout the country as Royal Oak Day, remembering the tree up which the king (Charles II) had secreted himself after his escape following the decisive battle of Worcester back in 1651. This was a commemoration of not only Charles's restoration to the English throne on that day in 1660, but also the general restoration of May Day celebrations, which had been banned for the previous 10 years by the Puritan Parliament of Cromwell's Commonwealth. The villagers gather at the church to attach sprigs of oak leaves and tree branches to its tower, which is then topped by a garland of wildflowers picked from fields around the village. A procession through the narrow, crooked streets is led by the Garland King (Robert Goodfellow/Puck) or a Green Man/Jack-in-the-Green type character and his female consort or 'Lady', essentially traditional figures of English May Day parades. It consists of lots of young girls dancing variations of Morris and maypole dances, with numerous stopping-off points, particularly the pubs! Is this an historical remnant or pagan corruption of the real legend of the local outlaw dressed in Lincoln green and 'Marian' maybe, who hid among the forest bowers of the Peak District?

One major early function of these Robin Hood Games was to foster the sport of archery for military purposes and the decline in the bow as a weapon of war with the advent of firearms mirrored the decline in the games. In a similar vein, communities were ceasing to use church 'ales' and May games as a means of fundraising for the needy in the parish, being replaced by a 'Poor Rate' or 'Poor Tax' and closely related to the decline in public 'misrule' in general. This decline in the games moved to the popularity of Robin Hood plays in the 16th century which in turn were replaced by the printed ballads and broadsheets with the wider advent of printing and literacy among the emerging middle class, in the 17th and 18th centuries.

69. Robin Hood in early 17th century May Day revels
(Note the use of contemporary clothing with no attempt to dress him for the
13th century)
Public Domain Image

This tradition of festivals, with which Robin was identified, died out a century after the Restoration, with the coming of the Industrial Revolution, expansion of towns, growth of the urban middle classes and more strictly polarised rural communities, but by this time the immortality of the Robin Hood legend had been assured. This was not, however, before poor old Robin was enlisted by the ruling class to the service of the Crown, which was desperately trying to re-establish its authority after the Restoration. Robin Hood, for so long a symbol of popular independence and resistance to authority by the lower classes, was quickly pressed into service, as he had been the century before, by Henry VIII. As part of the Coronation celebration at Nottingham in 1661 a short play was enacted in which Robin's supposed traditional loyalty to King Richard was carefully exaggerated.

'Robin Hood's nearly 3 centuries in the May Games. Stand, then, as the most important episode in the history of the legend...Robin Hood's role in the May Games made him one of the most spectacular heroes, historical and unhistorical, in English and Scottish history'.[695]

In the 1930s, an Egyptologist, historian and folklorist called Dr Margaret Murray wrote a book that became widely regarded as the definitive work on European witchcraft in the Middle Ages. In her book (*The God of the Witches,* Faber and Faber, 1933), she claimed that Robin Hood derived from a pagan deity worshipped by a witch cult. She went on to make all types of odd claims to do with the numbers of followers in his band, the colour green, the Plantagenets and paganism, the name 'Rabbin', and so on. Subsequent writers like P. Valentine Harris in the 1950s—*The Truth about Robin Hood* (1951) and more recently Steve Wilson—*Robin Hood: The Spirit of the Forest* (1993) have disparaged and discredited all these ideas, and no historical evidence was ever put forward by Murray to back up her somewhat fanciful claims which are now widely dismissed. In another wild claim in her book, Ms Murray presents her case, or more accurately 'notorious fantasies', to prove 'Divine Kingship' for Joan of Arc, Gilles de Rais, Thomas Becket and also, William Rufus, suggesting that there are many similarities between their respective deaths, and that each was a willing sacrifice—a divine victim. In William's case, she claims he was an adherent of the Old Religion (paganism and witches), and was a devil

---

[695] *'The May Games and the Robin Hood Legend', The Journal of American Folklore,* W. E. Simeone, Vol. 64, No. 253 (July-September 1951), pp. 265–274

worshipper. She claimed that apparently his dream the night before showed that Rufus knew of his impending demise, and went willingly as a victim in the afternoon after a pagan festival of fertility, Lammas. She ignores virtually all the contrary evidence and does not draw the obvious conclusion—that the death was indeed premeditated regicide. Although she gained some support in the interwar years for her 'Witch-Cult Hypothesis', today, Murray is regarded as a bit of a crack-pot and her works have been denounced by critics and historians.

Back to Robin, it seems that the most overriding evidence that this 'mythical' Robin is indeed, a myth, are the surviving stories themselves. In none of the ballads are Robin or his followers ever given supernatural powers. Surely if derived from mythical pagan forest spirits then some of the pagan motifs would be evident. Robin is not immortal, there are no curses, wands, spells, visions or prophecies, and any tangible connections to the gods of Norse mythology are absent. Although Robin is perhaps the greatest archer in England, this is not through having a magic bow like the supernatural powers of a King Arthur's sword, Excalibur. Indeed, until the popular British TV series in the 1980s, *Robin of Sherwood*, where he is cast as the son of the forest god, Herne the Hunter[696], no link has ever been made in the telling of the Robin Hood stories, unlike in the arthurian legends, with mythology, Holy Grails, dragons, witches, magicians or goblins. What I will concede is that the great royal forests represented mystery, especially to those not allowed to enter them. Robin's refuge in these woods was in open defiance to the laws and gave the woods a 'mystical' quality about them, even long after much of these woods had been cut down. According to John Bellamy, *"Woods like Sherwood Forest often had all kinds of ghost stories or other superstitions linked with them, the fact that an outlaw like Robin Hood could live in them, fascinated people."* [697]

The basis for the surviving stories generally sounds somewhat gritty and uncompromisingly real, with abundant references to secular life and existence, with only the most conventional references to religion. Robin and the other protagonists only seem to display a myriad of human emotions rather than anything to suggest a 'mythical forest-elf' as the foundation for our hero. The bottom line is there is no real evidence at all to support such a proposition.

---

[696] In fact, in English folklore, **Herne the Hunter** is a ghost associated with Windsor Forest and Great Park in the county of Berkshire, west of London adjacent to the royal castle and far removed from the leafy northern glades of Sherwood and Barnsdale!

[697] Bellamy, John, *Robin Hood: an historical enquiry* (Indiana University Press, 1985)

Appendix 11

Robin Hood and St Mary's Church...And Marriage?

Seemingly forever connected to the Robin Hood story is the folklore that he was the lover of Maid Marian and that at some point they became husband and wife, despite the fact that in none of the early ballads is there a singular reference to Marian or even wives, girlfriends or families, not just of Robin but of any of the Merry Men (Sir Richard at the Lee's wife is mentioned in *The Gest* and the sheriff's wife, with whom Robin flirts, appears in the Potters tale—Child Ballad 121). The only true link of a feminine nature is Robin's enduring love for the Virgin Mary.

The 2 village locations that cling to this 'lore', that their local church held the wedding of Robin and Marian, are St Mary's church, Edwinstowe, in Nottinghamshire on the southern edge of present-day Sherwood Forest and the late eleventh century church at Campsall, just 4 or 5 miles from Skelbrook, Barnsdale Bar and Wentbridge and the only St Mary's church in Barnsdale itself **(Appendix 1, Map Pins 17 and 13)**. The former is the most popular theory (though neither have provided a single piece of evidence to support their claims) and just supposing that he did marry in later life, then this location, if the time frame being suggested in this book is to be believed, is not a possible venue since the church at Edwinstowe is understood to date from about 1175 at the earliest, or nudging a hundred years later than is required for any matrimonials in the late eleventh century. The Campsall legend purports that their marriage took place there in St Mary's church. Admittedly this is the only St Mary's in Barnsdale, where Robin claims to have founded a chapel (*"I made a chapel in Barnsdale. That seemly is to see, It is of Mary Magdalene, And there to would I be."* (**'The Gest of Robin Hood'**, stanza 440), which clearly is the basis for its claim. However, historical record shows it was a building funded, not by Robin Hood, but by Robert de Lacy II (d.c.1130) Lord of the Manor (who also founded Pontefract Priory and built Clitheroe Castle) and son of the late, great Barnsdale baron and enemy of Robin—Ilbert de Lacy (d.1093). Given the close relationship between the de Lacys, the local sheriffs, barons and Peveril, it would have seemed a strange, unlikely, albeit cheeky, choice for Robin's wedding venue.

However, using Wentbridge, in Barnsdale, as a reference point (Appendix 1, map pin 6), St Mary's church, Edwinstowe, is about 35 miles to the south in Sherwood Forest, no doubt a geographic location at the core of its claim to fame. Stow(e) means 'holy place'; thus, in this case Edwinstowe is the holy place of Edwin. However, also 35 miles away south-east of Wentbridge, between Gainsborough and Lincoln, is the village of Stow (-in-Lindsay), Lincolnshire, where sits the Minster of St Mary, Stow (only 25 miles due east of Edwinstowe, Appendix 1, map pin 18). The Minster Church of St Mary, Stow, is one of the oldest parish churches in England, originally serving as the Cathedral Church of the ancient diocese of Lindsey, founded in the seventh century, and stands on the site of a much older one. There was a church situated in Stow even before the arrival of the Danes in 870, the year they are documented to have burnt the church down. The building remained in ruins, until an abbey was built in 1040, reputedly by Bishop Eadnoth III.

It was then refounded and re-endowed in 1054 by Leofric[698], the Earl of Mercia and his wife, Godiva. Leofric and Godiva were the grandparents of brothers, Earls Edwin and Morcar, co-rebels with Waltheof during the struggles of the late 1060s. During the currency of Waltheof and Judith's marriage (i.e. 1071–1075), the Bishop of Dorchester, Remigius de Fécamp, moved his 'See' to Lincoln and introduced monks at Stow. **Waltheof and Judith then made a most generous donation to the abbey, of land from their estates, namely the lucrative fifteen 'hide' manor of Leighton Bromswell in Huntingdonshire (today in Cambridgeshire).** However, it seems that shortly afterwards (post Waltheof's execution) the whole place went into decline for 15 years as later, in 1091, Remigius refounded it as an abbey and brought monks there from Eynsham Abbey, at the other end of his diocese in Oxfordshire, describing the church as 'having been a long time deserted and ruined'. However, Remigius died just a year later in 1092 and within 5 years his successor as Bishop of Lincoln, Robert Bloet, had transferred the monks back to Eynsham and from

---

[698] Domesday records that in 1066, Leofric's brother, Leofnoth, held thirty-six manors in Derbyshire, losing all after the Conquest, with most being granted to Ralph FitzHubert, including both Hathersage and Crich, onetime Castellan of Nottingham castle.

about 1097 St Mary's had become a simple, parish church, albeit now one of the largest and oldest in England and Grade I listed.

I quoted, above, Robin (from the *Geste*, verse 440) in which he is somewhat boastful of the chapel he has created[699], which I do not dispute but do not believe he married in. Did he, as a devout young teenager, during the short and maybe even happy times during Waltheof's marriage to Judith in about 1074–75, get them to contribute generously to the abbey's re-foundation? Granted Stow is not in Barnsdale but this was, of course, prior to his outlaw days, but then again, neither is Edwinstowe.

70. The 20th century Robin Hood statue outside Nottingham Castle and the 'Green man' carving on the 12th century font at Stow Minster— the same caps?
Photo Credit (l): David Ross and Britain Express
Photo CredI(r) by J. Hannan-Briggs, creative commons licence, ShareAlike 2.0 Generic (CC BY-SA 2.0)

---

[699] Someone funding the building of a church does not seem to ring true as the same man as the groom porter of King Edward leaving with a retirement gratuity of 5 shillings.

As is obvious, the years just after the abbey converted to a parish church (1097–1103) fit the time frame perfectly, should Robin have chosen this location, not maybe for his marriage but for his investment in a new religious building. This was, after all, an establishment once generously funded by his father and is one of the leading examples of the fusion of part Norman, part Anglo-Saxon church architecture in the country. Although now just called 'Stow(e)', I suspect it might well have originally been called *Eadnoth's Stow*, or *Eadnothstowe* (holy place of Eadnoth), which does not sound, phonetically, totally unlike *Edwinstowe*, which is what people believed it erroneously to be in later times, after it became corrupted.

Just to add another smidgen of intrigue, the Norman font at Stow, which is hard to date precisely but thought to be 12th or 13th century (though it could well be contemporaneous with the church's foundation as such carvings are almost impossible to date accurately), features, in carved stone round the outside, the remarkable appearance of a pagan 'Green Man' on a Christian font (also a strange interlocking pentagram, a little serpent-like dragon and various foliate motifs)—in fact none of the images are Christian! Not only is this most incongruous, and unchristian, but the face is a distinctly human one and the man is wearing a cap. Fig.72. In fact, the headgear bears a striking similarity to that depicted on the well-known statue of Robin, by sculptor James Woodford, just outside Nottingham Castle and unveiled in 1952 (fig.69). However, the public were expecting an Errol Flynn-type interpretation, sporting a pointed cap with a jaunty feather. So a controversial debate was born that continues even to this day, with complaints being made about Robin's headgear being an authentic leather skullcap, albeit with an added feather, rather than the triangular pointed felted hat that Flynn wore and was so loved by Hollywood and toy shops.

Are these 900 year old carvings a nod from the stonemason to the connections at Stow to Robin Hood? Hidden messages and tongue-in-cheek depictions were widespread throughout medieval churches, so did the stonemason pick up on the connection between the Minster and the notoriously elusive forest outlaw, whose 11th century exploits were already assuming legendary status? Make of this what you will but it is food for thought and not a little fun.

Appendix 12

Robin Hood and the Crusades

In recent times, most filmatic and televised settings for the exploits of Robin Hood are generally placed during the latter part of the 12th century, during the reigns of King John and Richard the Lionheart and are firmly established as such in the general psyche of the public. This is around the time of the third Crusade and all seem to have latched onto this period since being placed there in numerous 19th century incarnations, none more famously than in the 1820 novel *Ivanhoe*, by Sir Walter Scott. Several films from the 1920s and 1930s further cemented this notion, in particular the 1922 classic with Douglas Fairbanks and the renowned 1938 film, *The Adventures of Robin Hood* with Errol Flynn and Basil Rathbone.

The iconic TV series of the 1950s that I recall from my youth also depicted Robin as a returning Crusader. In 1985, the TV series, 'Robin of Sherwood' introduced the Saracen assassin *Nasir,* who proved very popular with audiences. This inclusion was leapt upon by Hollywood as somehow a real part of the legend and the popular Hollywood blockbuster film from 1991, 'Robin Hood, Prince of Thieves' (1991, with Kevin Costner and *Azeem*—Morgan Freeman) followed by 'Robin Hood' (2010, with Russell Crowe) and Robin Hood (2018, with Taren Egerton and *Yahya*, are also placed in this crusading era with 2 of the 3 featuring a 'good' Saracen—though both played by African Americans, not Arabs!). The Costner film, in the seemingly time honoured fashion of changing the story to improve the entertainment, starts with Robin being made out to be a Crusader, escaping from a Saracen prison in Jerusalem and, accompanied by a Moor, returning to England. He does at least find his father murdered by the Normans and himself disinherited, which bears some vague similarity to my notion of the demise of his father, Waltheof!

Even the Russell Crowe movie (which omits a Saracen character) starts the action in France, when Richard I is killed in 1199 following his return from the

Crusades and in the Taron Egerton version, Robin is recruited by the Sheriff of Nottingham to take part in the 3rd Crusade and his commander is Guy of Gisborne!

John Paul Davis published a book, *Robin Hood: The Unknown Crusader* (Peter Owen, 2009) putting forward a case that Robin and his men were Templars who had escaped to the greenwood together, in the years following the violent dissolution of the order in the years after 1307. He suggests that many aspects of the Merry Men and Robin's lifestyle, piety, philanthropy, fellowship and martial skills reflect those of members of the renowned Christian military order of warrior monks. Although some have found this argument quite appealing it founders on the total absence of any evidence between the theory and the early ballad stories of Robin Hood which make no reference or illusion to crusading and, of course, the lingering issue of the many Robin Hood references pre-dating this era; as such it remains wild speculation. However, this general link with the Crusades, while oft-used, may still fit in with the timeframe being proposed between the covers of this book. Reference has already been made as to how this can work within a late 11th century setting, when discussing Sir Richard at the Lee in Part I, as within the confines of the hypothesis for Robin's identity and timeline laid out in this book, the last 5 years of his life would have overlapped with the very first 5 of the initial crusading movement.

Pre-dating the first actual Crusade, which departed in 1096 for the Holy Land and was ultimately victorious in 1099, were a group called the Knights Hospitallers, rather benevolent precursors to the totally militaristic 'warrior' Knights Templars that sprung from the Crusade itself. The Hospitallers were founded perhaps as early as 1050 by Amalfian merchants in Jerusalem, but only became formalised as a chivalric order under papal charter in 1099 and followed the Benedictine (Cluniac) monastic rules, hence black habits and a white cross, while the Templars were Cistercian based, thus a white habit with a red cross.

The Hospitallers adopted the white, eight-pointed Maltese Cross that is still its symbol today and represents the 8 beatitudes that Jesus pronounced in his Sermon on the Mount. Whereas the Templars provided armed protection for pilgrims and Crusaders, the original Hospitallers simply set up a network of 'rest houses', simple bed and breakfast establishments, for pilgrims on route from around Europe journeying to visit Christian holy sites particularly in the Holy Land and Jerusalem itself where they had opened a hospital served by the order of St Benedict. A convent was built in Jerusalem, which became the Benedictine monastery of St John the Baptist, and it was on the adjacent site that their first hospital was built about 1070, to provide shelter and free medical care to sick pilgrims of any race, creed or colour.

Their official monastic status was not confirmed by the Pope until 1113 and they were known as the Knights Hospitallers of St John of Jerusalem until 1309, the Knights of Rhodes from 1309 till 1522, and were called the Knights of Malta since 1530, an island they defended right up to 1798 when disbanded. The order partially revived in the mid-19th century as the Sovereign Military Order of Malta that today has a modern-day role largely focused on providing humanitarian assistance. They are the original basis of the UK's St John's Ambulance Service, a charity founded in 1877 devoted to providing free first aid and first aid training, whose emblem and volunteers are well recognised with their uniform having a white Maltese Cross on a black background.

The name changes came about following the various failed Crusades and the gradual retreat of the Templar Order firstly to Acre, then Rhodes and finally Malta, after being granted the main island and several smaller ones by the Holy Roman Emperor, Charles V, under the Act of Donation of Malta in 1530. In return, the Order made an annual payment of a single falcon, given on All Saint's Day. This annual rent was immortalised in the Humphrey Bogart movie 'The Maltese Falcon' and the arrangement lasted over 250 years, until Napoleon expelled them from the island in 1798.

It is my understanding that one of eleven such wayside houses in England was owned and operated by the Hospitallers at one of the sites where Waltheof's aula was perhaps located, a couple of miles from Locksley. The house, called Royds (Platts Farm?), is still extant and lived in to this day, even retaining traces of its 11th century origins, which is remarkable. *'This house, with eleven others, formerly belonged to the dissolved Priory or Hospital of St John, of Jerusalem; and was distinguished by an iron or wooden cross, fixed in some conspicuous part of the building'*—(Hunter's Hallamshire, 1825). In the middle of the twelfth century, they are also said to have built a hospital at nearby Castleton, providing medical care for pilgrims, this was at the invitation of Avice de Lancaster, the second wife of William Peveril's son (William Peveril II c.1080–1155).

In 1095, with Jerusalem in the hands of the Saracen 'infidels', the First Crusade was mooted by Pope Urban II when Byzantine emperors made appeals for assistance and the Pope, moved by stories of ill treatment of Christian pilgrims, delivered his famous address cum sermon cum call-to-arms, in the

Auvergne region of France, at the Council of Clermont to an audience of several hundred clerics who spread the word. In this, he exhorted Christendom to '*go to war for the Sepulchre*', regain control of the sacred city of Jerusalem and the Christian Holy Land from Muslims, promising that the journey would count as full penance and redemption. It was effectively a guaranteed ticket to heaven if you joined up.

Although Urban has long been credited for instigating the 1st Crusade, the reality is now thought different by some leading historians. He was actually responding to a quite limited request for some mercenaries from the Emperor of the Byzantine empire, Alexios I Komnenos, who was under threat from the Seljuq empire, a Turkish Sunni Muslim dynasty, which controlled vast areas of the Middle East including Jerusalem and whose capital was Isfahan, in modern-day Iran.

What started as a minor call for aid quickly turned into a pretty haphazard wholesale migration and conquest of territory outside of Europe by some 60,000 who took up the call. The first tranche of Crusaders, later known as *'The Peoples' Crusade,* were mostly untrained and with little central leadership left Europe in 1096. Somewhat shambolic, they were easily defeated by the Seljuqs in Turkey but greater success came later in the year with the second batch, now known as *The Princes' Crusade,* whose progress the Seljuqs could not stop. This second army included peasants from many different nations of western Europe, though surprisingly little input from England[700] but significantly nobility like Robert Curthose, his brother-in-law Stephen de Blois and his uncle, Godfrey of Bouillon (and his brother Baldwin of Boulogne who became the first King of Jerusalem in 1100) plus Bishop Odo of Bayeux, 1st Earl of Kent, who were the most senior, though Odo died on the way at Palermo in Sicily in January 1097.

It is said that the tax burden imposed by Rufus raised to pay his brother for Normandy, meant the nobles in England simply could not afford to fund themselves for the expedition and there is no evidence whatsoever that Robin ever went on crusade. In fact, English involvement in the crusading 'movement' as a whole was minimal throughout the next 2 centuries. Travelling over land and by sea towards Jerusalem, these first Crusaders first captured Antioch and then the great city itself in July 1099, establishing the Kingdom of Jerusalem and

---

[700] It is believed that the great barons of England had been wrung so financially dry by Rufus, in raising the cash to pay brother Robert for the Duchy of Normandy that it rendered them unable to fund any crusading ambitions.

the other Crusader states. The irony is that just prior to this the Seljuqs had already lost their control of the Holy Land itself and the city of Jerusalem to the Fatimids, a Shia Islamic caliphate, which spanned a large area of North Africa, from the Red Sea in the east to the Atlantic Ocean in the west. This dynasty ruled across the Mediterranean coast of Africa and ultimately made Egypt its centre.

Jerusalem eventually fell to the Crusaders in 1099 just 2 weeks before the death of Pope Urban II, the man who had started the whole shebang, though due to the slow communications of the day he never got to hear about the triumph before his death. Although it is now called the First Crusade, no-one then saw himself as a 'Crusader'. The term 'crusade' is a late 12th century term that first appears in Latin over 100 years after the 'first' crusade. Nor did the 'Crusaders' see themselves as being on 'the first', since they did not know there would be more. They saw themselves simply as pilgrims (peregrinators) on a journey (iter), and were referred to as such in contemporary accounts.

Although these gains lasted for fewer than two hundred years, the First Crusade was a major turning point in the expansion of Western power, and was, in fact, the only crusade—in contrast to the many that followed—to achieve its stated goal of capturing Jerusalem. Back in Western Europe, those who had survived the journey, the battles, disease and starvation to reach and capture Jerusalem and make it back home again (only about 10%), were treated as heroes. Among them, of course, was Duke Robert of Normandy, Curthose, who arrived back to find his brother Rufus dead and the English crown now on the head of his youngest brother, Henry…

Bibliography and Primary Resources

Baldwin, David, *Robin Hood: The English Outlaw Unmasked* (Amberley, 2010)

Barczewski, Stephanie, *Myth and National Identity in Nineteenth-Century Britain: The Legends of King Arthur and Robin Hood* (Oxford University Press, 2000)

Barlow, Frank, 1. *The English Church 1066–1154*: A History of the Anglo-Norman Church (Longman, 1979)

2. *The Feudal Kingdom of England: 1042-1216*, (Routledge, 2014)

3. *Rufus*, (Yale University Press, 2000, - first pub. 1983)

Barnett, Elnathan, *Family, Feud, and the Conduct of War in Anglo-Saxon England* (Master's Theses. 211. https://aquila.usm.edu/masters_theses/211, 2011)

Bellamy, John, *Robin Hood: an historical enquiry* (Indiana University Press, 1985)

Benison, Brian, *Robin Hood, The Real Story* (Benison, 2004)

Bildhauer, Bettina, *Medieval Blood*, (Cardiff, 2006)

Birrell, Jean, *Agricultural History Review. 'Deer and deer farming in medieval England'*, 1992. Vol 40, Part 2.

Boardman, Davies & Williamson, eds. *Saints' Cults in the Celtic World*, (Boydell Press, 2009)

Bradbury, J., 1. *The Medieval Archer (*Boydell Press, 1985)

2. *Robin Hood (*Amberley, 2010)

Brand, John, *Observations on Popular Antiquities: Chiefly illustrating the Origin of our vulgar Customs, Ceremonies and Superstitions*, Vol 1. revised by Henry Ellis (London, 1813)

Brebbia, C. A. , *The New Forest: A Personal View*. (WIT Press, 2014)

Campbell, Alistair, *Skaldic Verse and Anglo-Saxon History*, Dorothea Coke Memorial Lecture in Northern Studies, delivered at UCL, 1970 (H.K. Lewis for the College, London, 1971)

Cawthorne, Nigel, *Robin Hood, the True History Behind the Legend* (Constable & Robinson, 2010)

Child, Francis, *The English and Scottish Popular Ballads, Vol 3* (Houghton & Mifflin, 1888/89)

The Duchess of Cleveland, *The Battle Abbey Roll with some account of the Norman lineages*.- in 3 volumes (John Murray, London, 1889)

Cokayne's *Complete Peerage,* 2nd Edition, Vol. XI.

Coote, Lesley, *Robin Hood, the origins of a medieval outlaw*, (Reaktion Books, 2020.)

Cornish, C. J. , *The New Forest*, (Seeley and Co., London, 1894)

Crouch, David, *The Normans: The History of a Dynasty (*Hambledon Continuum, 2007)

Cox, Charles, *The Royal Forests of England*, (Methuen & Co. London, 1905)

Davis, John Paul, *Robin Hood: The Unknown Templar (*Peter Owen 2009)

Dobson, R.B., *Robin Hood: The Genesis of a Popular Hero* - paper from *Robin Hood in Popular Culture: Violence, Transgression, and Justice*; edited by Thomas G. Hahn. (D. S. Brewer, 2000)

Dobson, R.B. and Taylor, John, *Rymes of Robyn Hood: An Introduction to the English Outlaw* (Heinemann, 1976)

Dugdale, William, *Monasticon Anglicanum: A history of Abbeys and other Monasteries,.* (James Bohn, London, 1846.

Eastwood, Rev. J., *History of the Parish of Ecclesfield* (London, Bell and Daldy, 1862)

Ellis, Sir Henry, *A General Introduction to Domesday Book* (Public Records Office, 1833)

Entwhistle, William J., *European Balladry,* (Oxford/Clarendon Press, 1951)

Everett Green, Mary Anne, *Letters of royal and illustrious ladies of Great Britain* (H. Colburn, 1846)

Farjon, Aljos, *Ancient Oaks in the English Landscape.*(Kew: Royal Botanic Gardens, 2017)

William Farrer, ed. *'Outline Itinerary of King Henry I',* Reprinted from the English Historical Review, (Vol. XXXIV, July-Oct 1919)

Faulkes, Anthony, *Outlaws in Medieval England and Iceland*, (The Viking Society, 2009)

Fletcher, Richard, *Blood Feud: Murder and Revenge in Anglo-Saxon England* (Penguin, 2002)

Fowler, J. T. (Ed. 1893), *The Coucher Book of Selby, 2 Volume Set* (Cambridge University Press, 2013)

Freeman, E.A. , *The Reign of William Rufus and the Accession of Henry the First*, (Oxford Clarendon Press, 1882)

The History of the Norman Conquest of England: (Oxford Clarendon press, 1871)

Fröhlich, Walter, (trans.), *The Letters of Saint Anselm of Canterbury,* Cistercian Studies (Kalamazoo: Cistercian Publications, 1990-94)

Giles, J. A. ed., *Gesta Willelmi Ducis Normannorum et Regis Anglorum*, London, 1845

Gillingham John, 'French chivalry in twelfth-century Britain?' The Historian, pp. 8f (2014), available at: www.history.org.uk/student/resource/7591/french-chivalry-in-twelfth-century-britain

Golding, Brian, *'Robert of Mortain'*, Chibnall, Marjorie (ed.), *Anglo-Norman Studies XIII: Proceedings of the Battle Conference 1990,* (Boydell Press, 1991)

Gotch, Alfred, *The Growth of the English Country House*, (Batsford,1909)

Gough, Richard & Payne, Thomas, *Sepulchral Monuments in Great Britain*, (Vol 1. 1786, Vol 2. 1799 – paperback Hansebooks, 2016)

Douglas Gray, *'The Robin Hood Poems'. Poetica*: *An international journal of linguistic and literary studies,* 18, Tokyo, (1984)

Green, Judith, 1. *English Sheriffs to 1154,* Public Records Handbook No. 24 (London: HMSO, 1990)

2. *'David I and Henry I'*, *The Scottish Historical Review,* Vol. LXXV, No. 199, (Apr., 1996)

Green, Mary Anne Everett, ed., *Letters of royal and illustrious ladies of Great Britain*; (H. Colburn 1846)

Green, Monica, *'The Four Black Deaths'*, The American Historical Review, (Vol.125, Issue 5, Dec. 2020)

Harris, Valentine P., *The Truth about Robin Hood* (Private, London, 1951)

Harrison, John, *Exact and Perfect Survey and View of the Manor of Sheffield and other Lands*, 1637. Transcribed and Edited by J. G. Ronksley; (Privately Printed for Arthur Wightman, 1908)

Henry of Huntingdon, *Historia Anglorum* (first ed. *c.*1129. Cambridge University Press, 2012)

Hobsbawm, Eric, *Bandits,* (Weidenfeld & Nicolson; 2nd Revised edition, 30 Dec. 2010)

Hollister, W., 1. *'Magnates and Curiales'*, Viator: Medieval and Renaissance Studies,

Vol. 8 (University of California Press, 1977, p. 63-82)

2. *'The Strange Death of William Rufus'* , Speculum: A Journal of Medieval Studies, 48(4) (October 1973, p. 637-653)

3. *Henry I*, (Yale University Press, 2001)

Holt, J.C., *Robin Hood* (Thames & Hudson, 1989)

Hooke, Della, *Medieval Forests and Parks in Southern and Central England'*, (ed. Charles Watkins, New York, 1998)

Van Houts and Love, Eds and trans. *The Warenne (Hyde) Chronicle..* Oxford Medieval Texts. (OUP. 2013)

Huntington, Dr Joanna, *The Taming of the Laity: Writing Waltheof and Rebellion in the Twelfth Century,* Proceedings of the Battle Conference (Boydell and Brewer, 2009)

Huscroft, Richard, *The Norman Conquest: A New Introduction* (Routledge, 2013)

Jamieson, Robert, *Popular Ballads and Songs, from Tradition, Manuscripts, and Scarce Editions,* 2 vols. (Edinburgh, A. Constable, 1806)

Jørgensen, Dolly, *The Roots of the English Royal Forest'*: Anglo-Norman Studies: Proceedings of the Battle Conference XXXII, Edited by C. P. Lewis, (Boydell Press, 2009)

Joseph, Hunter, 1. *Hallamshire. The History and Topography of the Parish of Sheffield in the County of York* (Folio, 1819)

2. *Critical and Historical Tracts*, (London, John Russell Smith, 1850)

Kaufman, A. L, British Outlaws from History and Literature, Essays on Medieval and Early Modern Figures from Robin Hood to Twm Shon Catty (MacFarland, 2011**)**

Keen, Maurice, *The Outlaws of Medieval Legend* (Routledge, 1961)

Kelliher, Hilton & Knight, Stephen, *Robin Hood: The Forresters Manuscript: British Library Additional MS 71158* (D.S. Brewer, 1998)

Kingsley, Charles, *Hereward, Last of the English* (The Floating Press, 2016)

Knight, Stephen, 1. *Robin Hood, a Mythic Biography* (Cornell UP, 2003)

2. *Robin Hood: A Complete Study of the English Outlaw*, (Wiley-Blackwell 1994)

Knight, Stephen and Ohlgren, Thomas, *Robin Hood and Other Outlaw Tales* (Medieval Institute, 1997)

Knowles, David, *The Monastic Order in England* (Cambridge University Press 1940/2004)

de Lange, Joost, *The Relation and Development of English and Icelandic Outlaw Traditions.* (Haarlem, 1935)

Lees, Jim, *The Quest for Robin Hood* (Temple Press, 1987)

Leland, John, *Itinerary',* Edited by Lucy T. Smith, in 6 vols. (1906-1910)

Lewis, P., *Ancient and Modern State of the New Forest* (T. Payne, London,1811)

Lloyd, Arthur, *The Death of Rufus* (New Forest Ninth Centenary Trust, 2000)

Lysons, Daniel *The Environs of London: Volume 4, 'Tottenham' & 'Walthamstow',* (Originally published by T. Cadell and W. Davies, London, 1796)

Macfarlane, Charles, *The Cabinet History of England* (Charles Knight, 1845)

Manwood, John, *A Treatise and Discourse of the Lawes of the Forrest* (Wight and Norton, 1598)

Mason, Emma, *William Rufus, The life and mysterious death of William II* (NPI Media Group, 2005)

Matthews, John, *Robin Hood* (Amberley, 2016)

McGlynn, Sean, *Robin Hood, a True Legend*, (Sharpe Books, 2018)

Milford, H., *A Glimpse Into Sawtrys Past* (Caresco, 1998)

Morant, Philip, *The History and Antiquities of the County of Essex,* Vols. 1 & 2 (T. Osborne, J. Whiston, S. Baker, L. Davis, C. Reymers and B. White, 1763 and 1768)

Morris, Christopher J., Marriage and Murder in eleventh-century Northumbria: a study of De Obsessiones Dunelmi, Borthwick, Paper No. 82 (Borthwick Institute of Historical Research, University of York, 1992)

Morris, W.A., 'The Office of Sheriff in the Early Norman Period', *English Historical Review,*

No. CXXX (April 1918. pp. 145-175)

Mortimer, Thomas, *A New History of England: From the earliest Accounts of Britain to the Ratification of the Peace of Versailles, 1763* (Nabu Press, 2011)

Murray, Margaret, *The God of the Witches (*Faber and Faber, 1933)

Northup, G. T., *An Introduction to Spanish Literature* (University of Chicago Press, 1960)

Norton, Christopher, *St William of York*, (York Medieval Press, 2006)

Owen, Professor L.V.D. , 'Robin Hood in the Light of Research', *The Times, Trade and Engineering Supplement,* xxxviii (864), p.xxix (February 1936)

Palgrave, Sir Francis, *The History of Normandy and England, Vol.4 , 'Accession of Henry Beauclerc',* (Macmillan, 1864,)

Paris, Matthew, *Historia Anglorum,* c,1250, (British Library, Royal MS 14 C VII)

Parker, F. H. M., *The Forest Laws and the Death of William Rufus*, (English Historical Review, 1912)

Percy, Dr. Thomas, *Reliques of Ancient English Poetry*, (George Allan and Unwin, 1885

Phillips, Graham and Keatman, Martin, *Robin Hood: The Man behind the Myth* (Michael O'Mara, 1995)

Planché, R. 1. T*he Conqueror and His Companions, Vol. II*, (Tinsley Brothers, 1874)

2. *A Ramble with Robin Hood*, (paper read before the Lincoln Diocesan Architectural Society and published in their *'Transactions'*, Report of the Association of Architects 1864)

Pollard, A. J., *Imagining Robin Hood: The Late Medieval Stories in Historical Context* (Routledge, 2004)

Pommeraye, Jean-Francis, *Histoire de l'abbaye de St Amand de Rouen*, (Lallemant, 1662)

Poncelet, Yves, *Annales de Normandie*, 37e année, n°2, 1987 (Institutions ecclésiastiques de la Normandie ducale)

Poole, A. L., *Domesday Book to Magna Carta, 1087-1216,* (2nd Ed. , OUP, 1955)

Prestwich, Michael, *Edward I* (University of California Press, 1988)

Preston, F. L., *An Account of the Loxleys of Hallamshire*, (Local Studies Section of Sheffield City Library, ref. 929.2, 1966)

Prideaux, Col. W.F., *Who was Robin Hood?* Notes and Queries, 7th series (*November* 1886)

Raglan, Lord, *The Hero: A Study in Tradition, Myth and Drama* (Methuen, 1935)

Rennison, Nick, *Robin Hood, Myth, History and Culture*, (Oldcastle Books, 2012)

Reuel, Michael, *Robin Hood Existed,* (Rule Hard Publishing, 2016)

Rigg, J. M., *Anselm - a Biography*, (Methuen, 1896)

Riley, Henry, T., trans., *Ingulf's Chronicle of the Abbey of Croyland* (1854)

Rex, Peter, *English Resistance* (Amberley, 2014)

Hereward, the Last Englishman (Amberley, 2005)

Reynolds, Susan, Eadric Silvaticus and the English resistance, *Bulletin of the Institute of Historical Research,* no.54 (1981)

Ritson, Joseph, *Robin Hood: A Collection of all the Ancient Poems, Songs, and Ballads, now extant relative to that celebrated English Outlaw, to which are prefixed Historical Anecdotes of his Life* (William Pickering, 1832)

Round, Horace J., *Walter Tyrell and his wife, 'Feudal England'*, (1895 - new edition, Barnes and Noble, New York, 1964).

Rule, Martin, *The Life and Times of St. Anselm*, (Wipf & Stock, 2016)

Rule, Med. Eadmer, *Eadmeri Historia novorum in Anglia: Eadmer's History of recent events in England,* Rolls Series 81, London 1884. Trans. G. Bosanquet (Dufour, 1965)

Rutherford-Moore, Richard *The Legend of Robin Hood* (Capall Bann, 2001)

Seal, Graham, *Outlaw Heroes in Myth and History* (Anthem Press, 2011)

Schmitt, F.S. (ed.), *Sancti Anselmi Cantuariensis Archiepiscopi, Opera Omnia* (T. Nelson, 1946–63), ep.237, 4.144-45; translation and annotation from *The Letters of Saint Anselm of Canterbury,* trans. Walter Frohlich, *Cistercian Studies,* 97, 3 volumes (Cistercian, 1990–94), 2.213-14.

Scot, Reginald, *The Discoverie of Witchcraft*, with addendum *Treatise upon the Nature and Substance of Spirits and Devils,* (printer William Brome, 1584)

Simeone, William E, *'The Historic Robin Hood', The Journal of American Folklore;.* Vol. 66, No. 262 (Oct. - Dec., 1953)

Singman, Jeffrey L., *Robin Hood The Shaping of the Legend* (Greenwood Press,1998)

Southern, R. W., *Medieval Humanism.* (Harper and Row, New York, 1970)

Speight, Sarah *Family, Faith and Fortification: Yorkshire 1066-1250,* PhD thesis, 1993, University of Nottingham:
http://eprints.nottingham.ac.uk/11870/1/335917.pdf)

Stenton, Frank, *Anglo-Saxon England* (3rd ed.), (Oxford University Press, 1971)

Stredder, Eleanor, *Who was Robin Hood?* Notes and Queries, 7th Series, III (April, 1887)

Strickland, Mathew and Hardy, Robert, *The Great Warbow: From Hastings to the Mary Rose* (Sutton, 2005)

Suger, *Vie de Louis VI le Gros,* Waquet, H. (ed. & trans.) (Belles Lettres, 1929 & 1964) p. 12

Thierry, Augustin, *Histoire de la conquête de lAngleterre par les Normands [History of the Conquest of England by the Normans]* 3 volumes (Firmin Didot, 1825)

Thoroton, Robert, *History of Nottinghamshire: Republished with Large Additions by John Throsby*, Vol. 1 (B and J White, J Walker, London, 1797)

Tout, Thomas F., *Christina* (entry in Dictionary of National Biography, vol. 10, 1895-1900)

Underdown, David, *Revel, Riot, and Rebellion: Popular Politics and Culture in England, 1603–1660* (Oxford University Press, 1985)

Vaughn, Sally M., *Anselm of Bec and Robert of Meulan: The Innocence of the Dove and the Wisdom of the Serpent* (University of California Press, 1987)

Victoria County History: *A History of the County of Bedford,* Vol.I, (Victoria County History series, London, 1904.)

Victoria County History: *A History of the County of Essex,* Vol. 2 (Victoria County History series, London, 1907)

Victoria County History: *A History of the County of Hampshire,* Vol. 2 (Victoria County History series, London 1903)

Victoria County History: *A History of the County of Lincoln,* Vol. 2 (Victoria County History series, London, 1906.)

Victoria County History: *A History of the County of Nottingham,* 2 volumes (Victoria County History series, London, 1910)

Victoria County History: *A History of the County of York:* Vol. 3 (Victoria County History series, London, 1974)

de Vries, Richard, *On the Trail of Robin Hood* (Hightown, 1982/1988)

Wace, Robert, '*The History of the Norman People – Roman de Rou*', c.1165, Trans. Glyn S. Burgess, (2004).

Wager, Sarah, '*The hays of medieval England: A reappraisal*', (The Agricultural History Review, December 2017)

Walker, J.W., editor, *Abstracts of the Cartularies of the Priory of Monkbretton,* (Yorkshire Archaeological Society, Record Series, vol. LXVI, p.185, 1924)

Waltz, Robert, *The Gest of Robyn Hode: A Critical and Textual Commentary* (History. E-Books, 2013)
https://www.free-ebooks.net/ebook/The-Gest-of-Robyn-Hode-A-Critical-and-Textual-Commentary/pdf?dl&preview

Ward, Jennifer, *"Royal Service and Reward: The Clare Family and the Crown, 1066-1154", Anglo Norman Studies,* vol. XI, (Boydell and Brewer, 1987)

Weir, Alison, *Britain's Royal Families: The Complete Genealogy* (Bodley Head, 1999)

White, Francis, *History, Gazetteer and Directory of the County of Derby* (James Ward, 1857)

White, Geoffrey, H. *'The Household of the Norman Kings'* (Royal Historical Society, CUP, Vol. 30, 1948)

Williams, Ann, *The speaking cross, the persecuted princess, and the murdered earl: the early history of Romsey Abbey,* (Anglo Saxon 1, pp.221–238, 2007)

Wilson R. M., *The Lost Literature of Medieval England* (Philosophical Library, 1952)

Wilson, Steve, *Robin Hood: The Spirit of the Forest* (Neptune Press, 1993)

Wise, John R., *The New Forest, its scenery and history.* (Smith, Elder, London, 1867)

Wood, Michael, *In Search of England, Journeys into the English Past,* (Penguin Books, 2001)

Wright, Thomas, *Essays on archaeological subjects, and on various questions connected with the history of art, science, and literature in the Middle Ages* (Smith, 1861)